The Jewellery Box
Jorunn Veiteberg

In memory of Mogens Krabek (1949–2020)

The Jewellery Box

Jorunn Veiteberg

arnoldsche

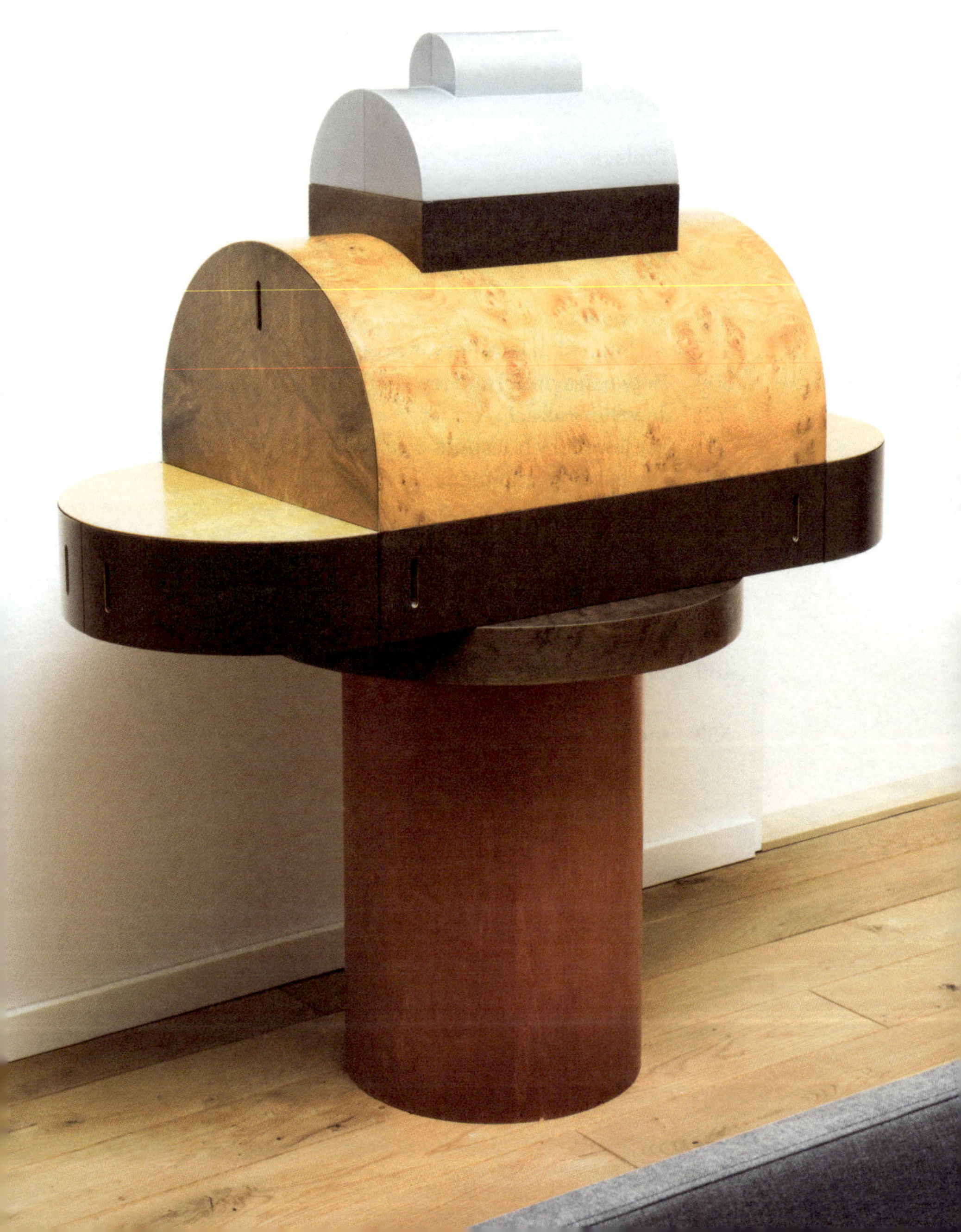
My jewellery box: The cabinet "Charlotte" designed by Martine Bedin for Memphis in 1987 [424].

Preface

Charlotte has been a true friend for many years. I made her acquaintance in February 1990 at Galleri F 15 in Moss, where I was working as a curator and editor. Striking as she was – and is – in every way, Charlotte attracted attention. But then, she is also from Italy. She came to F 15 on the occasion of the exhibitions *Memphis Milano* and *Meta Memphis*. Charlotte's mother is French-born Martine Bedin, and Bedin was one of the designers who helped to set up the Memphis group in Milan in 1981. At F 15 we showed some of Bedin's celebrated lamps, together with a vase – and "Charlotte", who happens to be a cabinet [424]. After the exhibition, that cabinet came home with me, and, ever since, she has served as a repository for my jewellery.

Wearable wealth. That is how jewellery has often been perceived. For many people, jewellery is all about luxury and flaunting one's status and position. While I wouldn't dispute that jewellery can serve such a purpose, it is a very narrow conception and one that is far too limited when it comes to *art* jewellery. Even the definition in the Oxford English Dictionary fails to capture the breadth of jewellery's many types: "Personal ornaments, such as necklaces, rings, or bracelets, that are typically made from or contain jewels and precious metal". Today's jewellery is often made from materials that could hardly be described as precious, and personal ornamentation is far from the only reason for making and wearing it. One of my strongest motivations for writing this book is the desire to expand our understanding of jewellery and what the term entails. I make no secret of the fact that this is also an exploration of a personal passion. The book deals with how I became a collector, why I focused on jewellery, and what jewellery can do for us.

There is a certain affinity between my jewellery box and the objects it contains. Memphis was the byword for a new freedom; it signified humour and vitality. Turning their back on functionalism, the designers of the group did as they pleased. Sadly, the fun was short-lived. When manufacturers began to complain that Memphis's designs were too expensive, too big and too difficult to package, they closed down. That was in 1988, but by that point the group was already known around the world. At the height of Memphis's popularity, I discovered there were jewellery artists who insisted on the same artistic freedom that Memphis stood for in the world of design. Although I was already wearing jewellery on a regular basis, the discovery of what I call art jewellery opened new horizons.

Today my collection contains some 550 items. It includes work by 210 jewellery artists from thirty different countries, although some pieces are made by unknown craftspeople or mass-produced by large companies. It is this collection that makes up my jewellery box. Here we find earrings, bracelets and finger rings, necklaces, hairbands and *bunad* jewellery, the brooches worn with Norwegian folk costumes. Jewels for everyday use and jewels for special occasions. A few cannot even be worn but belong in the box even so because they shed light on the cultural role of jewellery. Some could only be described as gewgaws, others as significant art. Conventional forms live side by side with experimental objects; political statements mingle with humorous asides. In my collection, there are no divisions in terms of whether items are made from cheap or precious materials. One of the things that fascinated me about art

jewellery in the 1980s was the fact that many of the leading
artists in the field made a point of reaching out to ordinary
people by making jewellery from plastic, paper, rubber or
other "poor" materials. The artist Kjartan Slettemark went
even further in reusing debris and transformed it into wearable art and sculptures. Plastic packaging was the material
he used when he portrayed me as a ptarmigan with a large
chain-like ornament.

It should also be said that a good collection does not
necessarily consist exclusively of "great" art. At least, not
if the artist Urs Fischer's criterion for what characterises
an interesting collection holds true: for him, the objects in
a collection must be *curious*. It is Erling Kagge who quotes
this point in his own book about art collecting.

For me, my jewellery box is more than just a storage
space. To open the lid is to be overwhelmed by memory.
Jewellery can be a vehicle for such a range of feelings. Some
carry memories of anniversaries and major milestones in
life. Others of people I have met and places I have visited.
My jewellery reflects who I am or would like to be, it points
to my interests and values, but it also reveals how I have
been influenced by trends and the historical period I have
lived through. Some of the pieces have ended up in the box
because gallery owners have talked me into buying them,
others because I have been influenced by fellow collectors
or by artists I have met. Not all these memories are equally
happy, and some hold secrets that should be allowed to
remain such. Even so, it is my hope that the book will have a
value beyond the merely personal story, namely a contribution to the recent history of crafts.

Throughout history, people have for various reasons
adorned themselves with jewellery-like objects. The cultural status of these objects has, however, varied. One place
where they are commonly encountered is in museums of
cultural history and ethnography. Jewellery's value usually depends on the materials it is made from, who made
them or whether a particular item is categorised as art or a
commercial product, design or craft. This unstable identity

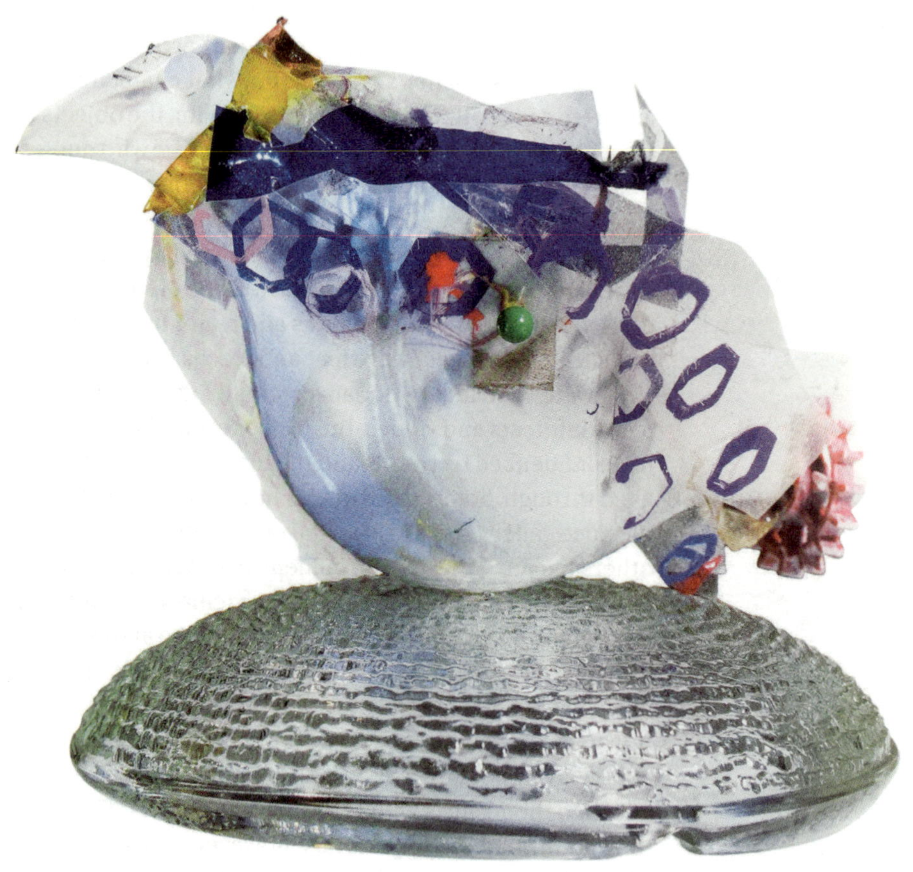

"Magister Jorunn Veiteberg", portrayed as a ptarmigan with an imaginary necklace, by Kjartan Slettemark, ca. 1992–94.

would appear to be one of the reasons why art jewellery has been largely, if not completely, overlooked in general introductions to art history. Apart from artist monographs, no book on contemporary jewellery has been published in Norwegian since the 1995 catalogue *Nordisk smykkekunst/ Nordic Jewellery*, to which I myself contributed. I therefore hope that the current publication will add a further link to what we could describe as the chain of art history. The choice of this metaphor is by no means accidental. In his book *The Shape of Time* from 1962, Georg Kubler describes the history of art as "a broken but much repaired chain made of string and wire" connecting "occasional jewelled links". My own thread stretches over fifty years and links together trends and themes that have interested me as an art historian since my student days in Bergen in the 1970s.

For many years, "Charlotte" alone was big enough to house my collection, but by the early 2000s she had reached her limit. Since then, I have added sets of drawers from IKEA to form a "jewellery box extension". They now stretch from floor to ceiling like pillars. And for the most part, this is where my collection resides. There is a particular joy in pulling out a drawer in order to share its contents with guests. We tend to develop blind spots for the art that is always part of our home environment. But pulling out a drawer and thinking about what jewellery I should wear on any given day entails constant reunions and conscious choices. The following pages also make my collection available in printed form. A few words about the principles of the presentation may be in order here.

In the main section (pp. 17–280), The Collection, the jewellery is arranged not according to artist's name or year of production but roughly in the order in which the items entered my life. Each piece is represented with a full-size image. This means that for any item with dimensions bigger than the page, only a section can be shown. To compensate, the full list of works at the end of the book (pp. 492–551), with artists arranged in alphabetical order, includes pictures of complete items.

But I am not just someone who collects and writes about jewellery. I am also a user of jewellery. The absence of the body it is meant to adorn can be a problem when presenting jewellery, whether in an exhibition context or a book. It is therefore important to document these objects in use. The wearer's personality, dress style and mannerisms all influence the way jewellery is perceived by others. Large, ostentatious pieces sometimes give me a sense of being a walking gallery, but most of the time I use jewellery as a medium for more discreet and tacit messages. Jewellery's role as a means of communication has always mattered greatly to me. It is this dimension that is overlooked when the jewellery is defined as mere "ornament".

The idea for this book arose after I received an invitation to show my collection at Nordenfjeldske Kunstindustrimuseum in Trondheim in 2018. The collaboration with the museum, and not least with curator Gjertrud Steinsvåg, forced me to reflect in greater depth on the activity of collecting and my relationship with jewellery. My thanks to them for that opportunity. Even more important was that the plan to create an exhibition required me to register my collection in detail. Up to that point, this was a task I had shamefully neglected. Fortunately I had taken care of most of the receipts. A stay at the Nordic Artists' Centre Dale provided the calm I needed to catalogue each piece individually, and it was there the first pages were written.

The book would never have become what it is without the support of Guri Dahl and Rune Døli. I am indebted to them for helping to develop the concept. Guri has also photographed the entire collection, and Rune has been responsible for the graphic design. My thanks to them both. The one person I always enjoyed sharing my collection with more than anyone else was my husband Mogens Krabek. Sadly, he did not get to see the finished book. But he is very much a part of the story, and the book is dedicated to his memory.

Jorunn Veiteberg
Copenhagen 2021

The Collection
1970–2020

ock with love woodsto

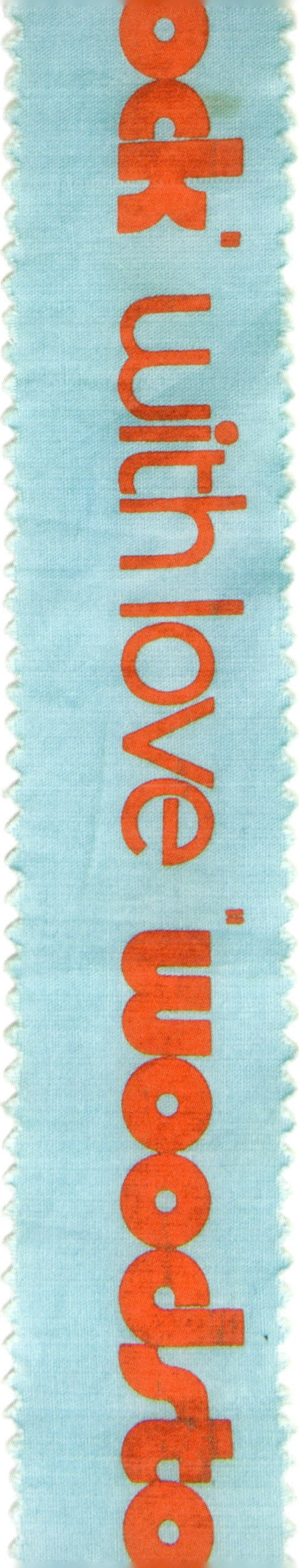

465

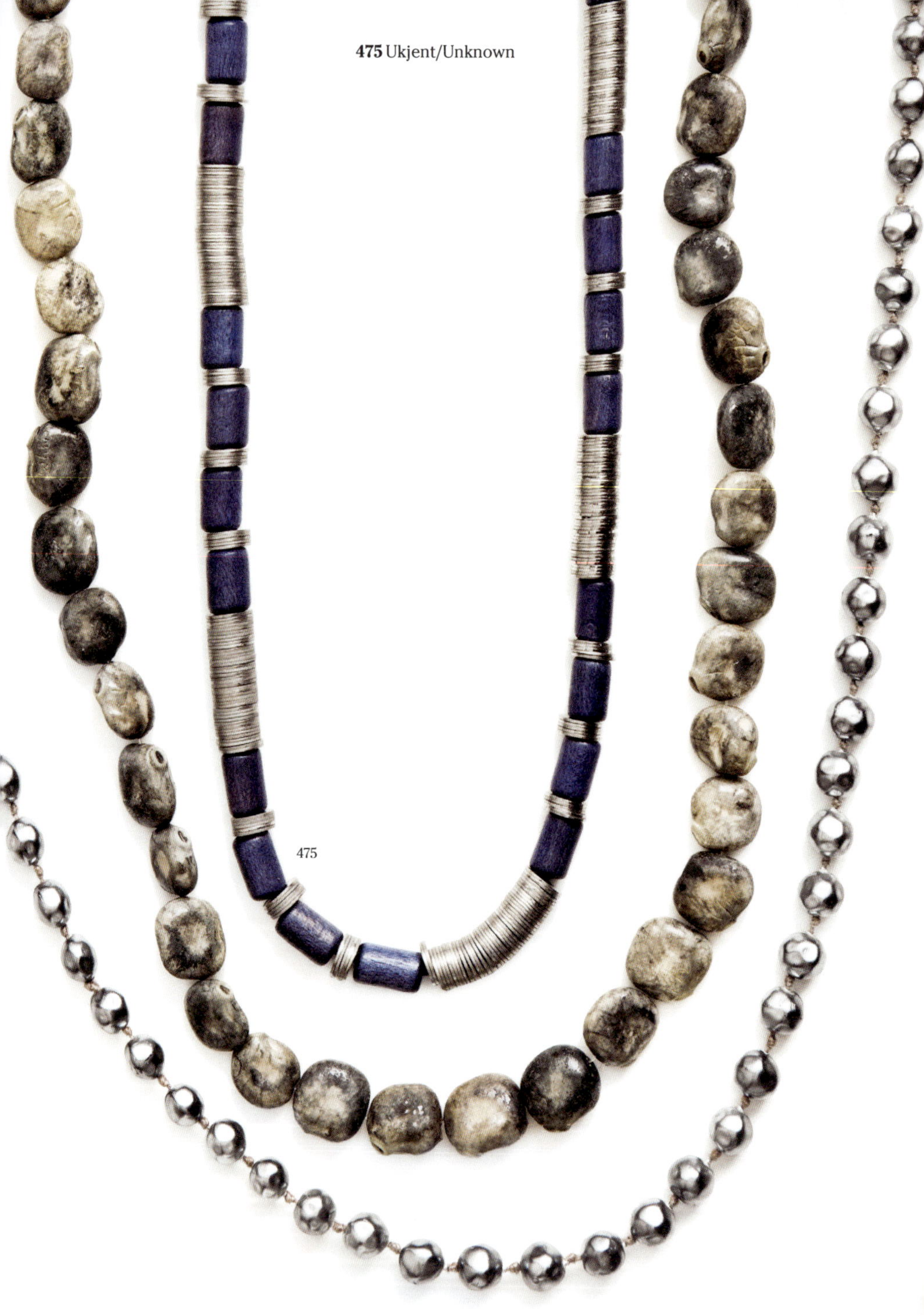

475

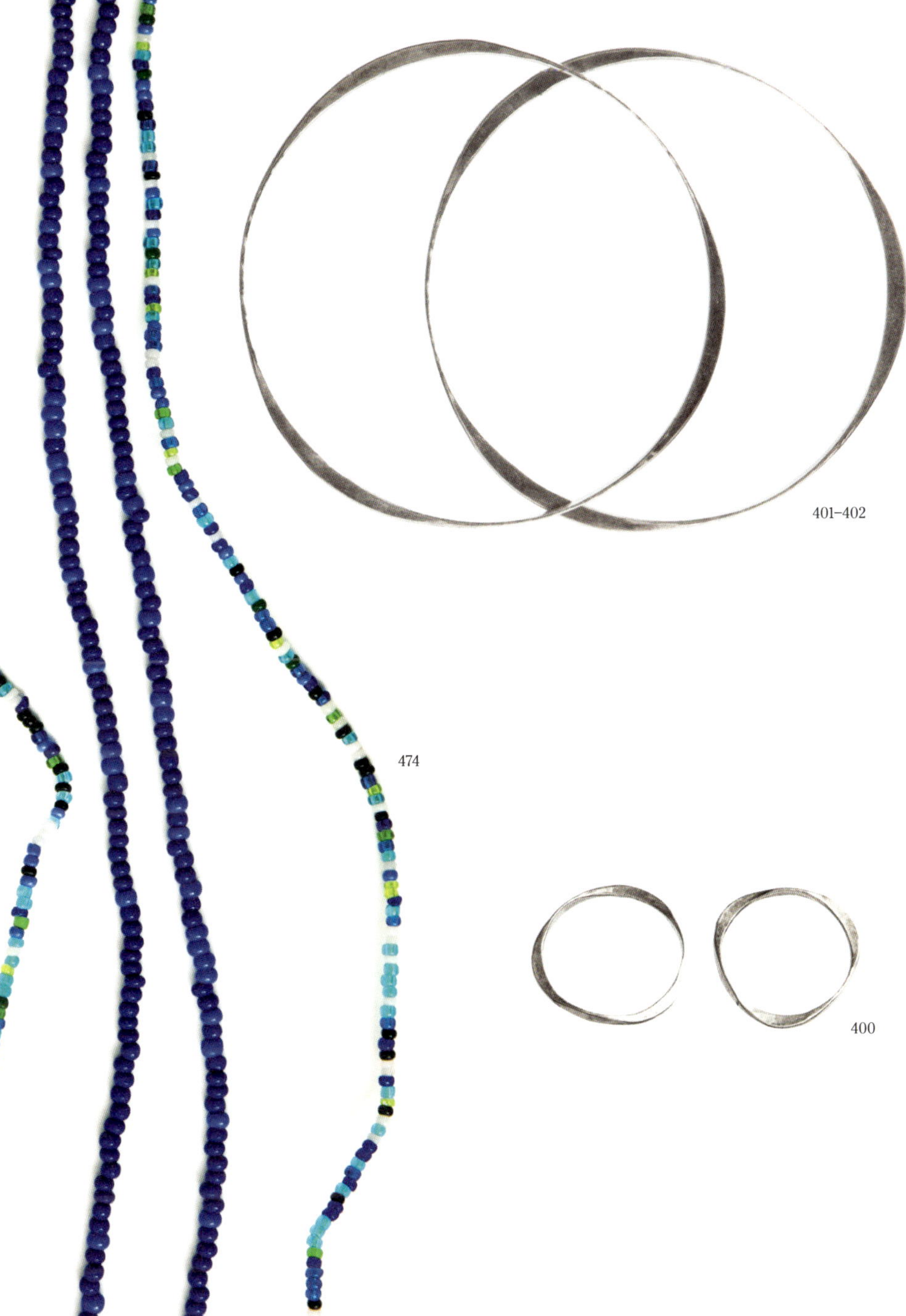

401–402

474

400

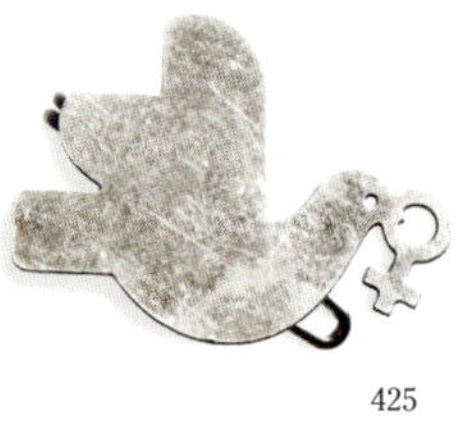

425

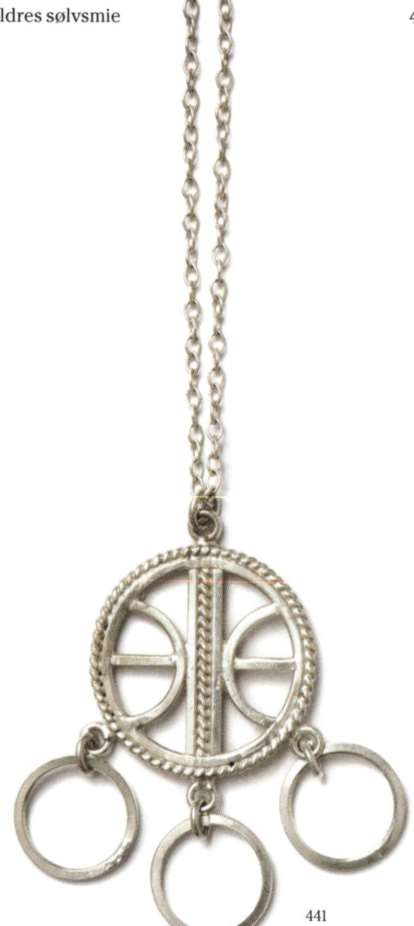

441

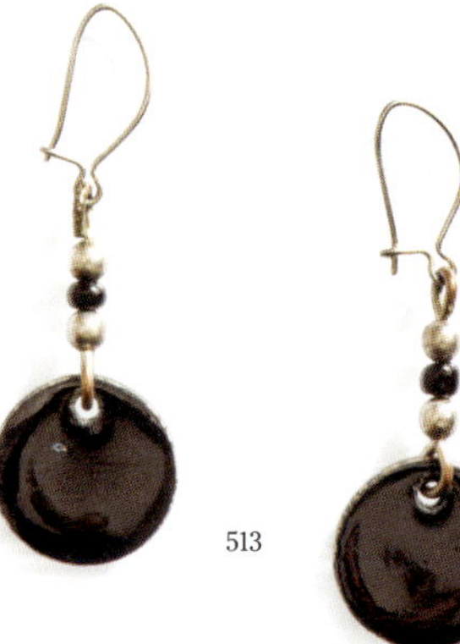

513

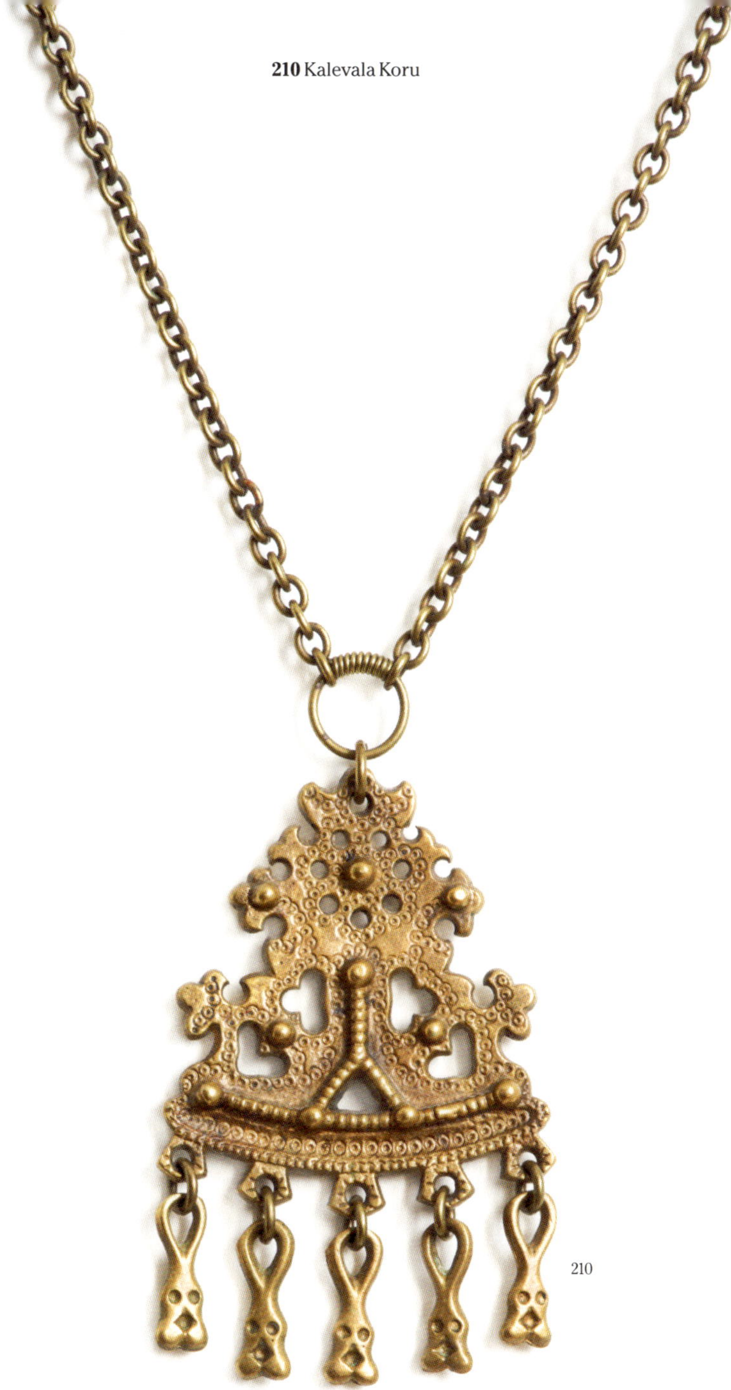

210

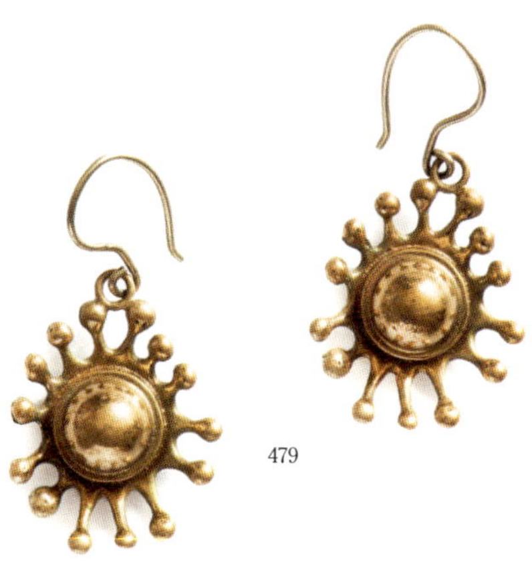

479

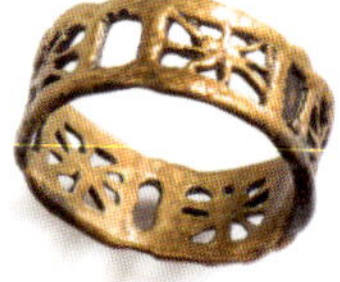

436

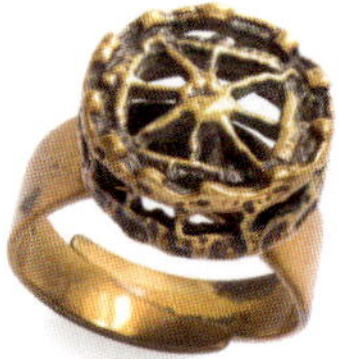

435

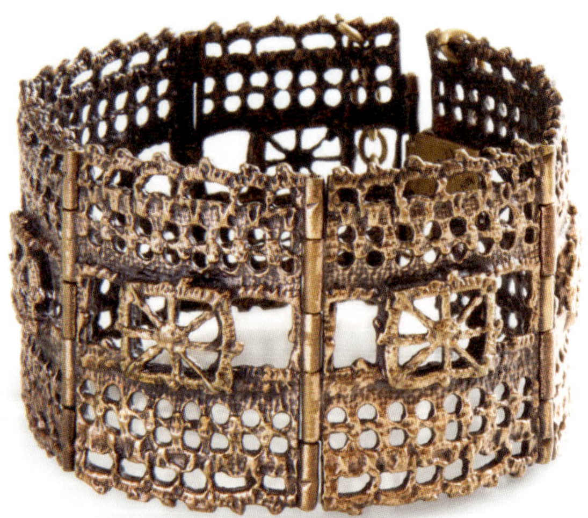

434

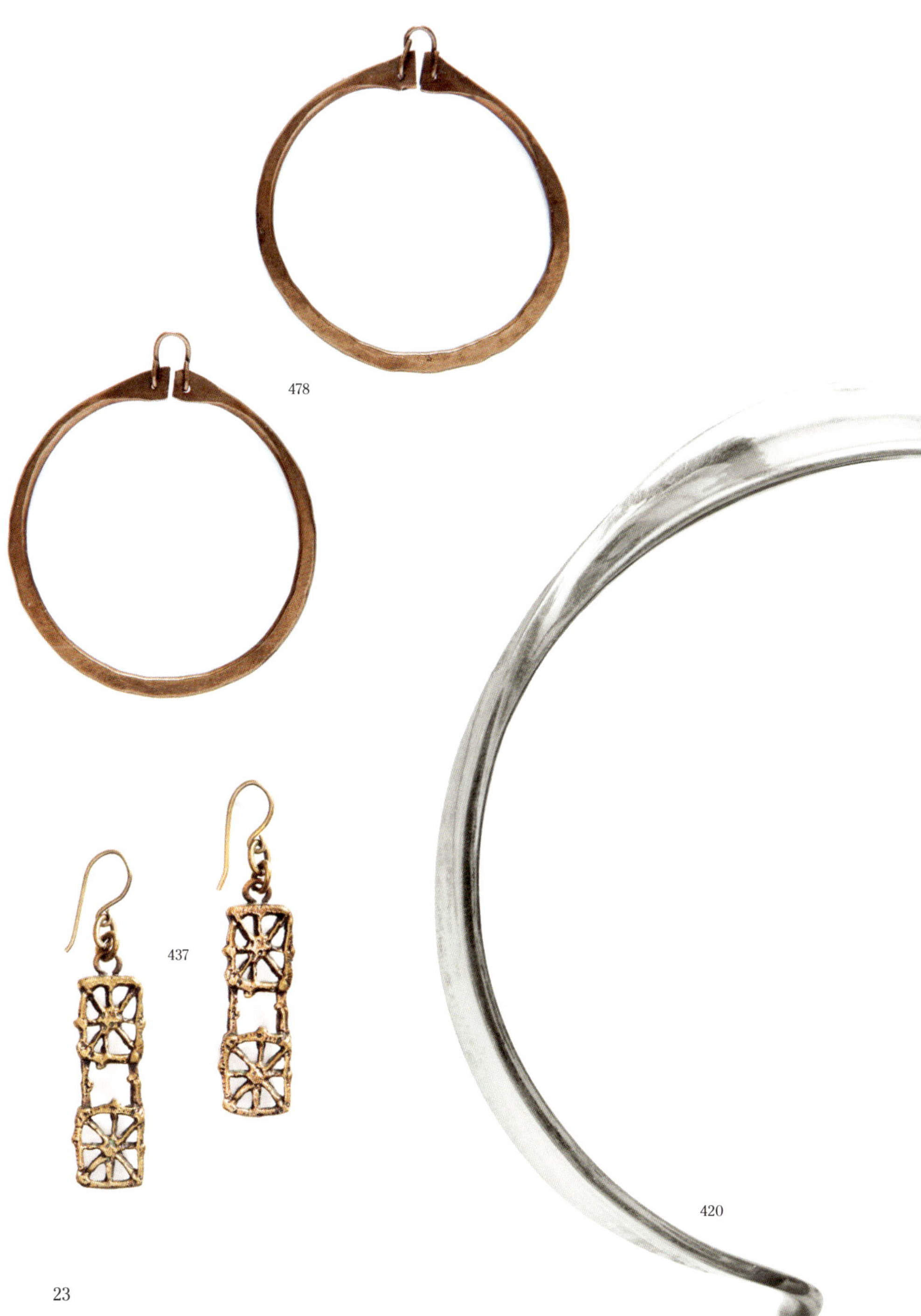

478

437

420

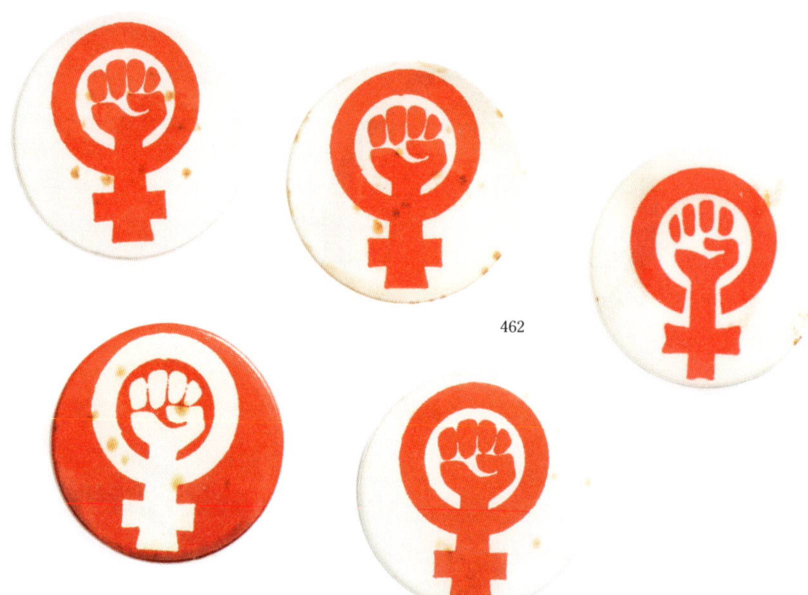

462

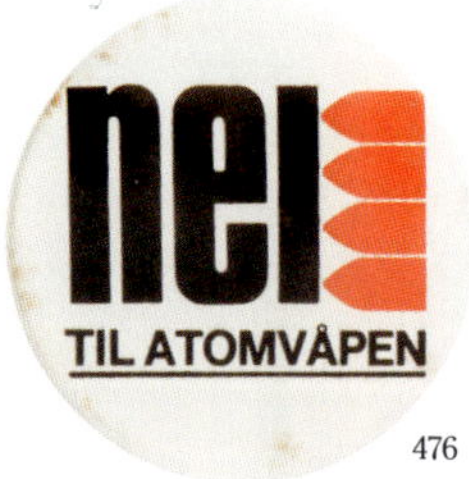

476

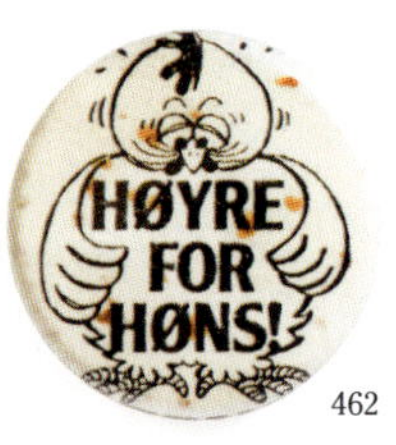

462

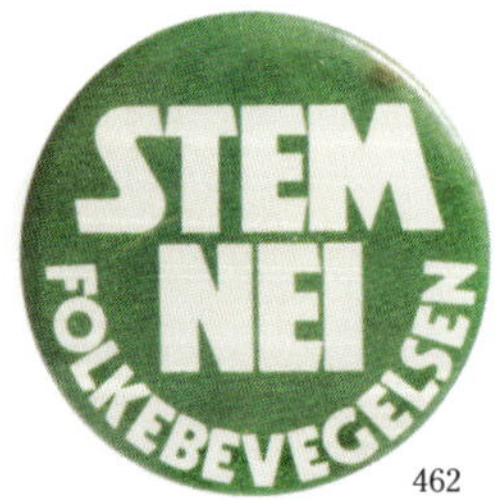

462

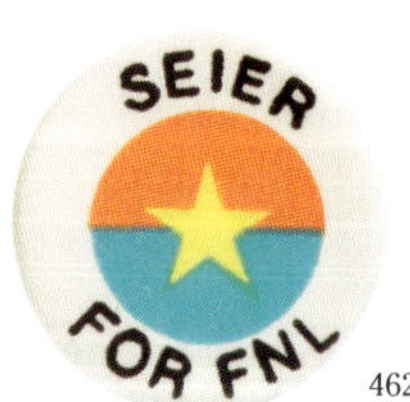

462

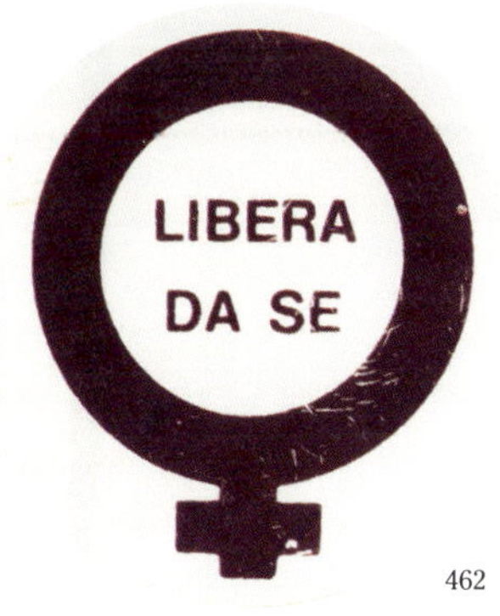

462

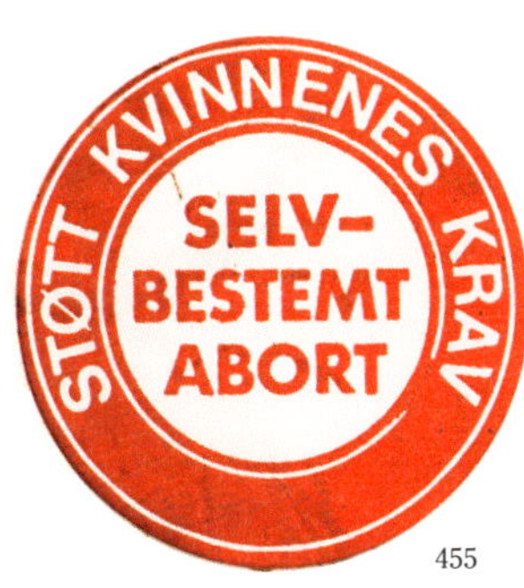

455

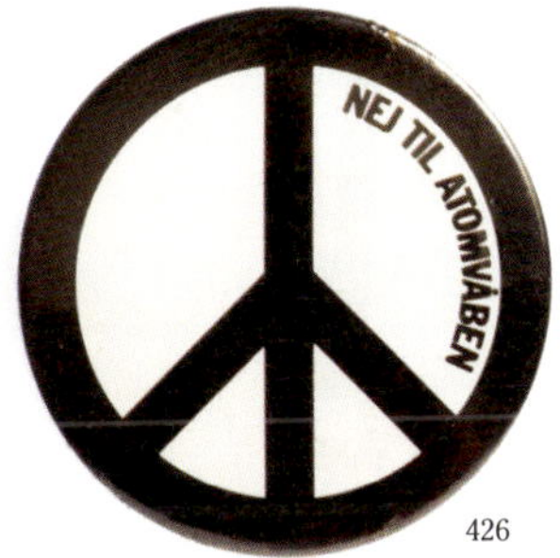

426

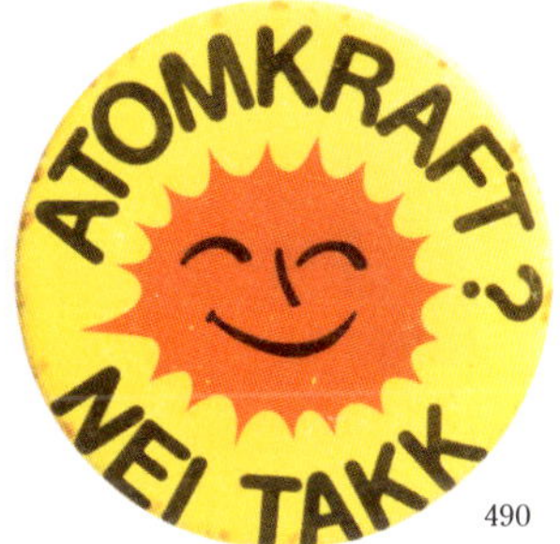

490

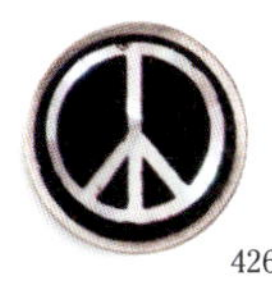

426

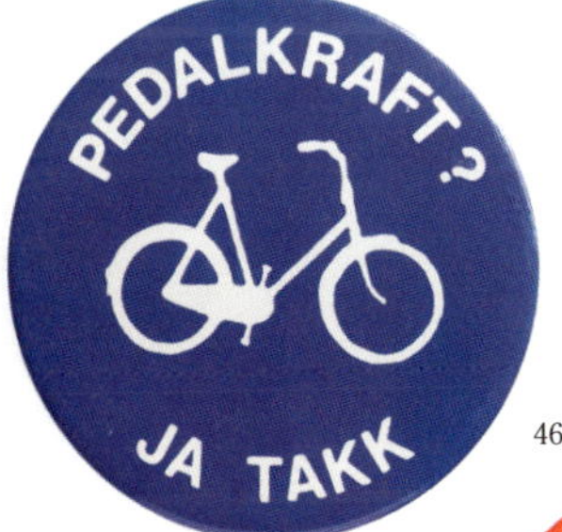

462

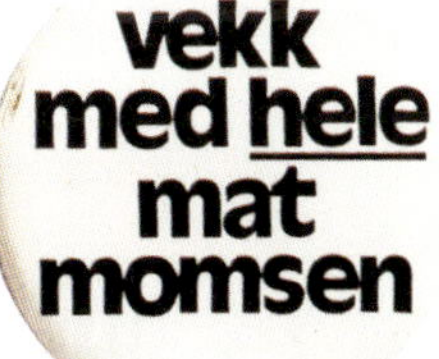

462

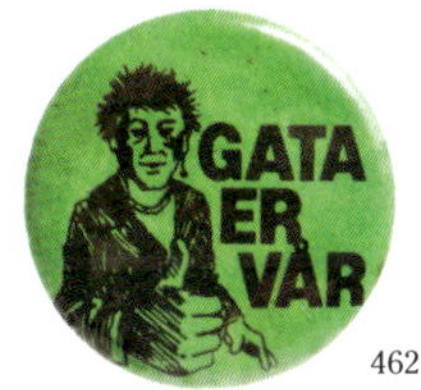

462

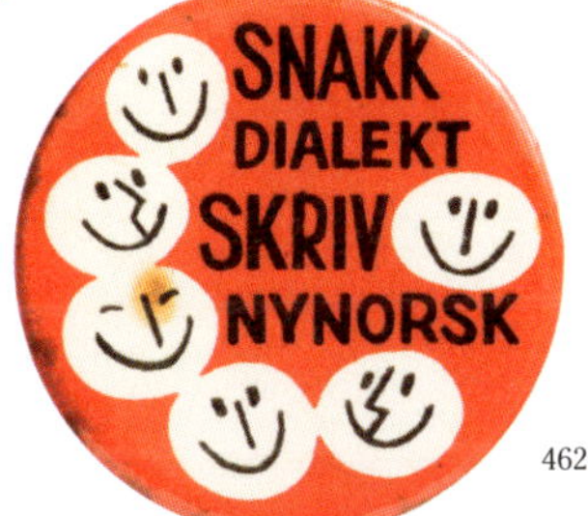

462

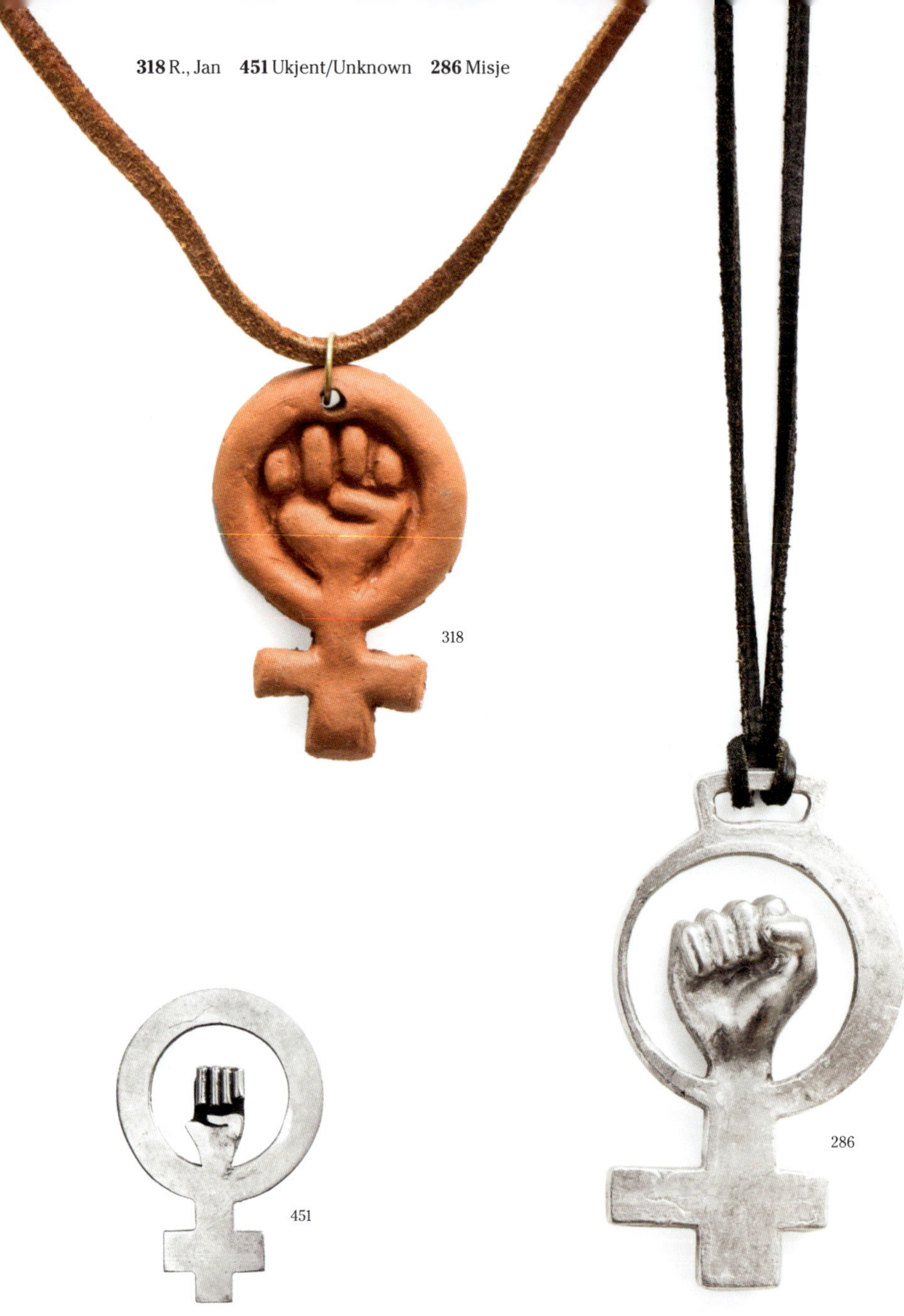

318

451

286

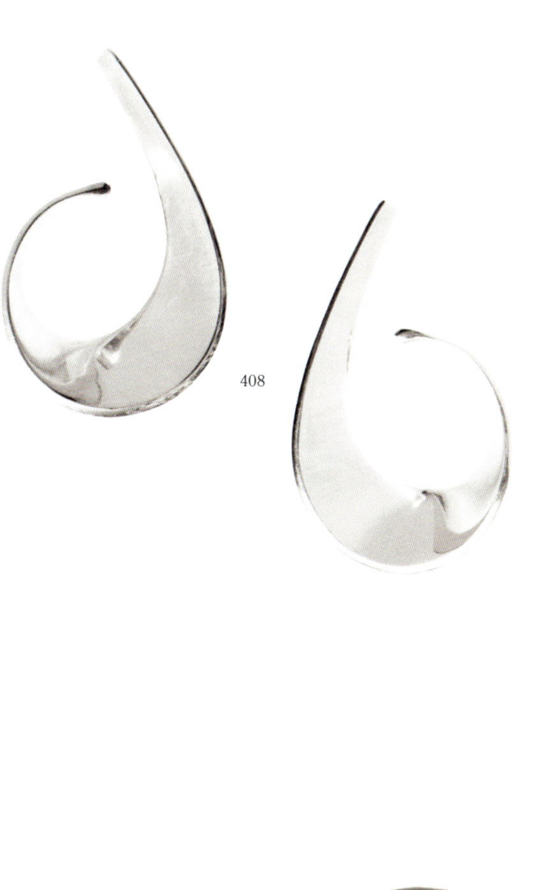

408

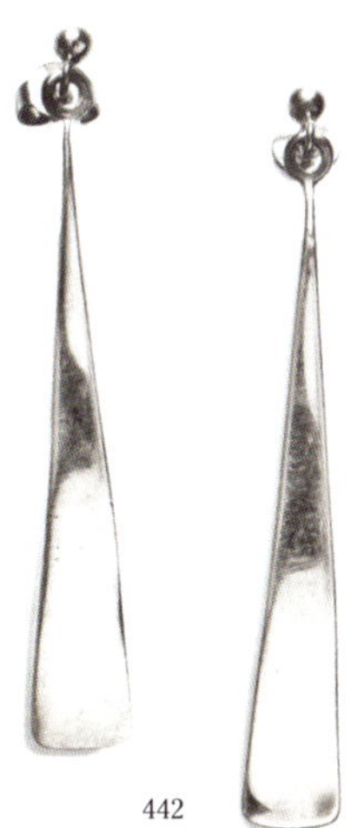

442

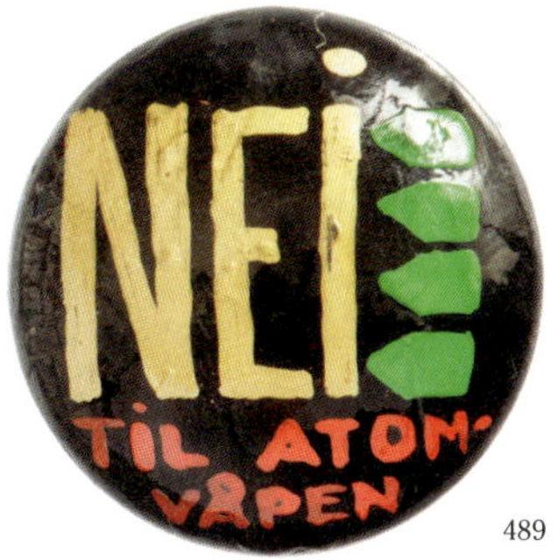

489

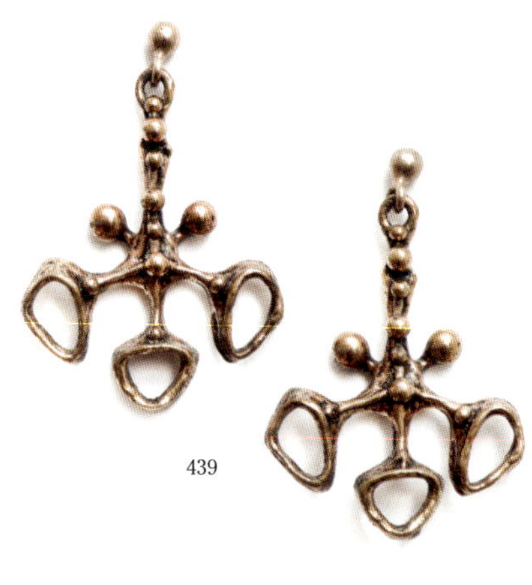

439

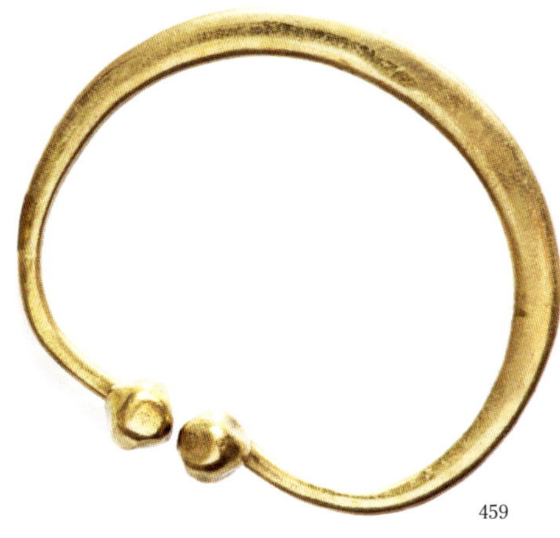

459

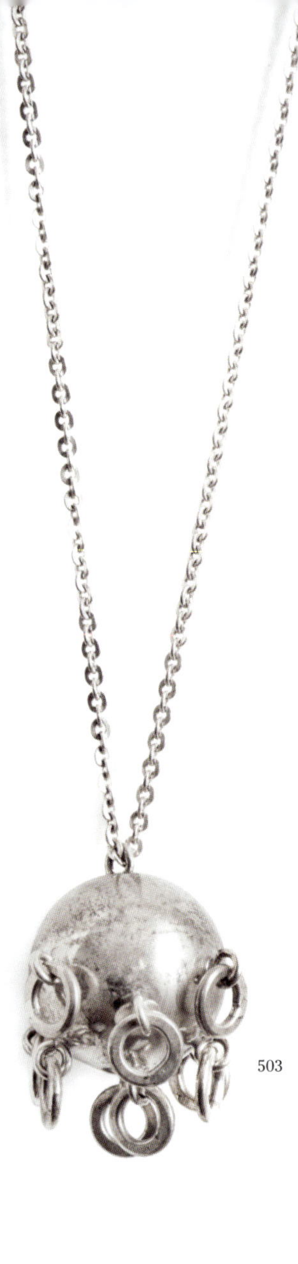

503

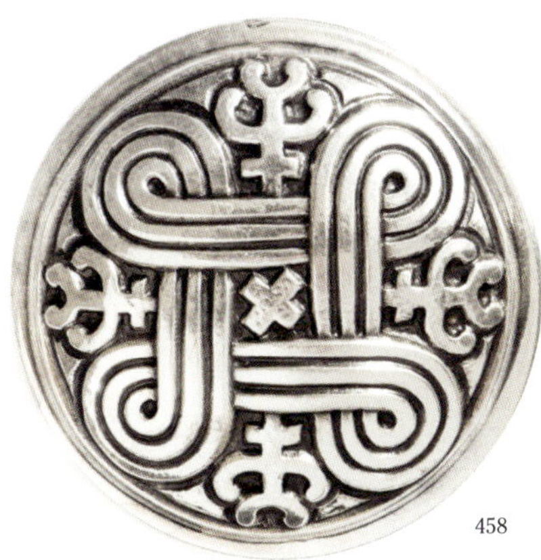

458

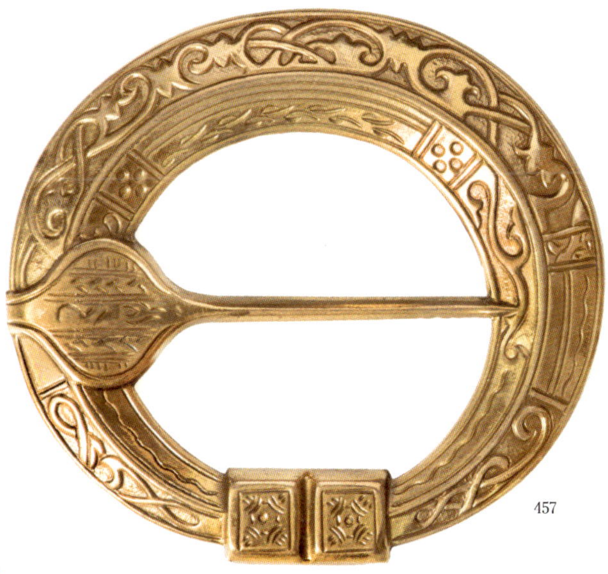

457

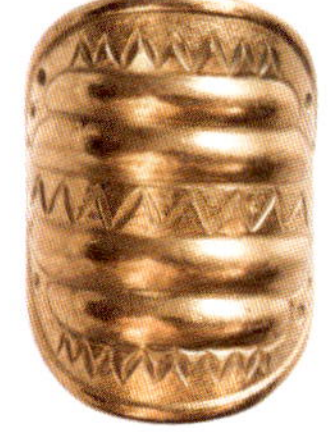

440

553

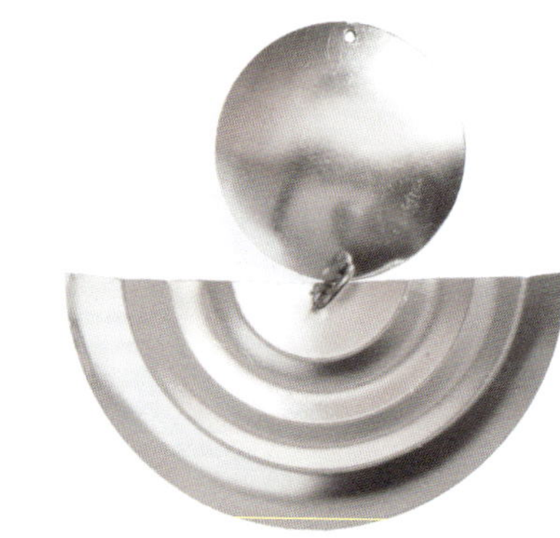

480

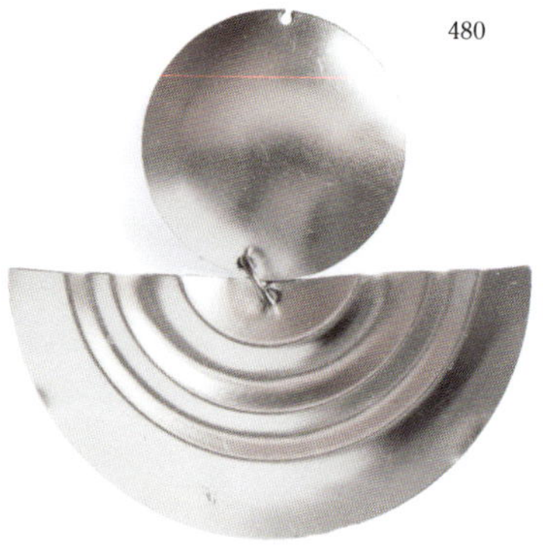

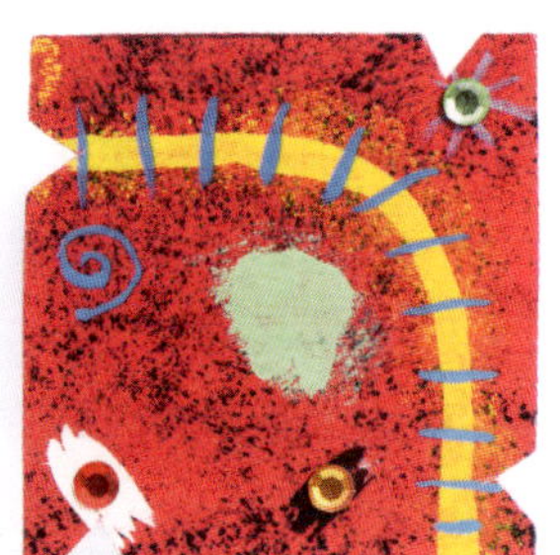

352

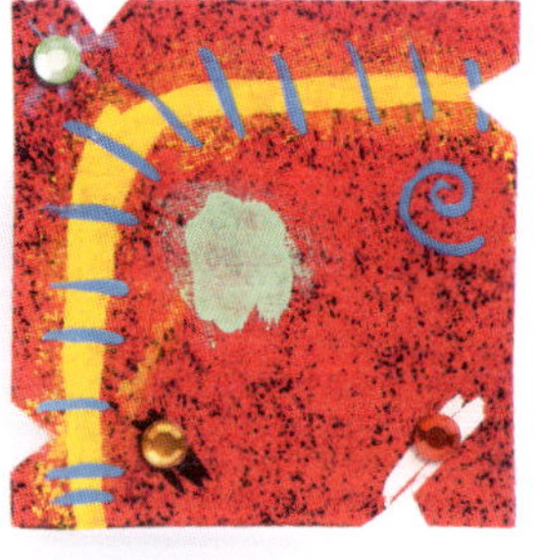

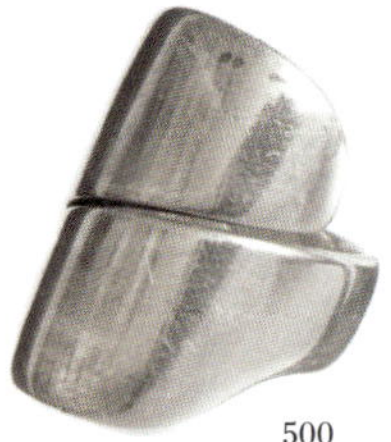

500

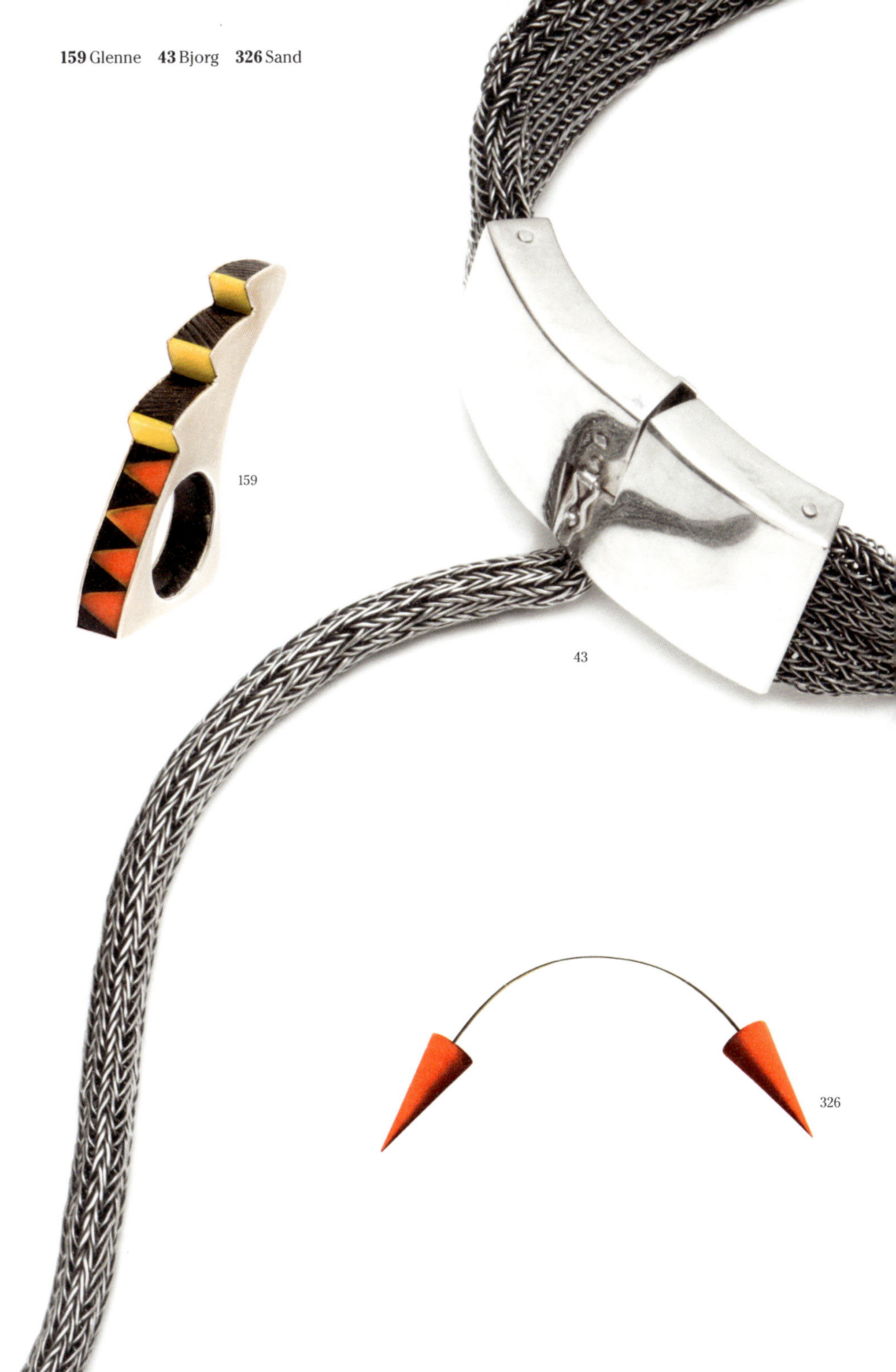

159

43

326

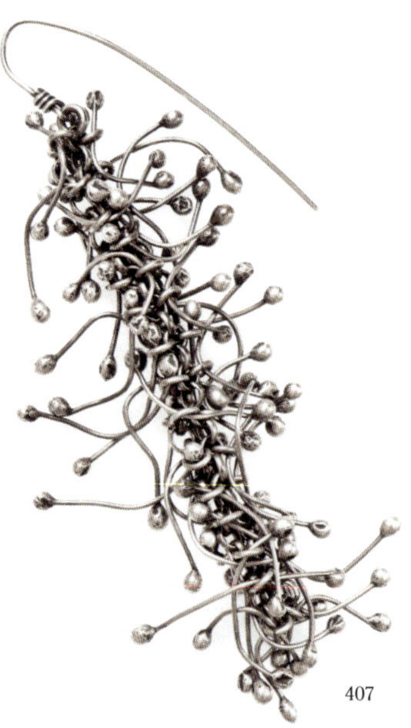

407

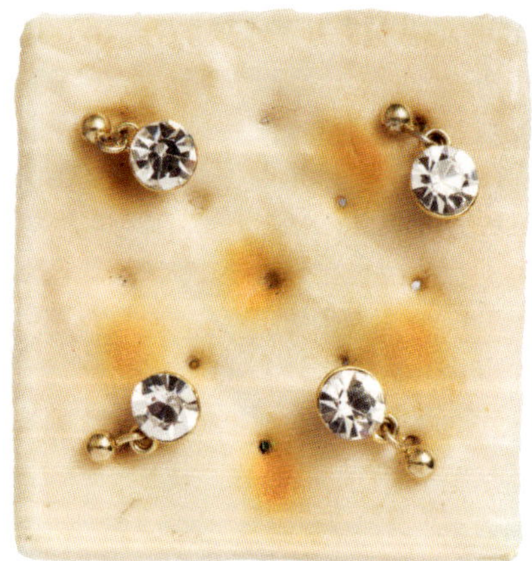

502

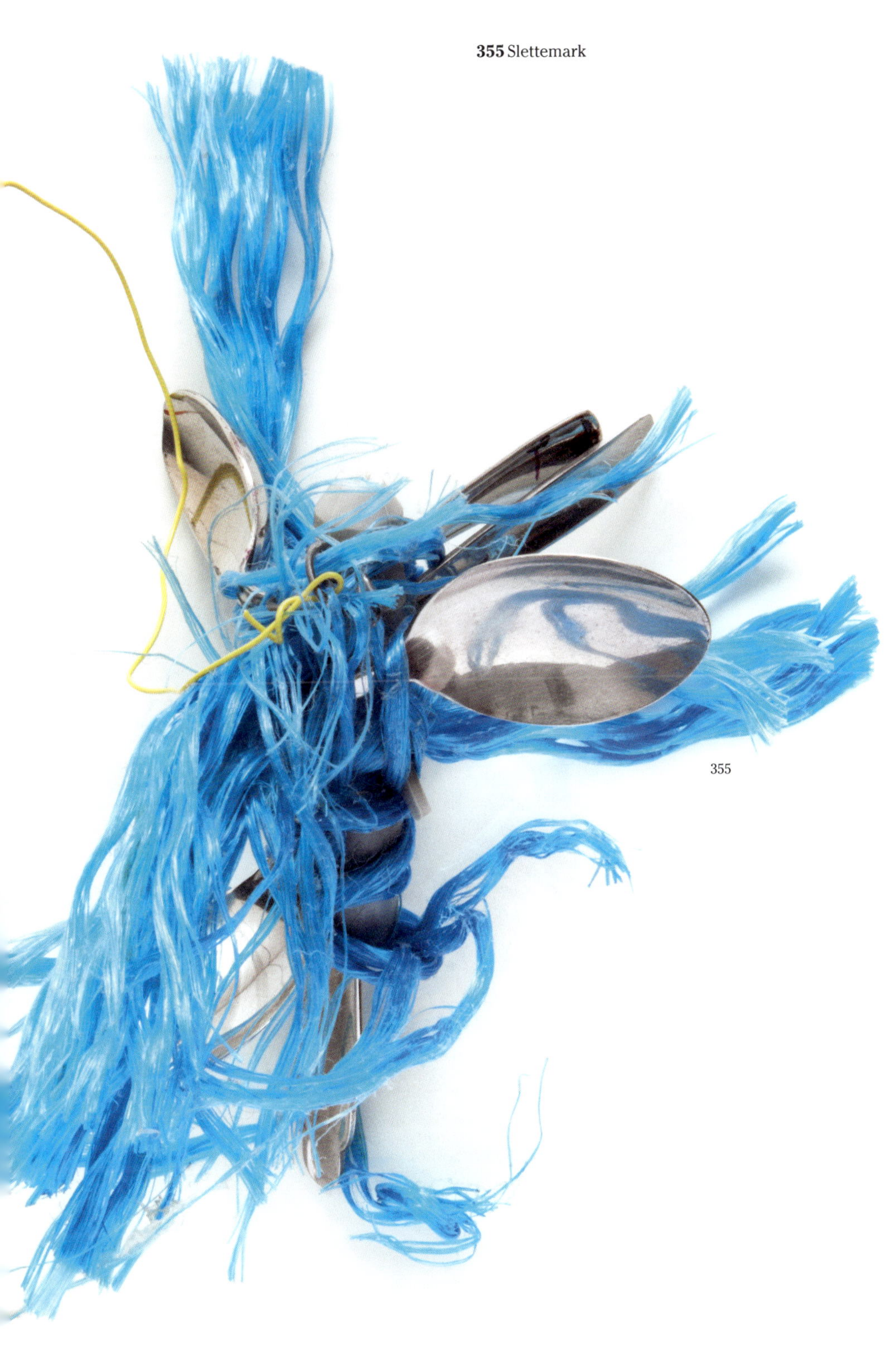

355

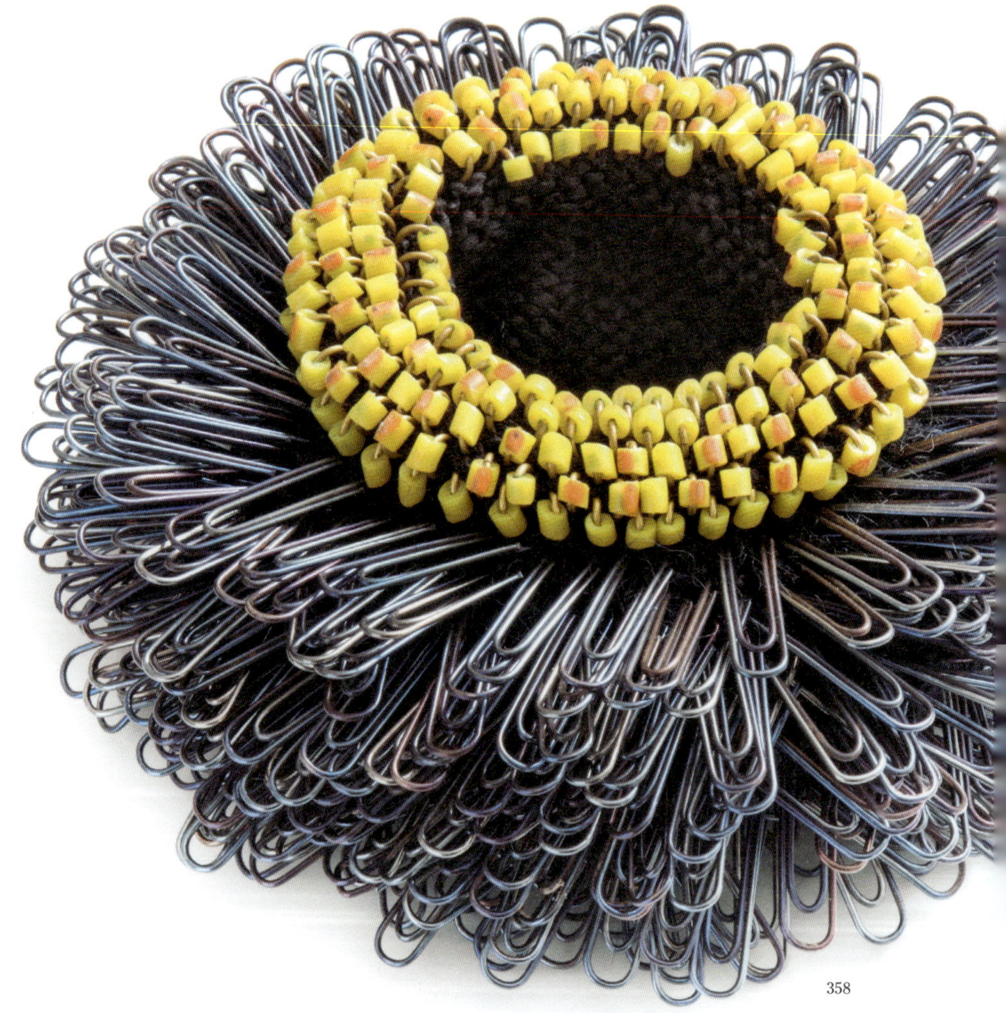

358

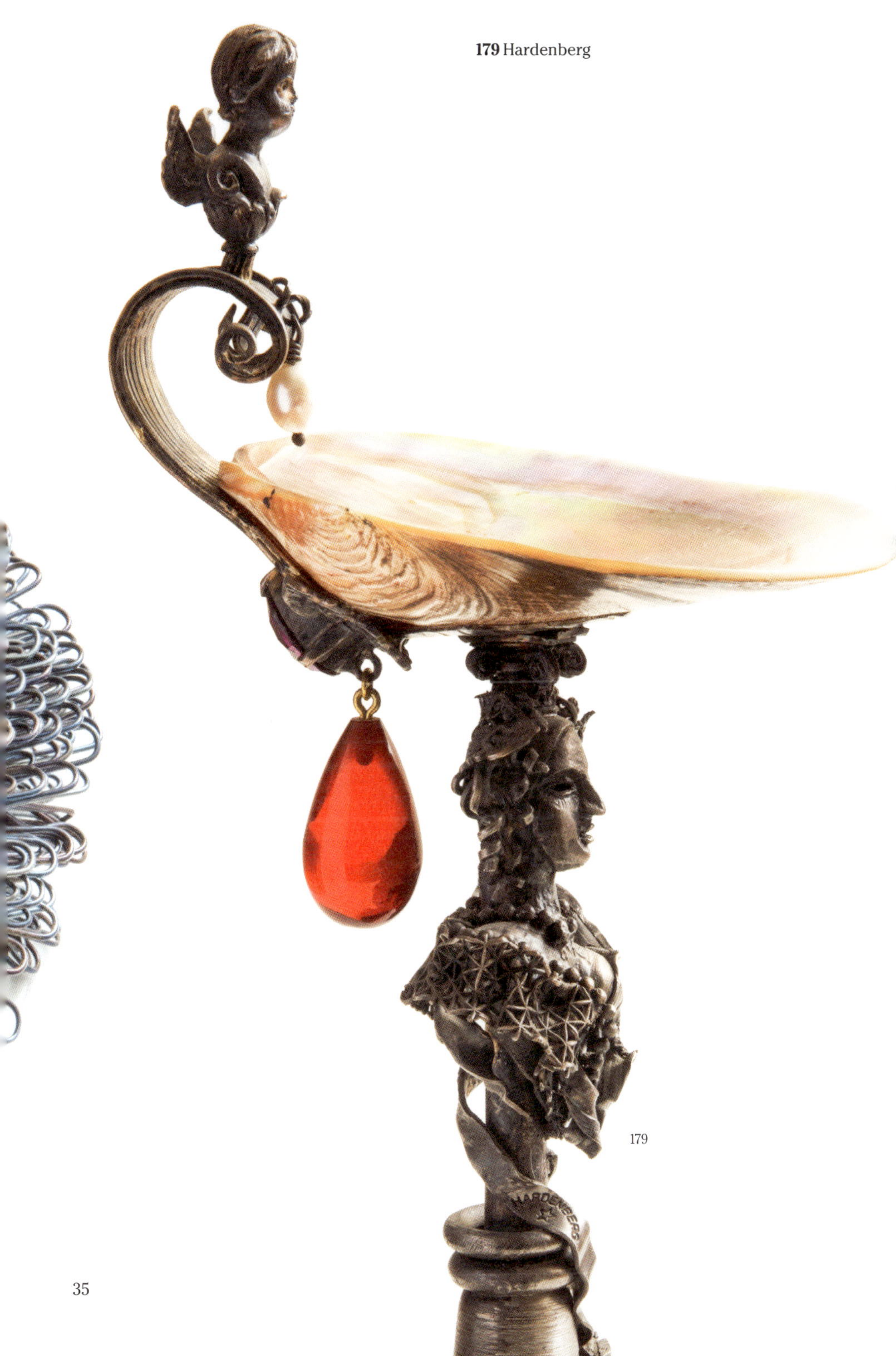

179

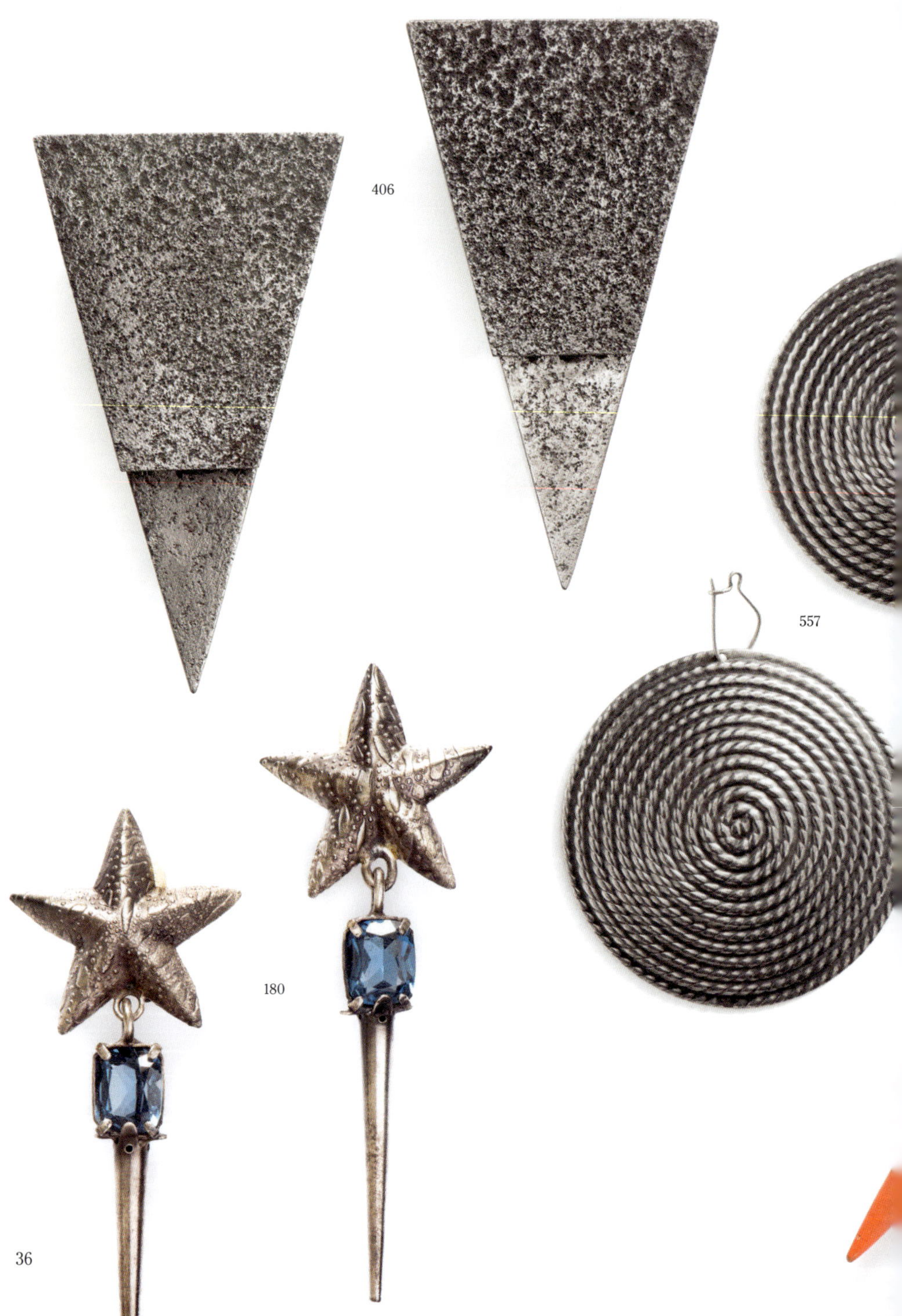
406
557
180

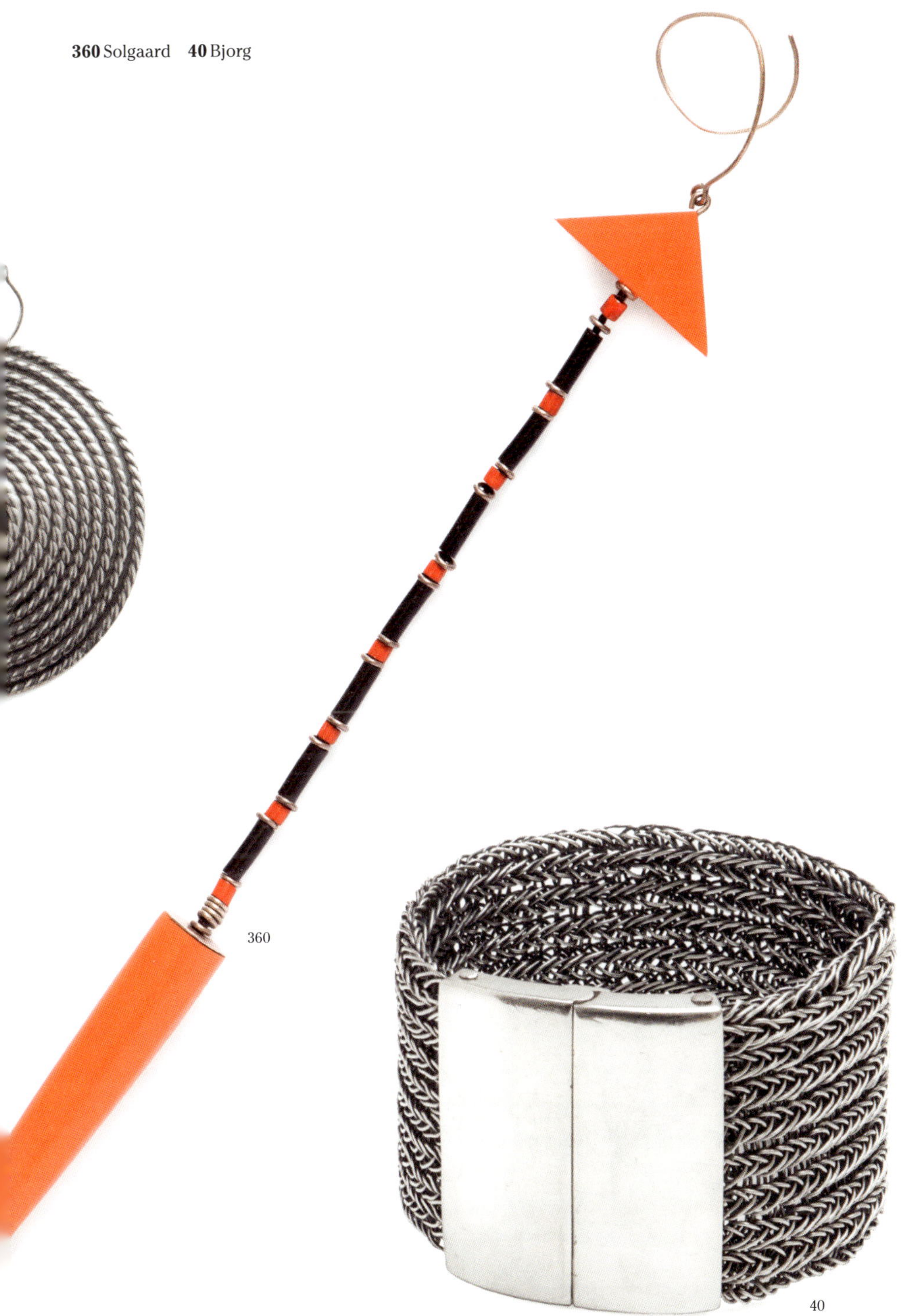

360

40

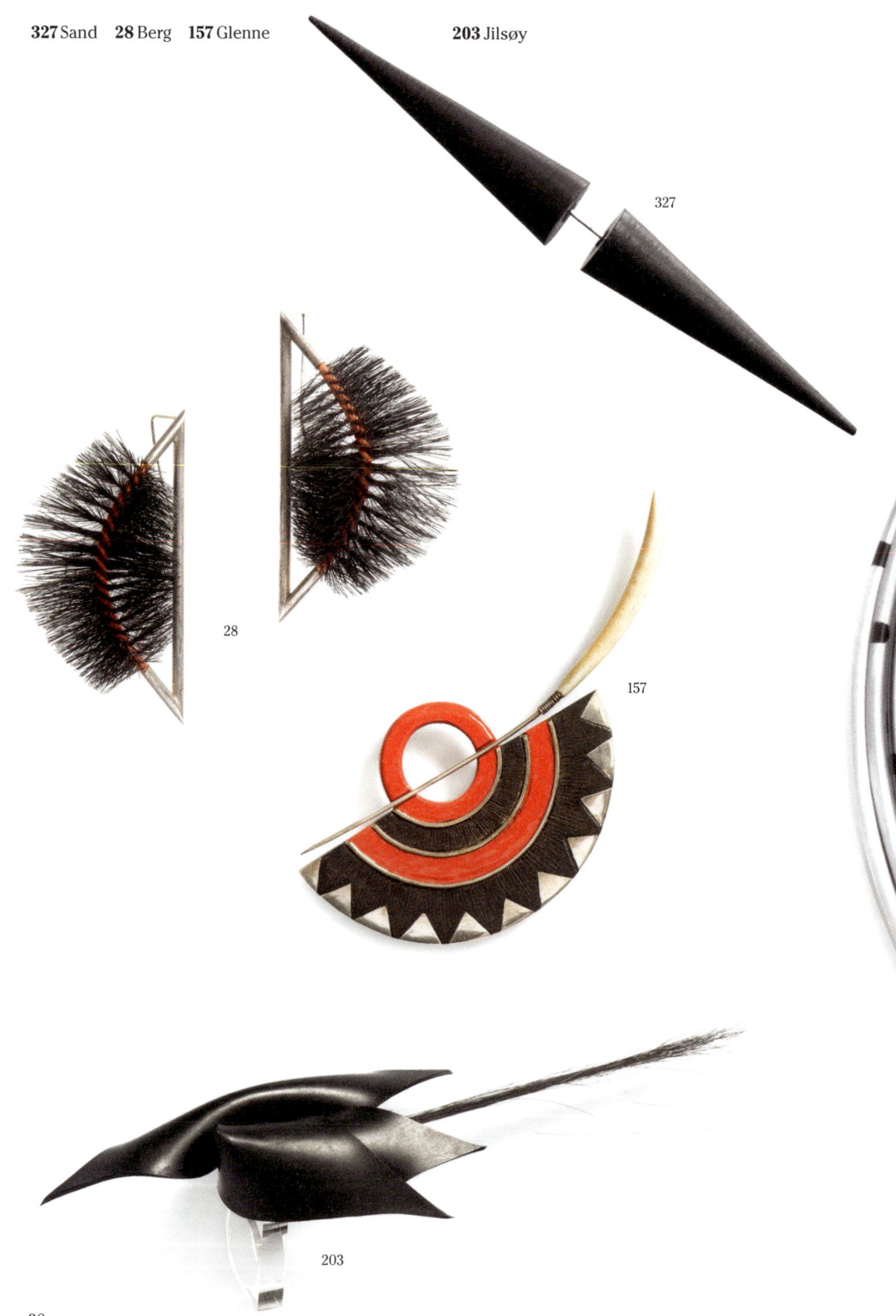

327
28
157
203

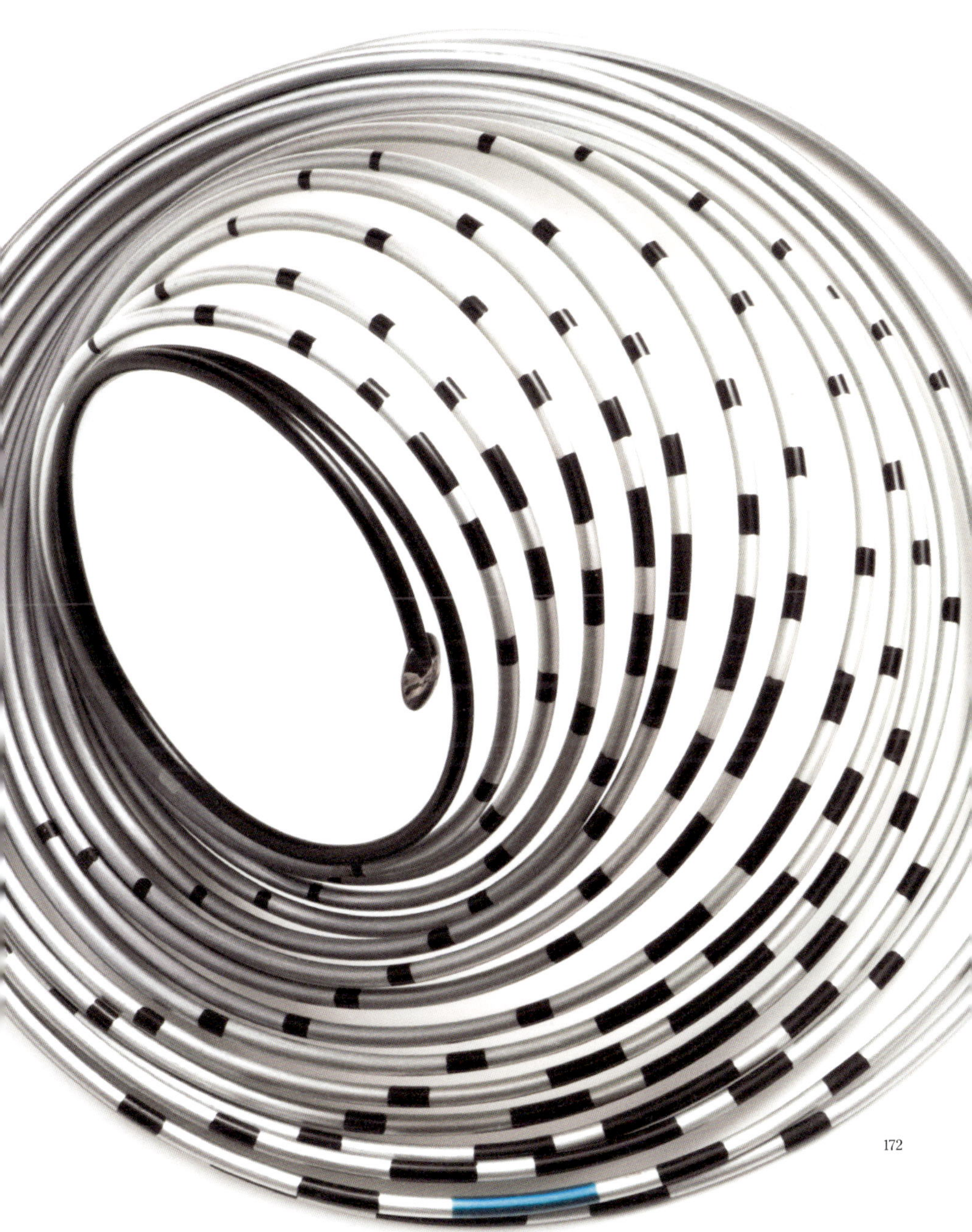

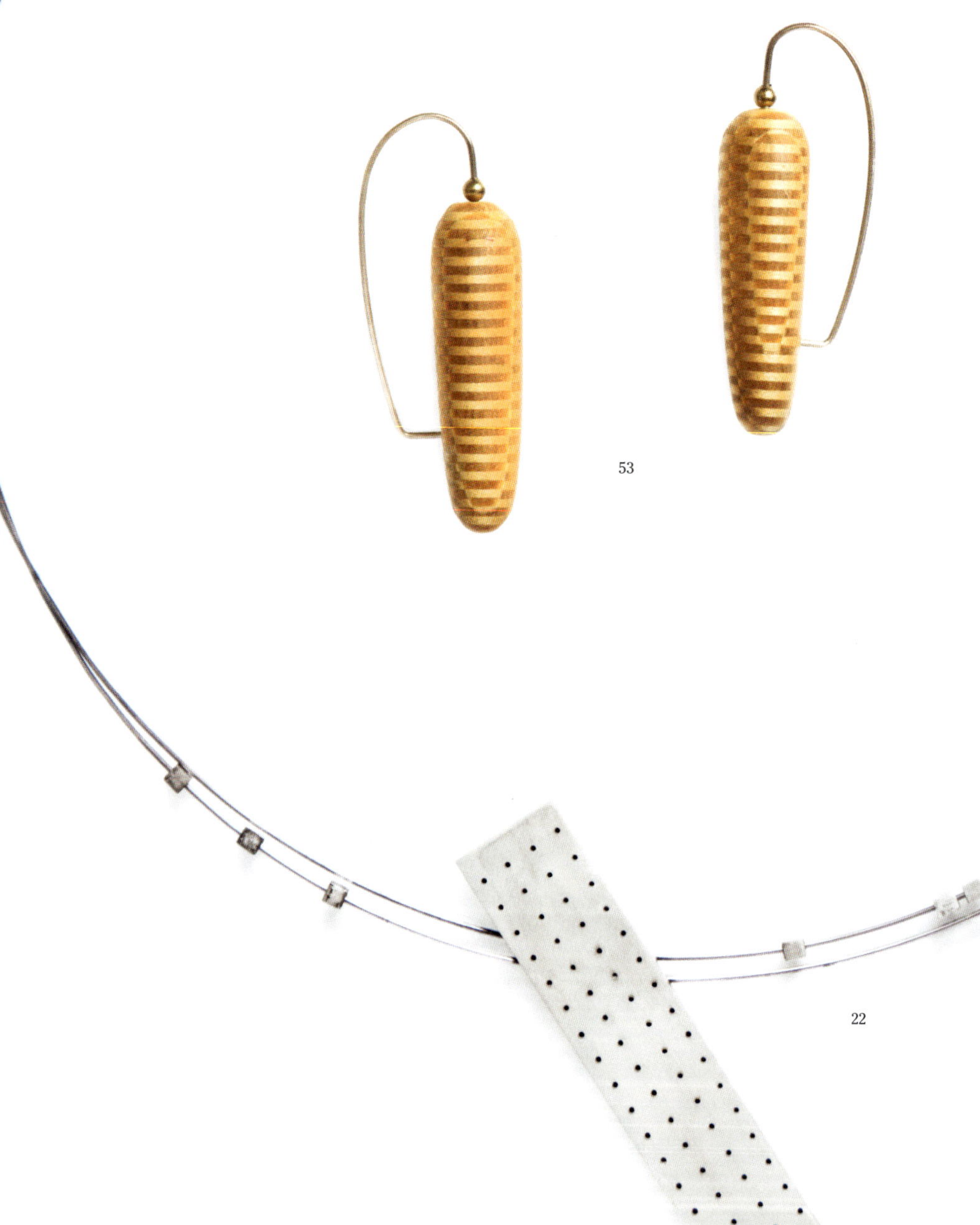

53

22

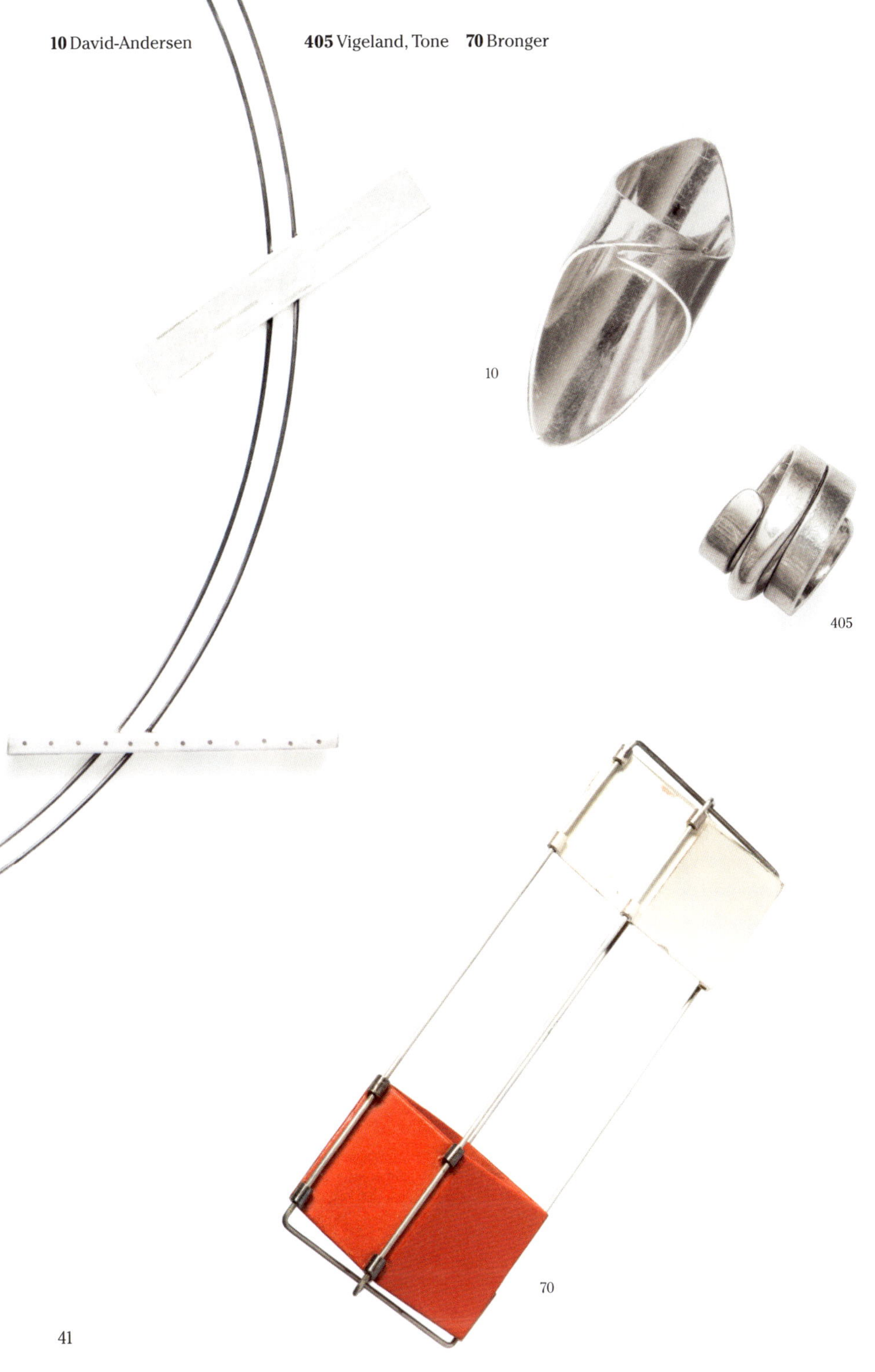

10

405

70

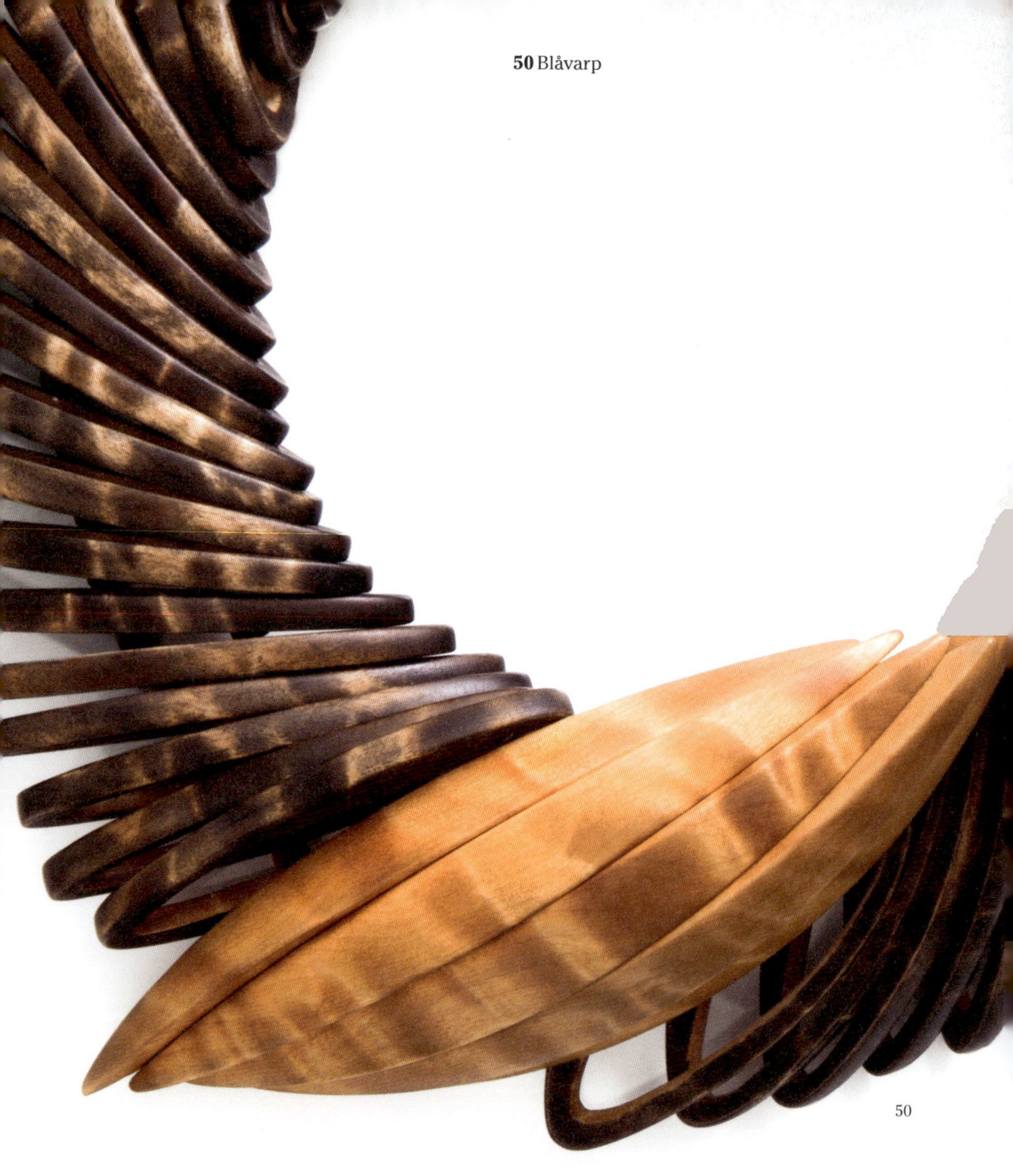

50

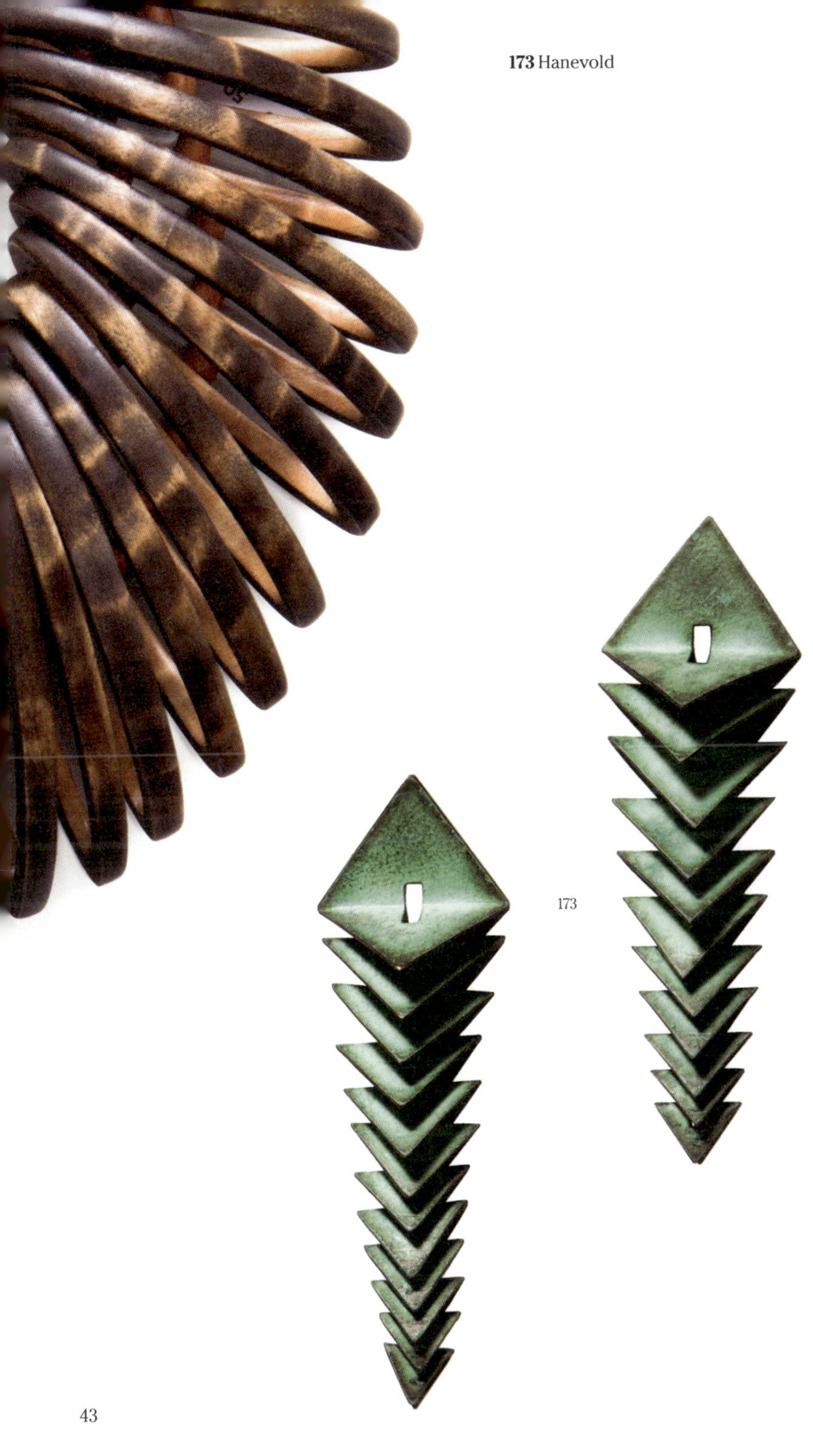

173

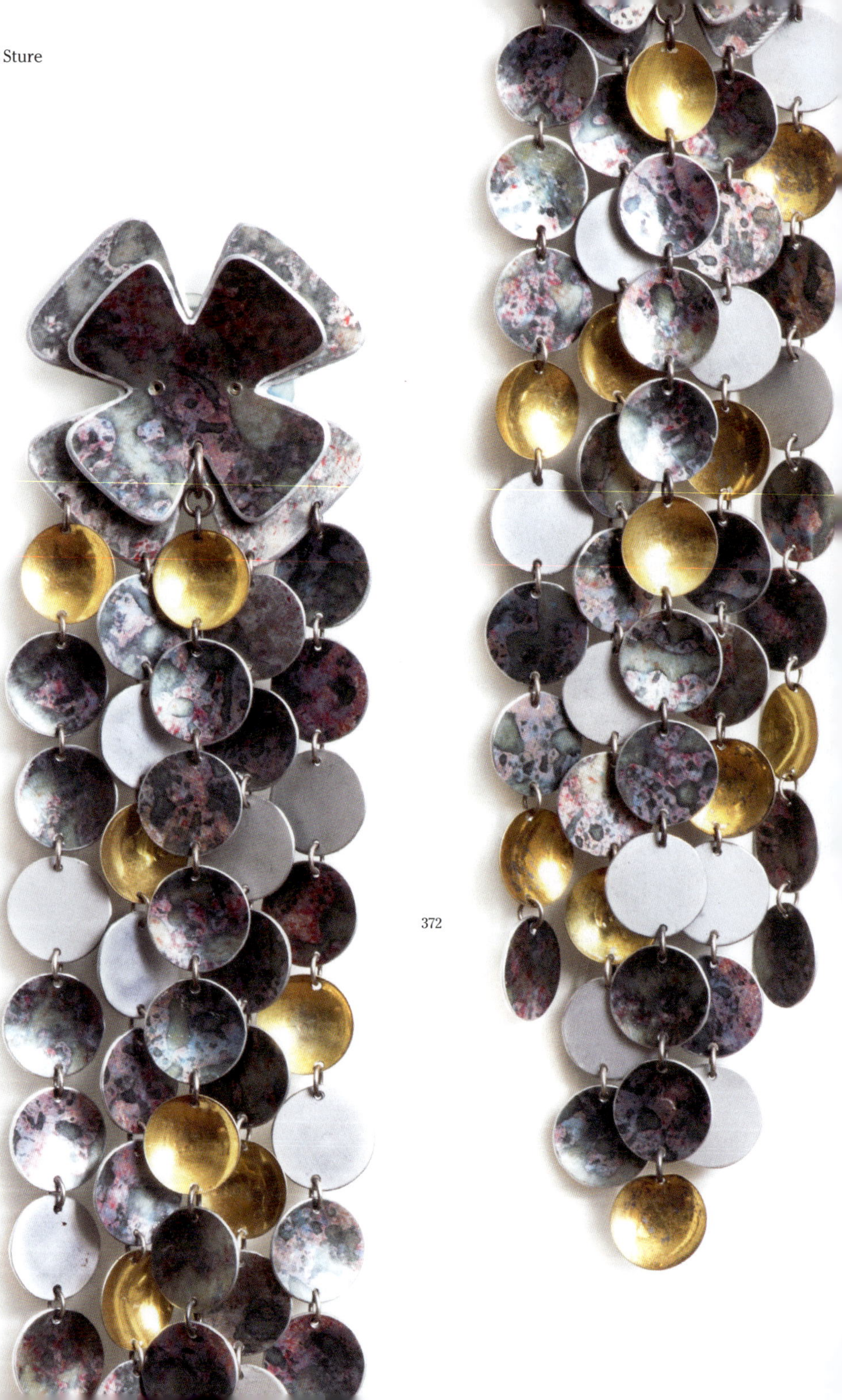

372

45

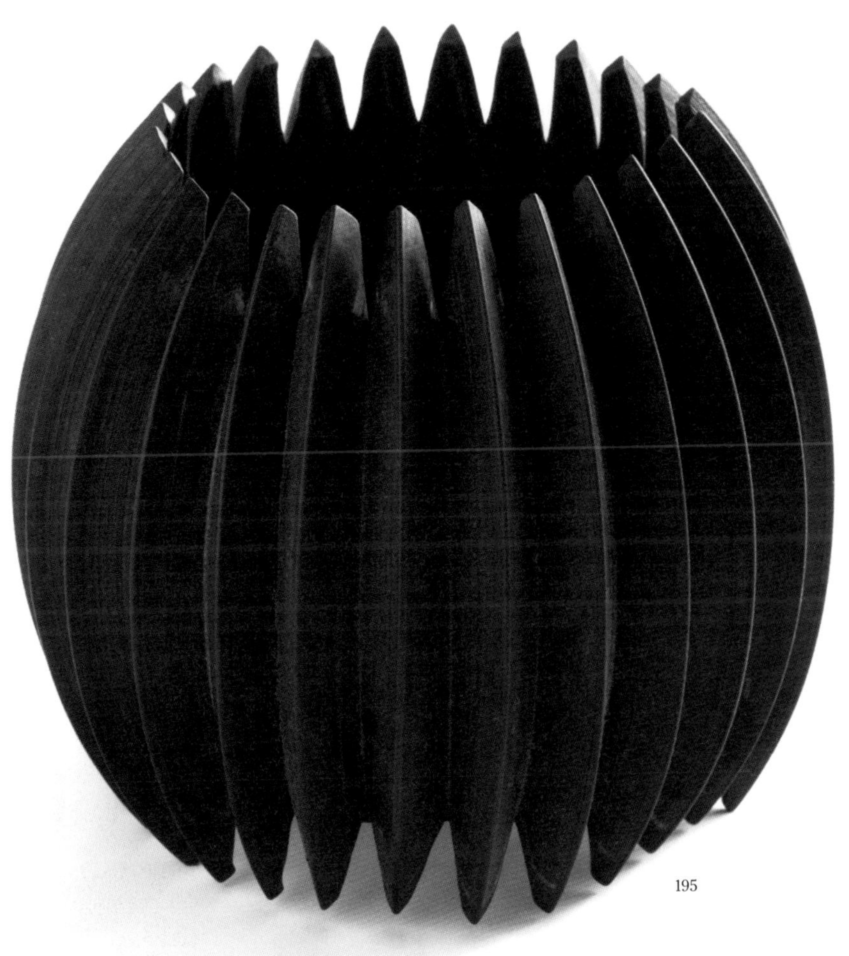

195

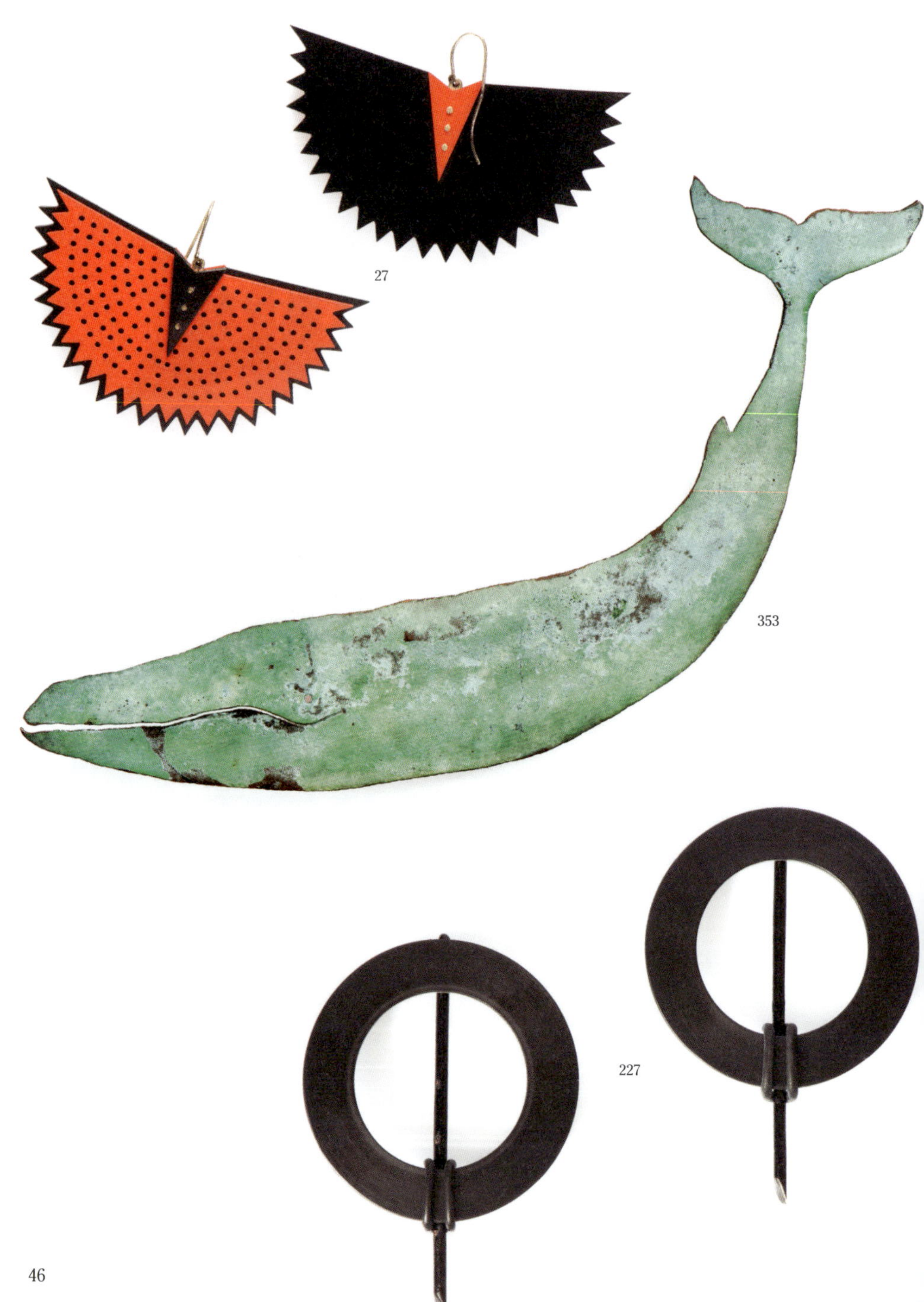
27
353
227

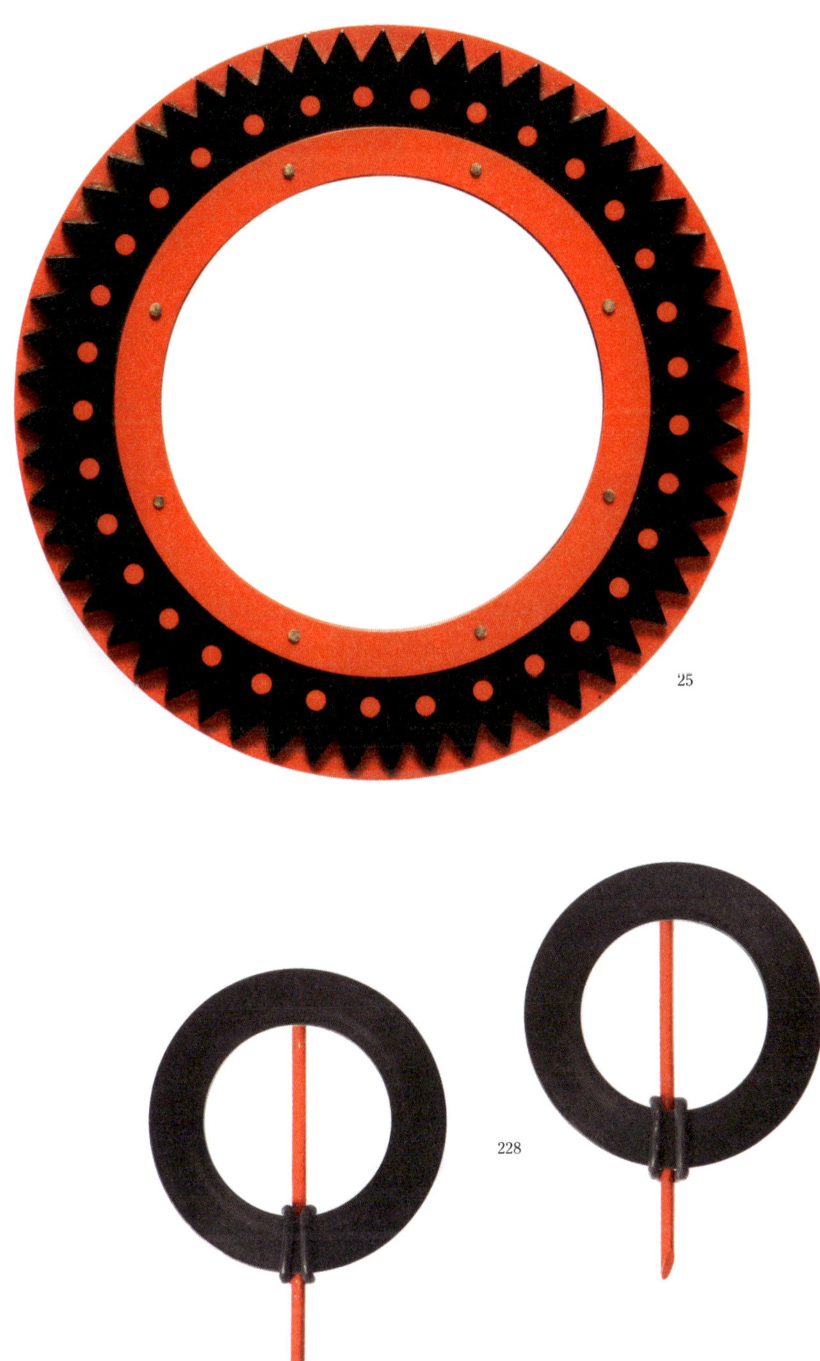

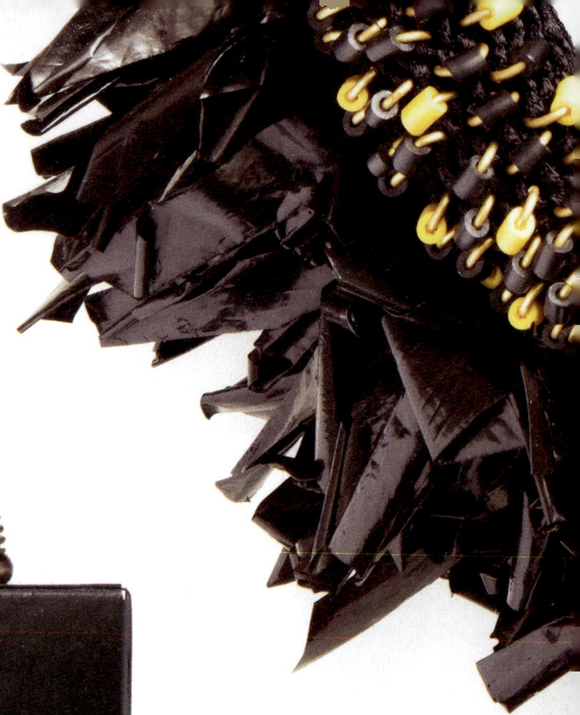

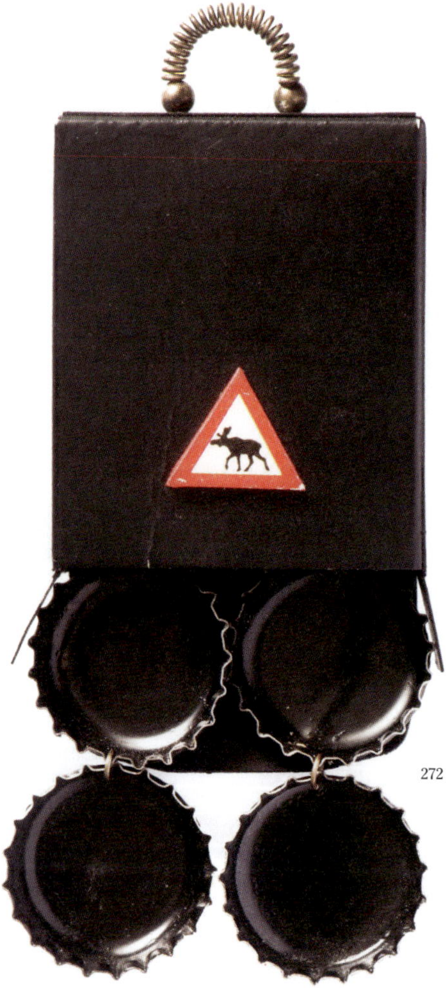

272

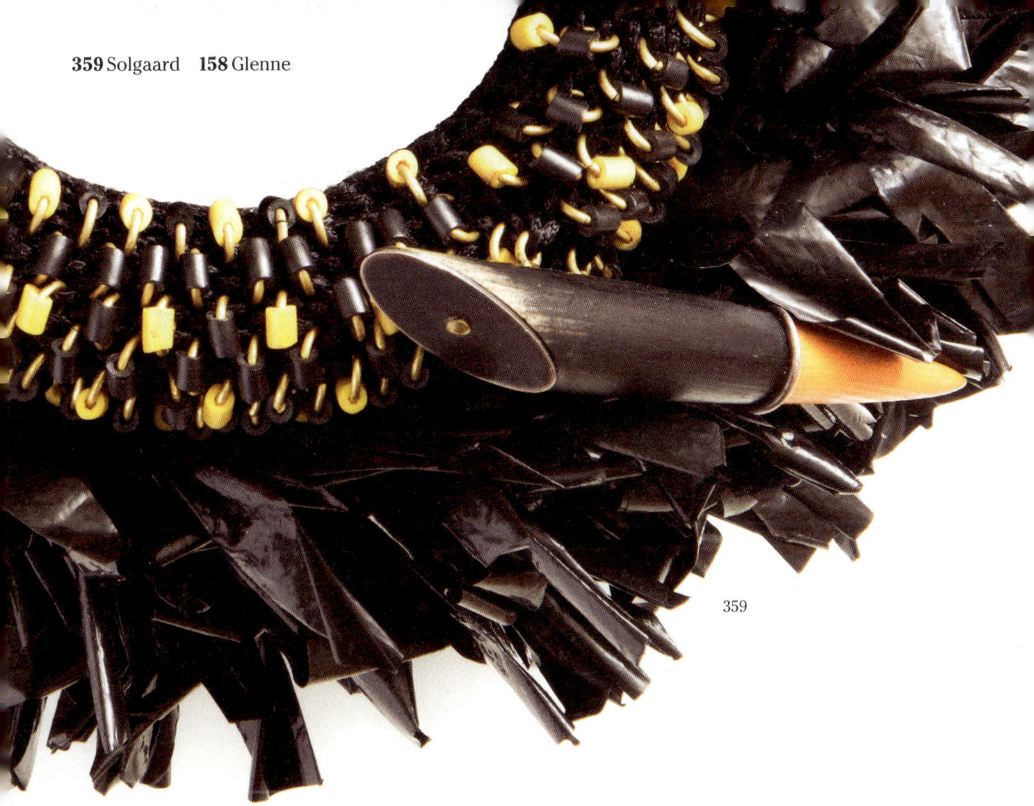

359

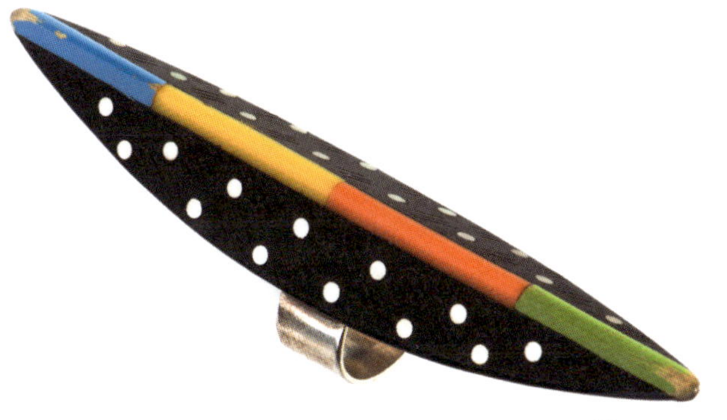

158

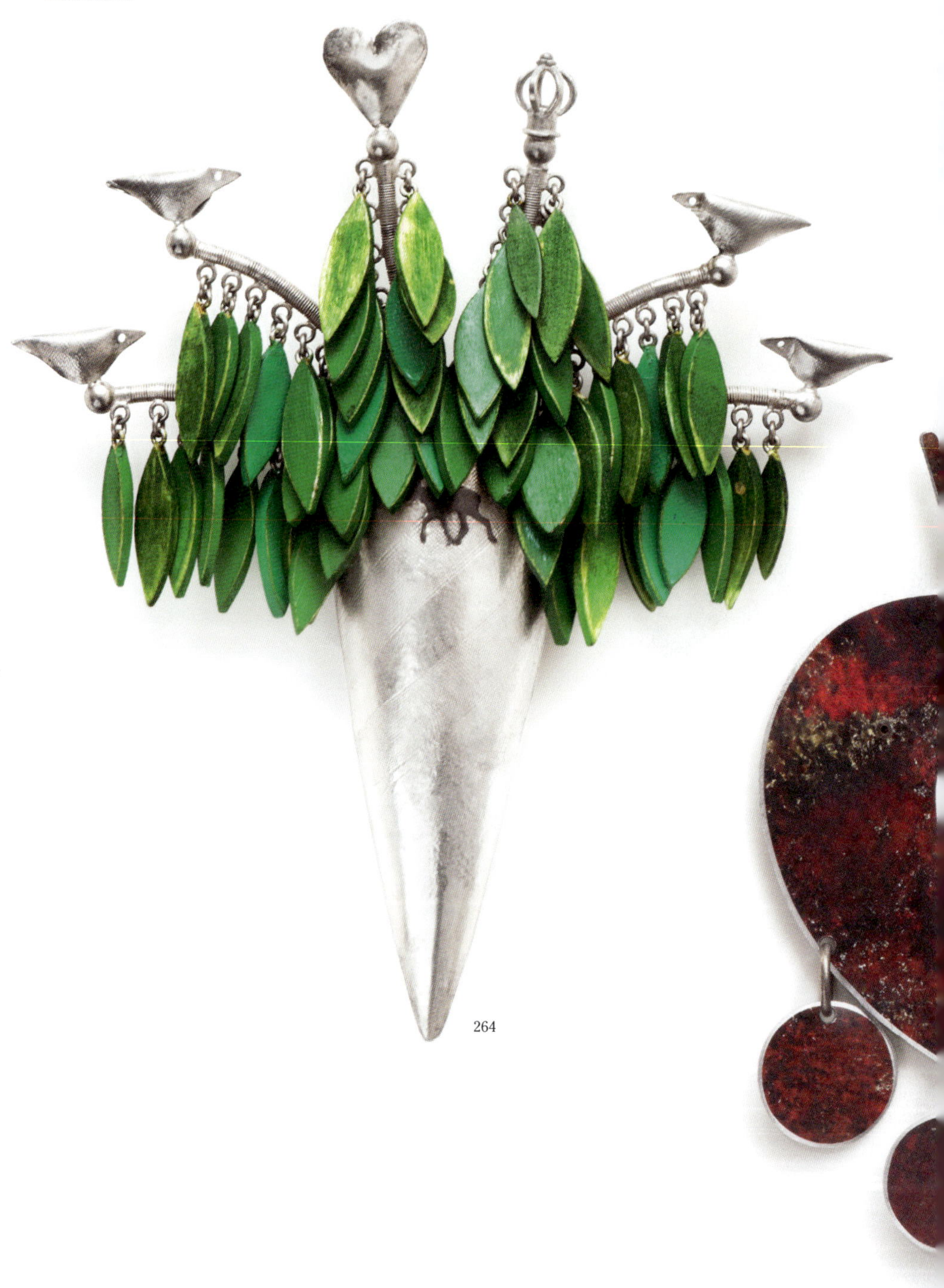

264

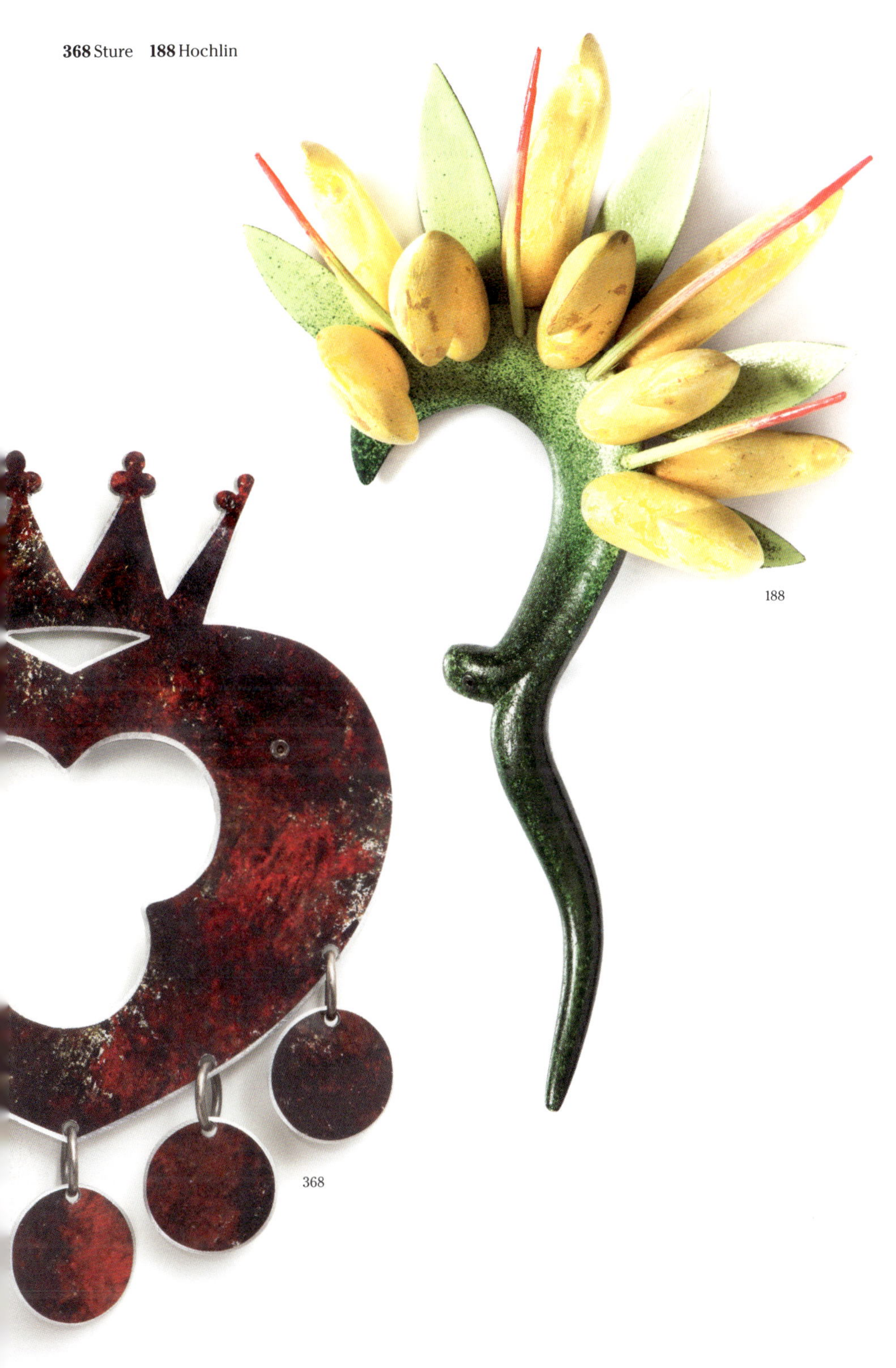

188

368

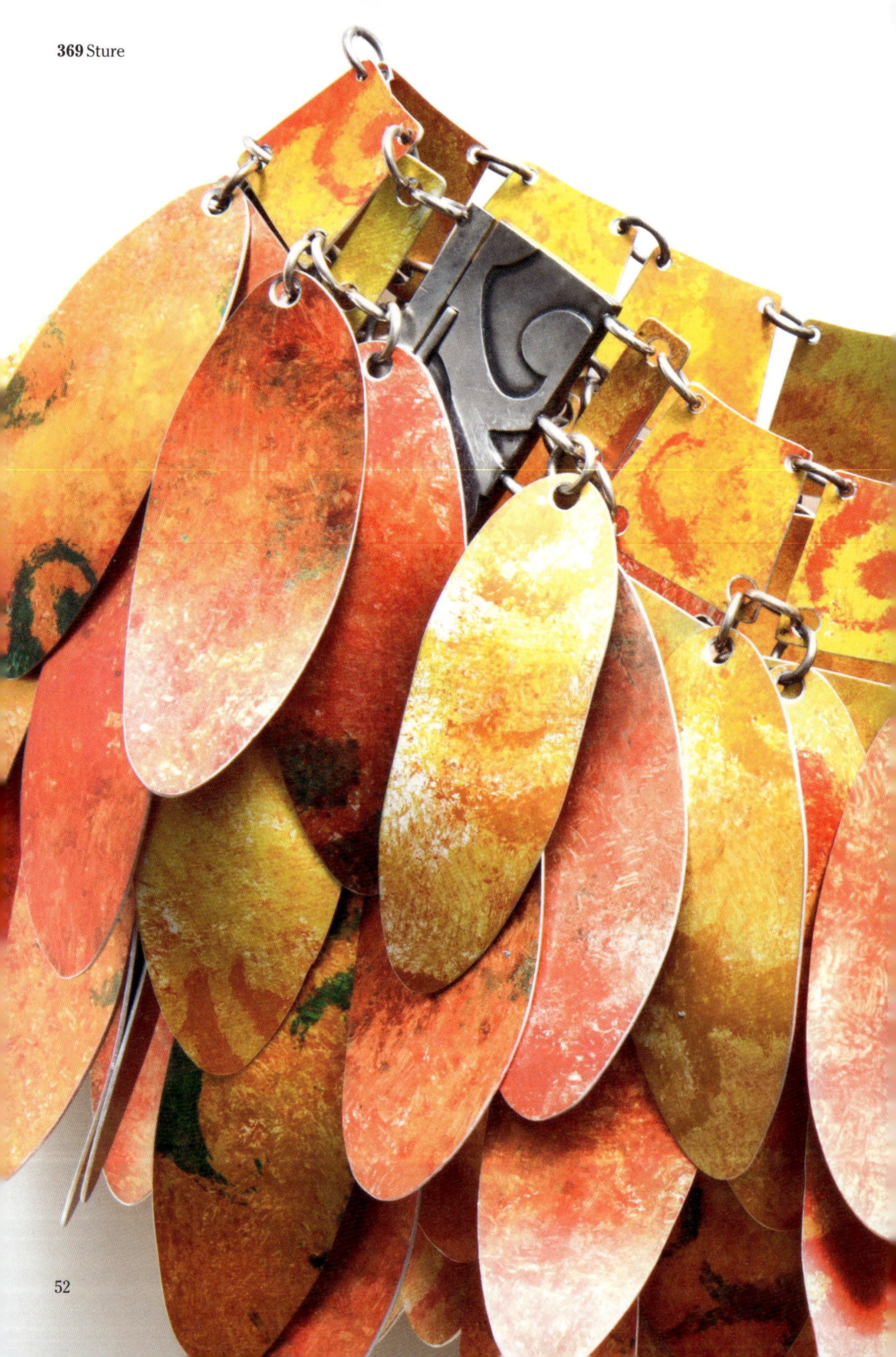

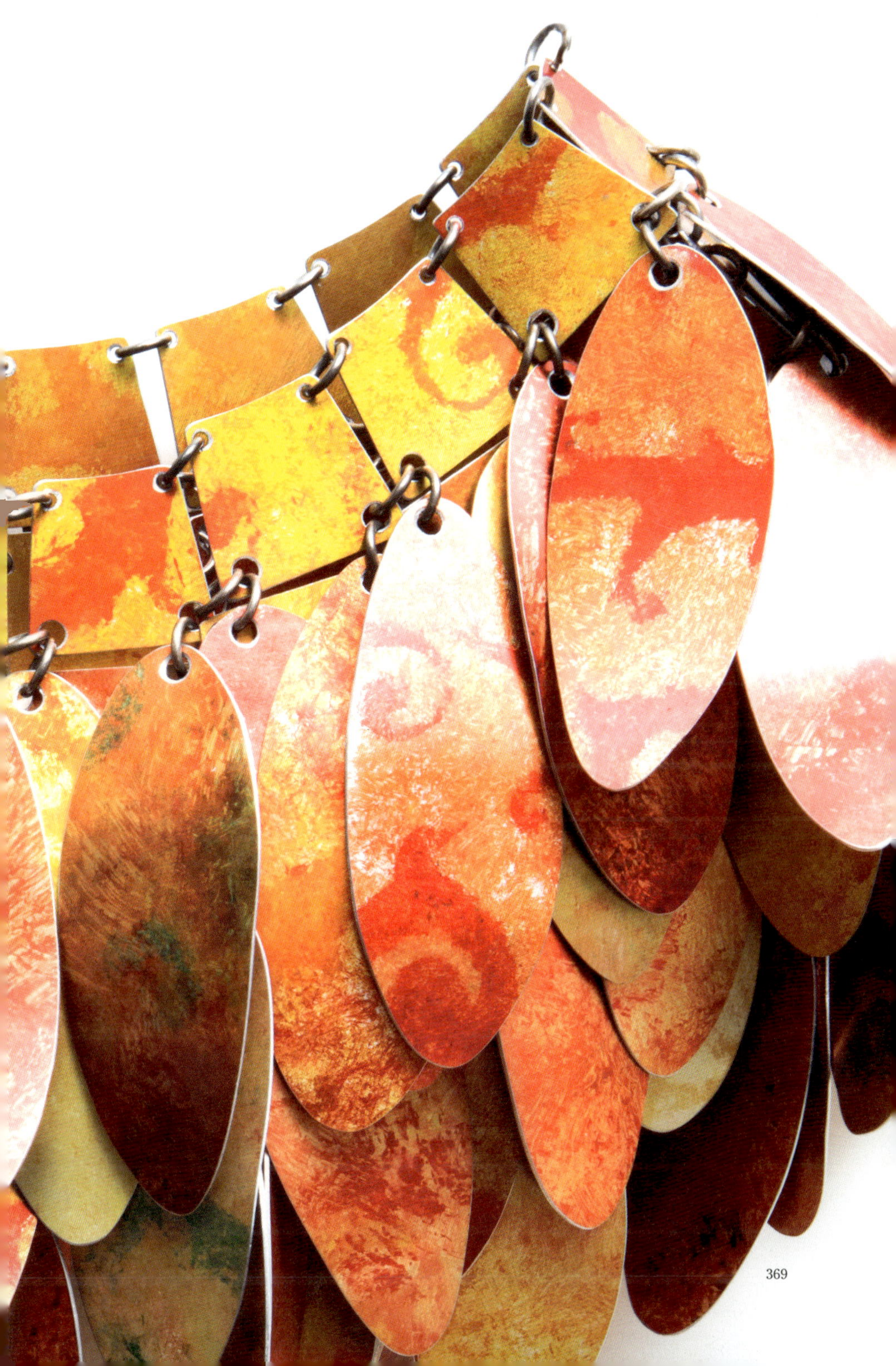

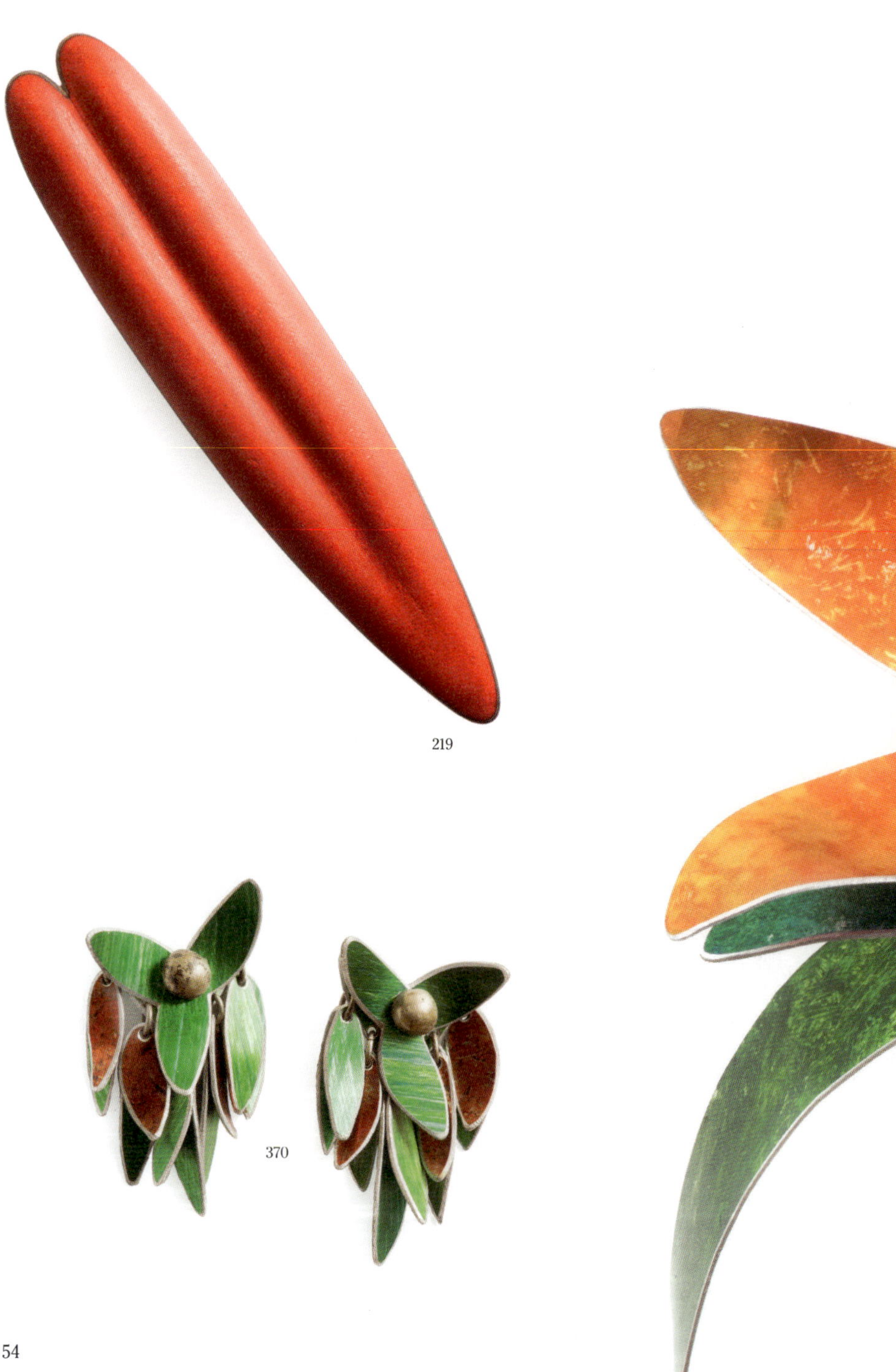

219

370

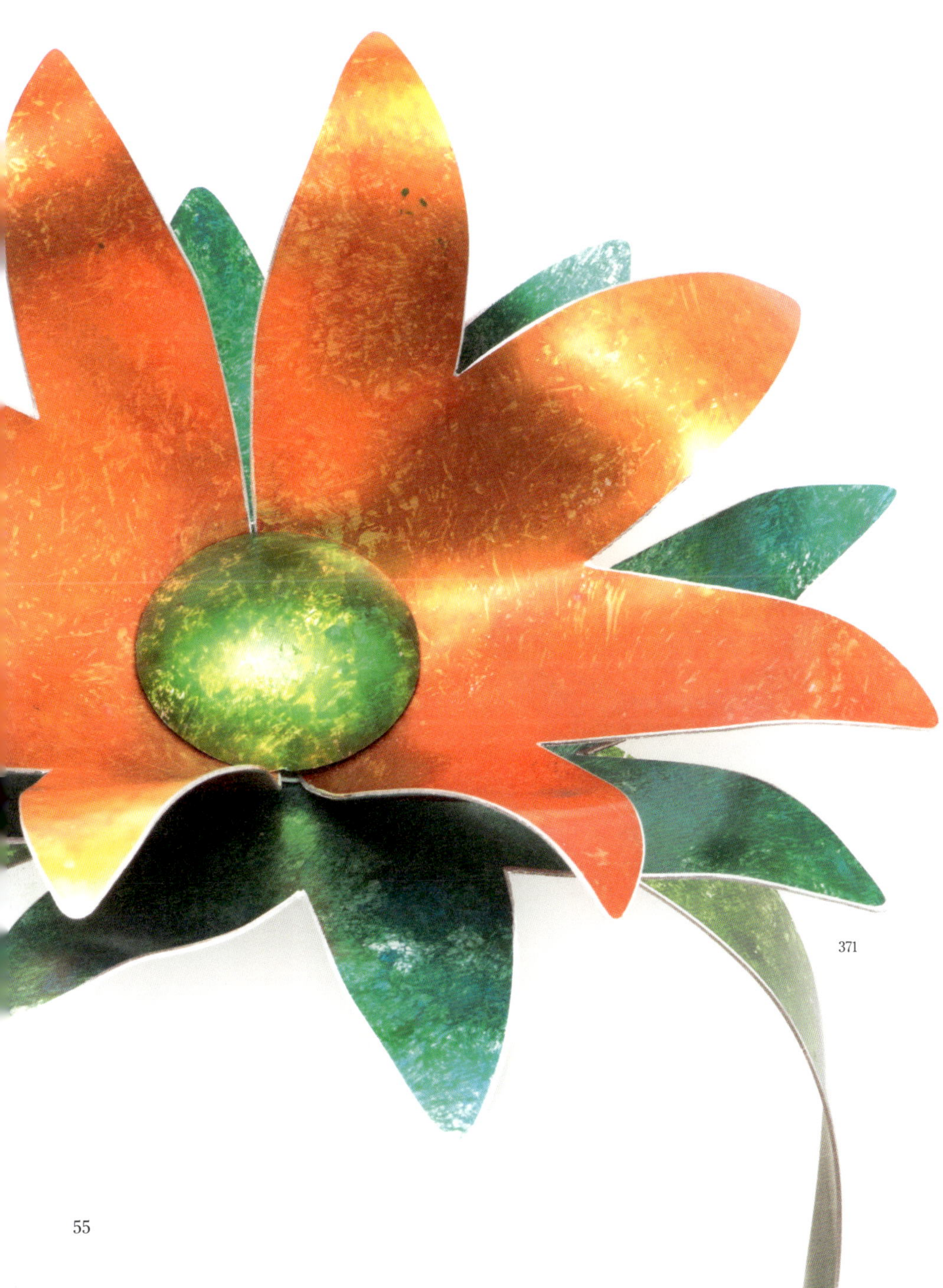

371

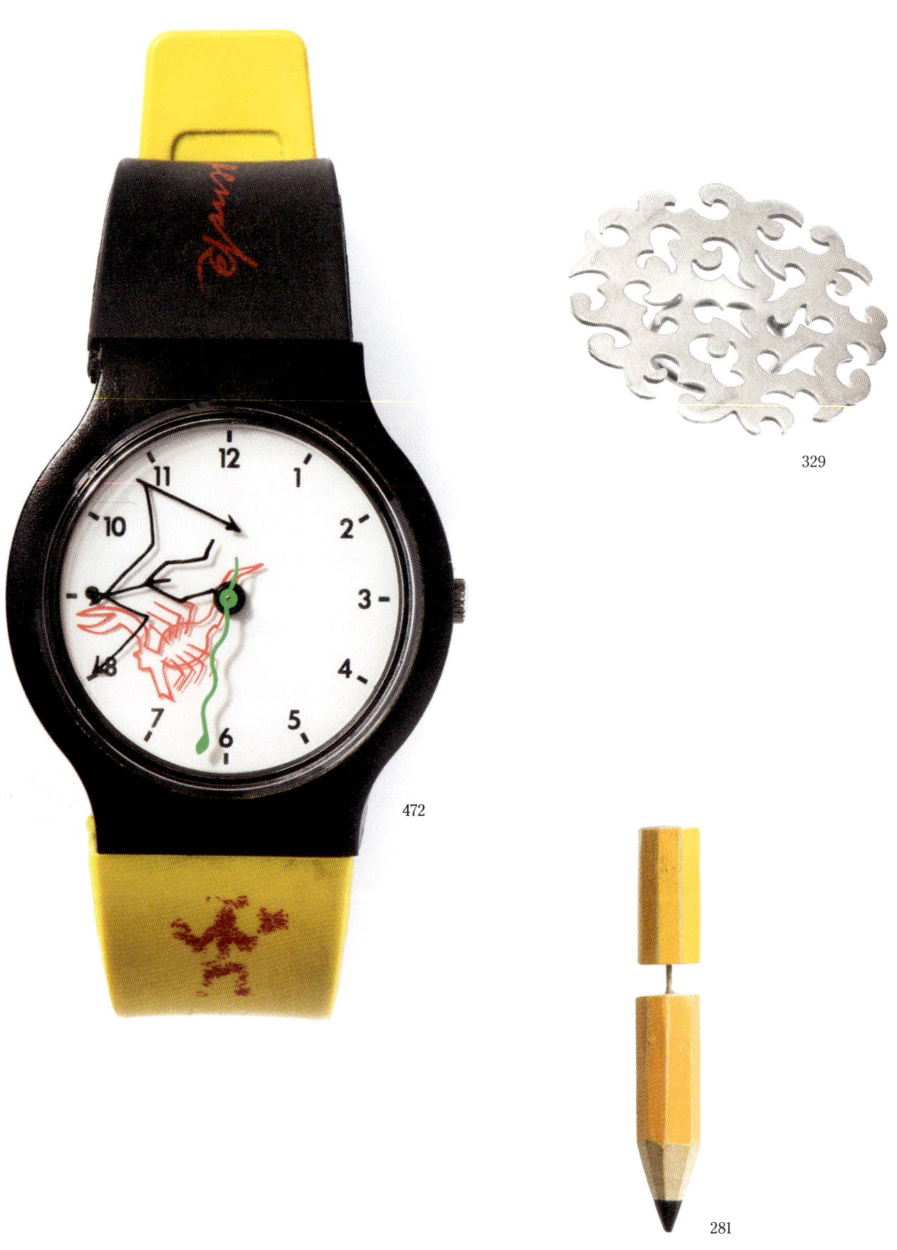

472

329

281

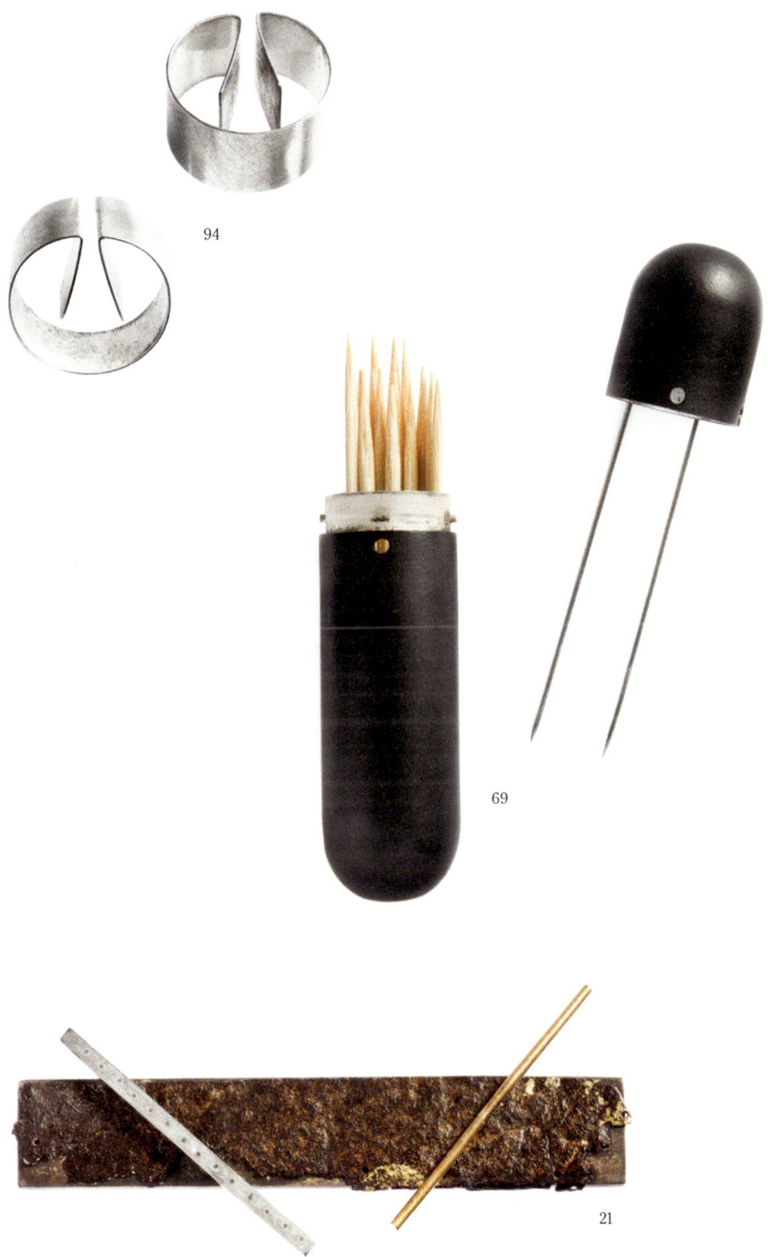

94

69

21

202 Ukjent/Unknown   **393** Vallejo

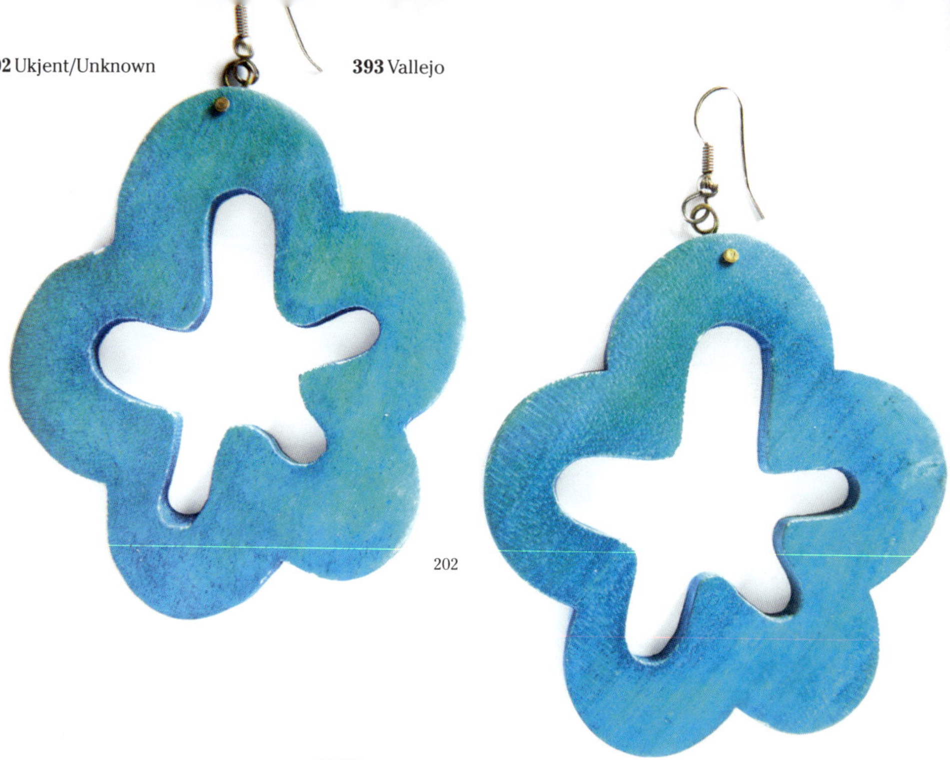

202

393

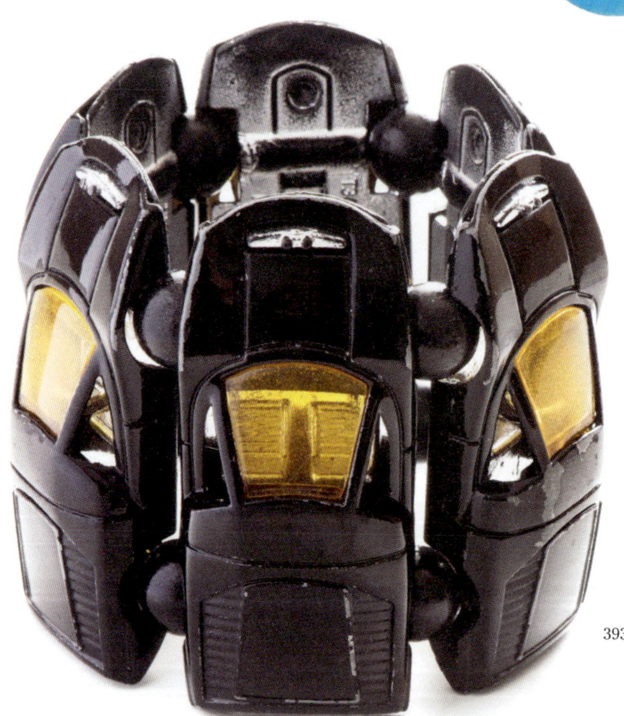

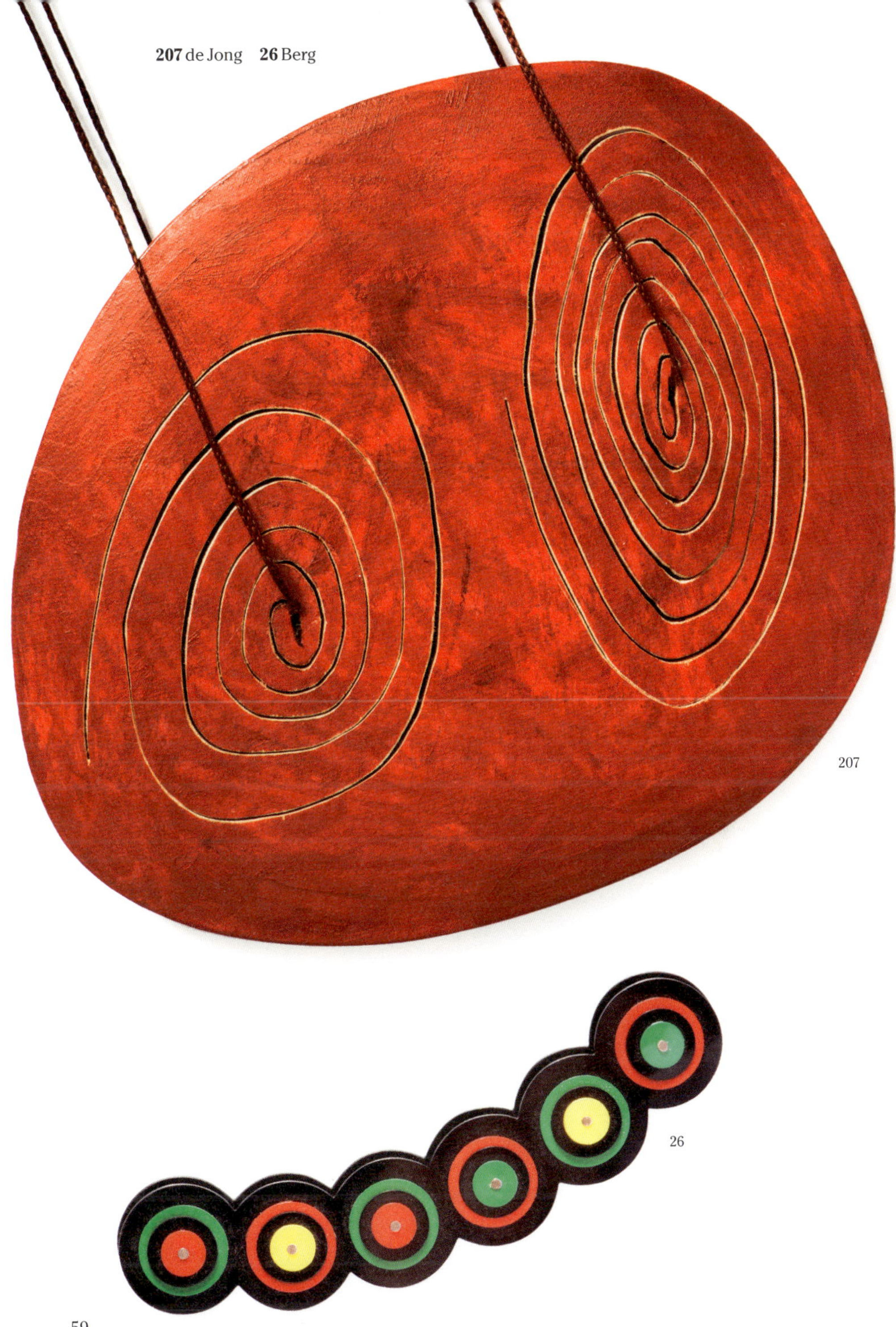

207 de Jong   26 Berg
207
26

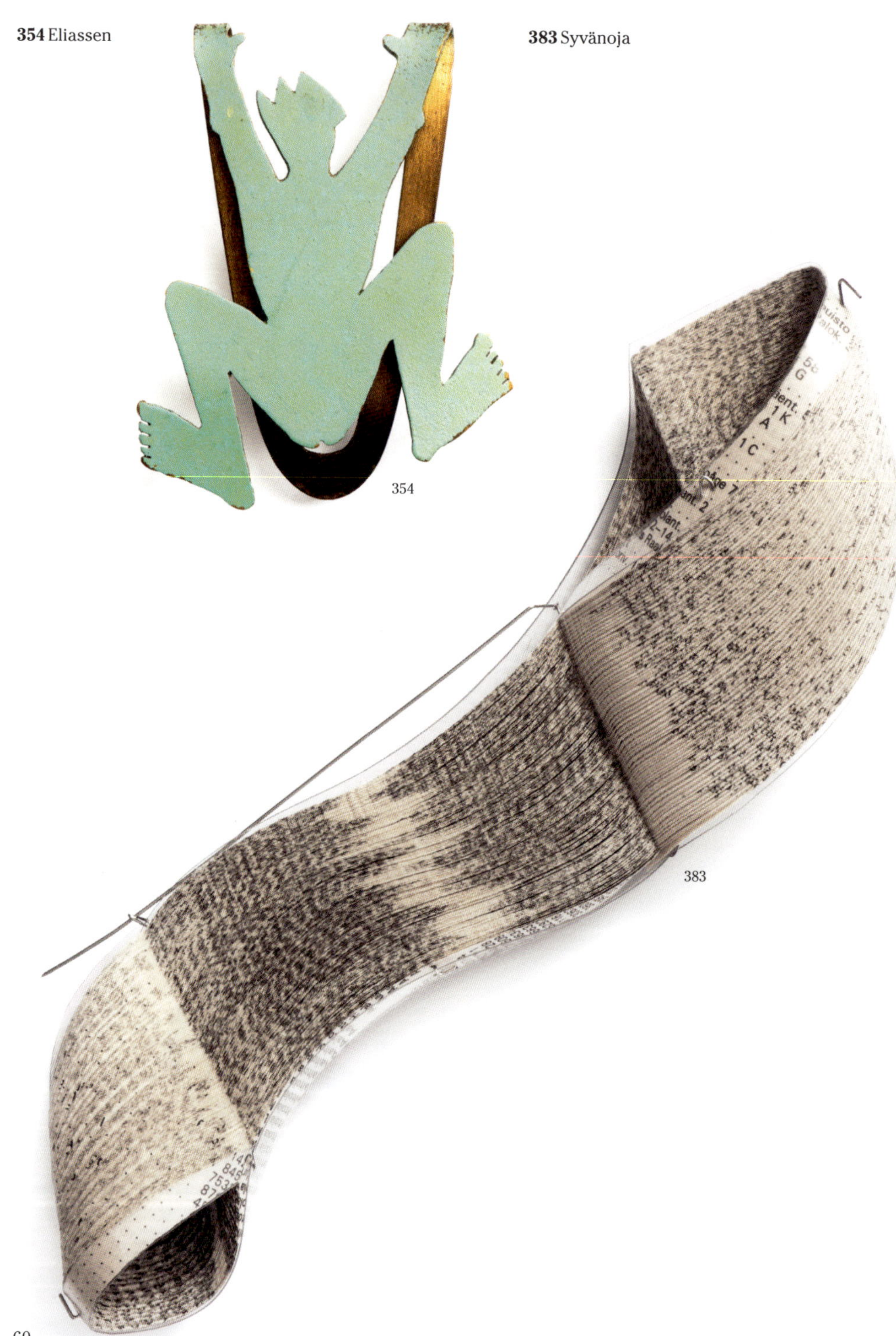

354

383

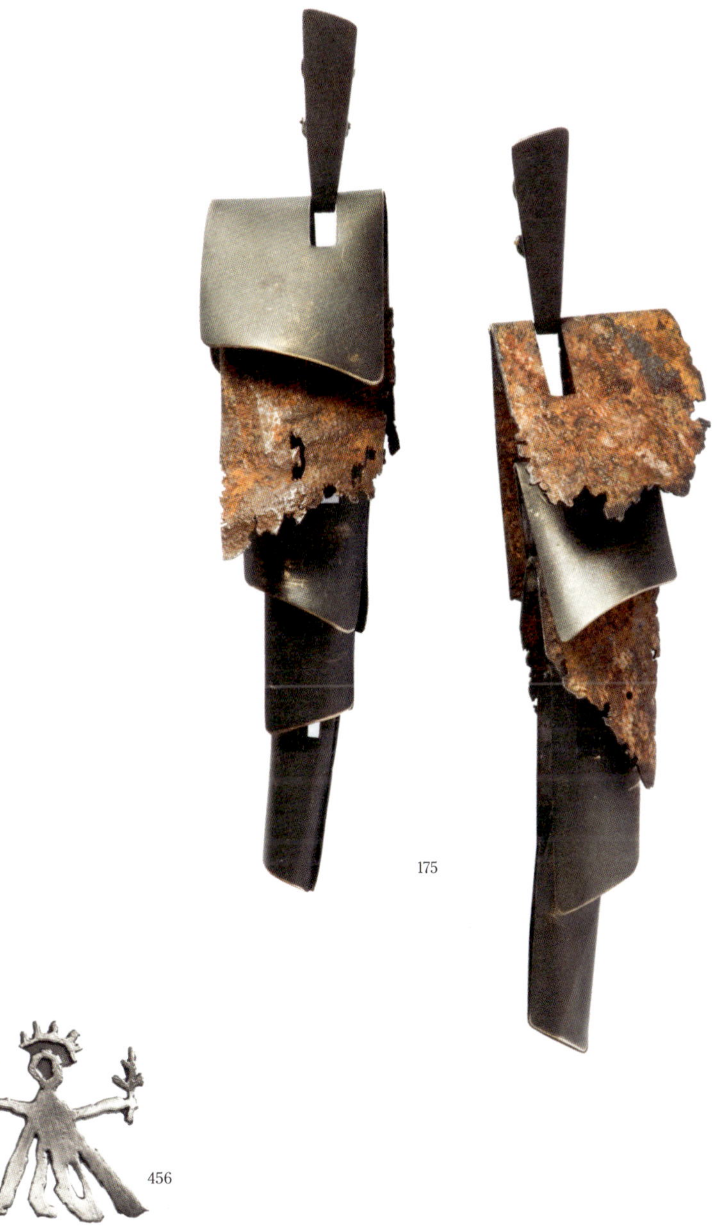

175

456

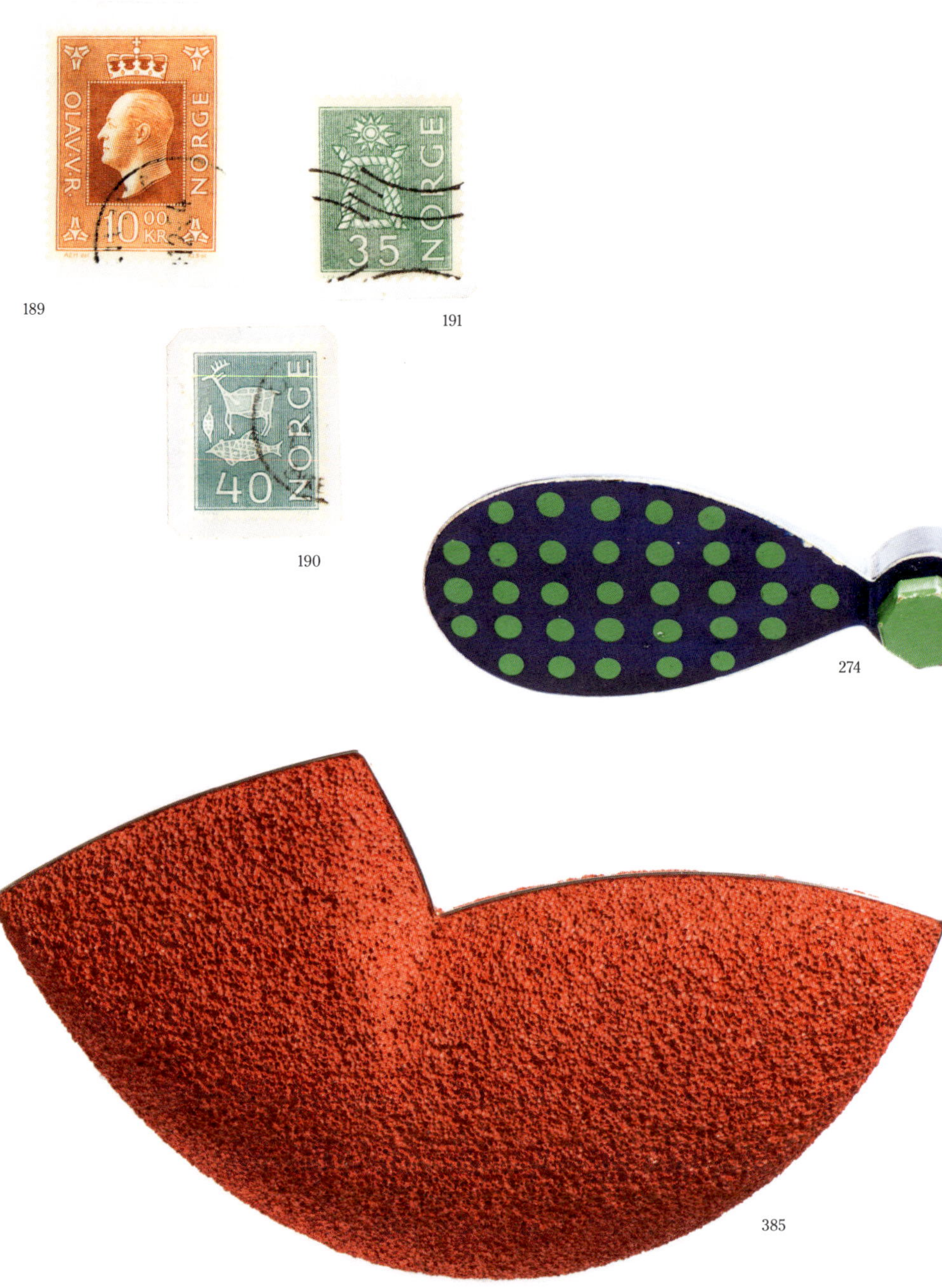

189

191

190

274

385

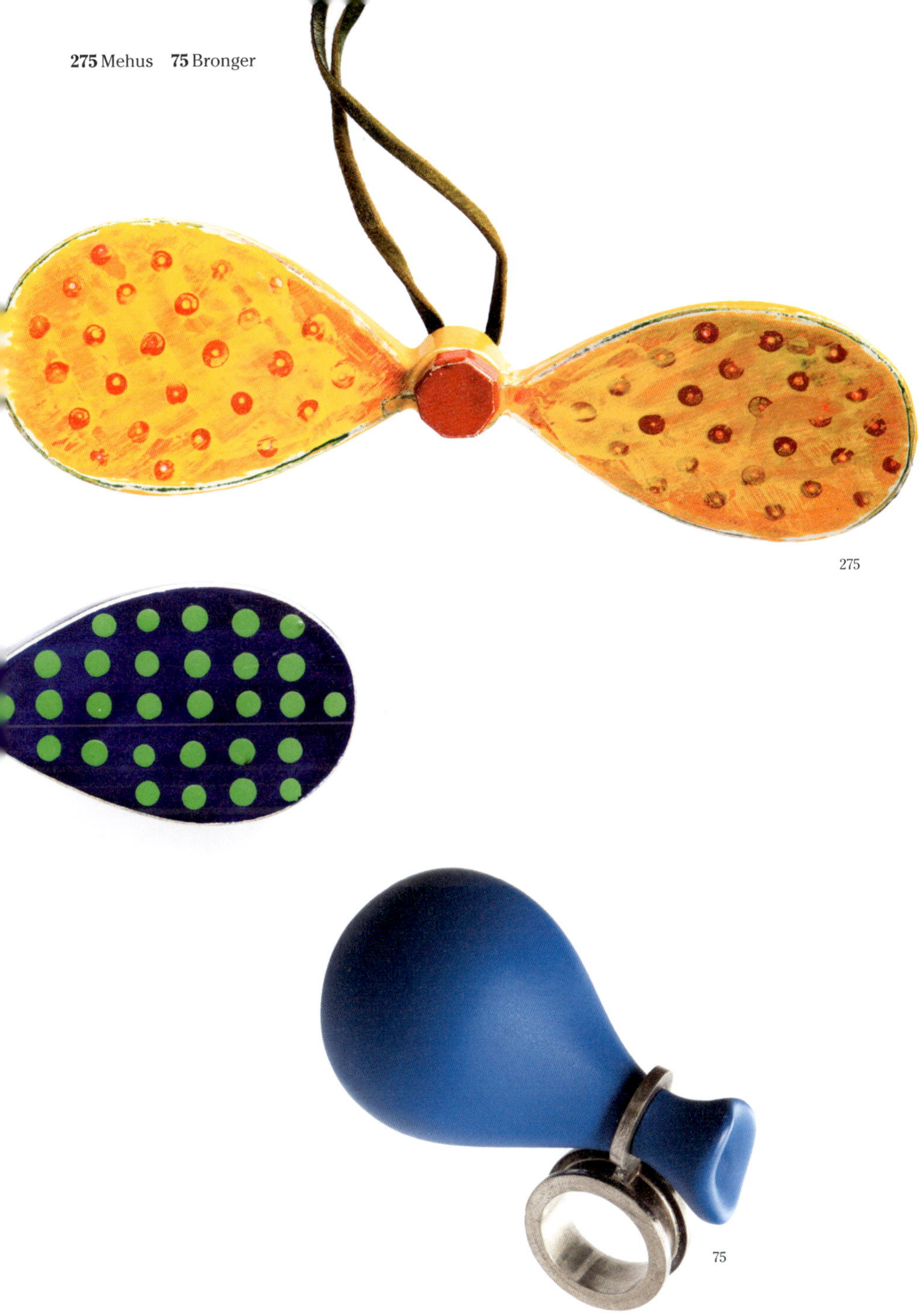

275

75

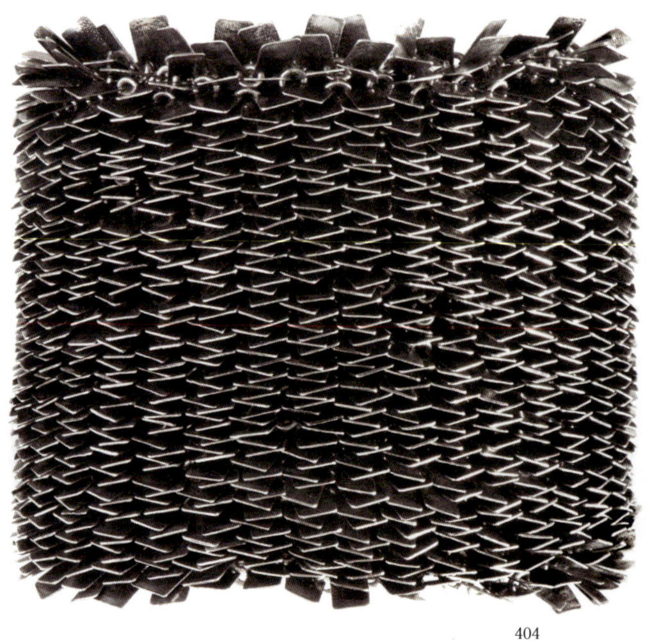

404

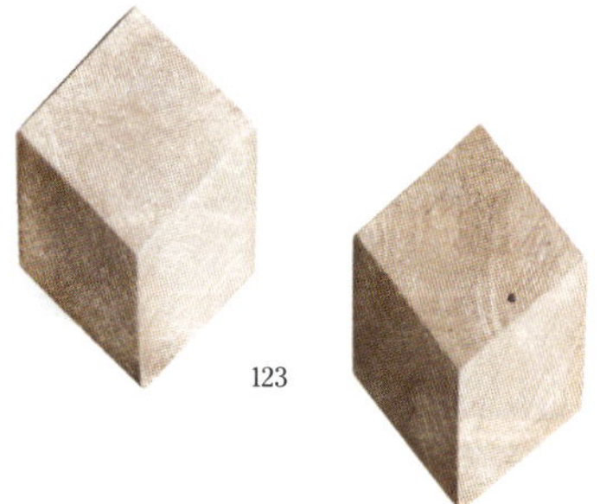

123

328

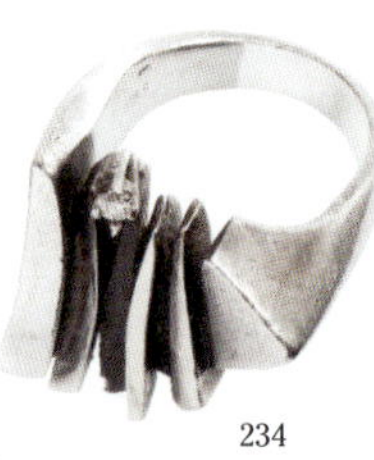

234

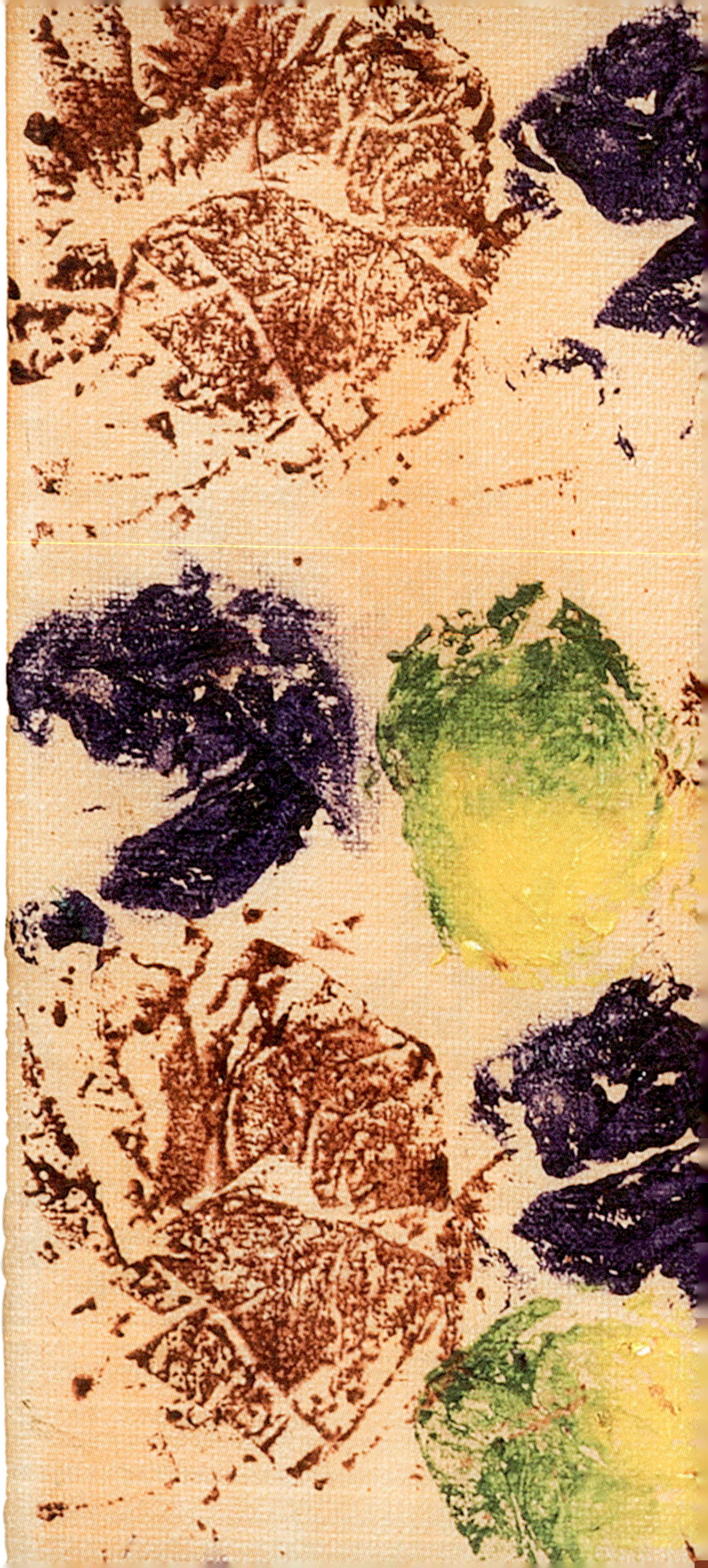

396

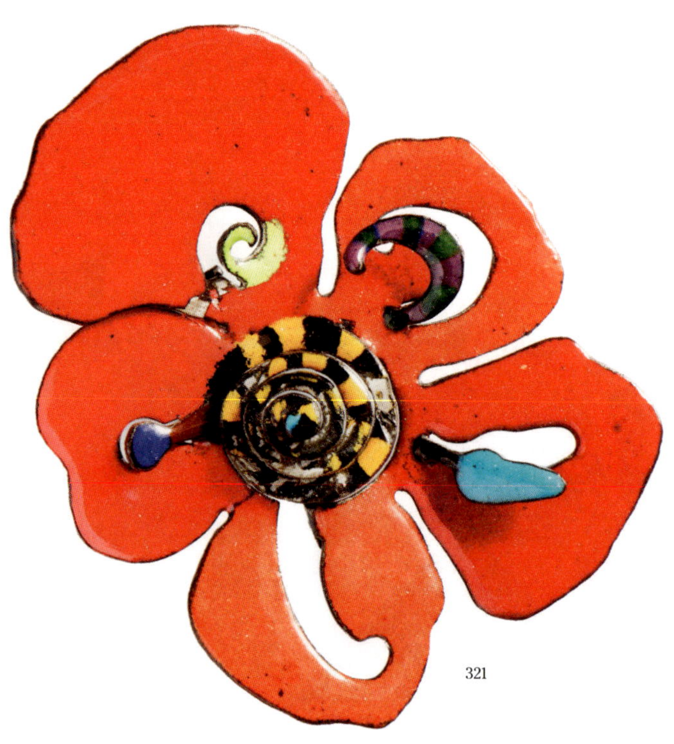

321

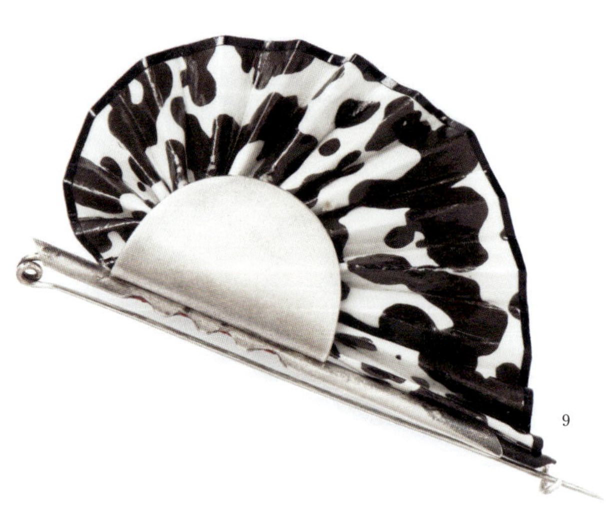

9

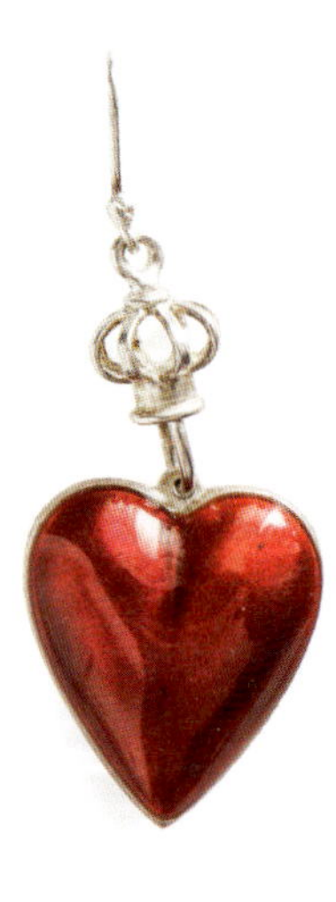

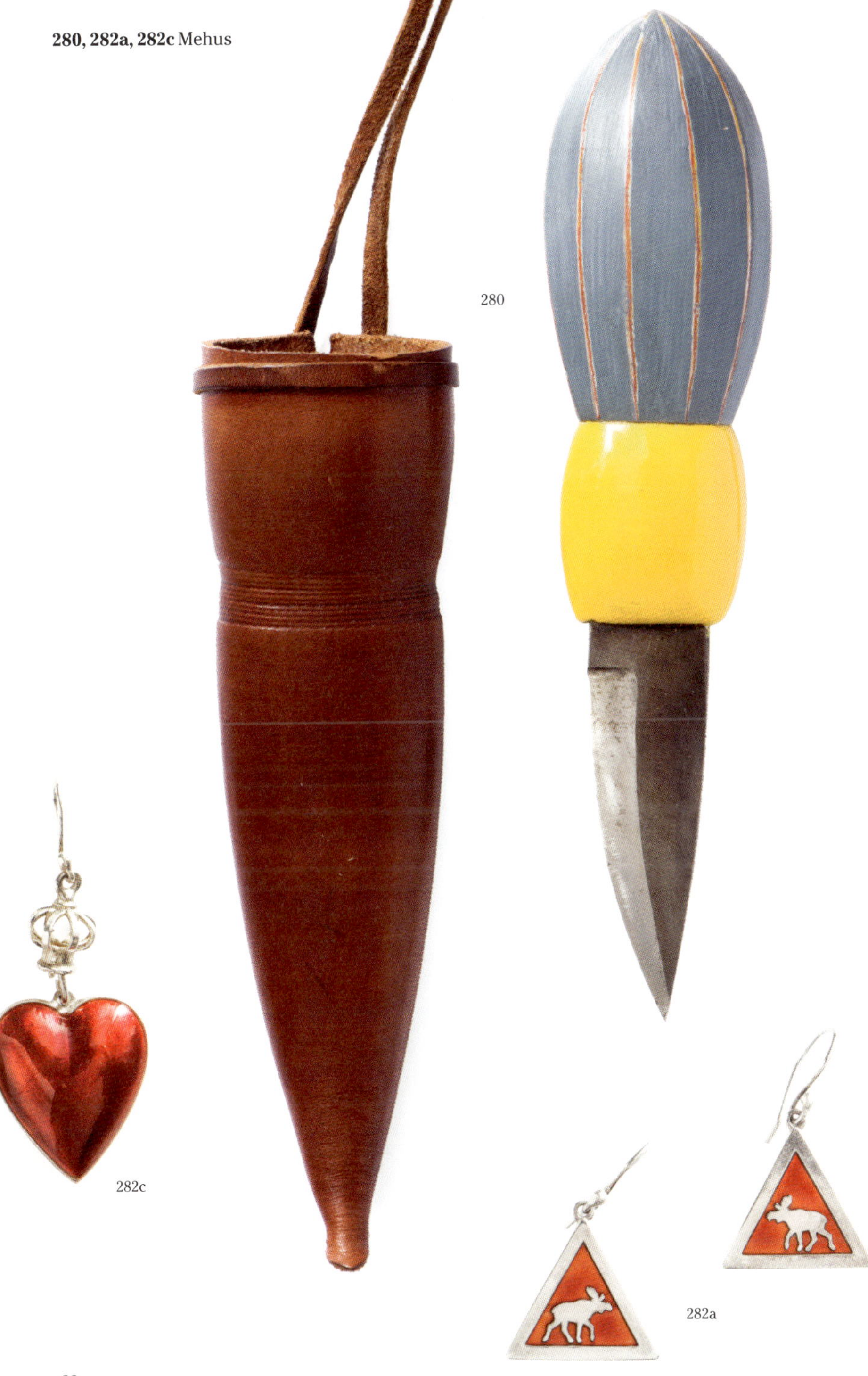

280

282c

282a

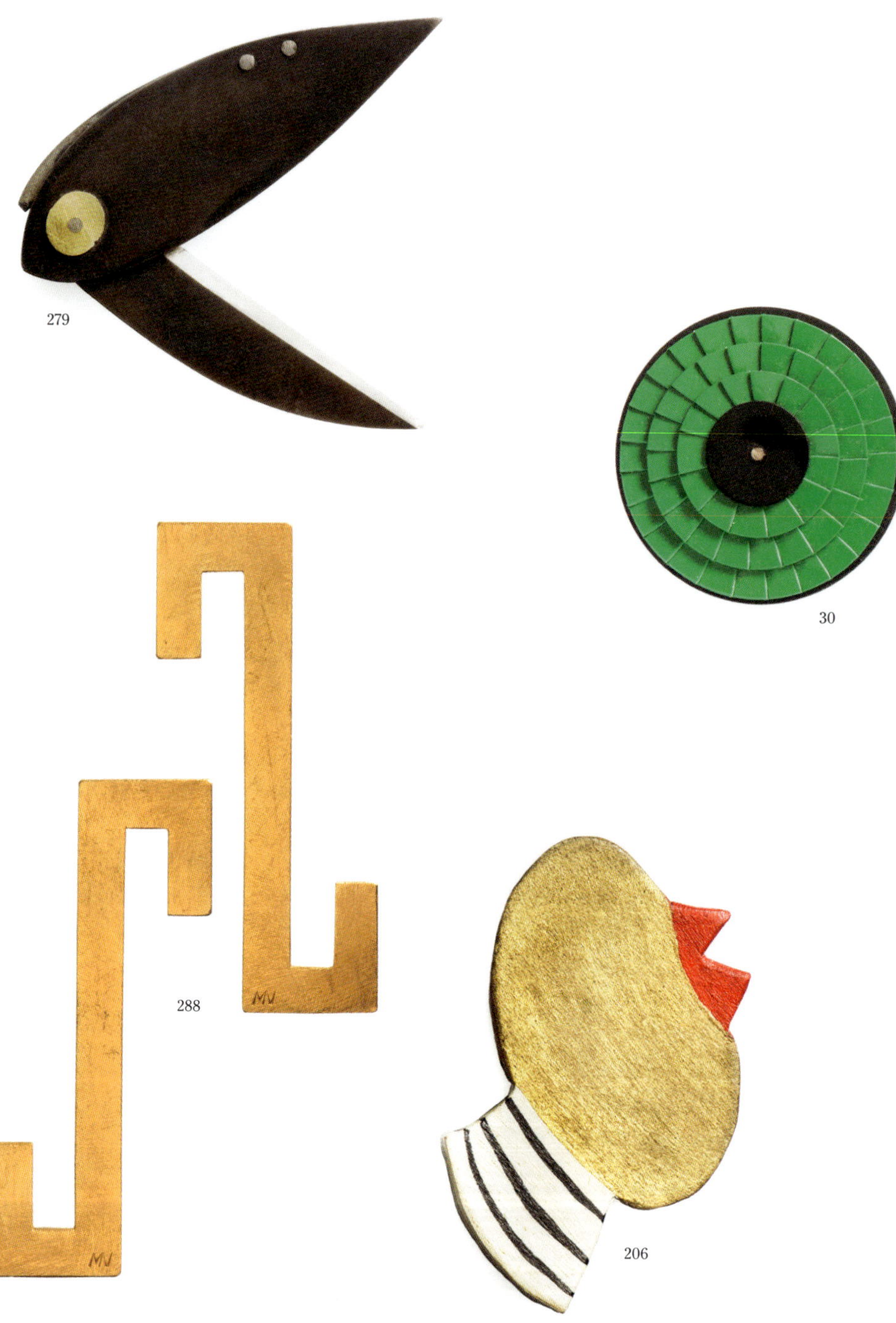

279

30

288

206

85

271

282b

71

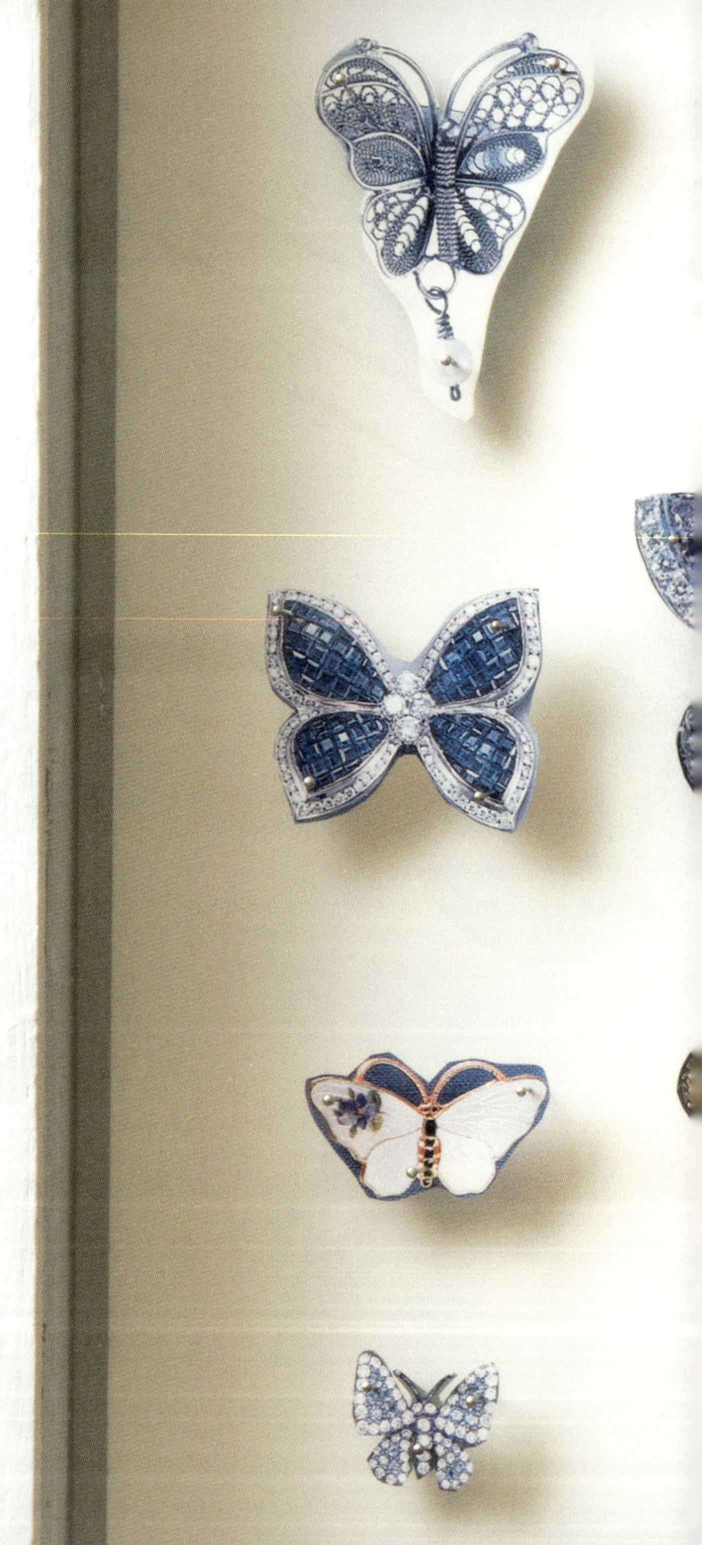

367

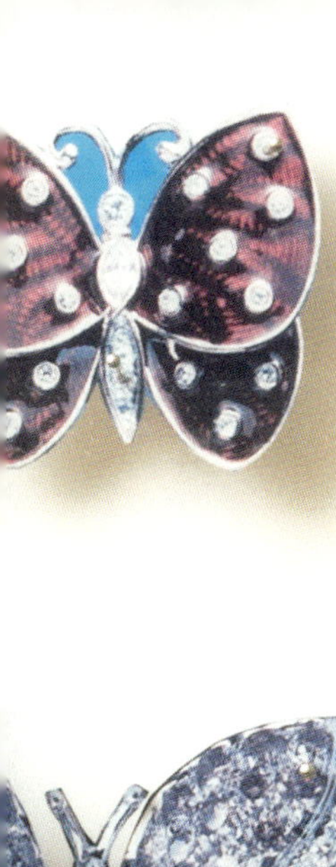
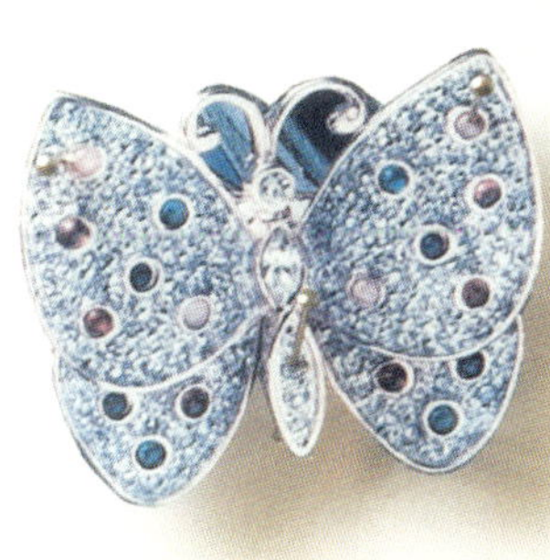
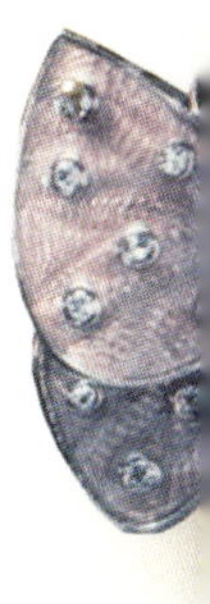
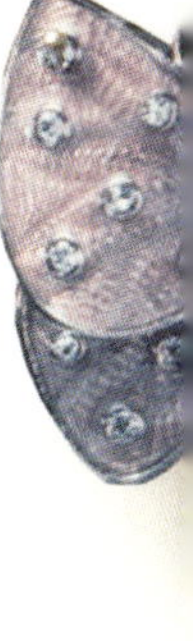
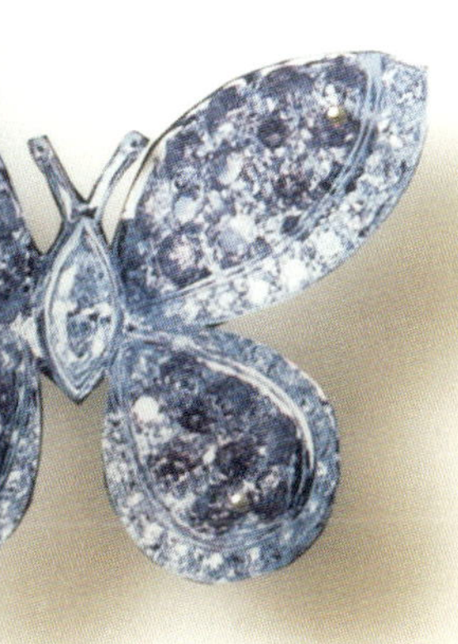
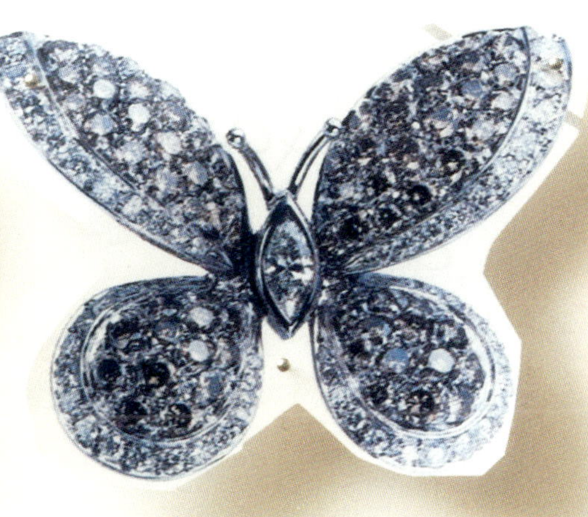
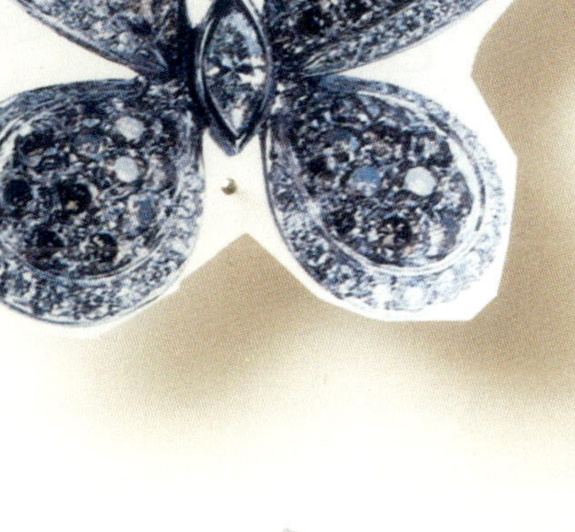
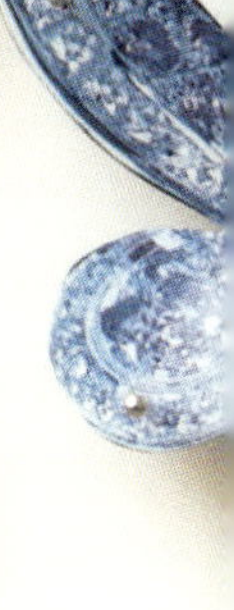
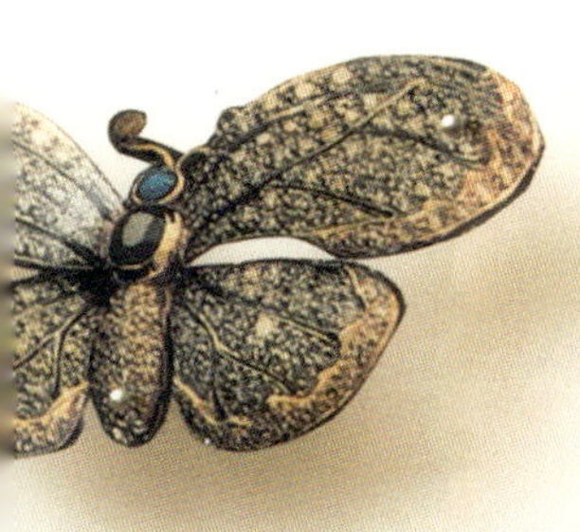
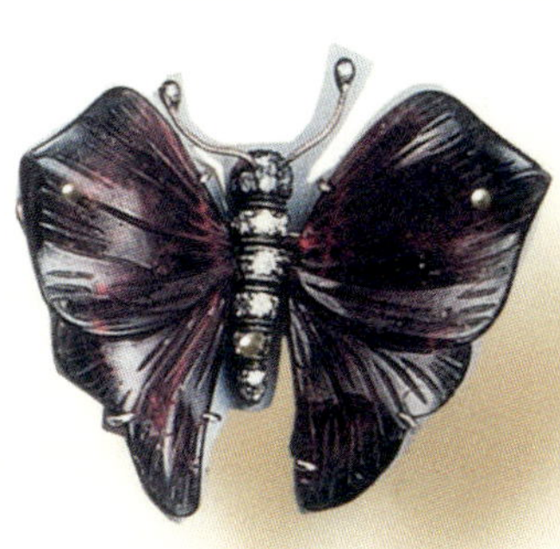
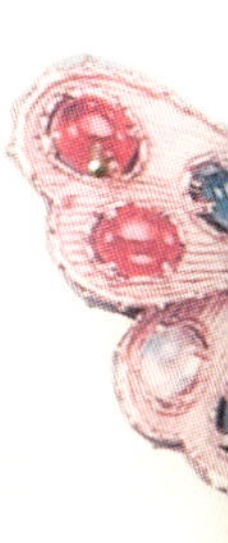
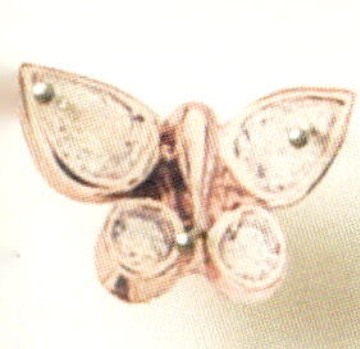
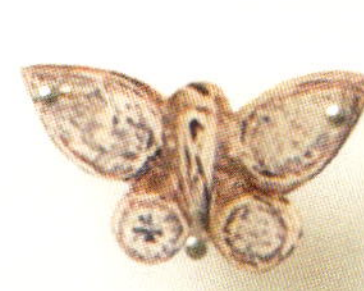
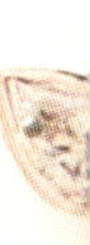

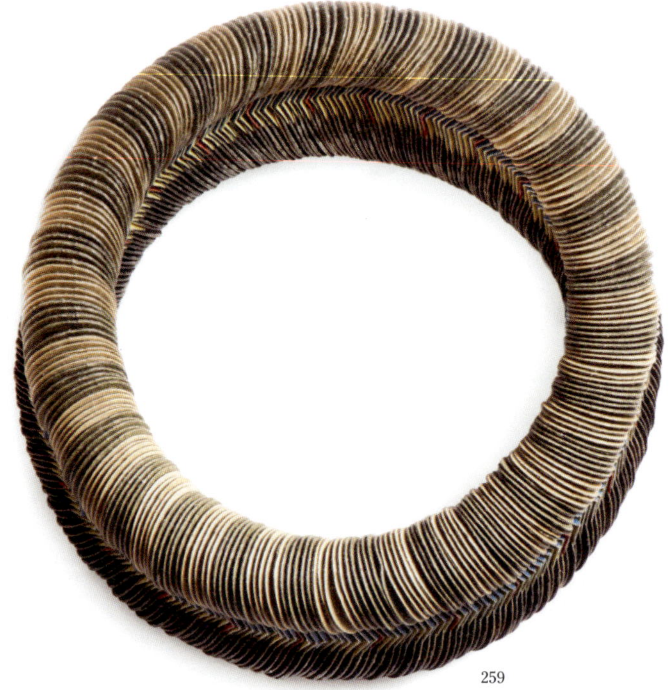

259

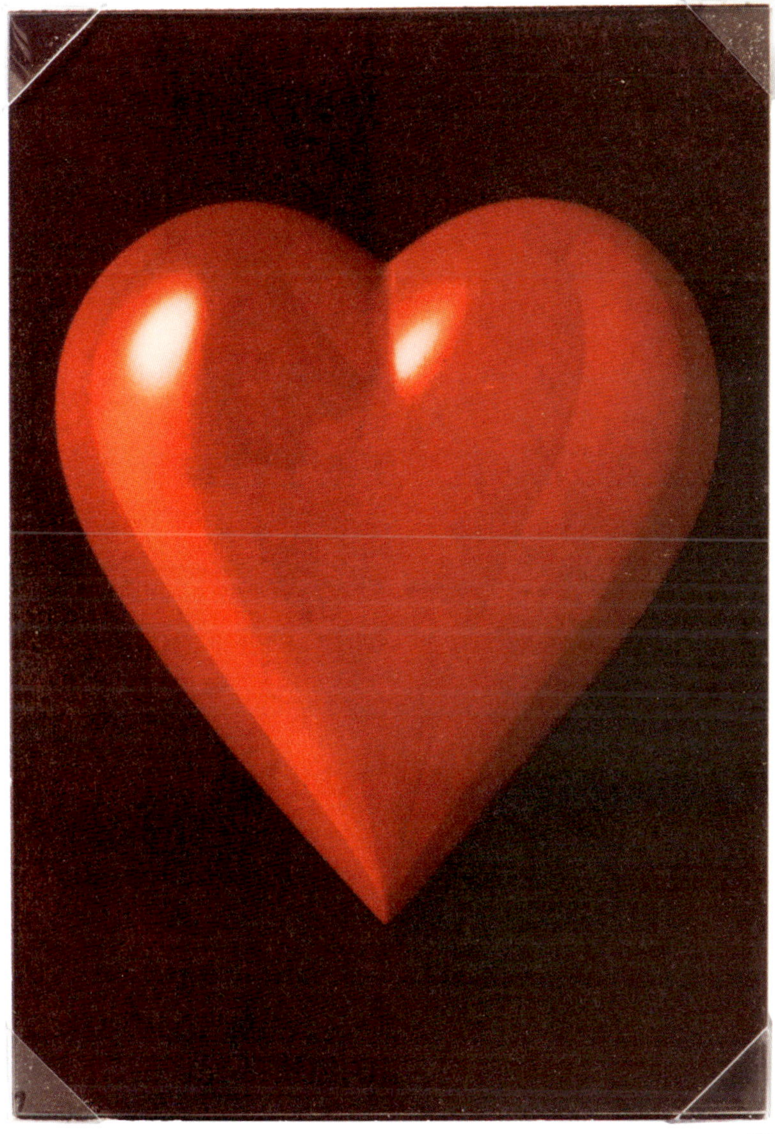

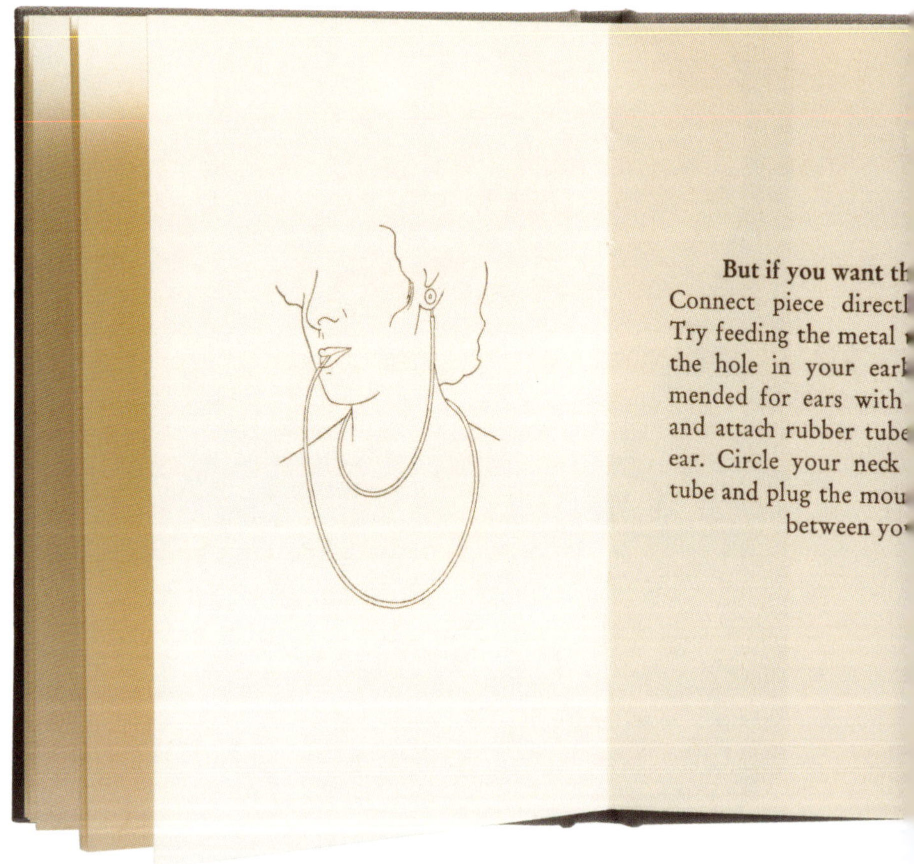

But if you want th
Connect piece directl
Try feeding the metal
the hole in your earl
mended for ears with
and attach rubber tube
ear. Circle your neck
tube and plug the mou
between yo

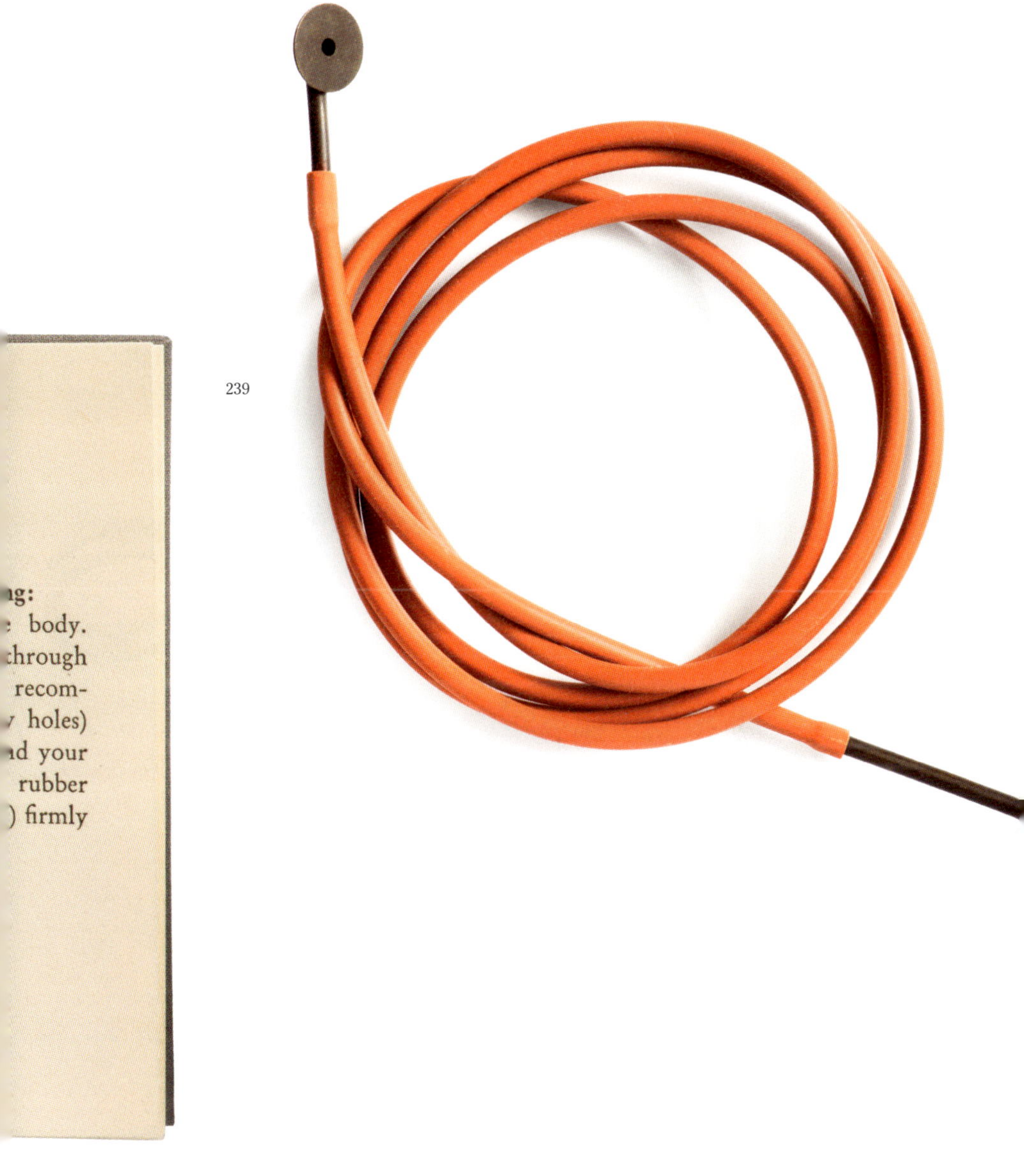

239

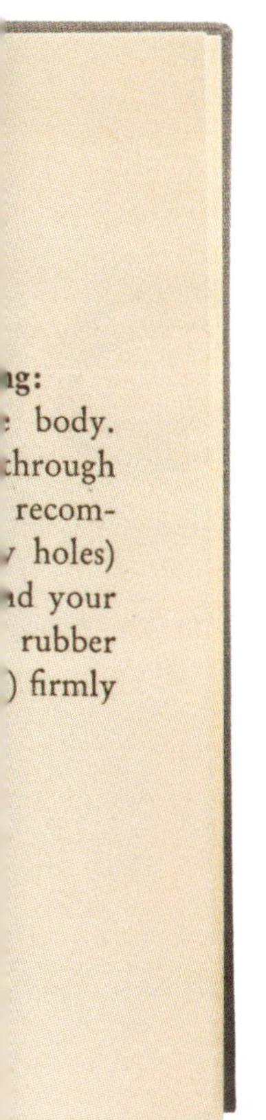

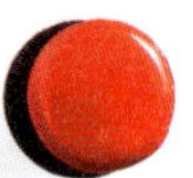

241

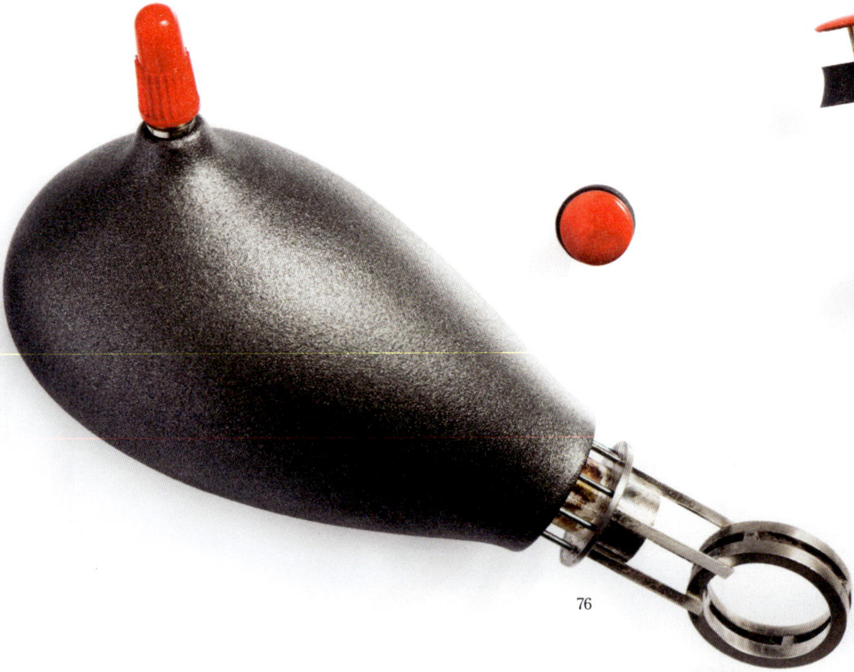

76

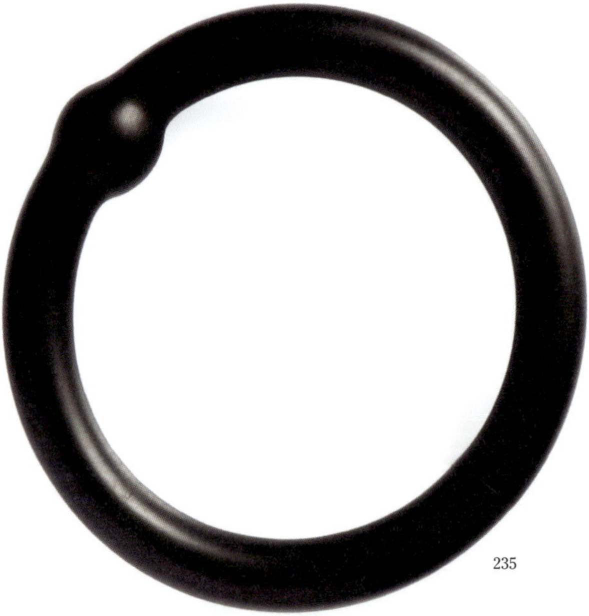

235

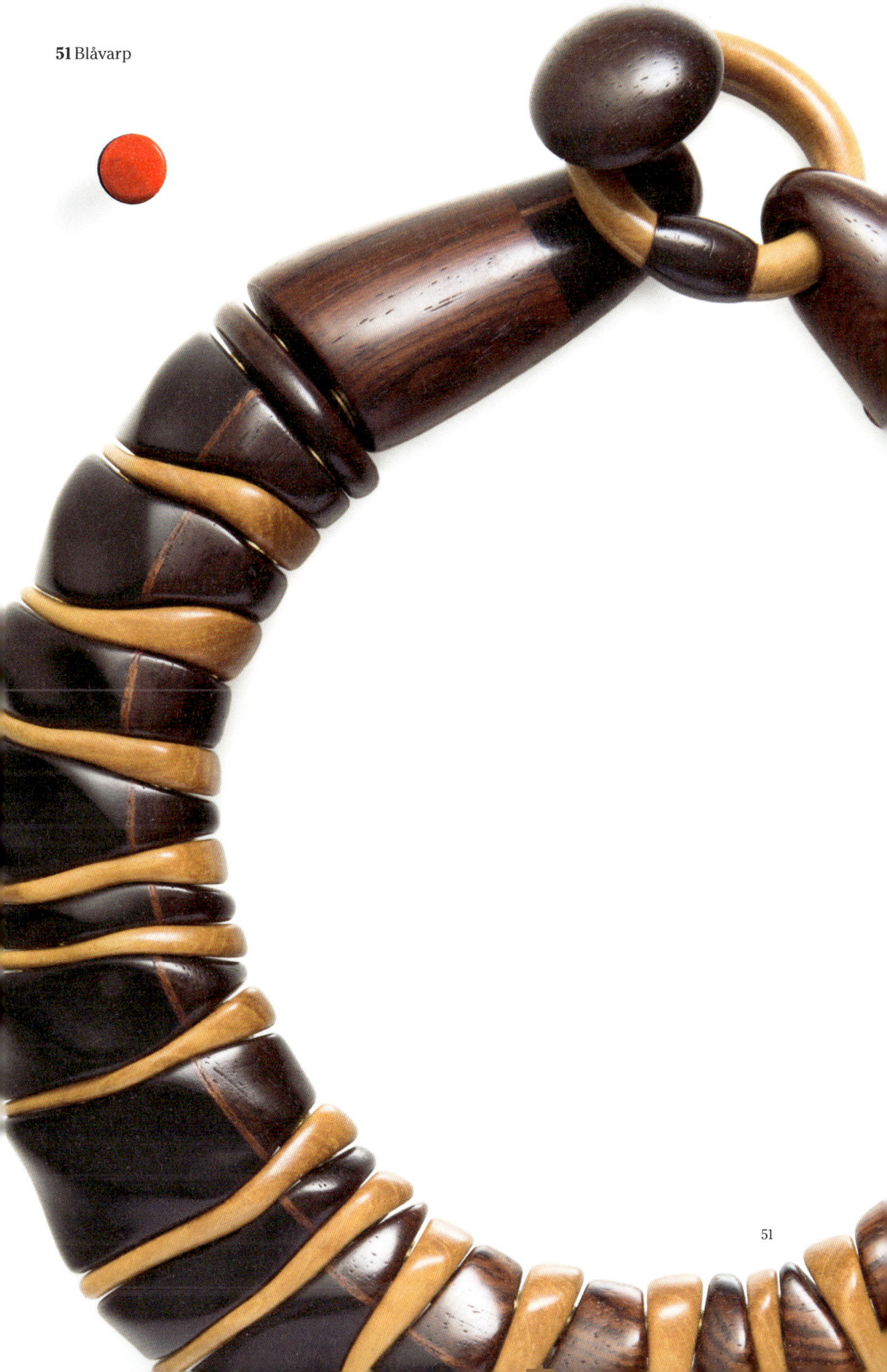

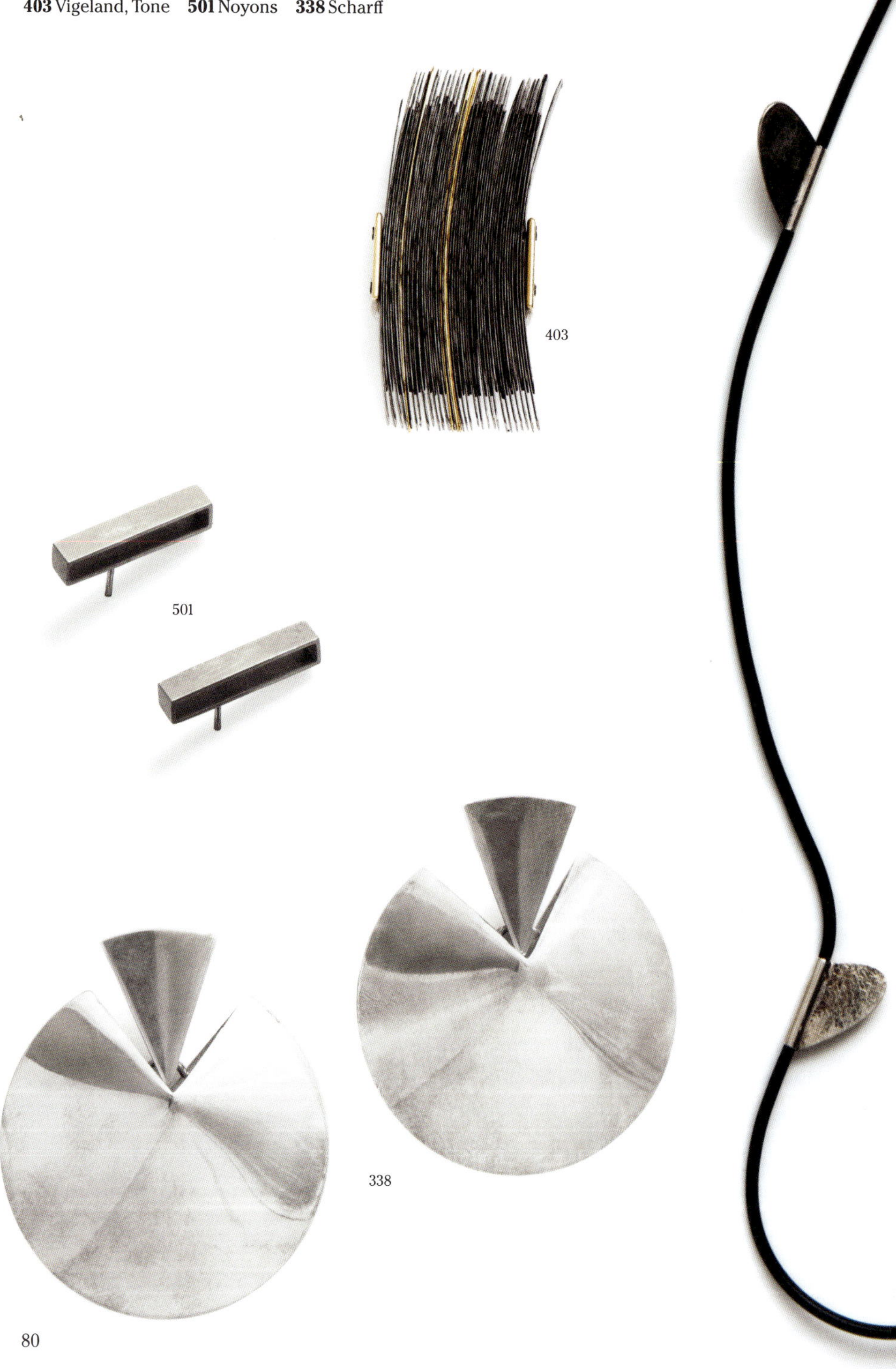

403

501

338

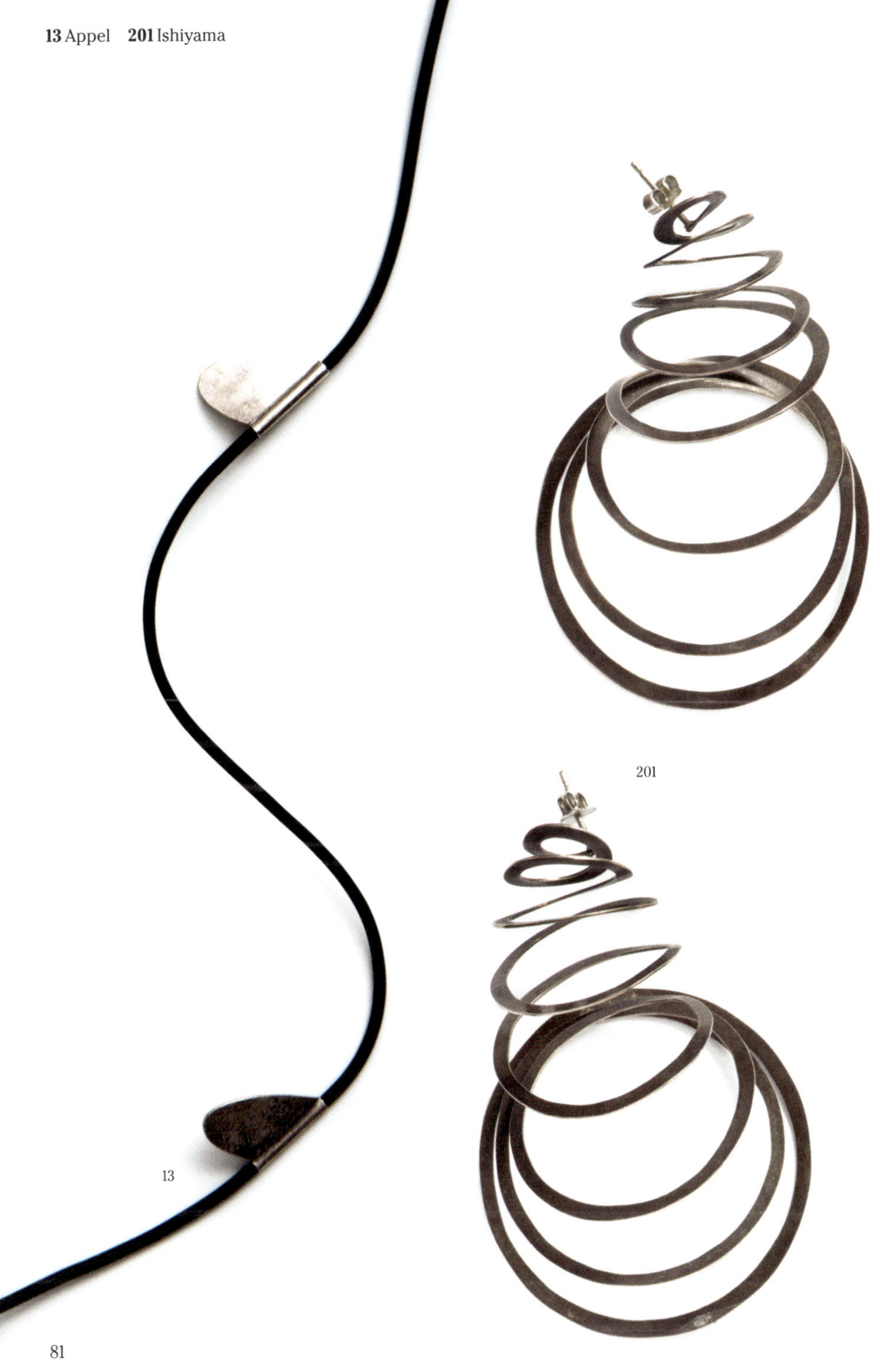

201

13

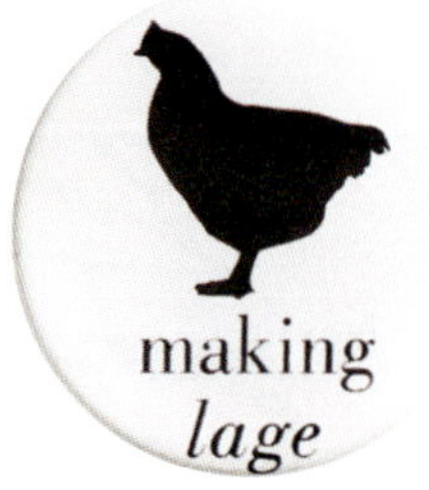

79

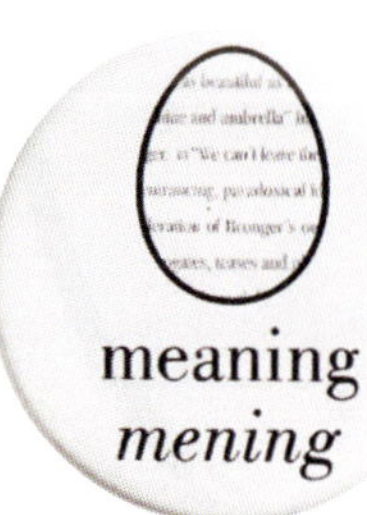

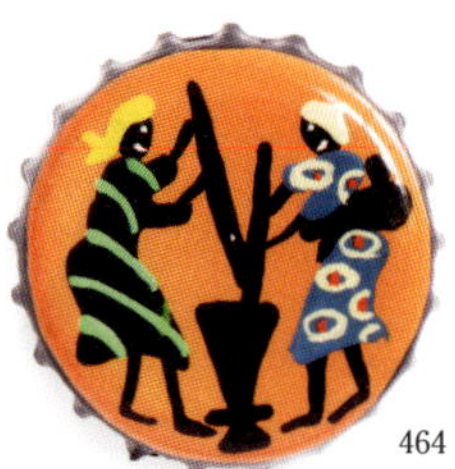

464

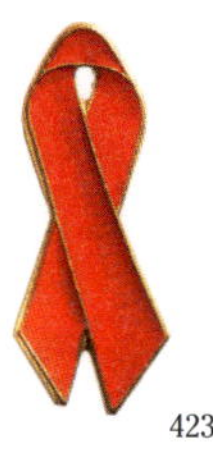

423

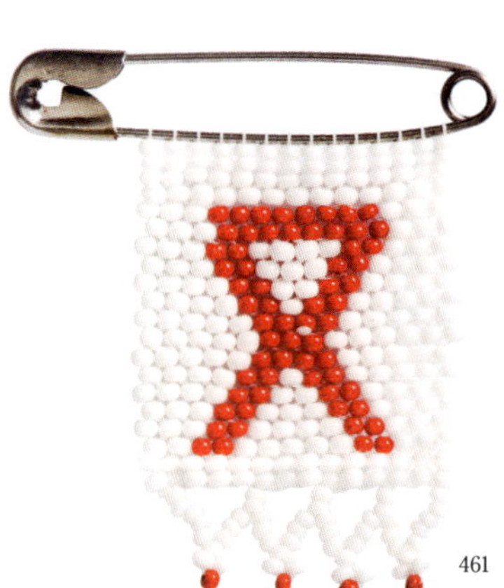

461

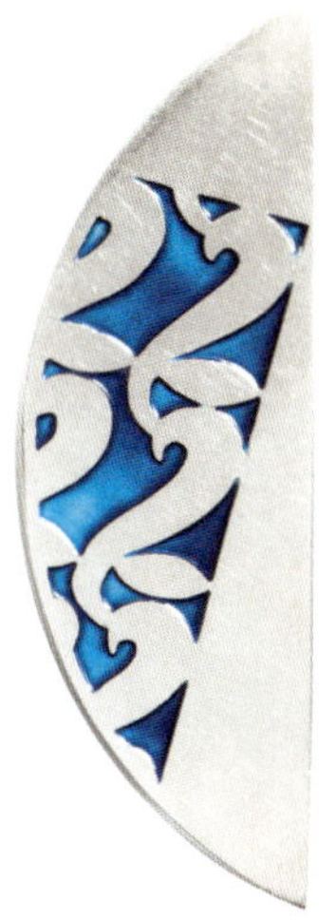 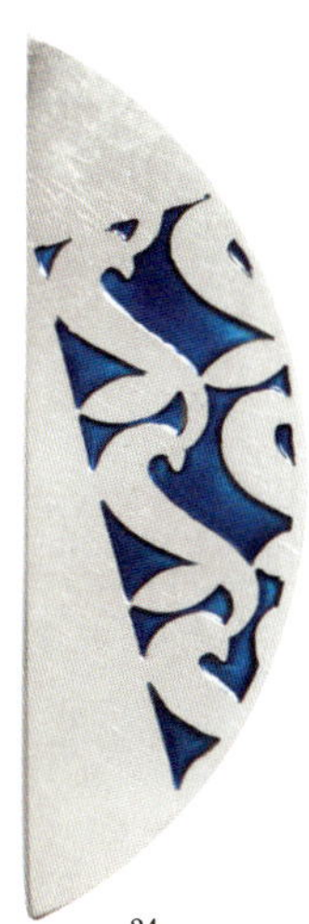

24

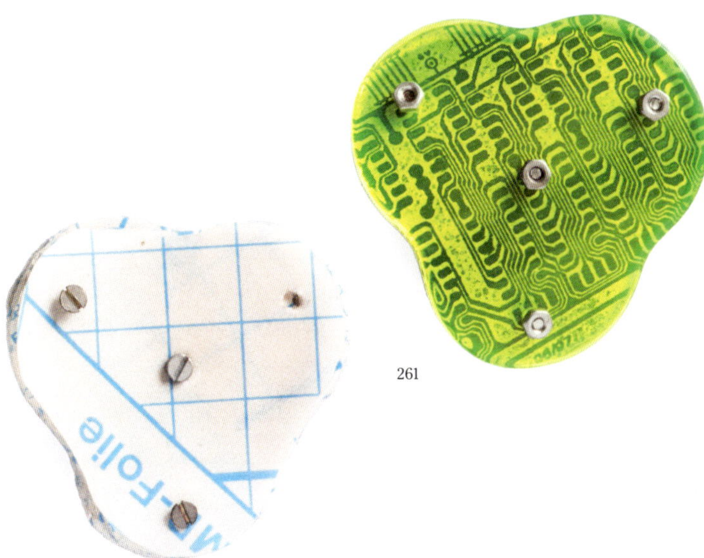

261

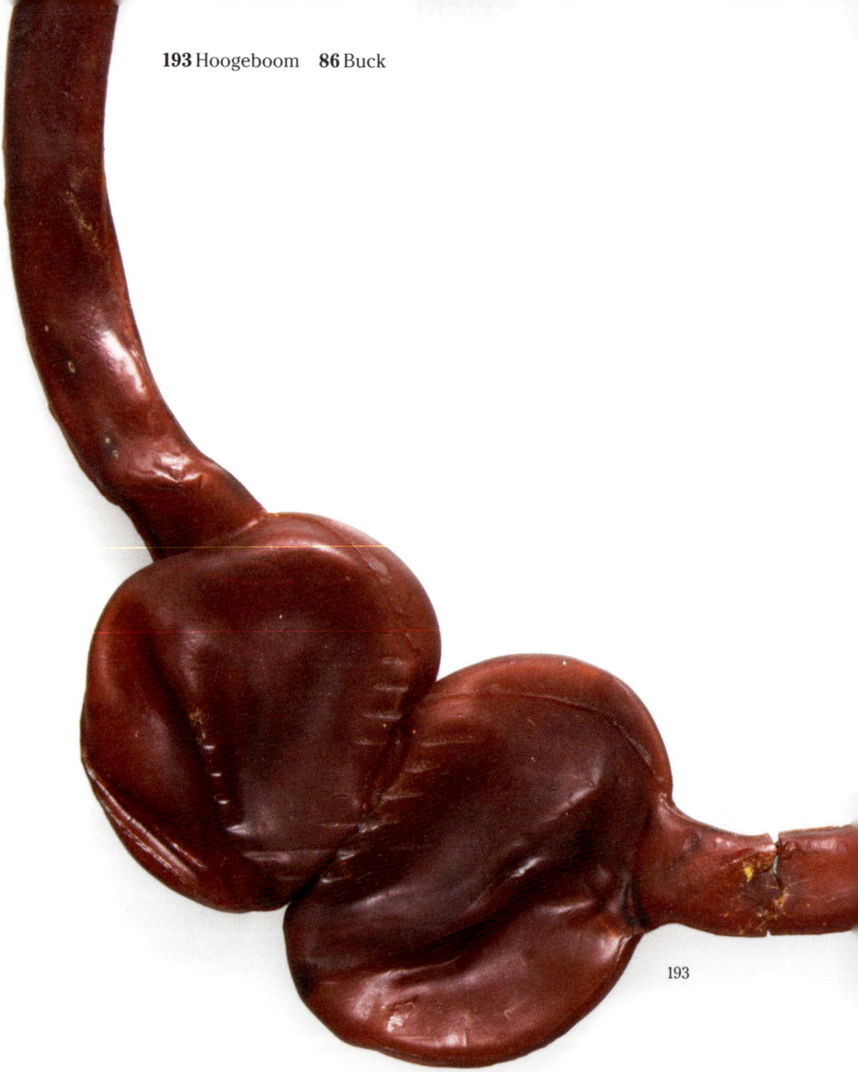

193

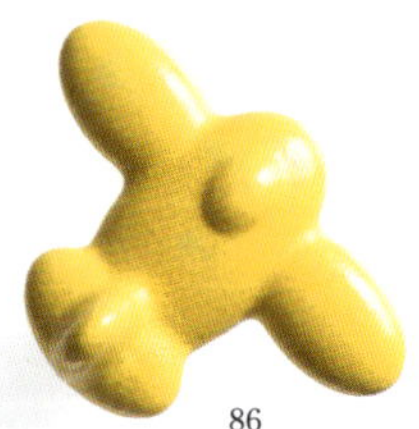

86

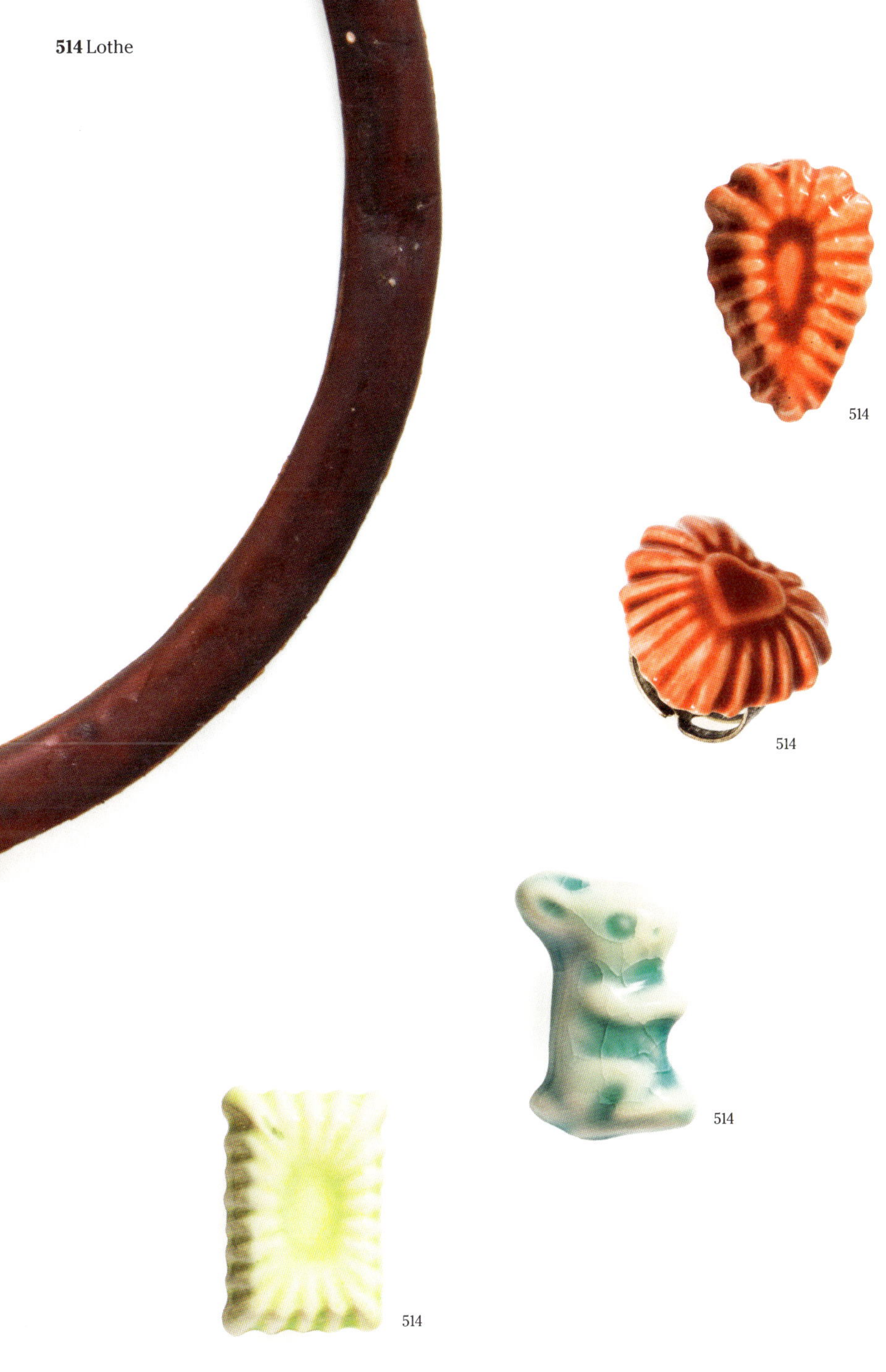

514
514
514
514

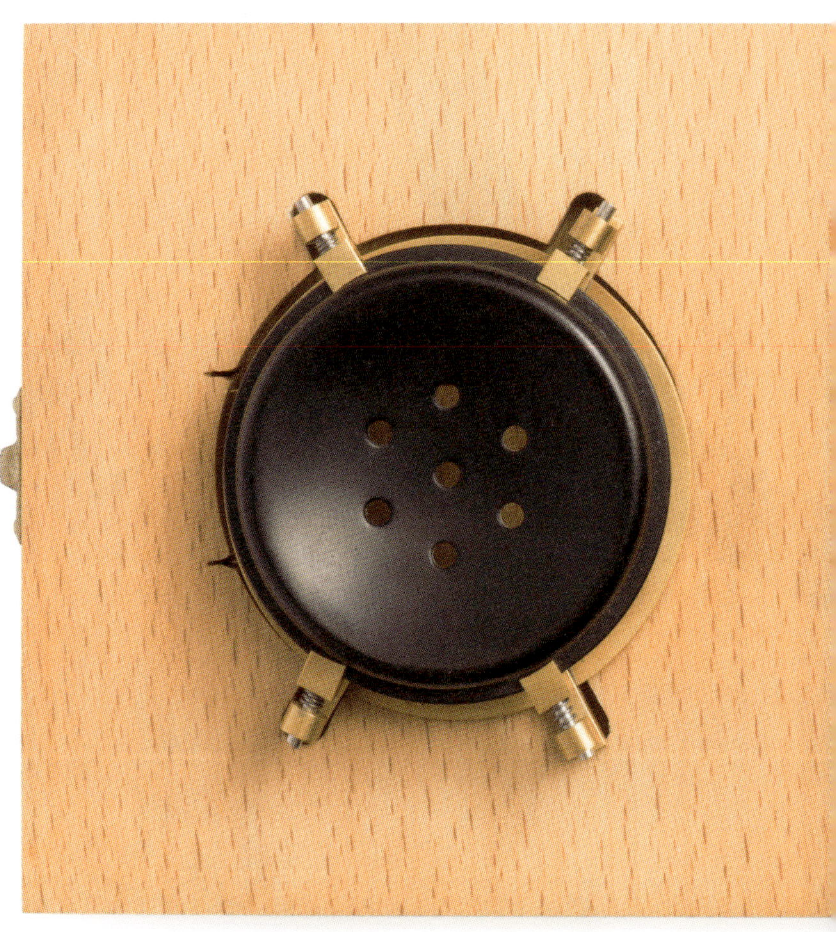

68

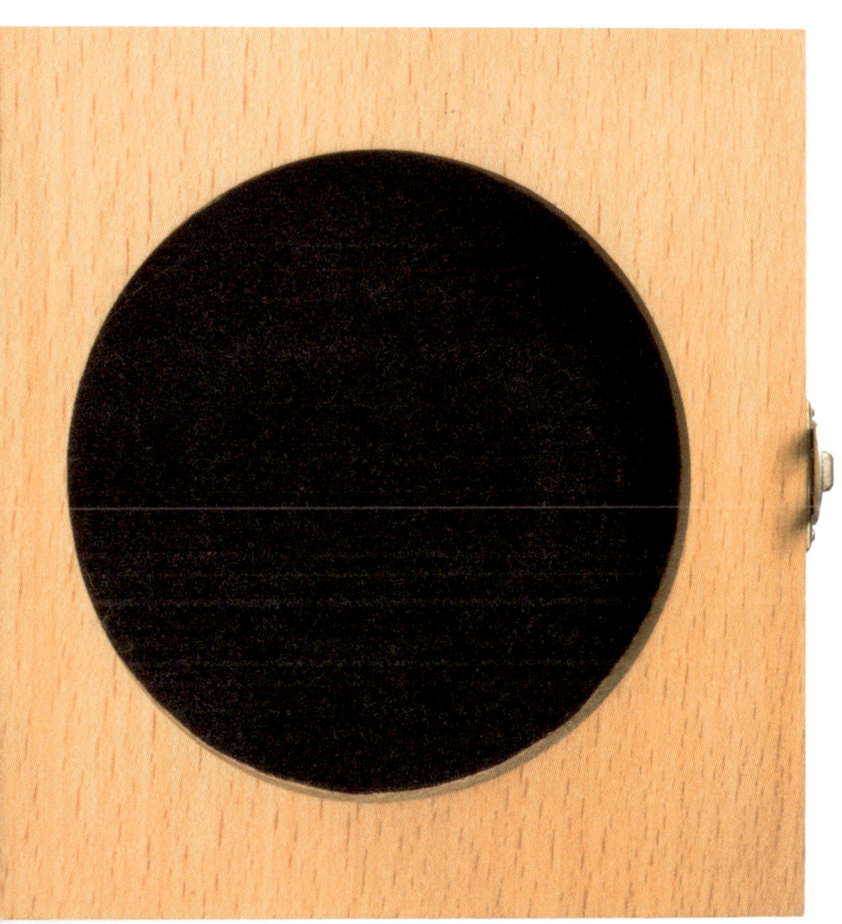

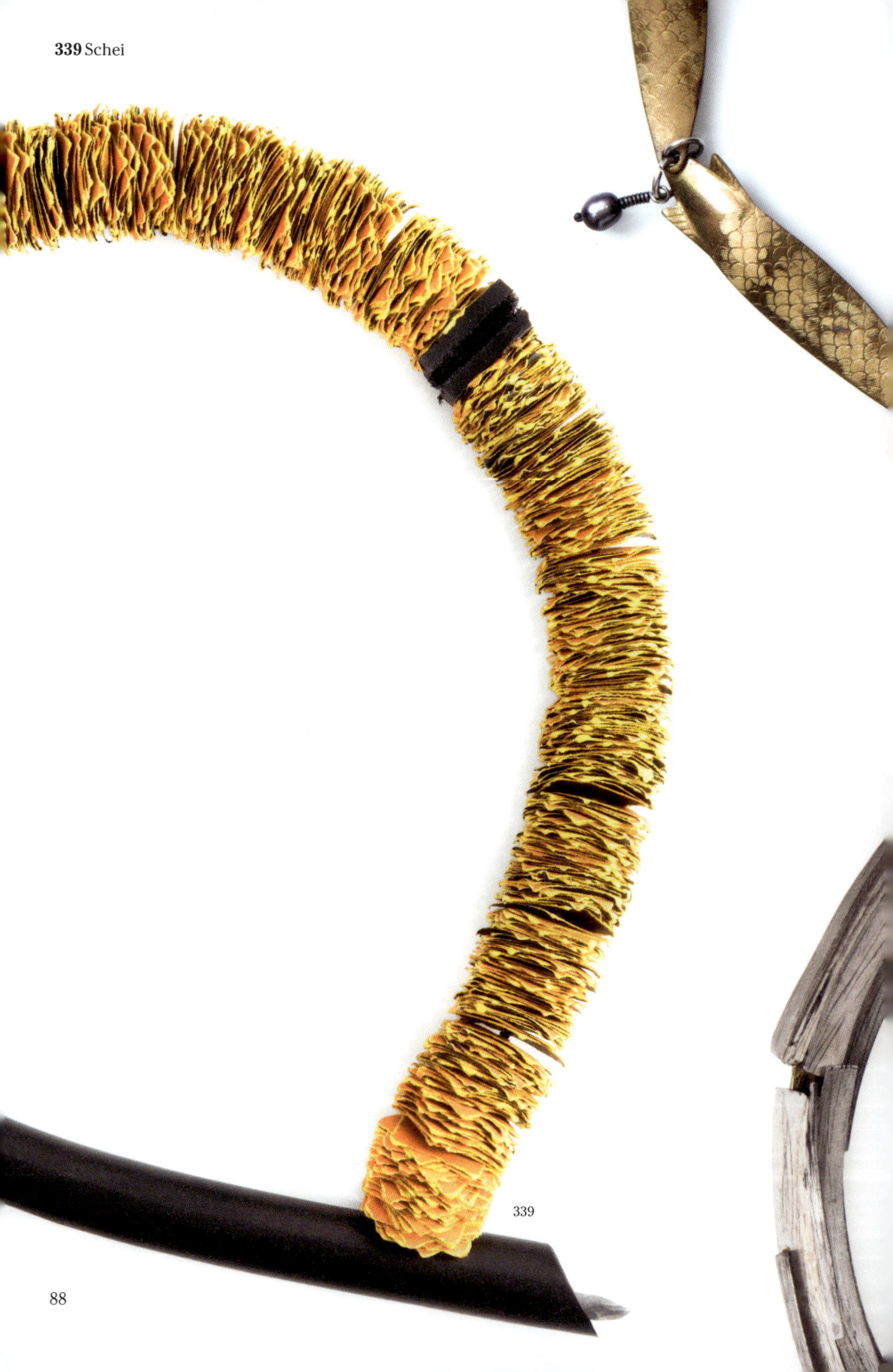

339

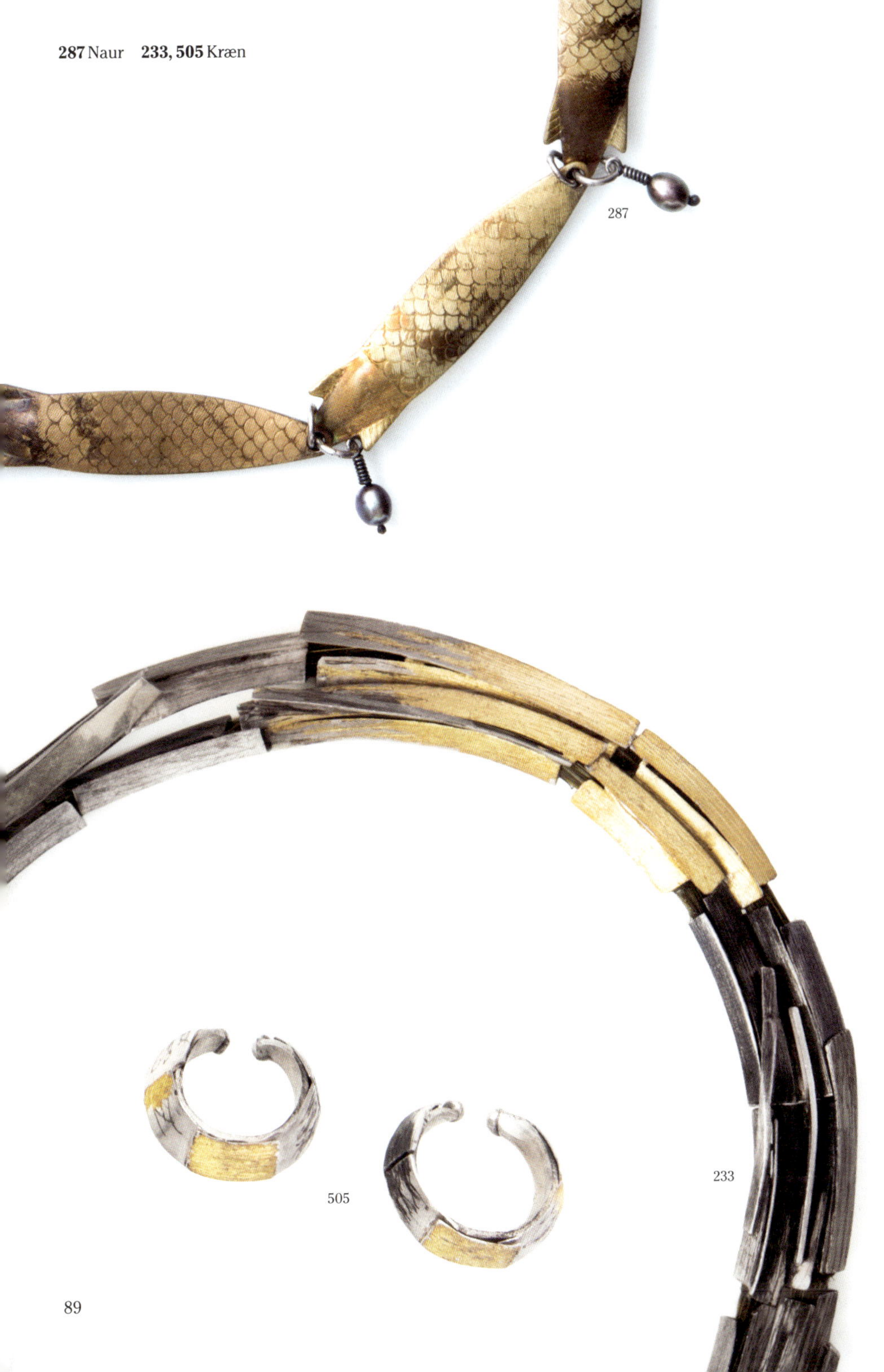
287
505
233

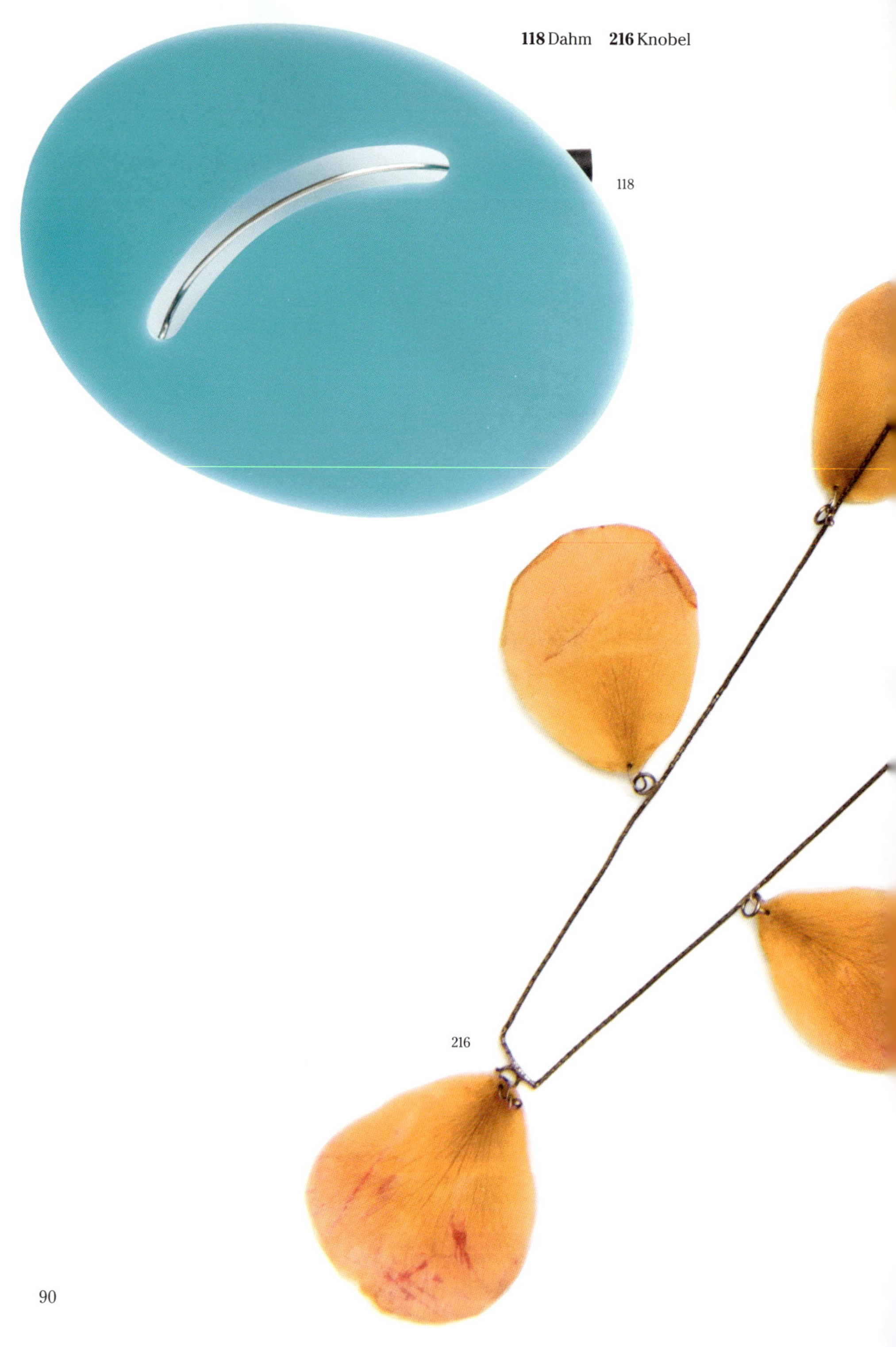

118

216

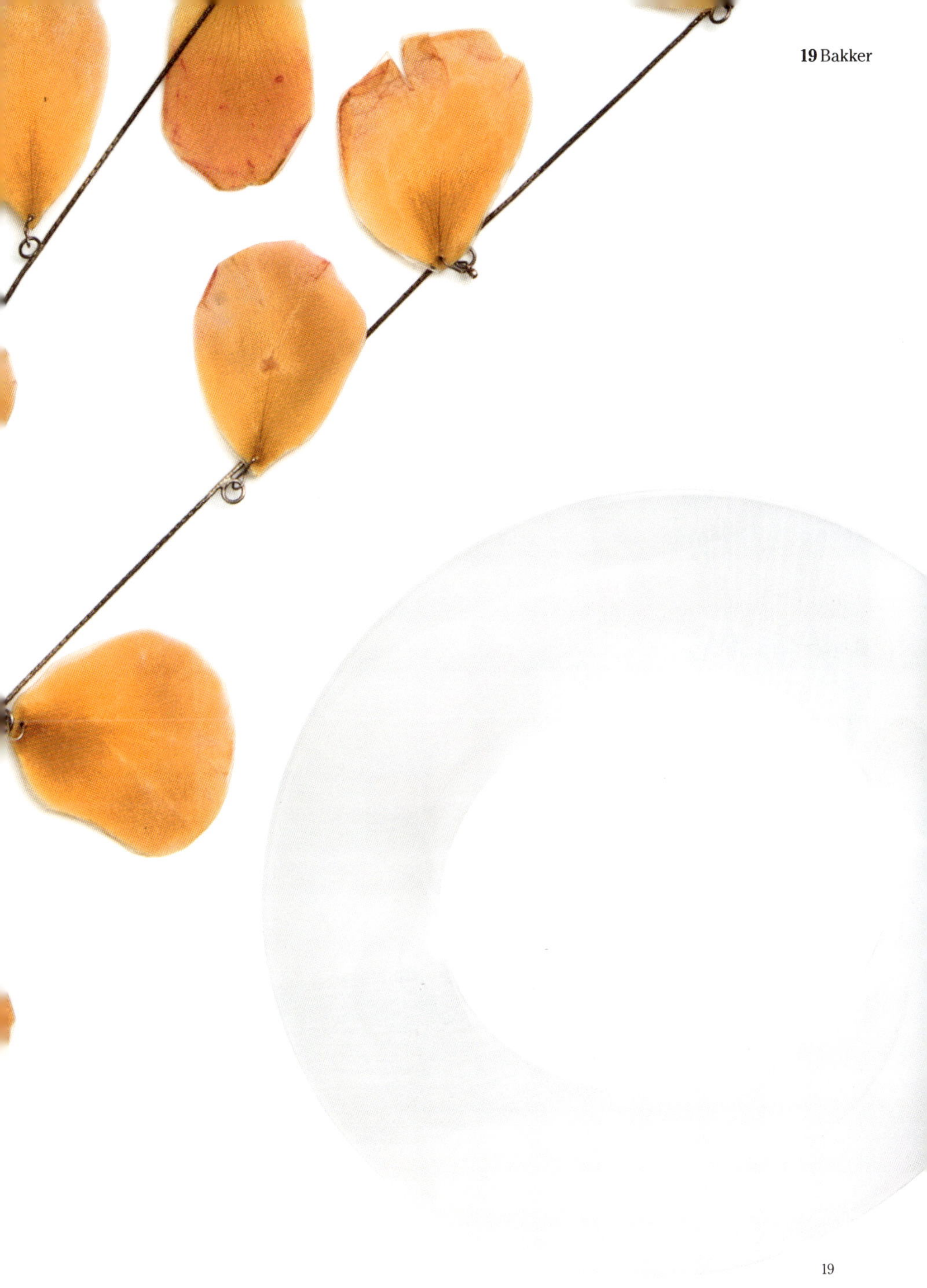

19 Bakker

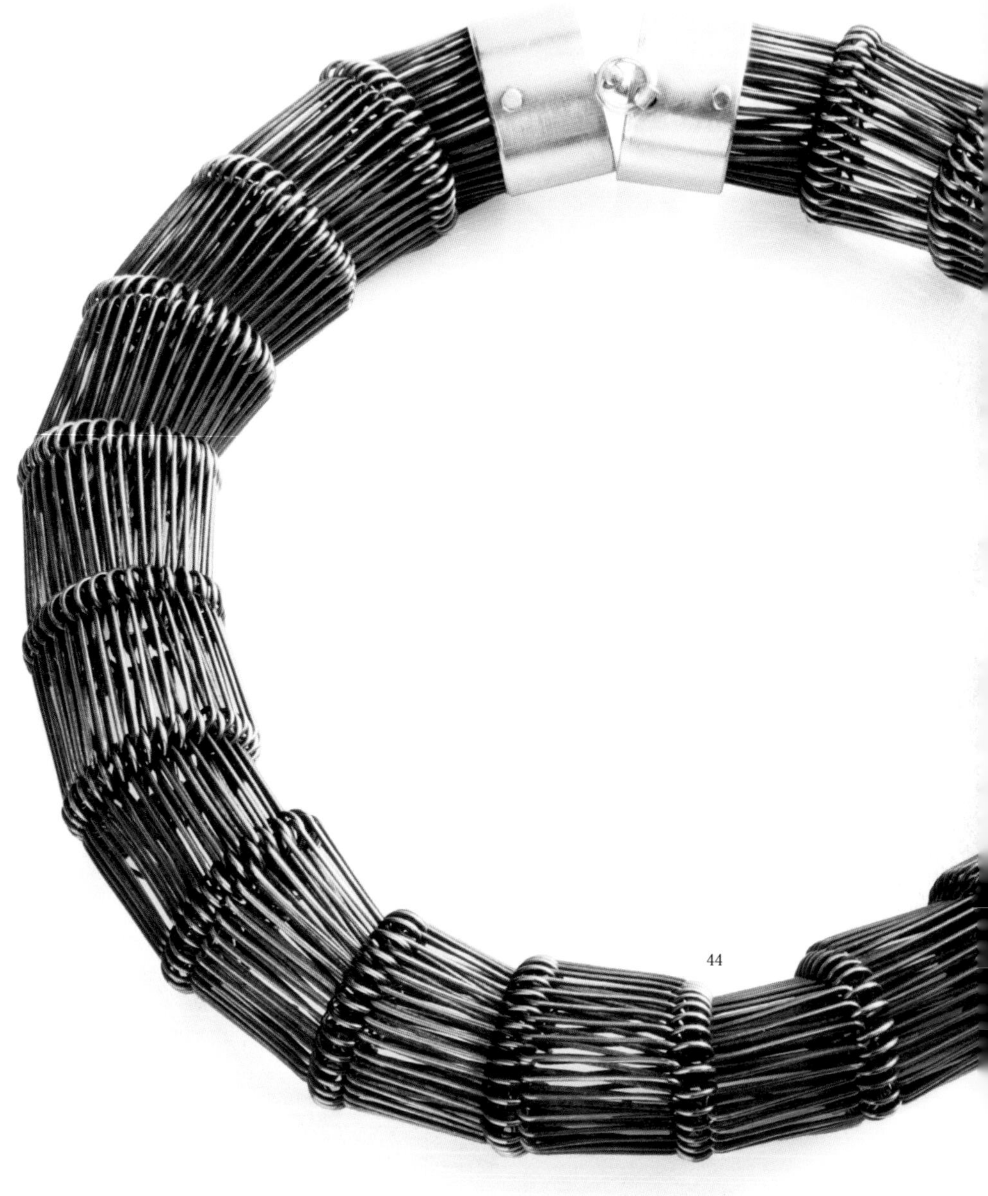

44

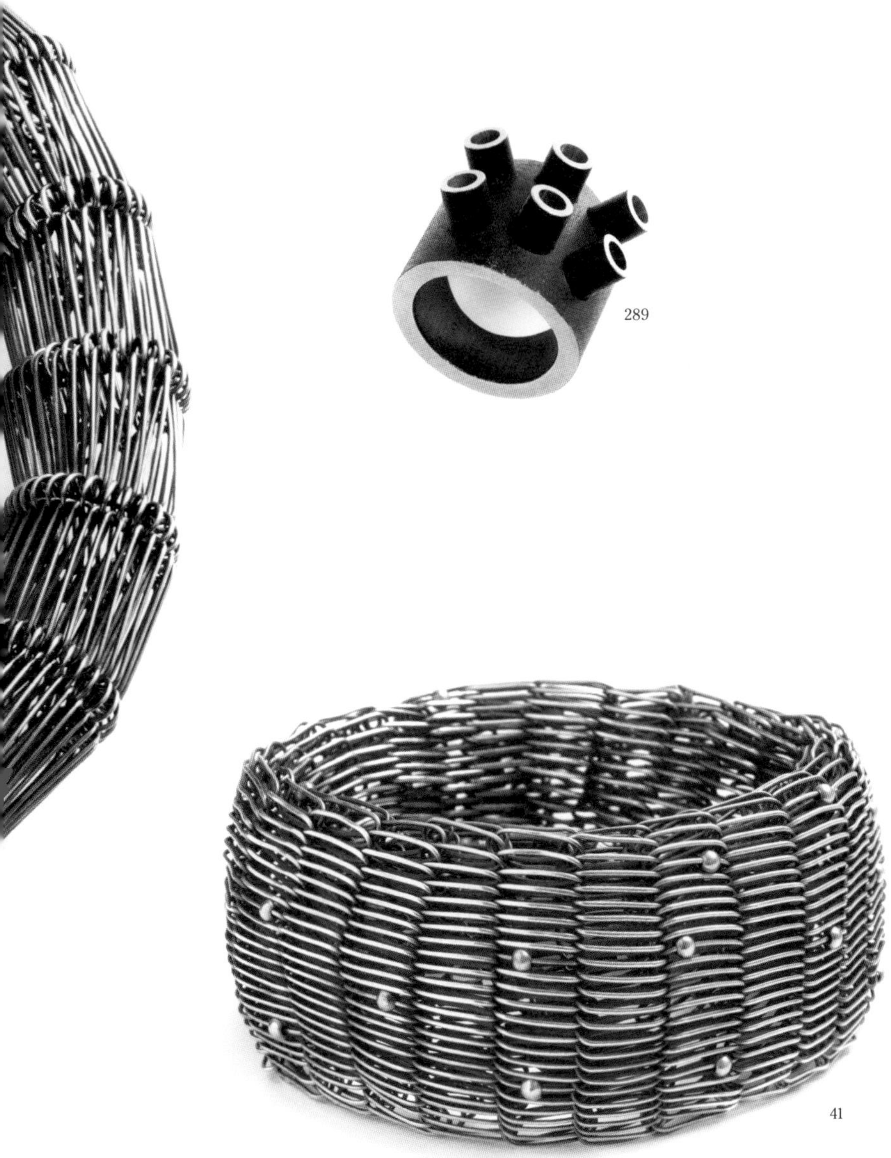

289

41

62

Valium 5 mg
25 tabl.
1 tabl.:
Diazepam. 5 mg
Lactos. 100 mg
Constit. et color (E.
Dr. Magnus
9.nr: 15 41 12
09/01/93
1 tablett ved behov
inntil 3 ganger
daglig.
HURUM Apotn
OPPBEVARES UTILGJENGELIG FOR BARN

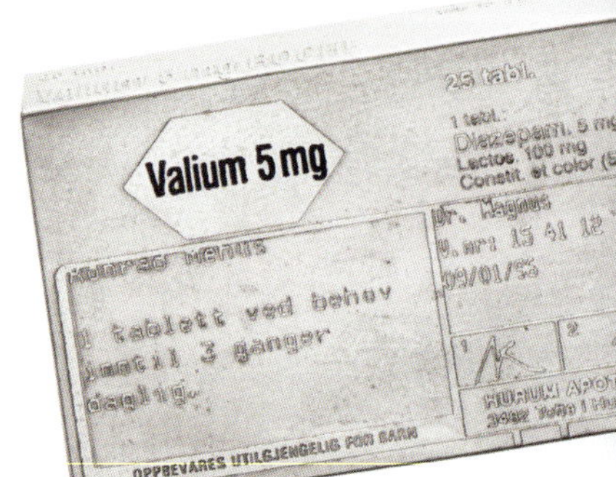

67

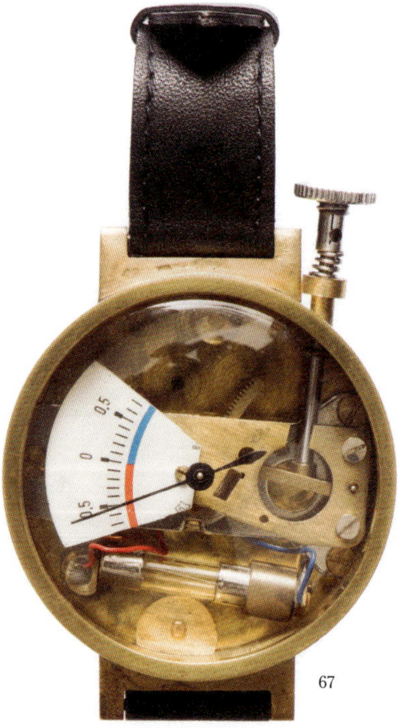

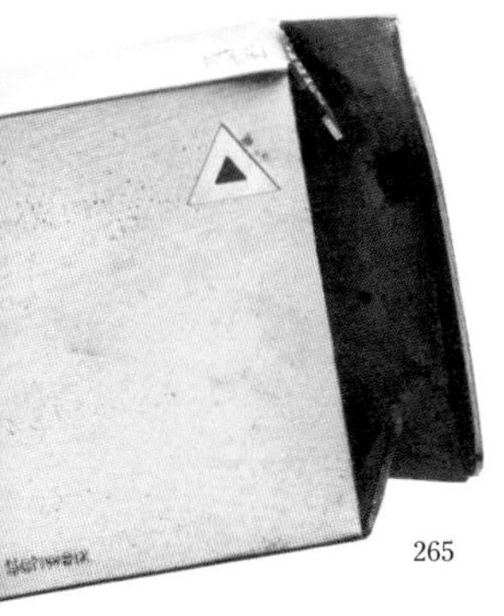

265

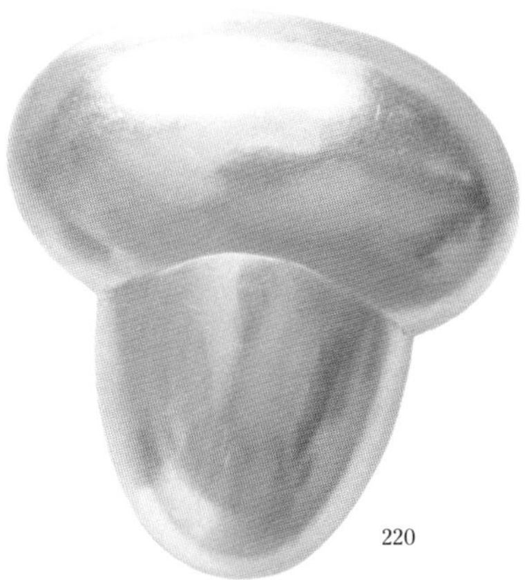

220

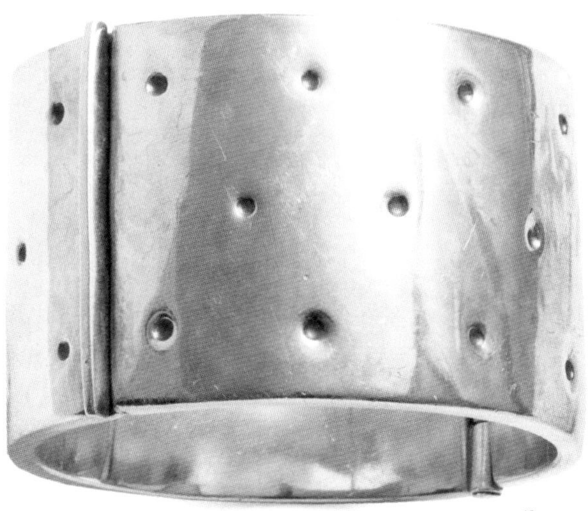

42

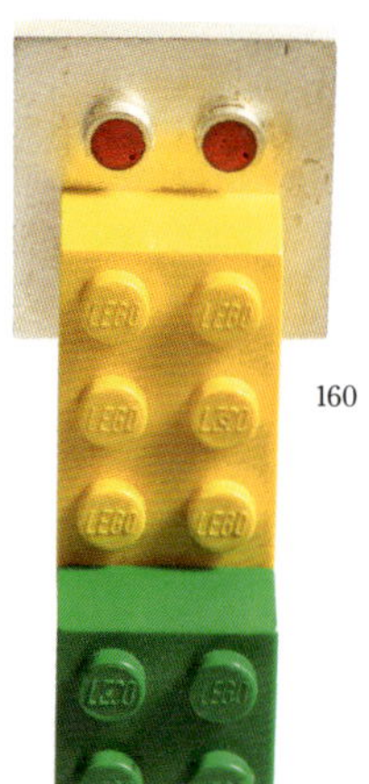

160

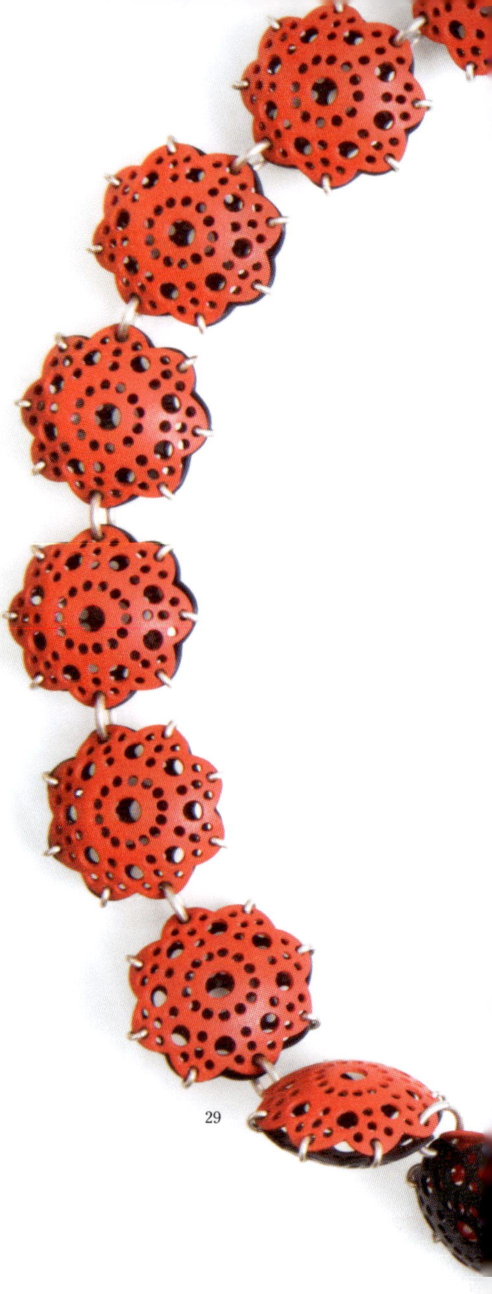

29

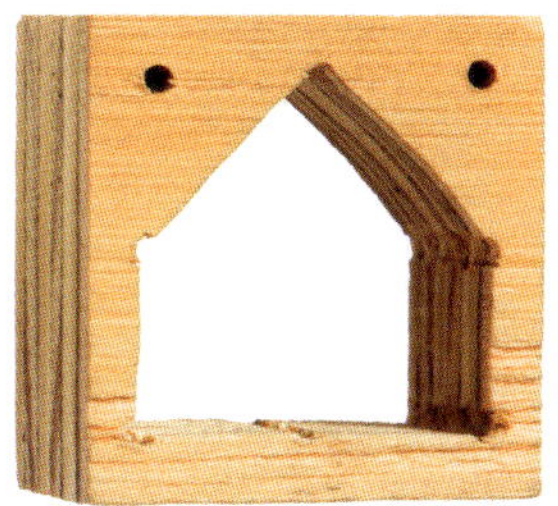 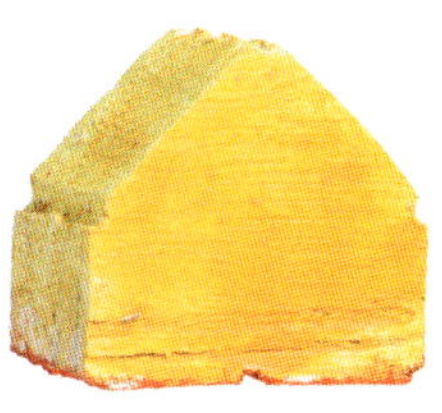

54

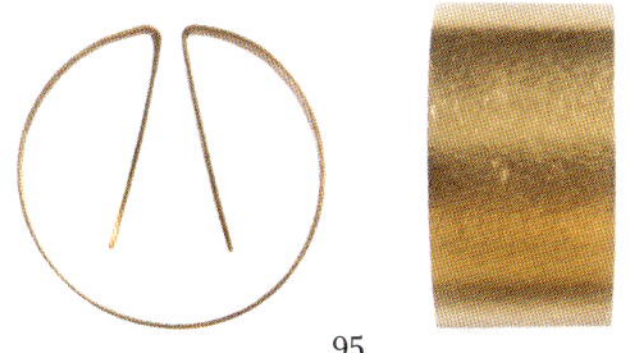

95

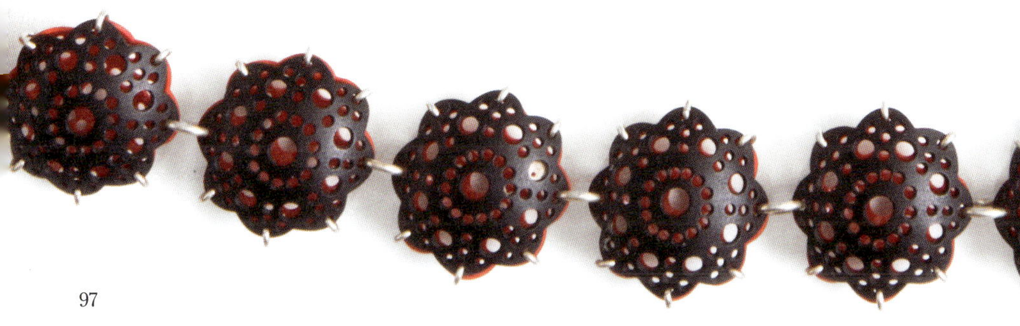

97

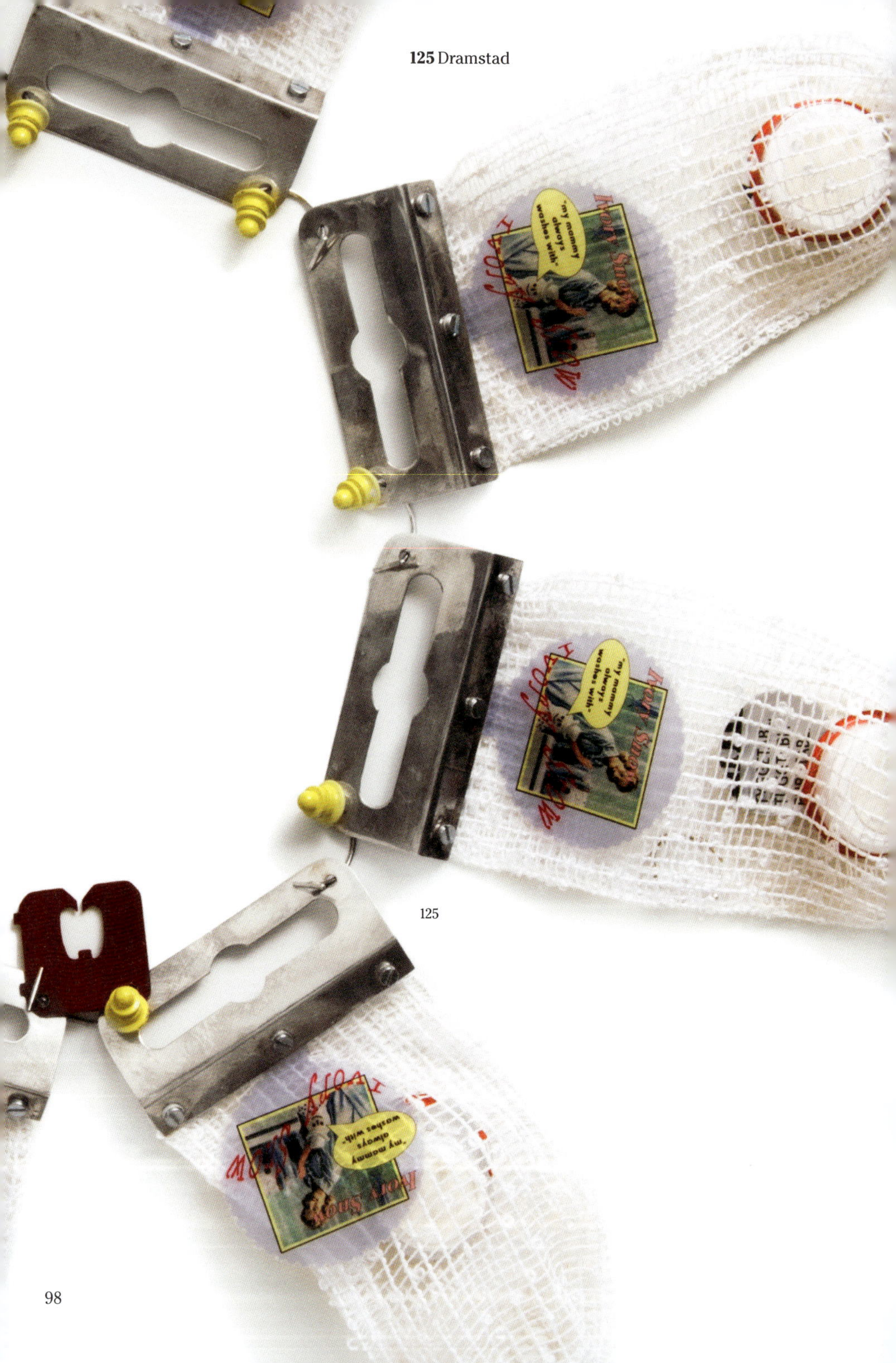

125

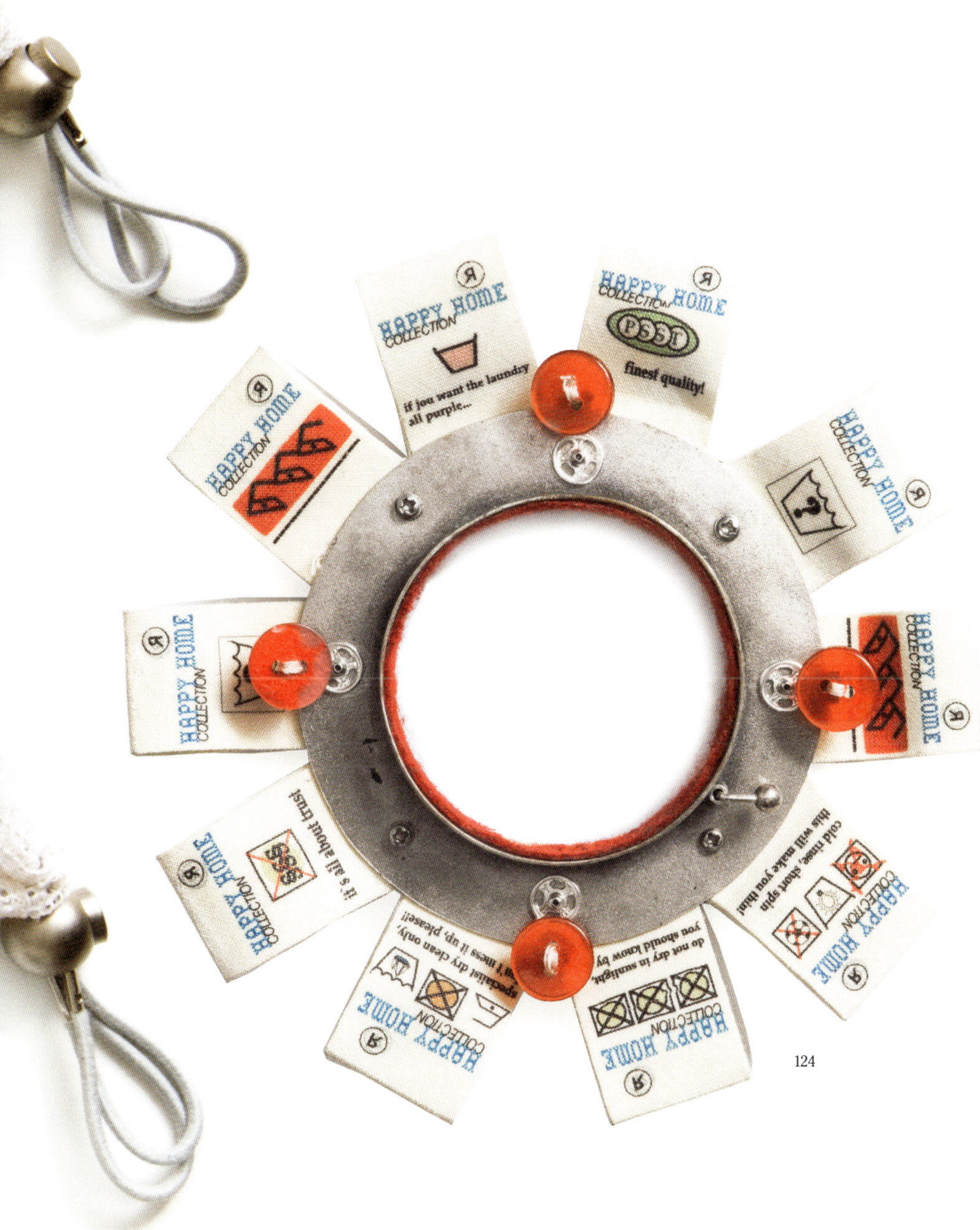

HAPPY HOME
COLLECTION
if you want the laundry
all purple...
HAPPY HOME
COLLECTION
finest quality!
HAPPY HOME
COLLECTION
HAPPY HOME
COLLECTION
HAPPY HOME
COLLECTION
HAPPY HOME
COLLECTION
it's all about trust
HAPPY HOME
COLLECTION
specialist dry clean only,
you'll need it up, please!
HAPPY HOME
COLLECTION
do not dry in sunlight,
you should know by...
cold rinse, short spin
this will make you blue!
HAPPY HOME
COLLECTION
124

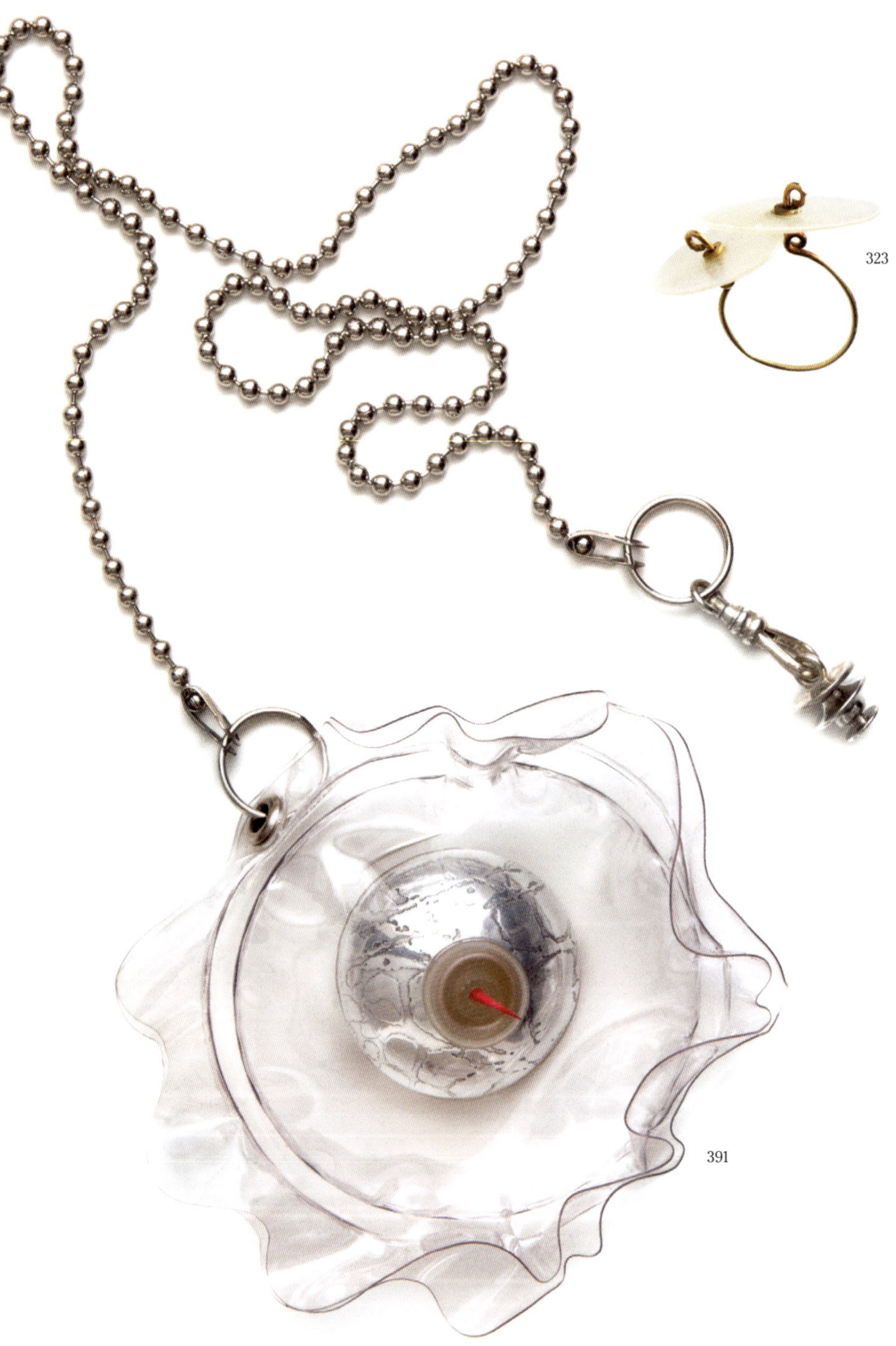

323

391

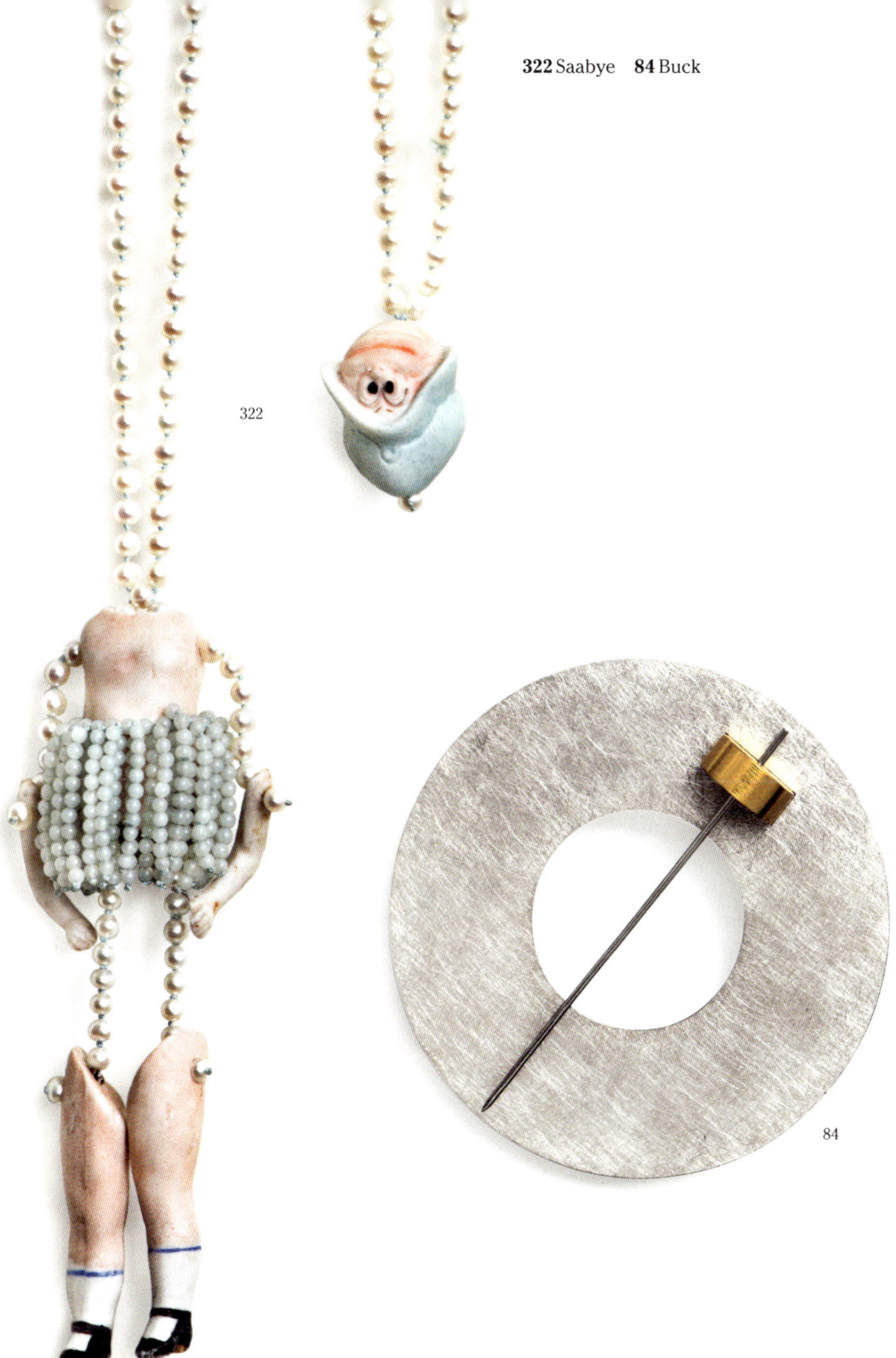

322

84

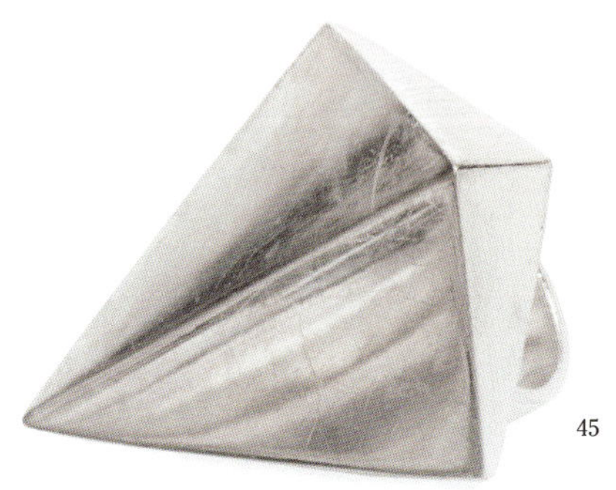

45

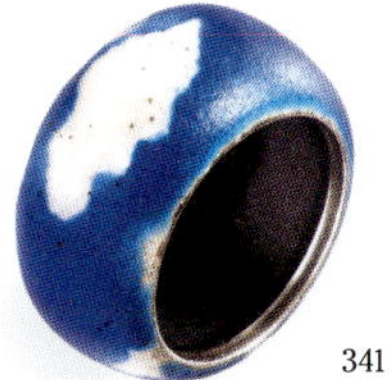

341

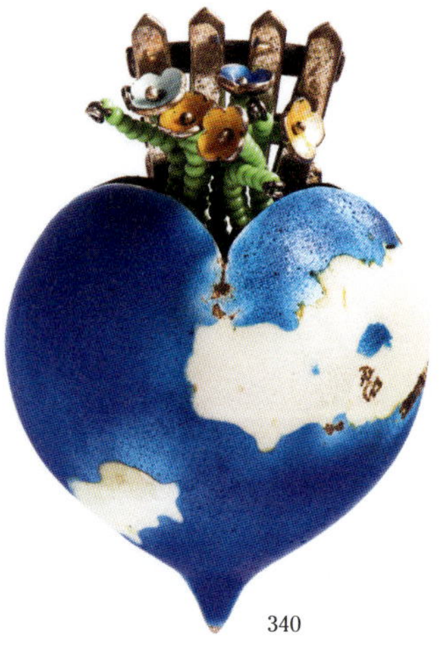

340

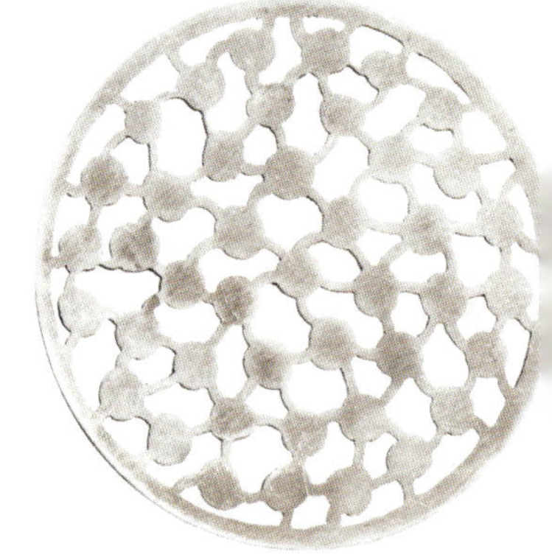

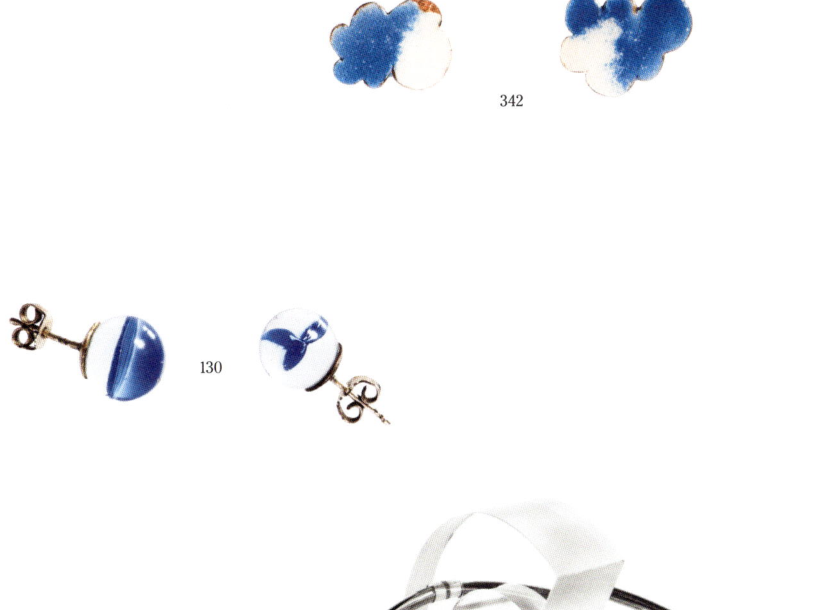

342

130

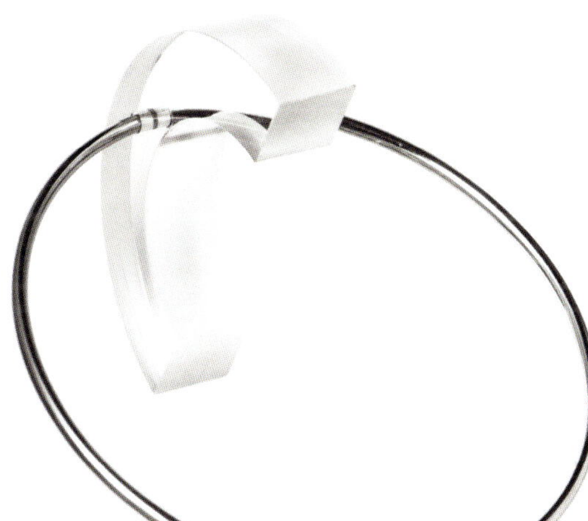

83

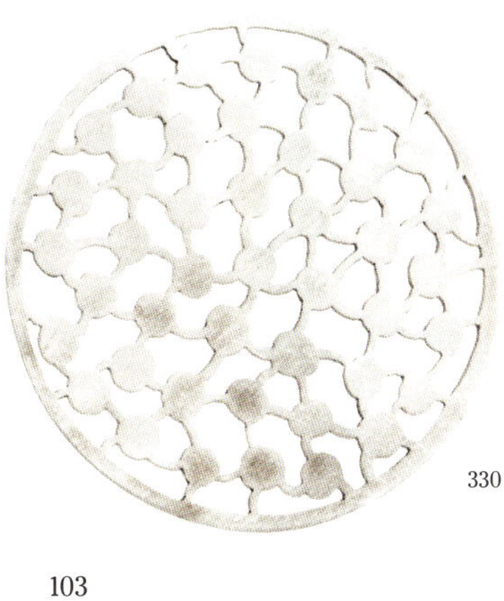

330

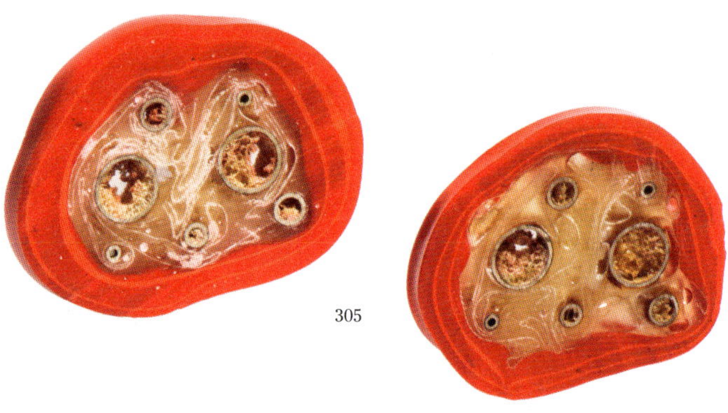

305

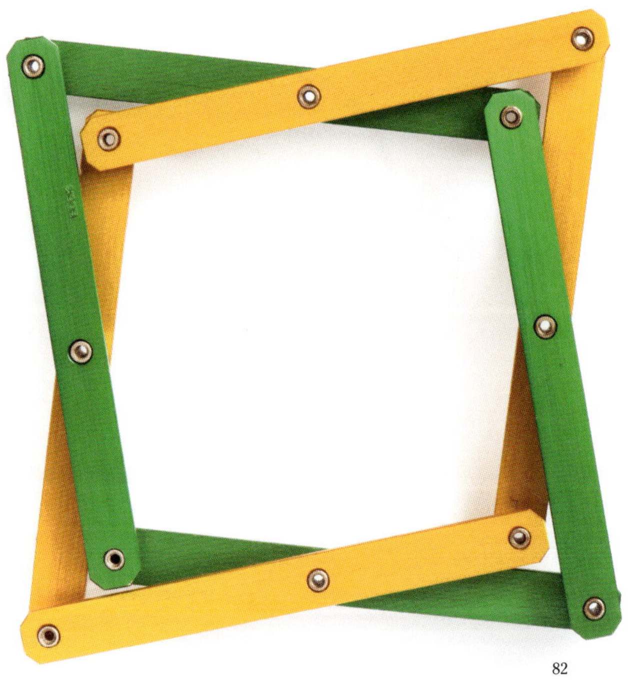

82

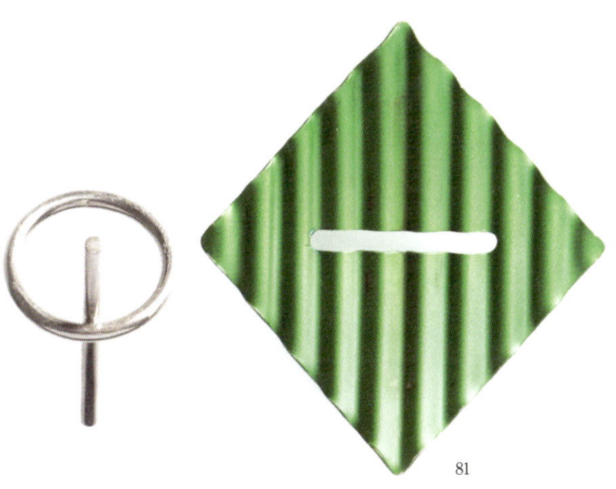

81

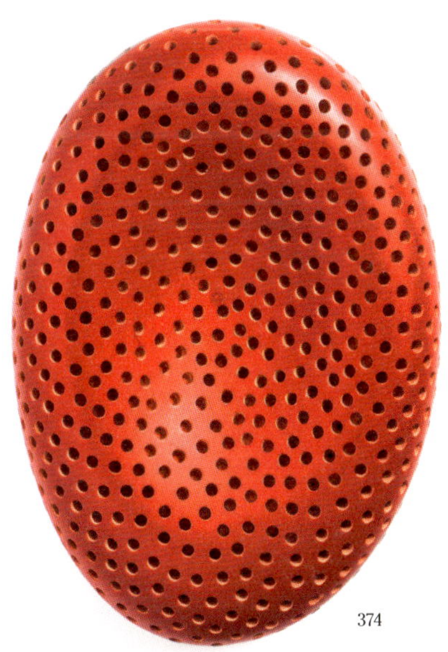

374

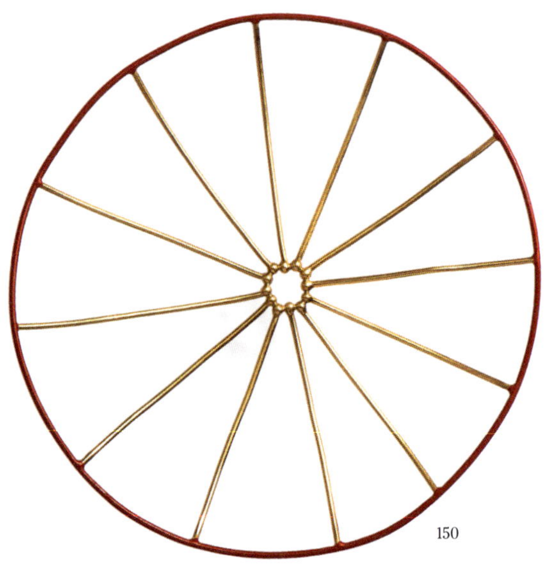

150

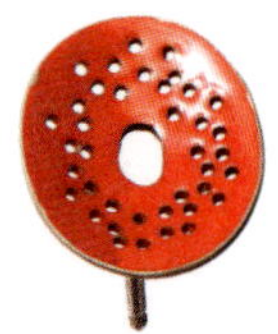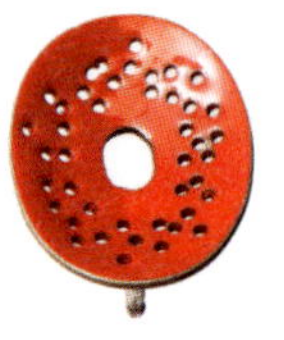

153

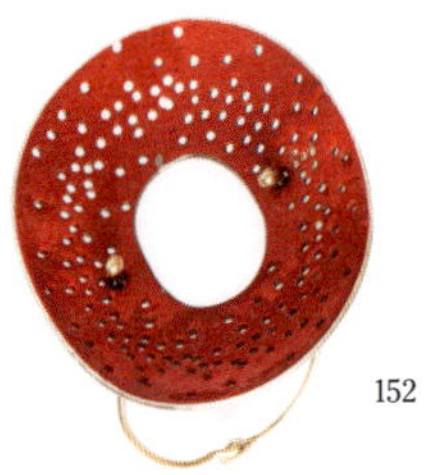

152

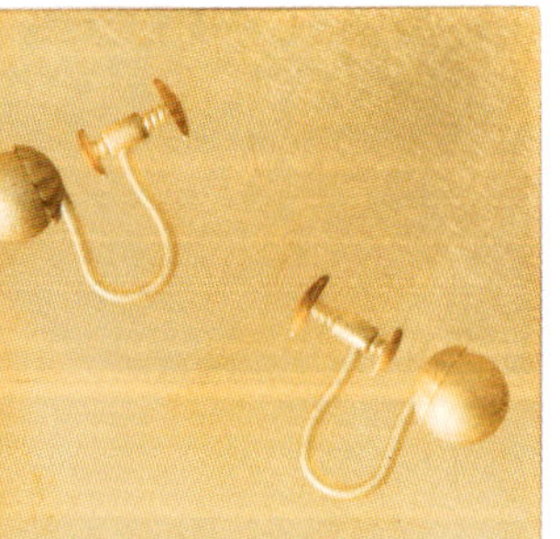

87

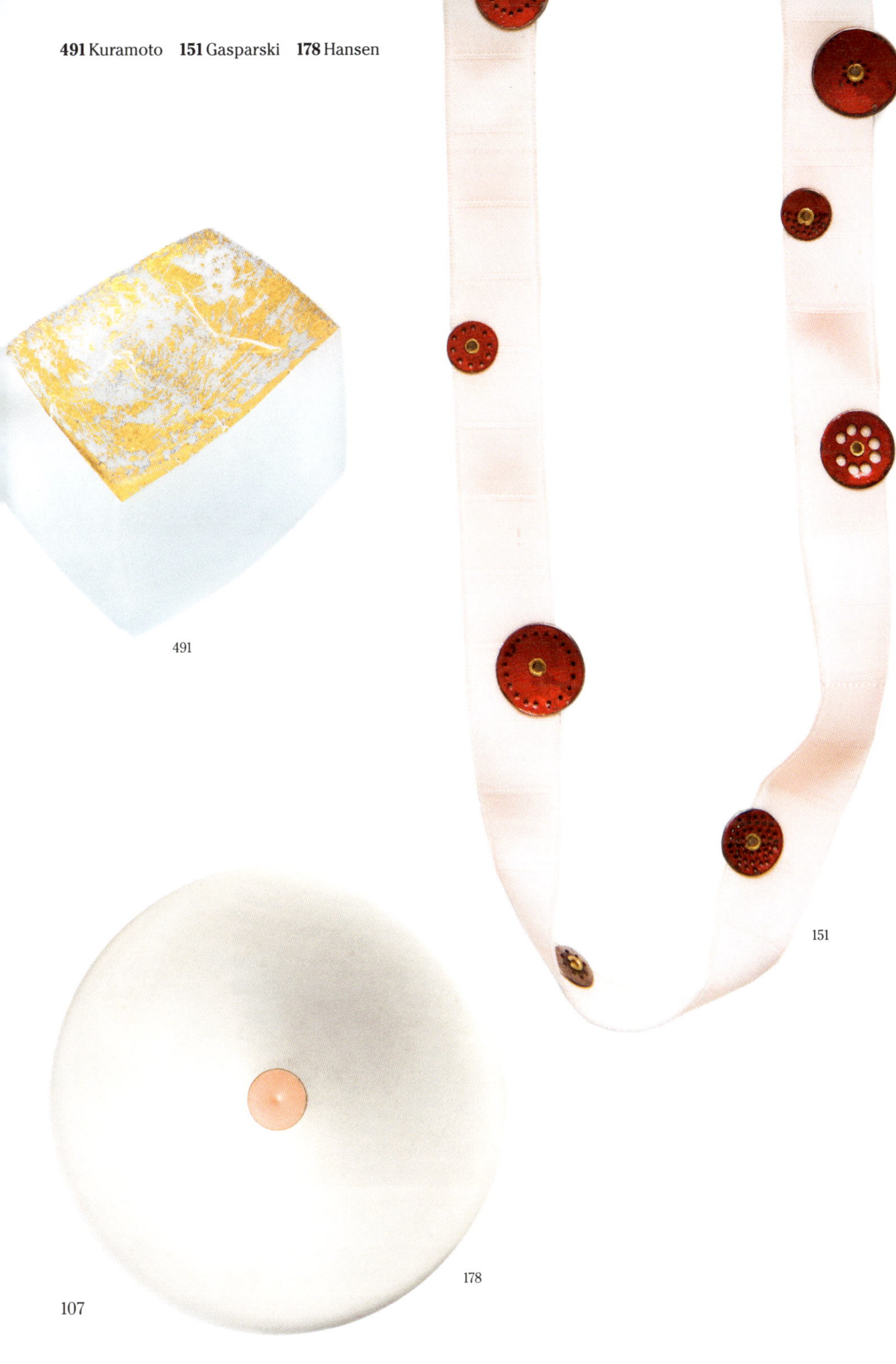
491 Kuramoto   151 Gasparski   178 Hansen
491
151
178
107

301

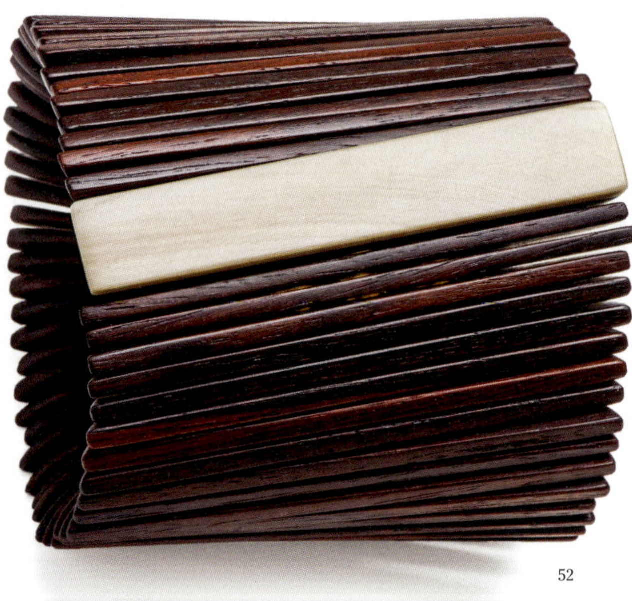

52

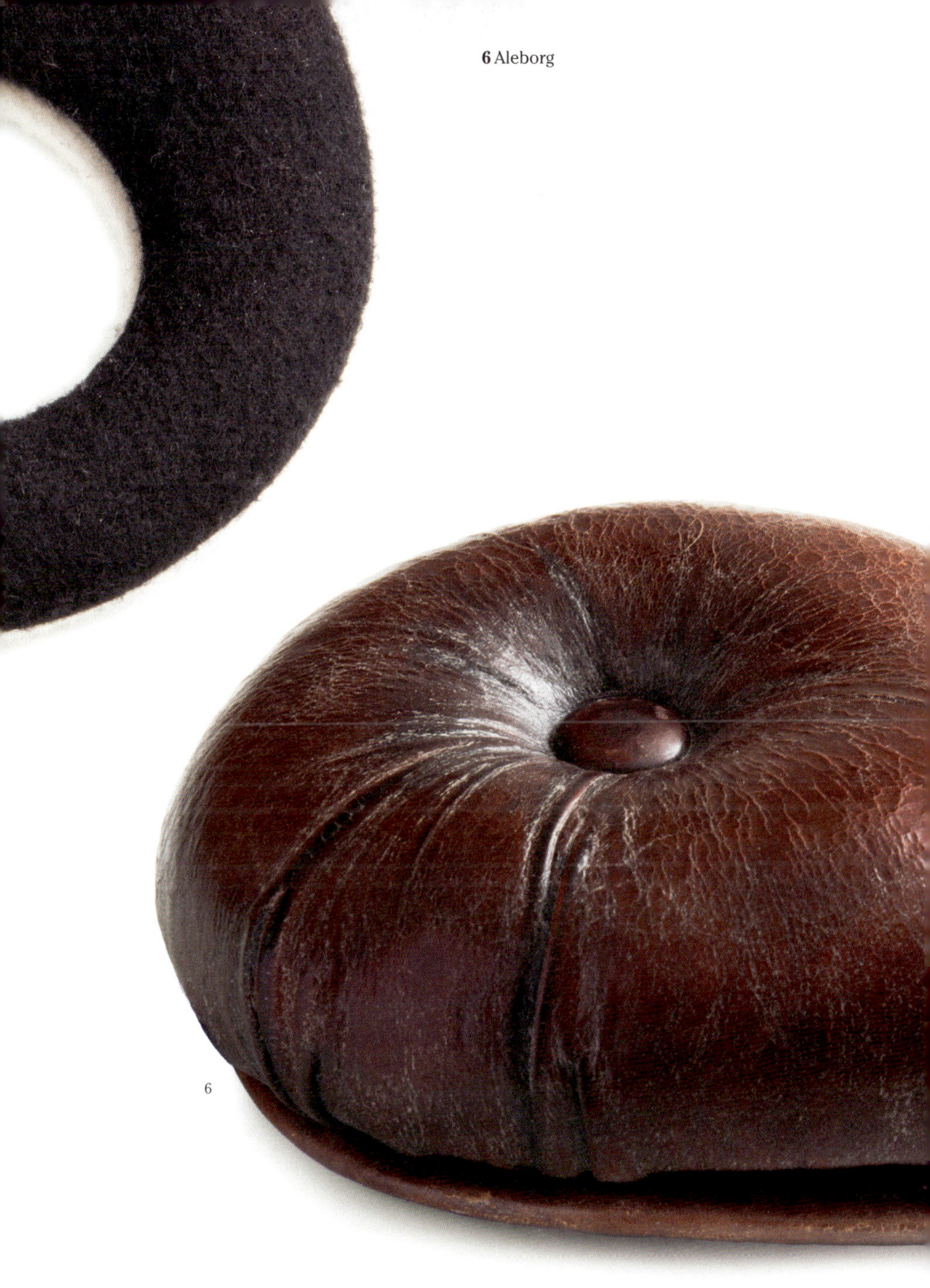

6

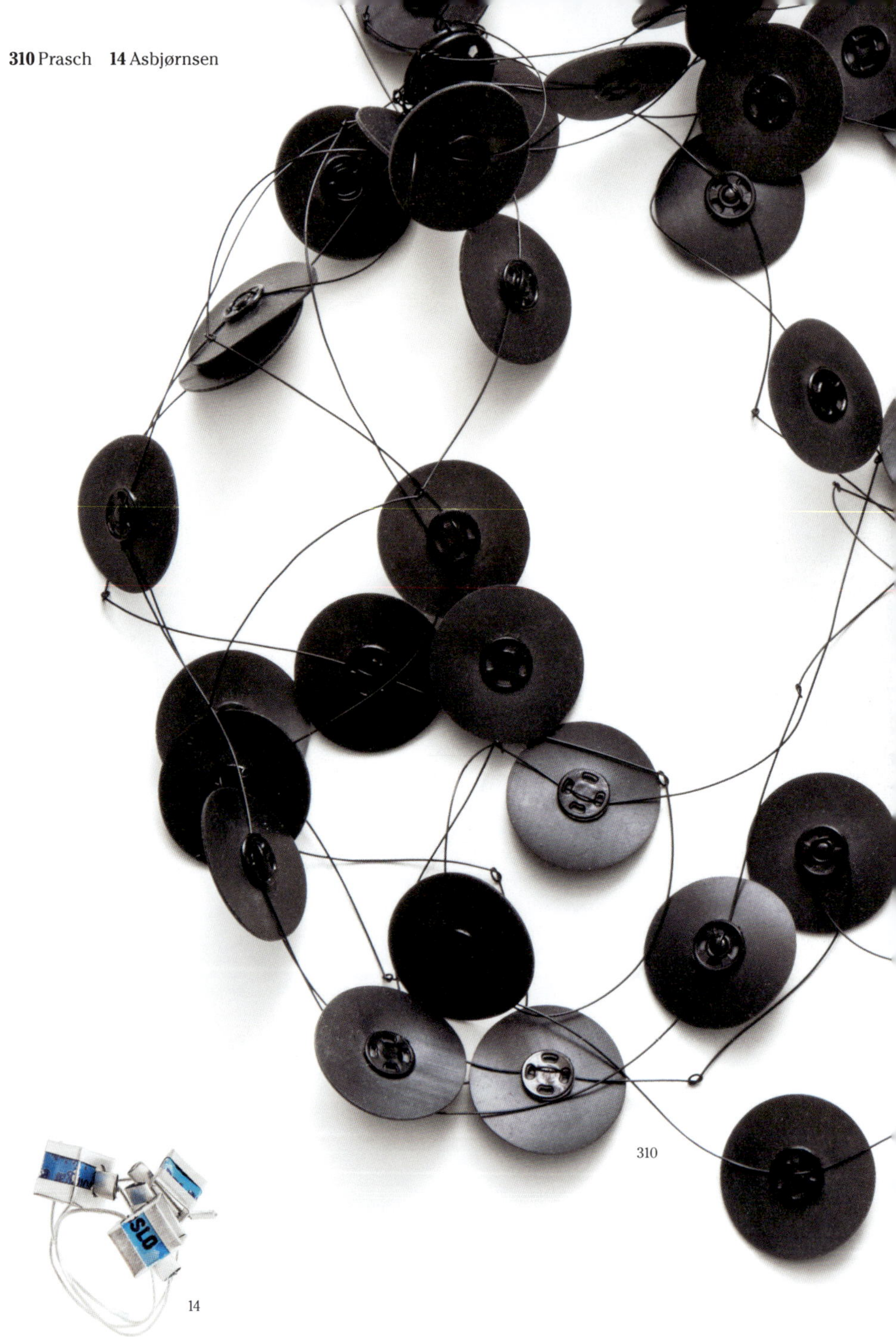

310

14

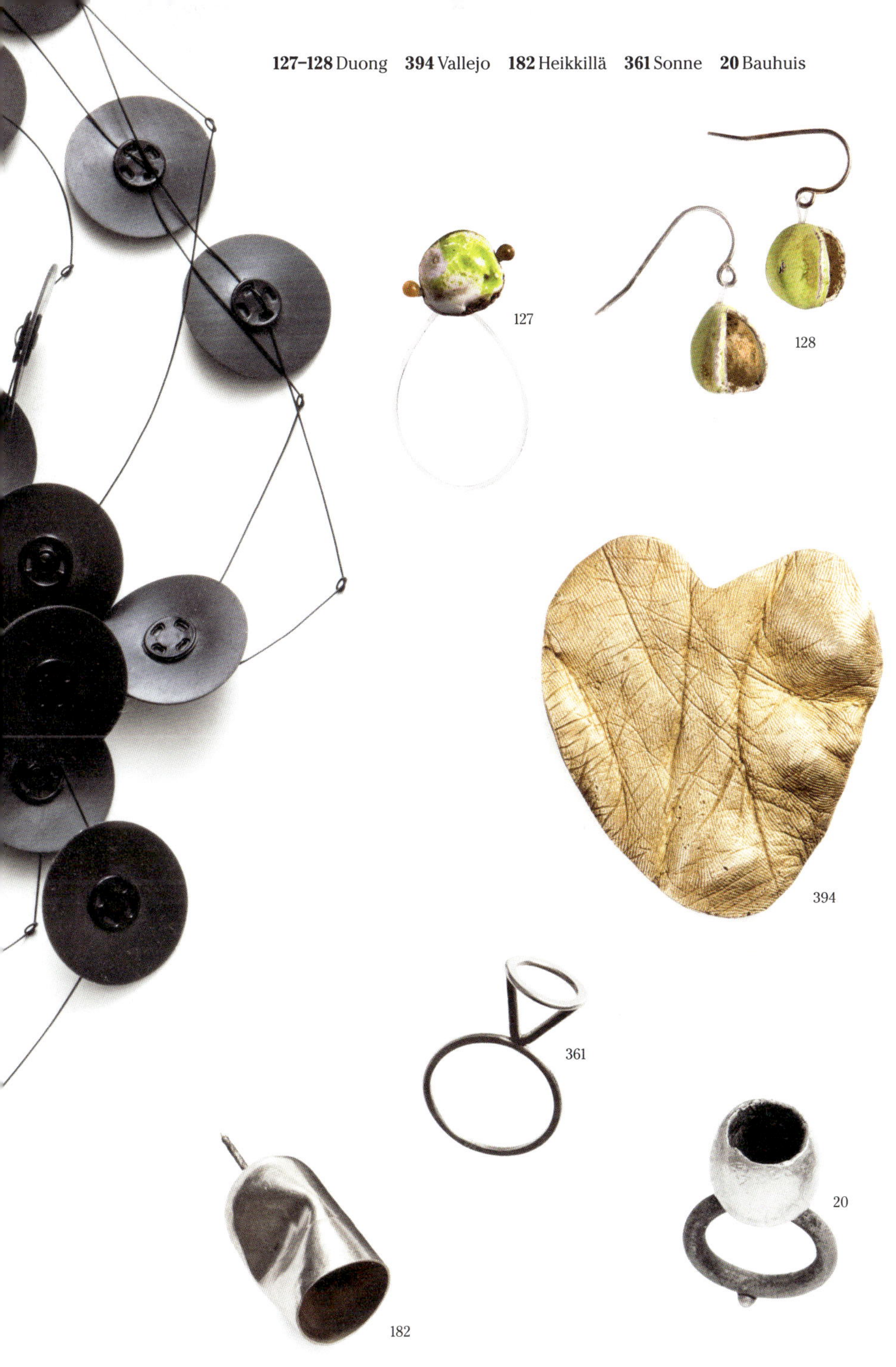
127
128
394
361
182
20

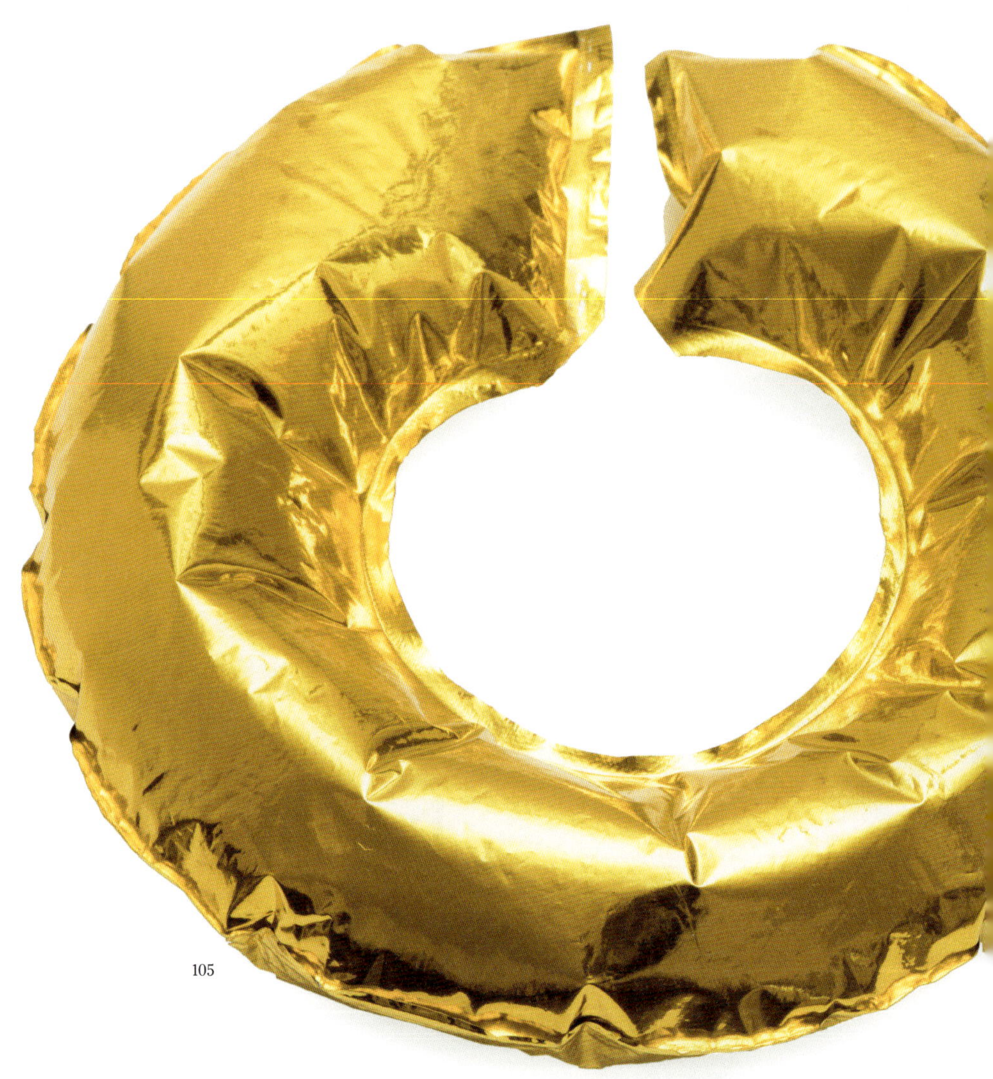

105

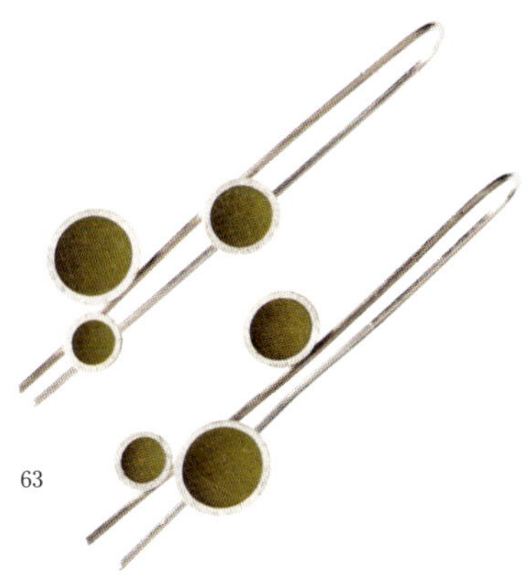

63

319

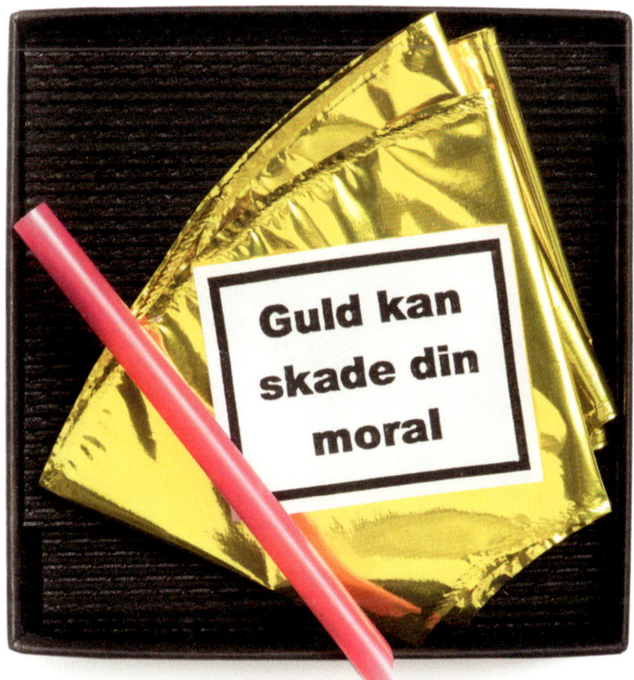

105

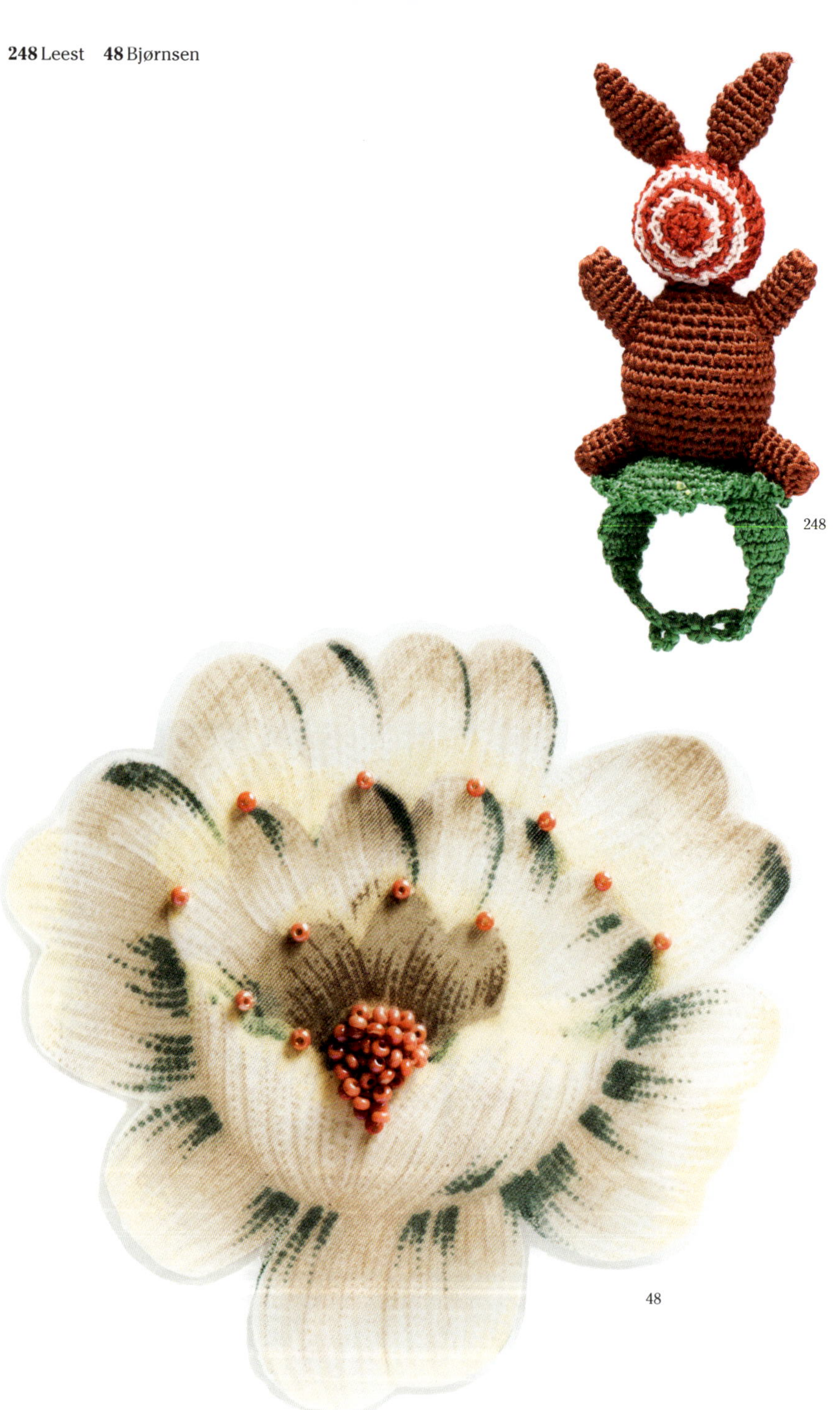

248

48

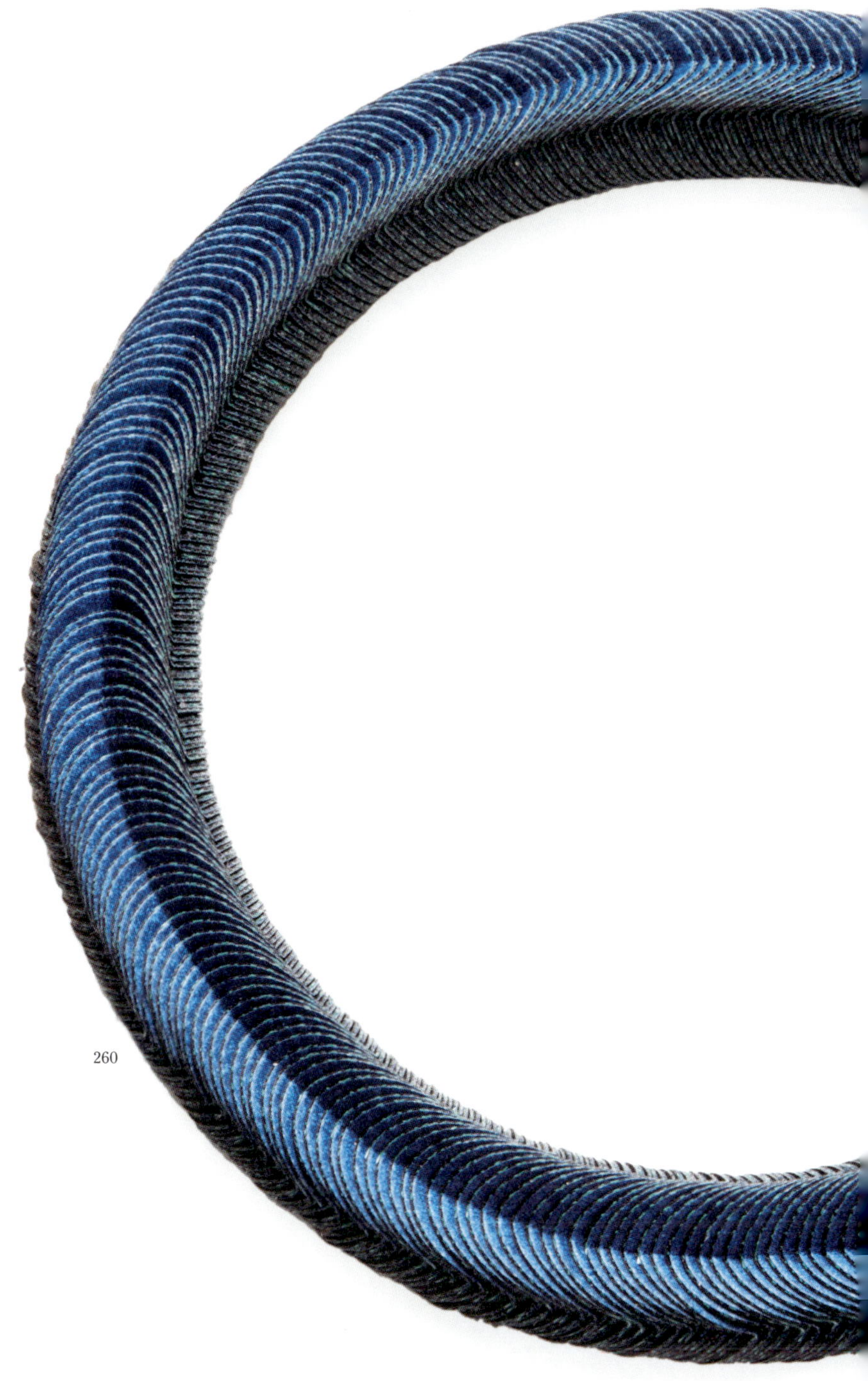

260

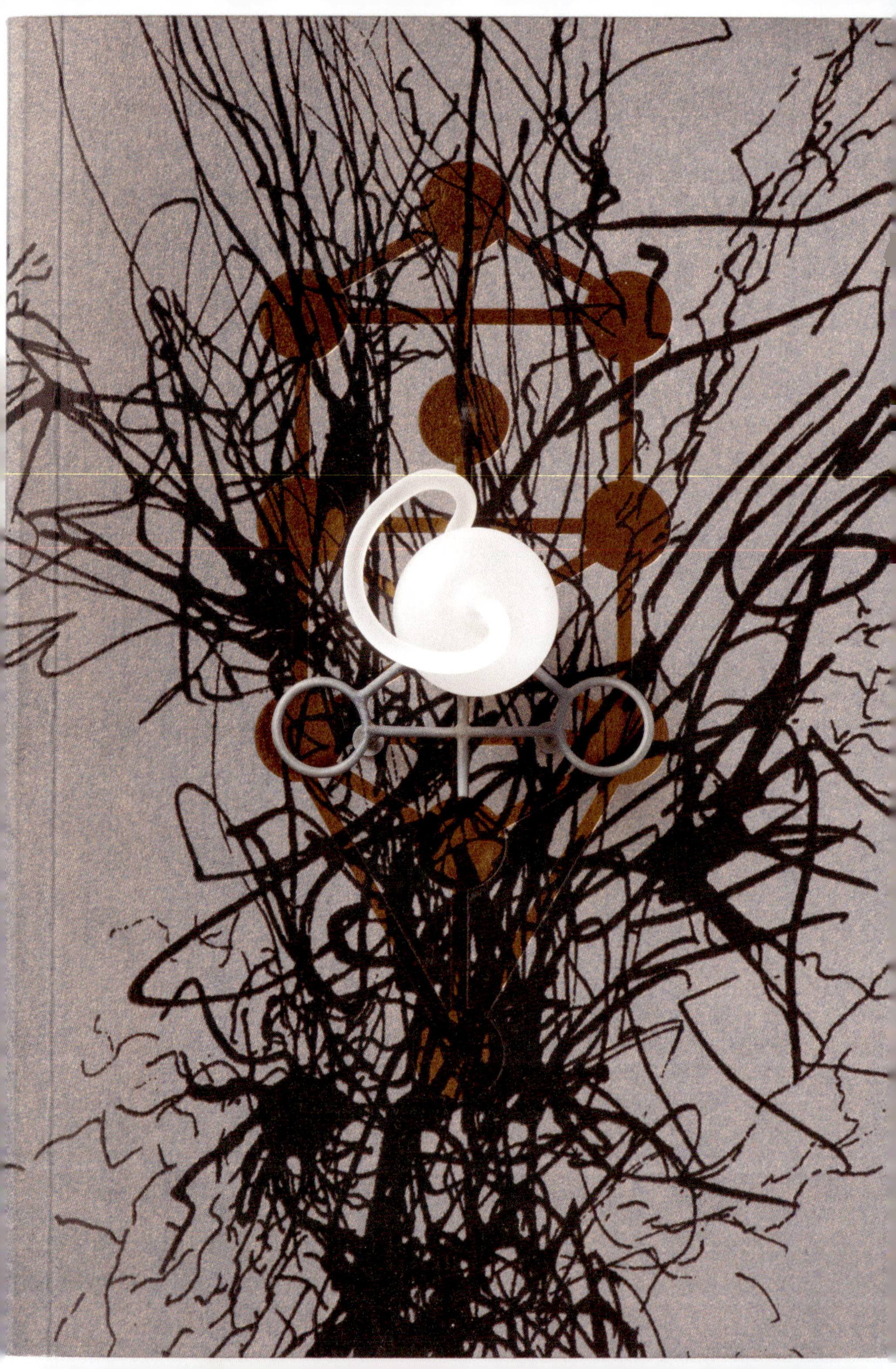

306

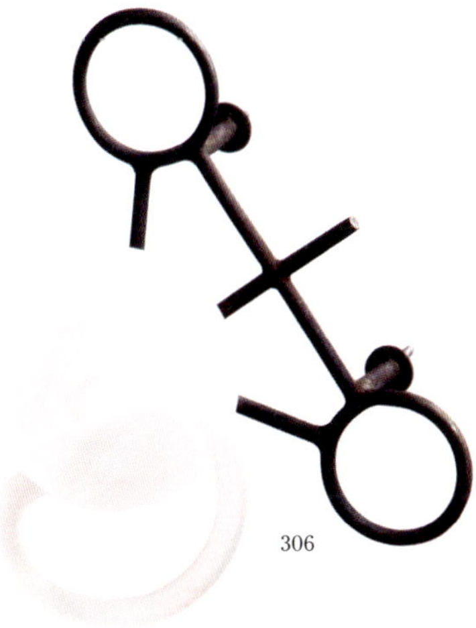

306

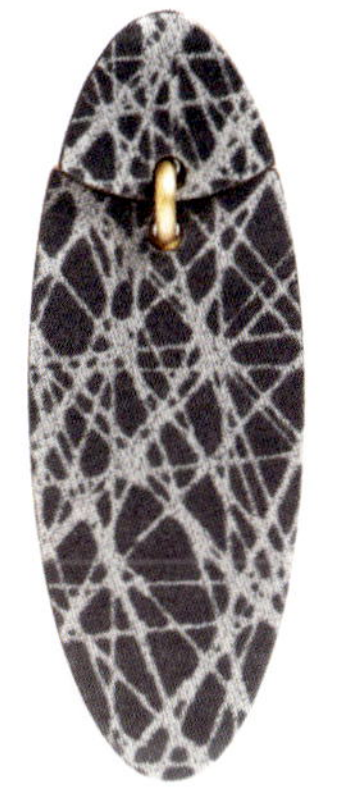
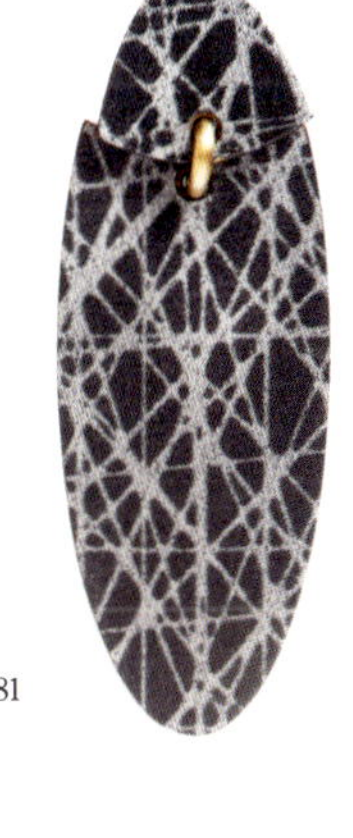

381

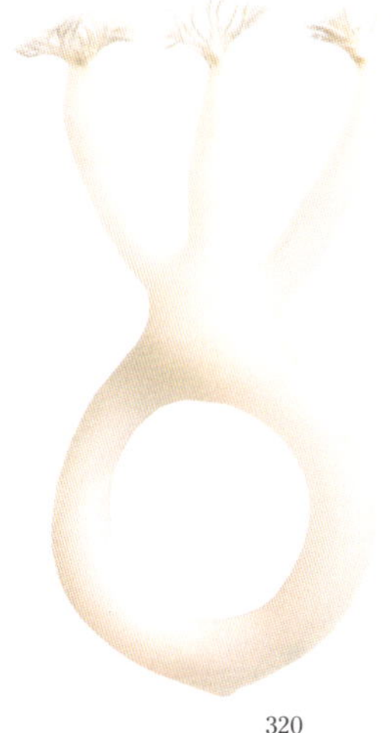

320

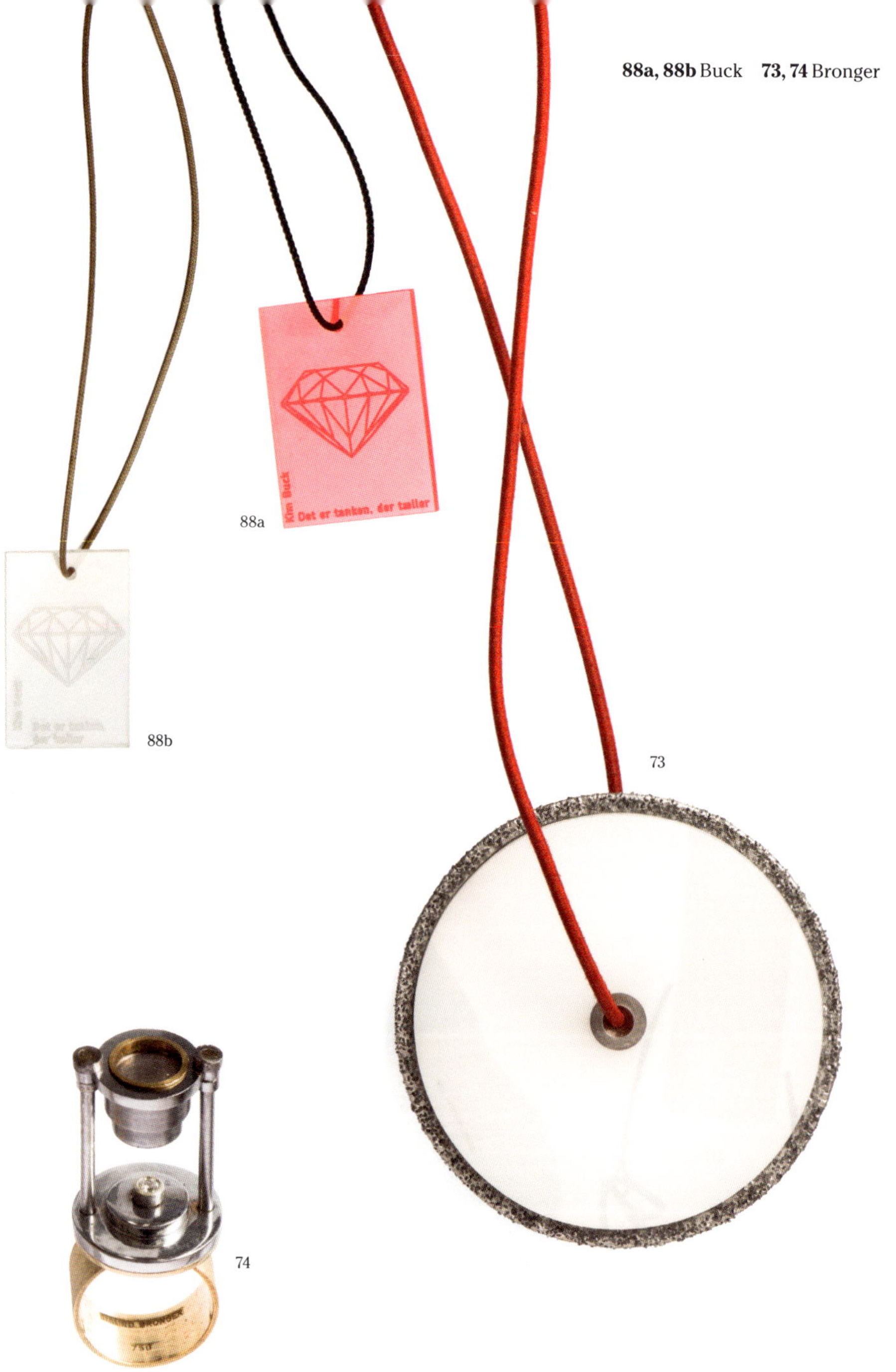

88a

88b

73

74

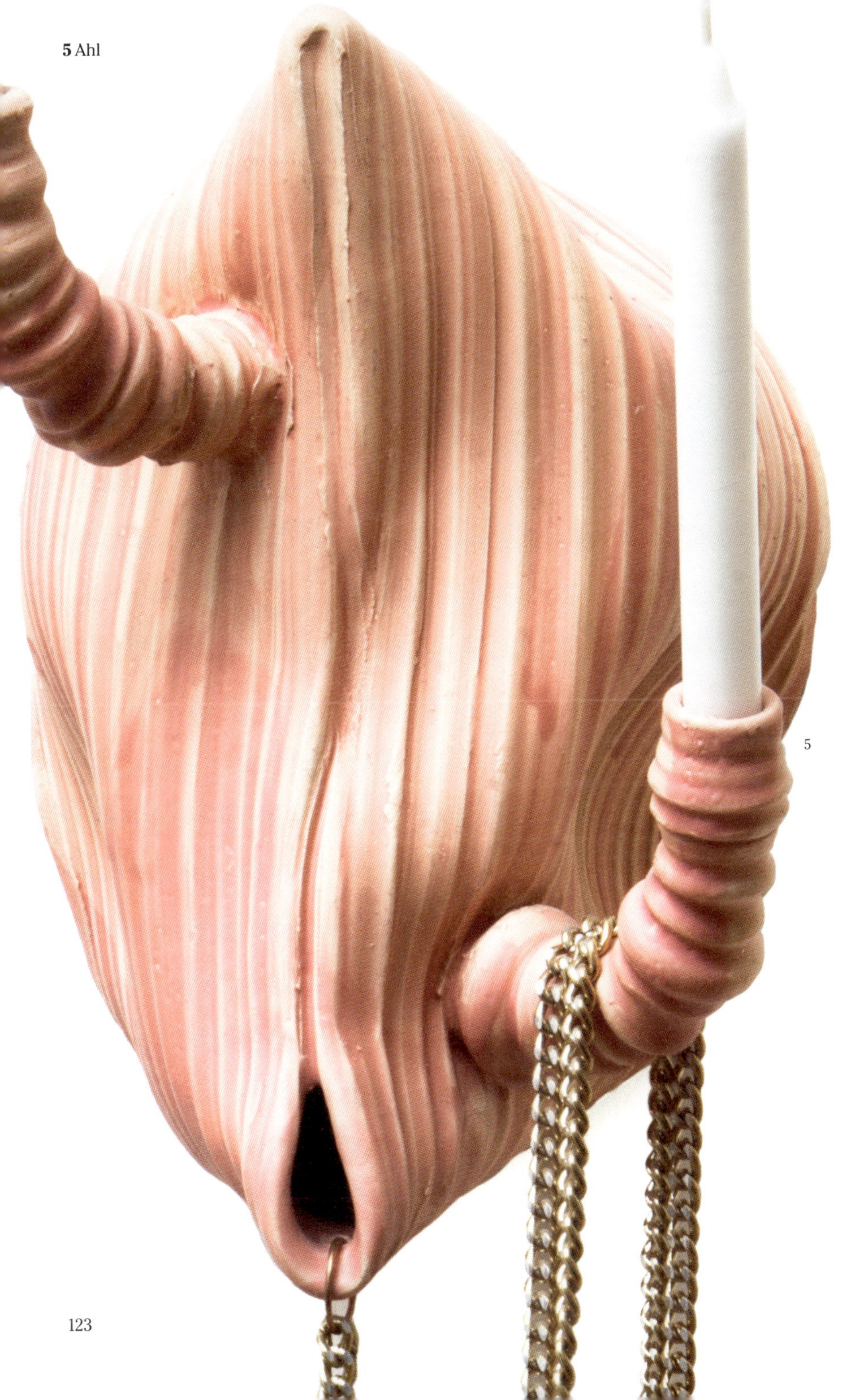

5

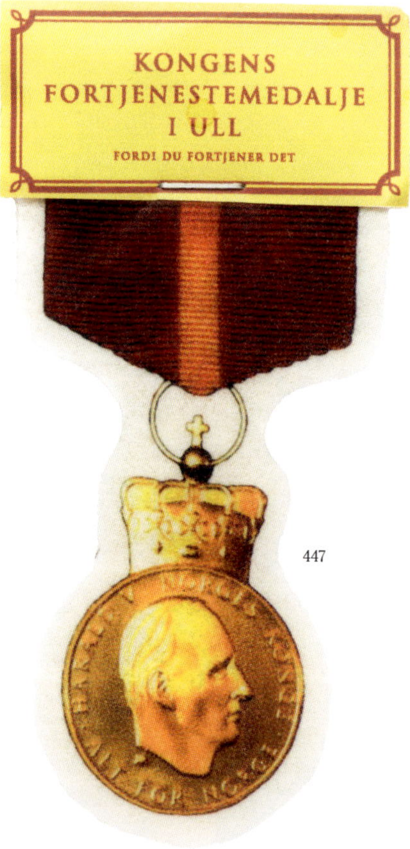

447

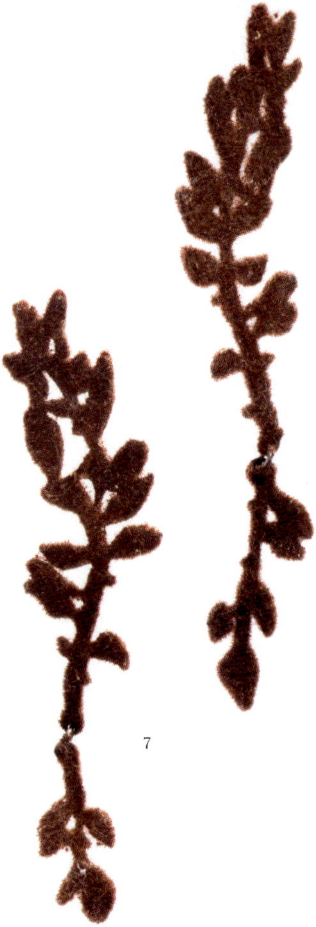

7

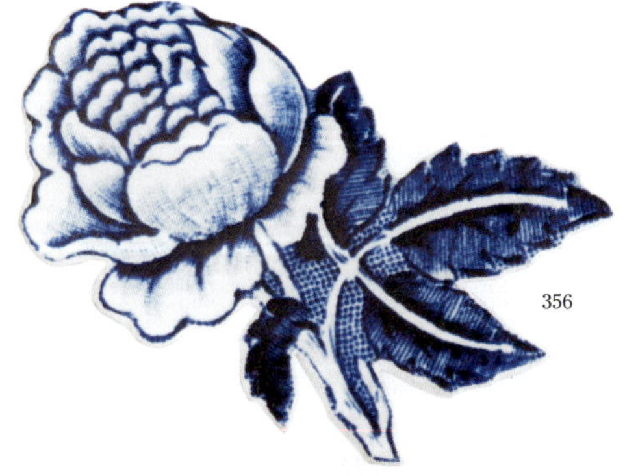

356

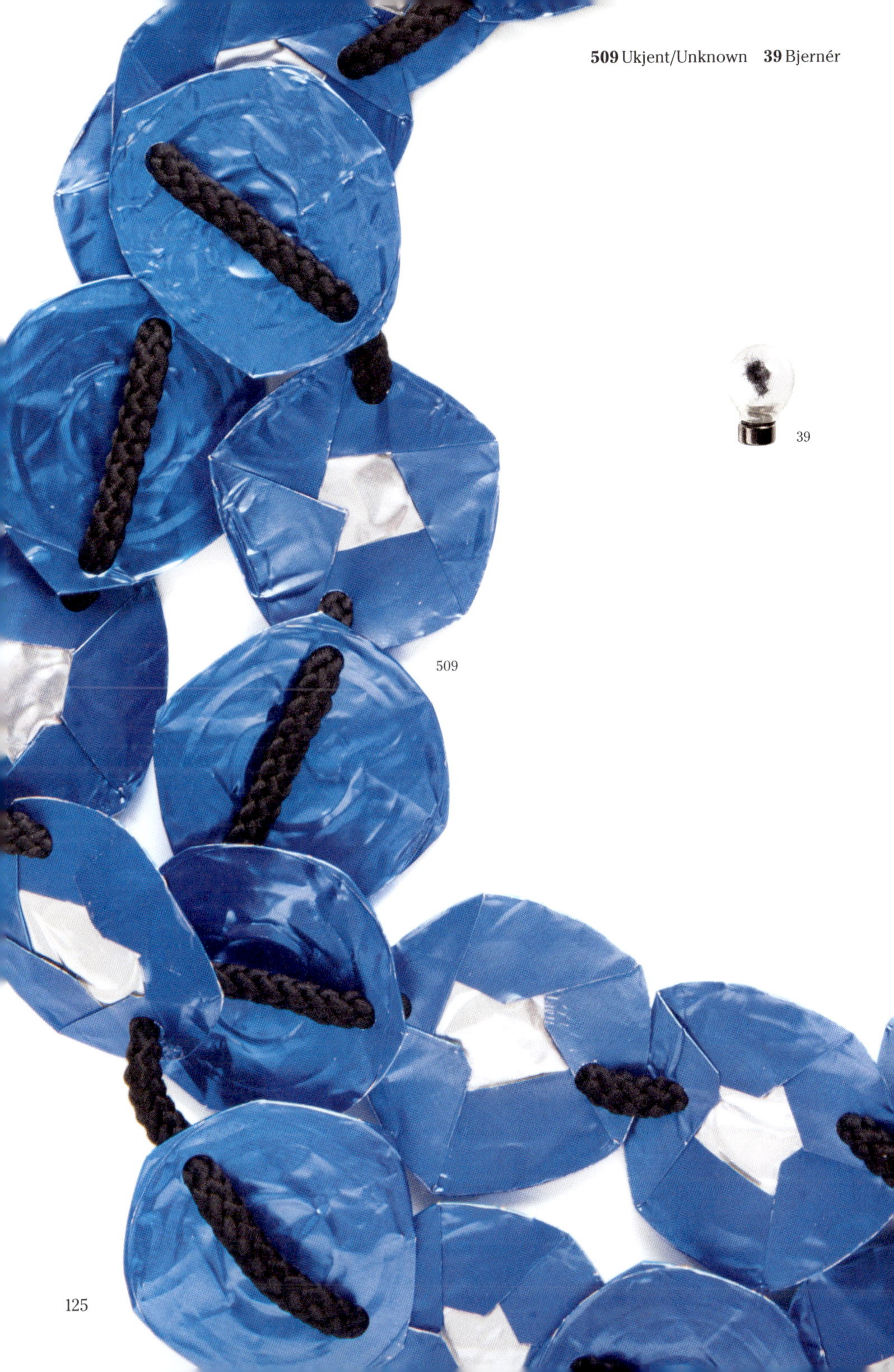

39
509

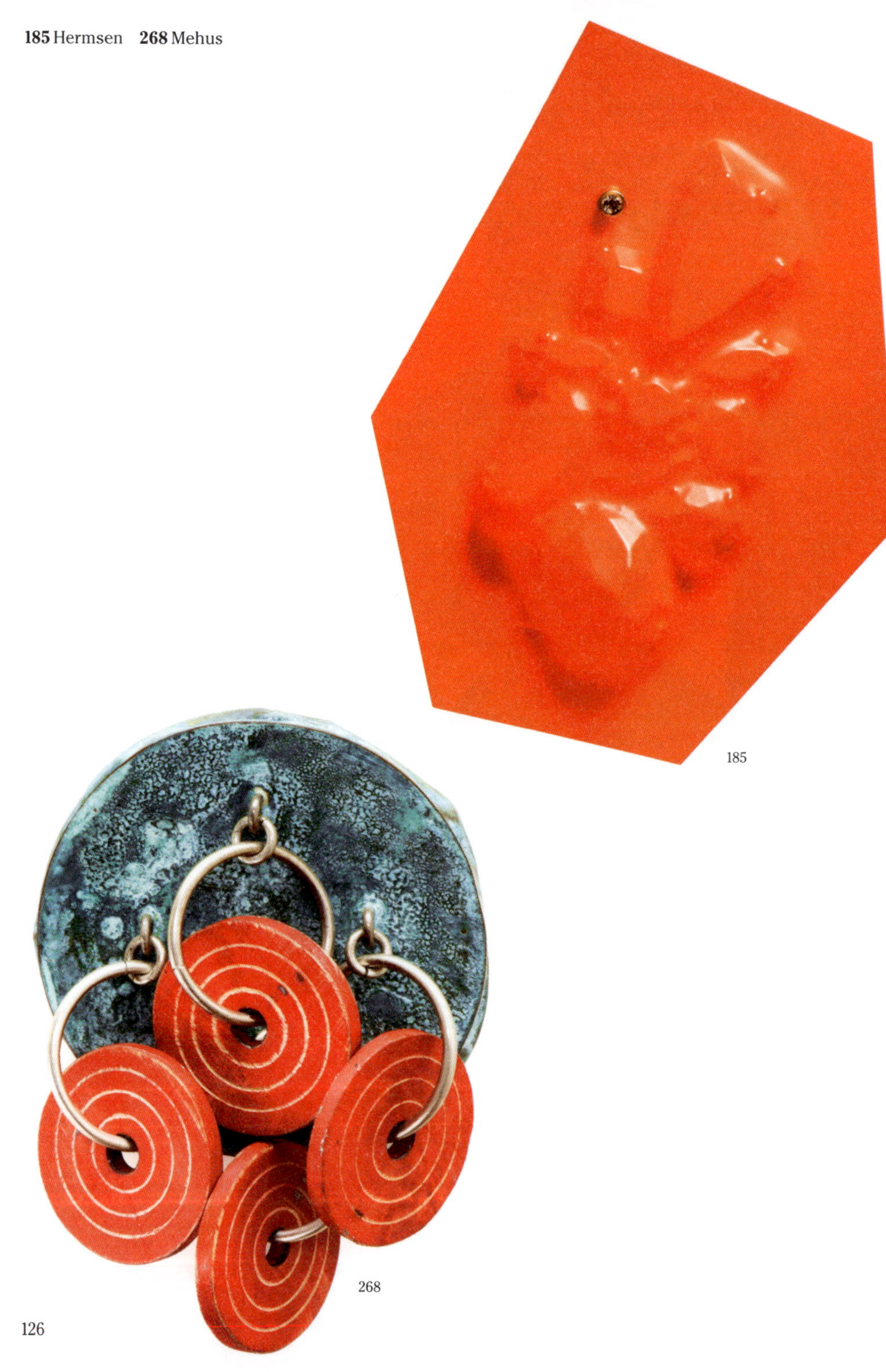

185

268

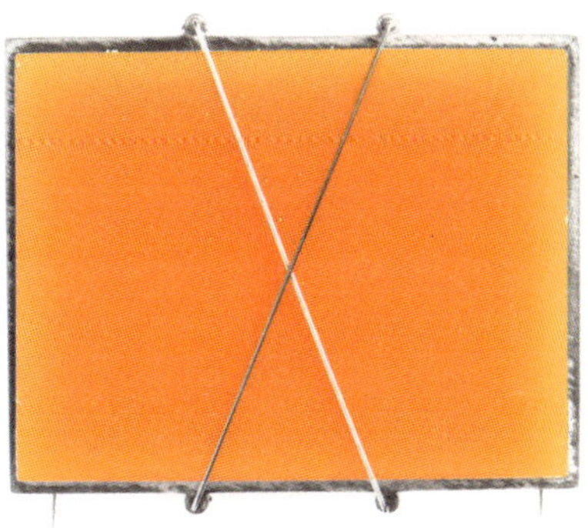

71

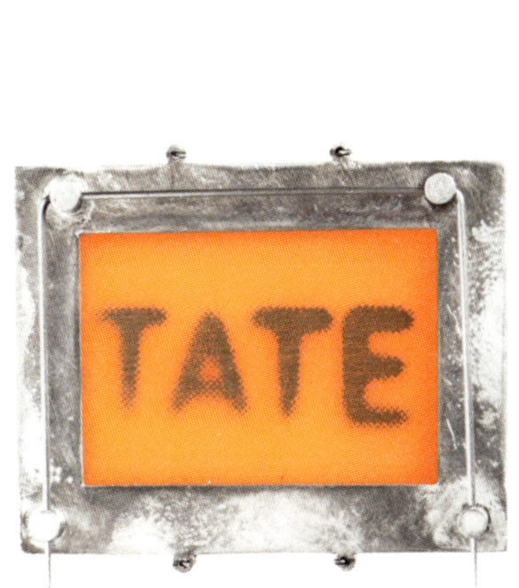

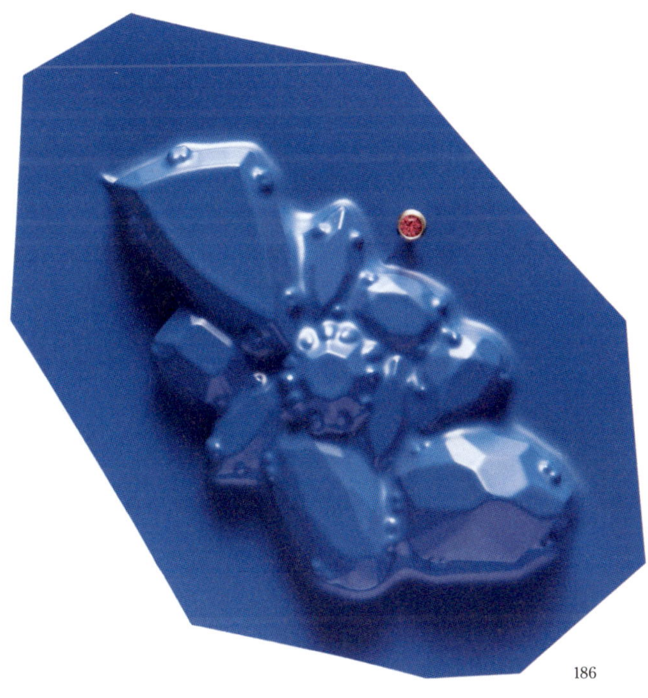

186

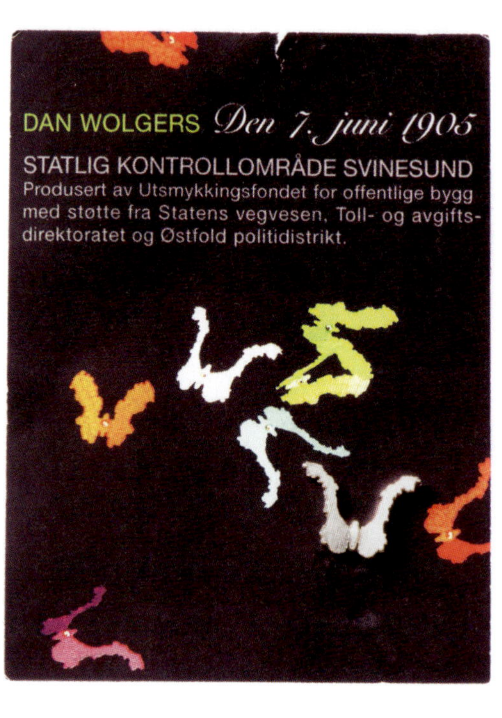

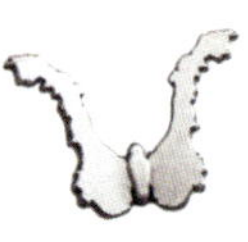

417

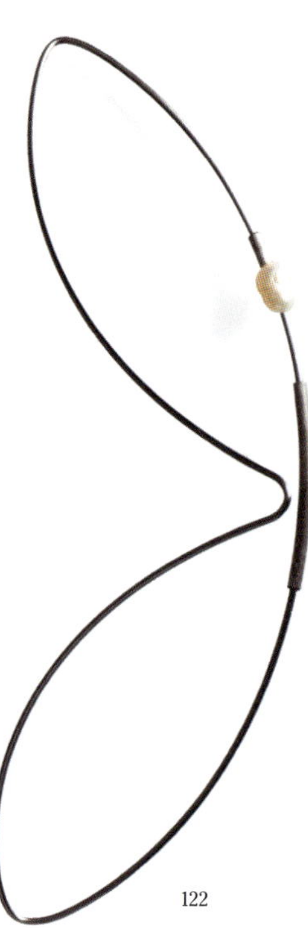

122

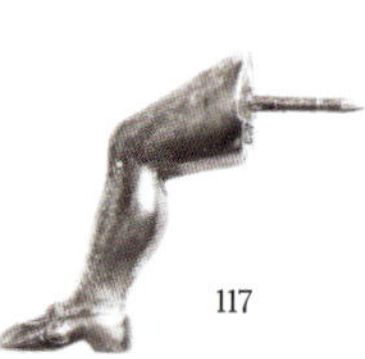

117

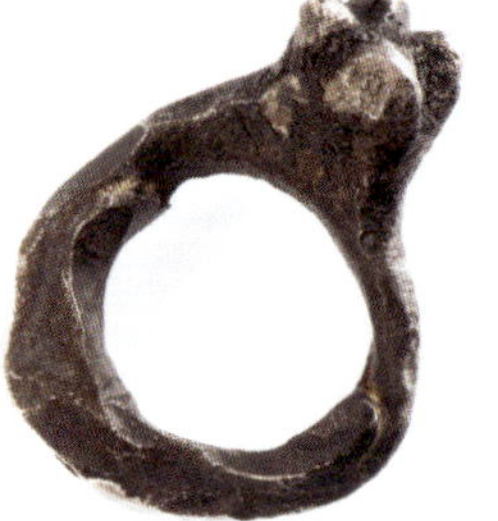

138

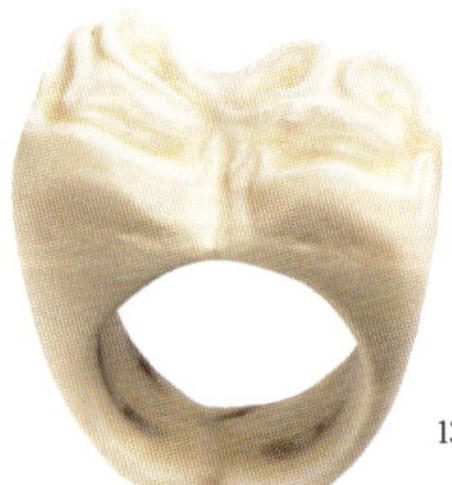

134

161 Grov   **126** Duong   **419** Zellweger

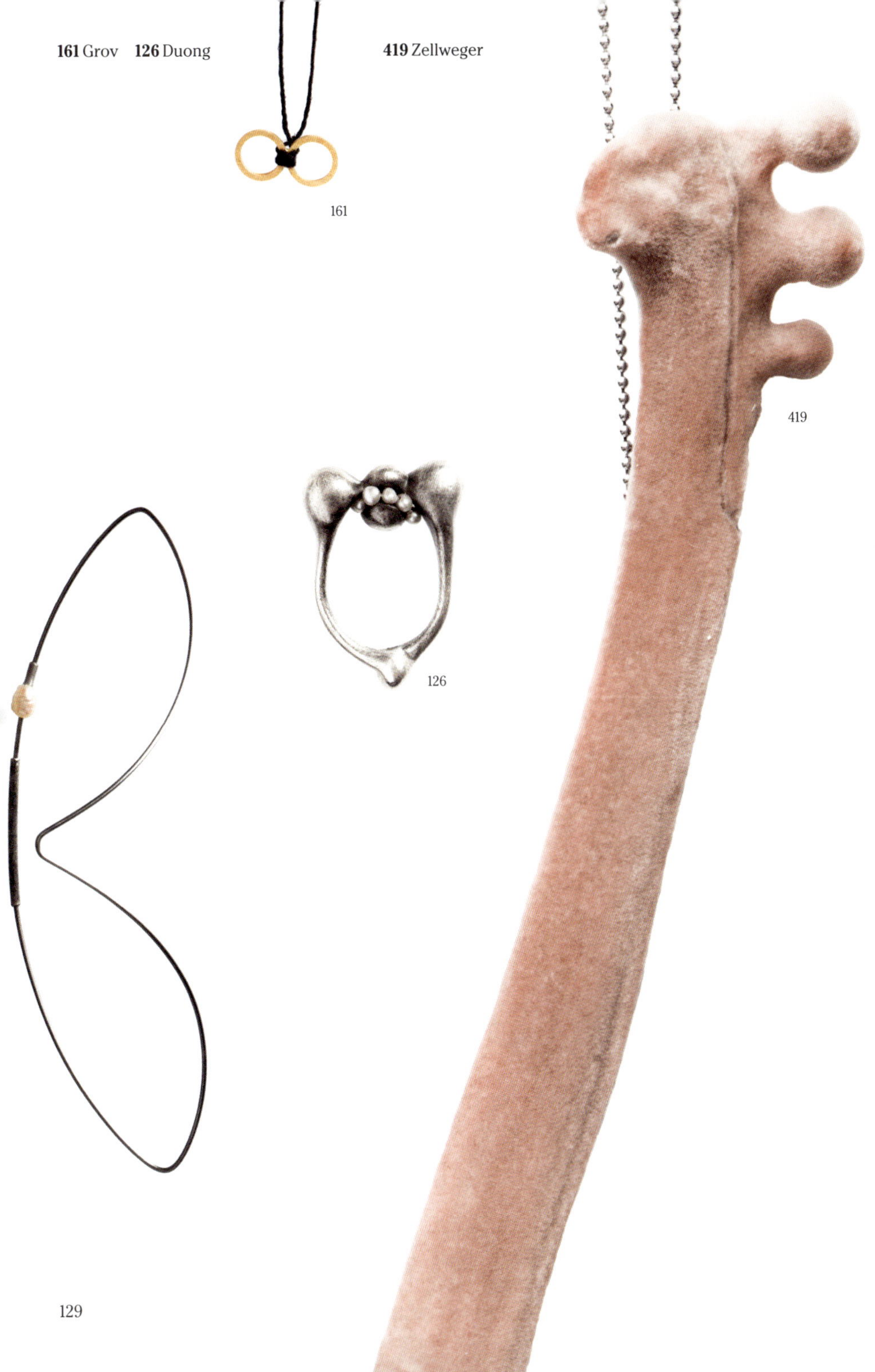

161
126
419

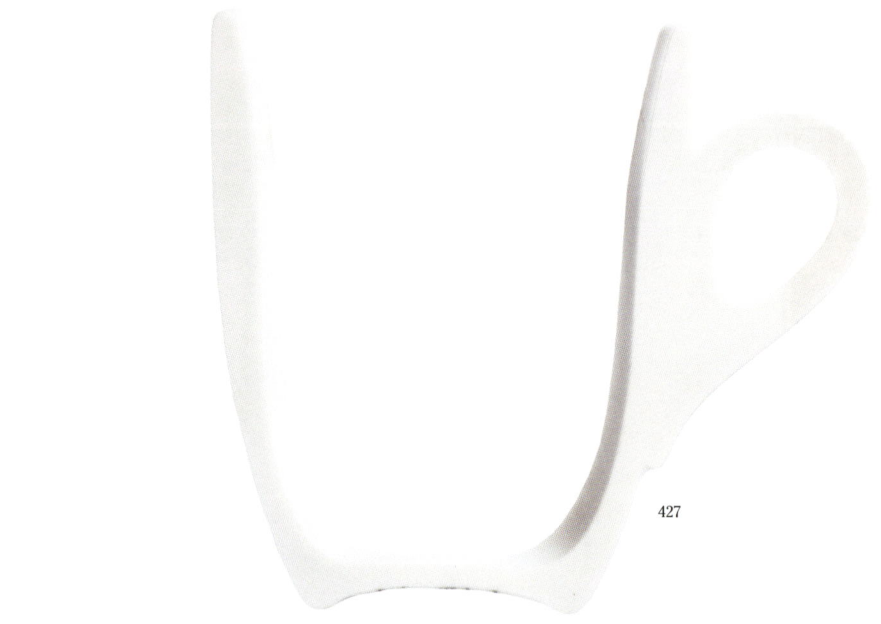

427

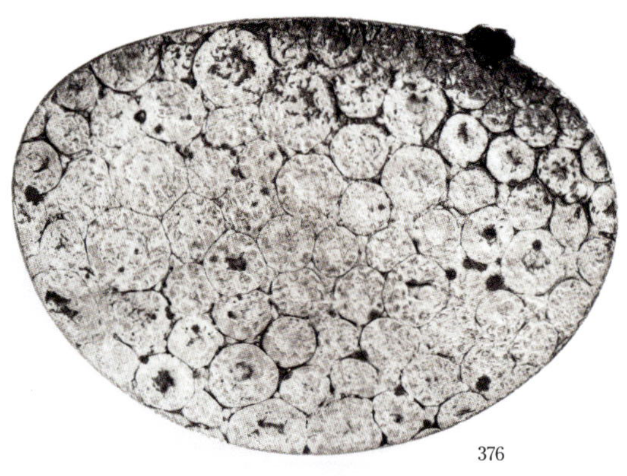

376

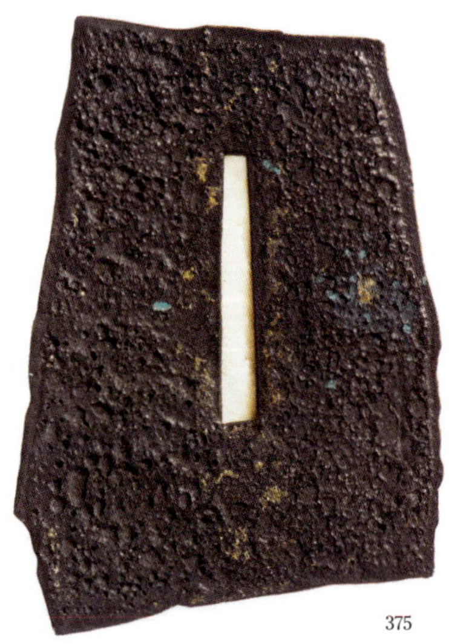

375

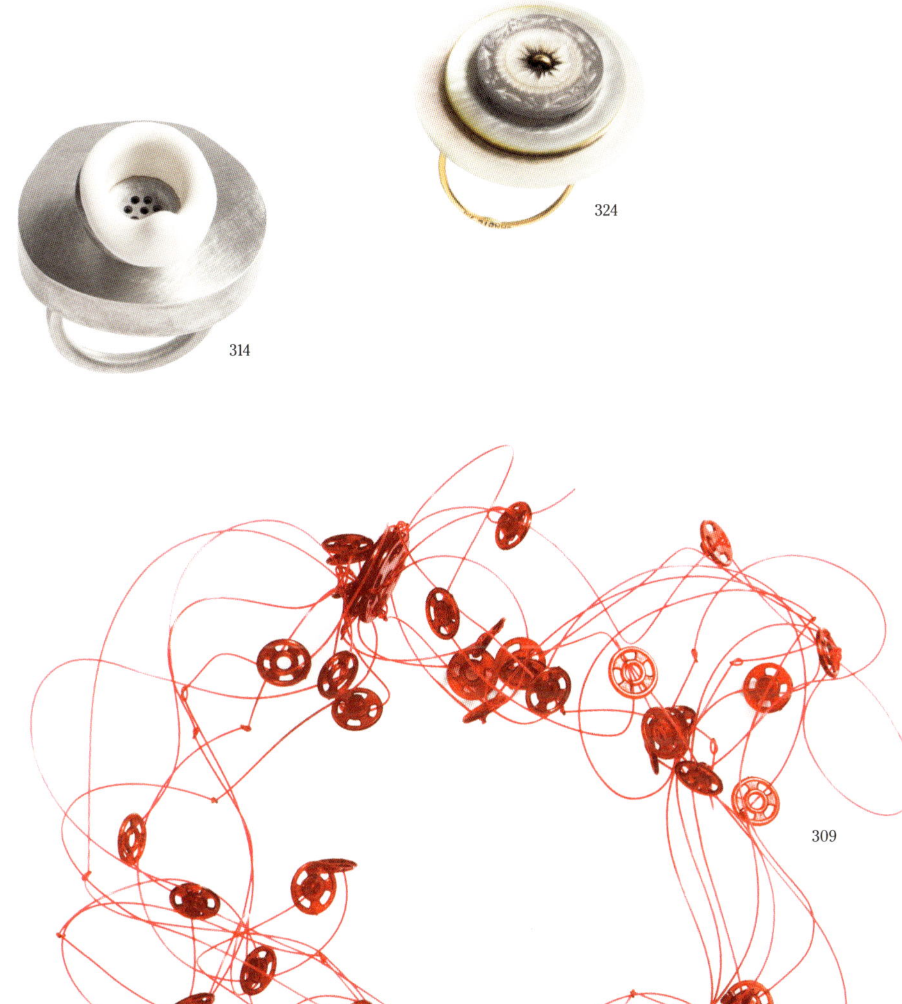

314
324
309

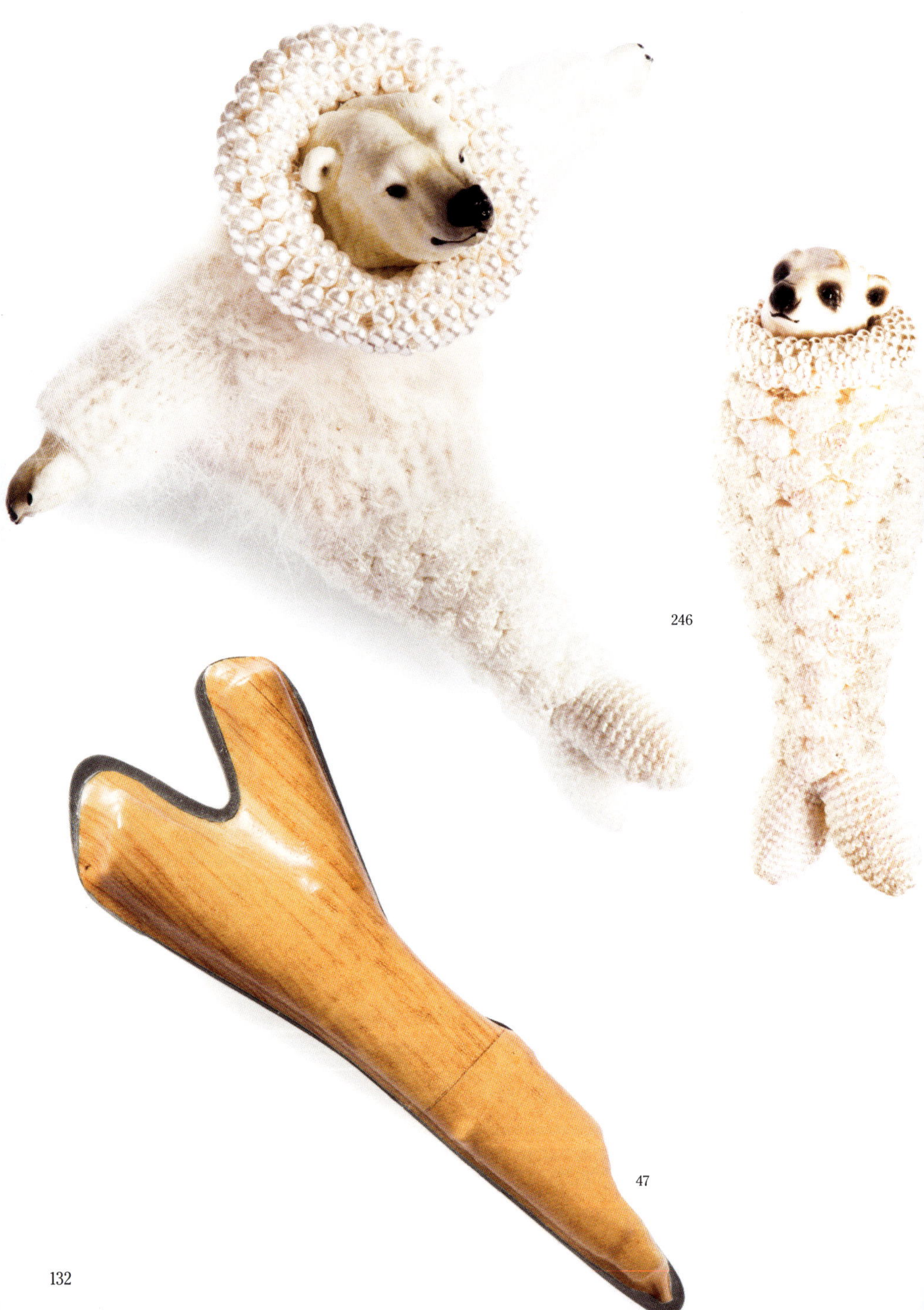

246

47

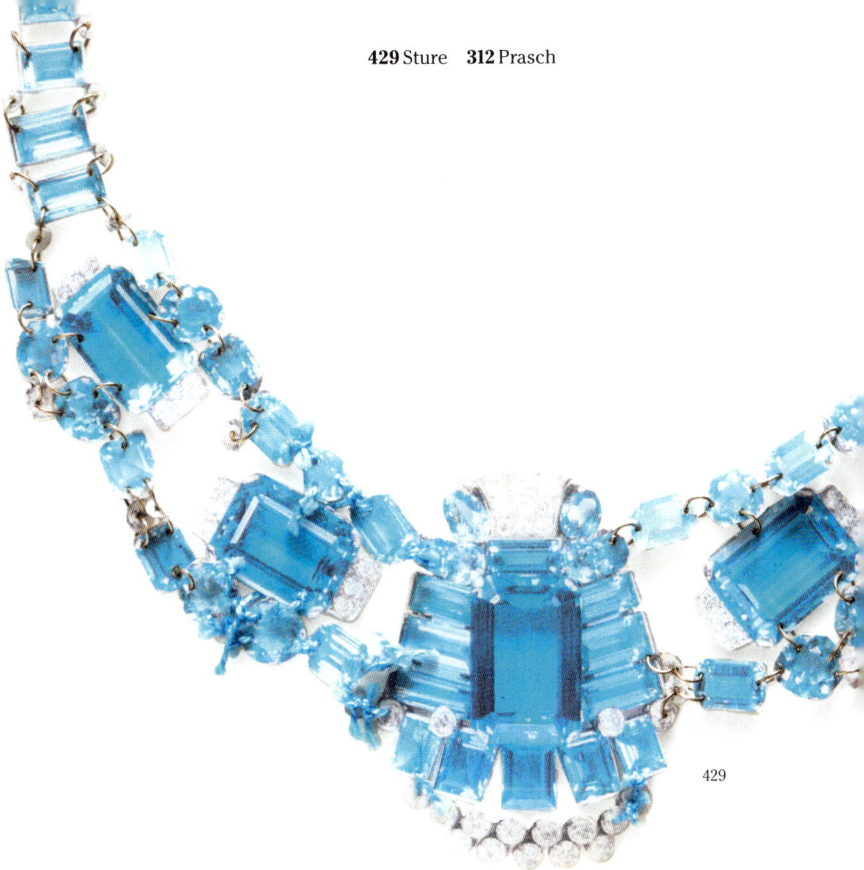

429

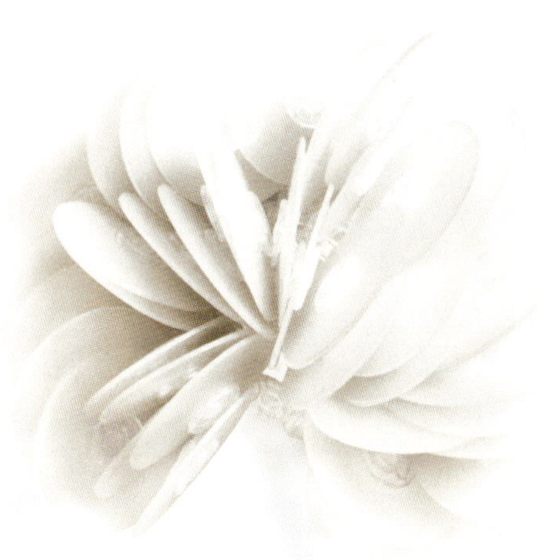

312

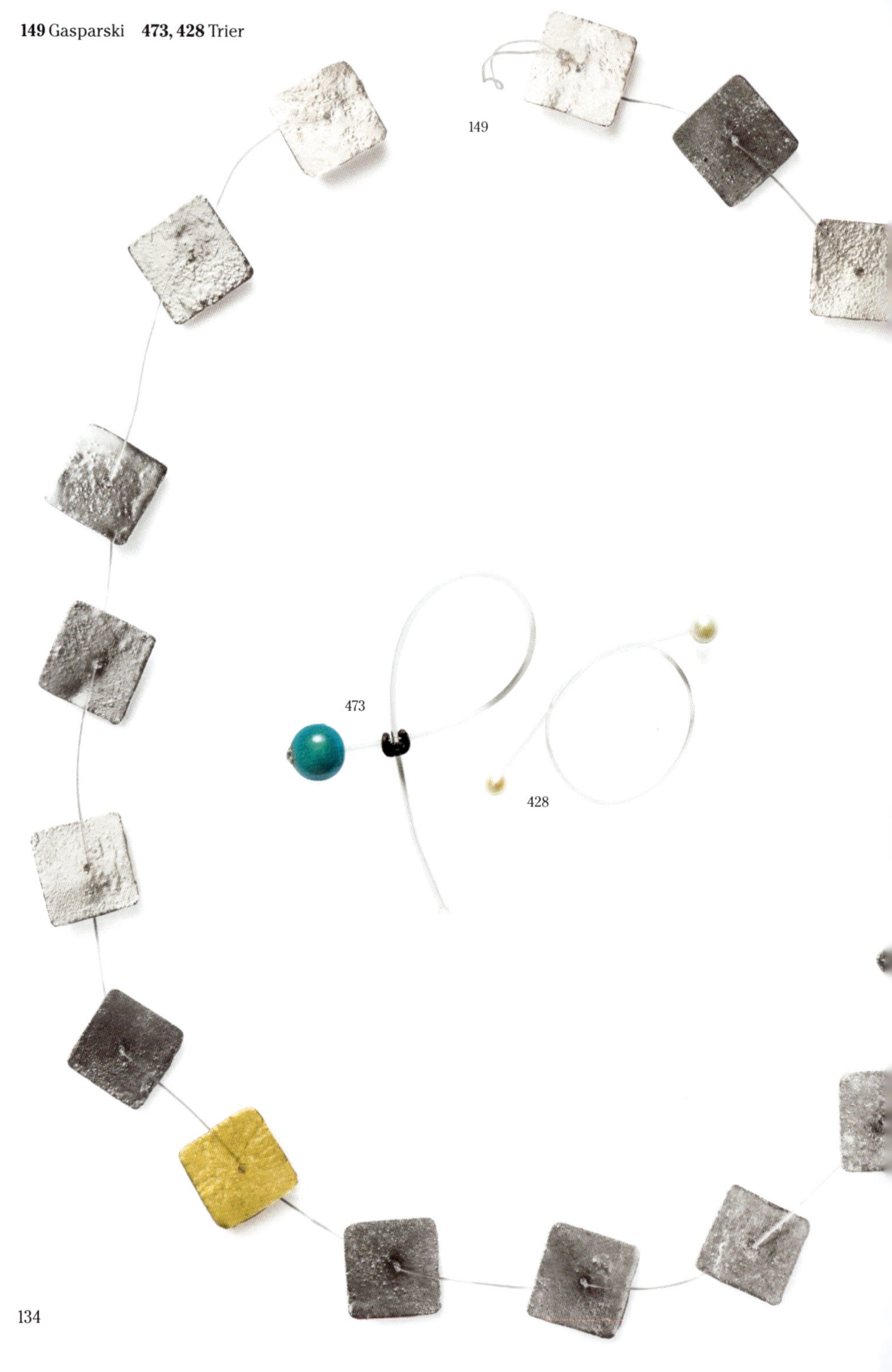
149
473
428

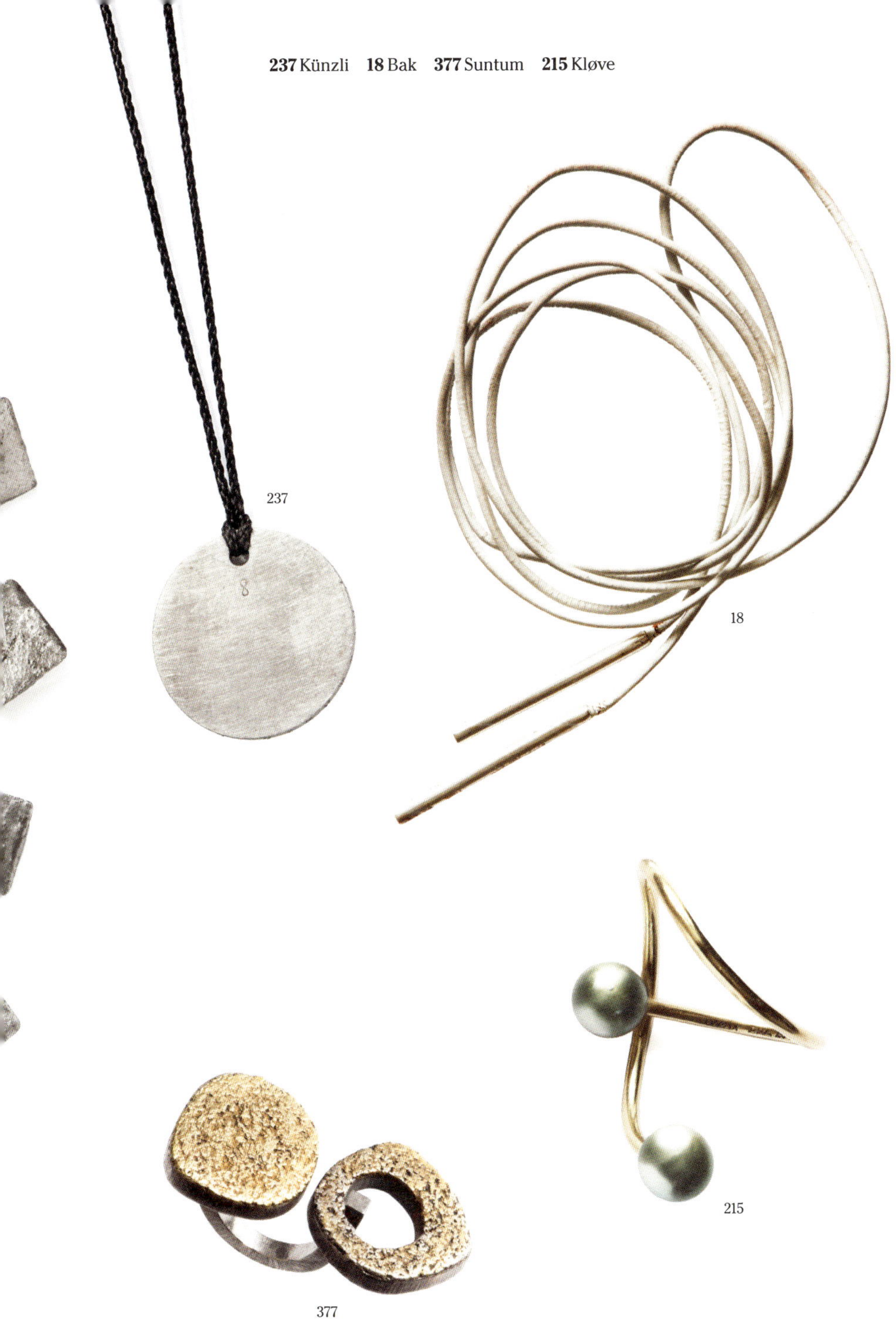

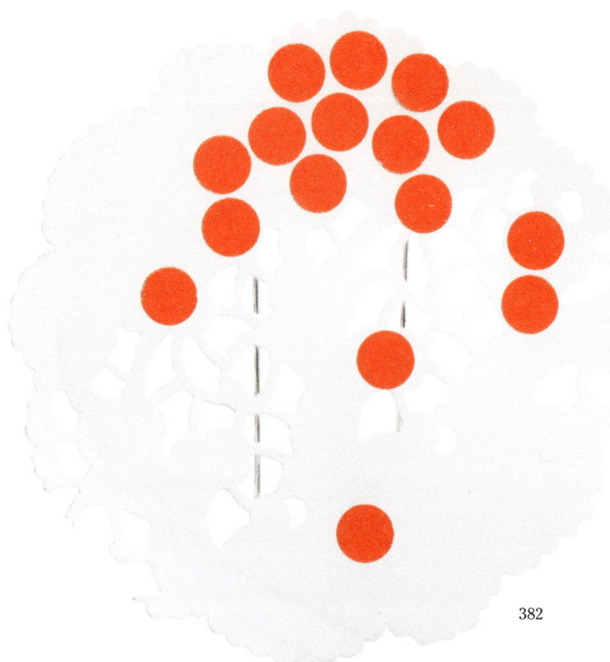

382

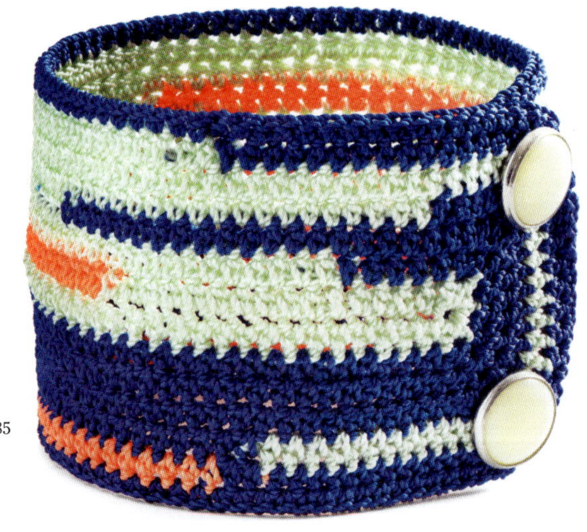

485

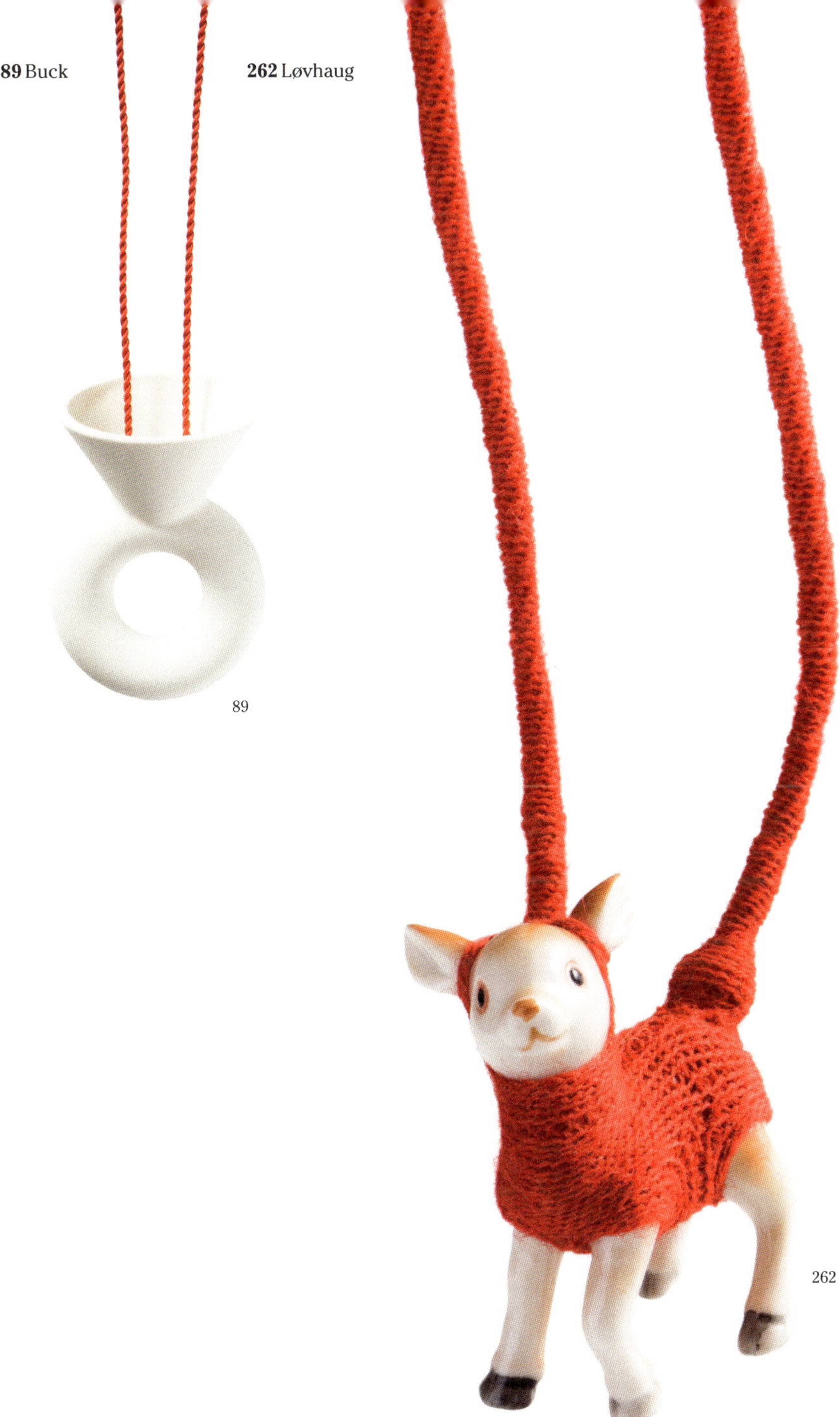

89 Buck   **262** Løvhaug

89

262

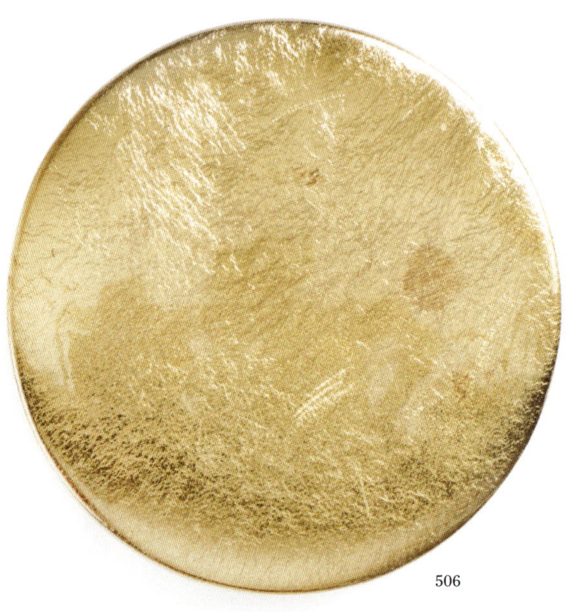

506

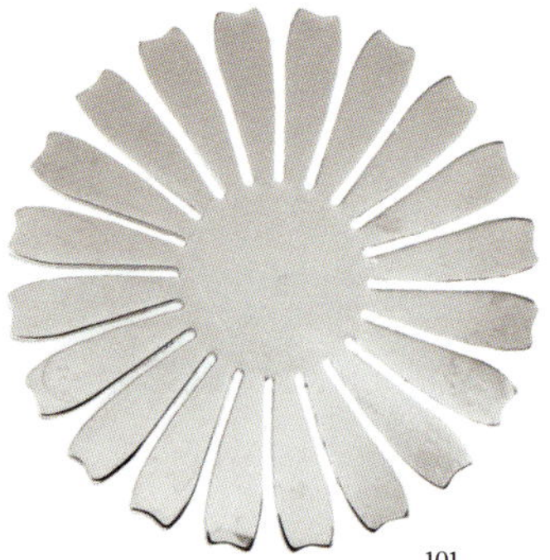

101

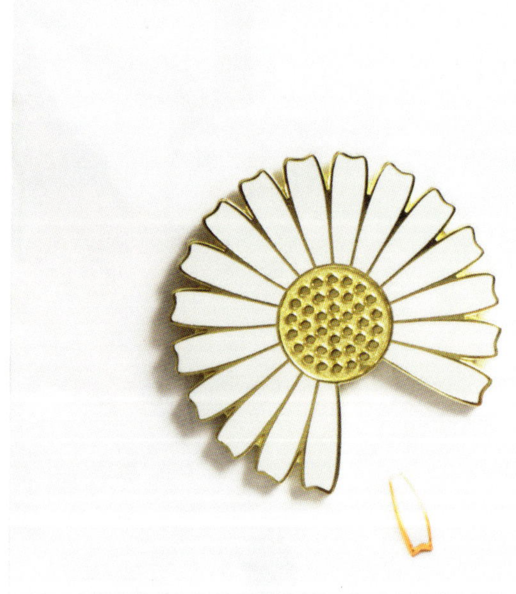

"Elsker, Elsker Ikke", Kim Buck 2007

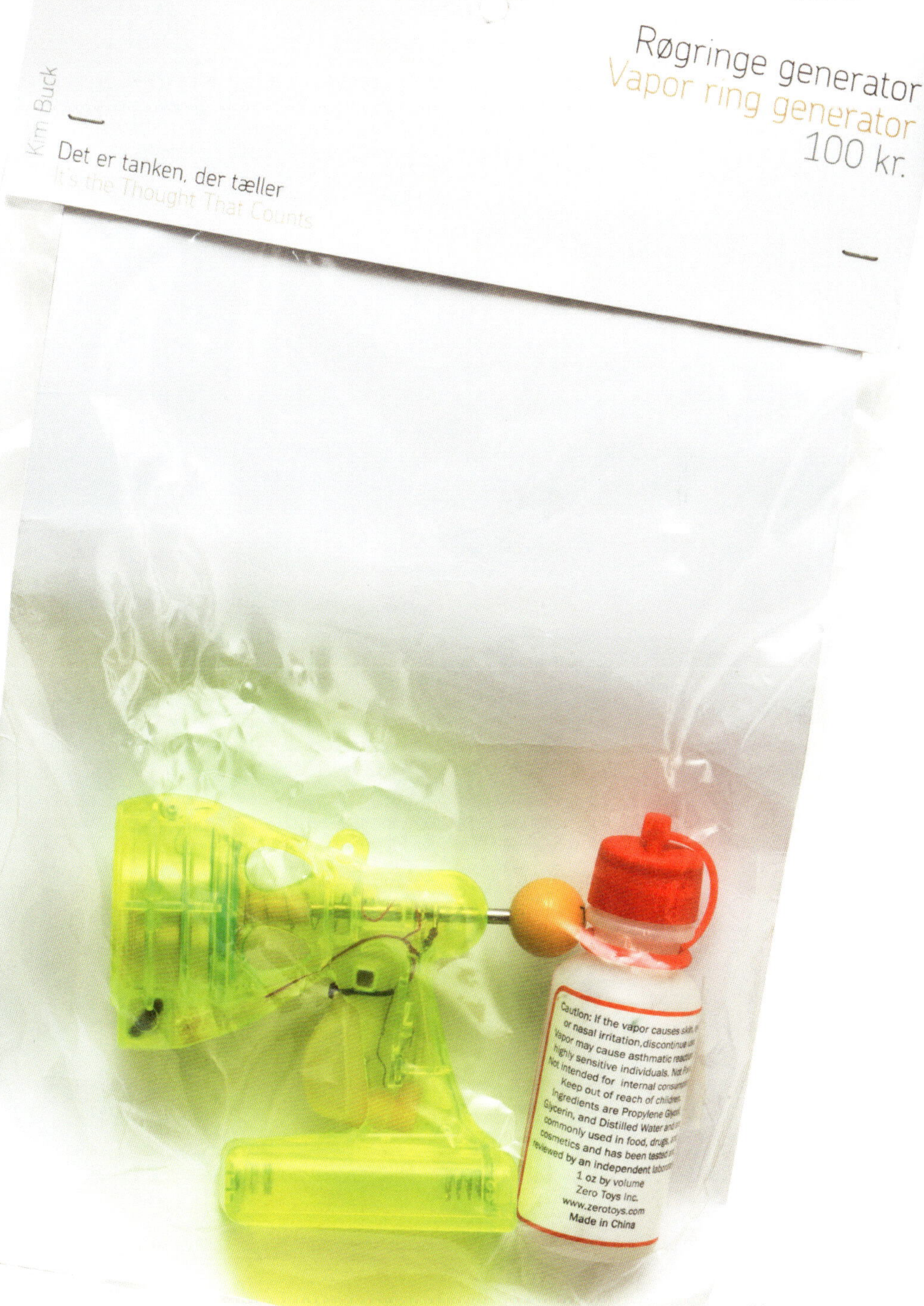

Røgringe generator
Vapor ring generator
100 kr.
Kim Buck
Det er tanken, der tæller
It's the Thought That Counts
Caution: If the vapor causes skin
or nasal irritation, discontinue use.
Vapor may cause asthmatic reaction
highly sensitive individuals. Not For
Not intended for internal consumption
Keep out of reach of children.
Ingredients are Propylene Glycol
Glycerin, and Distilled Water and
commonly used in food, drugs, an
cosmetics and has been tested an
reviewed by an independent laborator
1 oz by volume
Zero Toys Inc.
www.zerotoys.com
Made in China

Kim Buck

Det er tanken, der tæller
It's the Thought That Counts

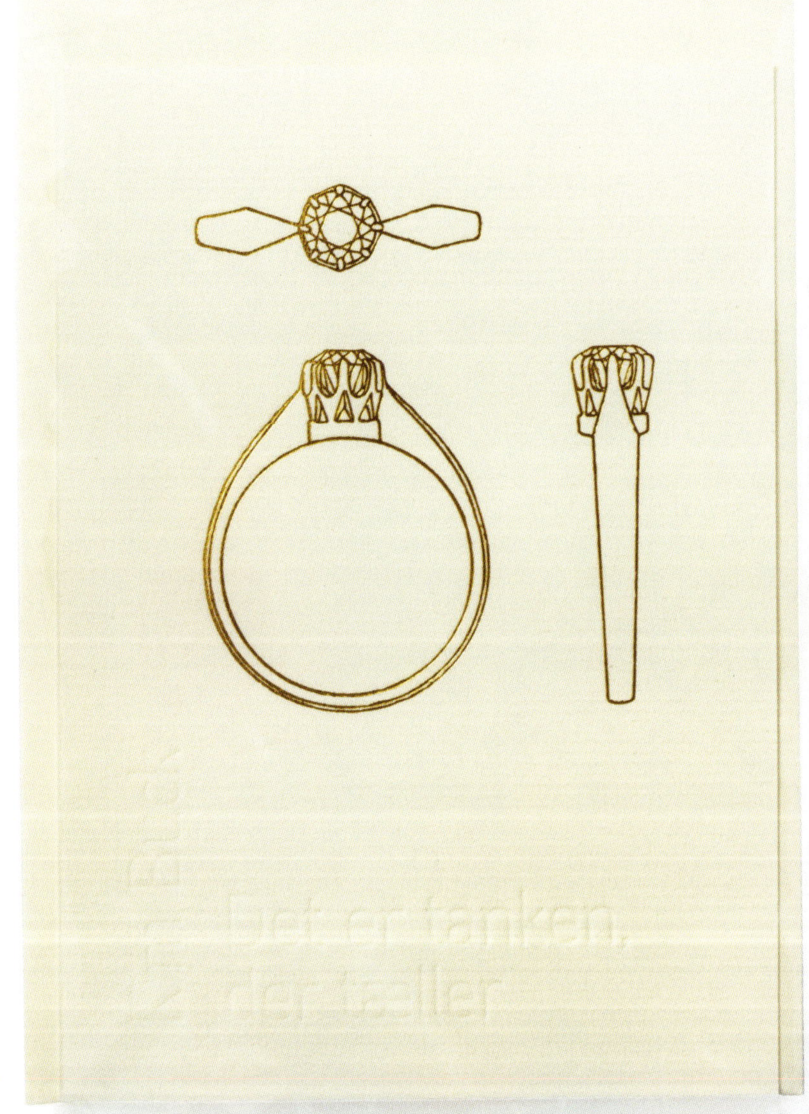

Elsker ikke.
Loves me not.
280 kr.

Det er tanken, der tæller
It's the Thought That Counts

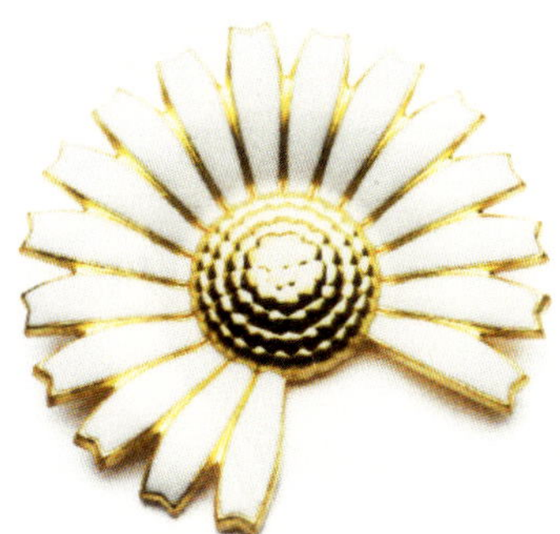

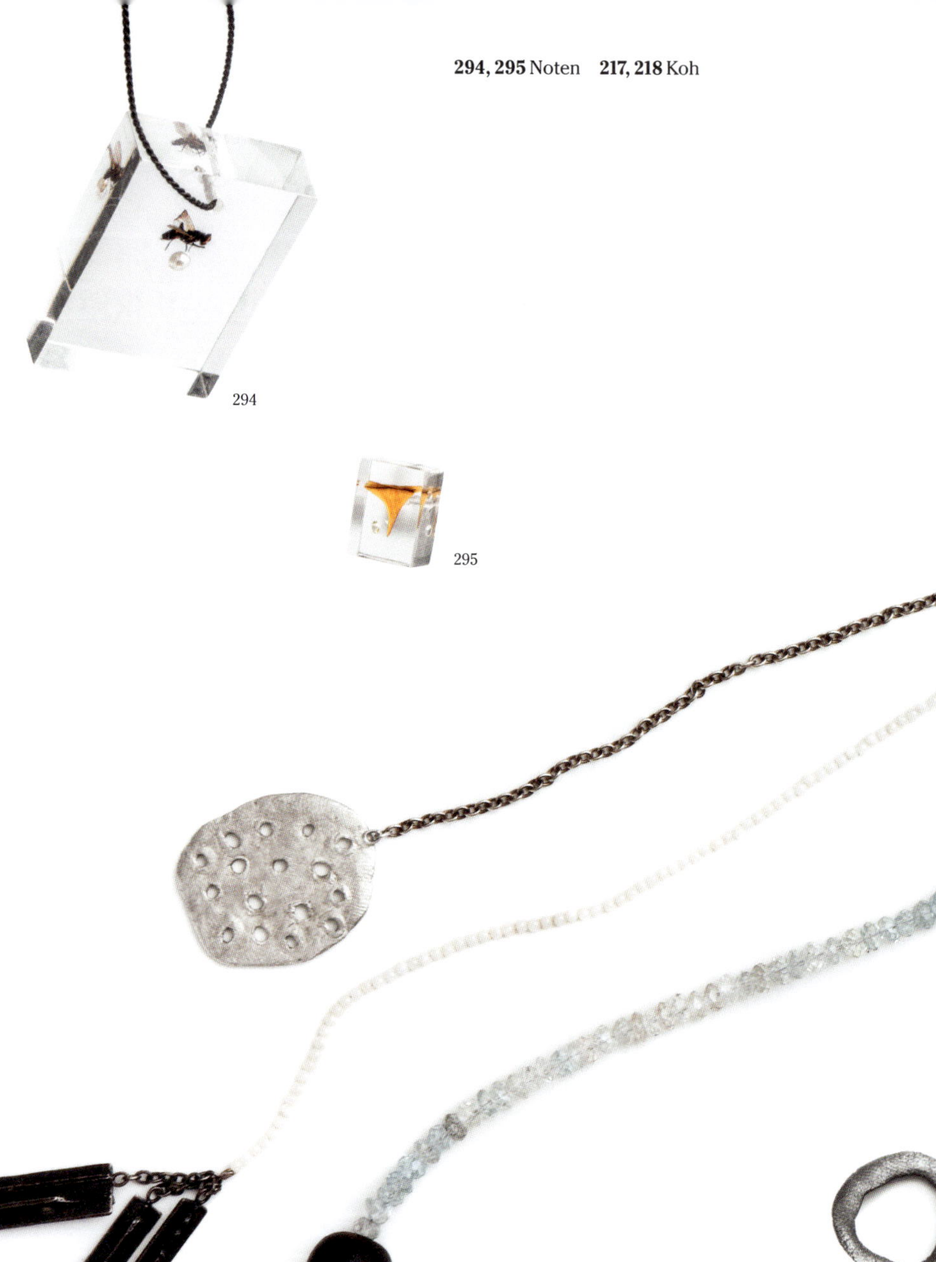

294

295

217

218

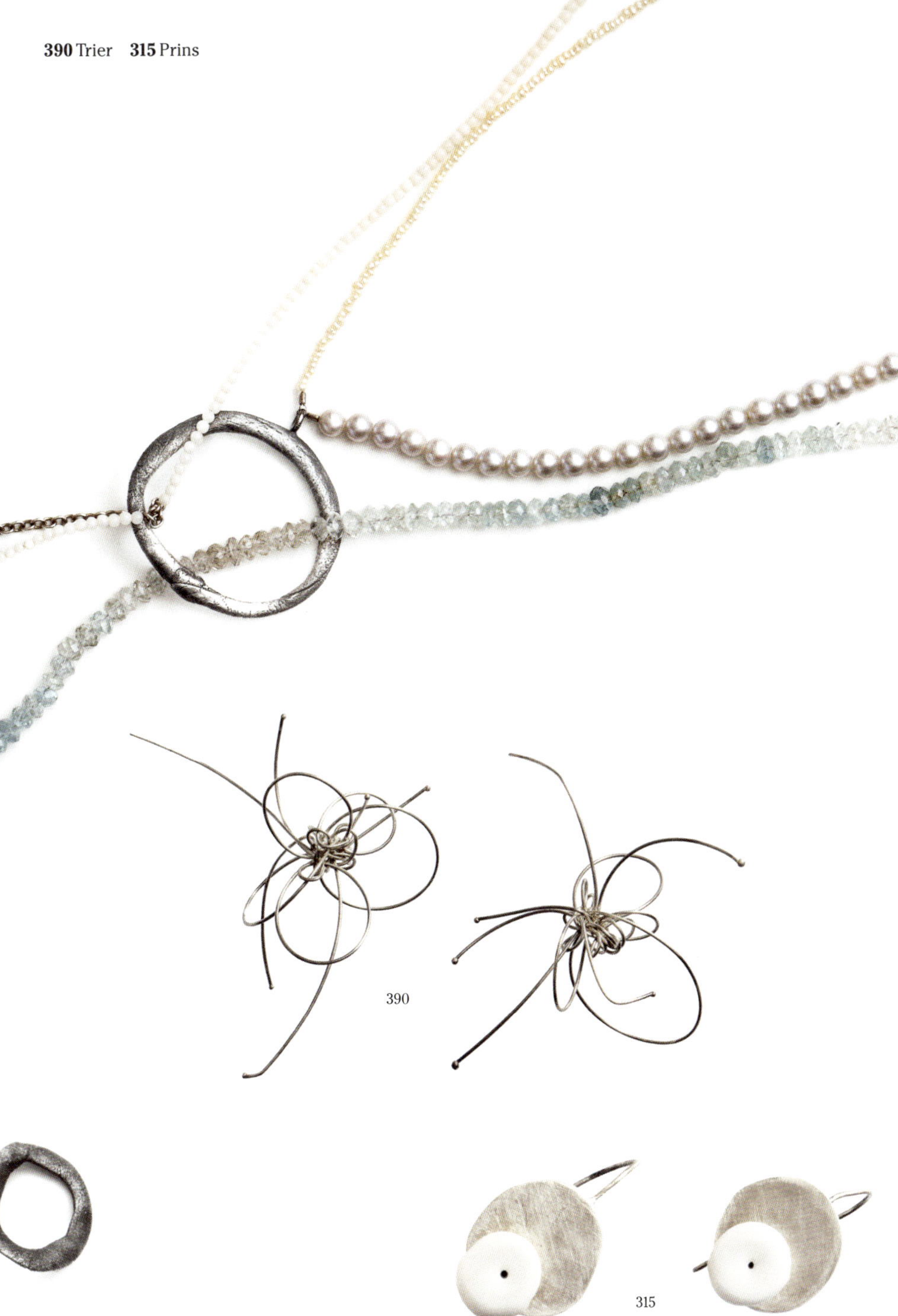

390

315

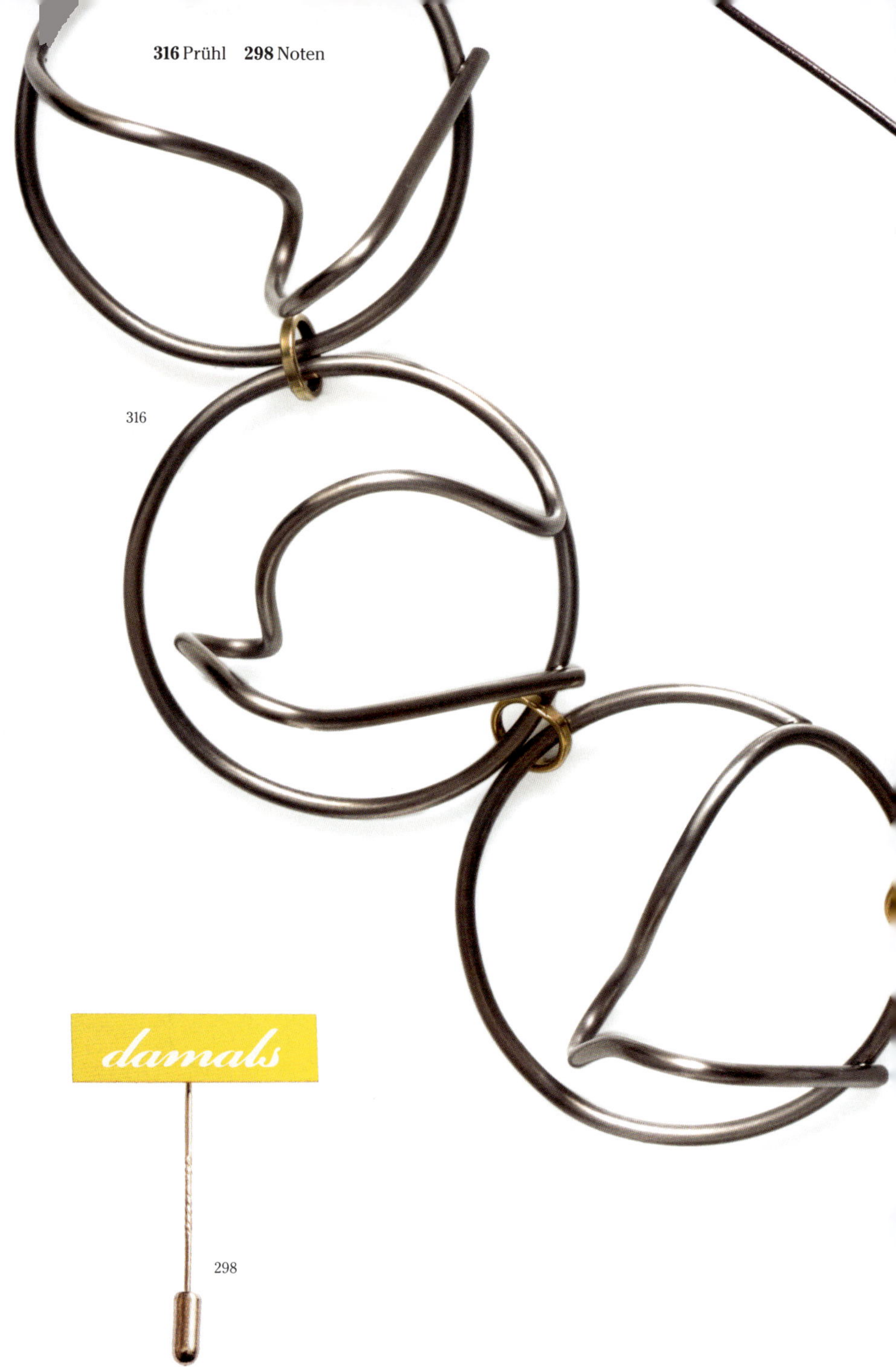
316
damals
298

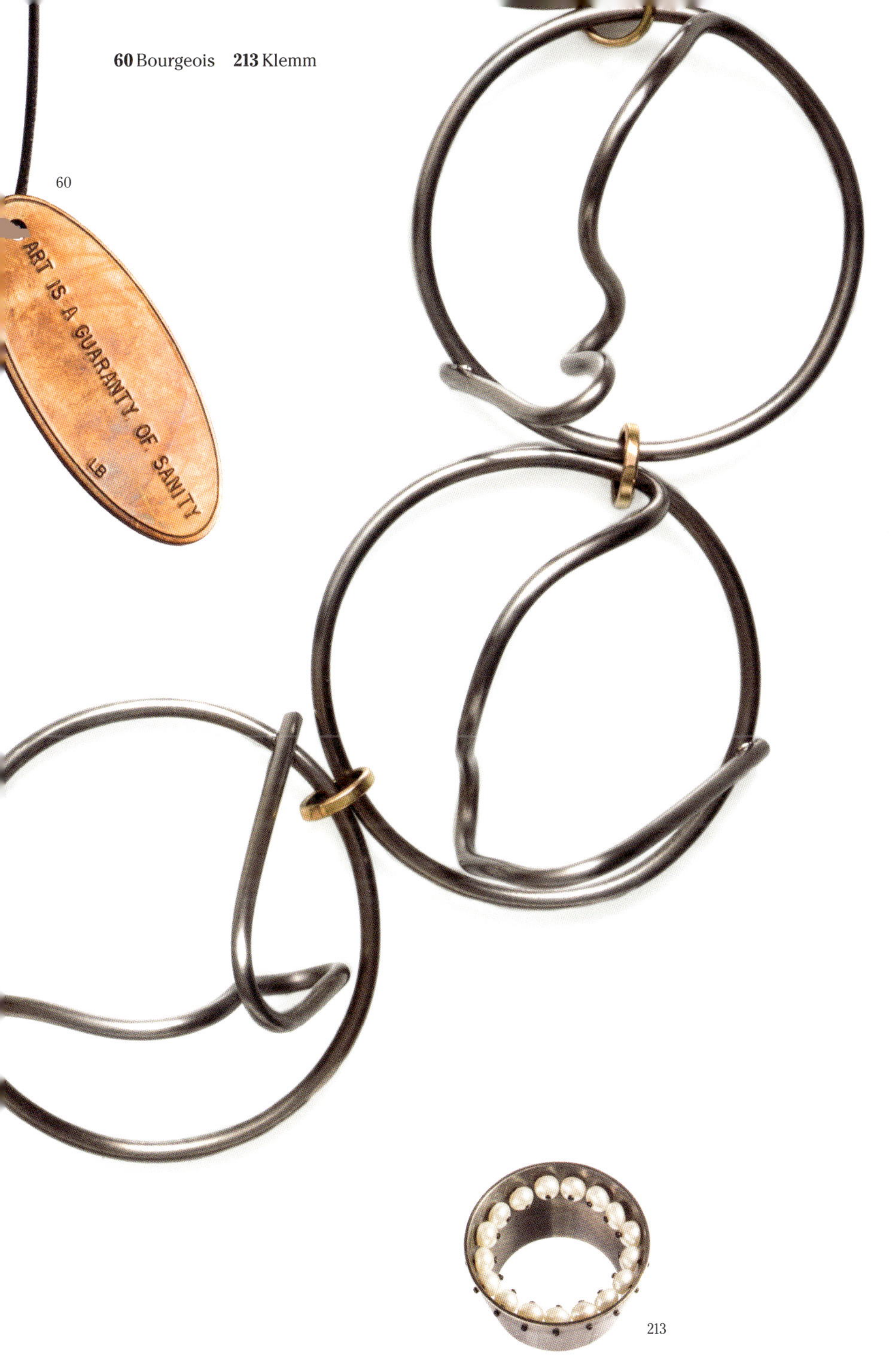

60

213

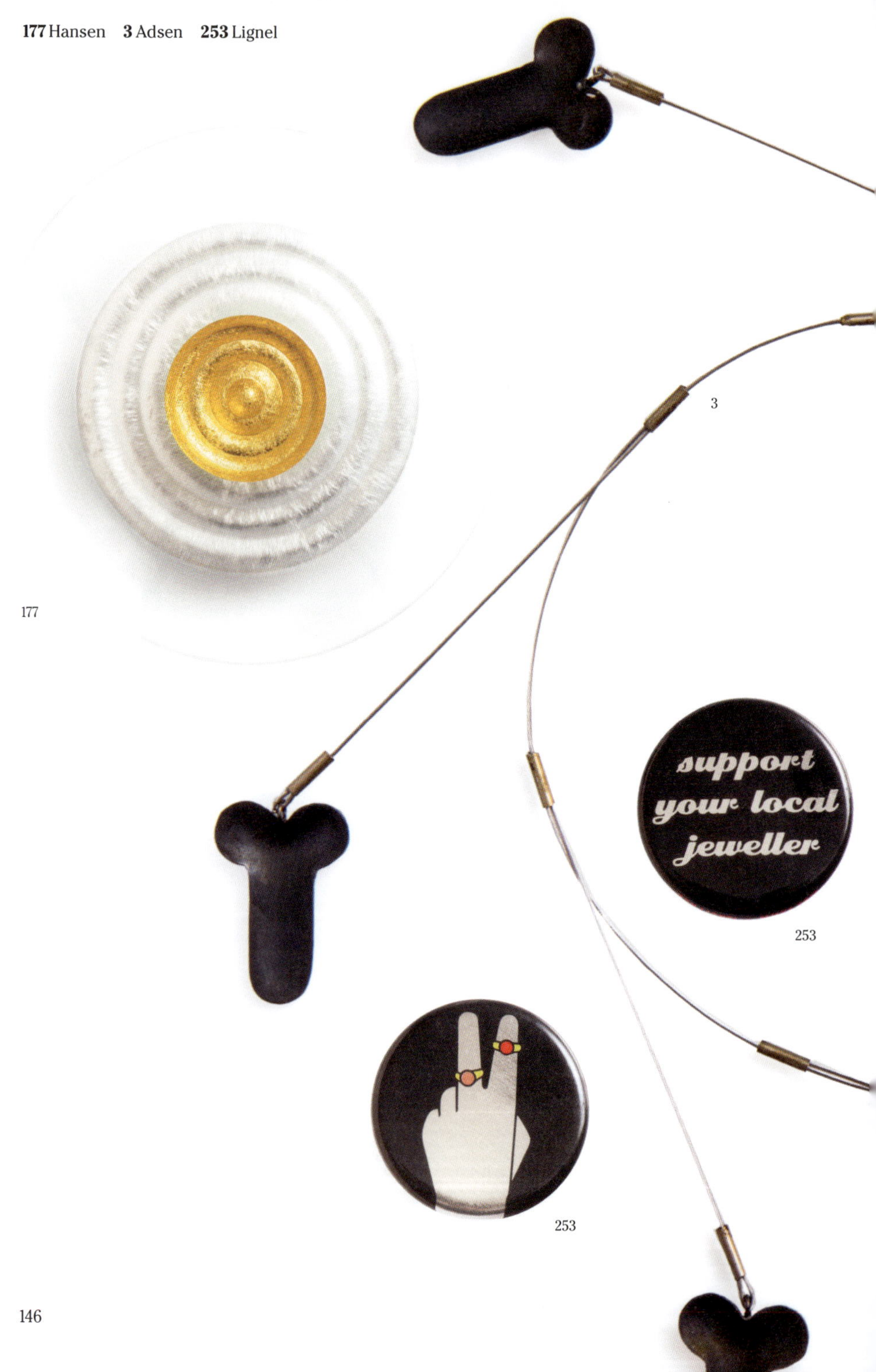

177

3

253

253

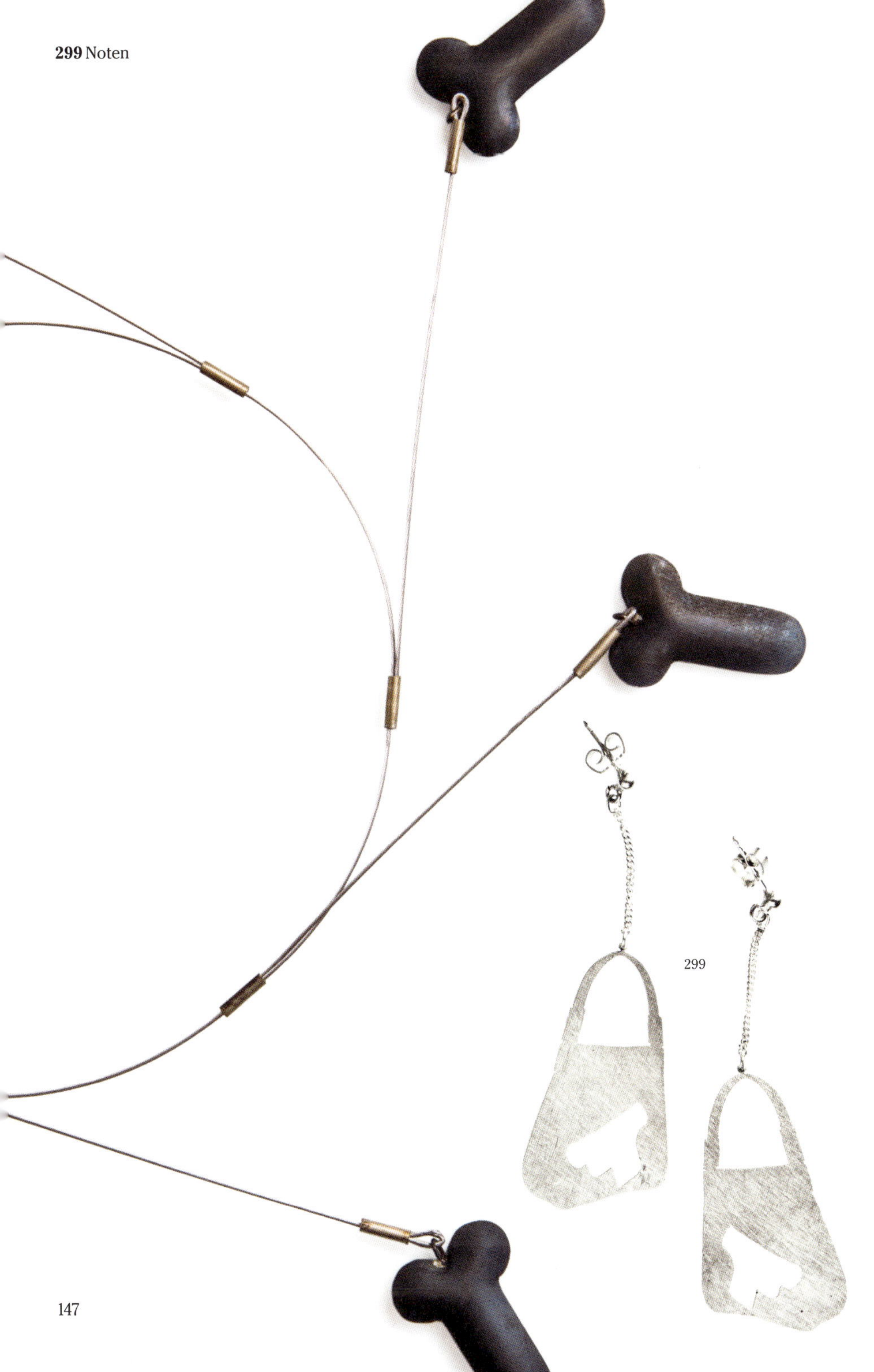

299

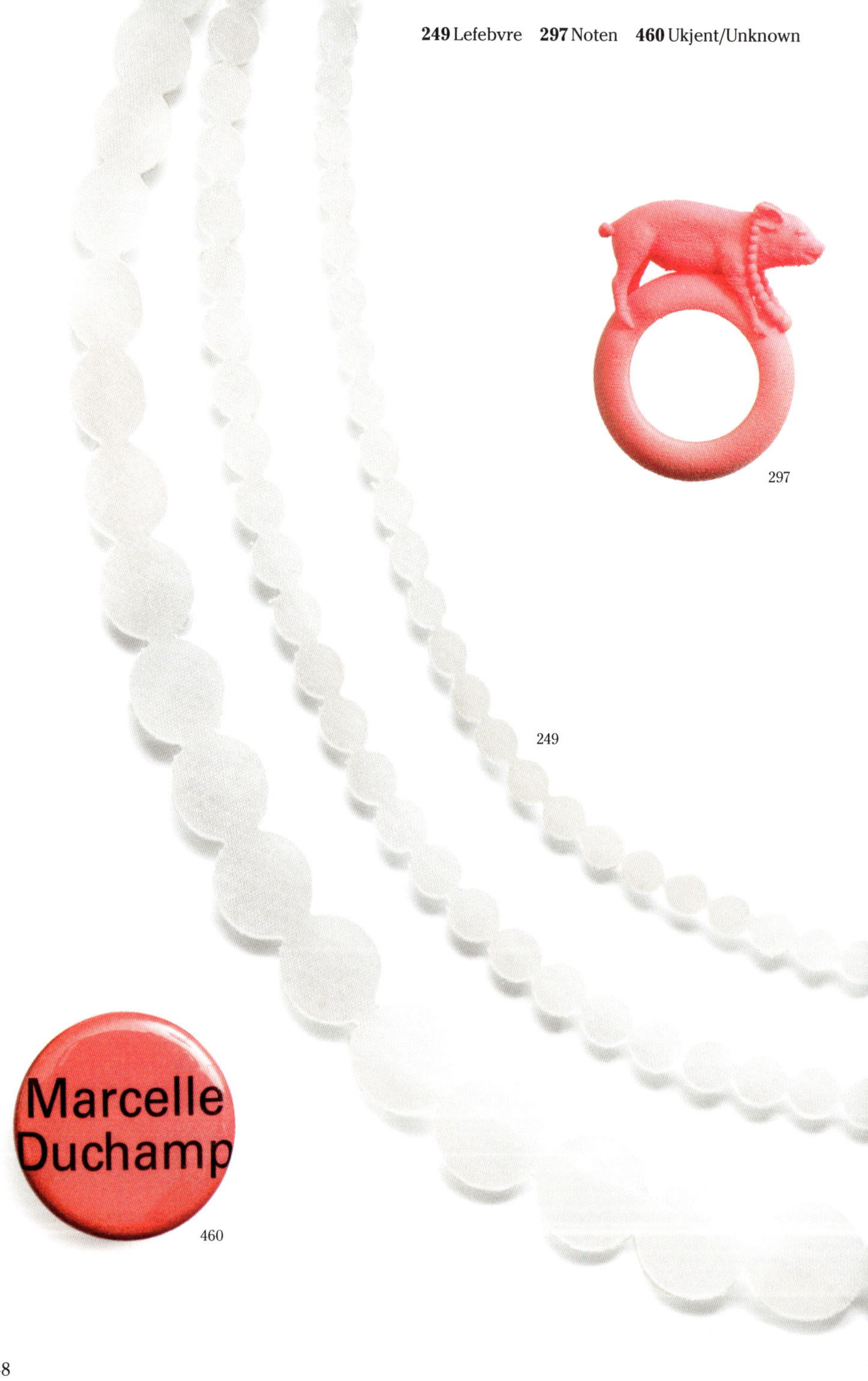

297

249

460

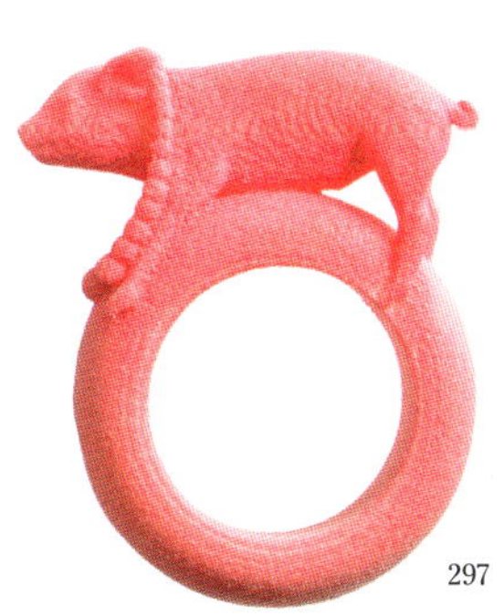

297

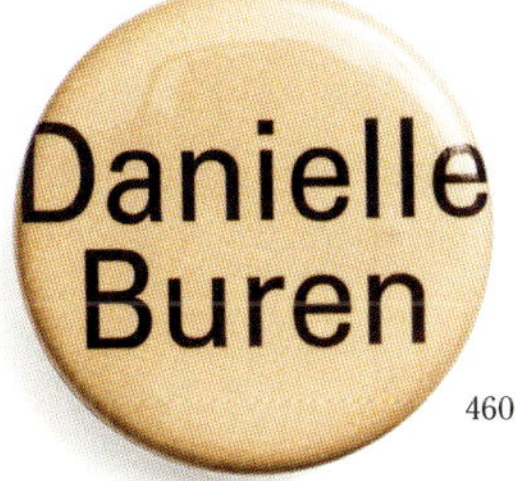

460

clémence
greenberg

460

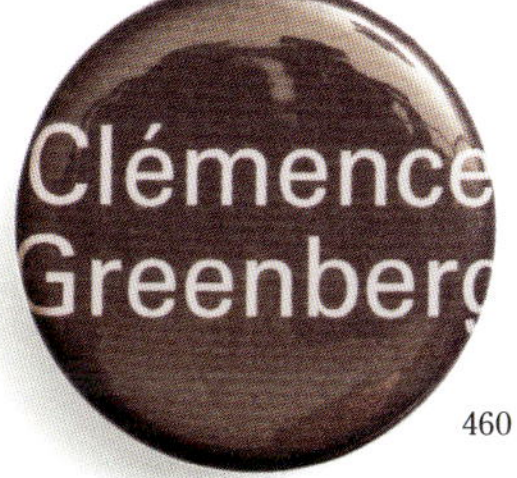

460

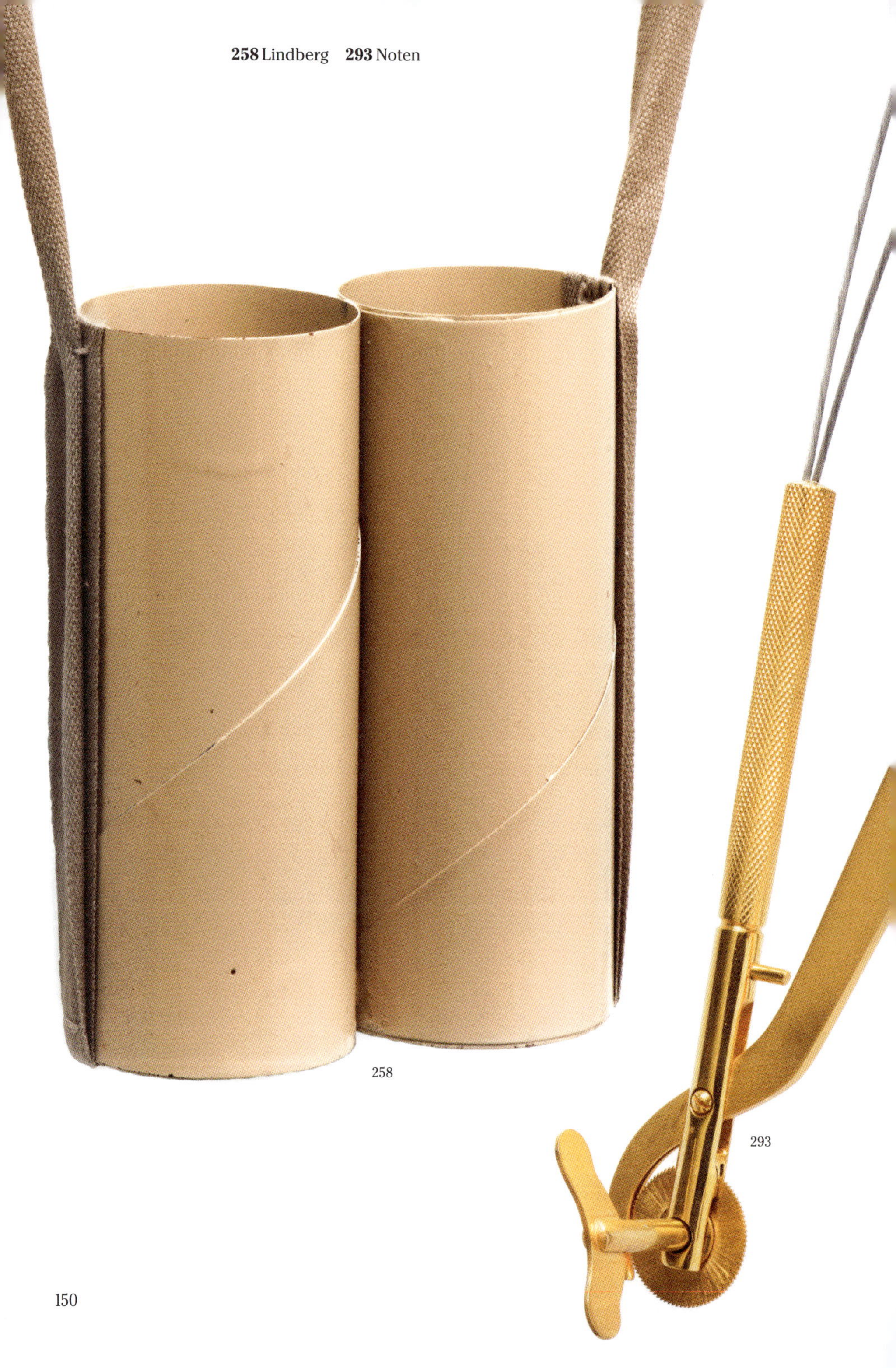

258

293

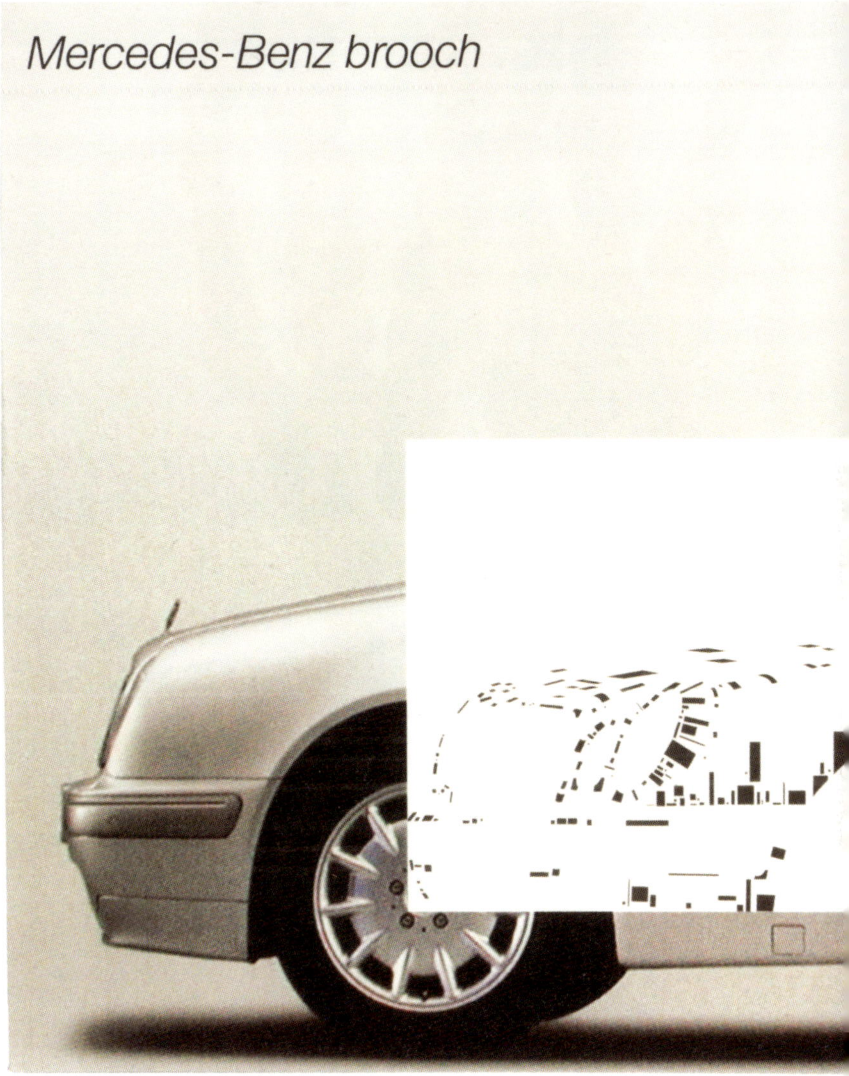

Mercedes-Benz brooch

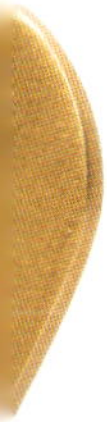

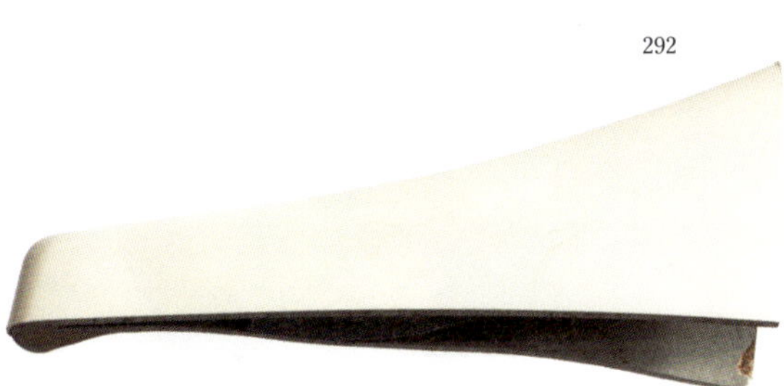

292

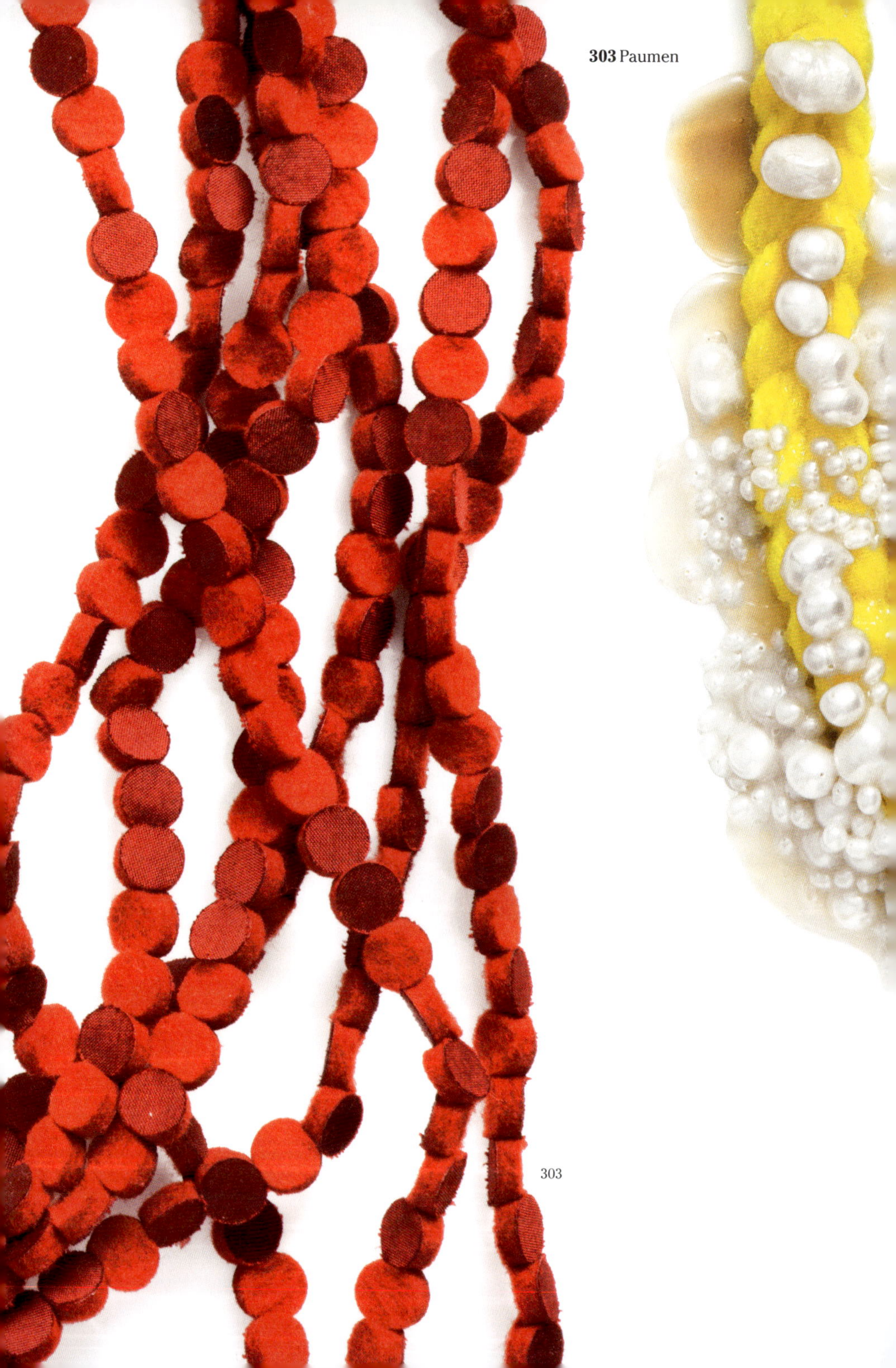

303

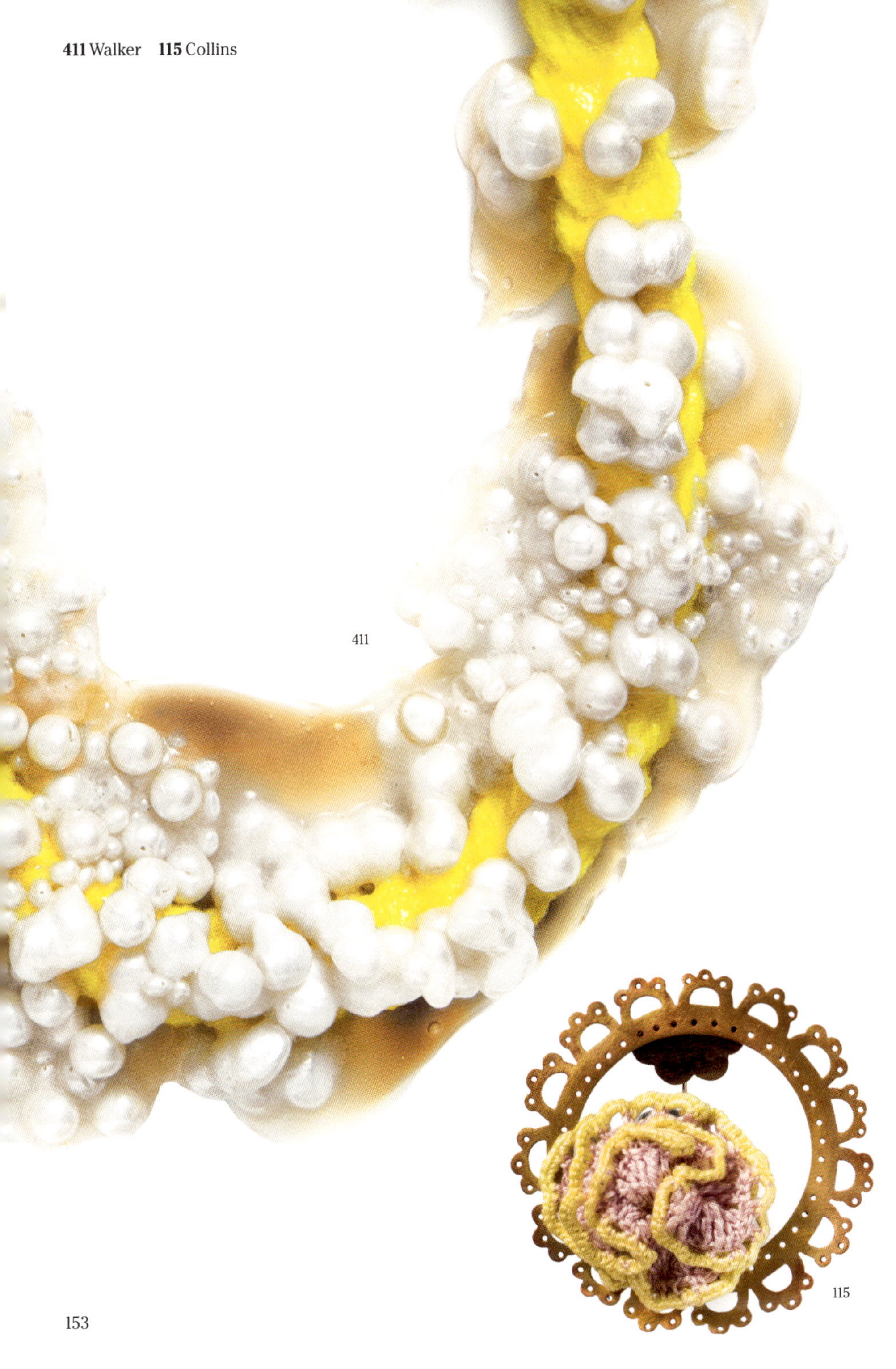

411

115

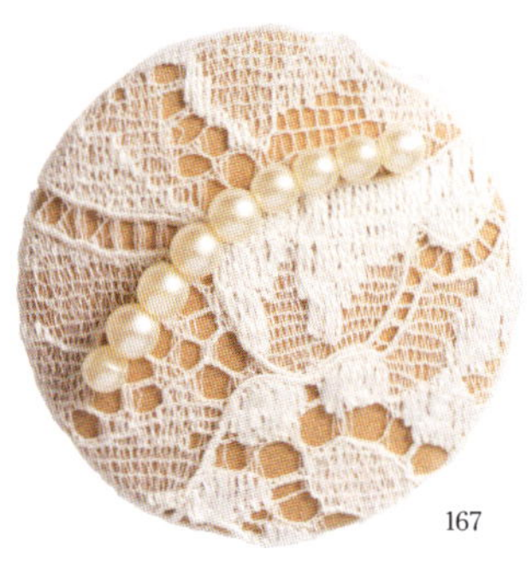

167

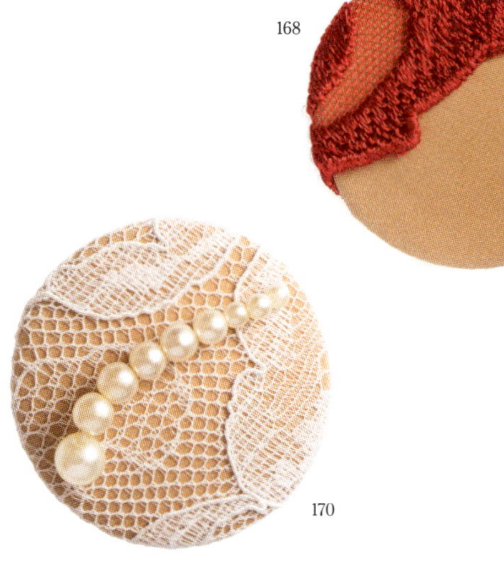

168

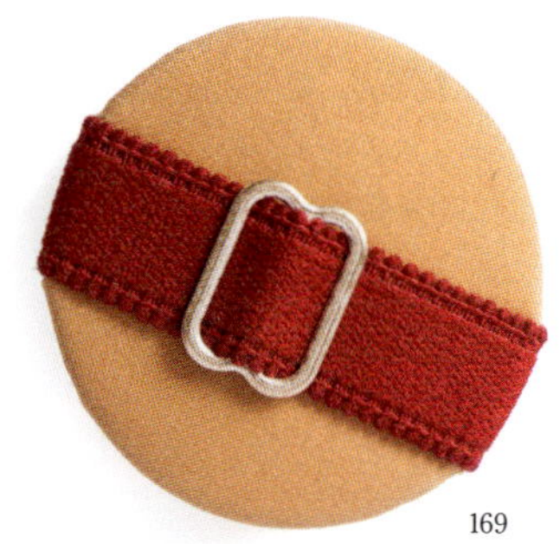

170

169

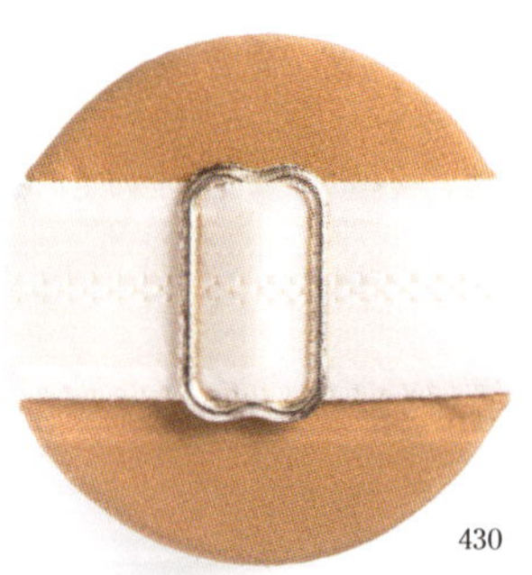

430

300

154

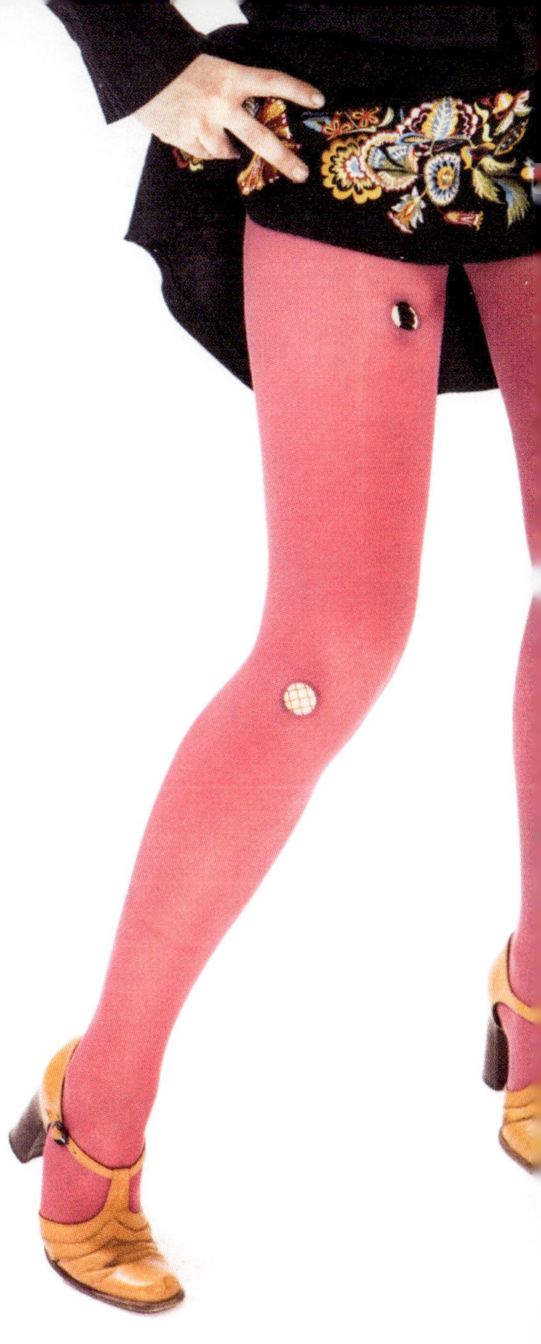

167 | Brooch: 925 silver, rubber, silk, fragments of unde

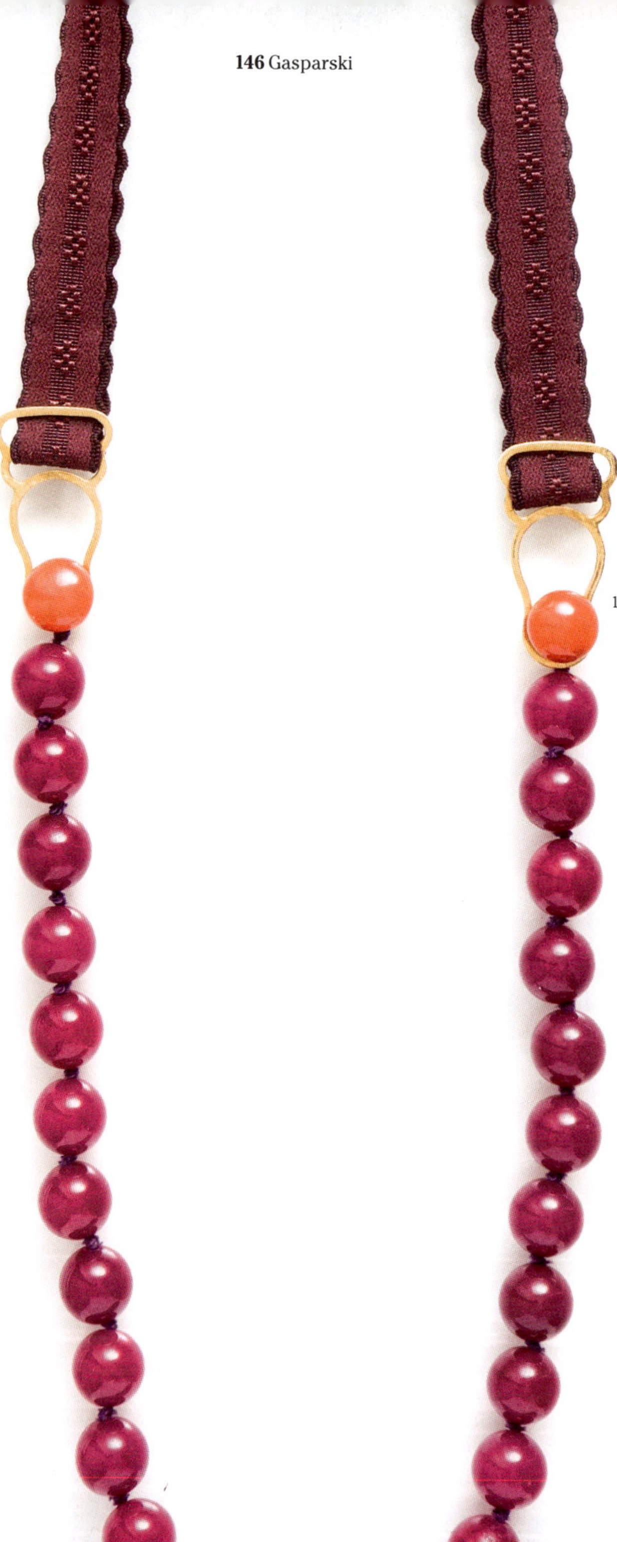

146 Gasparski

336 Sarneel

336

146

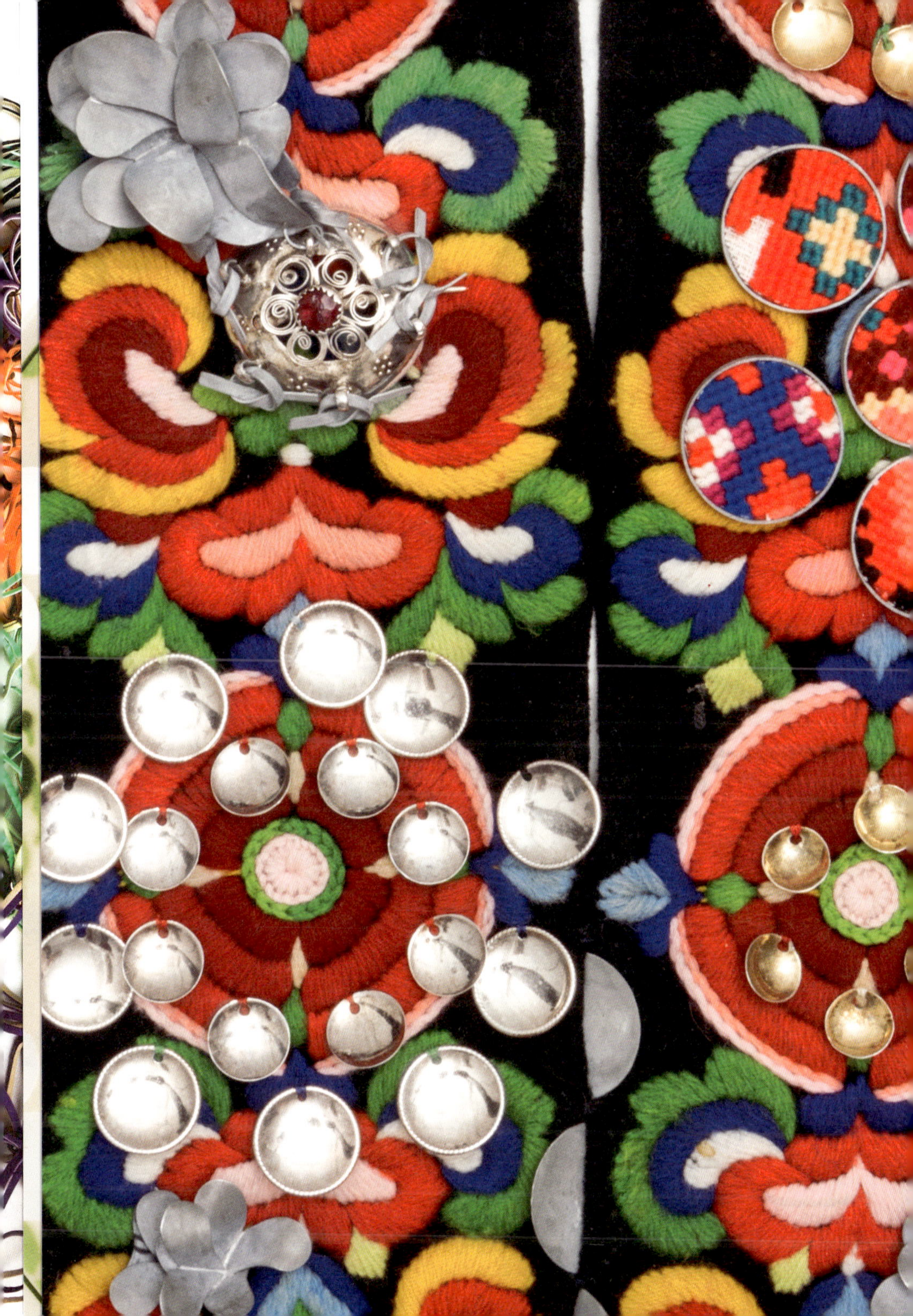

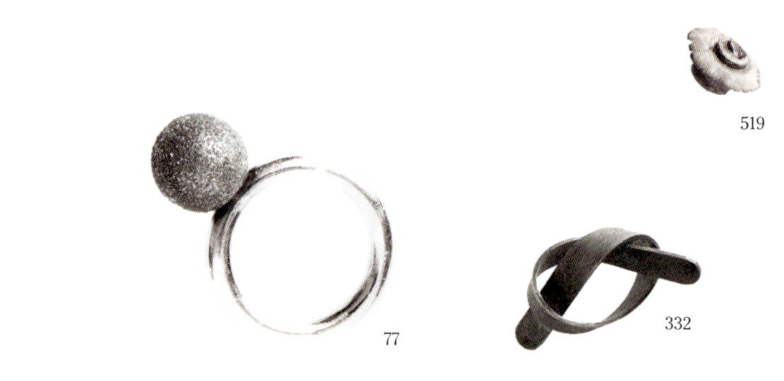

519

77

332

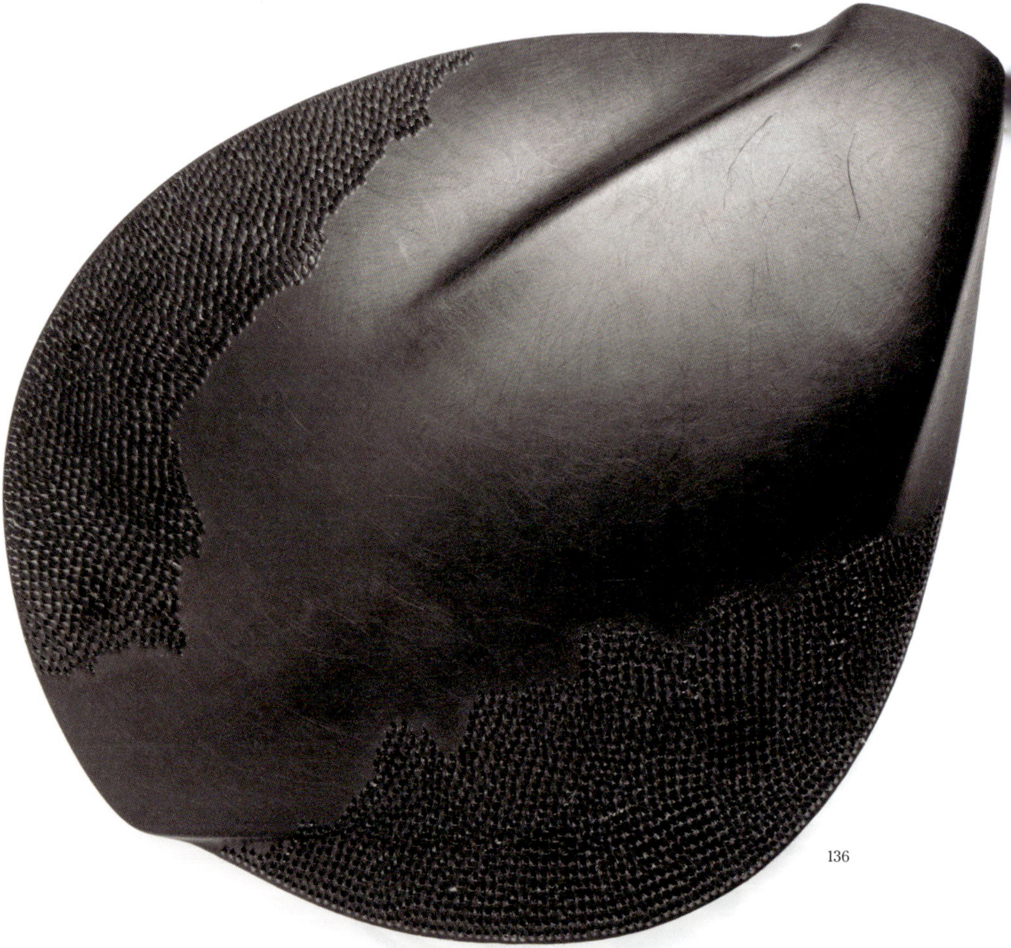

136

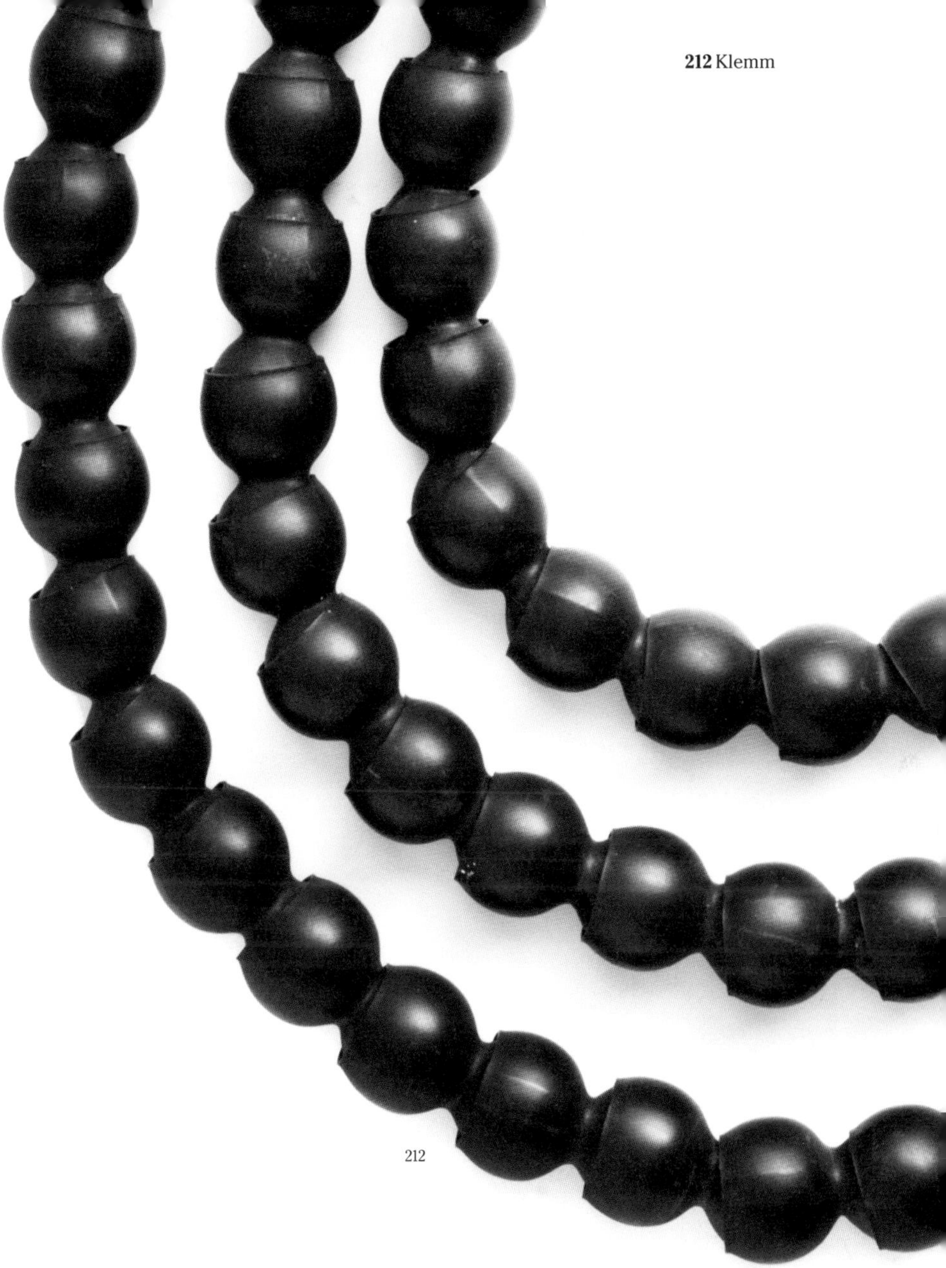

212

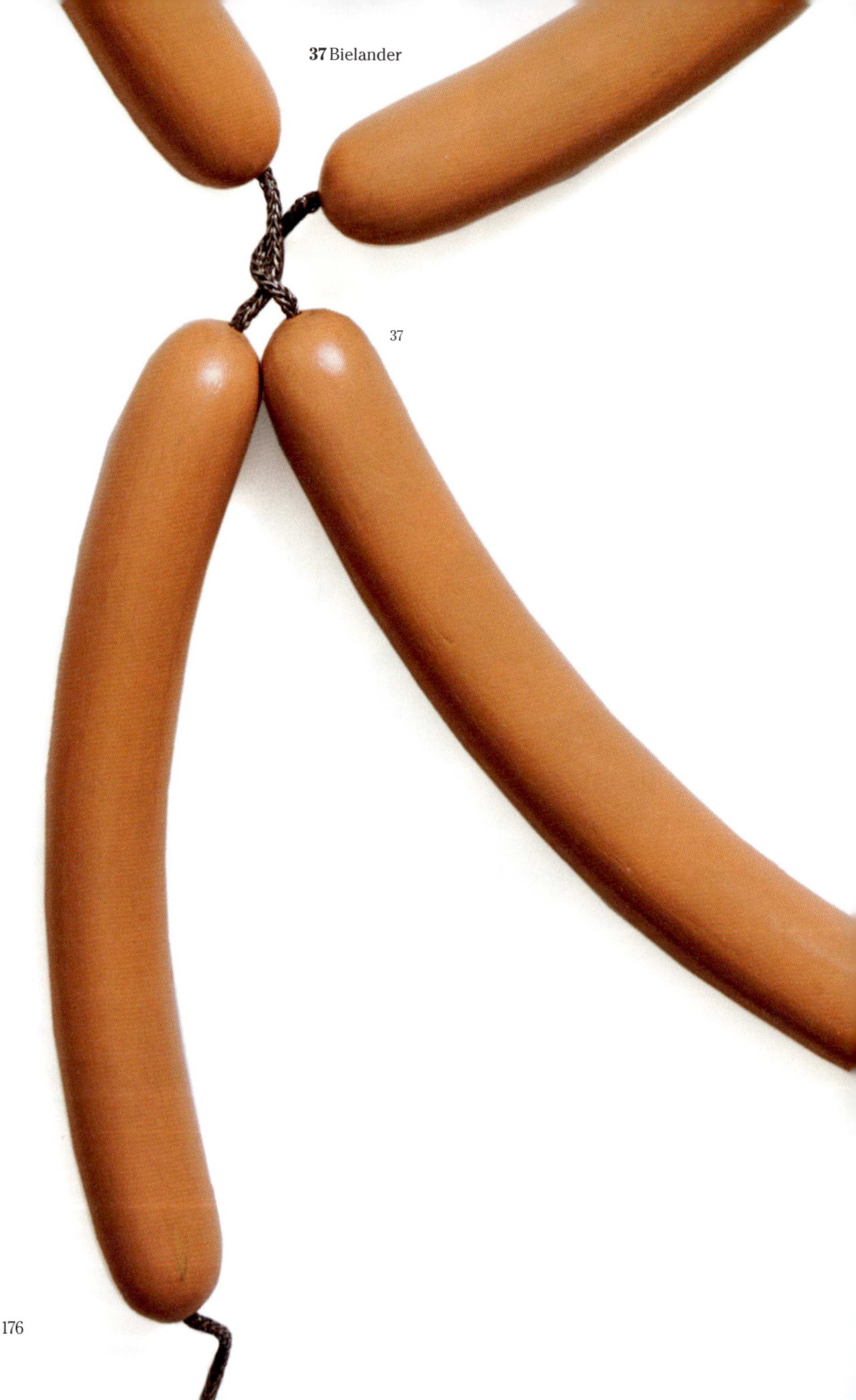

37

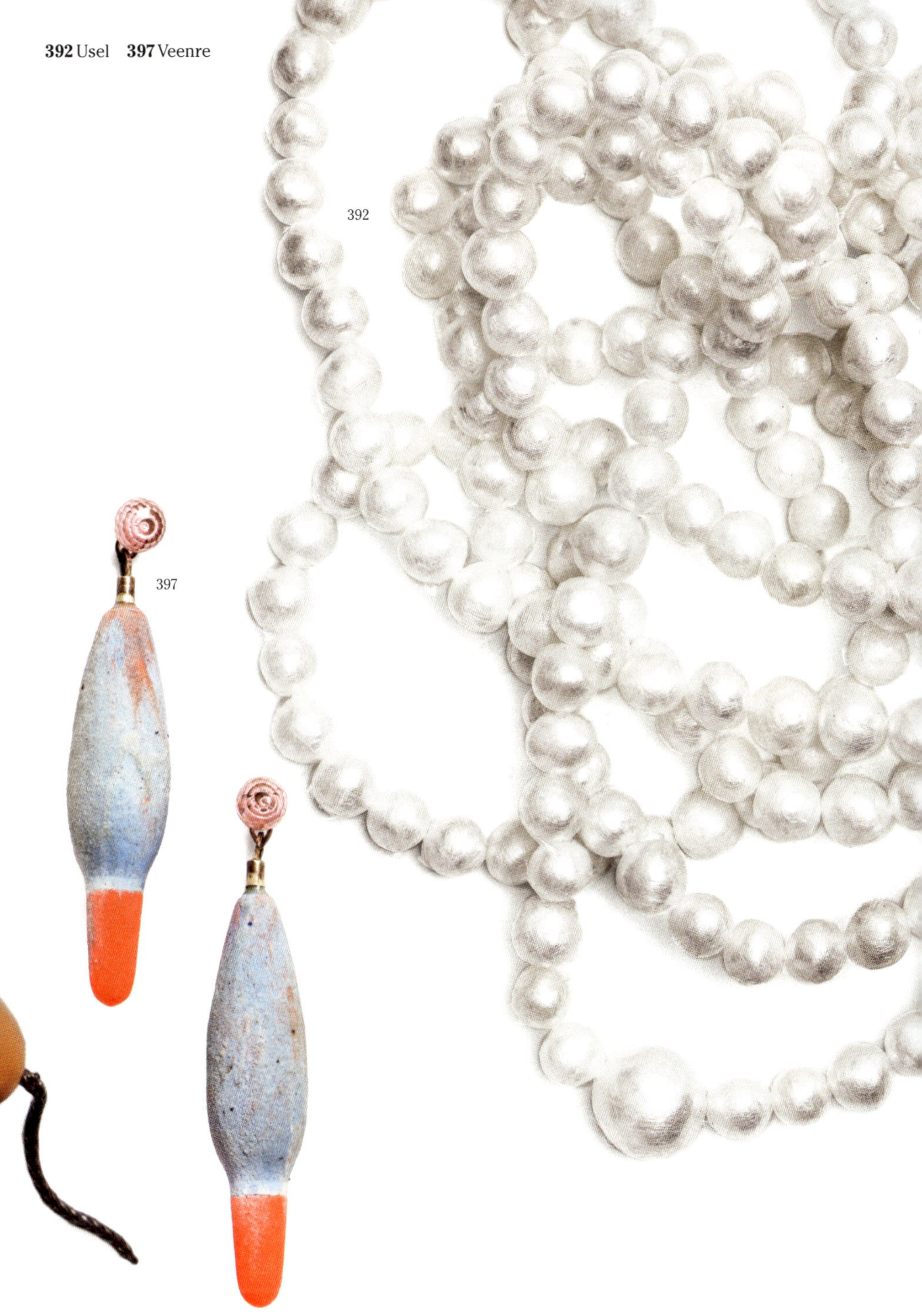
392
397

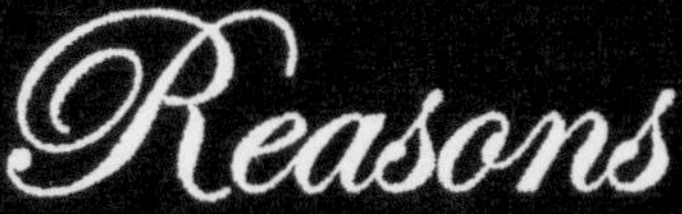
Reasons
(for wearing jewellery)
Limited Edition 70 / 170

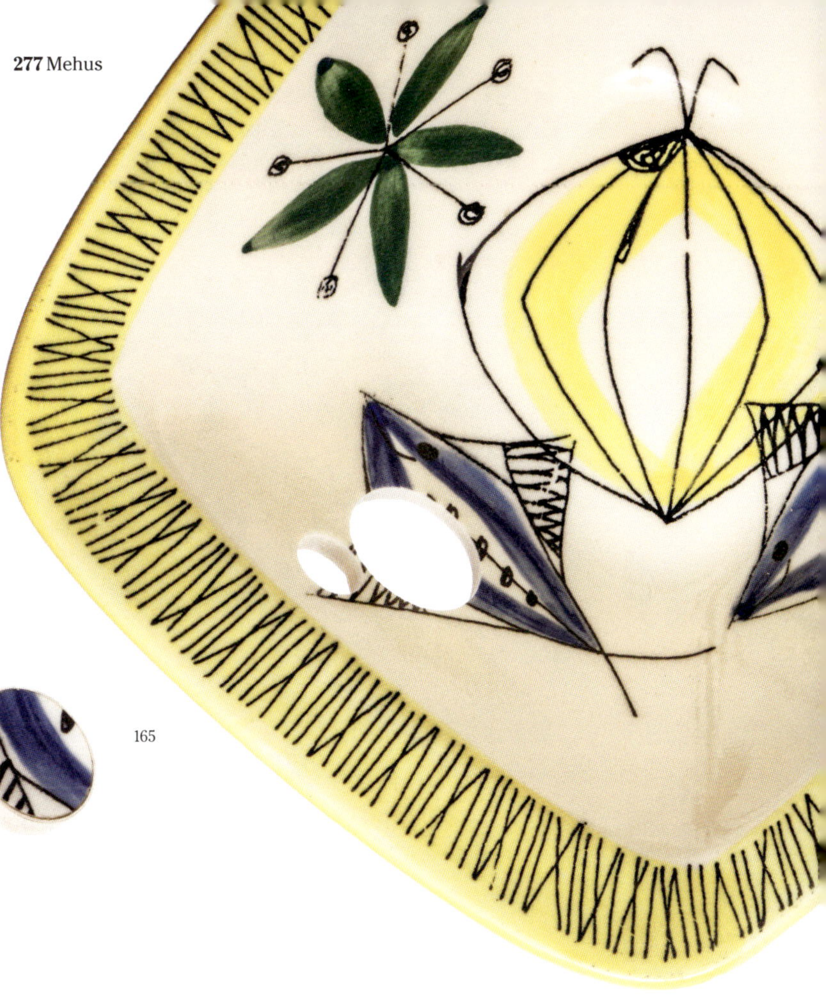

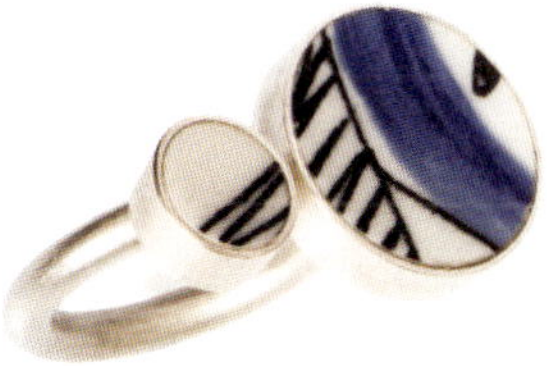

165

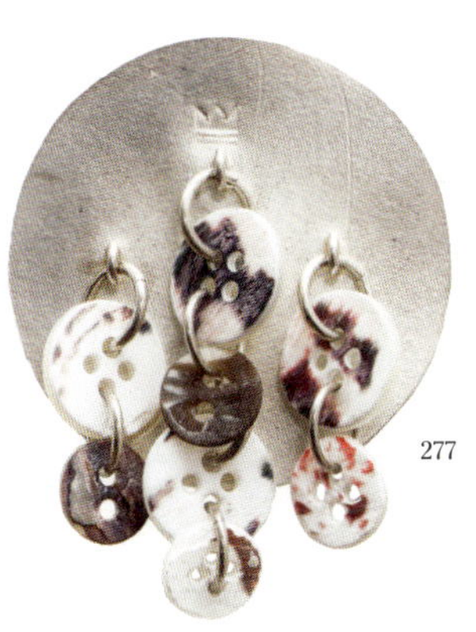

277

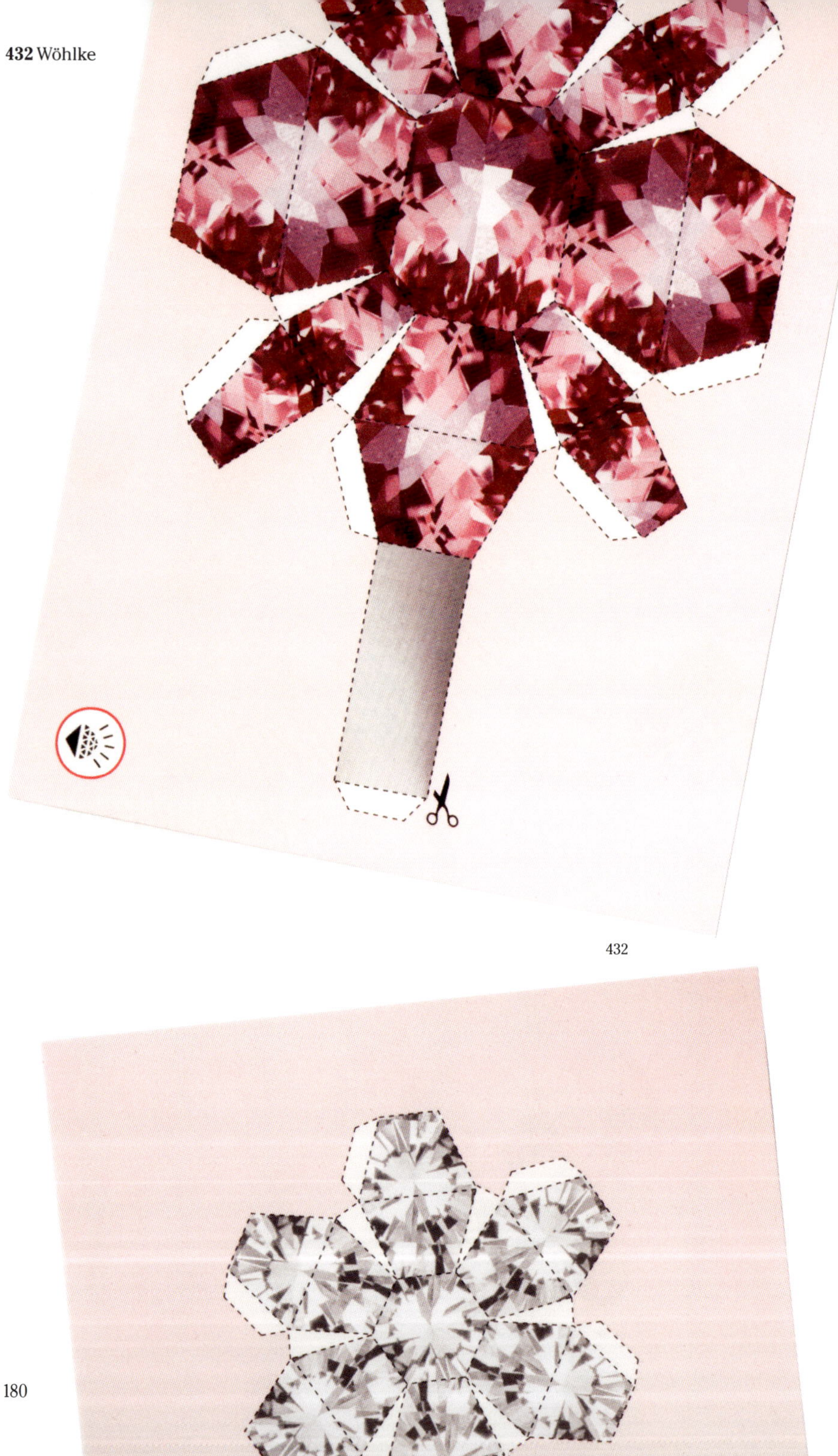

432

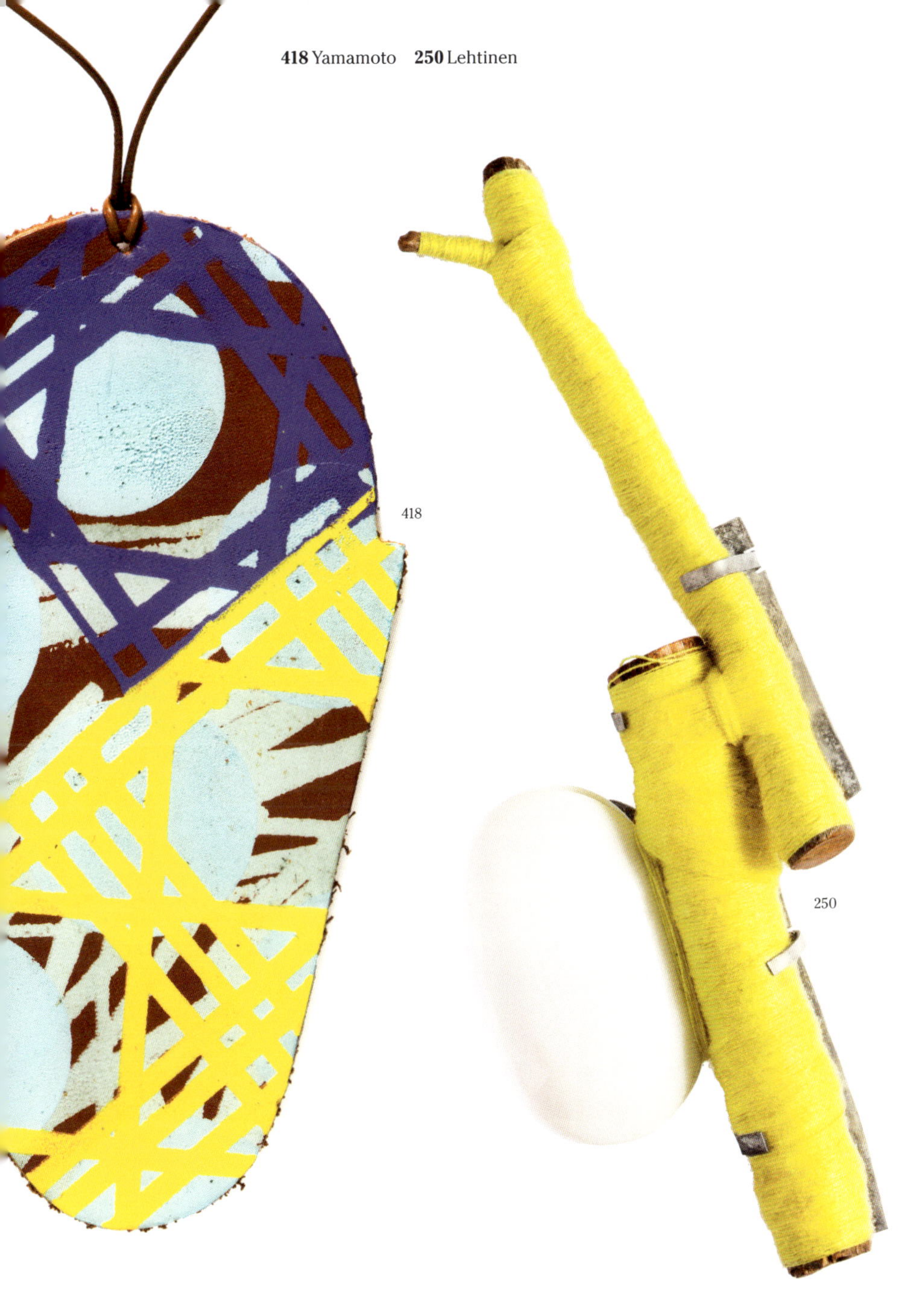

418

250

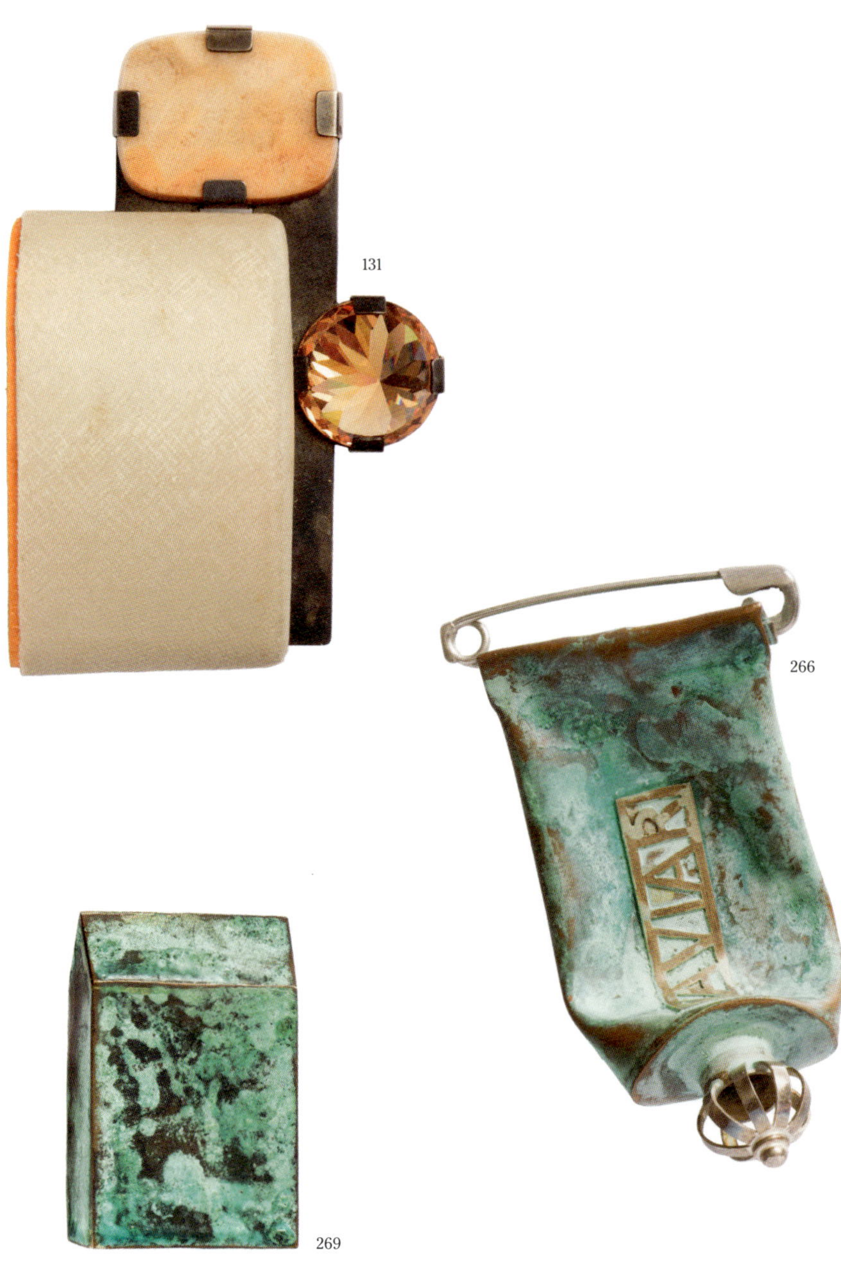

131

266

269

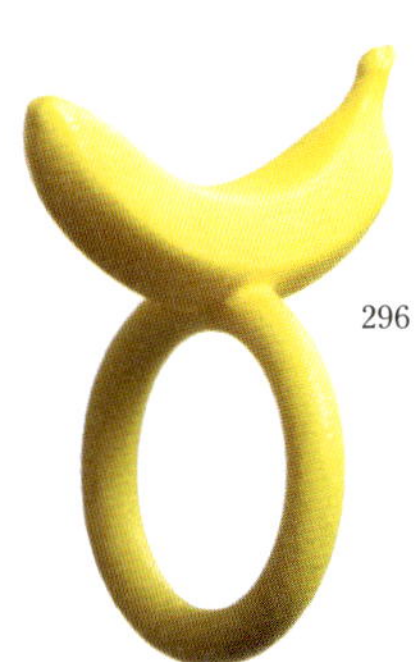

296

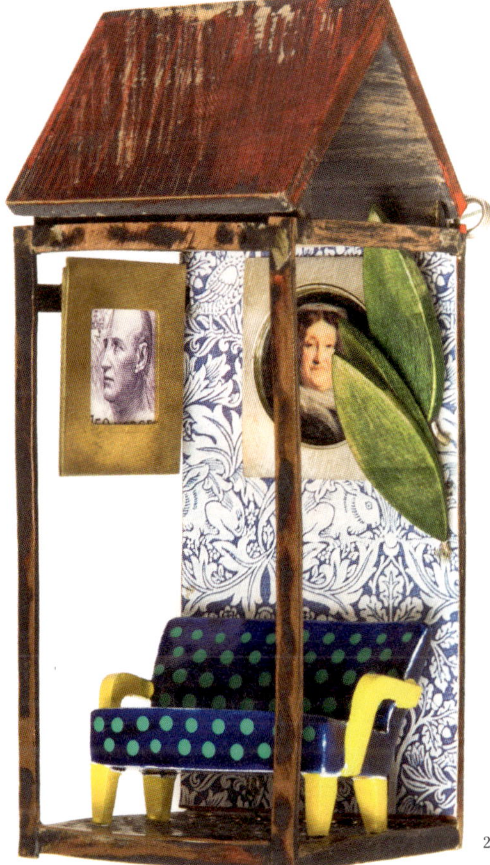

267

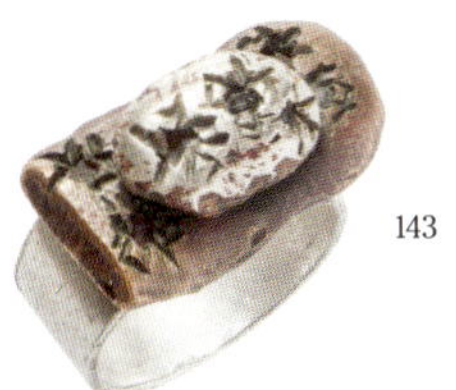

143

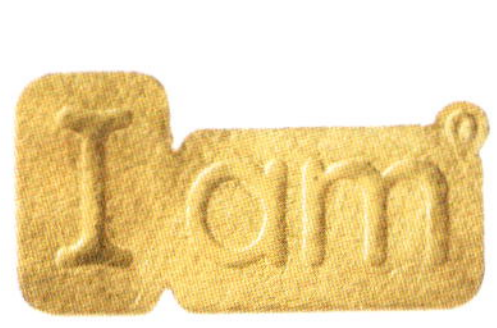

251

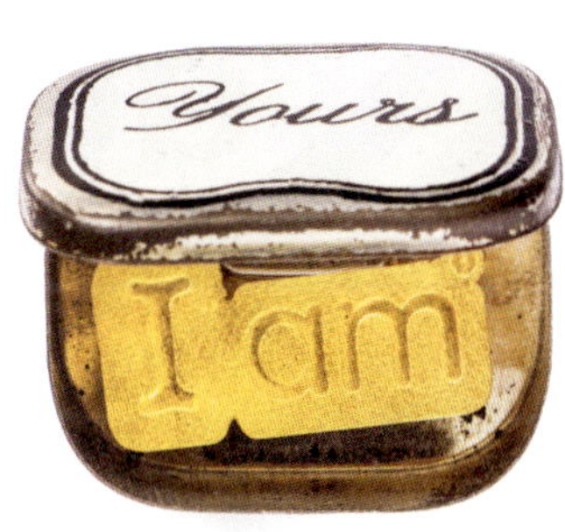

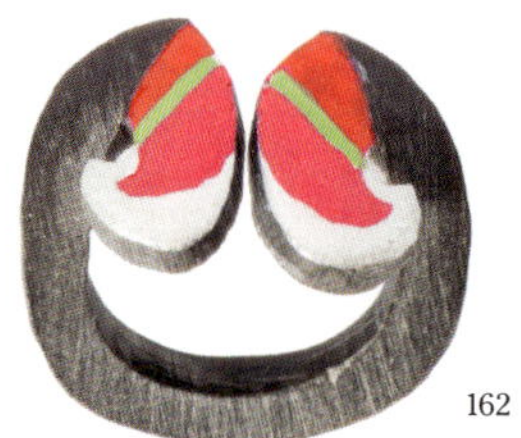

162

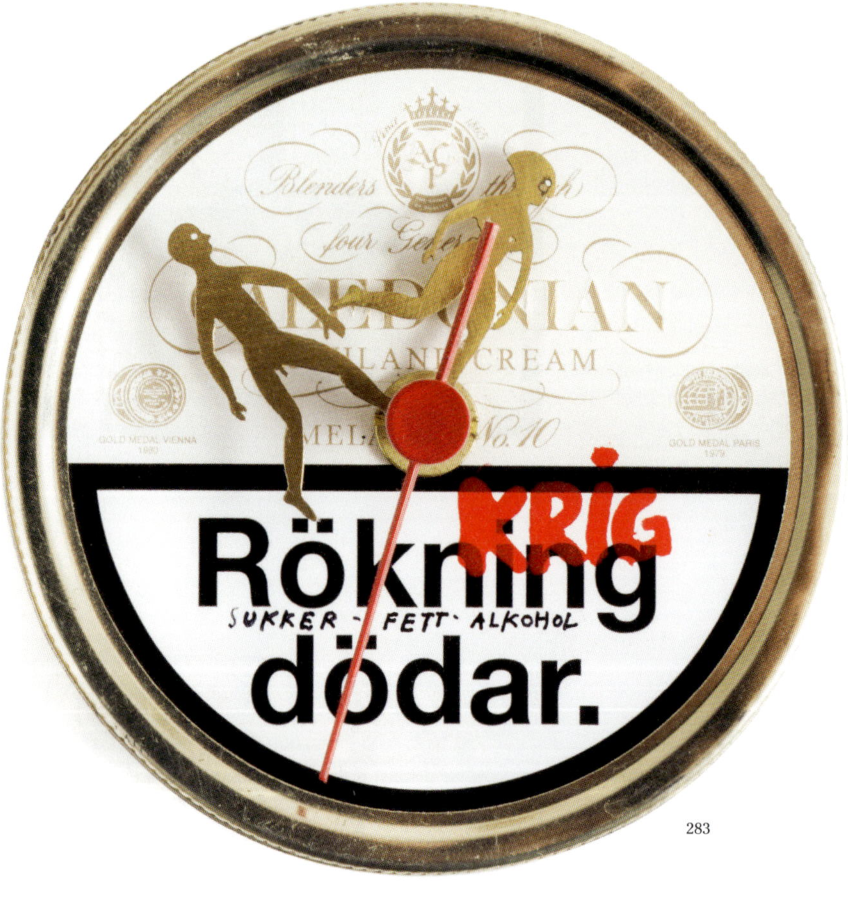

283

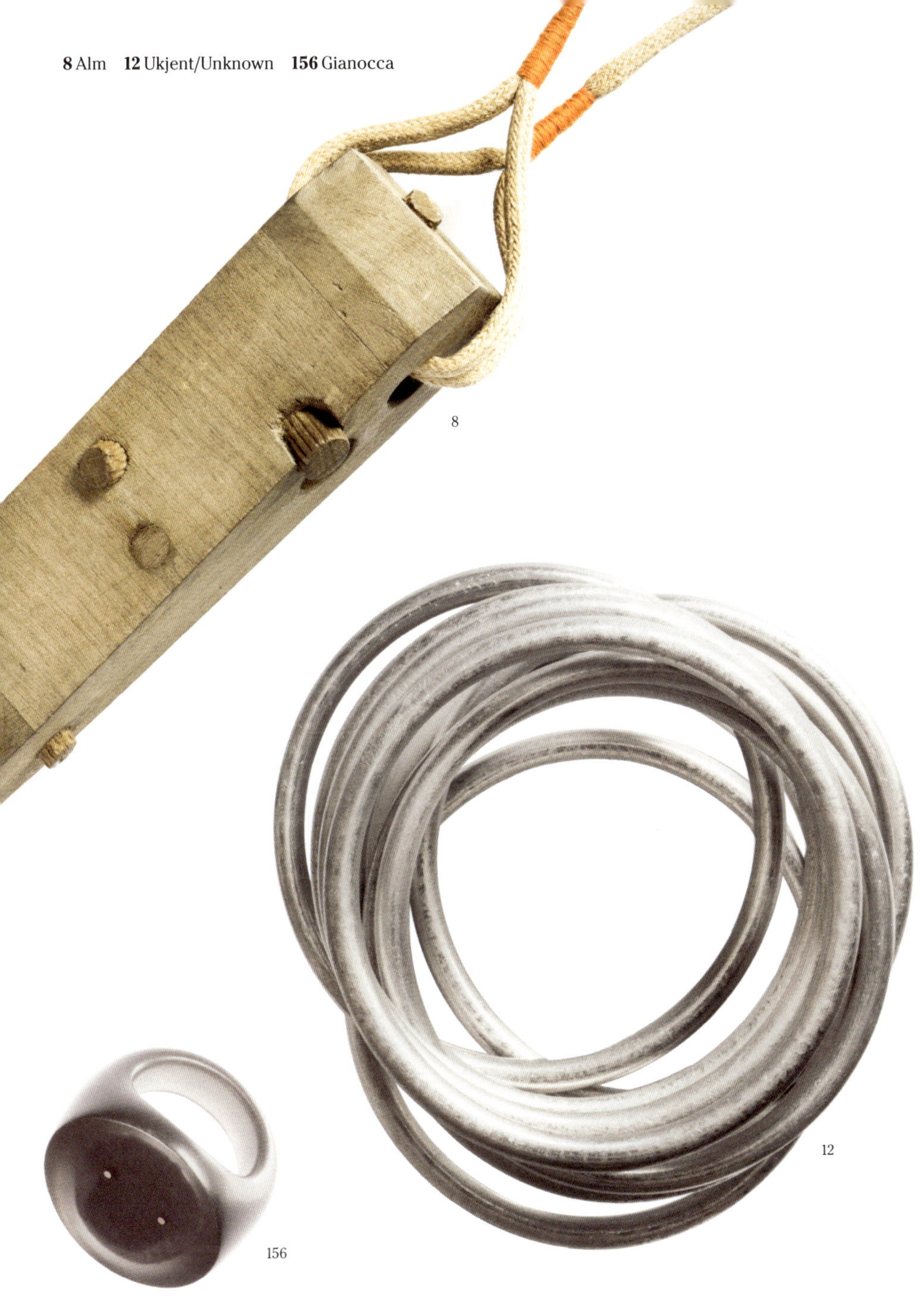

8

12

156

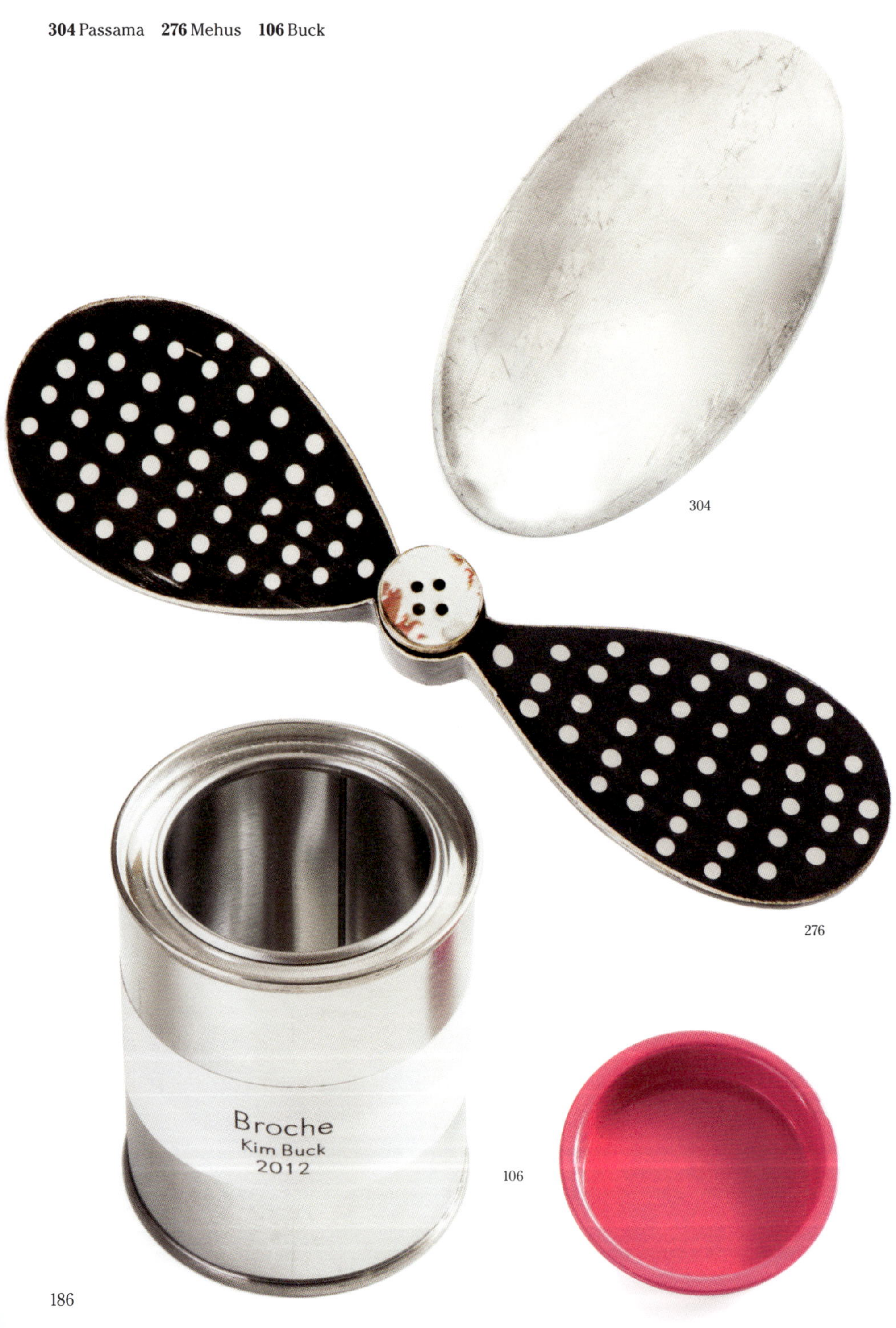
304

276

Broche
Kim Buck
2012

106

186

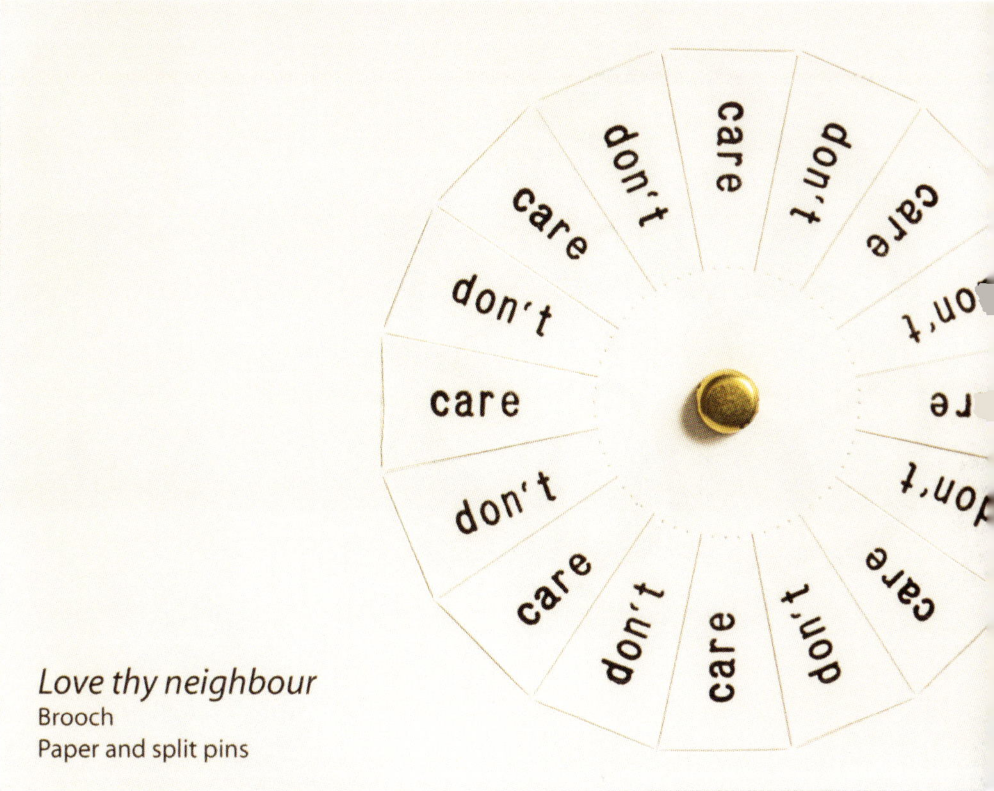

Love thy neighbour
Brooch
Paper and split pins

511

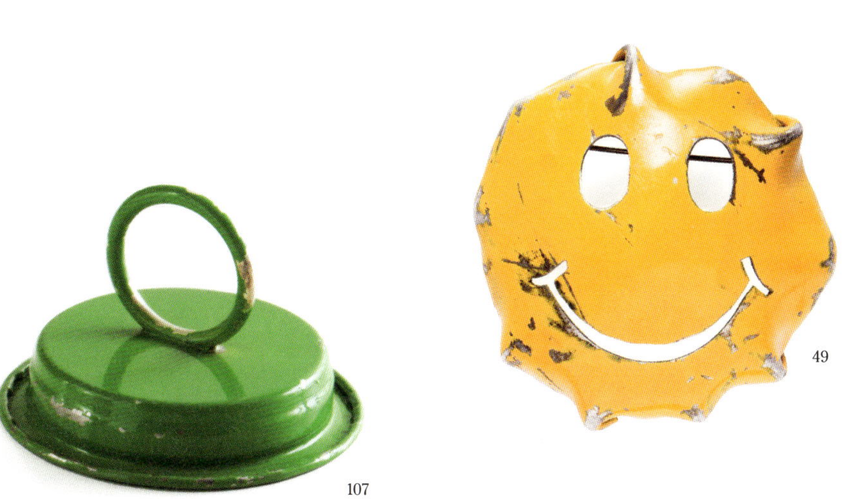

107

49

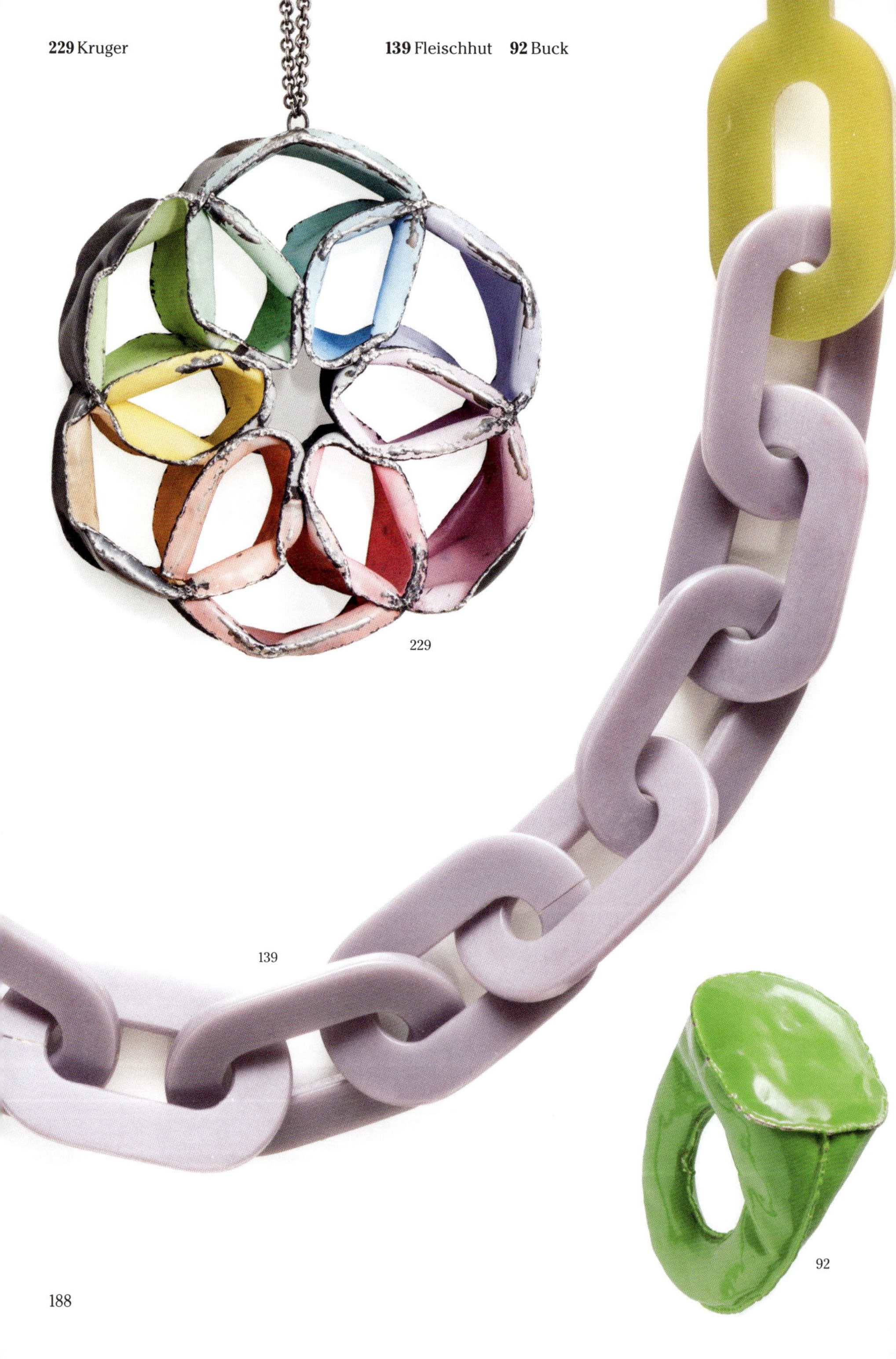

229

139

92

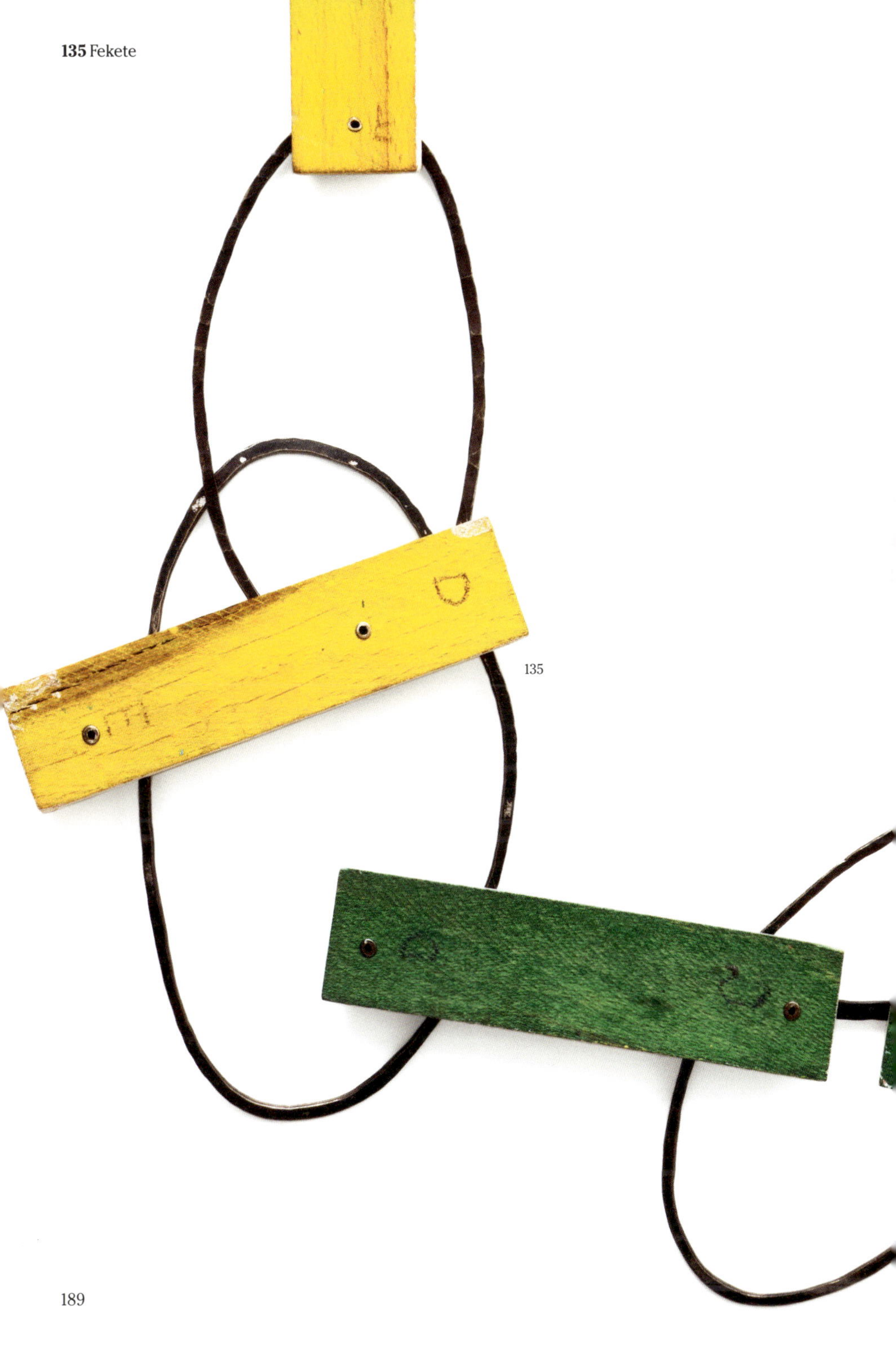

135

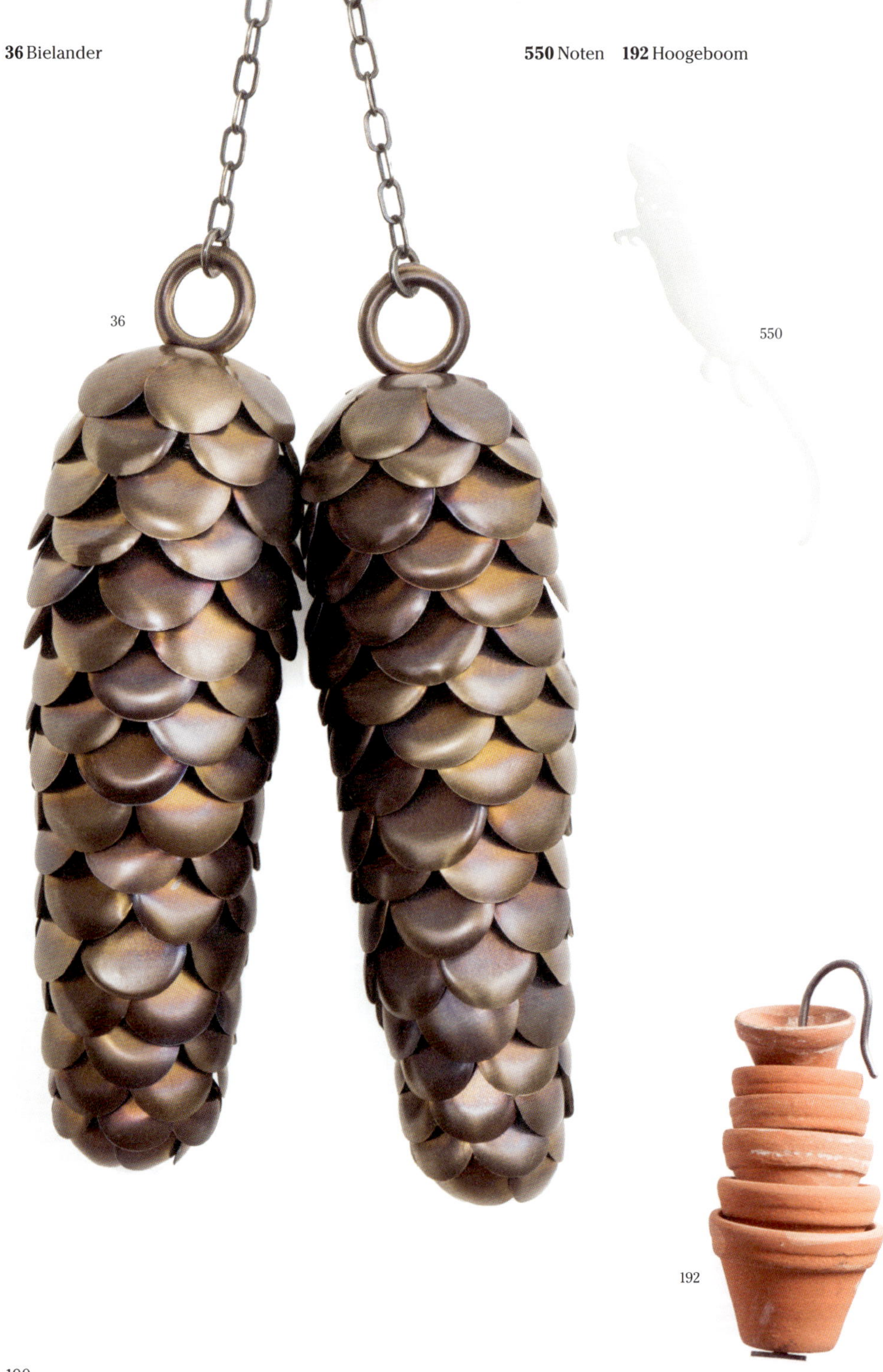

36
550
192

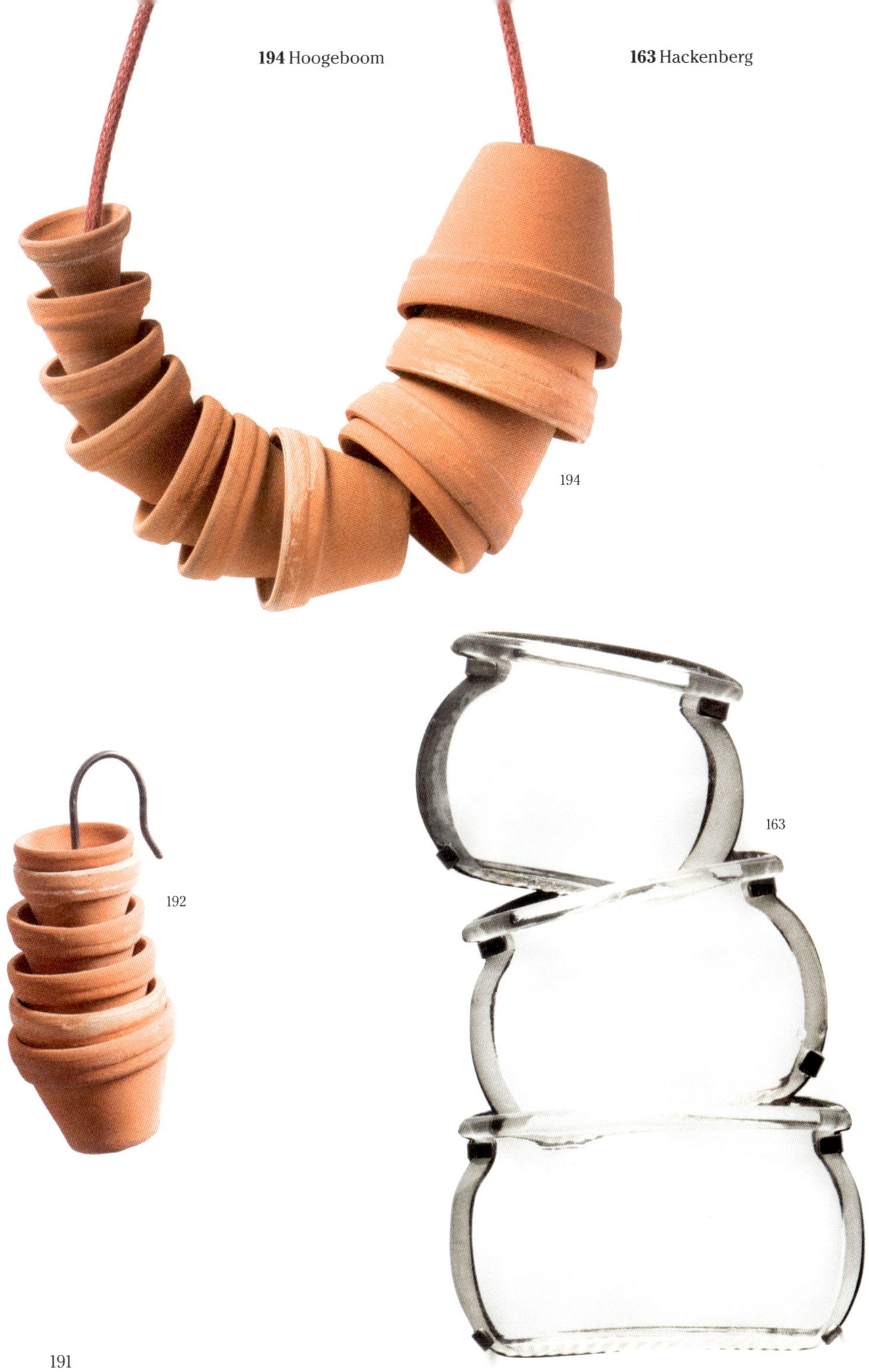

194 Hoogeboom
163 Hackenberg
194
192
163
191

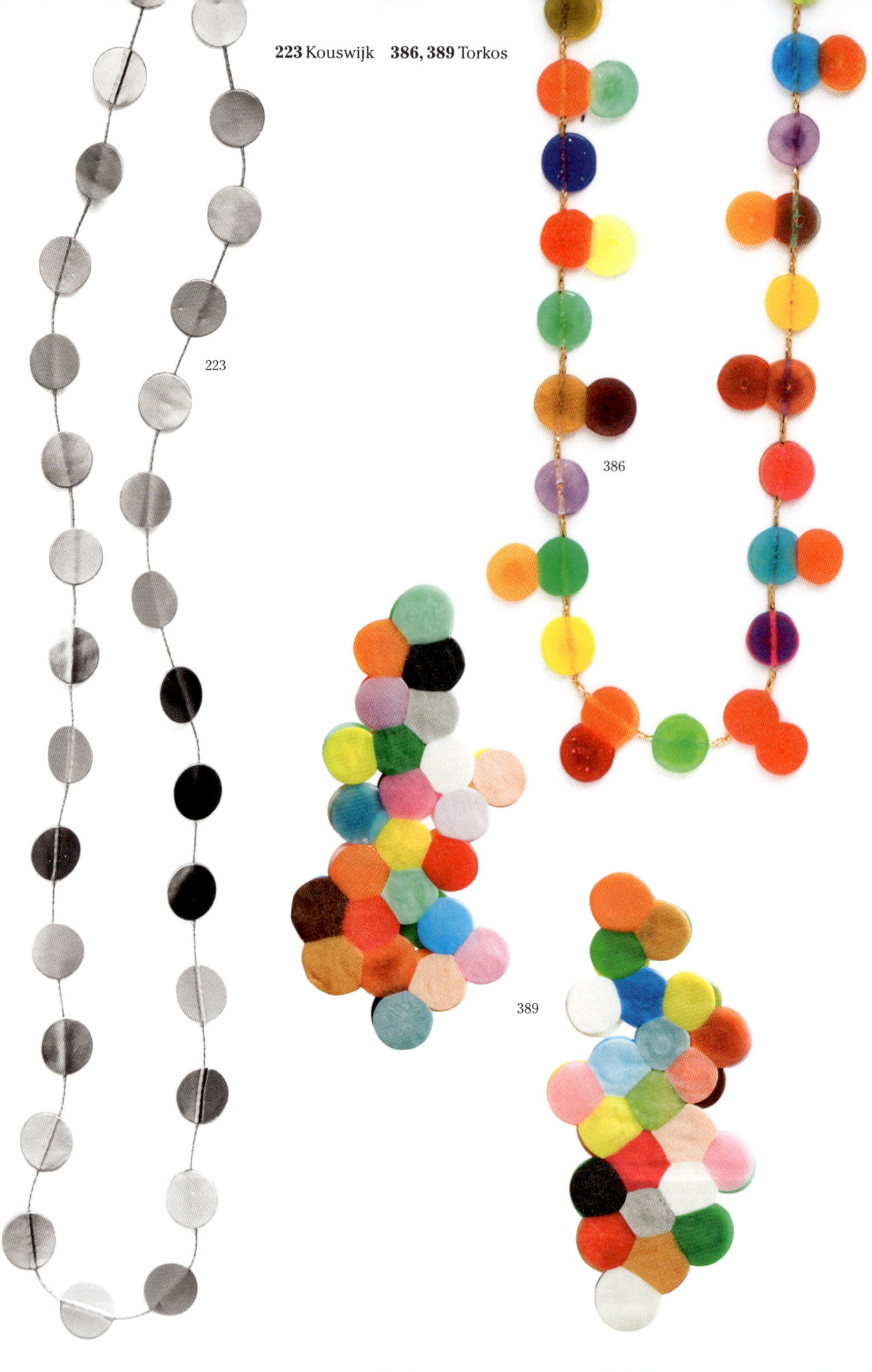

223 Kouswijk   **386, 389** Torkos

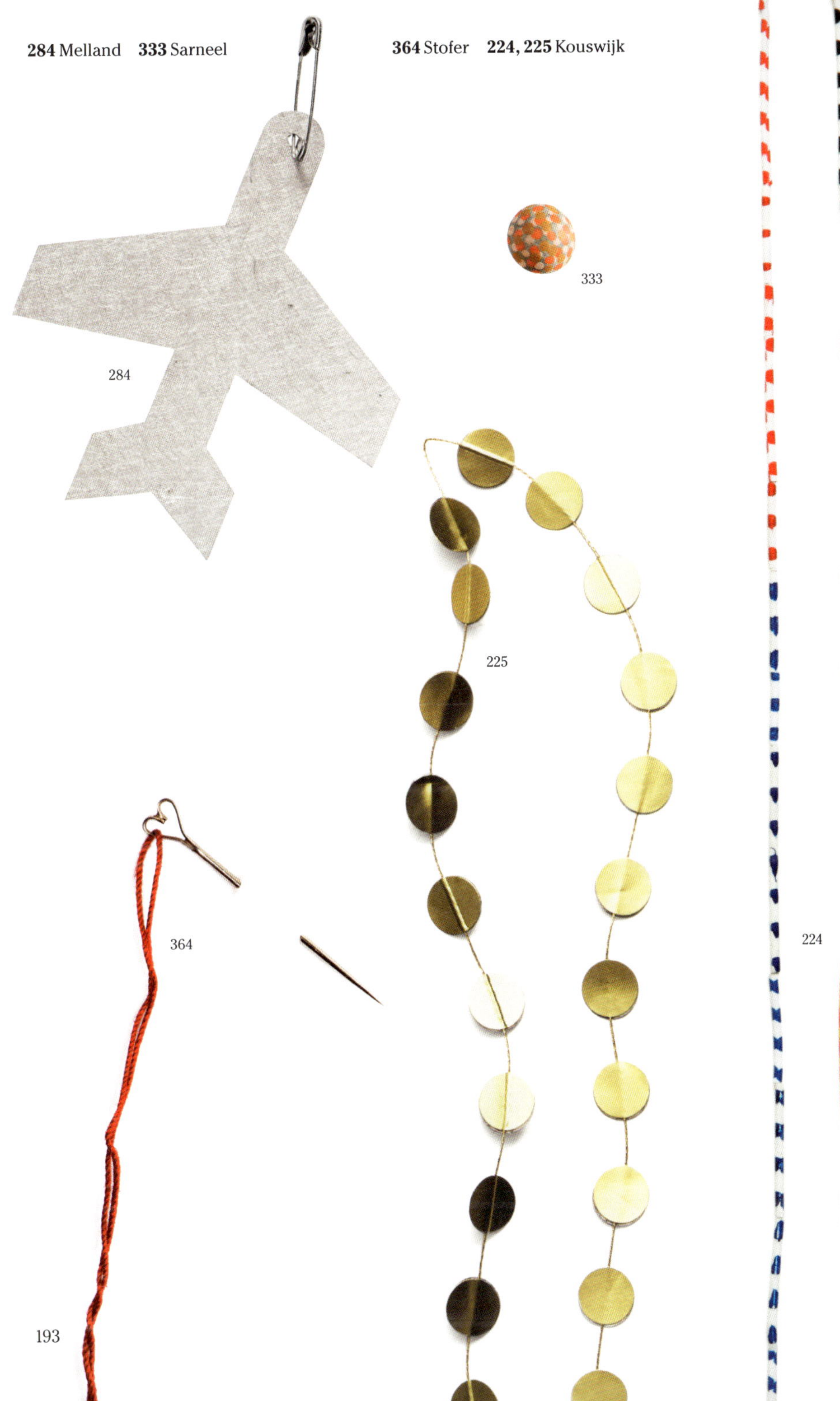
284
333
225
364
224
193

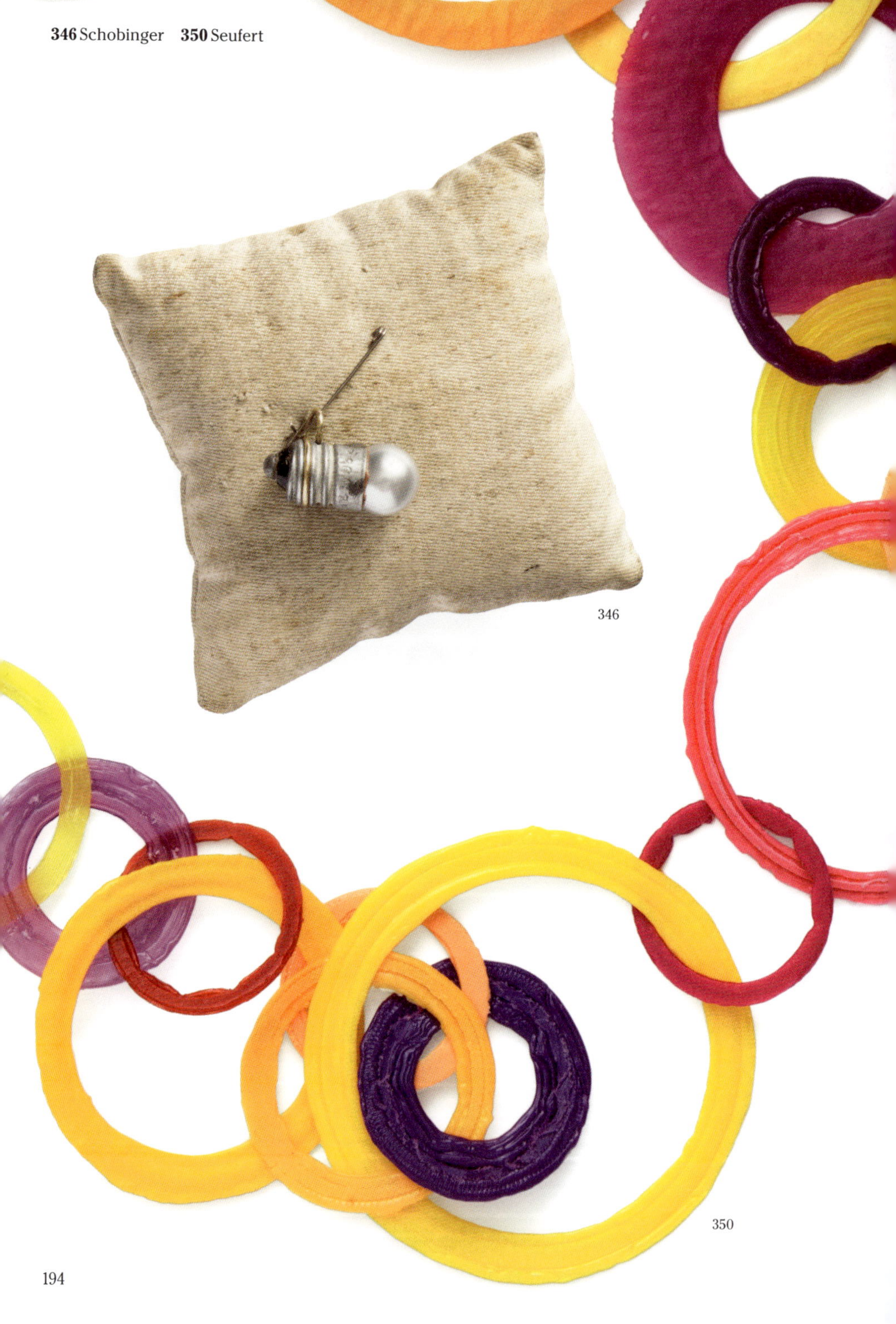

346

350

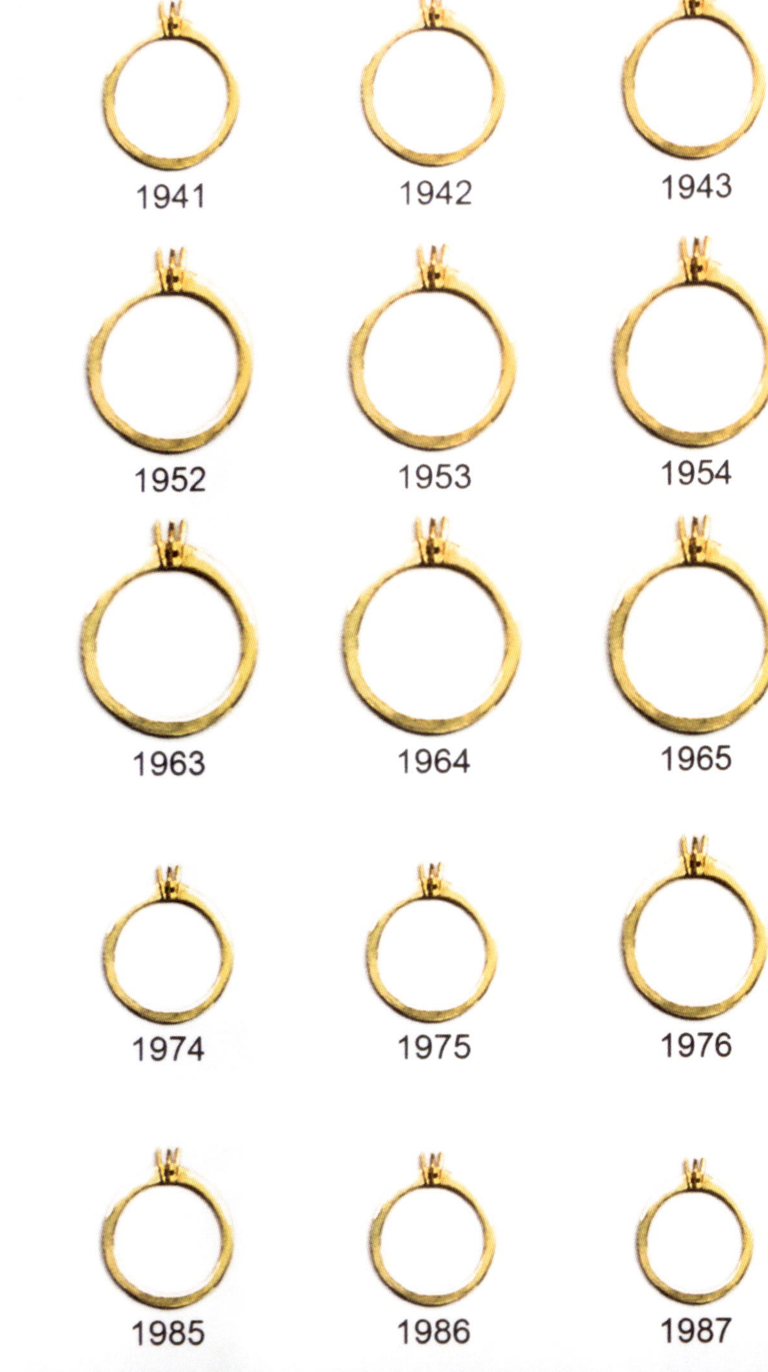

1941
1942
1943
1952
1953
1954
1963
1964
1965
1974
1975
1976
1985
1986
1987

204

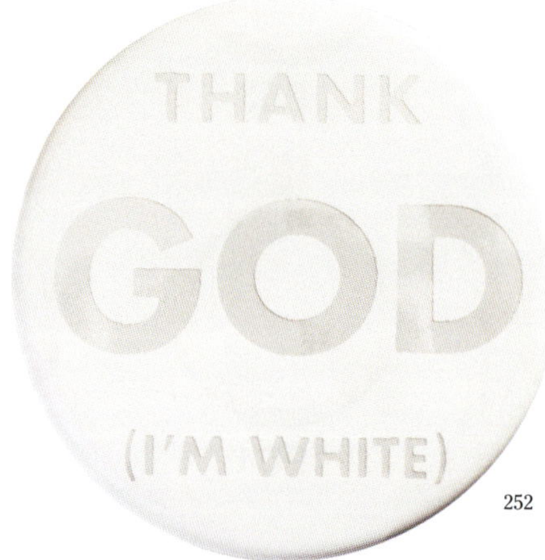

252

244

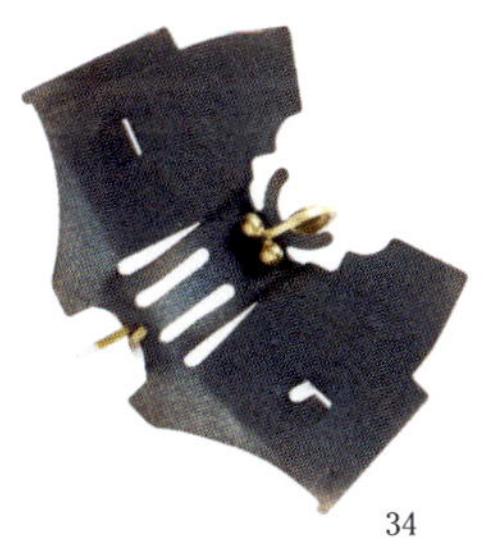

34

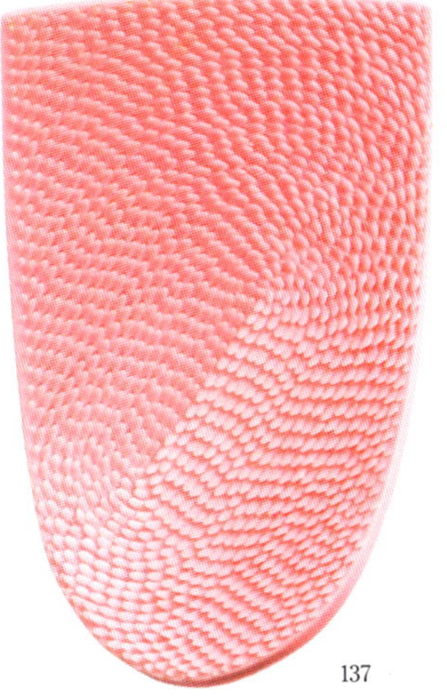

137

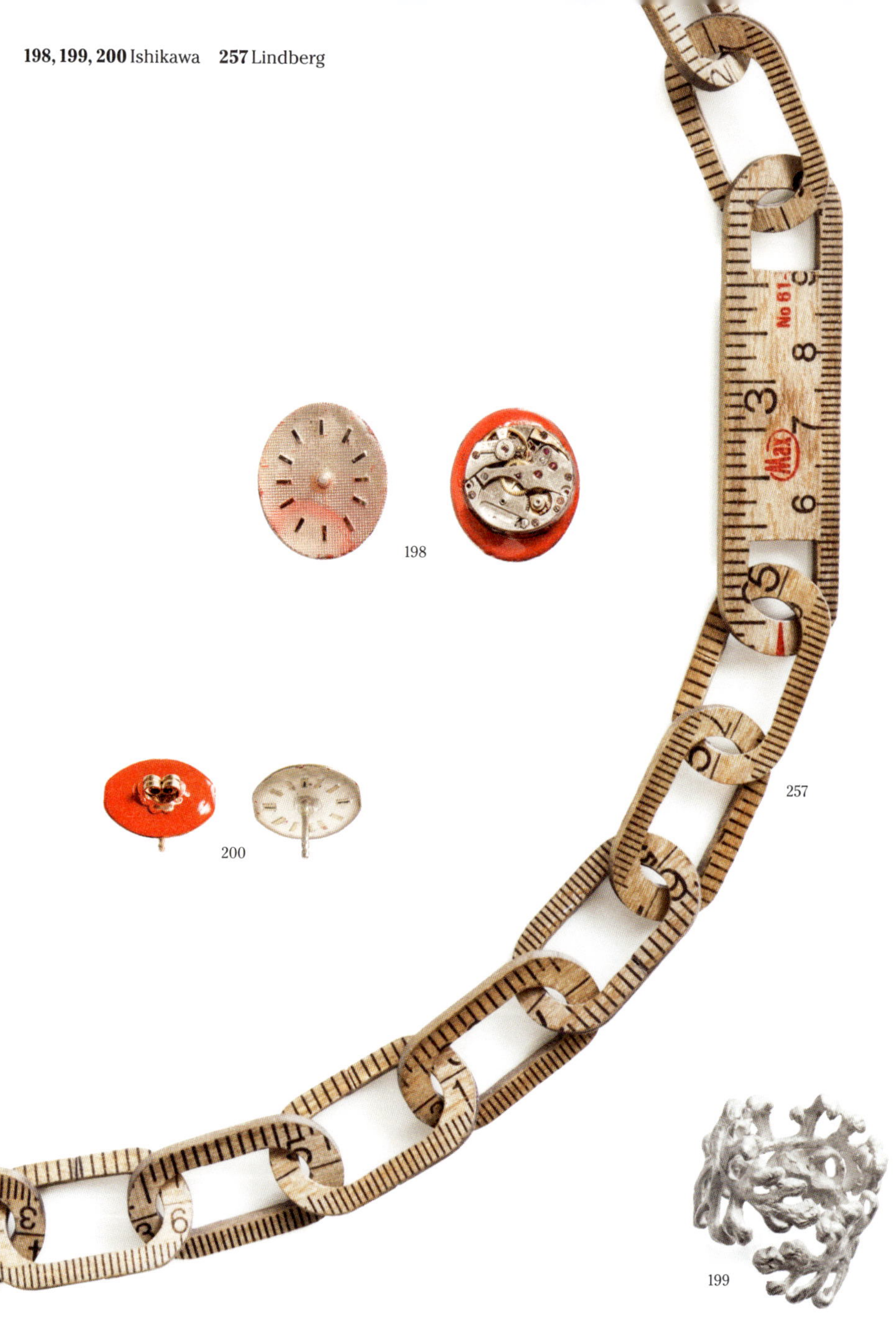

198

200

257

199

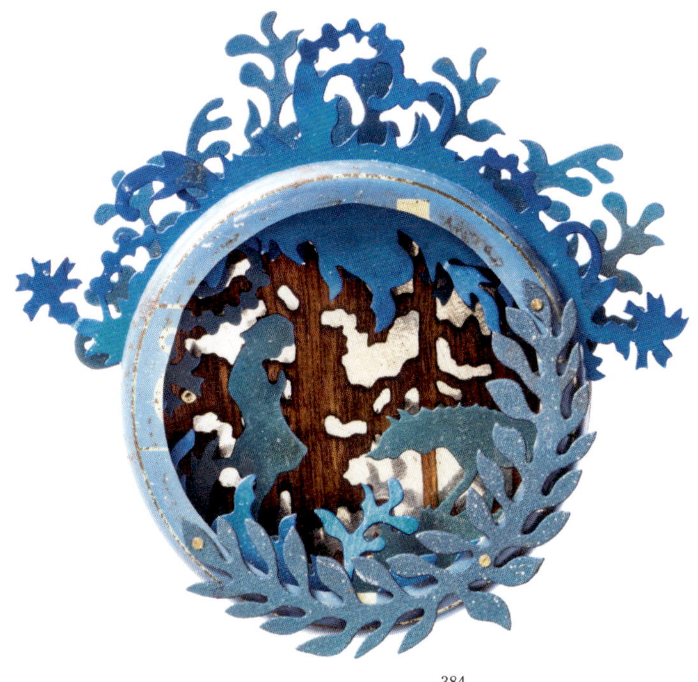

384

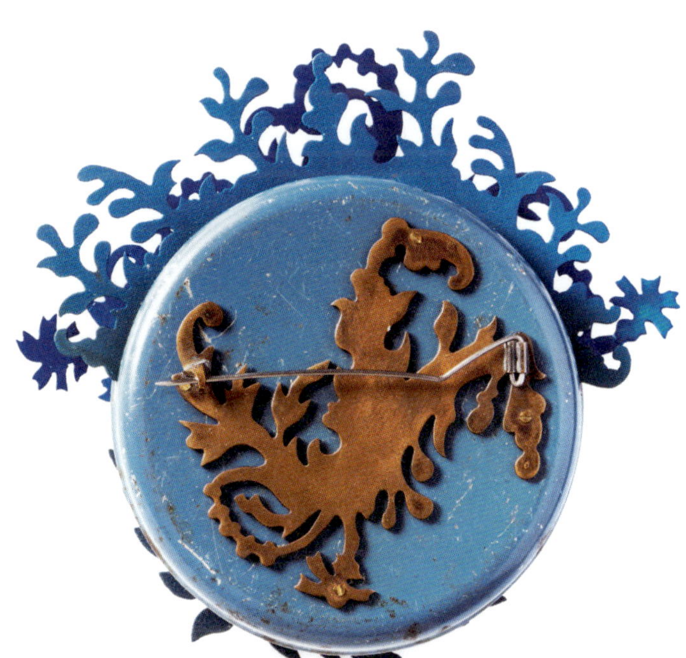

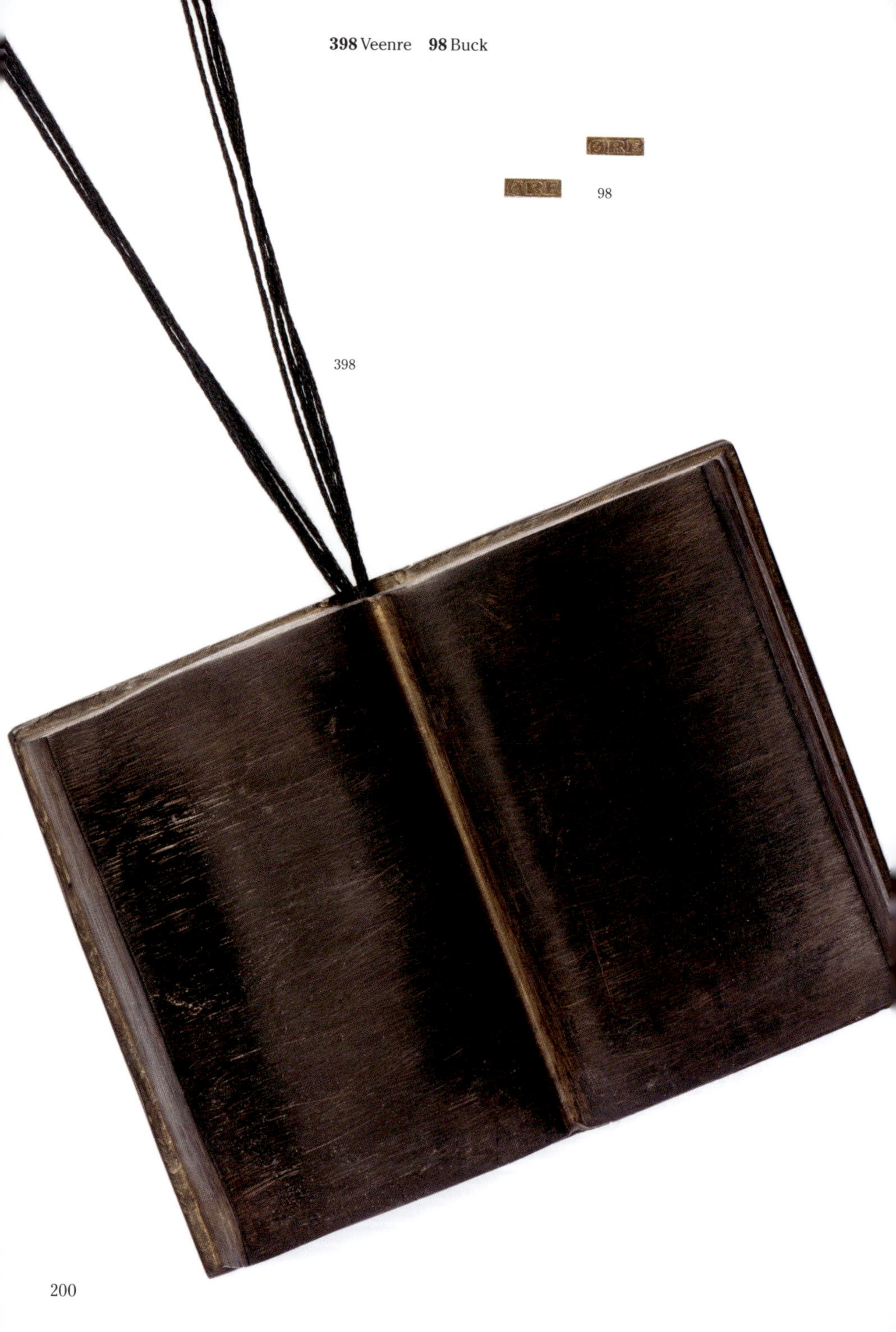
98
398

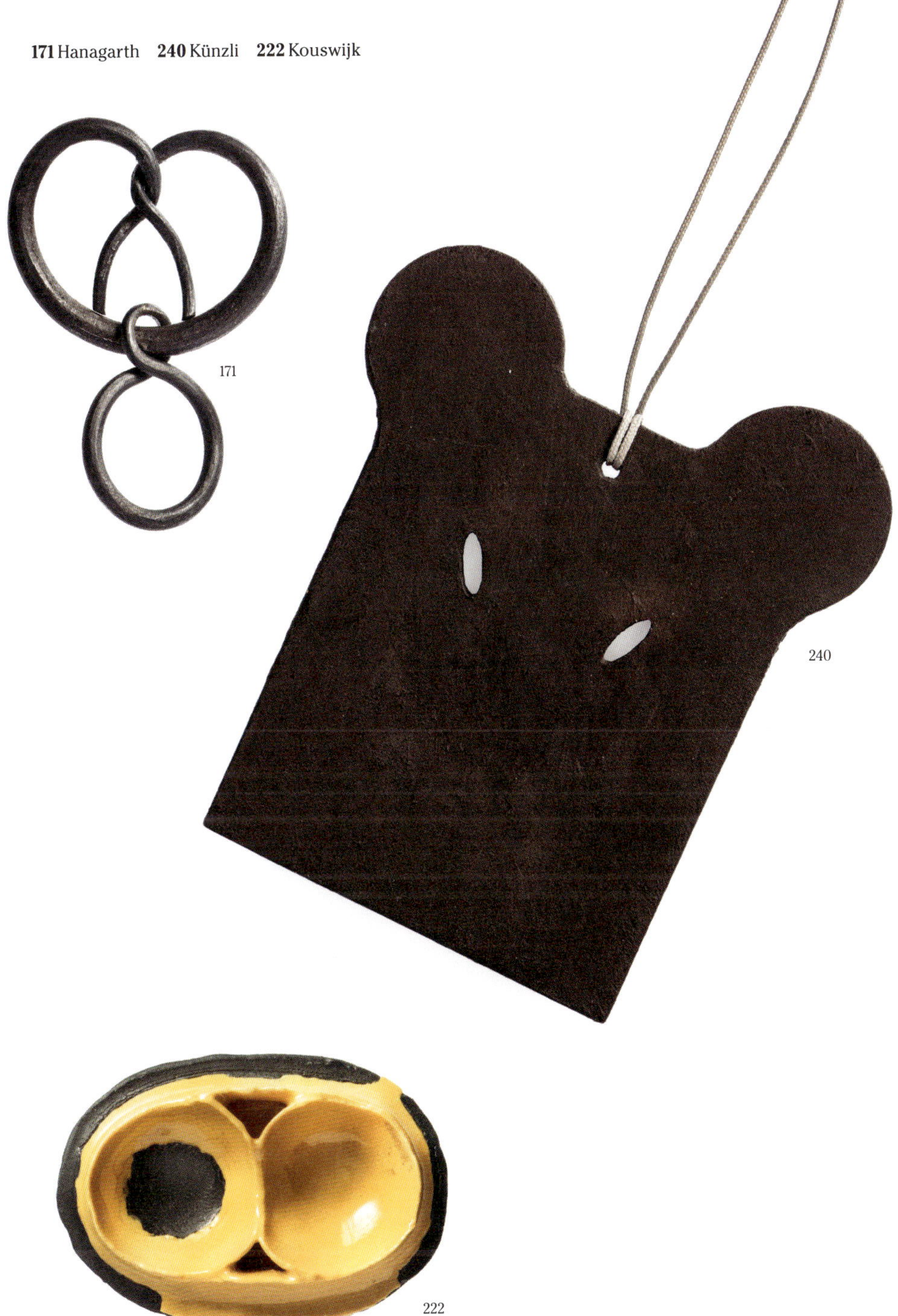

171

240

222

201

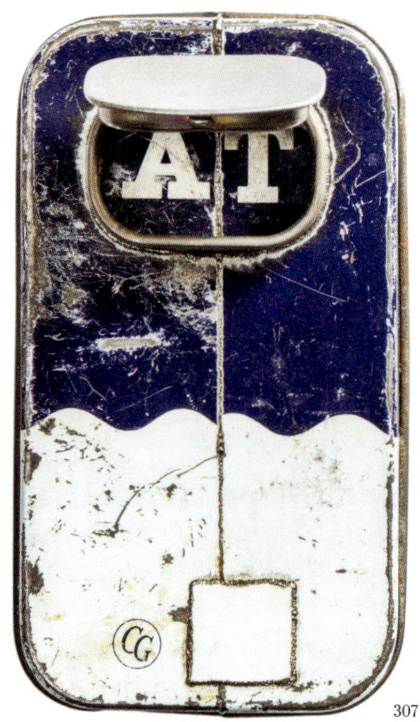

307

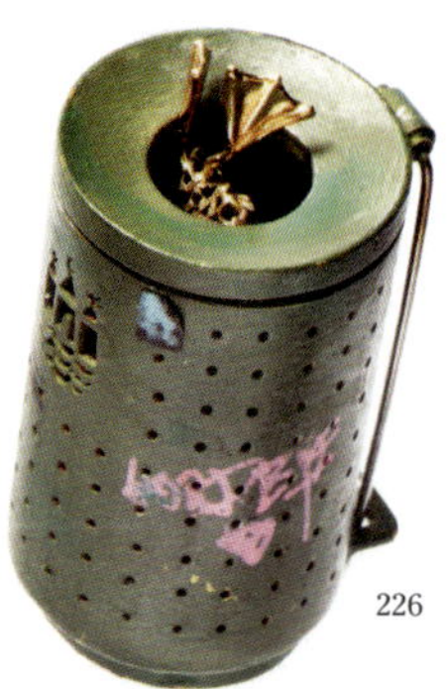

226

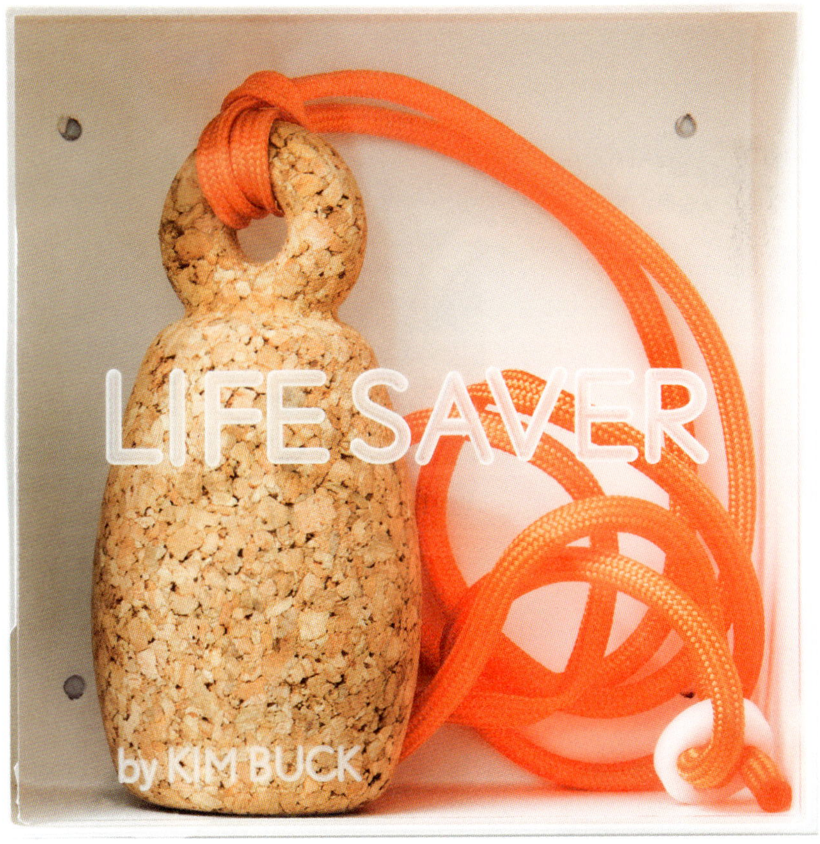

LIFE SAVER
by KIM BUCK

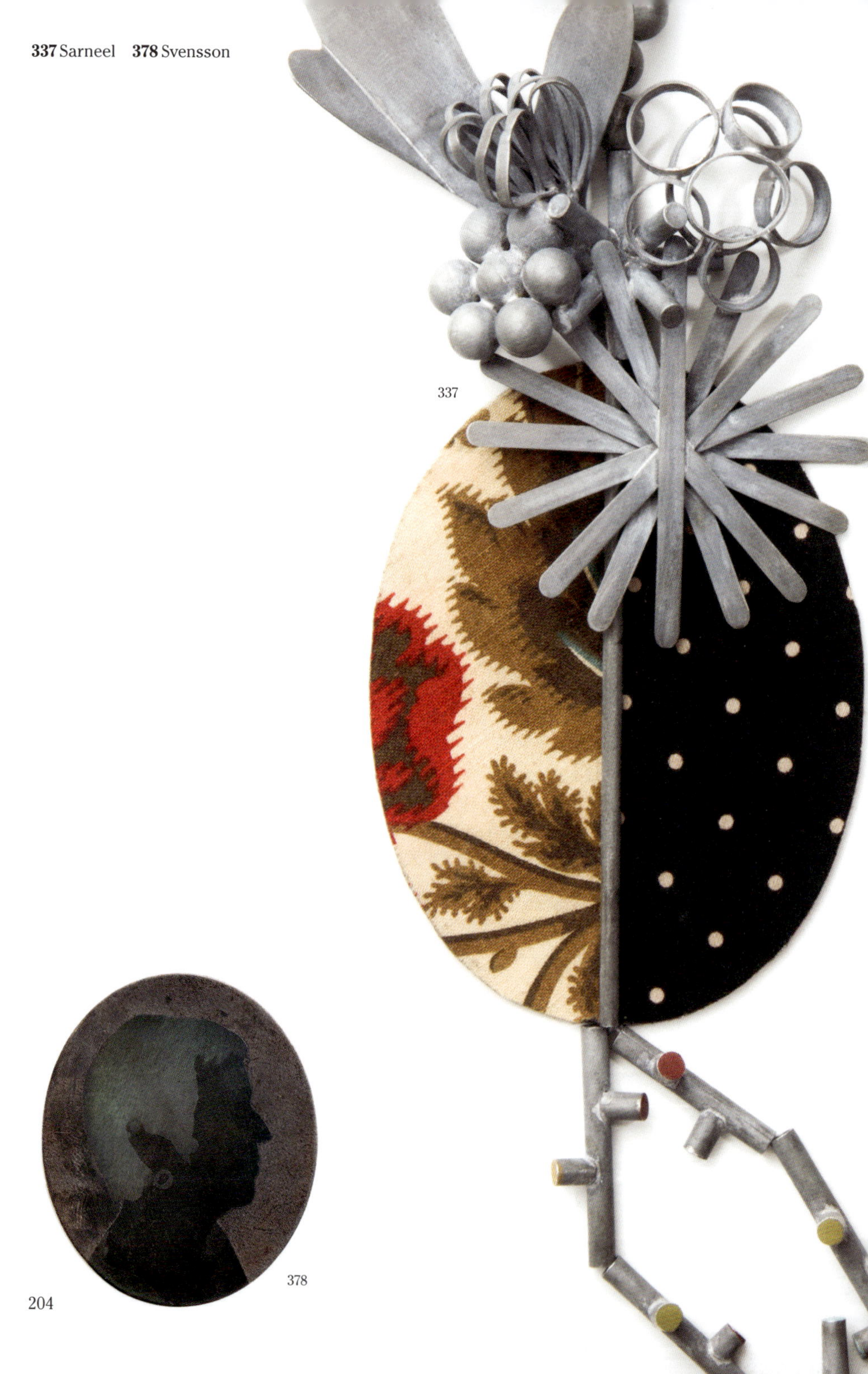

337

378

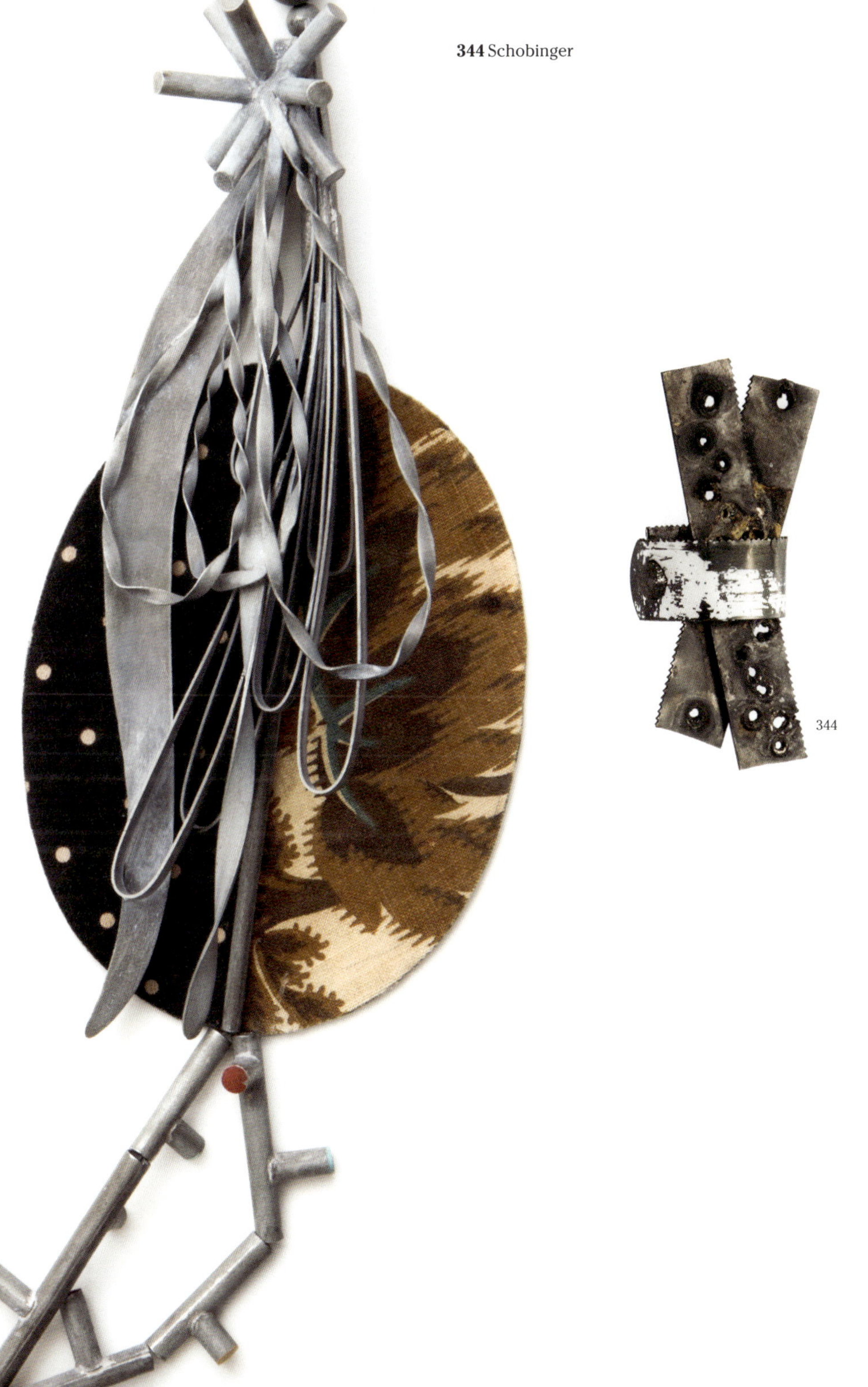

344

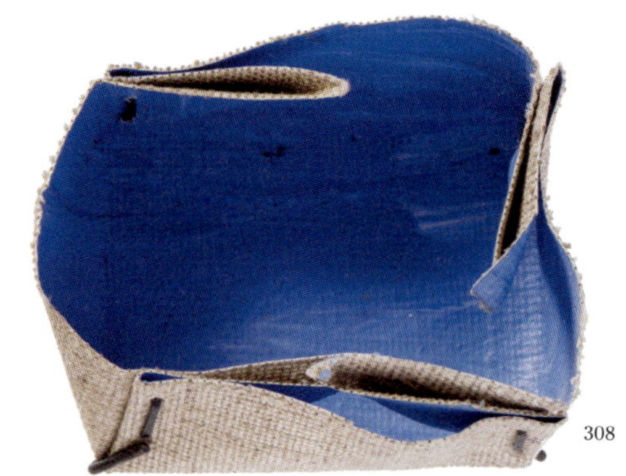

308

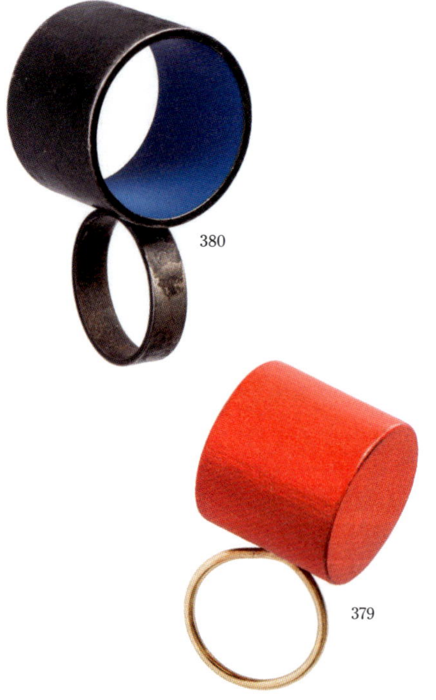

380

379

450

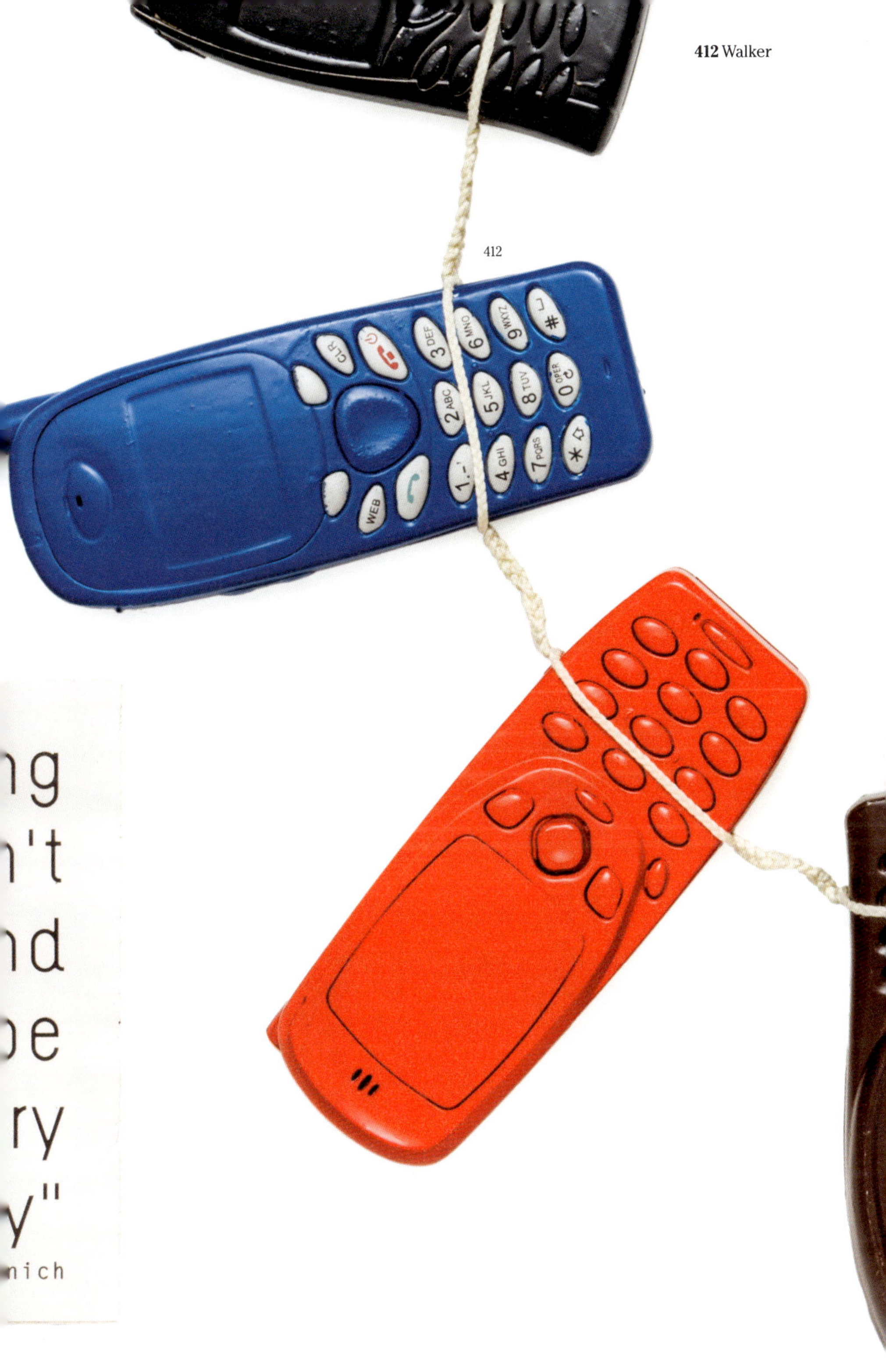

412

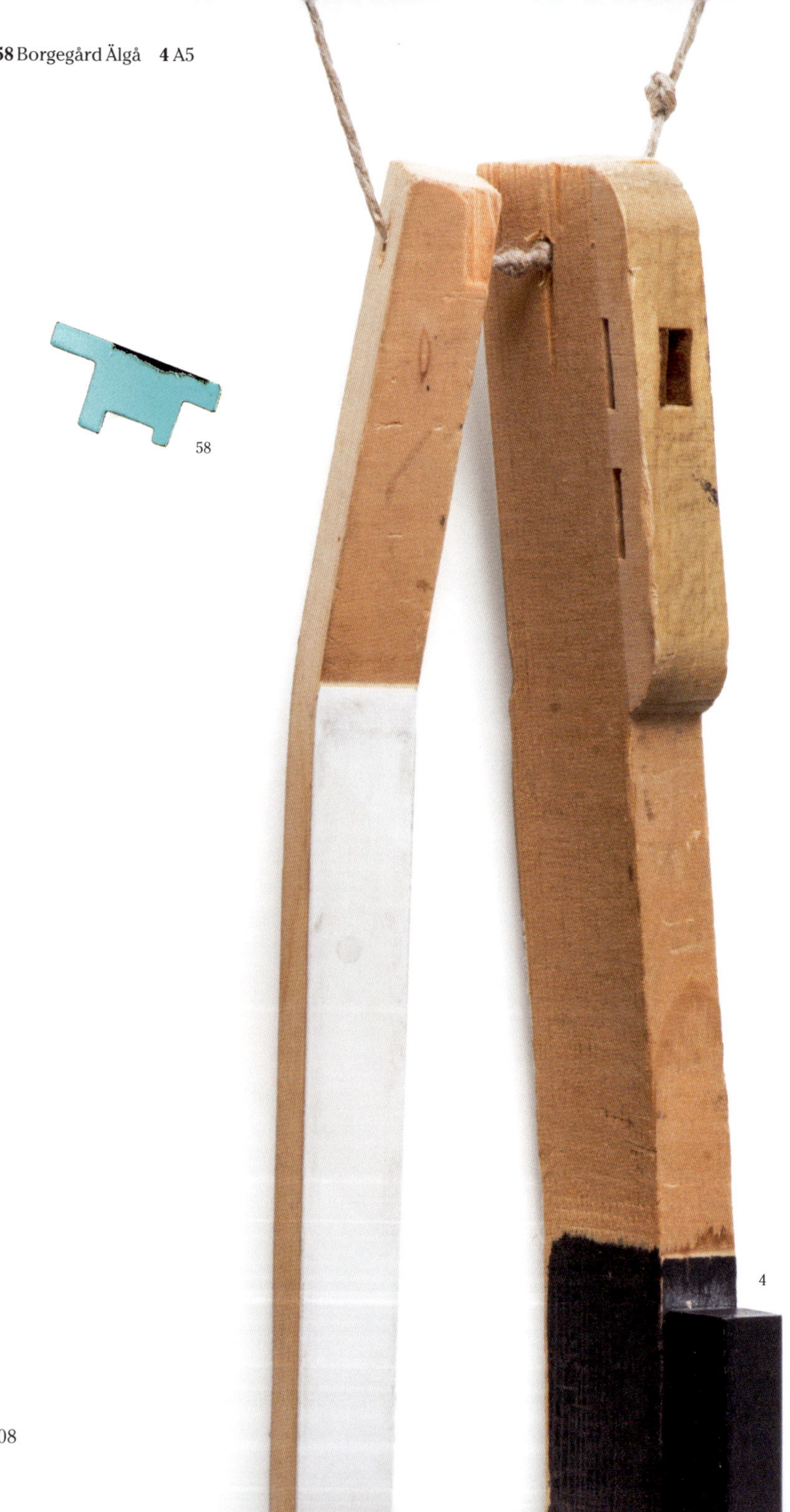

58

4

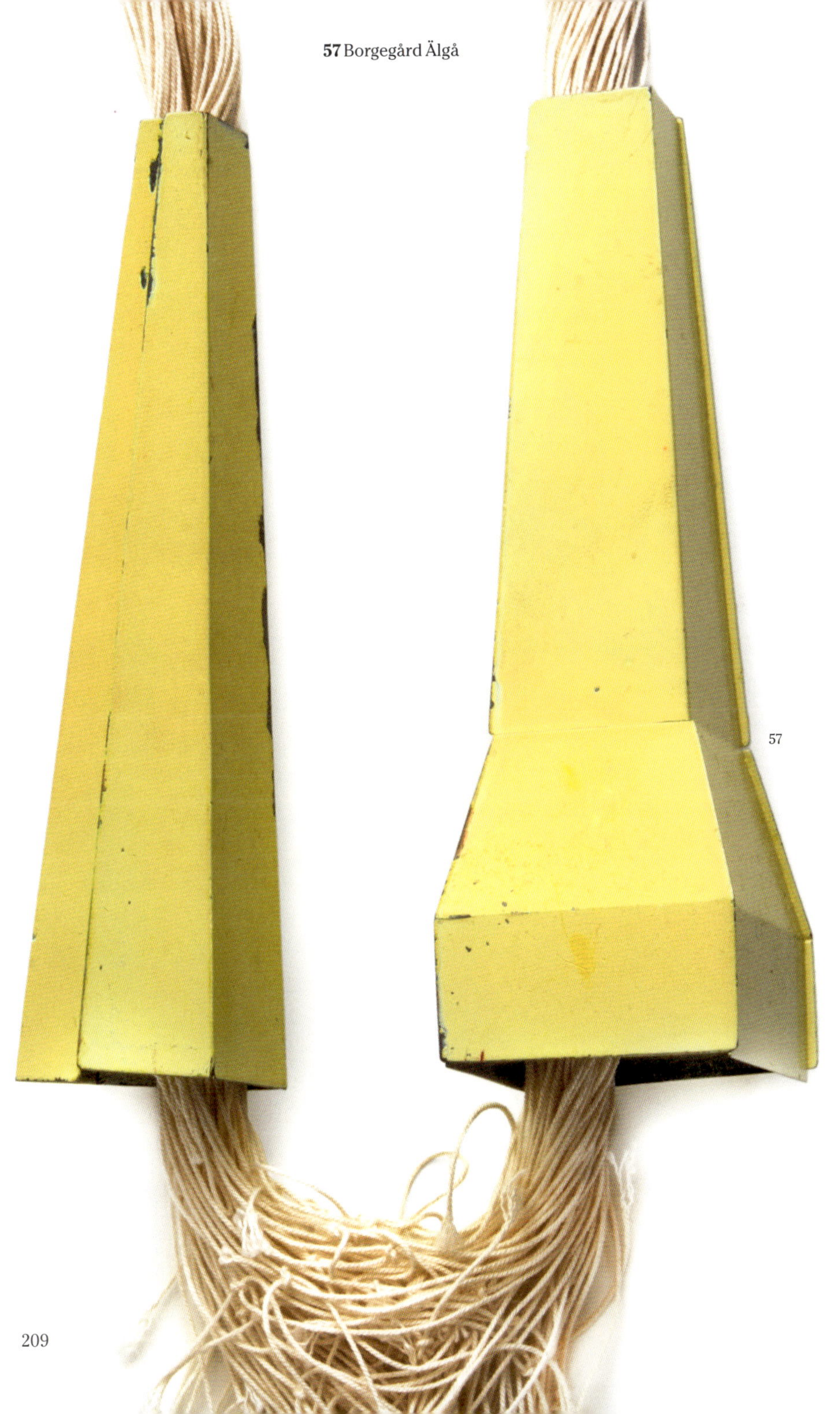

57

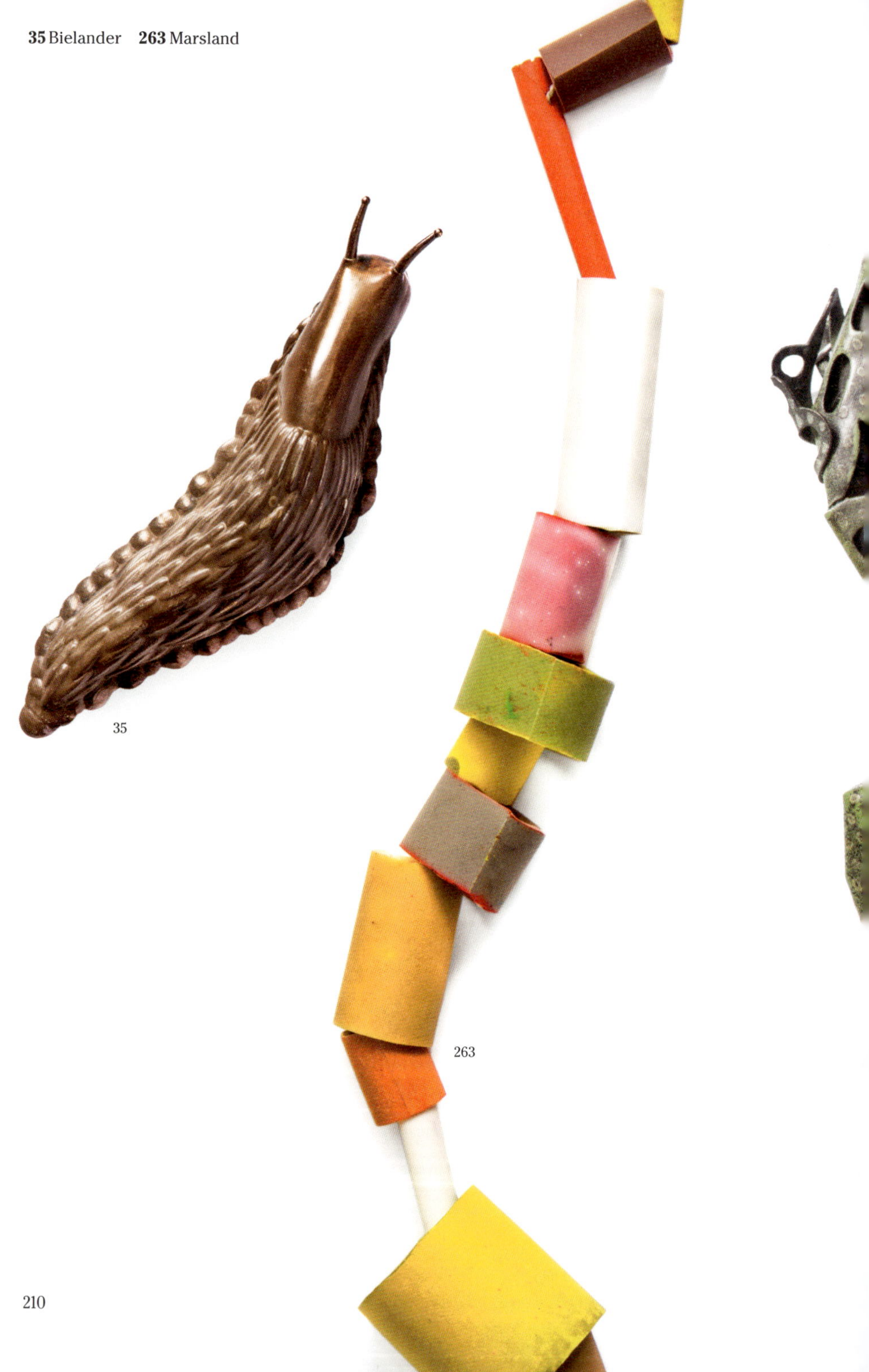

35

263

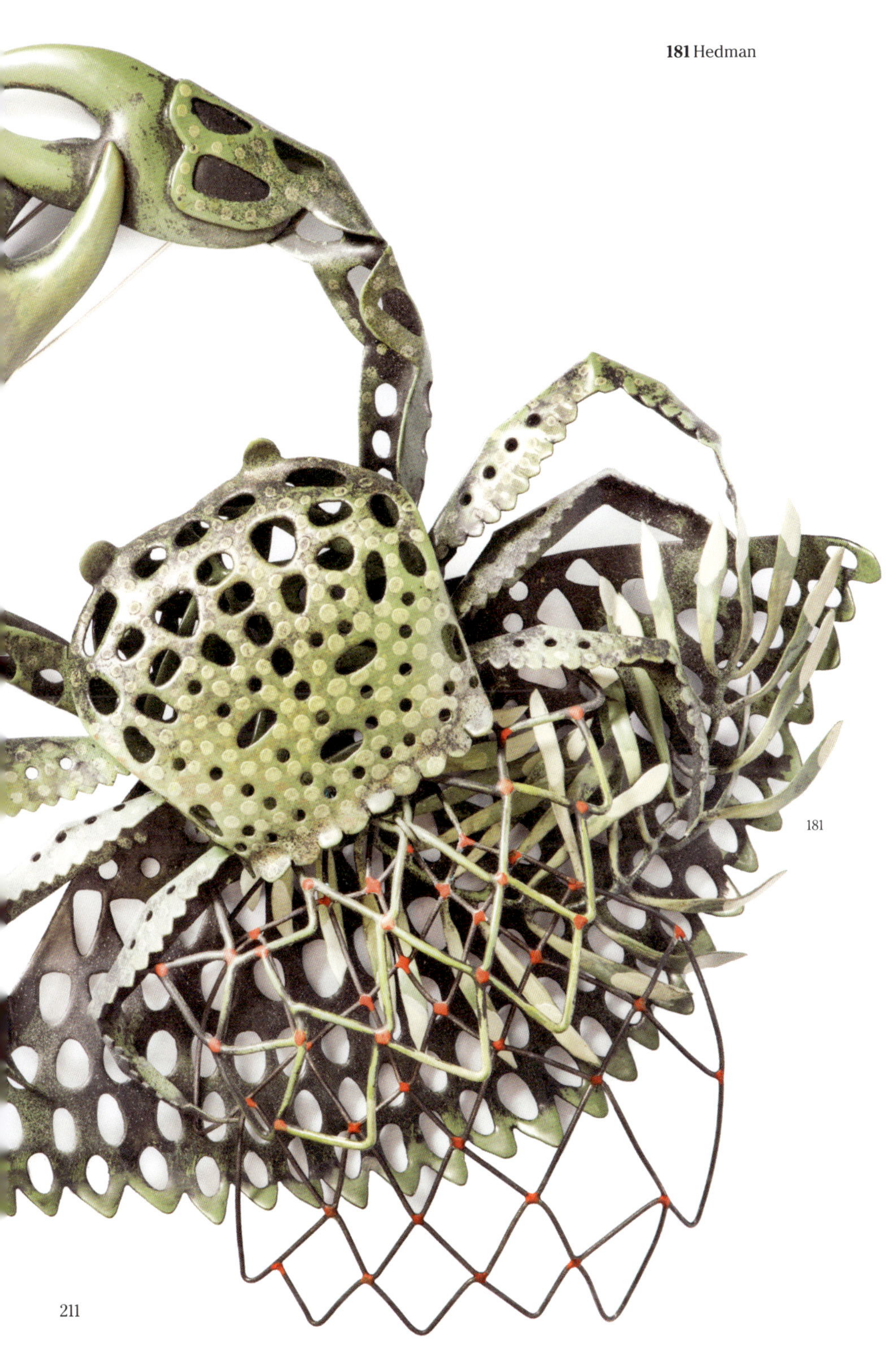

181

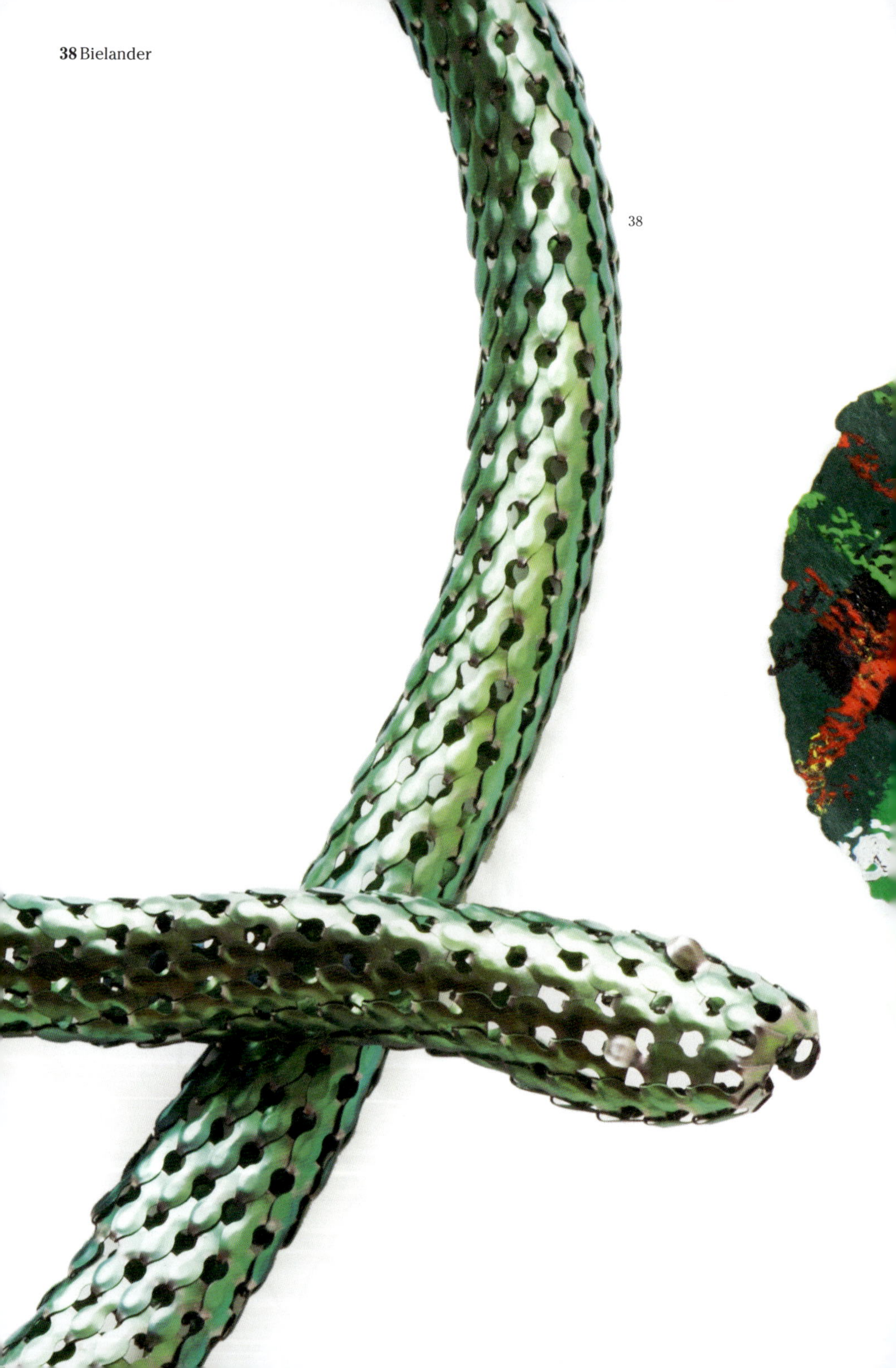

38

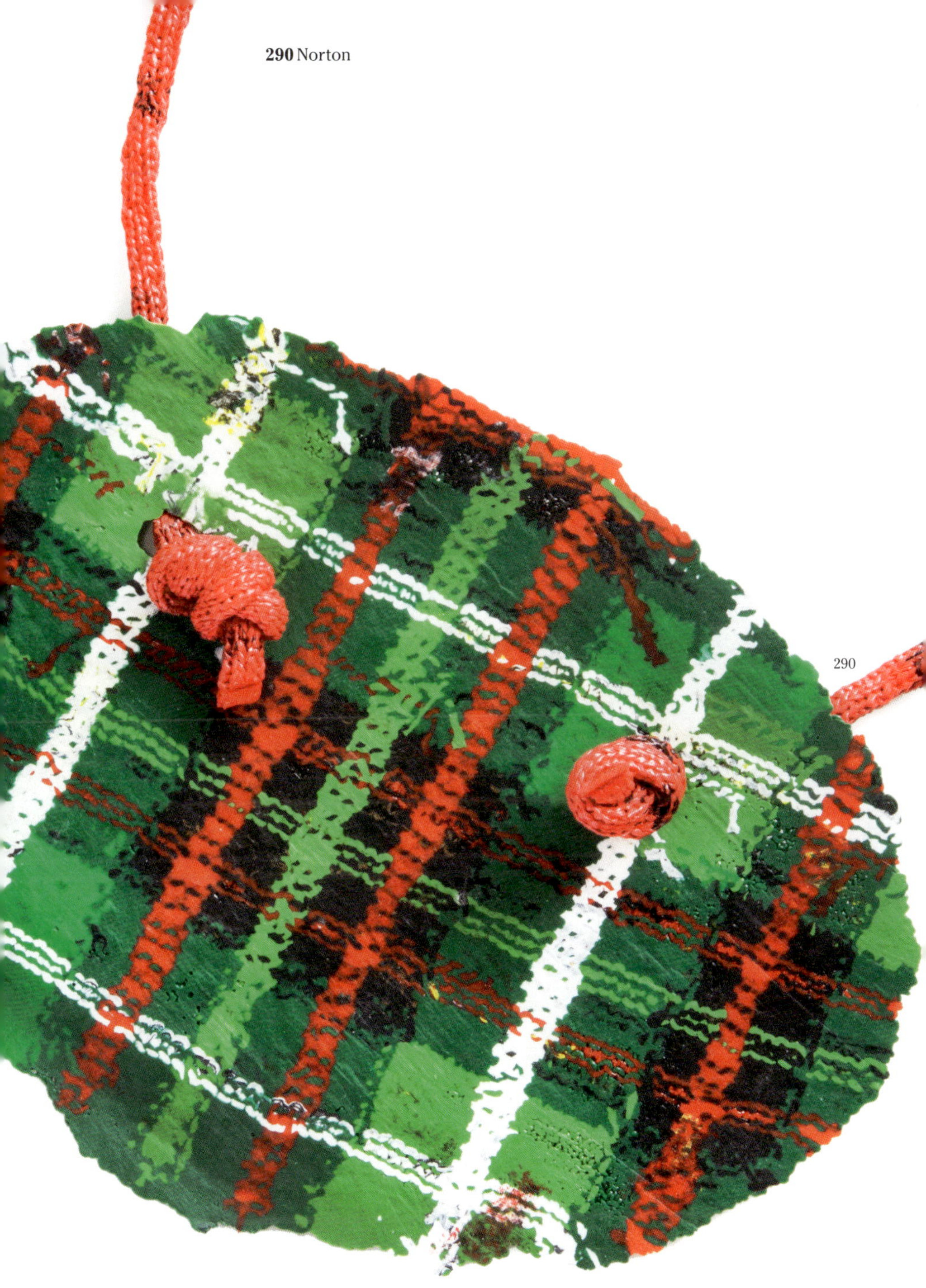

290

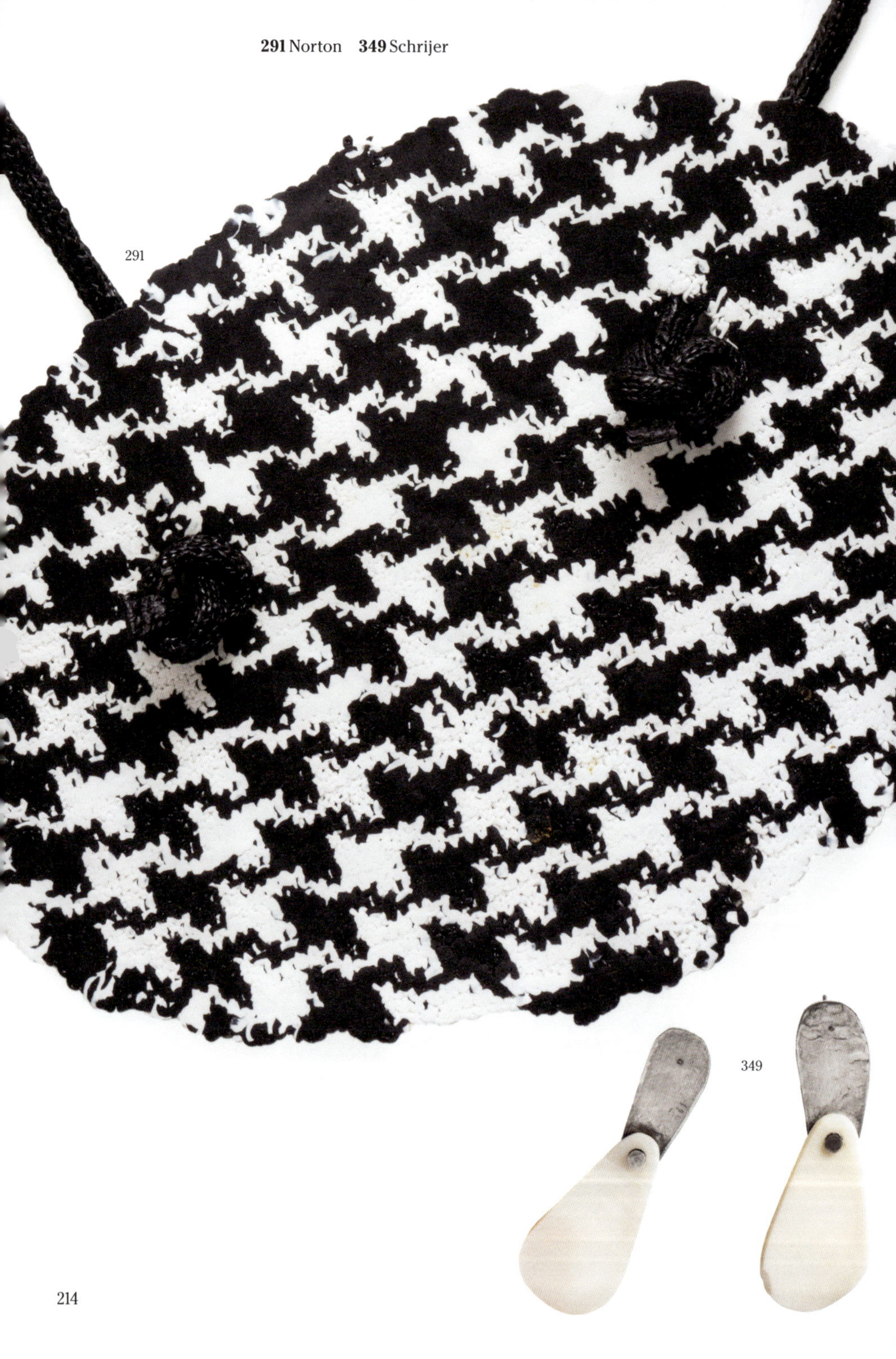

291
349

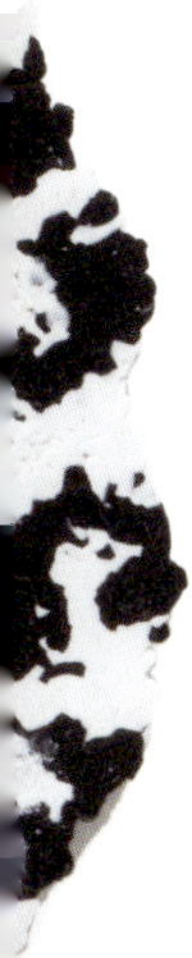

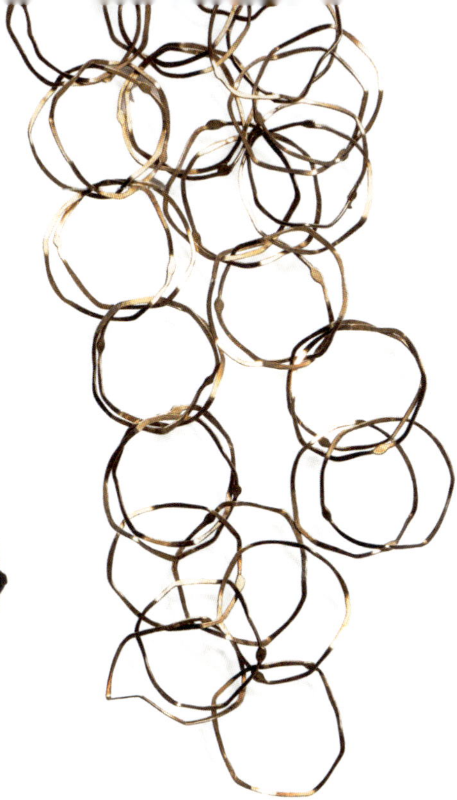

59

129

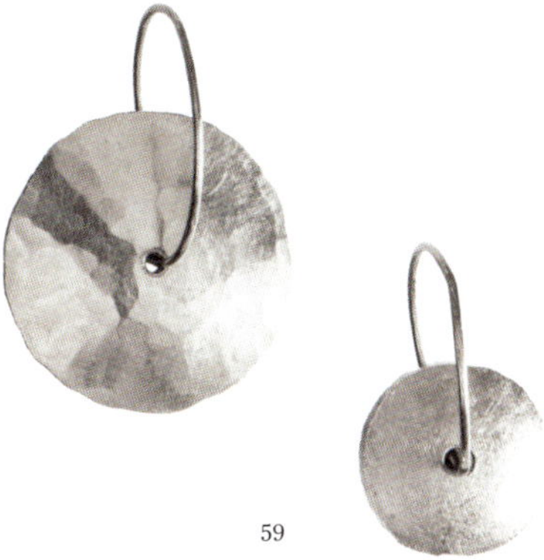

215

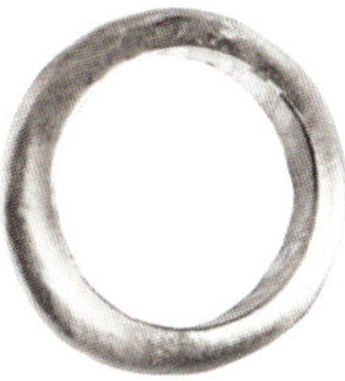

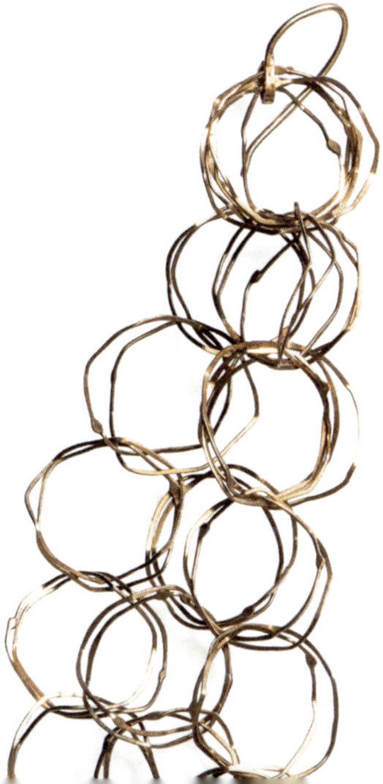

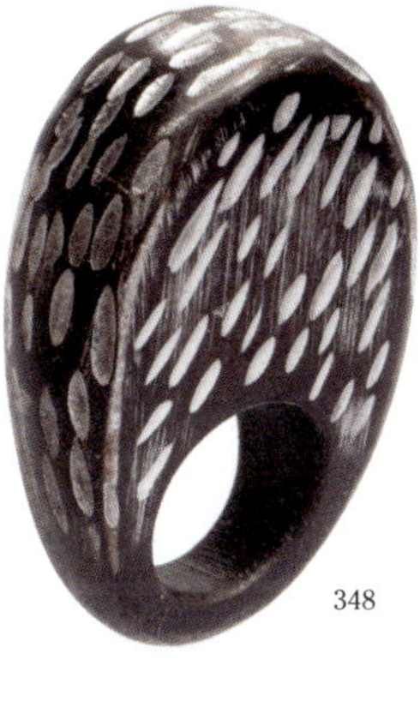

348

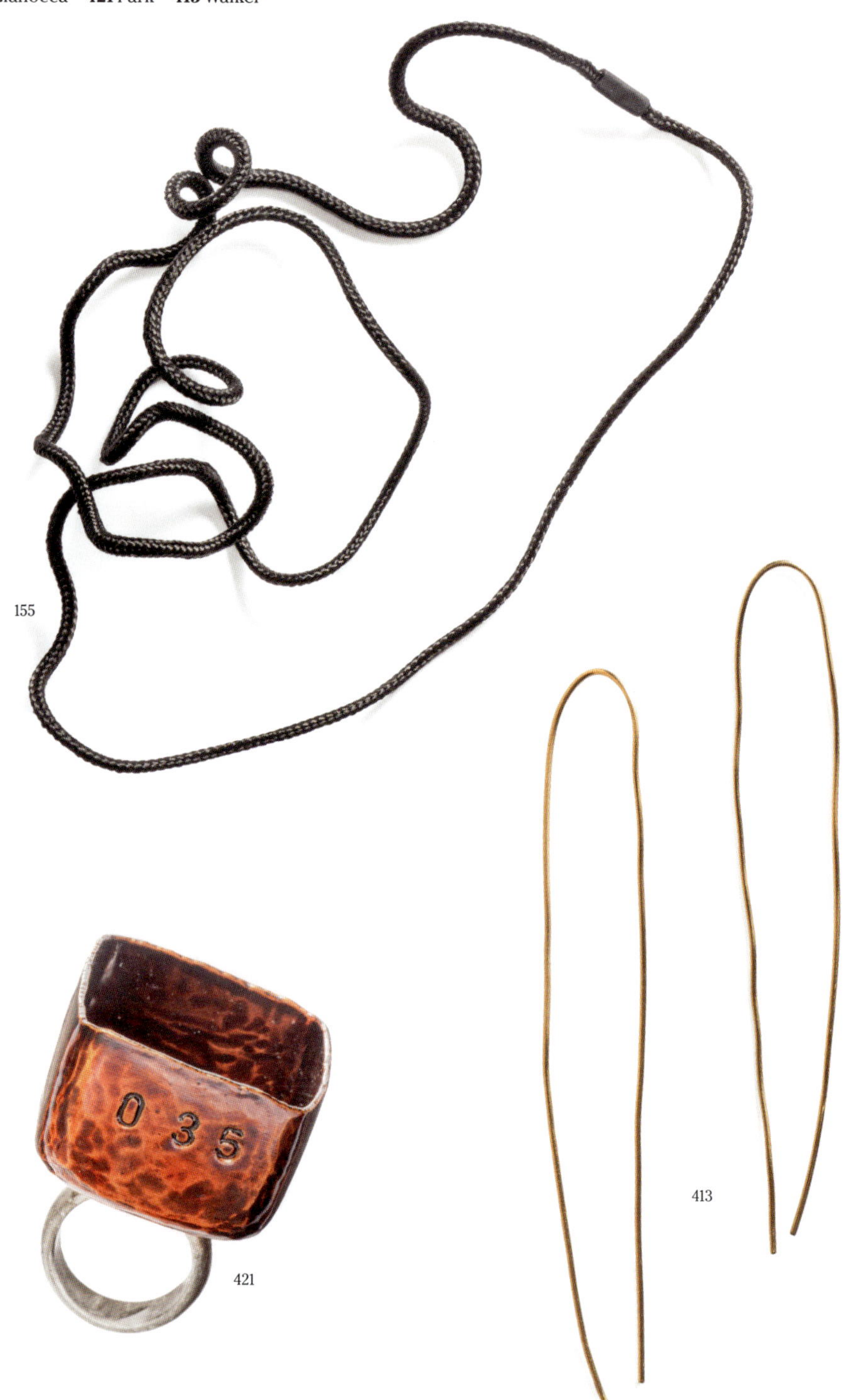

155

421

413

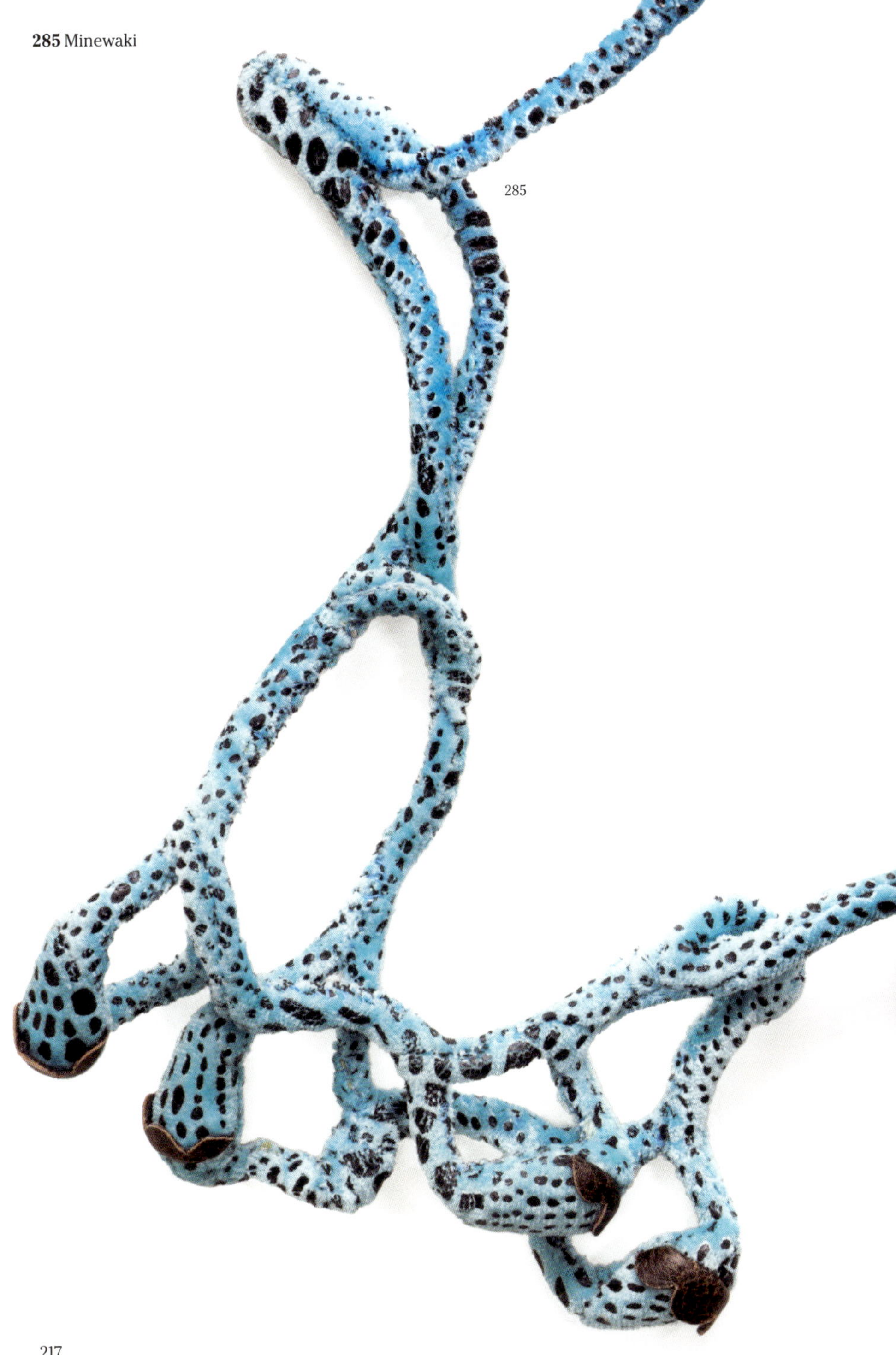

285

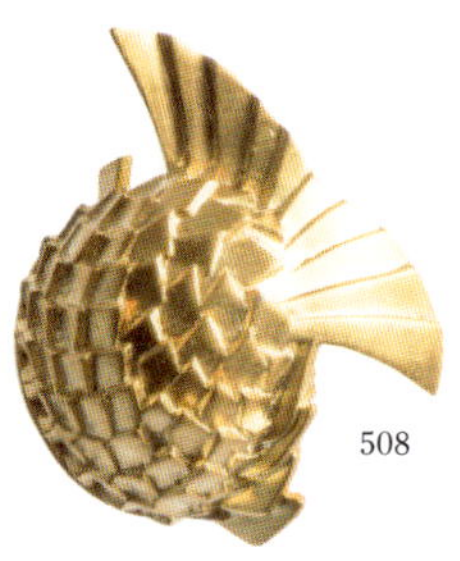

508

347

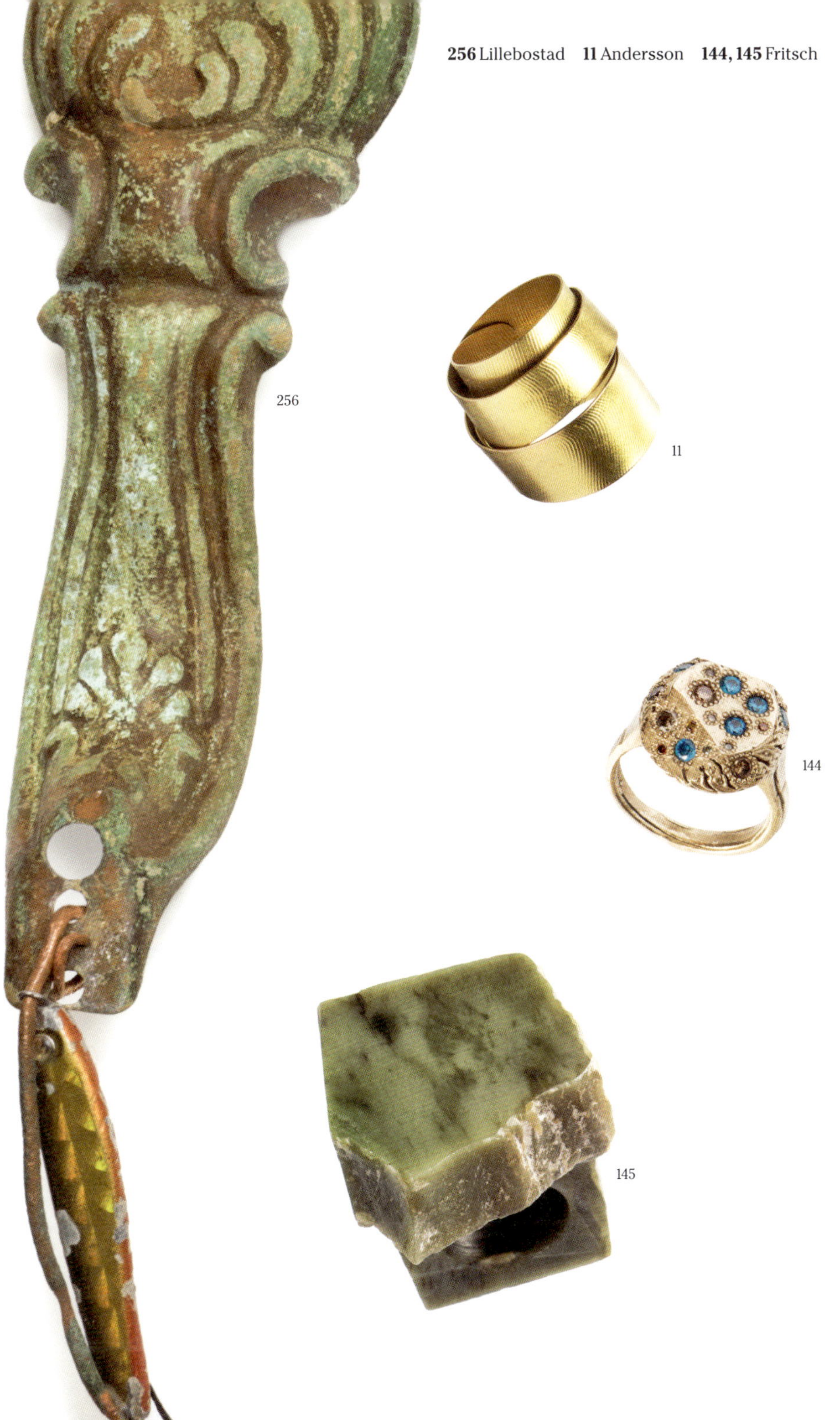

256

11

144

145

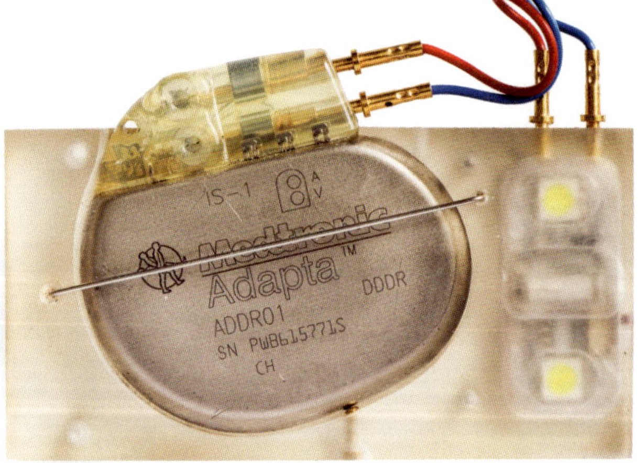

415

32

72

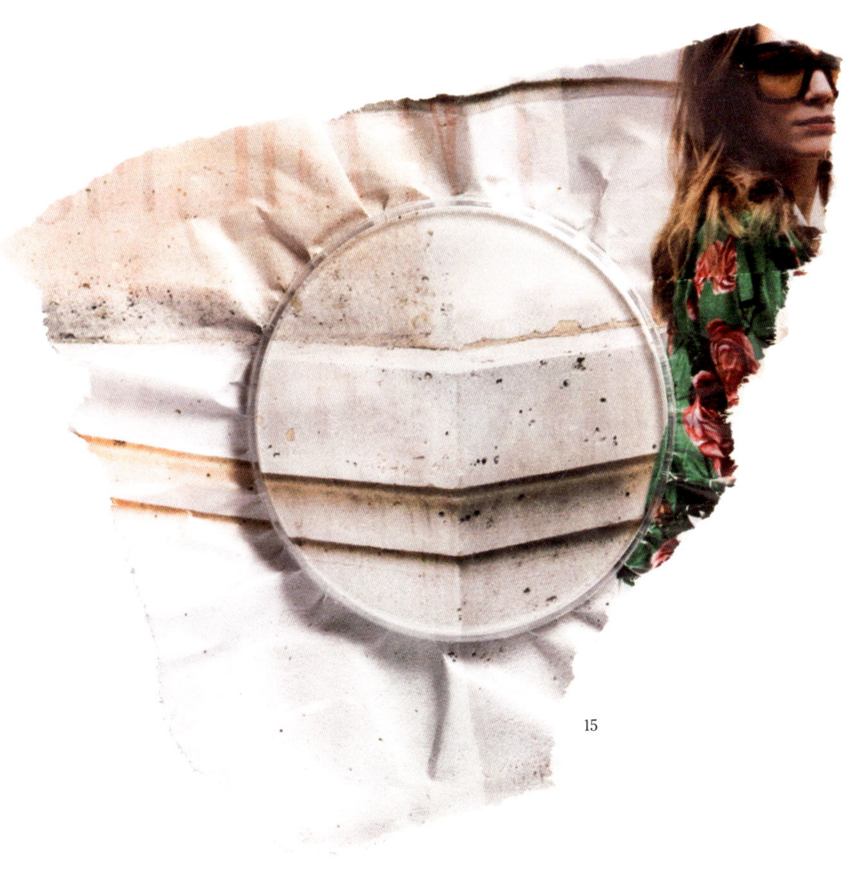

15

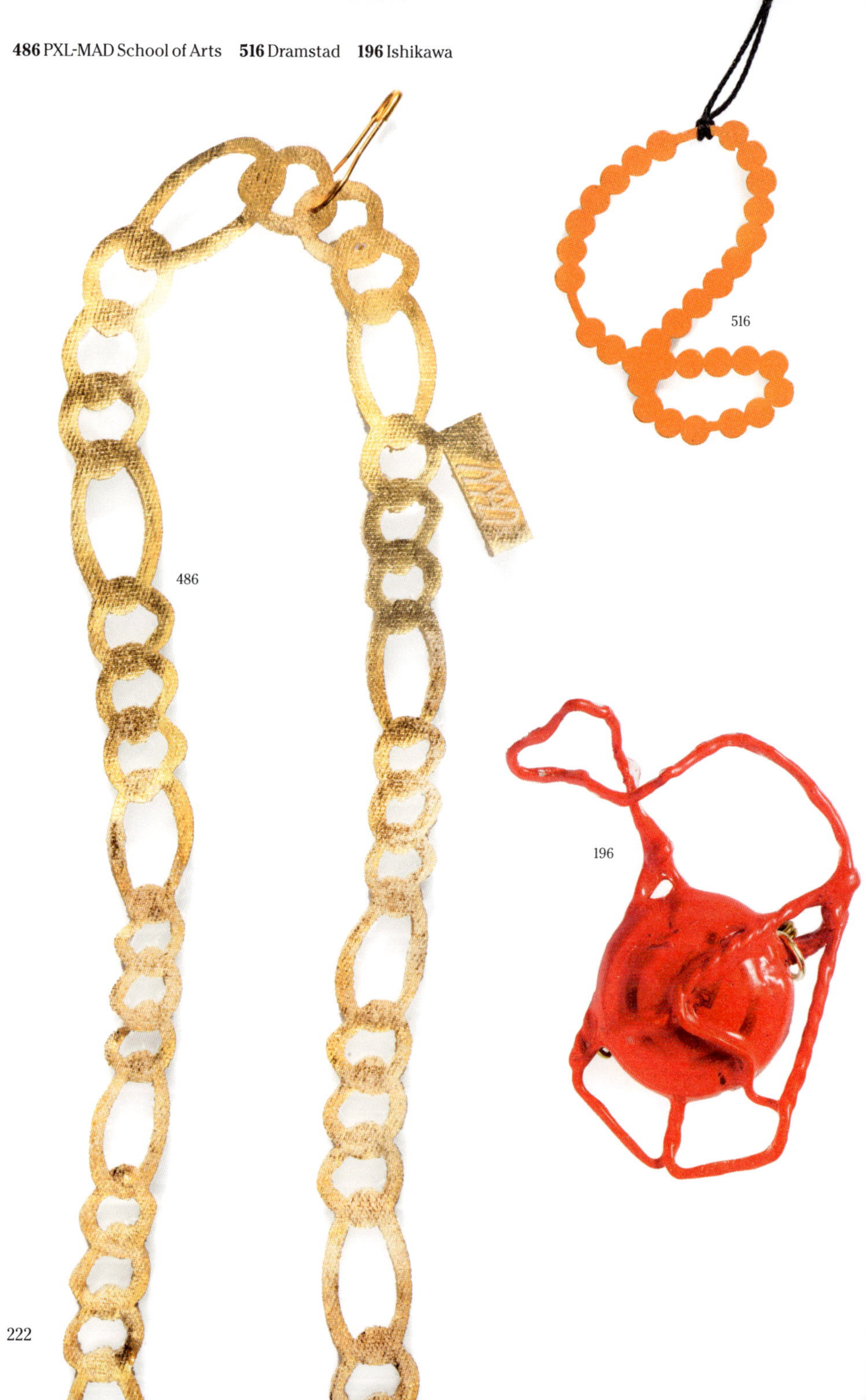

486

516

196

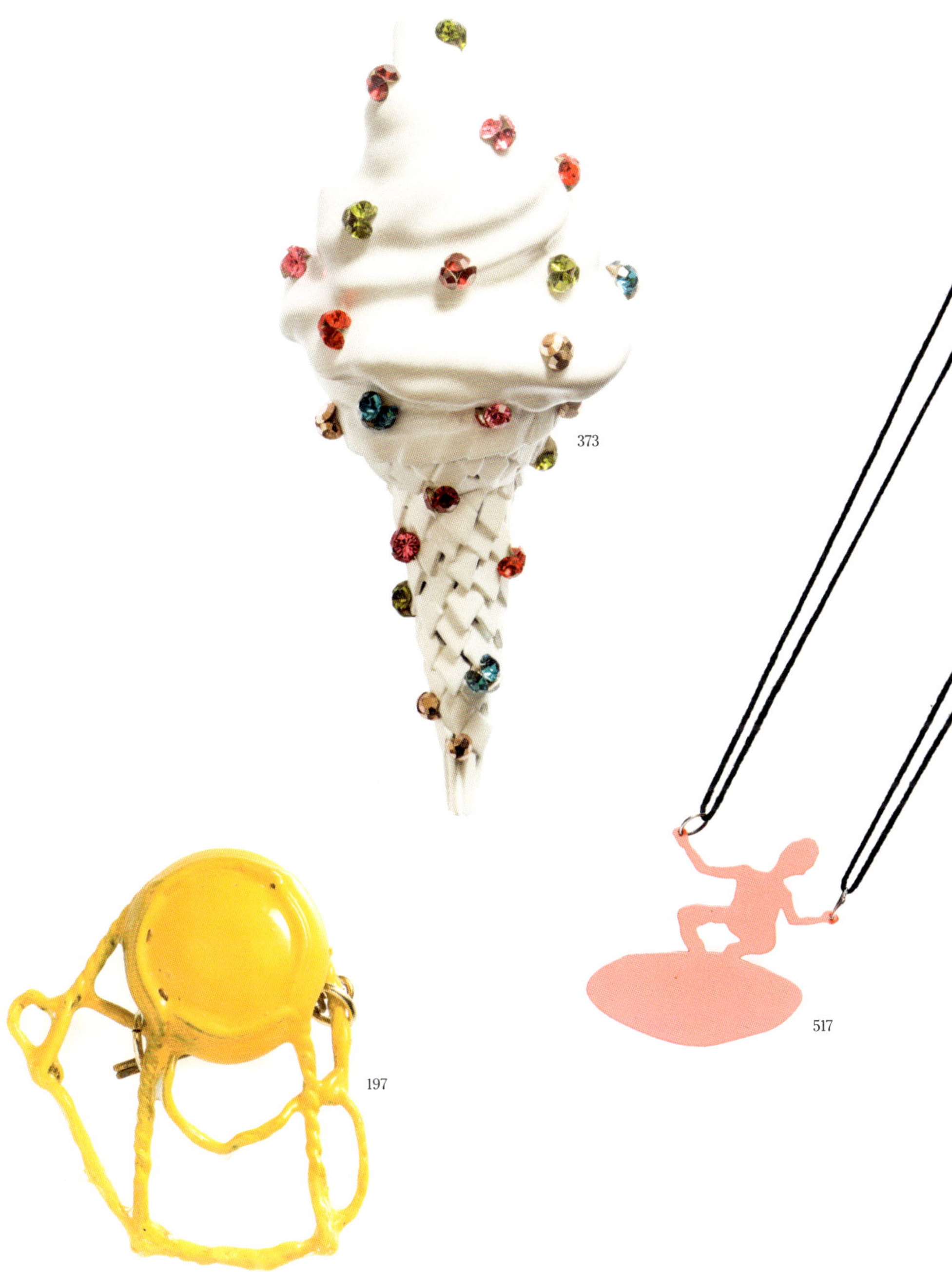

373

197

517

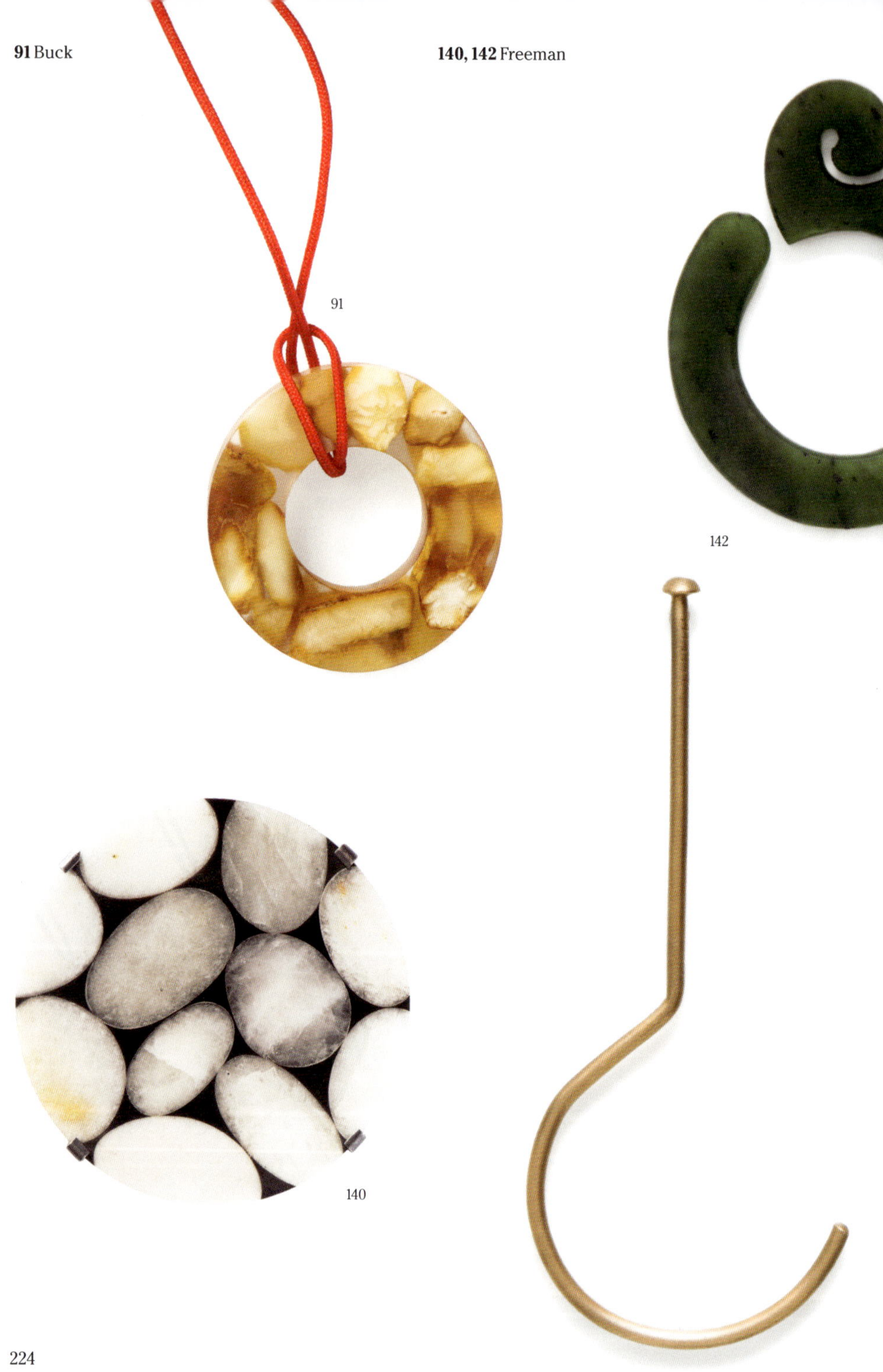

142

142

142

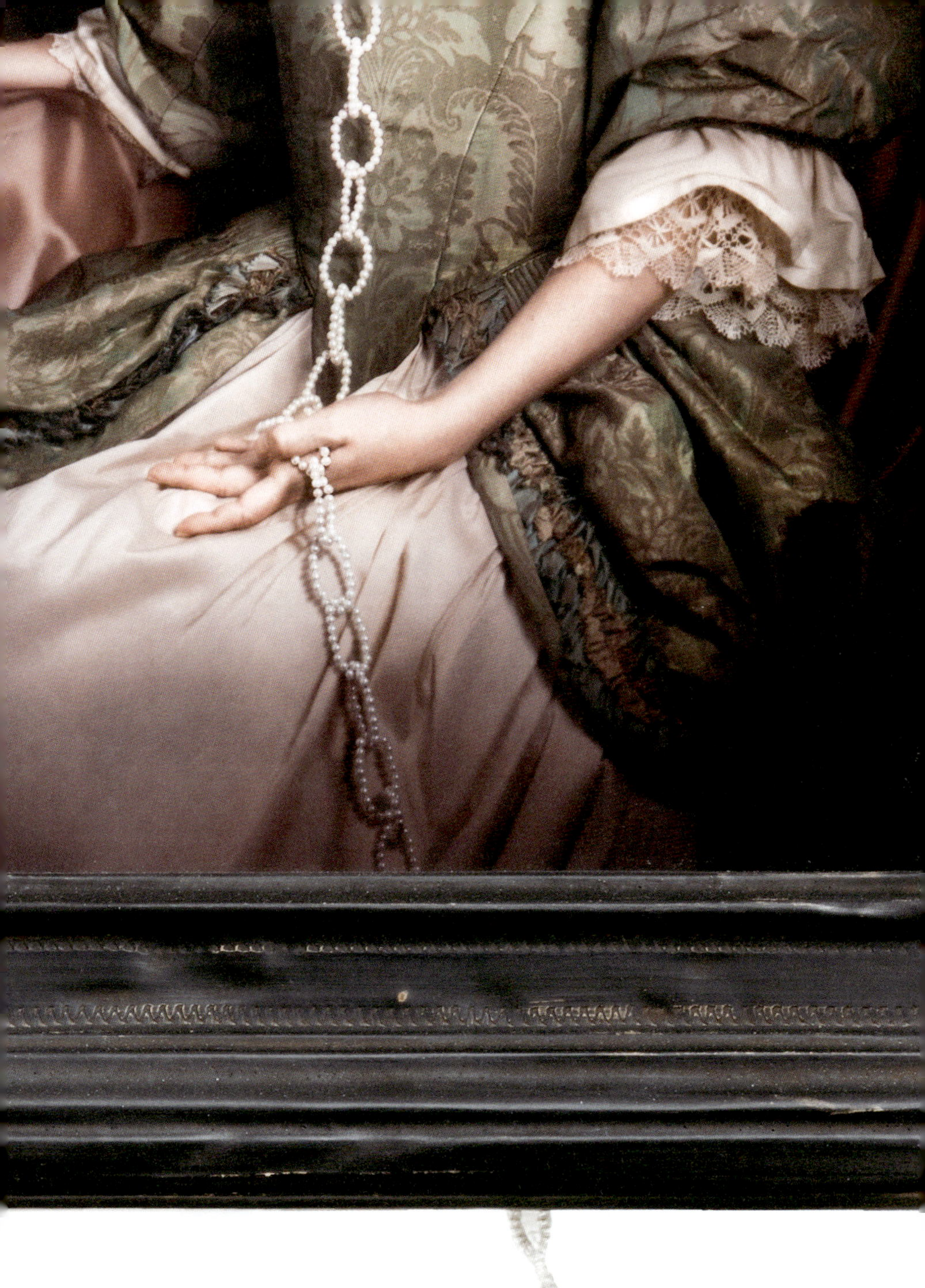

66

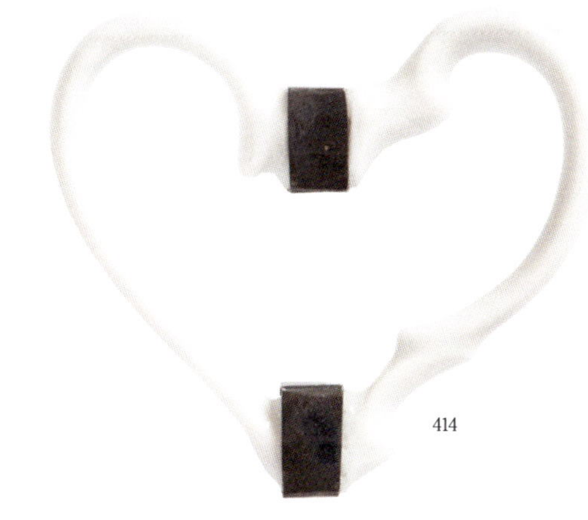

414

141

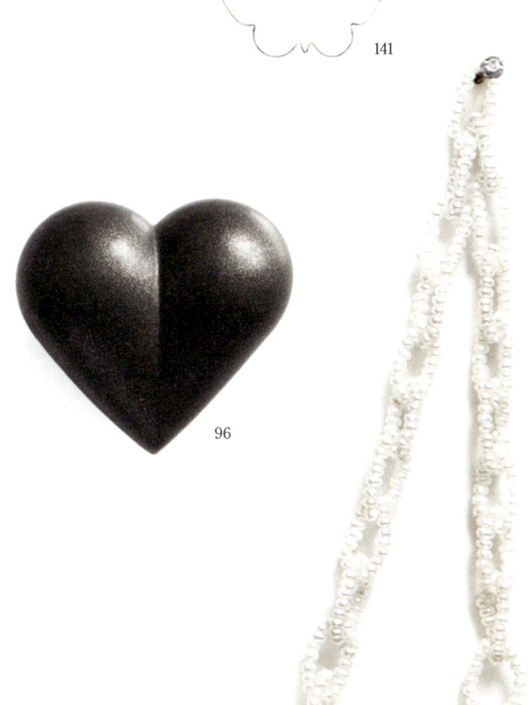

96

66

227

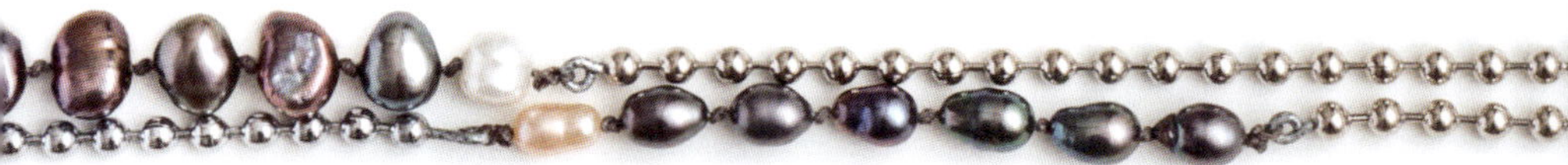

365

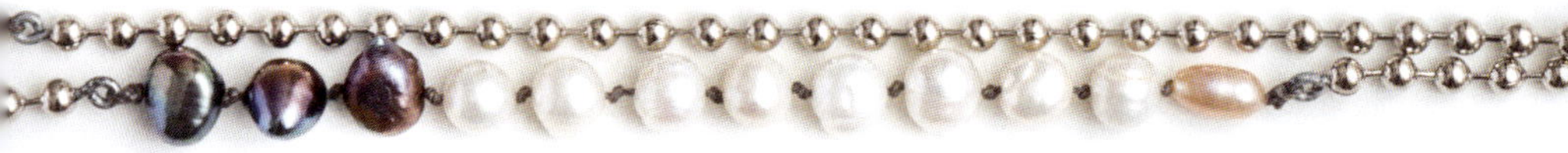

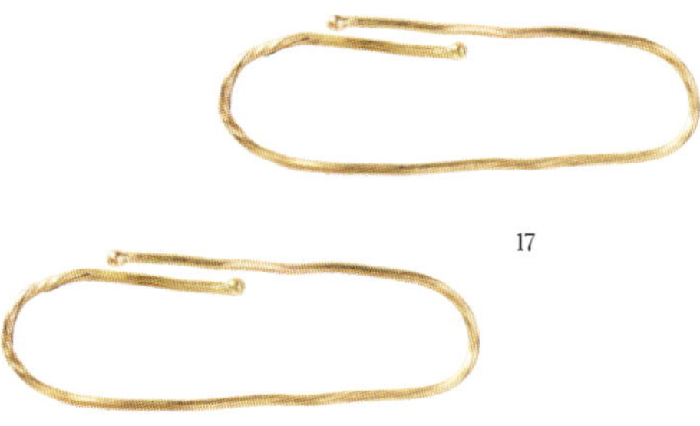

17

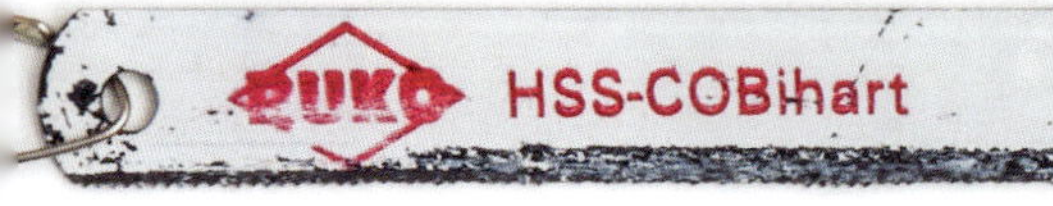

345

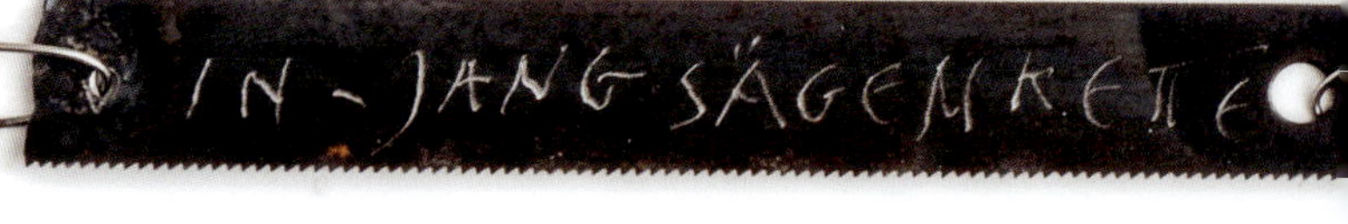

228

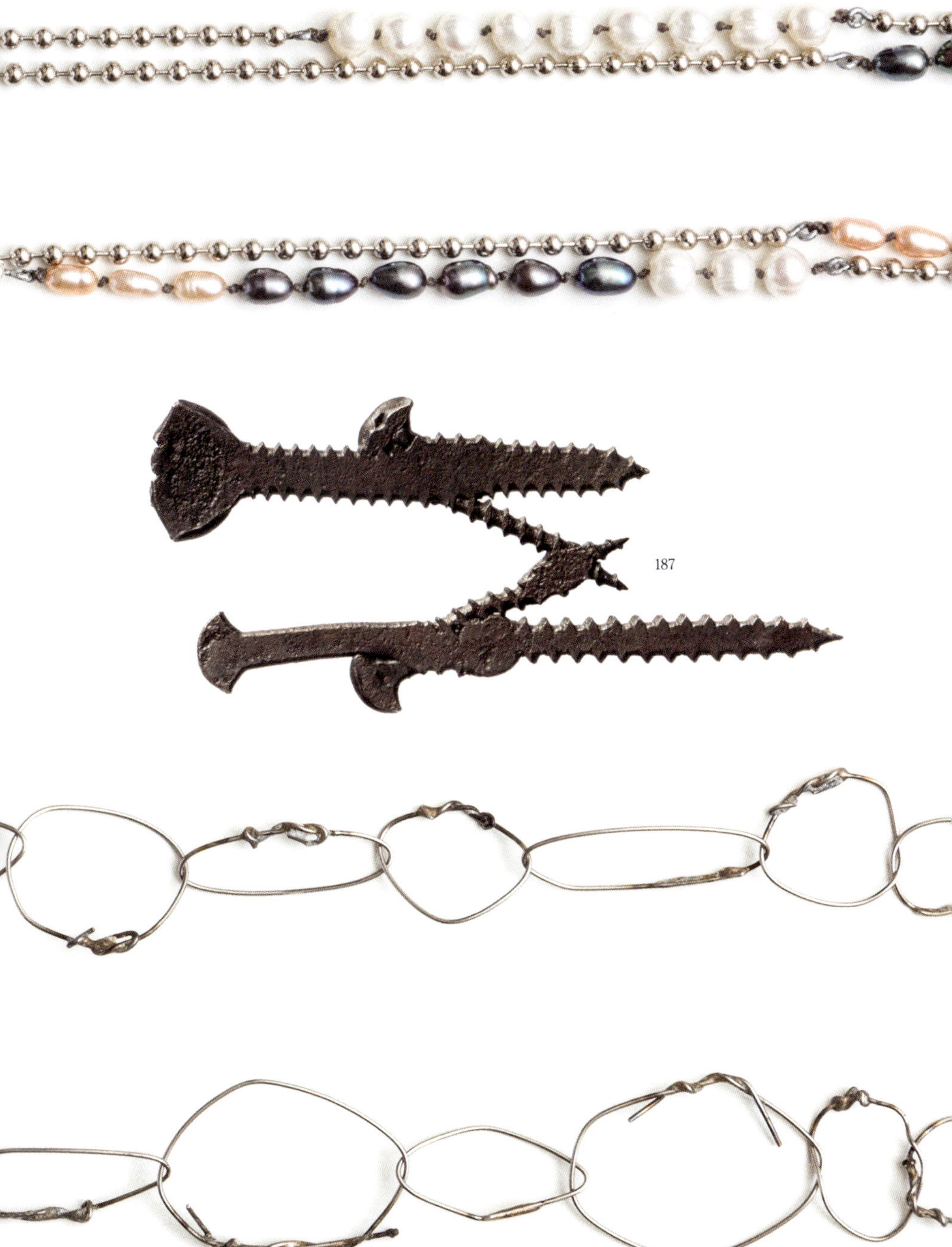
187

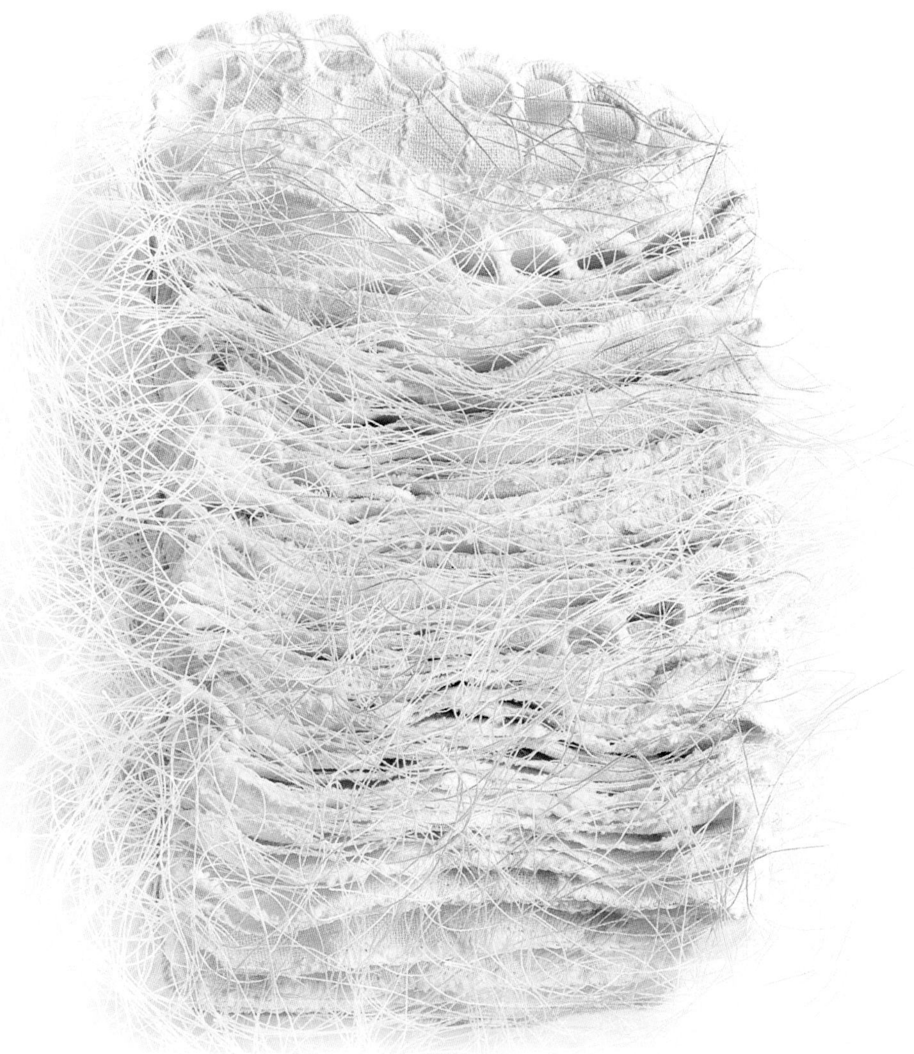

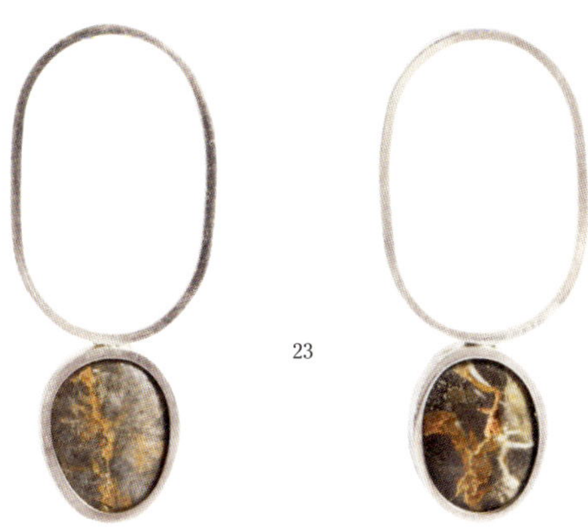

23

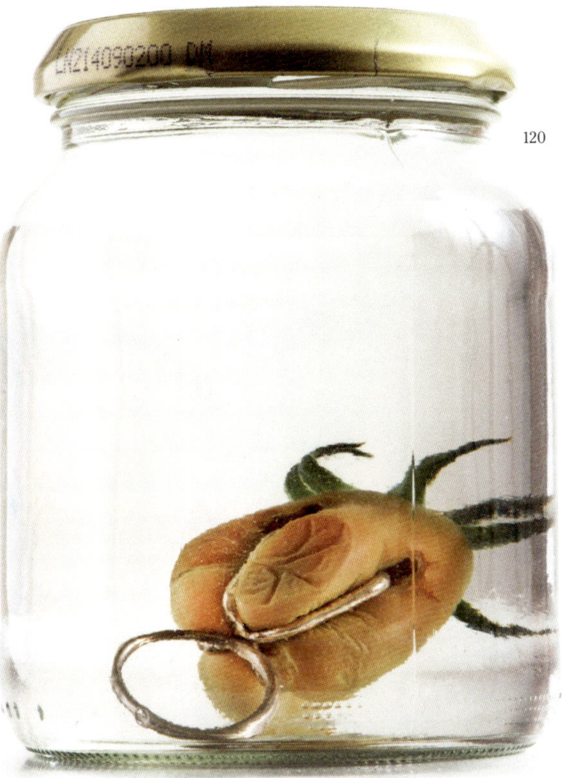

120

154

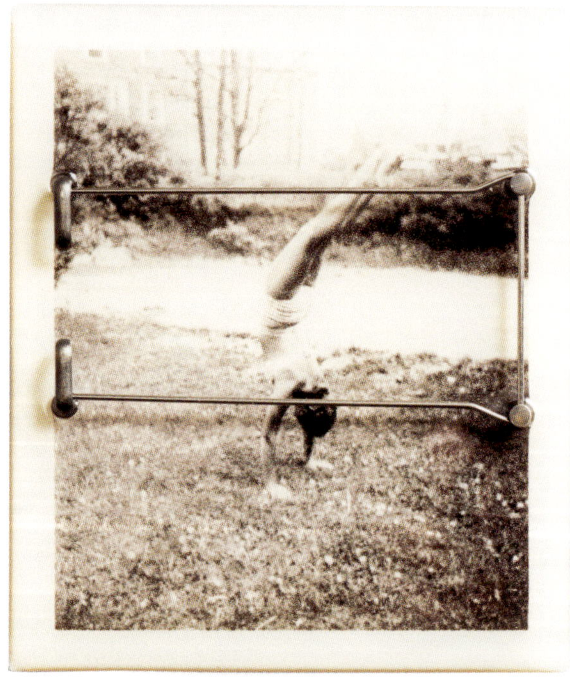

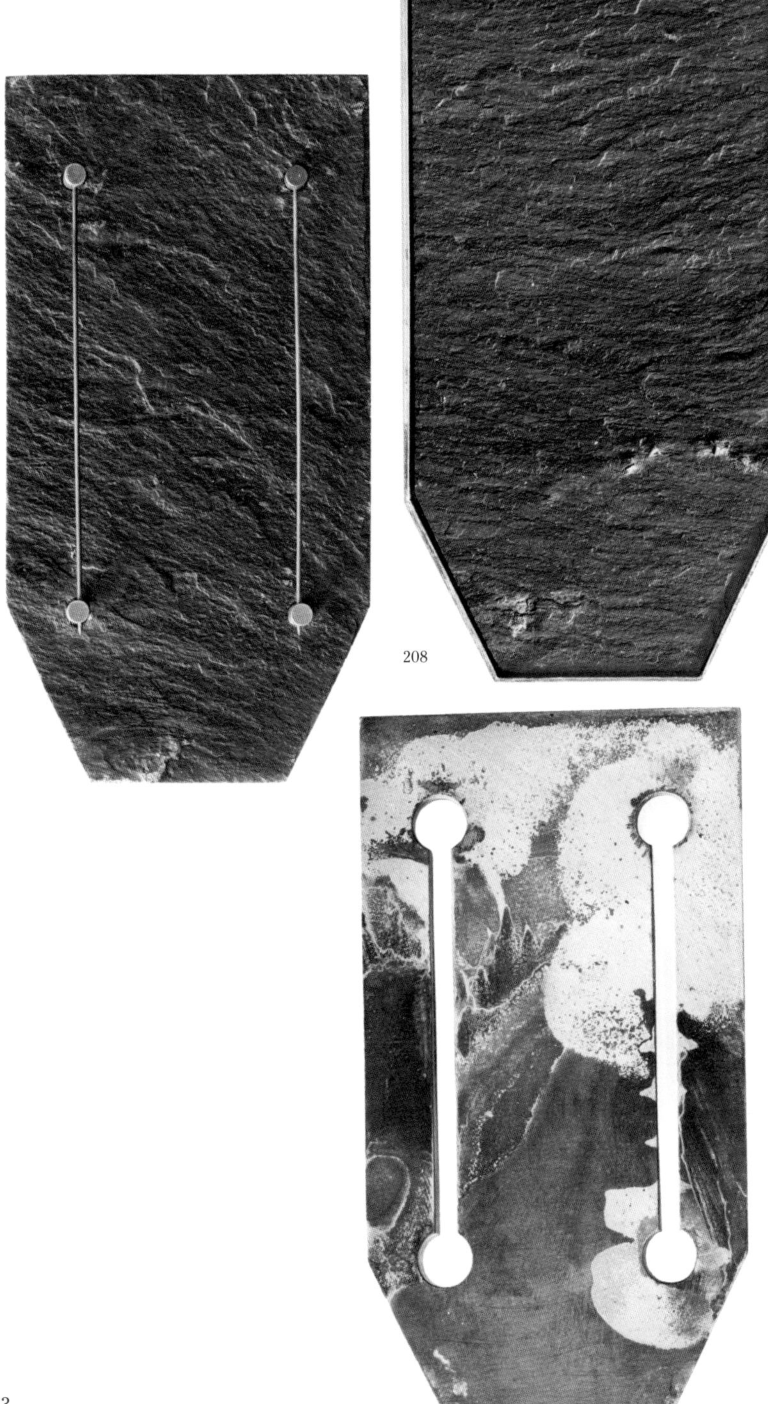

208

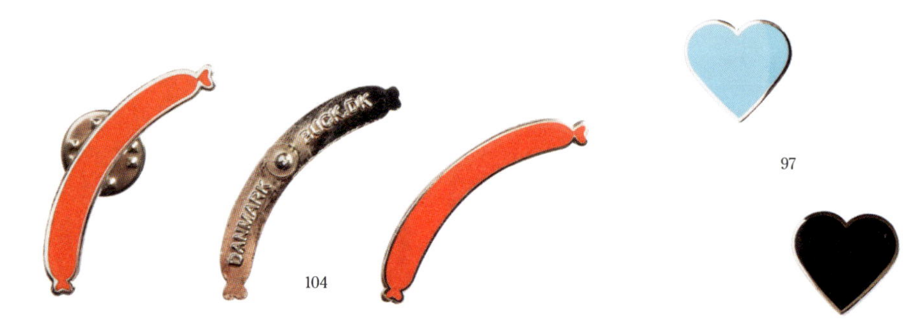

97

104

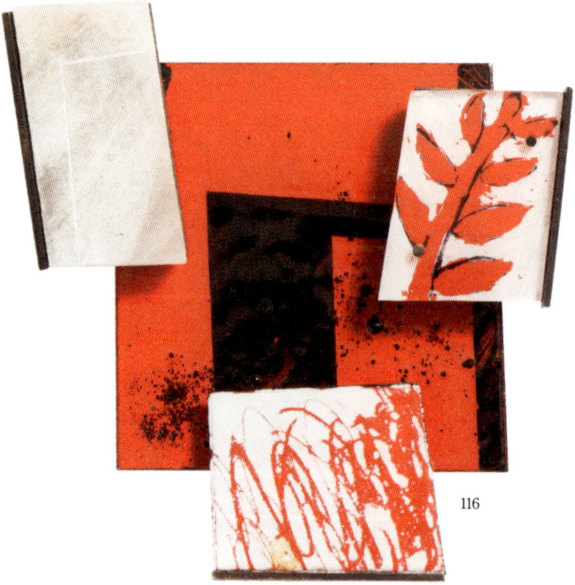

116

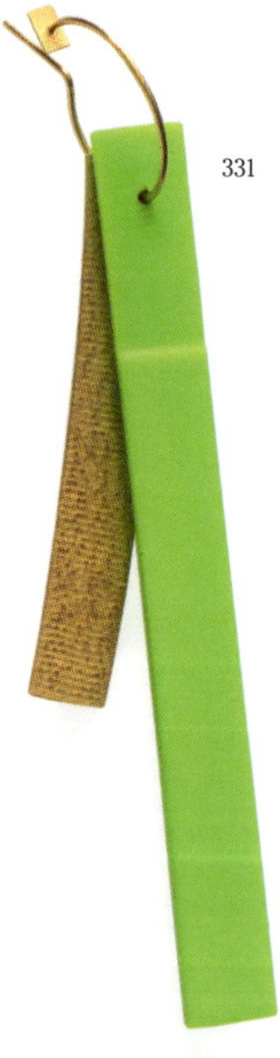

331

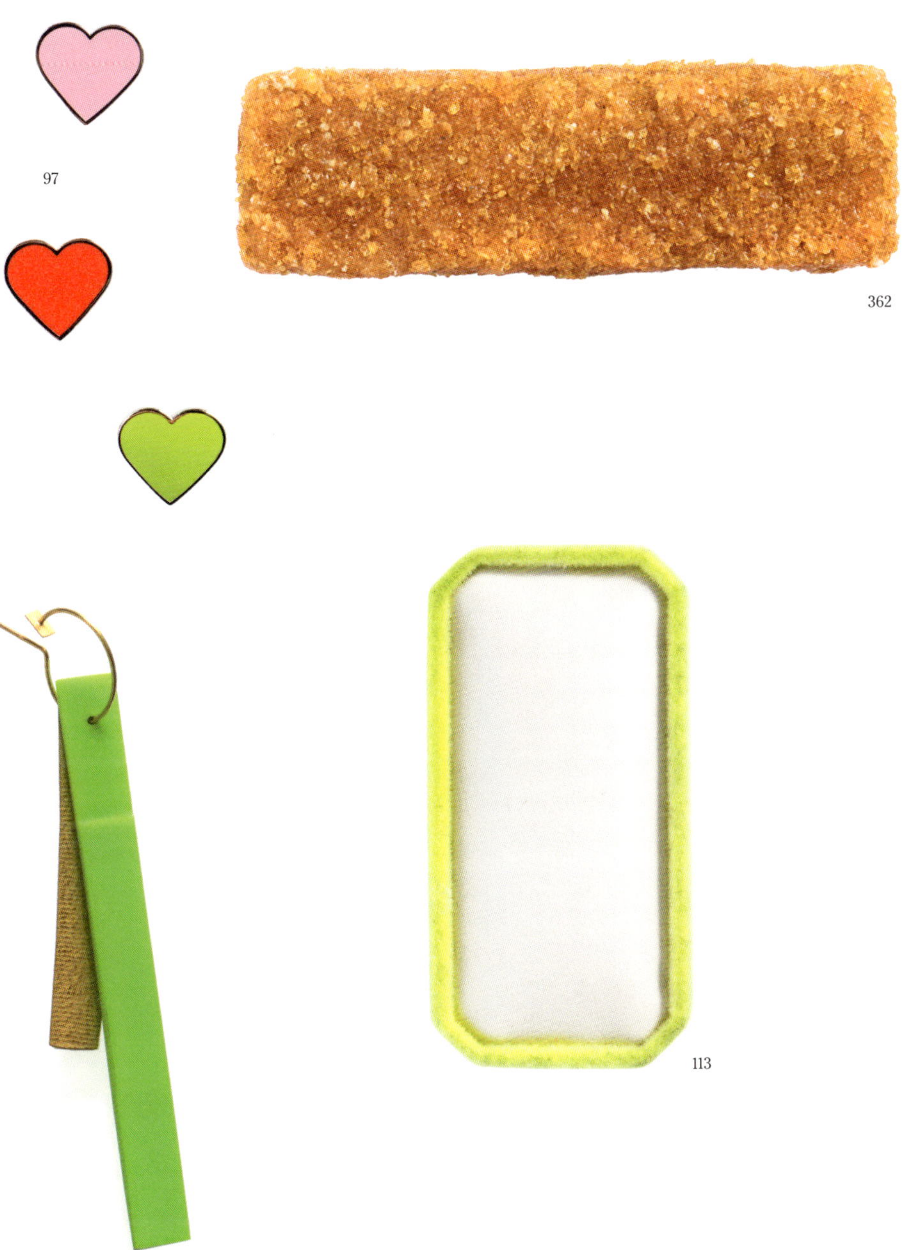

97

362

113

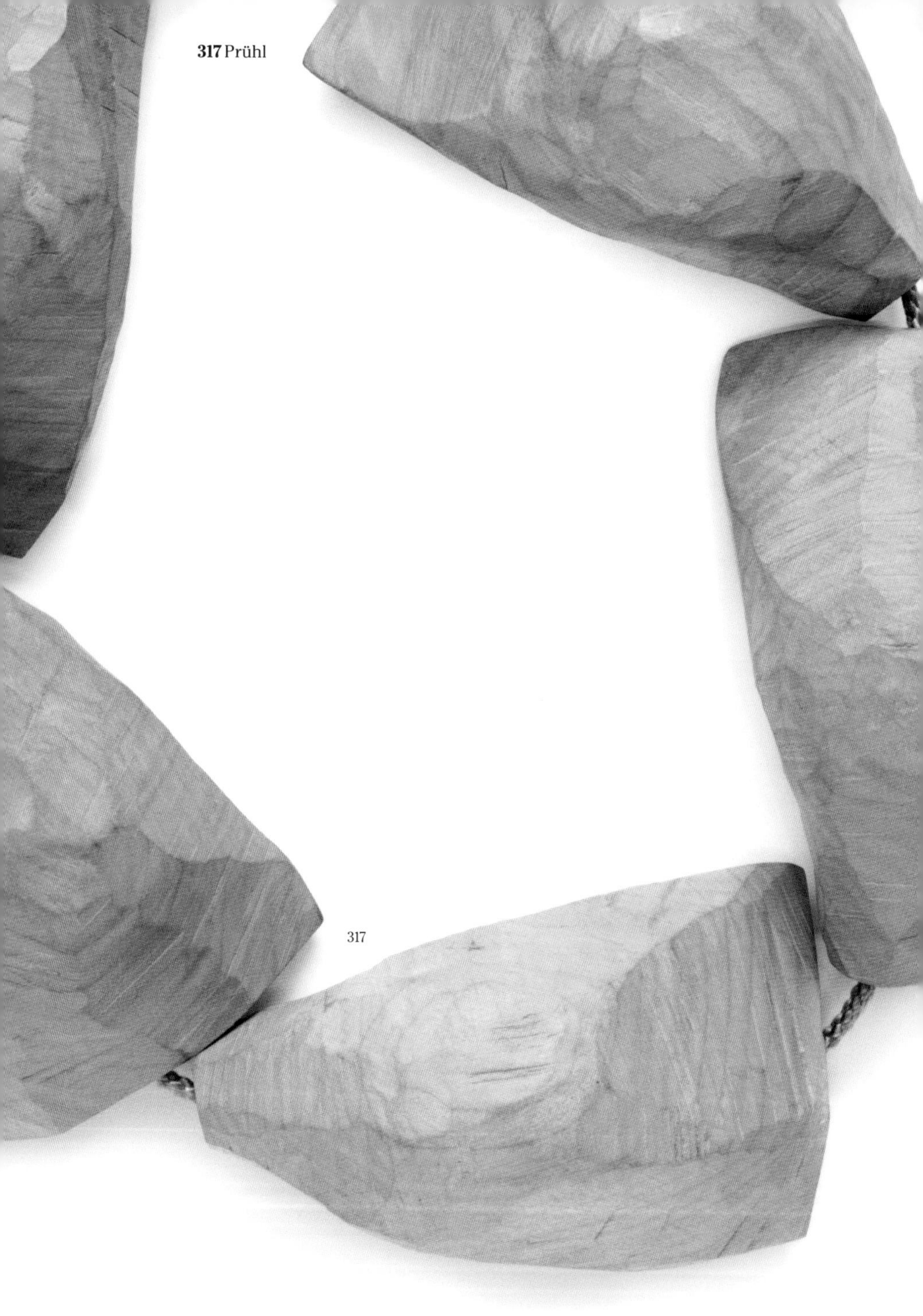

317

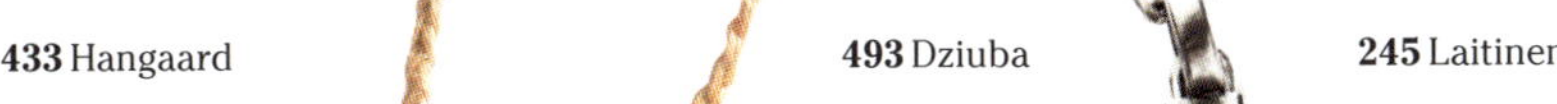

433

Detta är inte ett järnrör

245

493

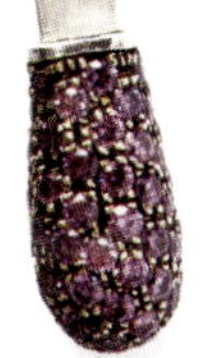

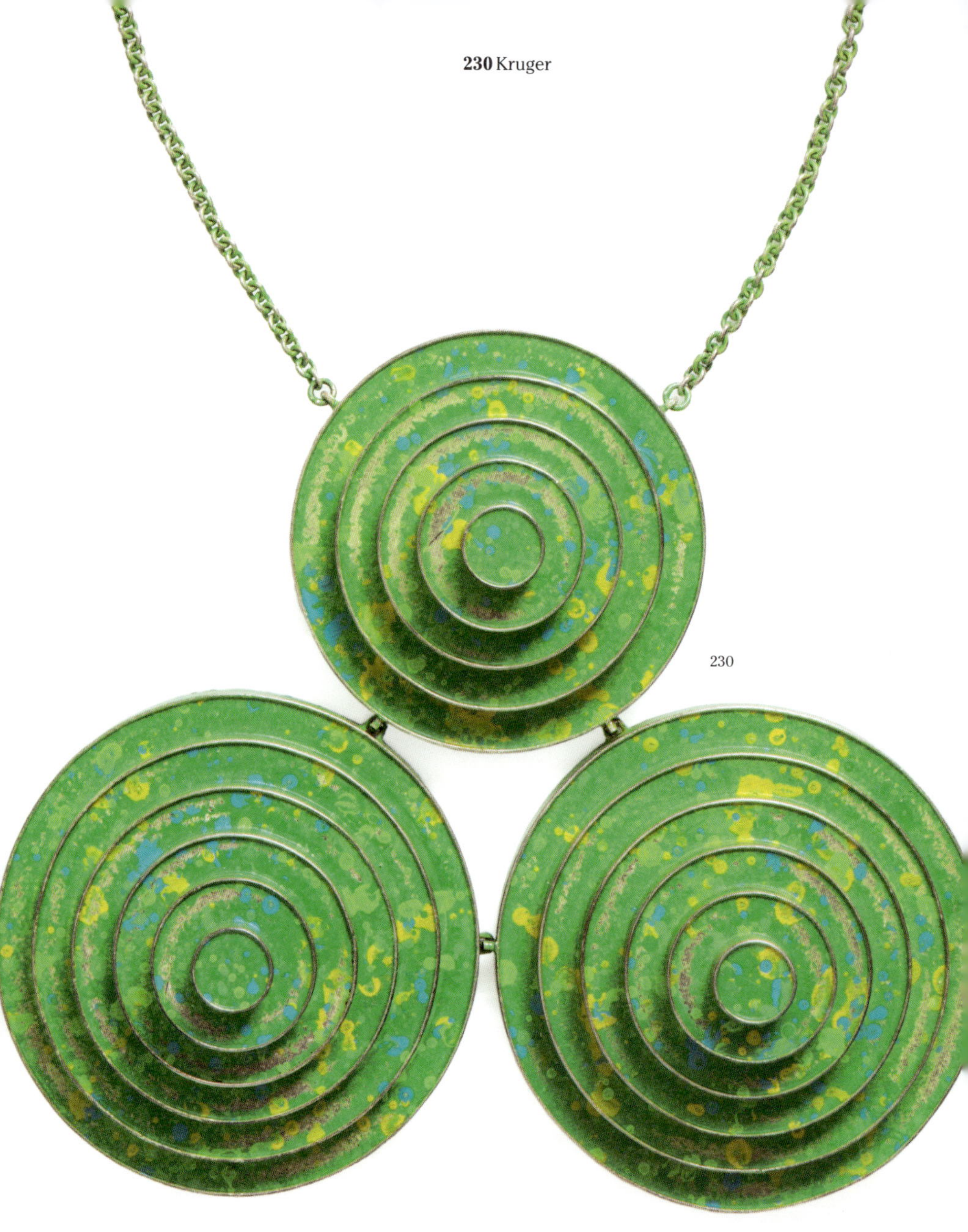

230

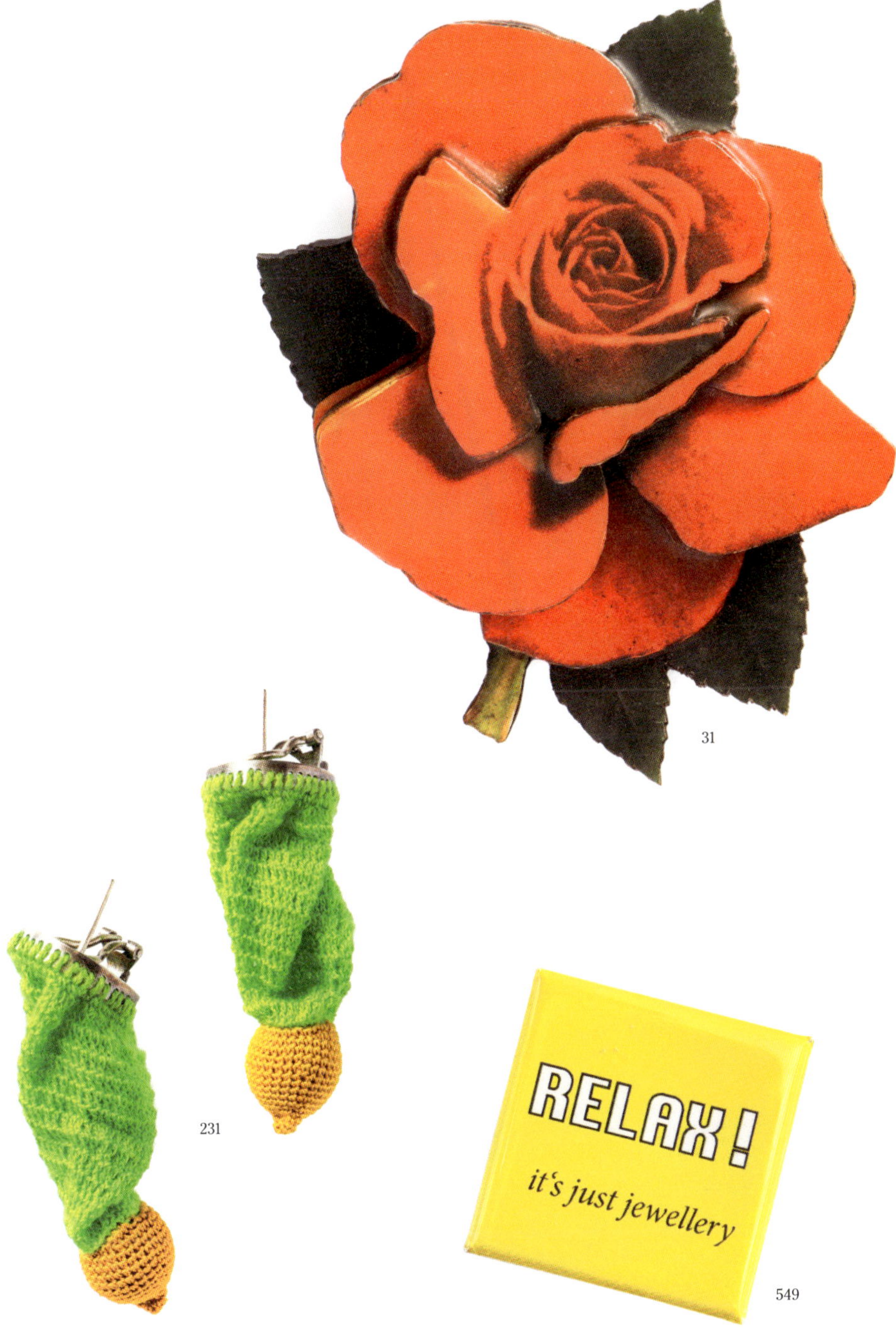

31

231

549

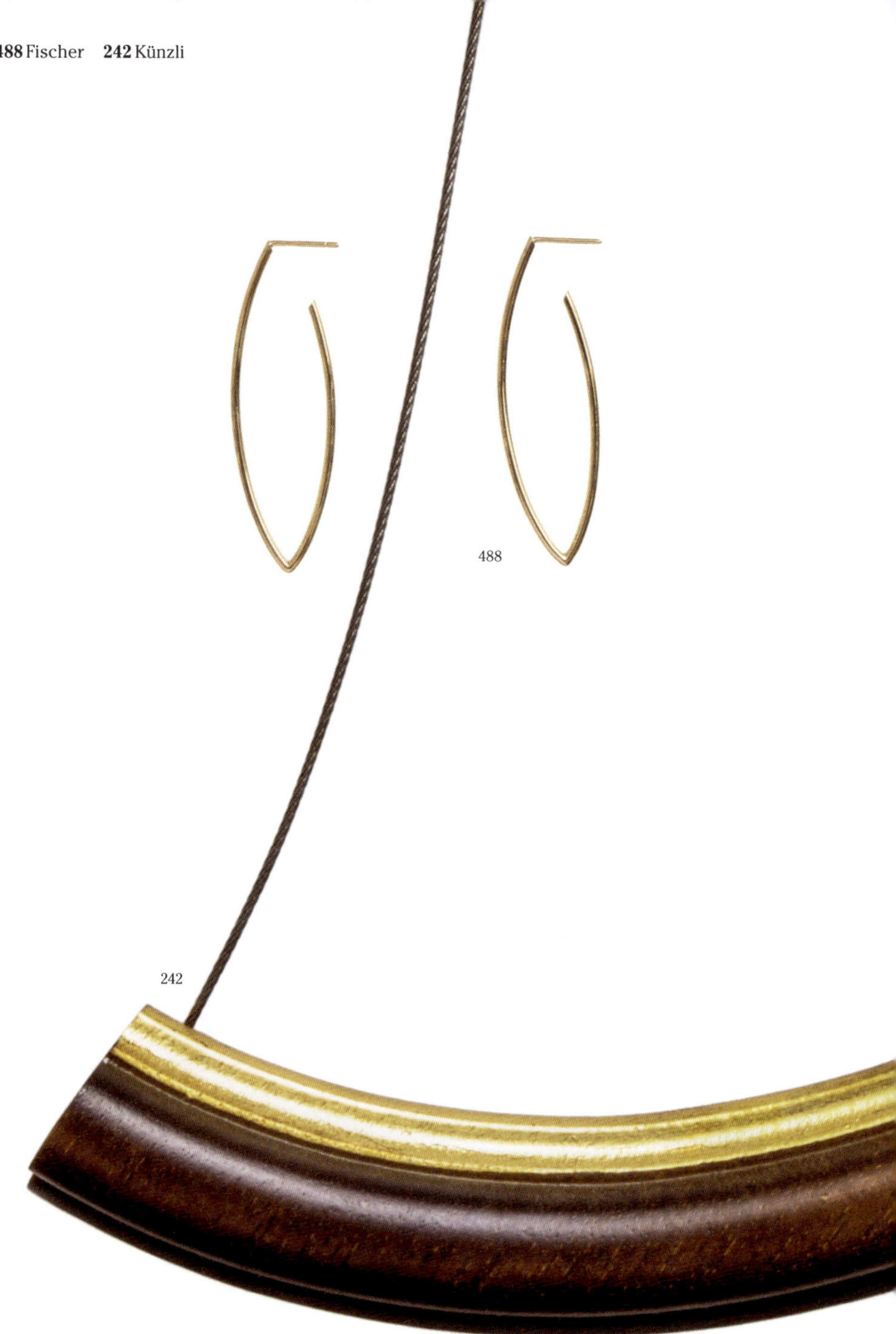

488

242

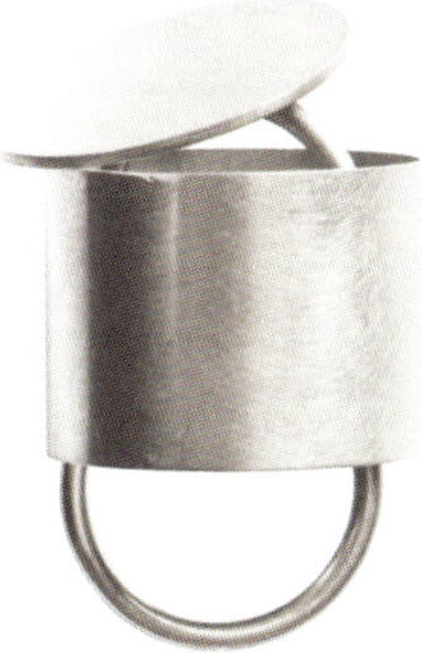

209

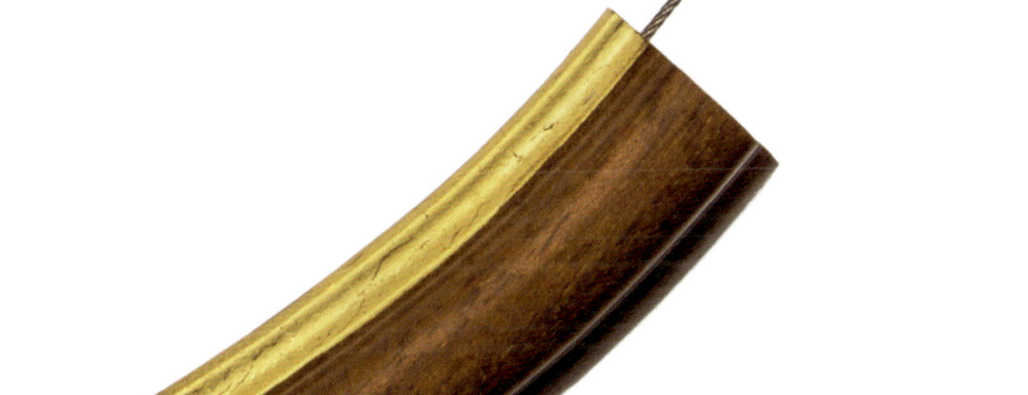

443

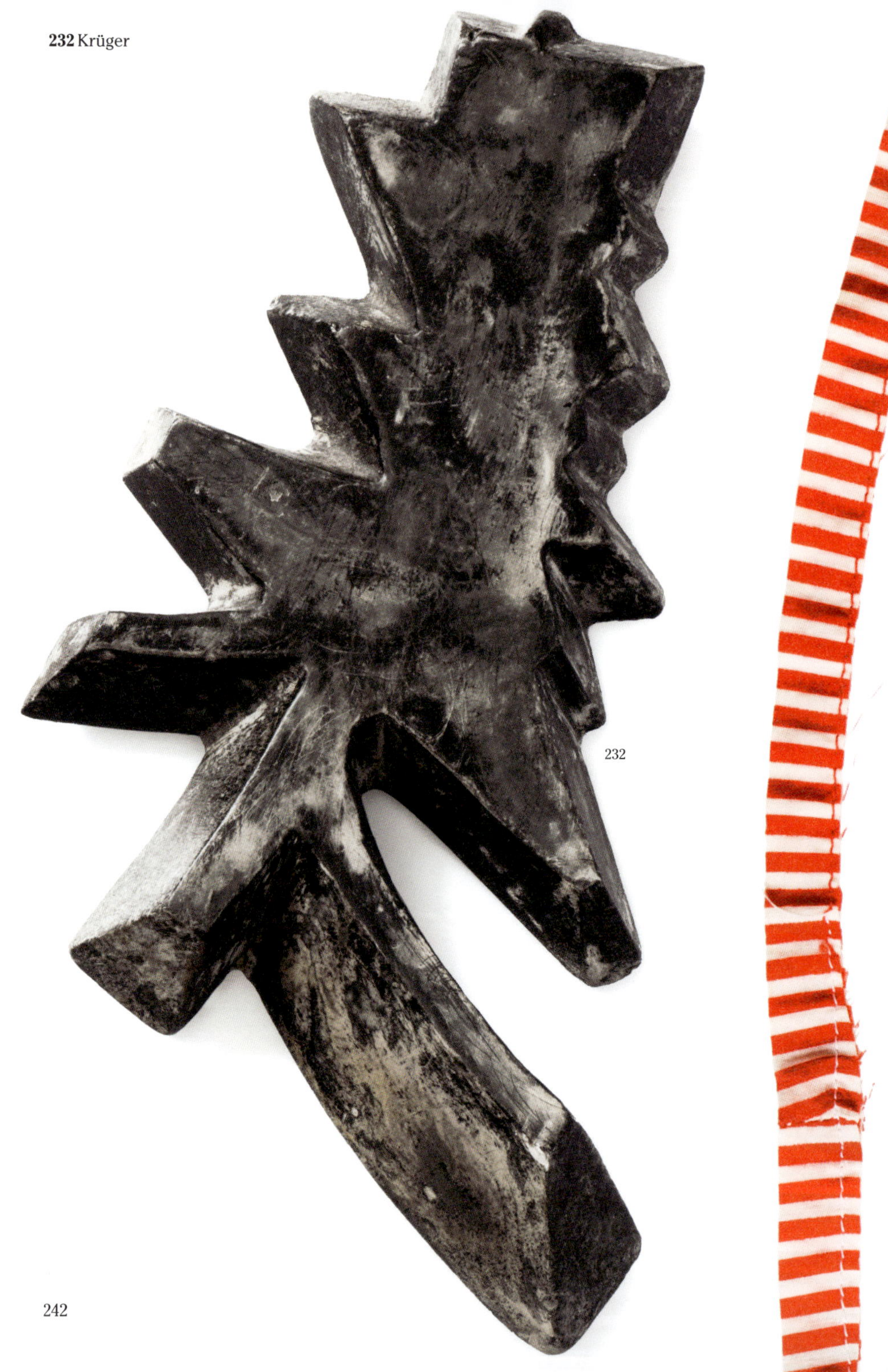

232

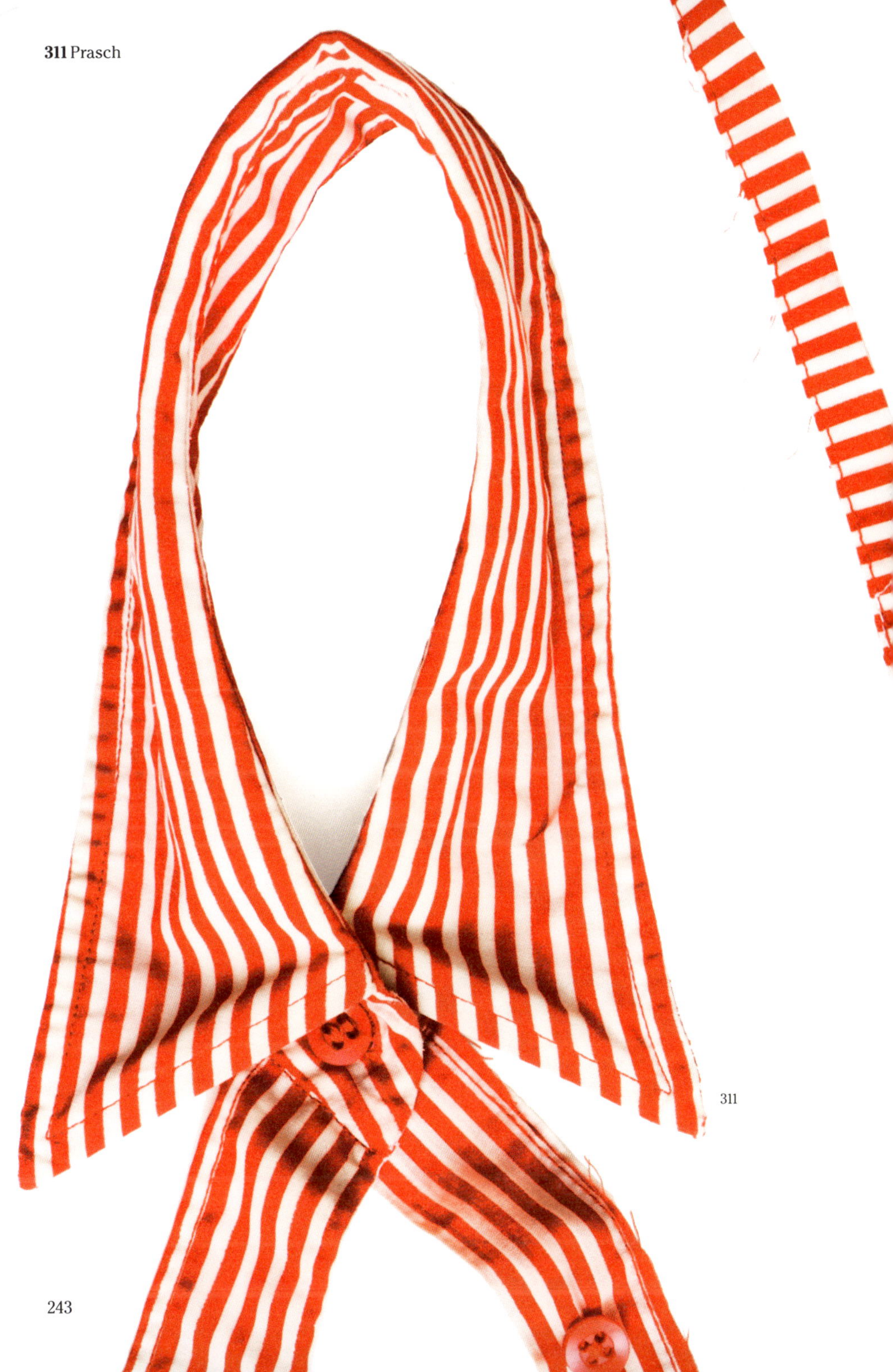

311

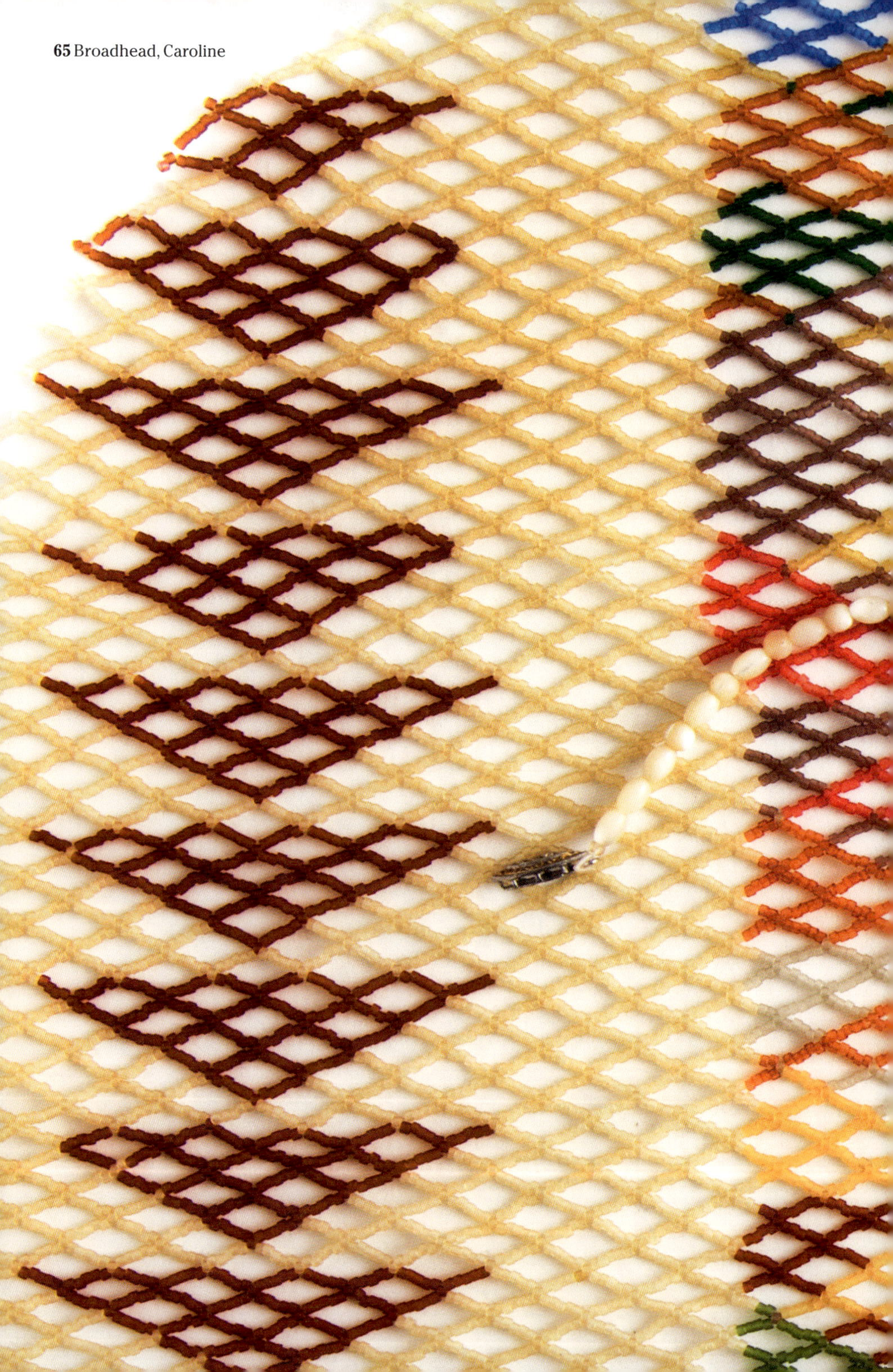

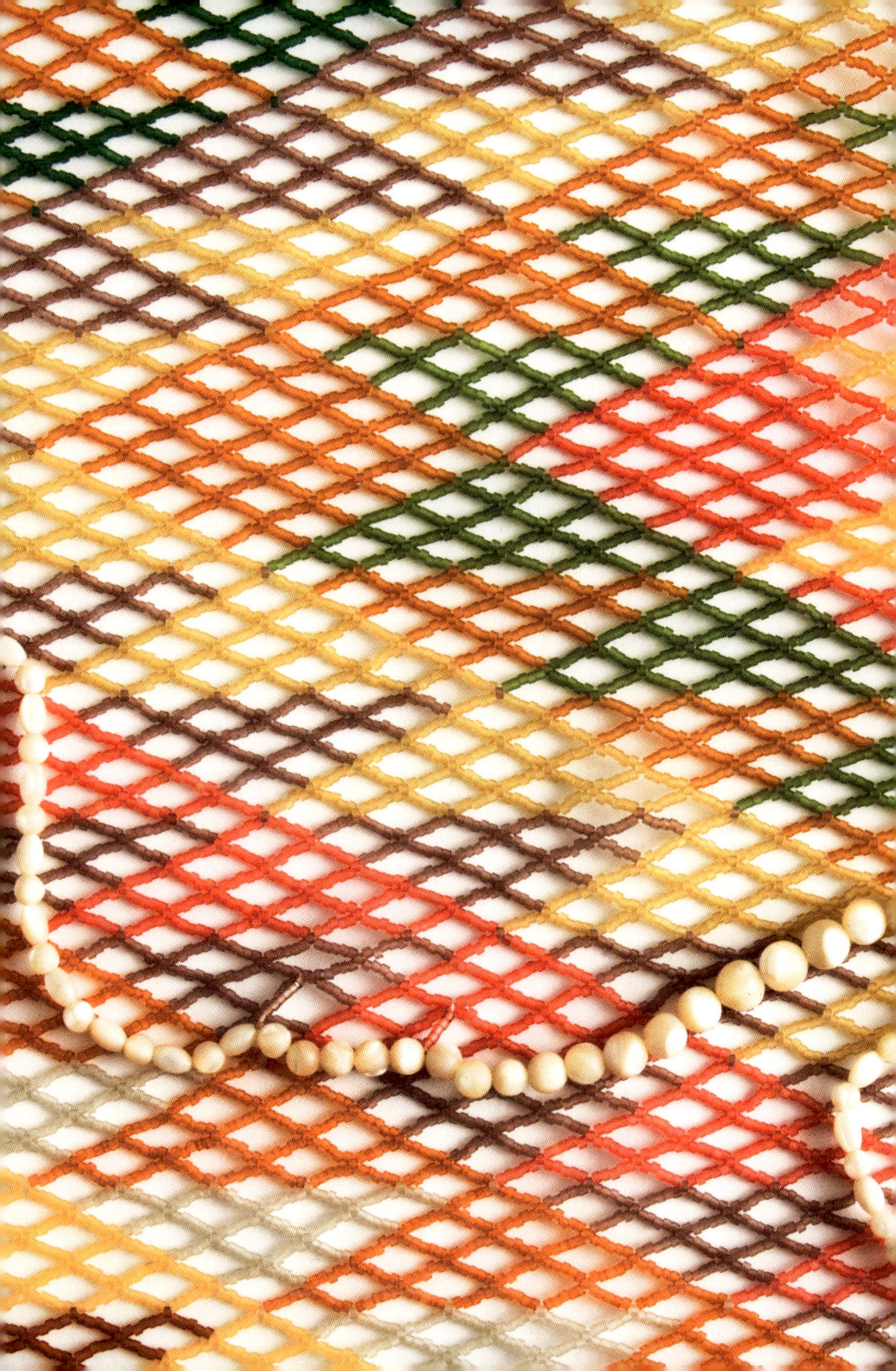

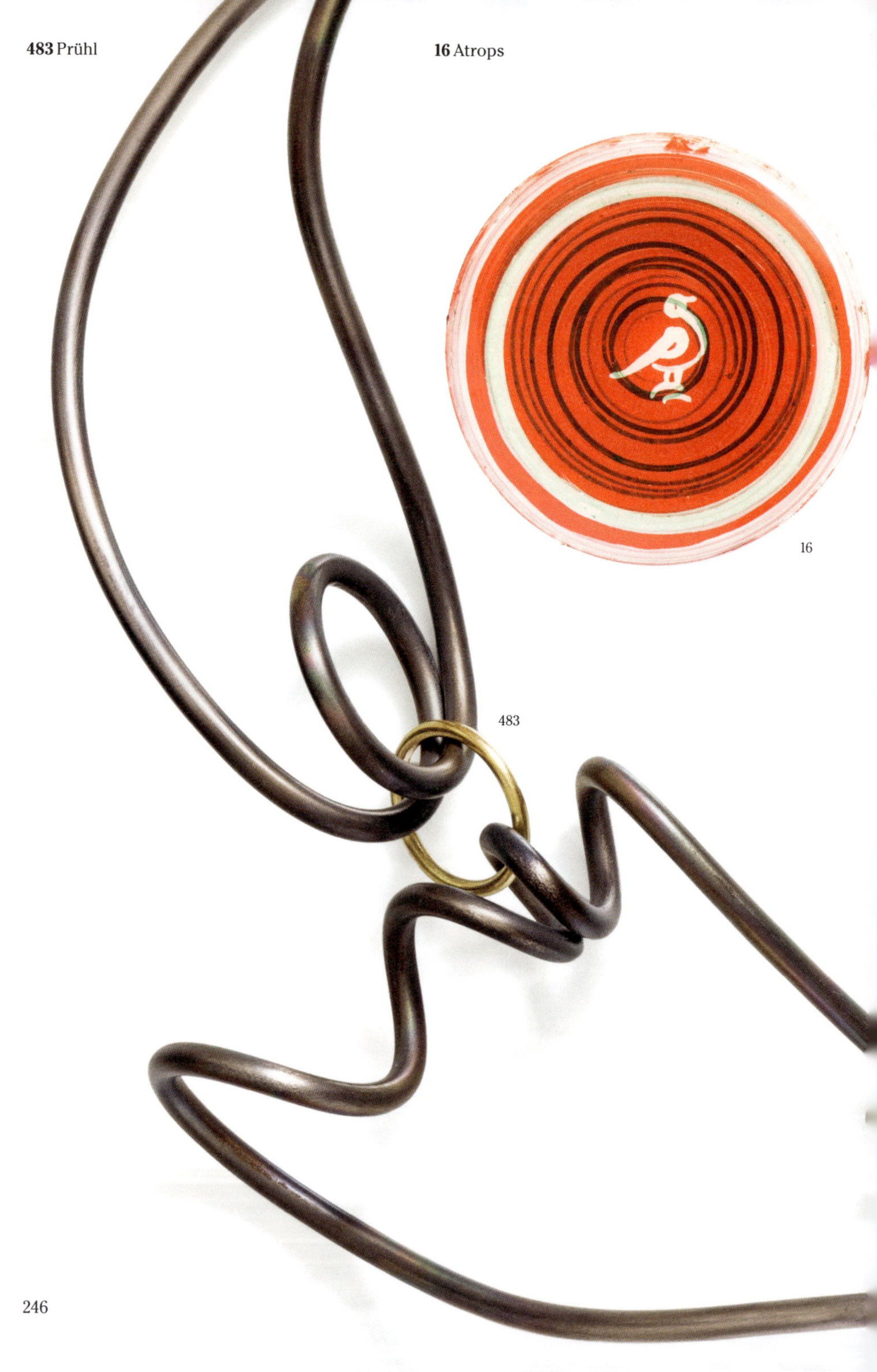
483 Prühl
16 Atrops
16
483

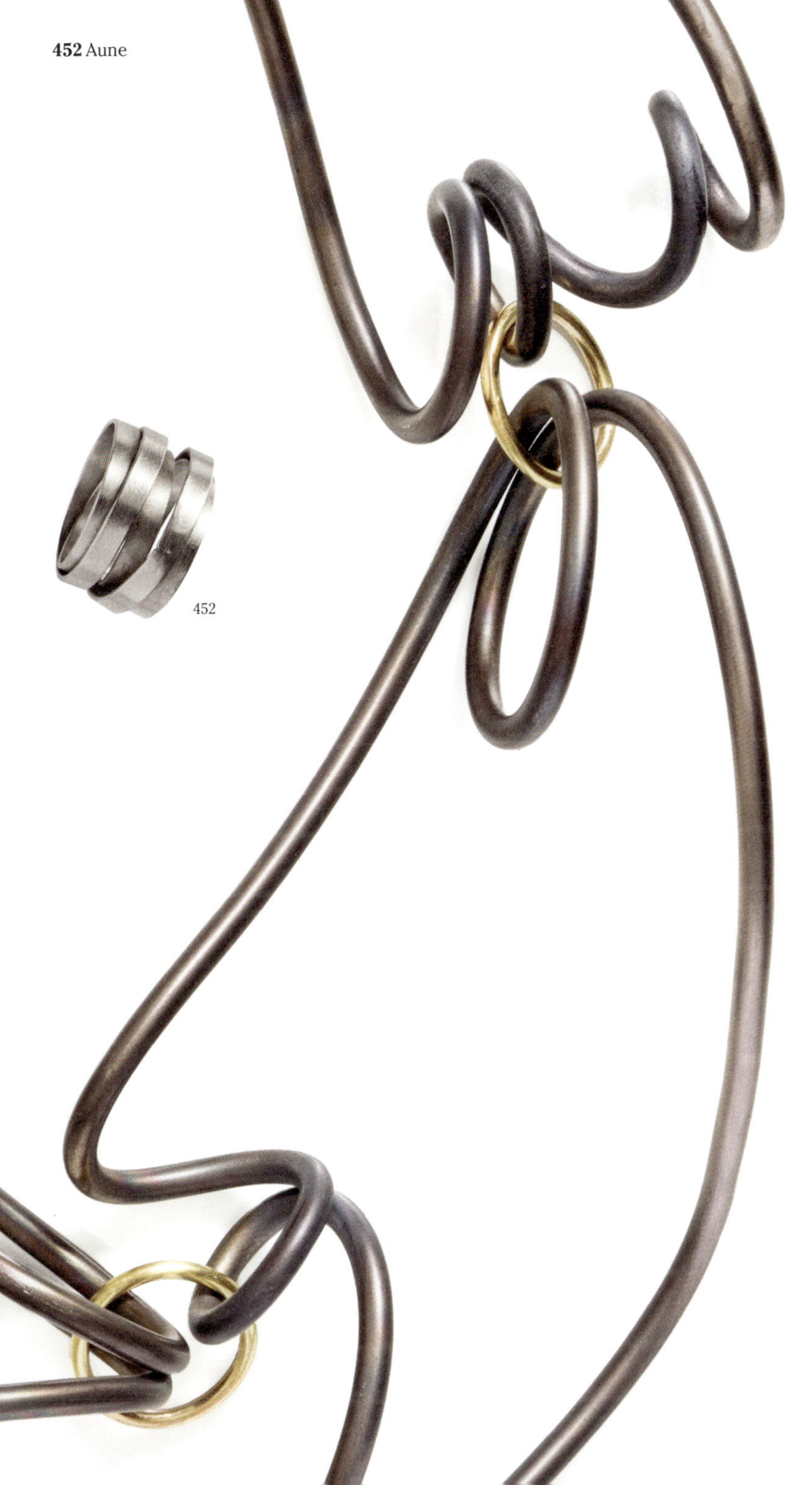

452

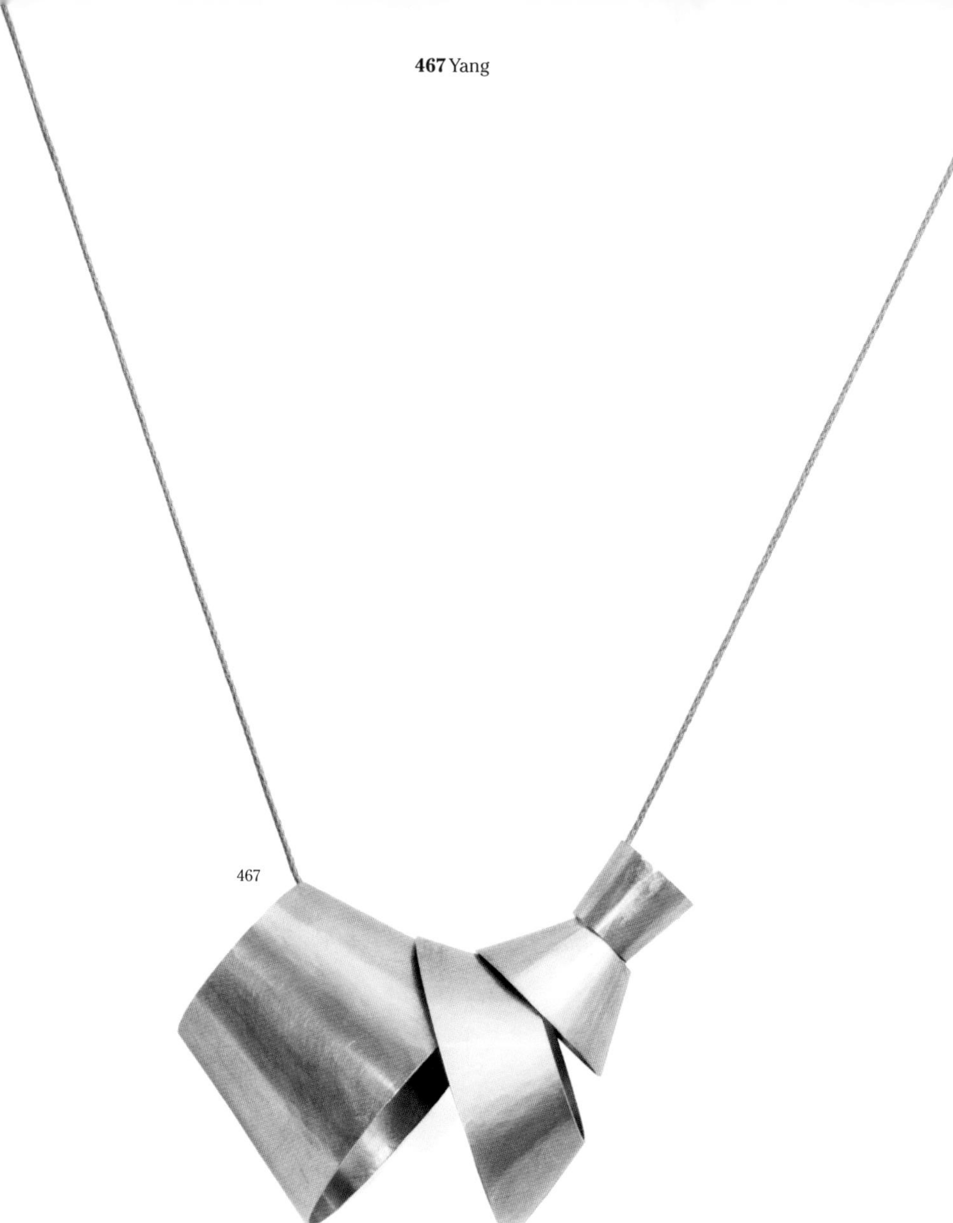

467

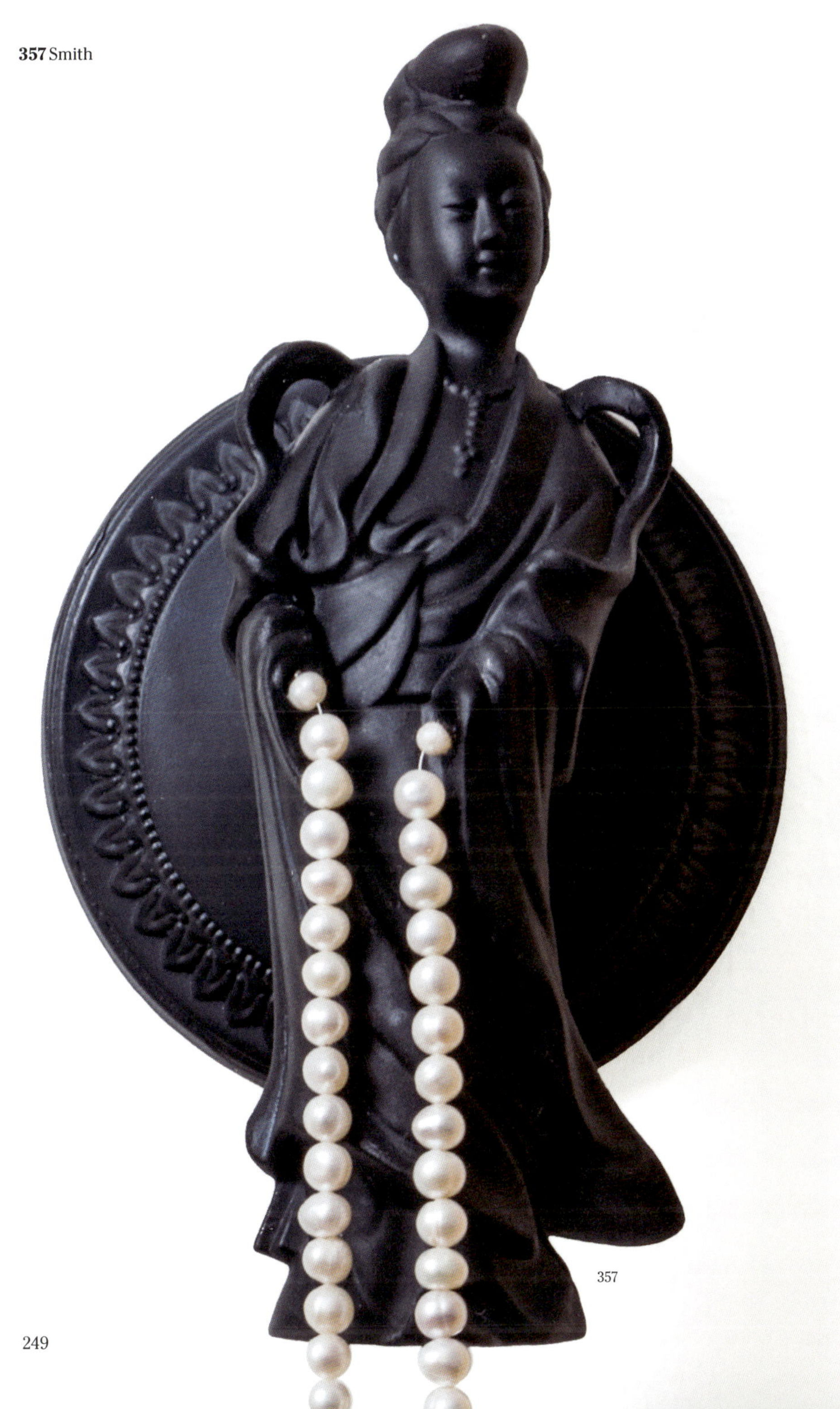

357

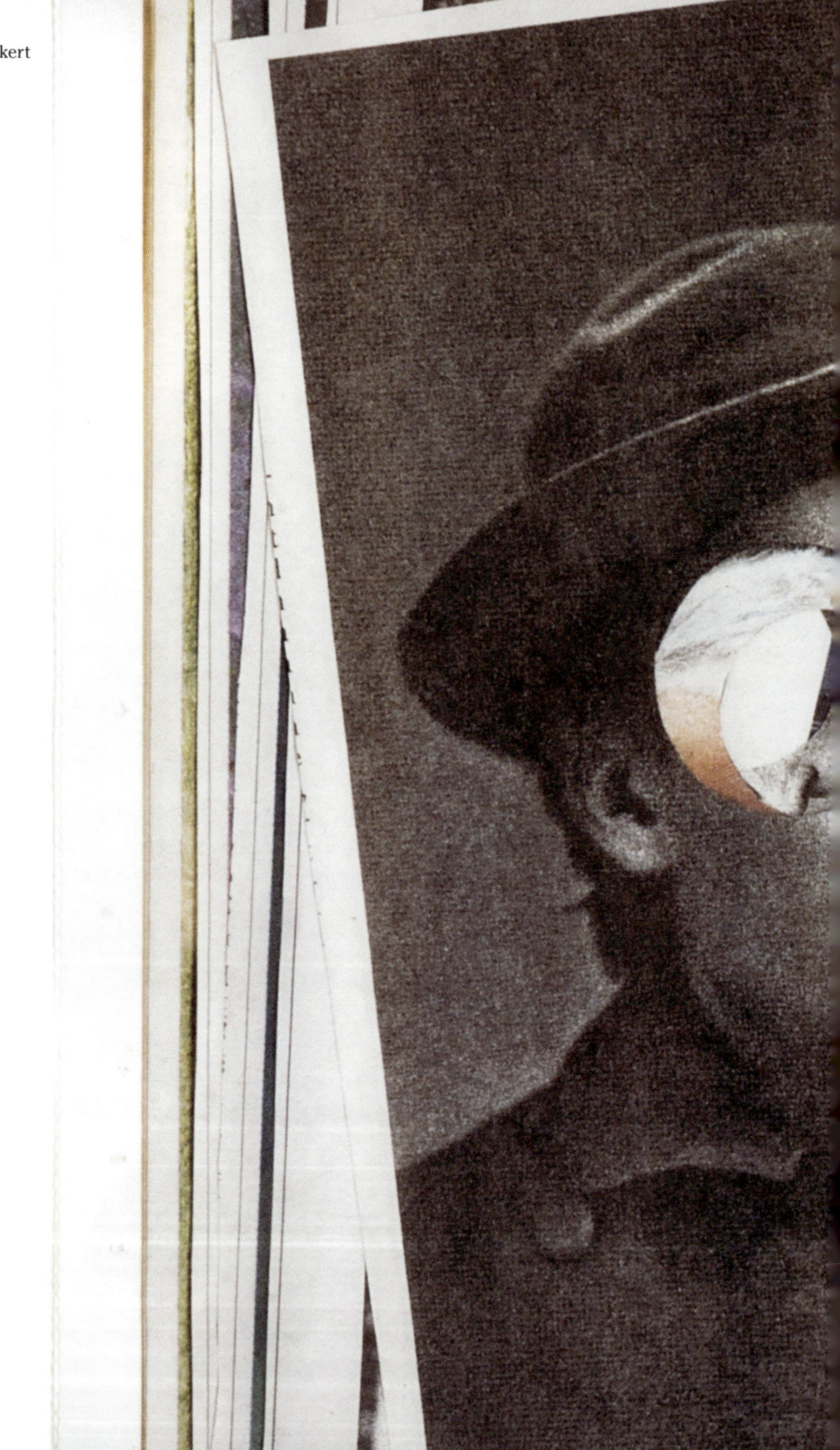

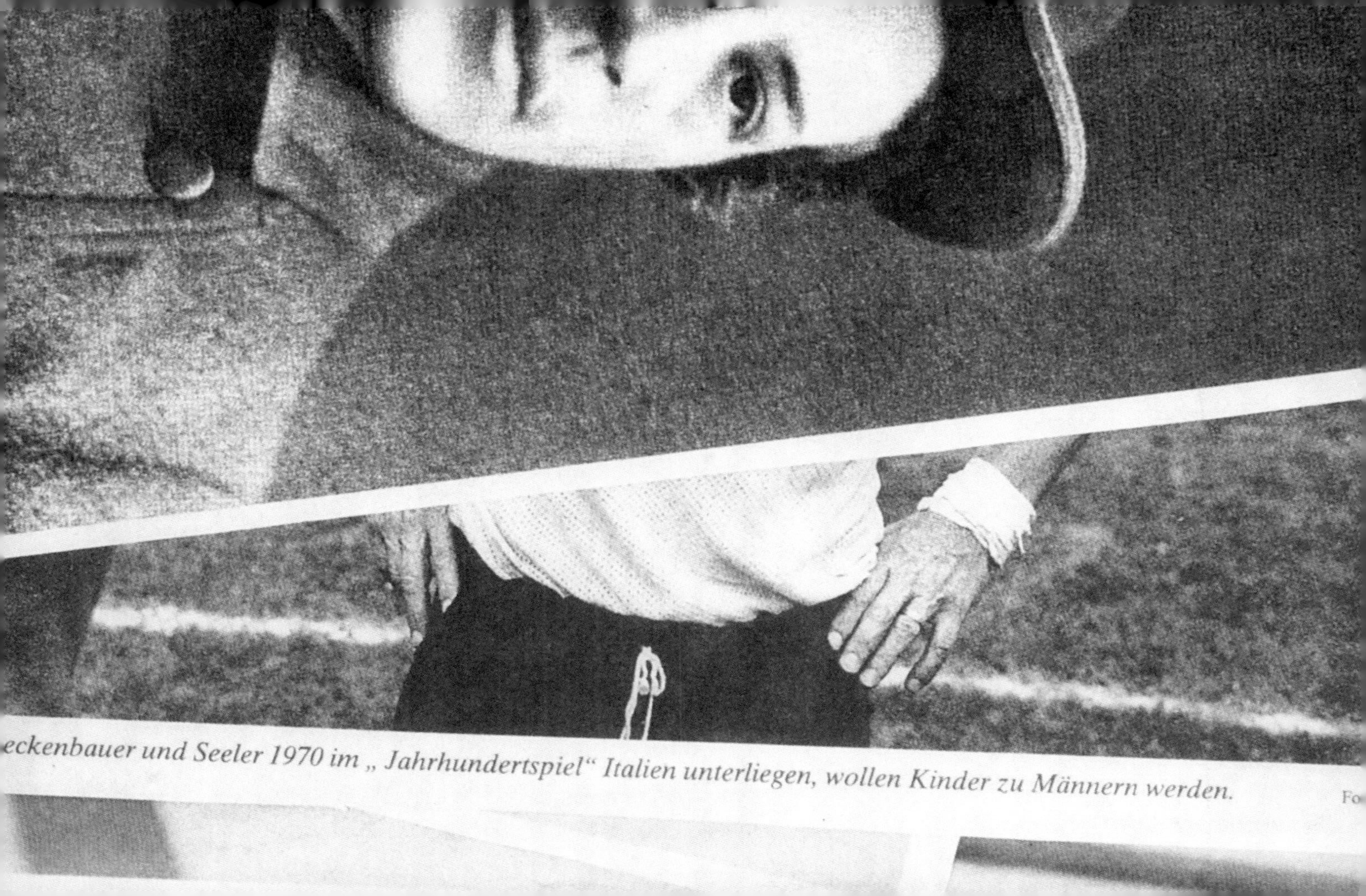

...eckenbauer und Seeler 1970 im „Jahrhundertspiel" Italien unterliegen, wollen Kinder zu Männern werden.

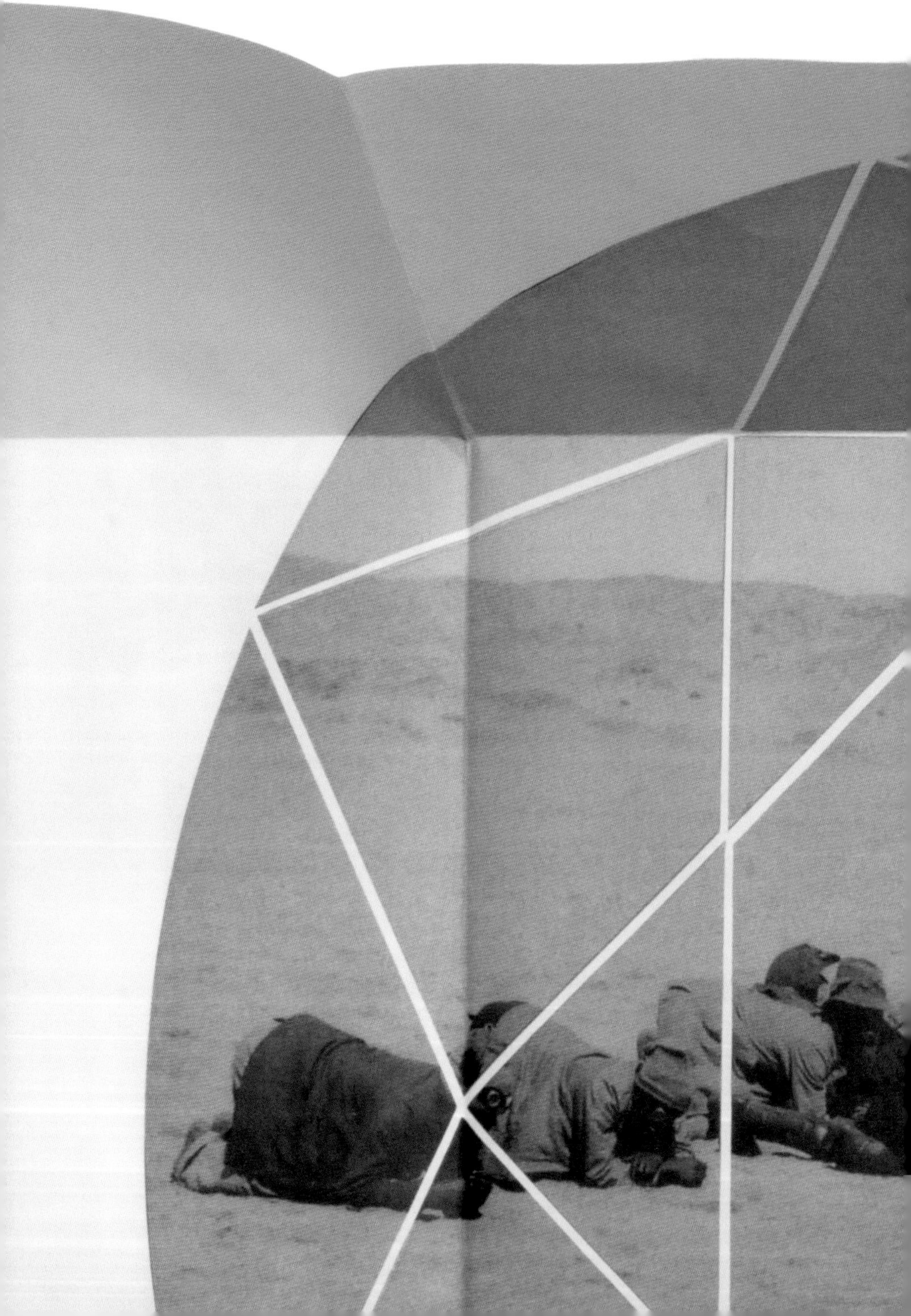

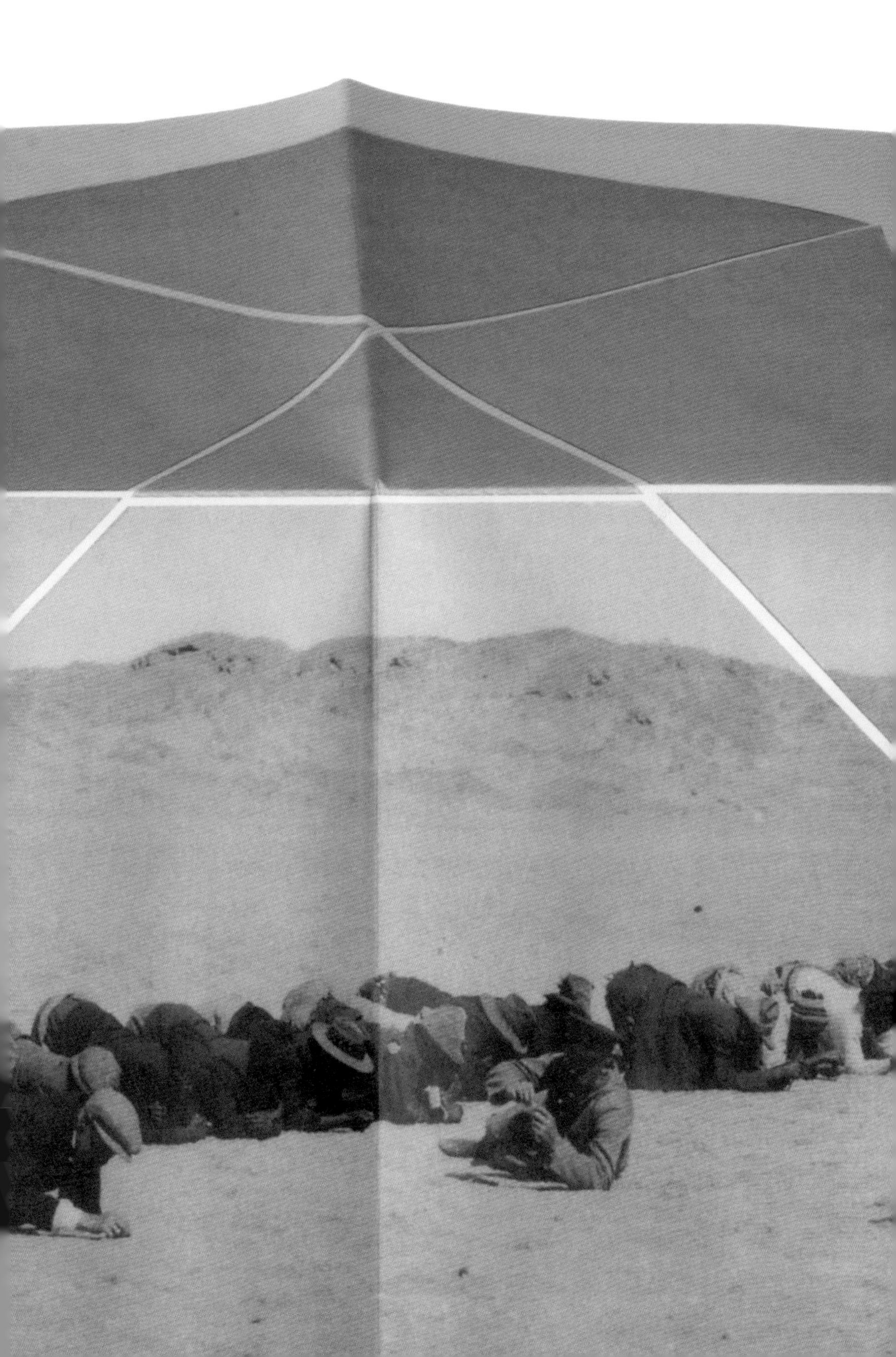

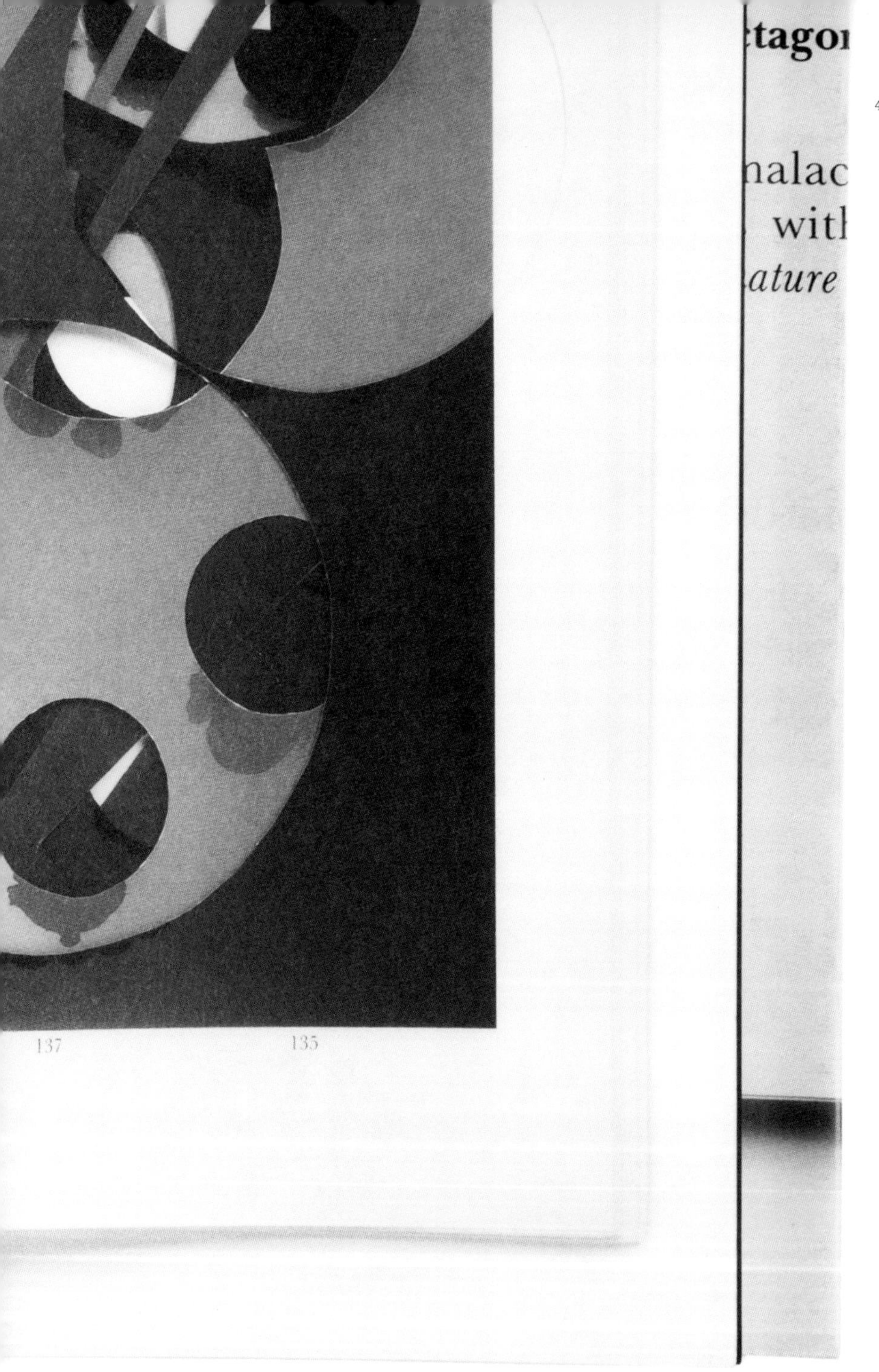

halac
with
ature

137   135

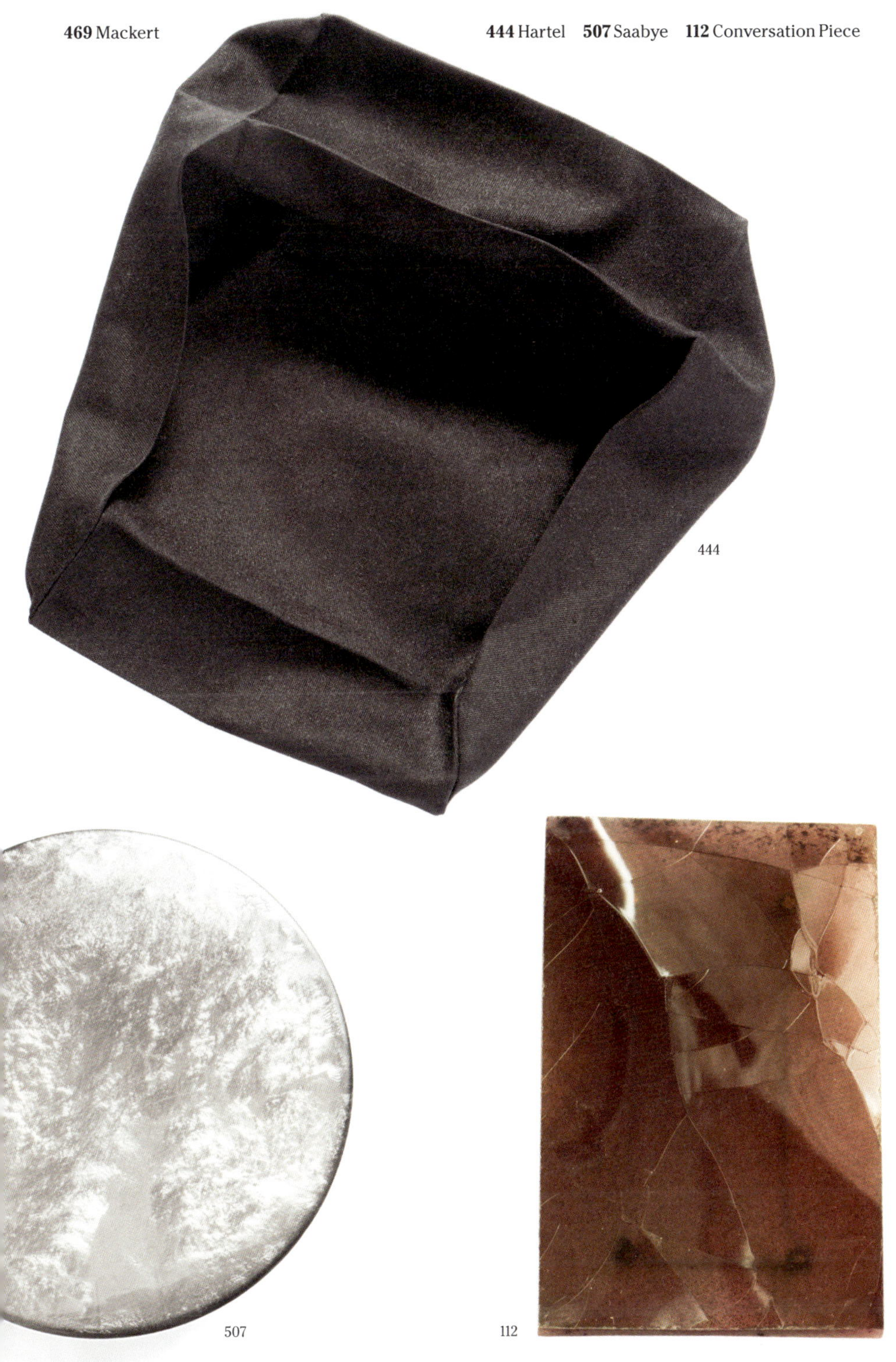

444

507

112

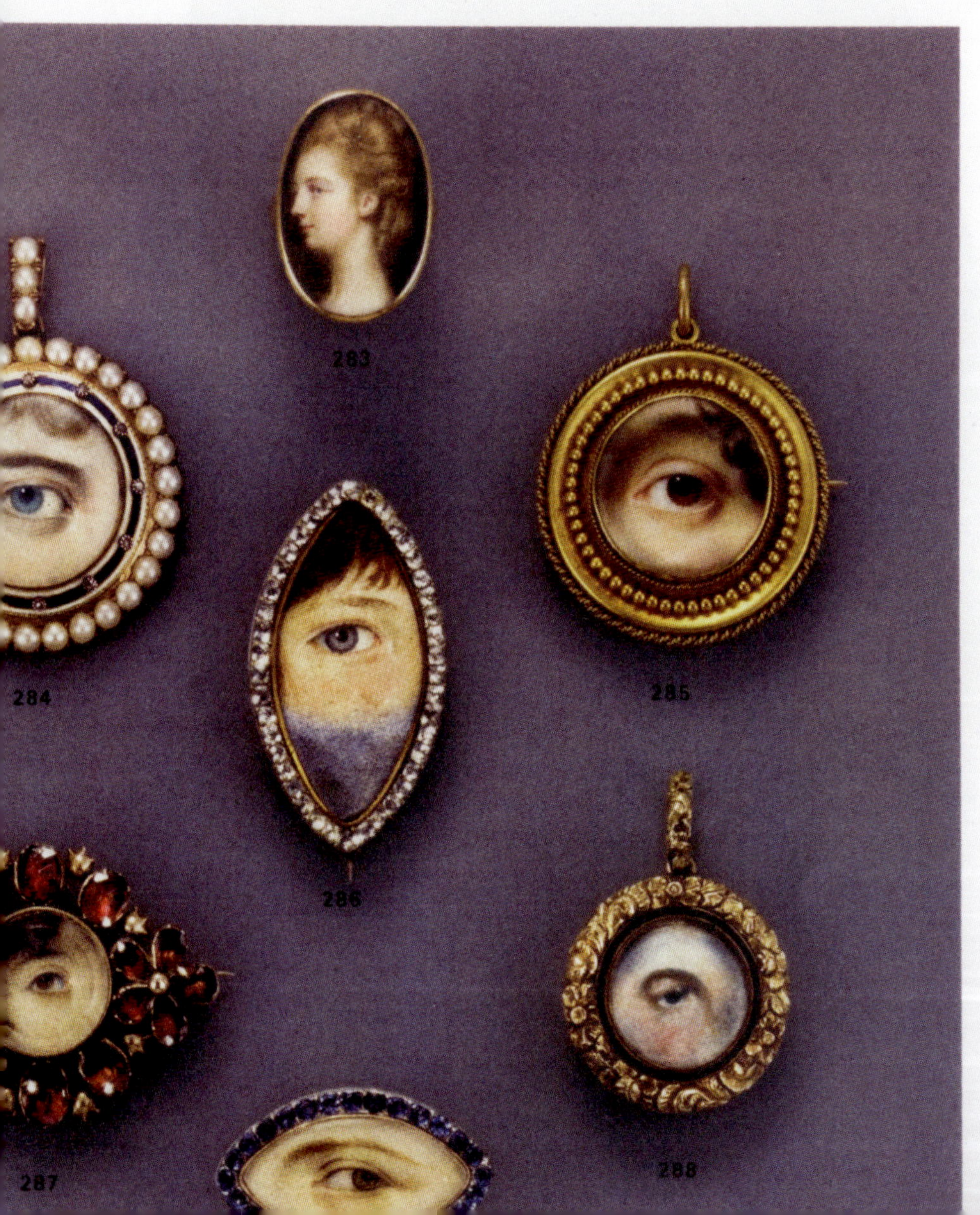

283

284

285

286

287

288

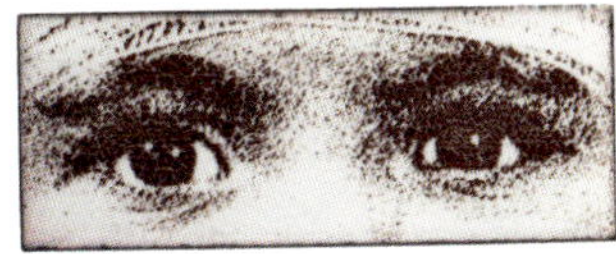

471

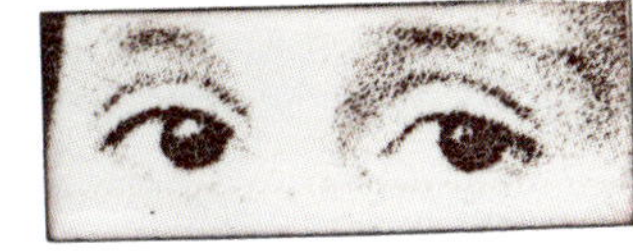

482

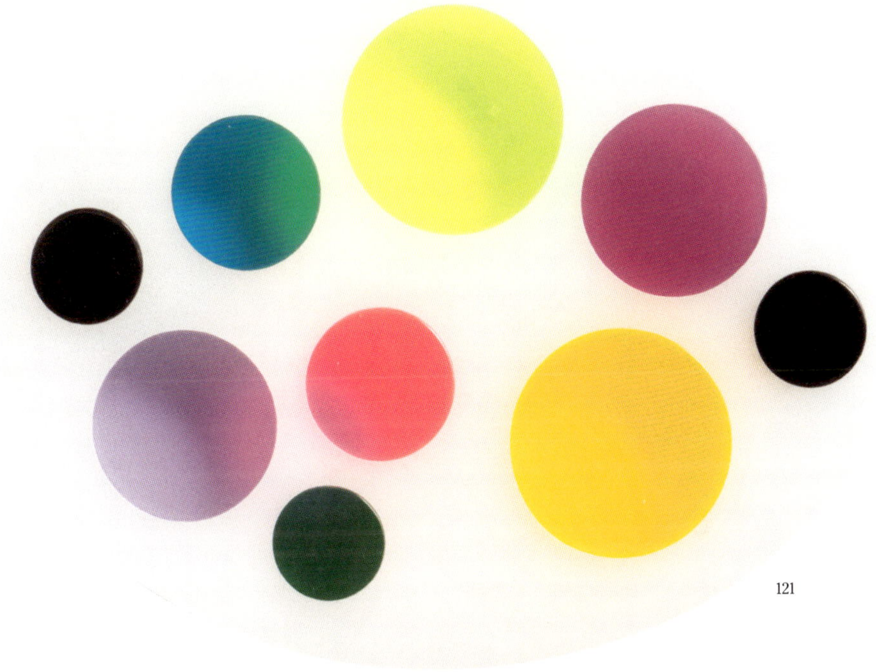

121

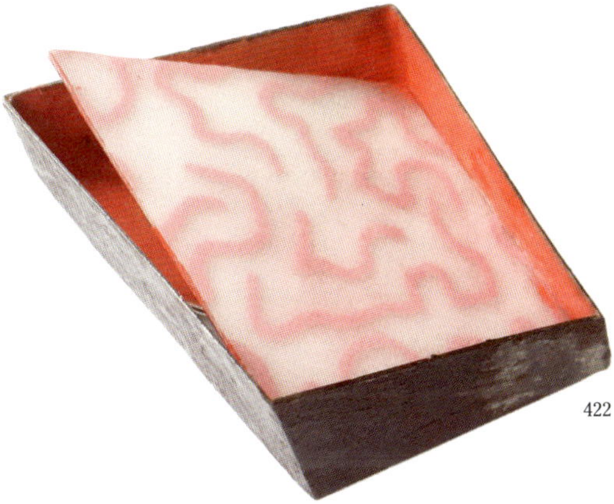

422

257

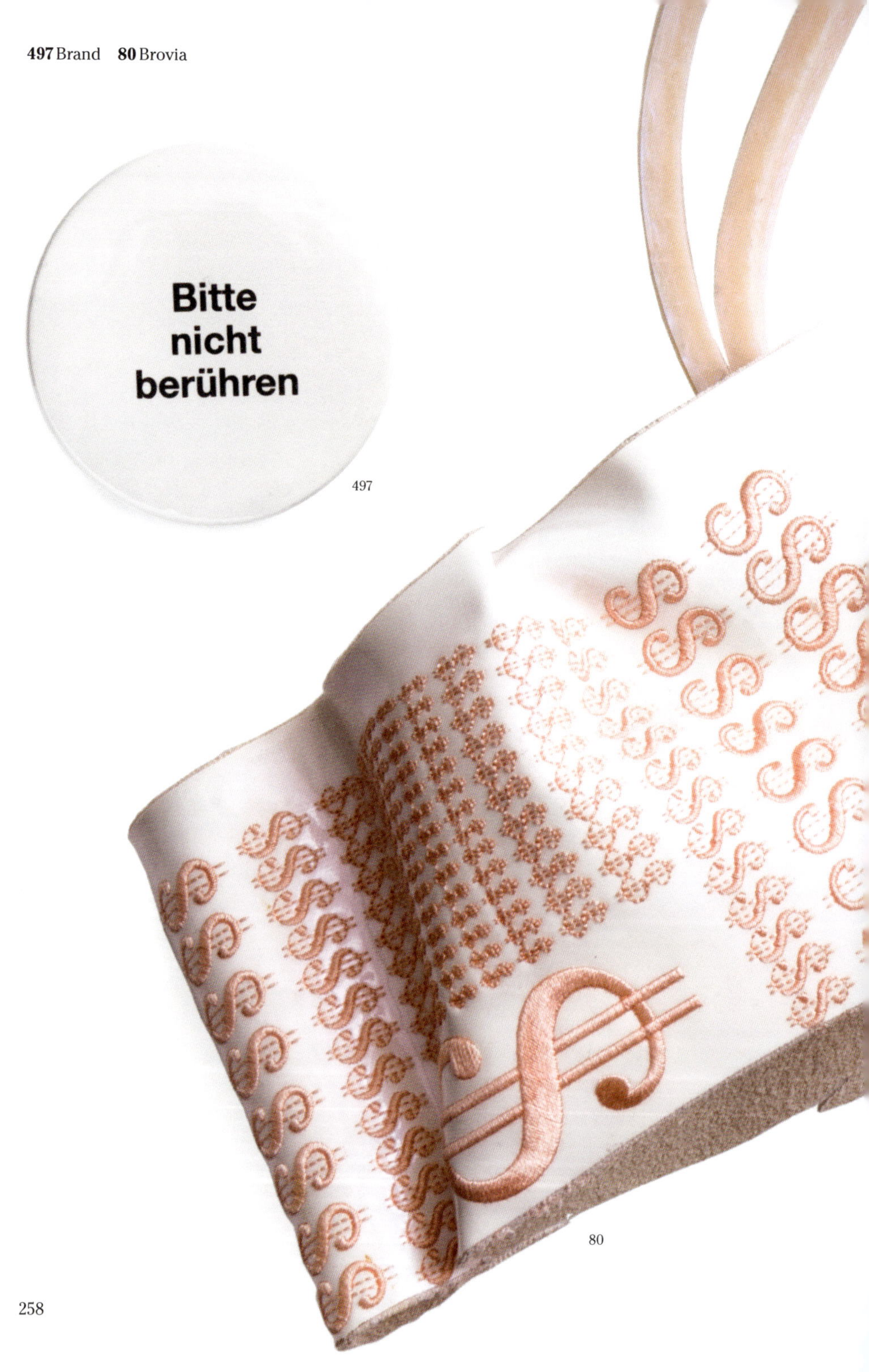

497

80

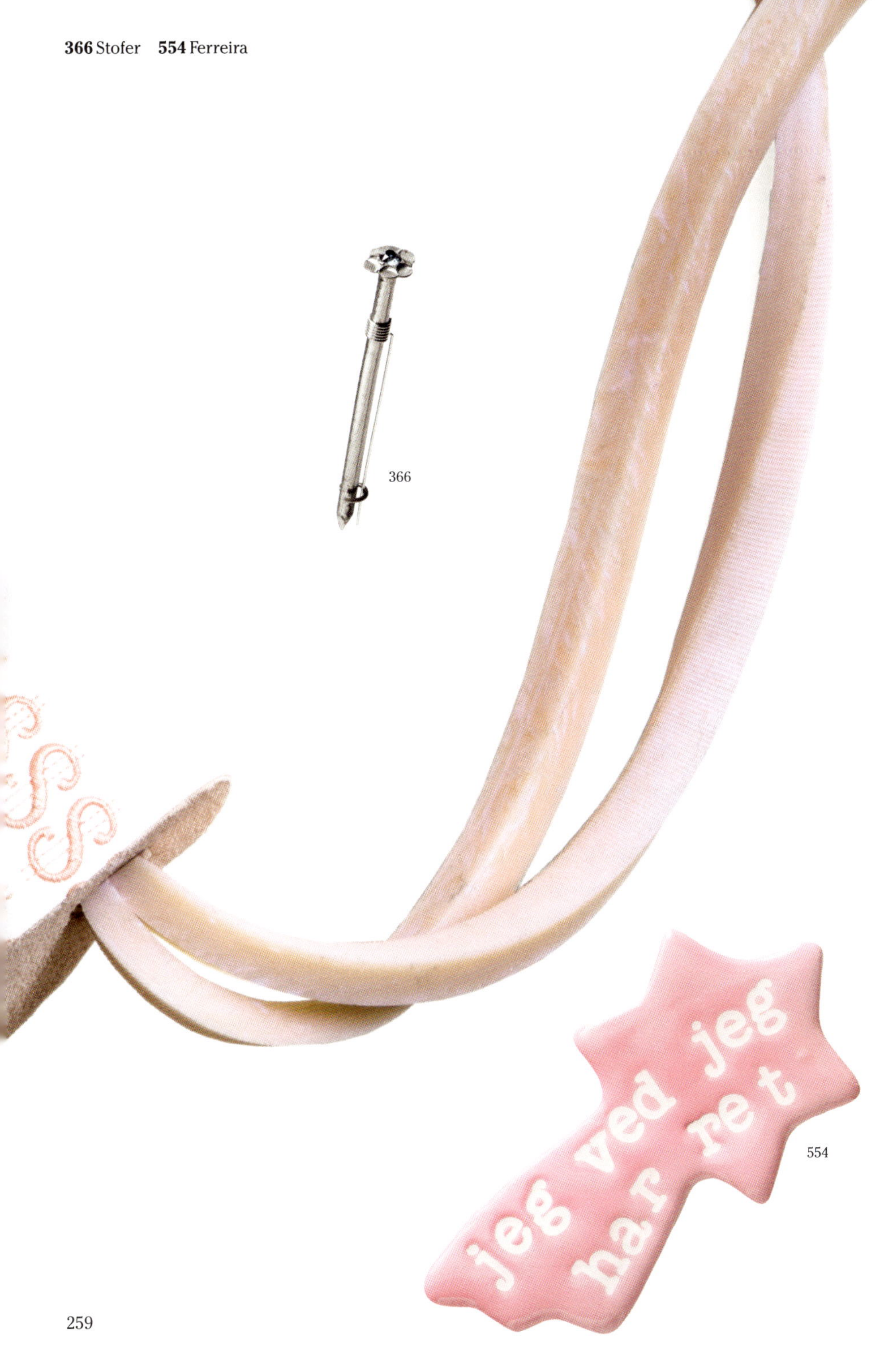

366

554

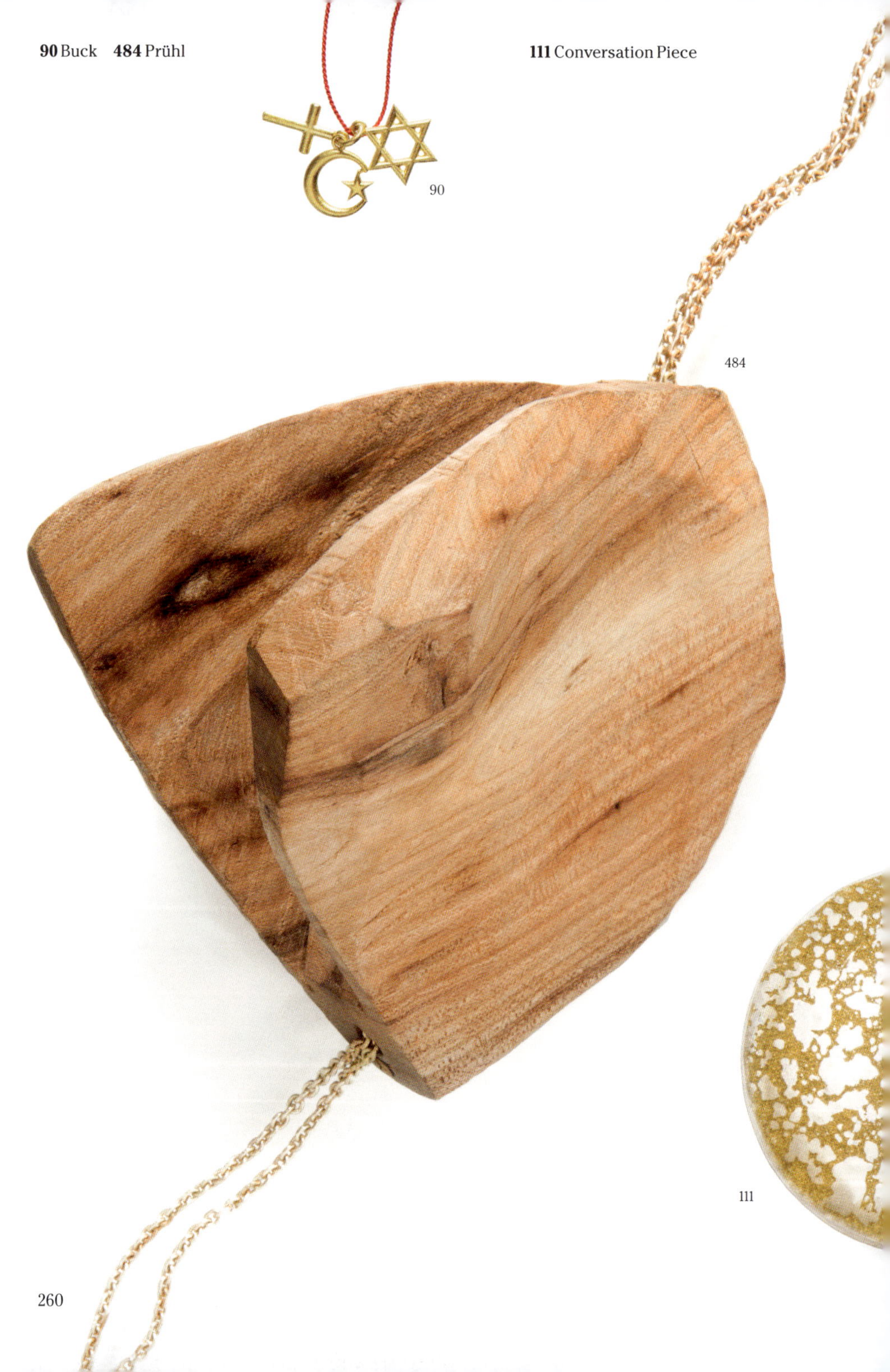

90

484

111

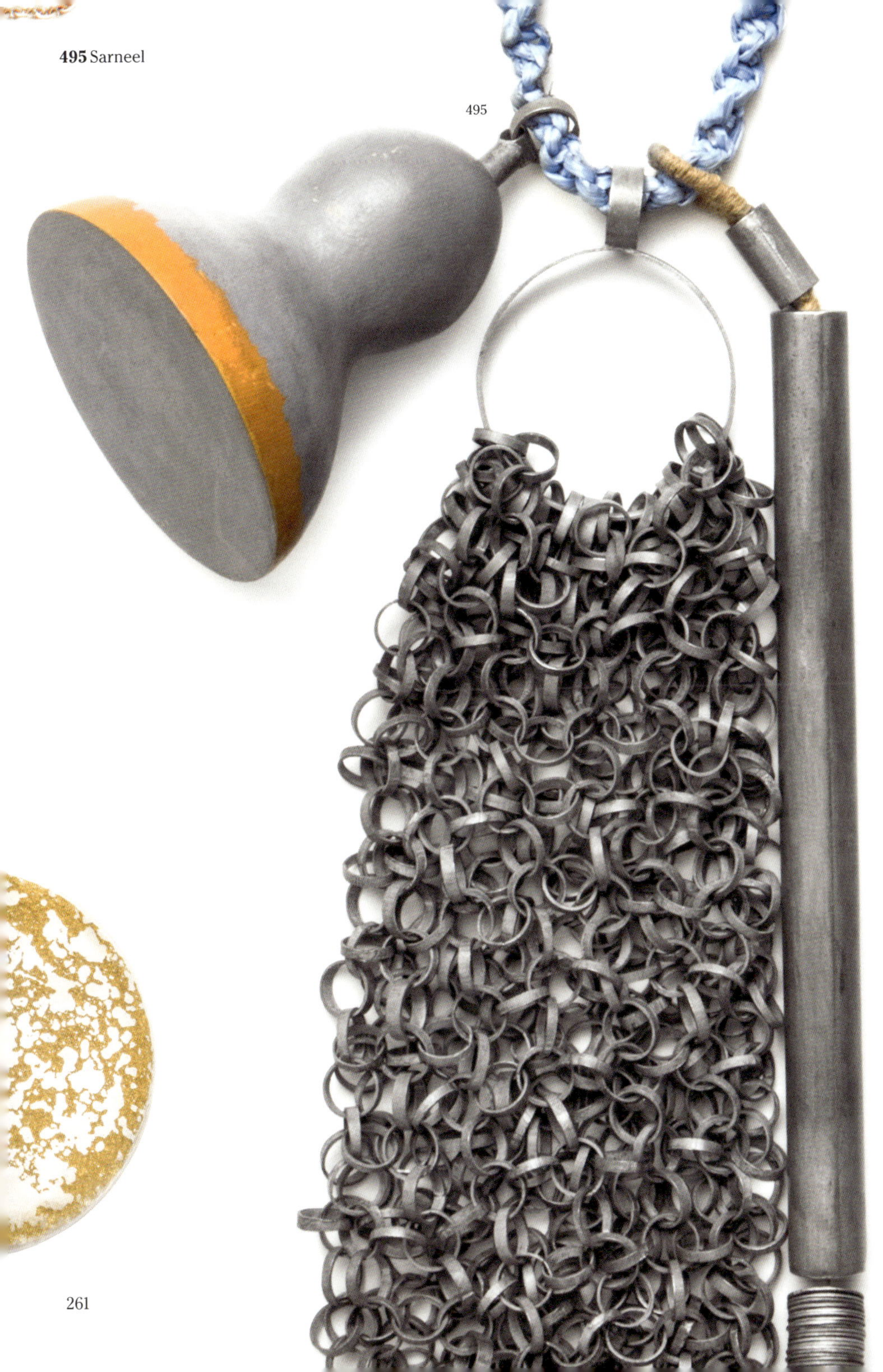

495

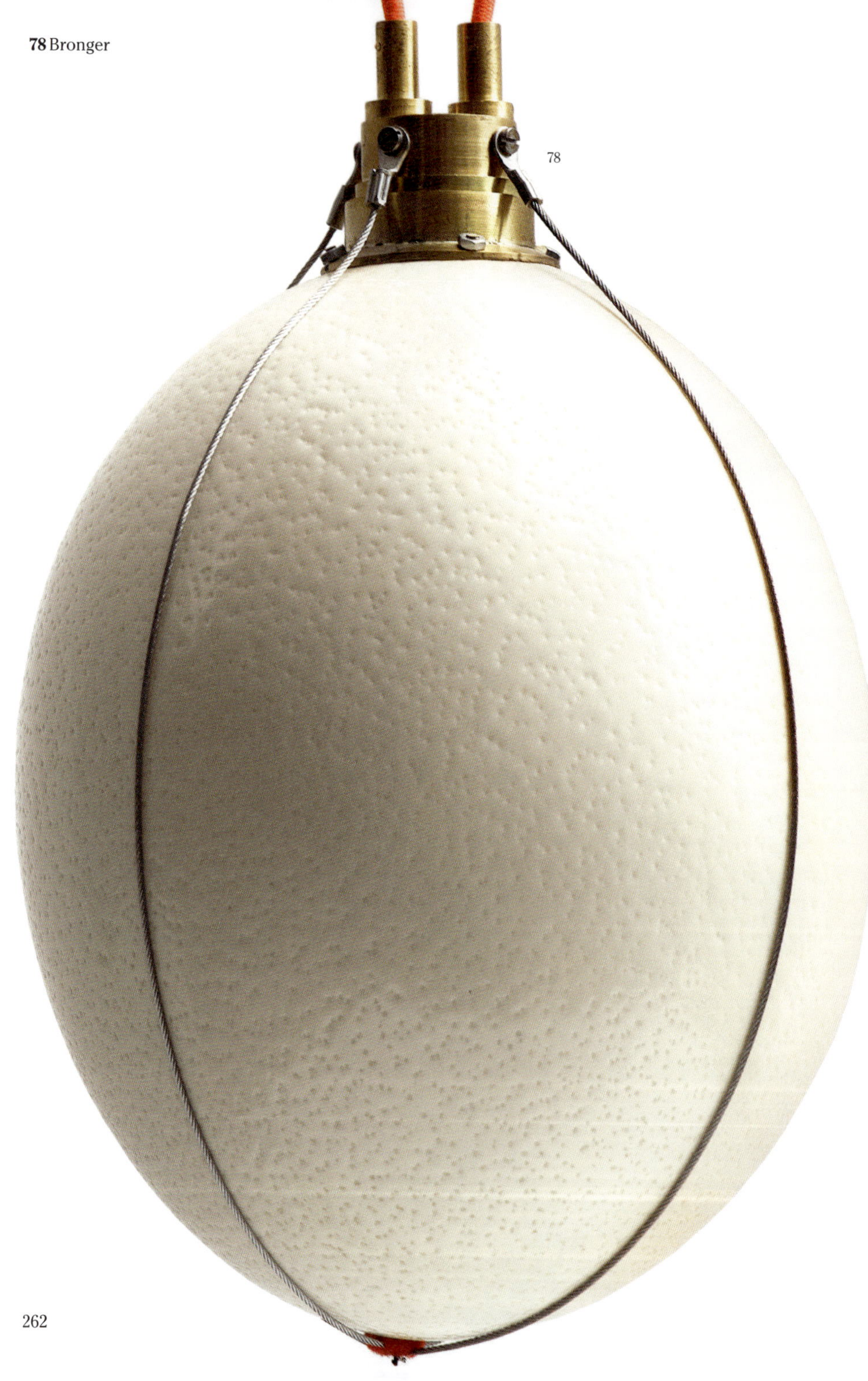
78

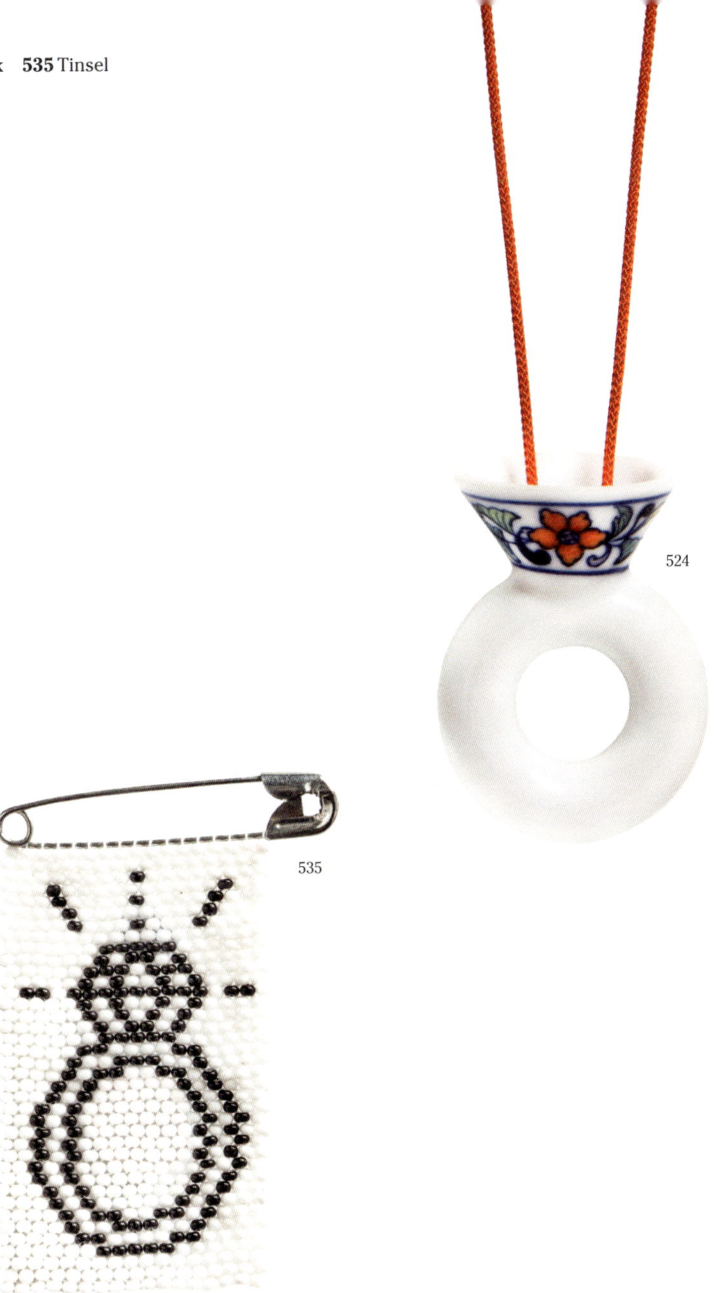

524

535

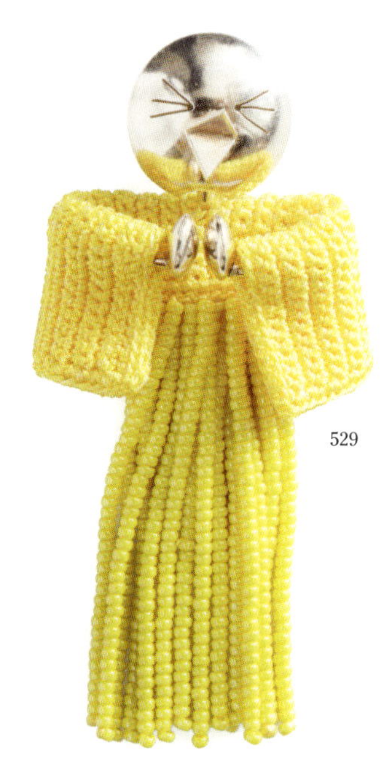

529

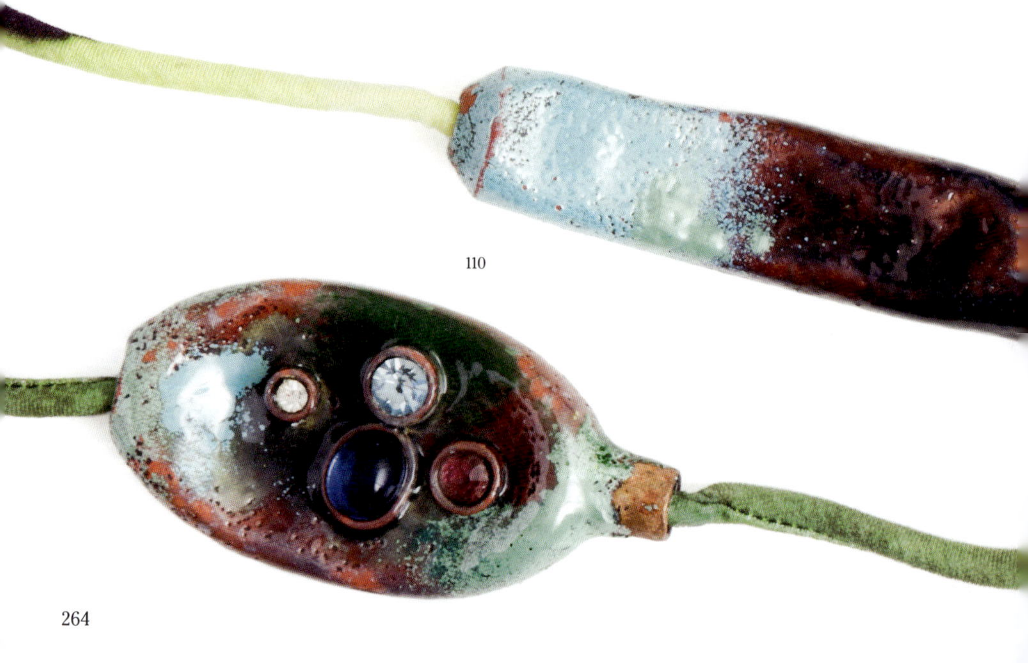

110

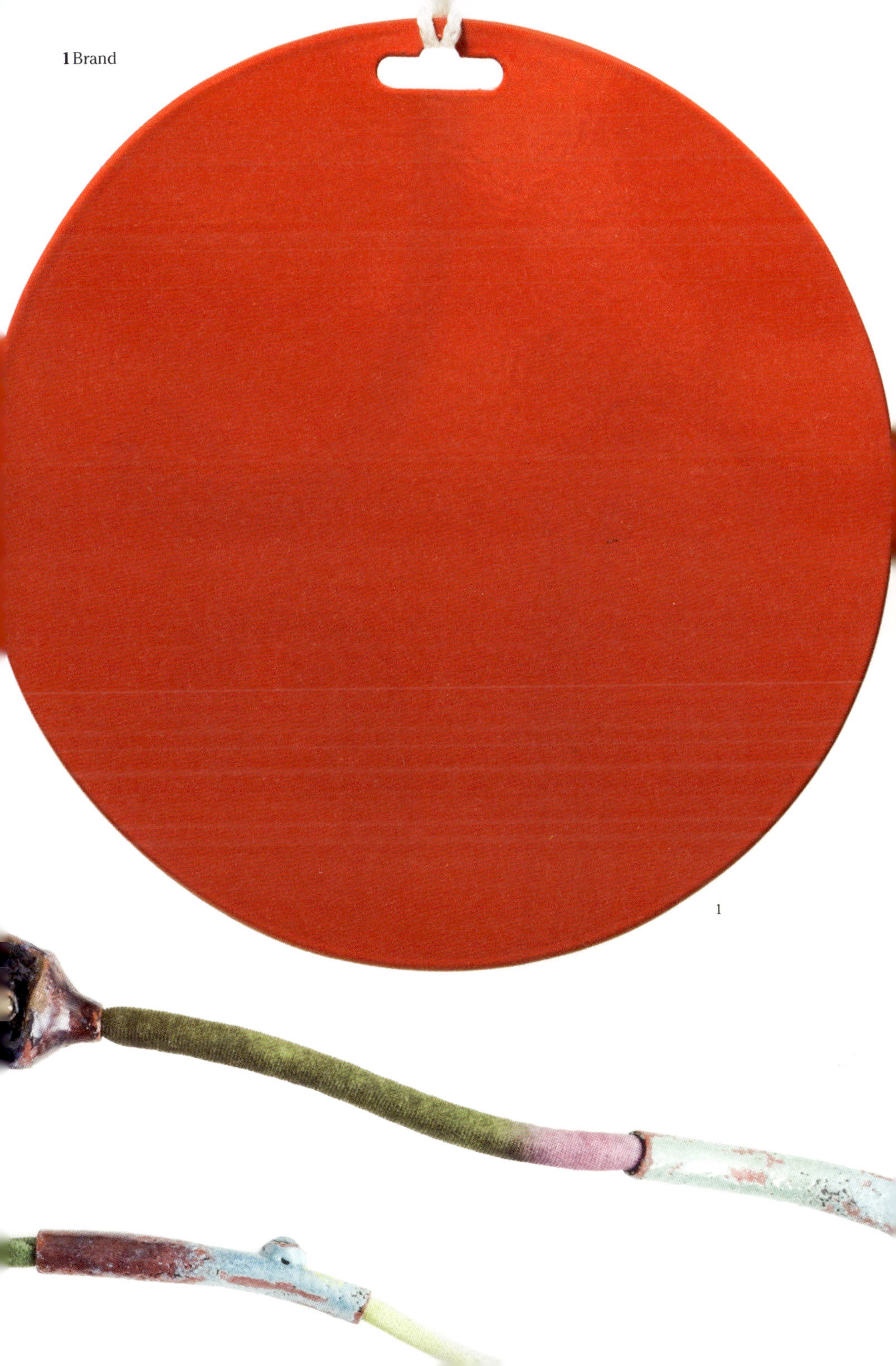
1 Brand
1

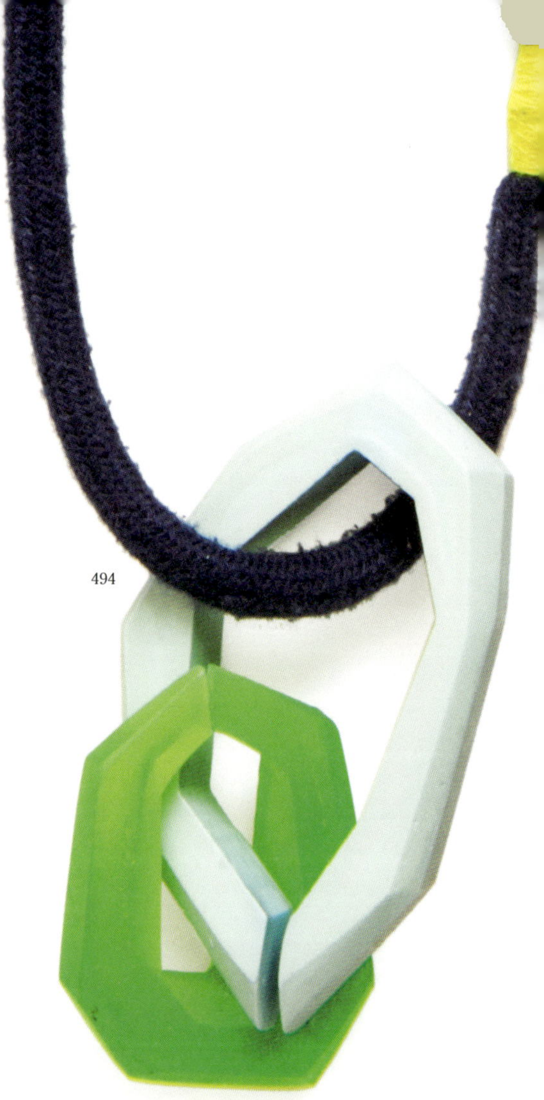

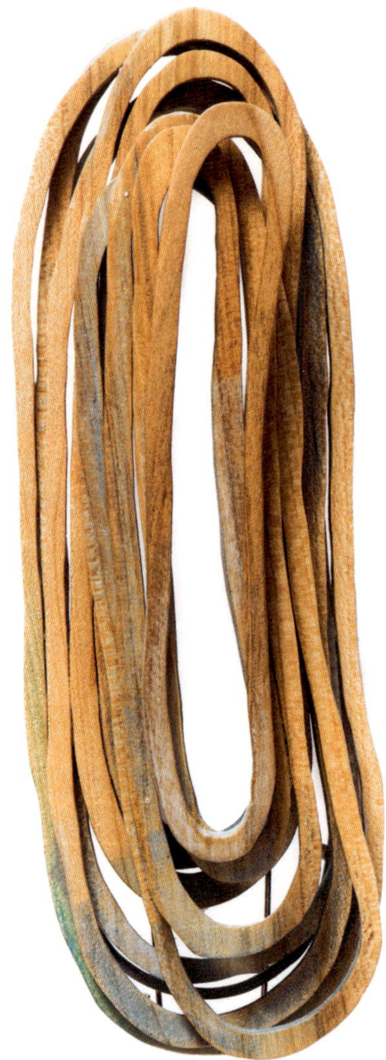

494

492

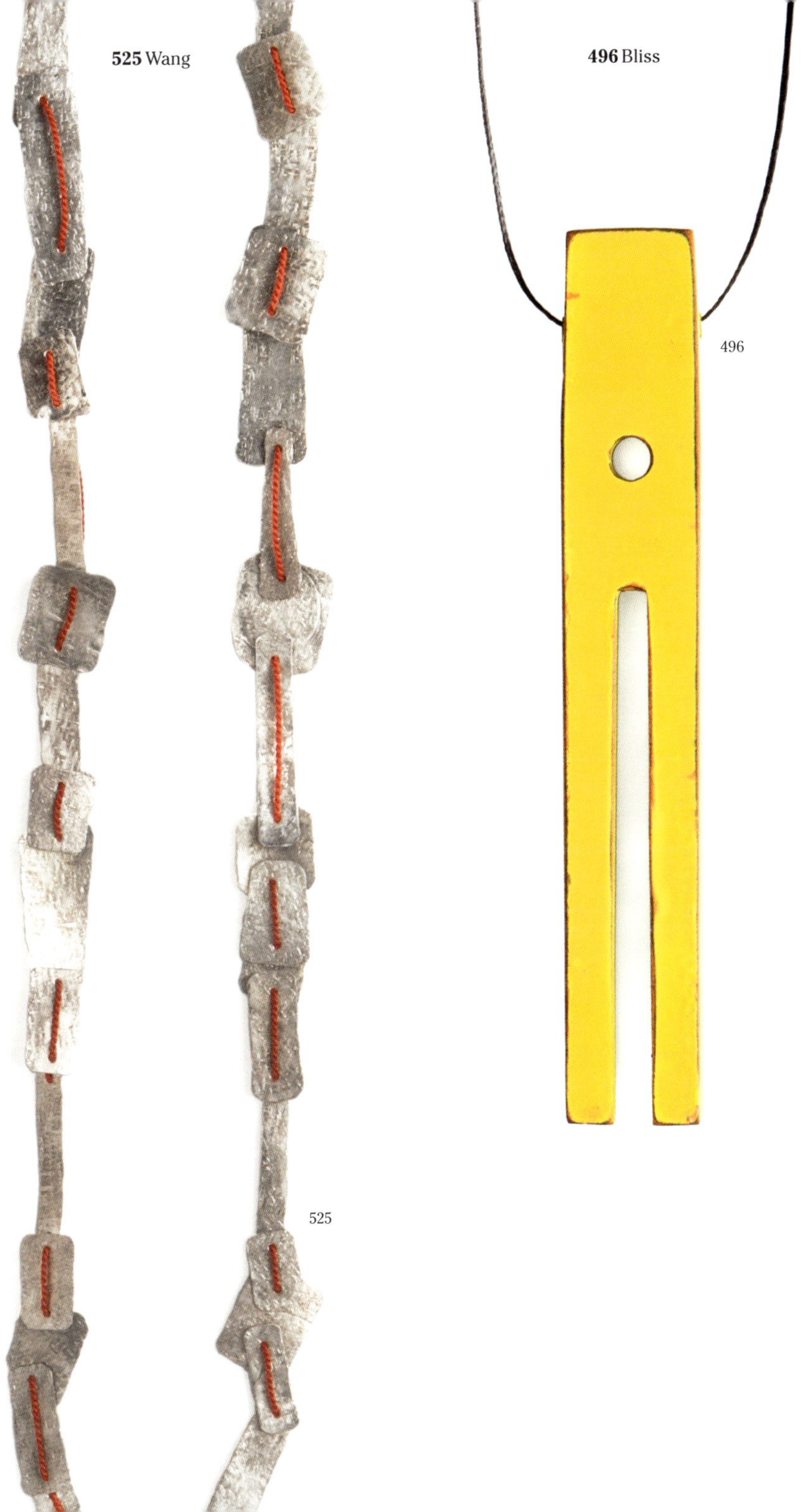

525 Wang
496 Bliss
496
525

205

445

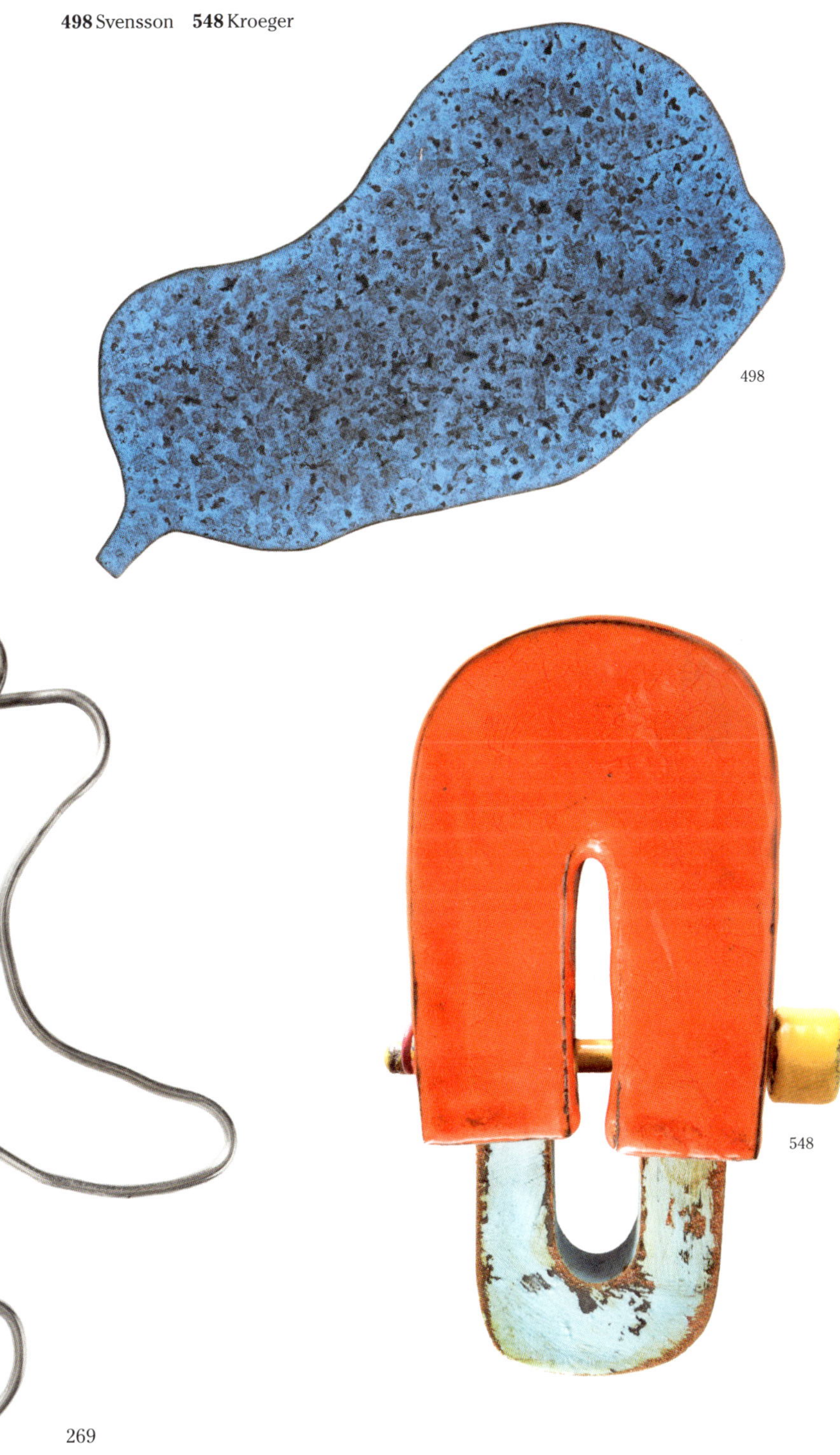

498

548

521

522

523

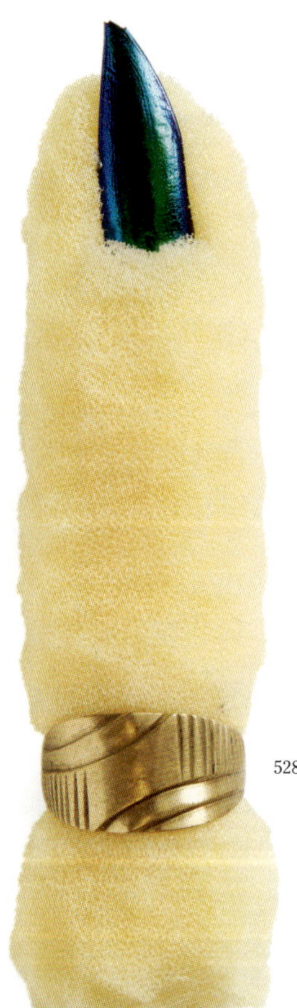

528

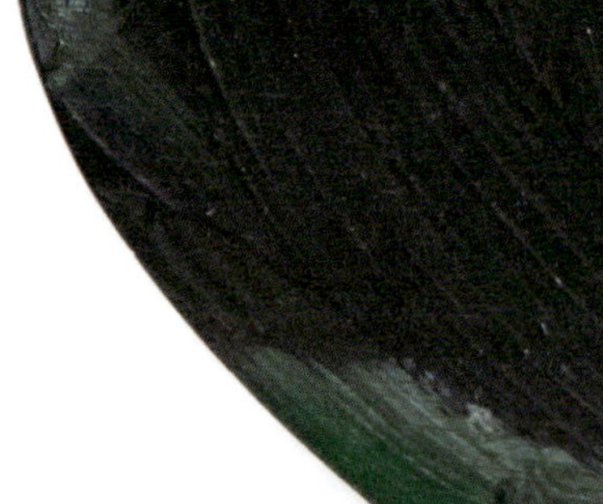

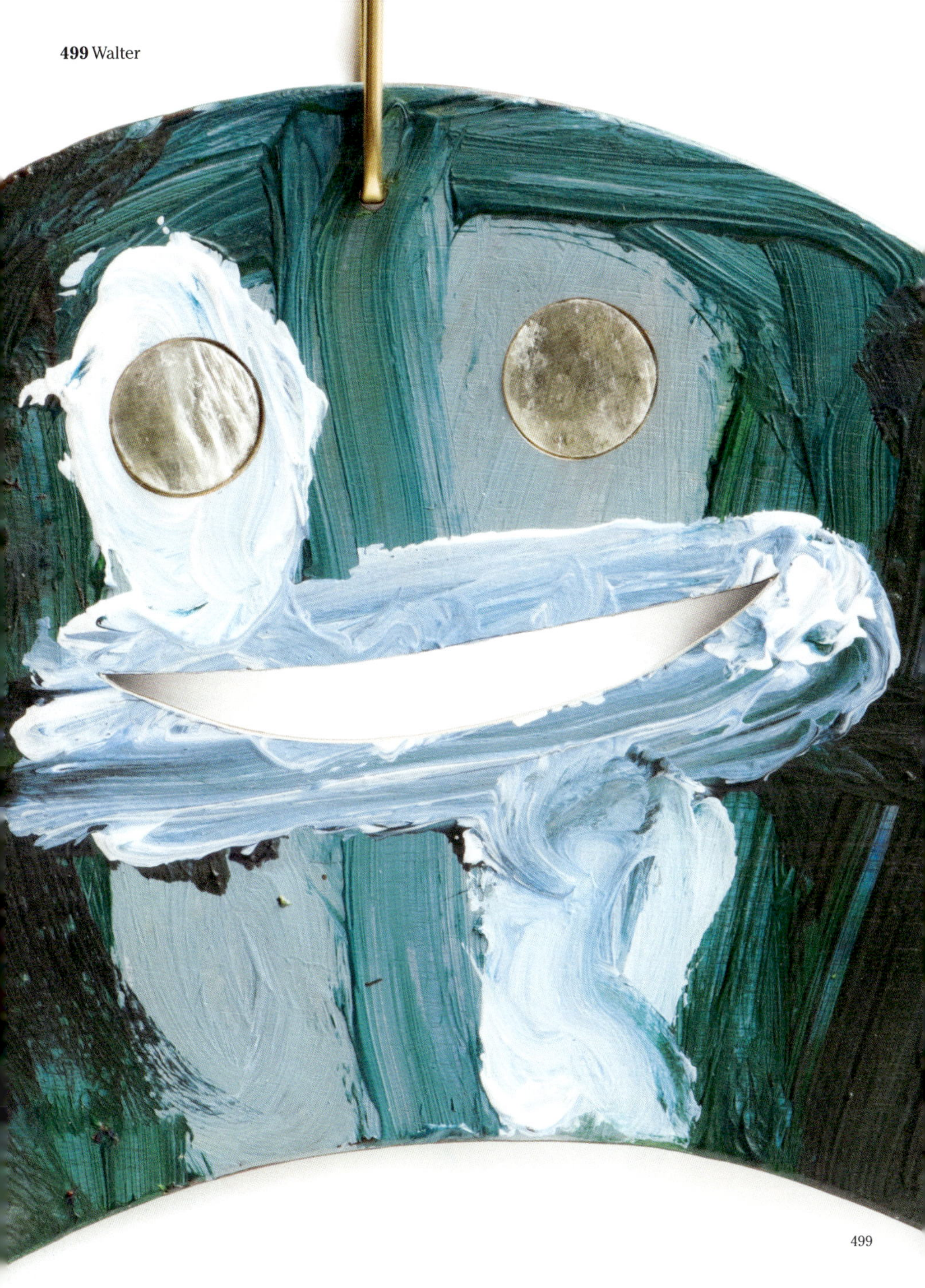

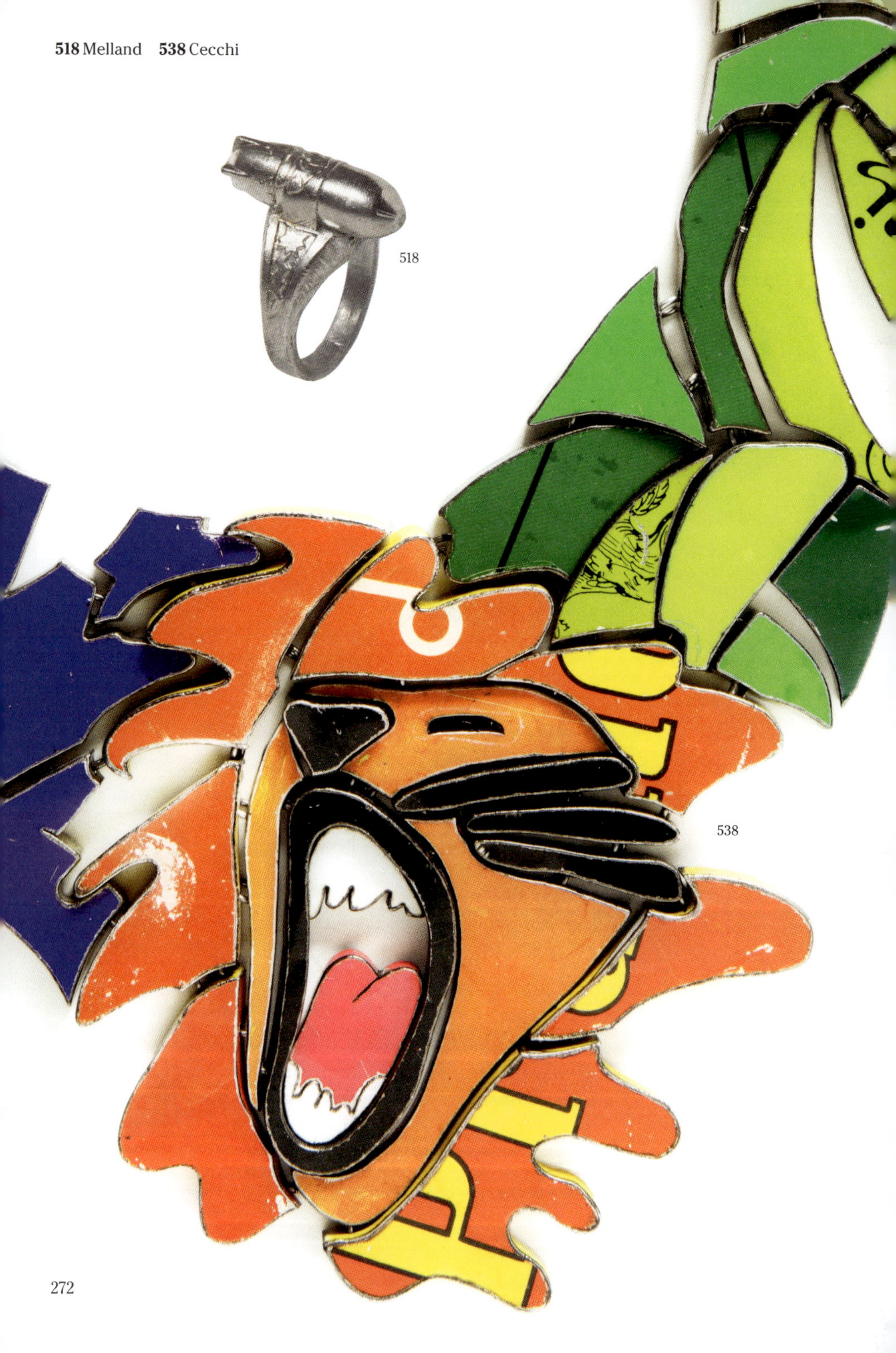

518

538

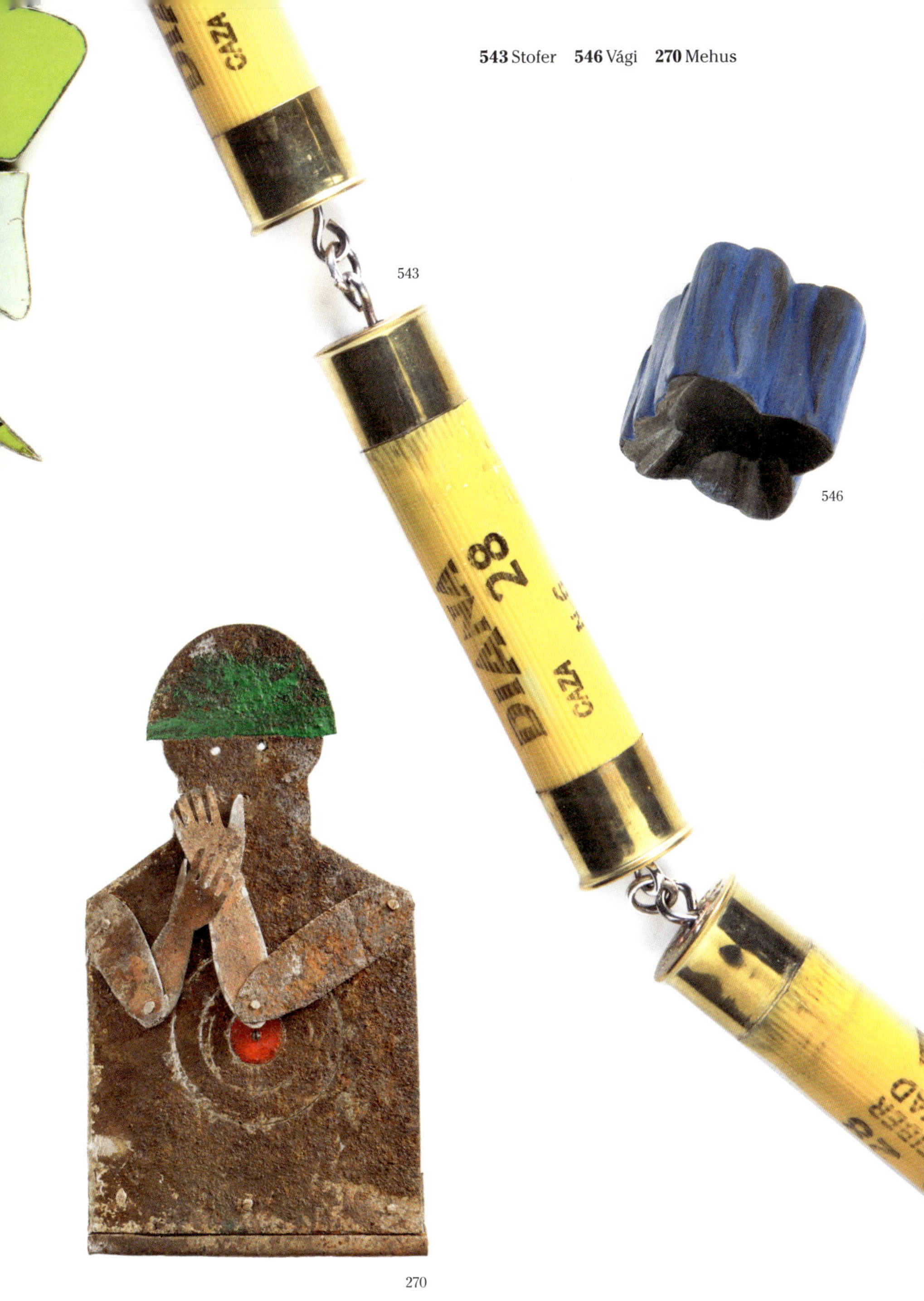

543

546

270

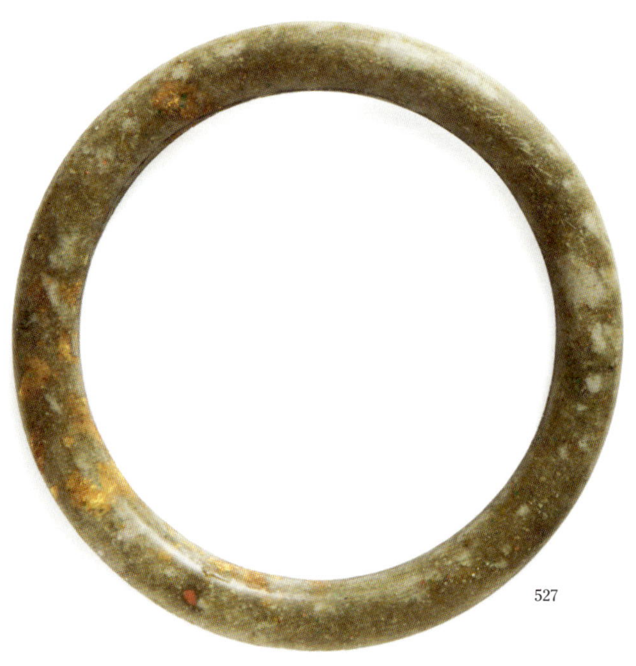

527

534

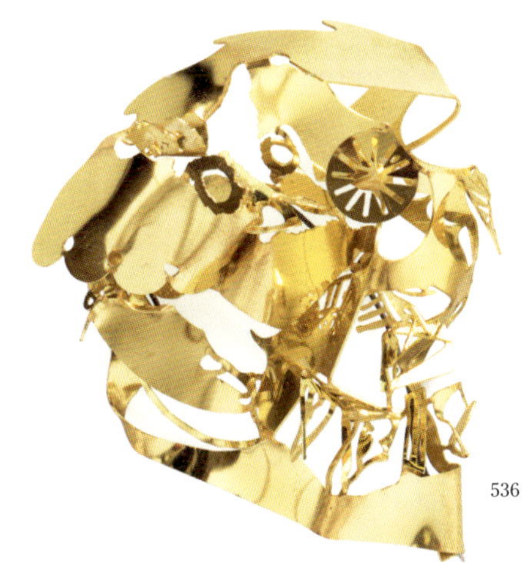

536

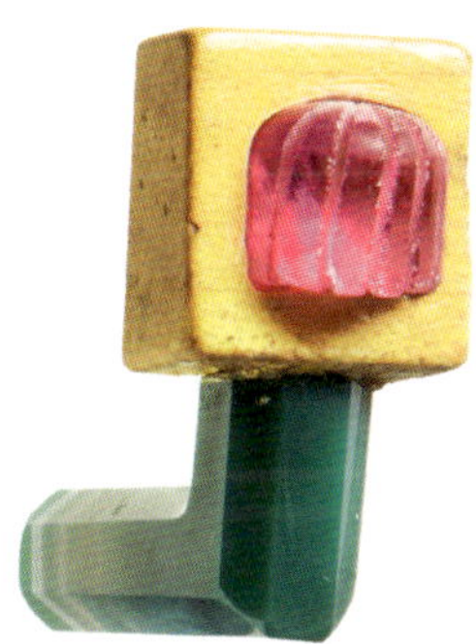

2

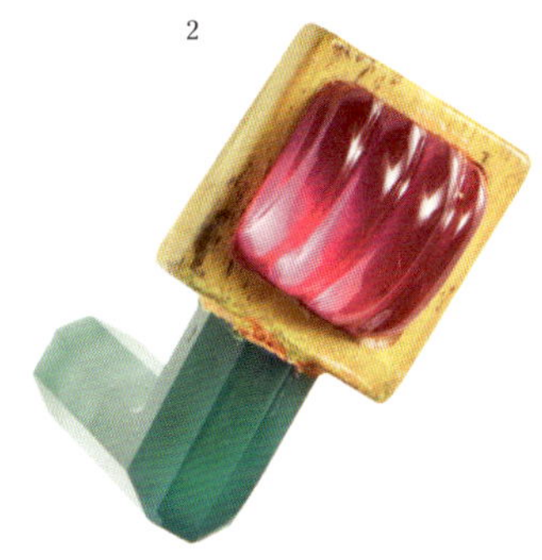

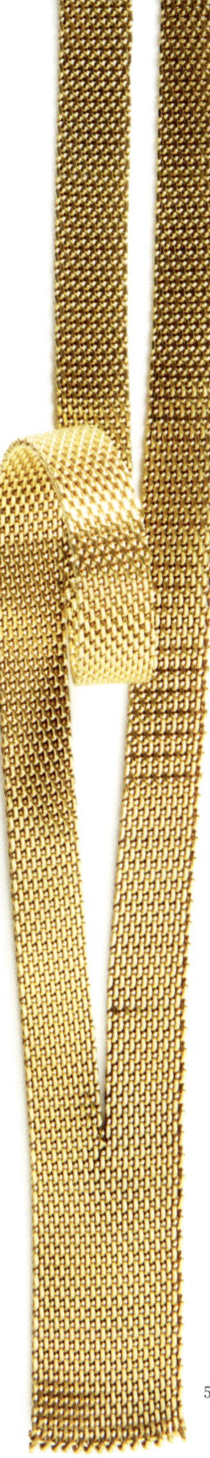

539

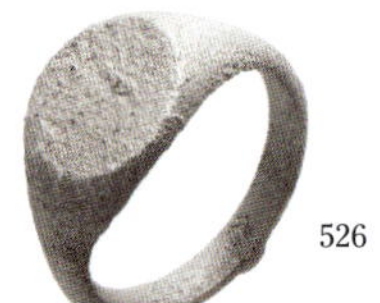

526

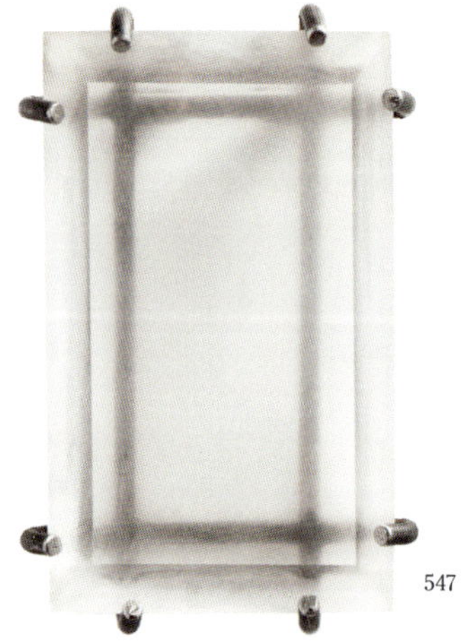

547

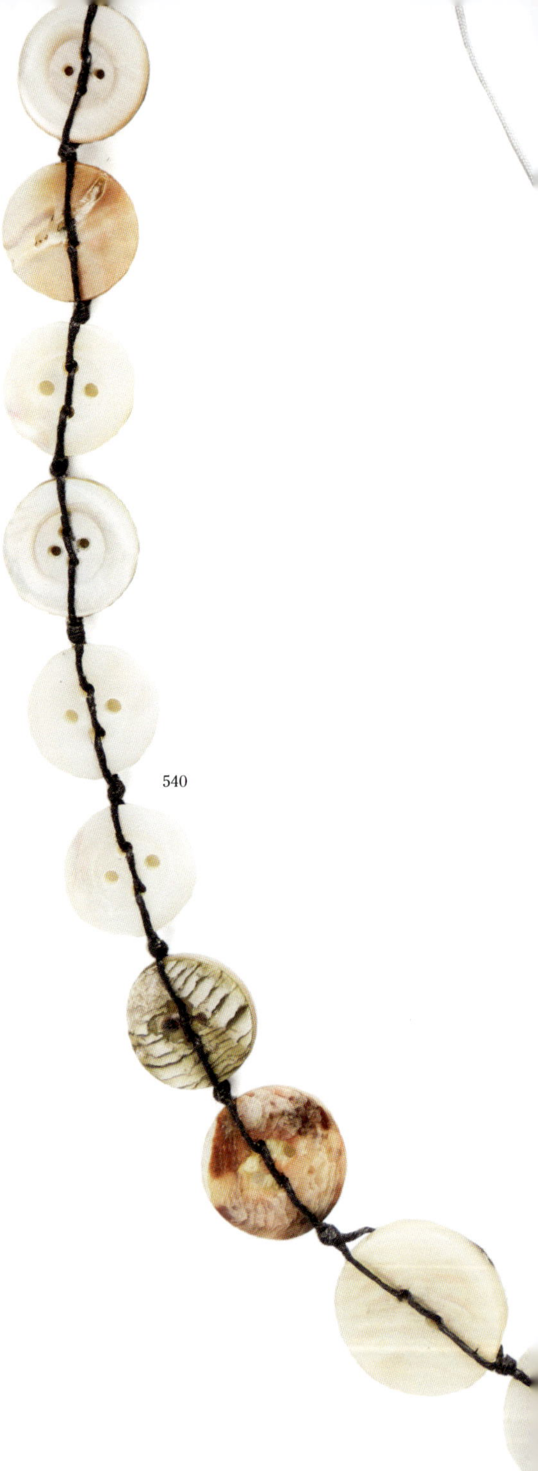

540

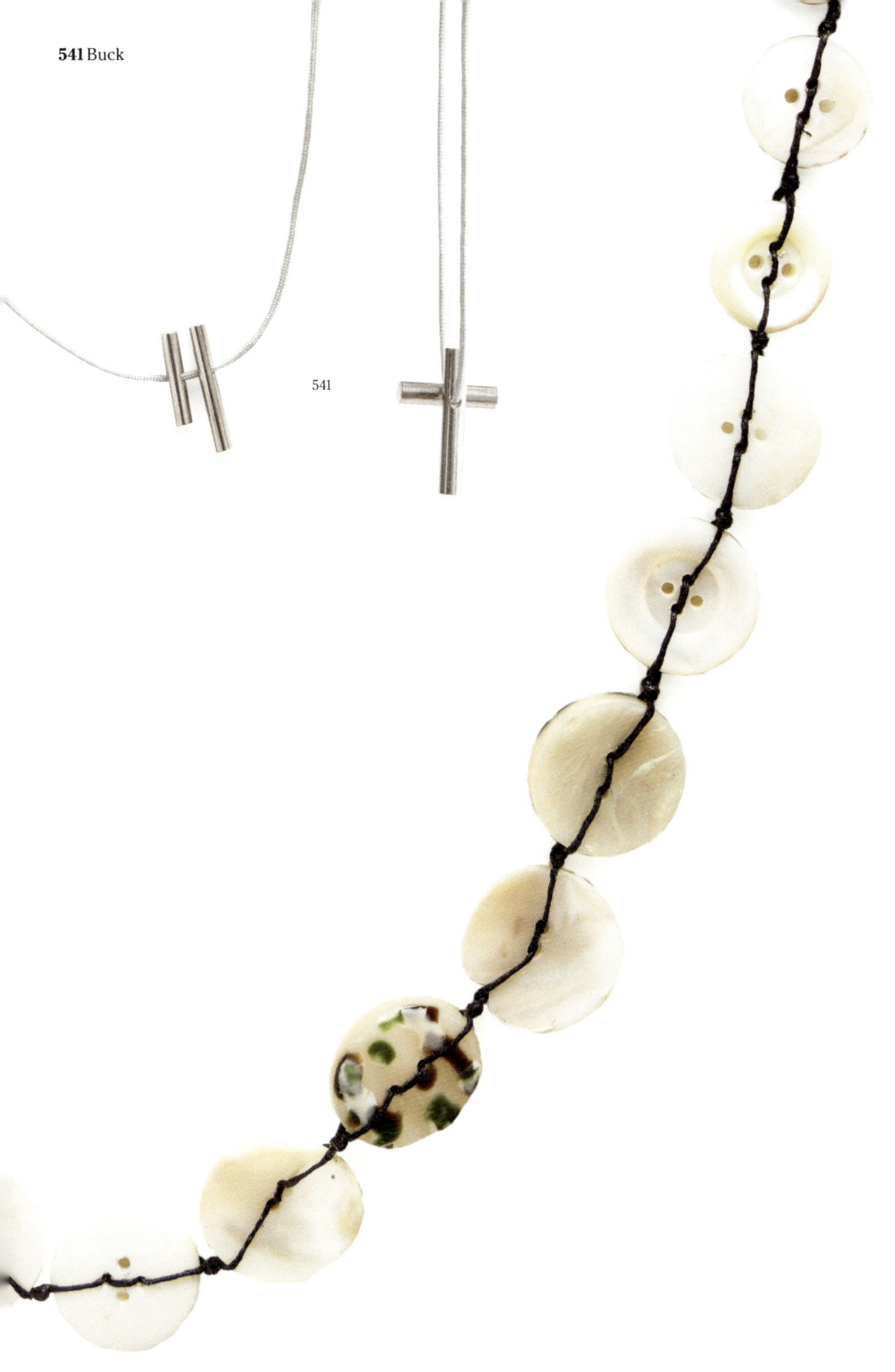

541 Buck
541

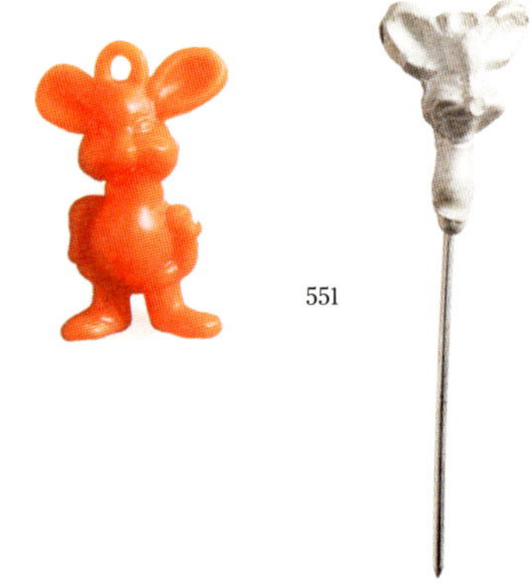

551

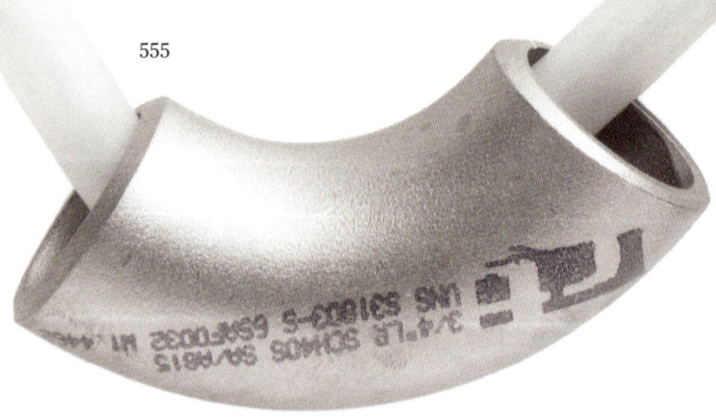

555

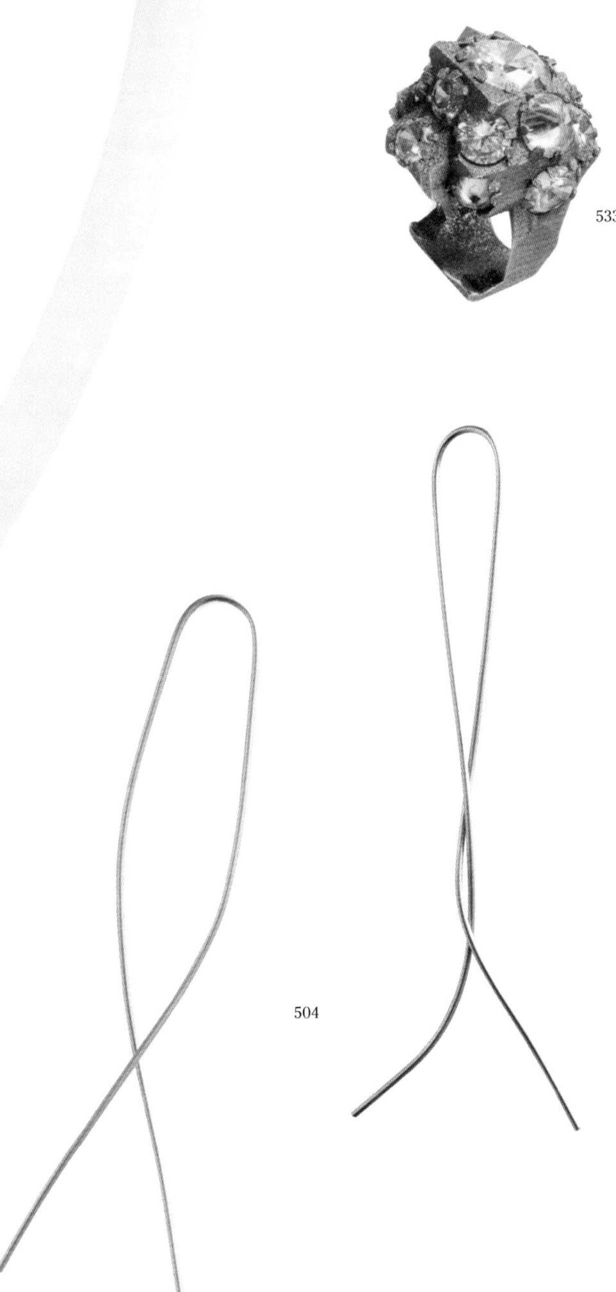

533

504

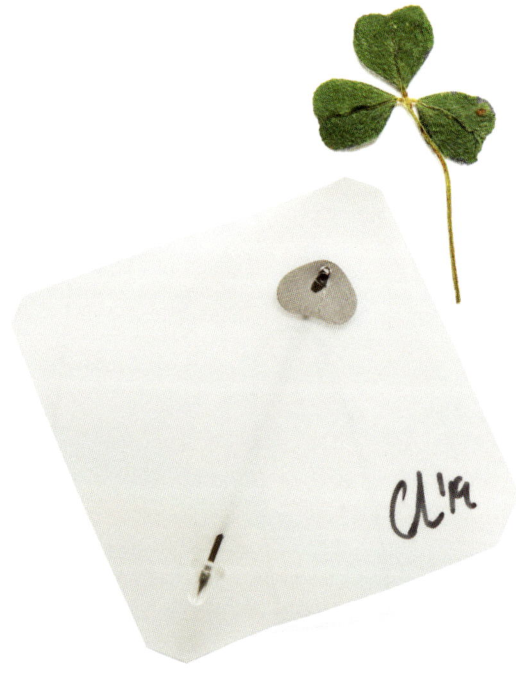

Collecting is a form of practical memory.

— Walter Benjamin[1]

For as long as I can remember,
I've always found collecting
things oddly comforting. […]
It makes me happy.

—Elton John[2]

To collect

I have always collected things. There are those who claim that the urge to collect starts in childhood. I still have albums and boxes full of glossy prints I collected as a young girl in the 1950s and 1960s. A bag of choice marbles and seven stamp albums have also survived countless moves, whereas a collection of paper napkins is now lost. As a student, I started collecting postcards of Marilyn Monroe and things that feature the Coca-Cola logo, and not least books and magazines. All these projects came to a halt when I succumbed in earnest to the enchantment of art jewellery. But although I started buying jewellery in my teens, it took a long time before I began to see myself as a collector. For me, jewellery was – and is – first and foremost something to be used. As the years progressed, however, the jewellery accumulated in such quantities that I was forced to confront the question so many people kept asking: Are you a collector?

It has been said that if you have more than three objects in a single category, then you're a collector. If you have only one version of a thing, it will always seem useful. When you acquire a second version of the same thing, however, one of the two will seem redundant. But this can be changed by acquiring a third version, for then you have the start of a collection.[3] This process, whereby one object

influences the meaning of others, is something I recognise
in the activity of collecting. But many of us own much more
than we absolutely need without thinking of our belongings
as a collection. So the question is: When does the tendency
to accumulate things turn into the activity of collecting?
I myself would argue that one can only talk about a collection when the quantity exceeds what can be justified in
terms of practical use or what space one has to store it in. As
a rule, one only reaches this point after a fairly protracted
period. At least, that's how it was for me. I had been buying
jewellery for many years before I began to regard the accumulation as a collection or myself as a collector.

A passion

It was in conjunction with the exhibition *These are a few of
her favourite things. Jorunn Veiteberg's jewellery collection*
at Nordenfjeldske Kunstindustrimuseum in Trondheim in
the autumn of 2018 that I first began to think seriously about
what drives some people to become collectors. Beneath the
surface was a fear that my own interest in collecting could
spiral out of control, possibly leading to financial commit-
ments I couldn't afford. What I discovered was that much
of what is written about collecting is comparable to psychiatric diagnoses. Although I like to think I have my behaviour
under control, I recognise in myself many of the traits that
characterise more clinical conditions. This is true of the
impulse or the supposed need to augment the collection
with yet another new object. It is a trait that is central to
the collector's way of thinking. Werner Muensterberger,
who has spent many years studying collectors from both
anthropological and the psychoanalytical angles, claims
that repetition is an essential factor. As he puts it: "Repetition
is mandatory."[4] If it were just a matter of acquiring something
that brings joy, then one butterfly or one work of art would
be enough. Consequently, the constant urge to add new
material indicates something happening on a deeper level.

Accordingly, Muensterberger suggests that collecting

is a means to cope with inner uncertainty and to curb anxiety and depression.[5] The collector often remains unaware of these motivations because they operate on an unconscious level. Muensterberger goes on to say that a common feature of many collectors is a more or less pronounced narcissism. A collection is something that inherently asks to be looked at, and hence it becomes a means to draw attention and to impress others. While I do not reject such psychological explanations, it isn't exactly pleasing for me to think of my own activities in this light. Even so, the idea that collecting art might help to alleviate depression is easy to grasp. One of the virtues of good art is that it gives to both the soul and the senses. It is not hard either to accept that someone would find satisfaction in the social status that art collecting can bring. It would appear that collecting and self-assertion are two sides of the same coin.

At the same time, it must be said that there is no clear answer to the question of what drives the collector. Is it a kind of mania, addiction or passion? Could collecting be compared to the physical urge to satisfy a craving? Or might it be an expression of the need to take care of things or to own them? Whatever the driving force, collectors often speak of a strong emotional identification with their treasures. Feelings of particular intensity are associated with the moment of acquiring a new object. But the collector is never fully satisfied. If there is one thing I recognise in Muensterberger's psychological account of collecting it is his description of the restlessness that can only be assuaged by a new discovery.[6] It is this that keeps the collector going.

Fortunately, there are different types of collectors. Some are like a bold, voracious lion, others like a wily ferret. What these animal metaphors suggest is that collecting is comparable to a hunt and the collected objects to trophies. For this type of collector, what counts is the actual hunt and not possession. The determination to capture prey can approach madness. The Swedish author Fredrik Sjöberg has written eloquently about the "psycho-pathology of collecting". But in his international bestseller *The Fly Trap*, he

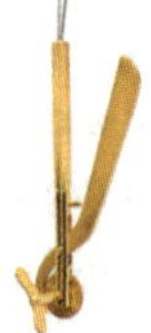

claims there is a substantial difference between collecting insects and collecting art.[7] Even so, I dare say any collector will recognise the passion he describes as fundamental to their activity. It is the equivalent of love. It is this driving force that I too identify with, and many art collectors would say the same. In his own book on collecting art, publisher and adventurer Erling Kagge writes that the first rule for anyone wishing to become a collector is to "be passionate", because "collecting art is about passion."[8]

Some jewellers have acknowledged this passion through their work. In 2003, Dutch artist Ted Noten made "My Most Criminal Piece" [293]. When I bought this neck-piece at Galerie Metal in Copenhagen in 2008, it had a different title: "Necklace for an Obsessed Ring Lover". The pendant element in this work is a tool used to cut rings off fingers. This is often used by undertakers preparing corpses for burial. The morbid reference in combination with the title appealed to the collector in me. The work plays on a widespread cliché about collectors – that they are the kind of people who would "step over corpses", i.e. do whatever it takes, to get what they want. The only change Noten has made to the tool is to have it gold plated. This modification changes the object's status from that of a useful gadget one carries around to that of something that serves as personal adornment. But the gilding is merely camouflage. The tool remains perfectly functional. If the temptation to steal a ring should ever prove irresistible, I dare say this jewellery would still function as intended.

Nevertheless, I would argue that for most collectors the act of collecting is a matter of pleasure more than madness. If the film star Elizabeth Taylor hadn't already used the title *My Love Affair with Jewelry*, I would have considered it for this book. Even for her, or so she tells us, jewellery featuring magnificent, rare diamonds had more to do with love than trophy hunting.[9] In presenting her book, she writes: "Here, in my own words and as I remember them, are my cherished stories about a lifetime of fun and love and laughter."[10] The joy she captures here is one I too have known. For me collecting has been an activity I equate first and foremost with happiness. On buying a new object, my primary emotion is elation and the immediate impulse is to share the experience with others and to show off my latest acquisition. This exhibitionist aspect of collecting is perhaps especially pronounced in collectors of jewellery. And not least if the collector is also a wearer of jewellery – as I am.

Thanks for the memory

In the literature on collecting, one often reads that for the collector the utility and usefulness of the objects she collects is immaterial. In other aspects of life, it is important that things perform the functions for which they were designed. But in the case of objects that are deliberately collected, they become detached from this utility requirement. Nowhere is this view better expressed than in the work of the philosopher Walter Benjamin. Written between 1927 and 1940, his *Passagenwerk*, posthumously published in English as *The Arcades Project*, includes a text about the collector. In this he writes: "What is decisive in collecting is that the object is detached from all its original functions in order to enter into the closest conceivable relation to things of the same kind. This relation is the diametric opposite of any utility."[11] Instead, the collection becomes its own universe, one in which the objects it comprises enter into dialogue with each other. The crucial factor is that they all belong to this one entity – the collection. This I can confirm from my own experience. Once I began to think of myself as a collector of art jewellery, it became irrelevant whether or not the jewellery was capable of being worn or whether it was practical. Instead, I began buying jewellery on the basis of certain themes or jewellery whose component materials expressed values that matter to me or which I felt had a place in my particular collection for some other reason.

It is interesting to note that, for a Marxist, Benjamin also wrote eloquently about the magic of owning things. On the one hand, he views the collector as a victim of the com-

modity fetishisation that characterises modern capitalism.
On the other, the collector represents a form of opposition
to consumer society, because, for the collector, objects
are more than just a commodity with the potential to be
exchanged for others. In a collection, each object becomes
irreplaceable, with its own identity and history. Its story is
personal: Where was the item bought, and when? Who was
one with? Where was one living, and how did one feel at
the time? And so on. But it is also objective: Where was the
object made? By whom? What motivated the maker to make
it? What defines it? And so forth. "Everything remembered
and thought, everything conscious, becomes the pedestal,
the frame, the base, the lock of his property. The period,
the region, the craftsmanship, the former ownership – for
a true collector the whole background of an item adds up
to a magic encyclopedia whose quintessence is the fate of
his object."[12] This quote is from Benjamin's "Unpacking My
Library. A Talk about Book Collecting," originally written in
1931, a text in which he describes how the reunion with his
books reawakens old memories.[13] Thus he establishes a link
between collecting and remembering. So for the collector,
Benjamin claims, owning represents the deepest relationship one can have to things, because it involves inhabiting
them.[14] It is this dimension of collecting that I identify
with most strongly. Built up over a long time, a collection
becomes a witness to one's life. My jewellery has become
part of my biography. It captures stories of journeys and
meetings with people and places. It is a record of different
phases of life, a set of symbols for events large and small
that I have experienced. Consequently, what makes a piece
of jewellery valuable to me is something very different
from its commercial or material value. Moreover, what it
symbolises for me generally has little to do with the original
intention of the goldsmith or jewellery artist in making that
work. Items of traditional jewellery often transport emotions more readily than other genres, because they tend
to be associated with important rites of passage, such as
baptism, confirmation and marriage.

Among so much else, my jewellery box contains my
parents' wedding rings. They stayed together to the end
of their days and never removed these simple, thin gold
rings. I have also preserved the gold rings from my own first
marriage and the wedding ring of the ex-wife of another
former partner. Sometimes I take them out and think about
all the conflicting emotions that are gathered within them.
Few have written more eloquently about the importance
of objects as vehicles of memory and for the projection of
dreams and emotions than the author Orhan Pamuk. He has
even set up a museum in Istanbul dedicated to the phenomenon. The Museum of Innocence is based on his novel of the
same title. For the narrator in the novel, who also provides
a narrative framework for the museum, neither the world
nor his own life would have any meaning without these
objects.[15] For the collector, it is the secrets that accumulate
in things that explain their enduring fascination.

One of the essential virtues of jewellery and other
collectibles is that they help me to keep hold of memories.
How trustworthy these memories are is always open to
debate. Memory exists in the moment. Generally, it is only
in retrospect that we see patterns and create meanings, and
I am aware that memories do not always reliably reflect the
truth. Even so, I wish to insist on the cultural value of things
as vehicles for both memory and facts. A pair of metal earrings that look like the cut-out lids of tin cans will serve as
an example [480]. I bought them in a hurry at a street market
in London on 23 November 1985, just a few hours before
I was due to show the Norwegian Crown Prince and Crown
Princess around the exhibition *Art in Norway Today* at the
Royal College of Art. The earrings not only remind me of
all the curatorial work on this exhibition and all the festive
formalities that accompanied it, they also encapsulate my
own little protest against all the snobbery of the occasion.
They represent my personal values and norms at the time,
and, in this sense, the objects in my collection help to define
the sense of meaning in my life.

480

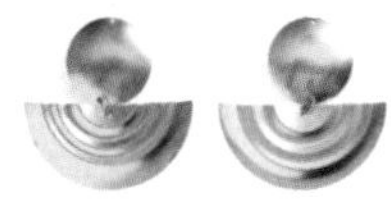

As a medium for memory, my jewellery plays both
a descriptive and a revelatory role in the current attempt
to recreate the period in which each item was made and
how I have used it. At the same time, these memories have
helped to shape and influence my own story of who I am. As
the historian Ingar Kaldal has pointed out, the act of communicating a memory can in itself play a part in the process
of creating, defending and changing not just norms and
values but also behaviours, practices and life.[16]

A study

In the 19th century, museums were not open to the general
public as they are today. One thing they offered in compen-
sation, however, was that they allowed bourgeois visitors to
study objects up close and even to handle them. Today this
is the prerogative of staff and researchers alone. Although
many museums hold what they call study collections –
accumulations of numerous similar objects from which one
can draw inferences about historical lines of development
and stylistic variations – these objects are almost always
kept under glass and hence inaccessible to close scrutiny.
Consequently I have often thought of my own collection as
a kind of private study collection. In having jewellery close
to hand, I can fetch out pieces whenever I please. I can turn
them over, feel their heft and texture, study signatures and
hallmarks with a magnifying glass and get a sense of what it
means to wear them.

"Collectors are beings with tactile instincts," Benjamin
tells us.[17] For the collector, it is not enough just to look; she
also needs to touch things. Few exhibitions make conces-
sions to collectors in this respect. Not only do most of
them prioritise the sense of sight, they also come with the
injunction "Do Not Touch". Whether shown in a gallery or a
museum, jewellery is usually displayed on pedestals or in
showcases. Such devices might raise things to eye level, but
they also place them out of reach. Ropes, lines and other
markings in the exhibition space constitute other kinds of

barriers, either imaginary or physical. And we are all familiar with the alarms that start screeching the moment we get too close or the guards who rush forward if we stretch out a hand in order to stroke an attractive surface. All these measures serve to underline what every Norwegian child learns from the song by Margrethe Munthe: "Bare se, men ikke røre!" (Look, but don't touch!).

I have nothing against showcases that isolate, enhance and create an exclusive space around jewellery. They highlight the fact that we are dealing with valuable and often delicate objects. But for most jewellery, this is an unfortunate form of presentation. The reason being that jewellery is made to be touched as much as seen. Most discussions about handmade objects stress this tactile aspect as crucial.[18] Even so, touch has become a taboo that most exhibition organisers and museums rigorously uphold. In one of the handbooks of the International Committee of Museums (ICOM), touching museum objects without permission is regarded as downright vandalism. In their list of the factors that motivate people to do this, they mention "a disrespect for or feeling of threat from the object" and "personal anger which a person satisfies by committing a violent or emotionally destructive act".[19] Evidently it never occurred to the authors of this handbook that a viewer might feel tempted to touch an object due to some positive tactile curiosity. Do such attitudes make it any easier to understand why I have assembled a collection of my own? Having done so, at least I am independent of the rules museums impose telling us what we can and cannot do. I do not have to take into account opening hours or geographical distances. It means a lot to be able to live with the objects over time. In the case of some works, it has taken me years to get to know them properly. "Collecting is a primal phenomenon of study," Benjamin writes, for the student is a collector of knowledge.[20] My jewellery collection is my visual library. With jewellery and books in the house, I am never alone.

A private collection is of course more subjective than that of a museum can afford to be. It is the personal that makes it something special. To understand how my own collection became what it is today, allow me to look back and retrace some of the steps on my own path to becoming a collector of art jewellery. Although some of my encounters with good art have entailed surprises that have changed my views on what deserves to be liked, the foundations for my taste were probably laid already at a young age.

Jewellery has always served
as an identity marker.

— Marjan Unger[21]

An interest in jewellery is born

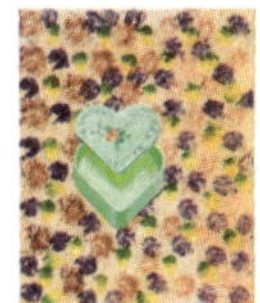

As a child, I was given a pink plastic jewellery box decorated with flowers, and in this I started collecting my jewels. I still have it. It resembles a box depicted by the painter Hilde Vemren in a series of memorabilia from the 1950s [396]. A few years later, one of my aunts sent a package from America which contained, in addition to a dress and stiff petticoat, a large, shiny medallion. I kept it in the jewellery box. It soon had the company of brooches and necklaces, received over several years as regular gifts from Lorentz in Oslo. This was cheap jewellery made of plated nickel or plastic. I never met Lorentz Larsen, but my mother got to know him while studying at the teacher training college at Sagene. During her student years in Oslo, she was a regular guest in the house of Albert and Ragnhild Holsen at Glads vei 68, in the district of Grefsen. A prison chaplain and active member of the Blue Cross charity, Albert was always a welcoming host. The couple shared their house with two of Ragnhild's siblings, one of whom was Lorentz, who was then in his forties. He was what one might describe as a "simple" soul, someone who appreciated it when others took the time to talk to him. My mother encouraged us children to send him letters and drawings, and he reciprocated by sending jewellery. Judging from photos of myself as a child, I evidently enjoyed wearing these items. Could it have been these gifts that triggered my interest?

Or was the ground prepared even earlier? When I was a child, it was still uncommon to travel abroad for holidays. I believe the first time I ever saw a person of colour was when I visited London as a fifteen-year-old, my first trip to a foreign country. But prior to that, I had attended many slide shows by missionaries returning home from Cameroon and Madagascar. The colourful clothes and bodily adornments of the indigenous people impressed me greatly. When I was just three or four, my favourite doll was black and exemplified all the current clichés about black Africans: she had frizzy hair, a bast skirt and gold earrings. I especially liked the earrings. The Barbie dolls that I progressed to later on did not come with earrings, but that was a deficiency I rectified with coloured pins. No one in my family wore jewellery in their ears, so from an early age I must have sensed that these adornments were somehow special. But in what way?

It could be that my interest in jewellery only really took root with the struggle to have my own ears pierced. It was something I wanted from the age of twelve, but my parents adamantly refused. It would have to wait until I was grown up. When I turned eighteen, and having long since moved away from home, I decided to take matters into my own hands. In short, I did the job myself with a darning needle. For me, this was an act of rebellion. A statement that I was choosing my own path, which did not coincide in all particulars with the one my parents wanted me to follow. It also marked a rebellion against the puritanical attitudes I had encountered in Sunday school and among members of my own family. In these circles, large earrings were symbolic of a worldly and possibly even sinful existence. It didn't bother me that the wearing of earrings should be viewed in this way. And consequently, I have worn jewellery in my ears every day since the age of eighteen, and preferably big pieces at that.

The rebellion that this action initially represented has become central to my understanding of jewellery's potential. "Jewellery is always about self-image and how people relate to one another," to quote Marjan Unger, an art historian who was herself a serious jewellery collector.[22] She compares the function of jewellery to that of a stage set in the theatre.[23] It is an element in the staging of the self. More than a century ago, the sociologist Georg Simmel was thinking along similar lines. The purpose of jewellery is to highlight the wearer, he claims.[24] It communicates a desire to stand out and is both egoistic and self-assertive. But more than that. The glitter of sparkling jewels is also a joy for others to behold. Pleasing others and relishing the pleasure one thereby gives is another key aspect of wearing jewellery: "One adorns oneself for oneself, but can do so only by adornment for others."[25] But might this represent first and foremost a modern Western attitude to jewellery?

Either way, jewellery can be an indicator of difference, or it can bind people into certain groups. In my teenage years, jewellery served to signal my rejection of established bourgeois tastes, and my identification with the ideals of the hippie movement and youthful rebellion.

Counterculture

In the summer of 1970, I attended a language school in Torquay, England. En route, I stopped off in London, where I saw the musical *Hair* and *Woodstock*, the cinema documentary about the rock festival of the same name which had taken place in the USA the previous year. On Carnaby Street I bought a ribbon with the inscription "'woodstock' with love" [465], and for a long time afterwards I wore it as a headband like a true hippie. In a class photo from my ninth school year at Stord ungdomsskule in 1971, I am the only one with a headband – one I had made myself using the tablet weave technique. I desperately wanted to be part of the scene which, from the late 1960s, became known as the counterculture. I showed this through my tie-died blouses, modified

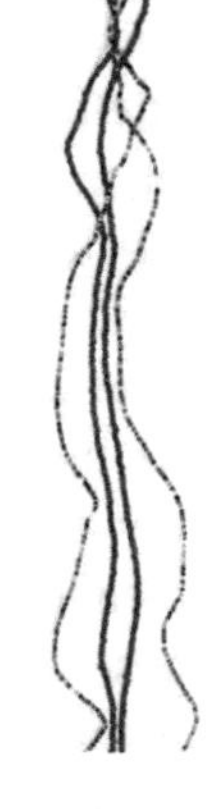

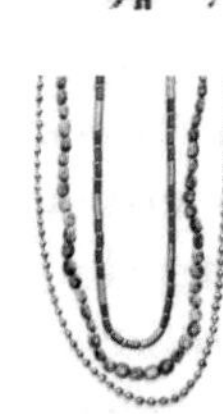

shirts inherited from my father and various garments rescued from my mother's wardrobe after she had discarded them. And not least, I showed it through my choice of necklaces. Inspired by photographs of Janis Joplin and others, I wore metre-long strings of the most varied materials, including some of glass beads that I had threaded myself [474, 475].

It didn't bother me that few in my social circle seemed to cultivate this style. It was in the literature that I found my most important friends and inspiration for alternative ways of living. This was also true in the autumn of 1971, when at the age of sixteen I moved from home to attend high school at Øystese in Hardanger. After several weeks at the new school, I noted in my diary on 5 September 1971:

> I stand out a bit for my choice of clothes. I run around in an old nightie that I've dyed green. It reaches to below the knee. In addition, lots of necklaces and velvet slacks. Or I come with a big shawl wrapped round my head, a sweater covered in patches, or a heavy pullover, size 54, popularly called the "house". And no bra. It's so wonderful to go without. Nothing that pinches. Why on earth would I want to wear a bra?

This anti-consumerist hippie was also becoming a fervent feminist.

My feminist convictions found expression in a variety of ways. Having long since discarded my bra, in the summer of 1976 I renounced make-up and cut my hair short. These were liberating steps that gave me a strong sense of expanding my scope to act as a woman. I was deeply influenced by the fundamental questions posed by Simone de Beauvoir in *The Second Sex*. The most famous is: What is a woman? Another is: "What circumstances limit woman's liberty and how can they be overcome?"[26] Among the things de Beauvoir lists as limiting a woman's chances to achieve transcendence are high-heeled shoes, make-up and jewellery. These lead to a petrification of the face and body, she claims, and serve to transform the woman into an idol and object of male desire:

> Woman becomes plant, panther, diamond, mother-of-pearl, by blending flowers, furs, jewels, shells,

> feathers with her body; she perfumes herself to spread
> an aroma of the lily and the rose. But feathers, silk,
> pearls, and perfumes serve also to hide the animal
> crudity of her flesh, her odour. […] In woman dressed
> and adorned, nature is present but under restraint, by
> human will remoulded nearer to man's desire.[27]

The yearning for emancipation that permeates *The Second Sex* greatly impressed me, and I too wanted a life that encompassed it all: work, love and thus freedom. But did it have to entail a rejection of adornment? After a while, it began to bother me that the ways I had chosen to express my ideal of emancipation always seemed to involve denying everything that had previously been labelled as feminine in favour of forms of behaviour that were coded as masculine. I could no longer accept that things associated with an aesthetic or decorative aspect should be dismissed as superficial and useless, just as I also rejected the idea that the bodily aspect of life was inferior to the intellectual dimension. I began to find it more interesting to create confusion by mixing elements of the feminine and the masculine. Jewellery proved useful to this end. Traditionally, it is women who wear the most jewellery, reflecting the expectation that she should "look good". Meaning, of course, for the male gaze, as de Beauvoir stresses. The use of jewellery is associated with this notion of femininity, but, at the same time, the type of jewellery that I was using conveyed counterculture and the yearning for emancipation. It was also encouraging to discover that the suffragettes had actively used jewellery. They had special badges produced to honour their leaders, while those who had been imprisoned for demonstrating received personal "Jailed for Freedom" pins. In addition, they sold jewellery in the suffragette colours of green, white and purple as a way to raise money for the movement. "These usages all show early feminists embracing the power of jewelry and of their femininity, not shying away from it, and co-opting it for their own ends," as the jewellery artist and feminist Rebecca Ross Russell puts it.[28]

Family heritage

Although I had no contact with jewellery artists in the
1960s and 1970s, at least I inherited an interest in crafts and
design. In my eighth year at school, we had a practical week
to get a feel for working life. In my diary, I noted my dream
jobs as interior designer or craftsperson. I doubt whether,
back then, there would have been professionals in either
sector on the island of Stord in Sunnhordland, where I grew
up, so most probably my interest in these fields had been
stirred by the books and magazines my father kept in the
house. I remember that both he and I were diligent readers
of *Bonytt*, which, in the 1960s, was an important channel
for modernist applied art. My father, Karl Veiteberg (1918–
2006), worked as an arts and crafts teacher at the teacher
training college on Stord, and I too had him as a sloyd
teacher during my fifth and sixth school years. We visited
many art exhibitions together, and he was always passionate about the art that he felt captured the spirit of our own
day and age. He had little time for historical nostalgia. When
travelling, it was always the contemporary art we went
looking for.

In our own home, on the other hand, it was other types
of visual stimuli that dominated. My father was from Jølster,
the home turf of the painter Nikolai Astrup (1880–1928),
many of whose best-known paintings hung as reproductions on our walls. My father could name the mountains
and the farms that Astrup depicted, but the picture he dwelt
on most was *Gethsemane*. The theme here is the dramatic
episode of Christ's betrayal from the story of the Passion,
but Astrup had set the event in his native landscape of
Jølster. It was a radical reimagining that fascinated my
father. Although Astrup was later joined by Ludvig Eikaas
(1920–2010), my childhood home featured little contemporary art. The exceptions were several silhouette cut-outs
on Sami themes by Sigrid Marie Riise (1911–1955) and two
large watercolours from 1953 by the Dutch artist Enno
Brokke (1919–2007). A fellow resident of Kautokeino in the
years when my mother worked there, Brokke delighted in

scenes of Sami children romping around on skis in their colourful *kofte* jackets. They were a daily reminder of the exciting, independent life my mother, Ragnhild Veiteberg (1926–2015), had led before she married in 1954.

As a newly graduated teacher, my mother moved to Finnmark in 1947, where living conditions were still very tough after the devastation wrought by the Second World War. As a result of her own experience of the war years, and later from her work in refugee camps in Berlin and Vienna in the summers of 1950 and 1951, peace work became a matter of passionate interest. She became actively involved in politics and organisational work, not least within the Church of Norway. Like my father, she was also firmly committed to the New Norwegian language movement and the temperance movement. In her work for the community, she occasionally encountered misogynistic attitudes, and she fostered in me and my sisters a feminist perspective from early on. It was only as an adult that I fully appreciated how unusual it was to have a mother who was interested in neither needlework, cooking nor gardening but who made up for it with her deep commitment to working life. For my first three years at school, my mother was also my teacher. Later, she improved her qualifications as a mature student and herself became a lecturer in educational science at a teacher training college.

My mother was from Hol in Hallingdal, a background that left an identifiable trace on our home in the form of rose-painted furniture and utensils she had inherited or otherwise acquired. Folk art and the question of which aspects of this tradition could be considered alive or dead was a subject I and my father discussed frequently. These discussions prepared the ground for my interest in forms of jewellery that reinterpret traditional motifs in free and respectful ways [368]. My folk costume is also a legacy from Hallingdal. The decorative ribbon was hand-embroidered by my grandma Ågot Tufto (1894–1992). When she died, I inherited many fragments of embroidery from her, which I later had made into a necklace [336].

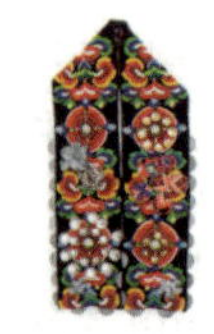

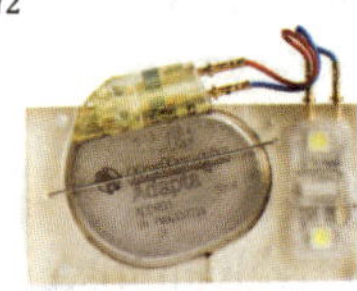

For my mother, jewellery was of little interest. I never saw her wear anything on her fingers other than her wedding ring, and when she did need to dress up, she almost always resorted to the same modest necklace my father had given her as an engagement gift. But although she had little jewellery to pass on, at least I was able to acquire her pacemaker when she had it replaced. Although it was a device that extended her life, it remained invisible to others while hidden under the skin. Today I use it as a brooch, which serves as a visible sign of the bond between us and as a symbol of life [72].

It is easy to see that I have inherited important values from my parents, but the extent to which my aesthetic tastes were shaped by my childhood home is harder to assess. Might the physical landscape in which I grew up have influenced me in this respect? This is something I learnt to view through the words *furet* (craggy) and *værbitt* (weather-beaten) in Norway's national anthem. Vast, wild and bleak is the kind of nature I like best. The writer Torborg Nedreaas paid tribute to the island of Stord with the words: "There is something truly barbaric about this extravagant lack of order, this profuse accumulation of the many kinds of beauty Norwegian nature is capable of." She even uses pearls as a simile, comparing the island to a piece of jewellery: "If it were a pearl necklace, Stord would be a barbaric and highly irregular creation."[29] That comparison could apply to the full length of Norway's coast. It is a barbaric nature that binds us together, and a barbaric landscape we have learnt to see as beautiful. Quite possible, then, that this has helped to shape my aesthetic tastes.

First fascination: Finnish bronze
When I was around sixteen or seventeen, my father gave me a necklace that absolutely thrilled me. He had been to Finland to attend a course, and his present was the work of the Finnish company Kalevala Koru (*koru* is the Finnish word for jewellery). A large, vigorous piece, back then it struck me

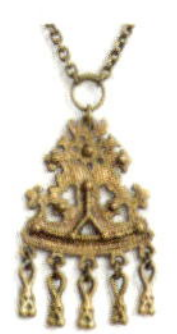

434

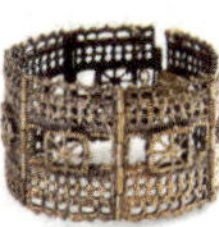

435

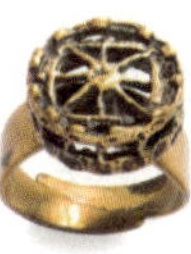

436

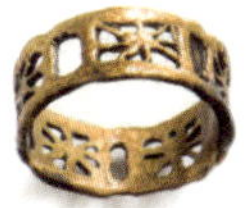

437

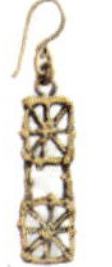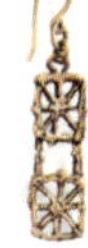

as distinctly modern [210]. I later found out that it is a copy of an item found in a burial ground dating back to somewhere between 400 and 900 CE in the Karkku region. The original is now in the National Museum of Finland. I find it very gratifying that a gold-plated version of the same item was once given as a gift to Eleanor Roosevelt. The donor on that occasion was the founder of the Kalevala Women's Association, the author Elsa Heporauta (1883–1960). Kalevala Koru was and still is owned by that association, which channels the profits to good causes. The jewellery project started with Heporauta's plan to erect a statue in honour of Finnish women. In pursuit of this aim, Heporauta assembled a group of like-minded women, and together they developed the idea of producing and selling jewellery based on historical finds as a means to finance their statue project. They named their company after the famous Finnish national epic, the *Kalevala*. With my awareness for Finnish design aroused by my father's gift, I began buying Finnish bronze jewellery myself.

This activity took off in earnest when at the age of eighteen I received my first wages from a holiday job as an assistent at Valen Psychiatric Hospital. Back then, wages were handed over in cash in transparent envelopes. With a new sense of wealth, it was time for a trip to Diversen, a shop on Stord. Among the gift items on offer were examples of Finnish bronze jewellery. Thus I celebrated my first pay packet with a bracelet designed by Pentti Sarpaneva (1925–1978). The pattern is inspired by lace [434]. In the years that followed, I supplemented it with two different rings and a pair of earrings based on the same pattern [435–437]. Could this have been the seed of a collection?

It is not uncommon for women to invest their first earnings in jewellery. Those who study the use of jewellery have noted as much. Another typical phenomenon is that women hang on to these pieces even after they have stopped wearing them. The memories they carry, and the hard work required to afford them, give them enduring significance.[30] In my own case, it became customary to mark the receipt of larger sums of money, such as a pay packet, a scholarship

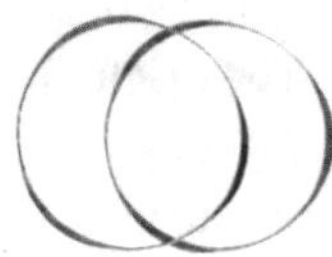

401

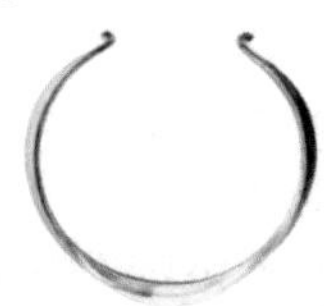

420

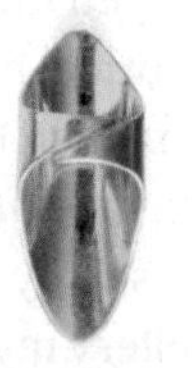

10

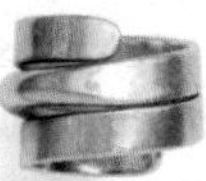

405

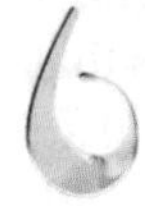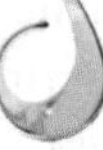

408

or some unexpected monetary gift, with the purchase of jewellery. As a student at the University of Bergen, from the autumn of 1974 until I graduated with a doctorate in 1982, I had to exist on a tight budget. But on receiving my student grant in the autumn, I couldn't resist a trip to the shops that sold jewellery inspired by Viking finds. And when Pål Vigeland set up his workshop in Lille Øvregaten in Bergen in 1981, that was my preferred destination. One year it was a fine ring of hammered silver, the next a bracelet [401]. Hand-made hippie jewellery and the heavy Finnish bronze pieces now had competition from simple, elegant silver jewellery in the Scandinavian Design tradition, signed by jewellers such as Bjørn Sigurd Østern [420], Uni David-Andersen [10] and Tone Vigeland [405] [408]. This was jewellery suitable for both everyday use and special occasions. For a long time, it was only rings and earrings that interested me. With one major exception: pin badges.

Say it with buttons.

— Jo Freeman[31]

Between symbol and jewellery: pin badges

A badge (UK), button (US) or – more technically – pin-back button is an item "that can be temporarily fastened to the surface of a garment using a safety pin, or a pin formed from wire, a clutch or other mechanism", to quote one simple lexical definition.[32] Pin badges are used prominently in promoting political slogans and symbols. In the USA, this is an old tradition, but in Norway it was in the 1970s that pin badges really caught on. I myself flagged up my opposition to Norwegian membership of the EEC (now the EU) and support for the Viet Cong by sticking badges on my clothes. In other words, pin badges are a medium for declaring one's stance on issues relevant in the here and now. Whether or not they should be regarded as jewellery is another matter. I have included them for two reasons in particular: they are an important part of my own biography, and they serve as a crucial point of reference in the work of certain artists. What appealed to me in my youth was the power of these small markers to express attitudes. For some ten years, I wore them with enthusiasm. And especially those that supported women's rights.

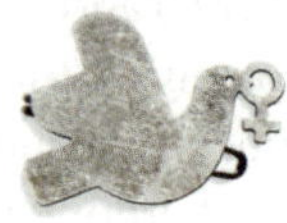

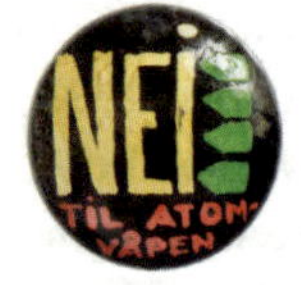

The women's struggle

Designated International Women's Year by the UN, 1975 was a busy year for the Women's Liberation Movement. I myself was active in Nyfeministene – a Norwegian version of the Redstockings in New York – in Bergen, and showed it by always wearing a badge with the Woman Power symbol. As the American feminist Jo Freeman put it in the magazine *Ms.*: "Symbol-making is a necessary part of any social movement; it provides a quick convenient way of proclaiming one's views to the world."[33] It was a view I shared, and few pin badges can claim such international success as those with the Woman Power symbol – a fist set in the centre of the biological symbol for female [462]. According to Freeman, it was designed by author and activist Robin Morgan for a demonstration against the second Miss America Pageant in 1969. In the original version the emblem was dark red on a white field. During International Women's Year, many variants began to appear. I have the device as a silver brooch and as a ceramic pendant, but my personal favourite is another pendant, this time of pewter, of a size that makes it highly conspicuous [286].

No to nuclear weapons

Beside the women's lib movement, the cause that preoccupied me most in the 1970s was the anti-nuclear campaign. Bergen's Nyfeministene often coordinated with the Women's International League for Peace and Freedom, and their own logo, a peace dove combined with the biological symbol for female, was something I frequently wore [425]. But my favourite from the early 1980s is a hand-painted badge in support of No to Nuclear Weapons [489]. This Norwegian campaign group was founded in the autumn of 1979, with my second cousin, Jon Grepstad, as one of the initiators. Grepstad also designed the logo that features on the badge. He described how that came about in a memoir:

> I designed the logo in the office of Folkereisning mot
> krig [Popular Uprising against War] in Gøteborggata

one afternoon in October 1979. I took the warheads
from the symbol of the "Campaign against the arms
trade" in an ad in the magazine *Peace News*. The "NEI"
[NO] was written with Letraset. The background for
this was that No to New Nuclear Weapons had formu-
lated a declaration that would be printed in several
daily newspapers the following day, and we urgently
needed a logo of our own.[34]

The No to Nuclear Weapons logo has stood the test of time.
The word NEI stands as an effective bulwark against the
four warheads. The colours in my own version are different
from those that Grepstad used. It was probably made for a
1981 peace march, organised by a group of Nordic women,
which started in Copenhagen and ended in Paris forty-five
days later. To my great regret, I was unable to join the march,
but I followed the news of its progress with intense interest.
In the 1980s, the Cold War was still very real. Campaigning
for peace was synonymous with campaigning for nuclear
disarmament.

A red bow

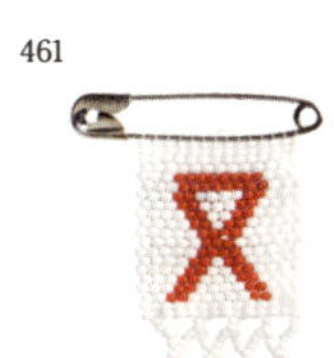

461

In the early 1980s, the first cases of HIV and AIDS were
diagnosed, triggering widespread fear. There was an urgent
need for information, and, since 1988, 1 December has
been internationally designated World AIDS Day. In 1998
I was in Johannesburg in South Africa for World AIDS Day,
which was marked by a big procession in support of people
affected by the disease. I took part and bought an AIDS
badge designed to resemble a classic Zulu love letter [461].
Among the Zulus, it is traditional for young women to weave
messages to their sweethearts from beads. Rectangular
in shape and using colours with specific meanings, these
"letters" can be attached to one's clothes with a safety pin.
My AIDS badge has a white background, which in the Zulu
lexicon stands for purity and fidelity. Set against this is a red
bow, the logo of the AIDS awareness campaign. The symbol
was launched in 1989 by a group of artists and activists in

New York who called themselves the Visual AIDS Artists' Caucus. Their aim was to devise a symbol that would signal empathy for people living with AIDS. The colour red was chosen for its connotations of blood, passion, anger and love. Significantly, they decided not to copyright the symbol, thereby making it freely available for use worldwide. Today, the red ribbon is internationally recognised as a symbol for the fight against AIDS. As a design icon, it has inspired many similar campaigns with bows in a variety of colours, often representing the struggle against other diseases.

A poetic stunt

In February 1985, some five thousand books were stolen from the Notodden public library. Those who had taken them were the Stunt Poets, a group of writers who fought for greater recognition of poetry in society. They declared they would only return the books once twelve demands had been met. One of these was: "The Minister of Culture must read a poem from the parliamentary lectern." The Minister of Culture at the time was Lars Roar Langslet of the Norwegian Conservative Party. Since he ignored the demand, the Stunt Poets removed the Ls from the minister's name and "donated" them to the working men's club at the Rosenberg shipyard in Stavanger. In conjunction with this action, they produced a "cult badge", a square pin badge that featured a large L and the name ars roar angset [553]. This they sold for fifty kroner a piece, donating the profits (with the approval of the club at Rosenberg) to the employees of Sydvaranger, a mining company in Kirkenes. The campaign was widely covered in the press. At one press conference, the poets were asked whether wearing the badge might not be interpreted as a gesture of support for the Minister of Culture. To which they replied: "This action is not political but fully and entirely poetical. The possibility that wearing Angset's L will be seen as an act of support for his policies is not something we fear. Neither do we fear Ars Roar Angset in

553

any way; we simply don't understand why he will not meet our demands."[35]

The Stunt Poets worked closely with Norway's best known and most controversial advertising agency in the early 1980s, Haugen and Maning. In 1985 one half of the agency, Per Maning, was due to make his debut as an artist in his own right at Bergens Kunstforening with the multimedia exhibition *Selevandring*. Two of the Stunt Poets, Thorvald Steen and Erling Kittelsen, had contributed texts for works in the exhibition, and I myself was the curator and had both the artist and several of the poets staying in my flat. Thus it was only natural that the group should use the exhibition as a setting for a public hearing. The event took place on Friday, 23 August at 7 p.m., and it was here that they announced the fate of the books they had taken from Notodden. The five thousand books were neatly stacked in Kunstforening's central hall and solemnly unveiled over the course of the tribunal. To publicise the event, we had handed out leaflets and drove around Bergen reading out poems from a car with a tannoy system. By that point, the Stunt Poets were already negotiating with Iceland as a possible destination for the book collection. Those taking part in the hearing included the poets Jón Sveinbjørn Jónsson, Erling Kittelsen, Thorvald Steen and Thor Sørheim. There was also an Icelandic delegate, who was said to be a direct envoy for Iceland's president Vigdís Finnbogadóttir. During the meeting, two resolutions were adopted: firstly, to send the books to Iceland and, secondly, to confiscate a further E from the name of the Minister of Culture. They concluded by issuing the statement: "Now we can LAUGH,[36] while all the Minister of Culture has left is ANGST."[37]

Artistic badges
Several jewellery artists have worked with the pin badge as a medium. My collection includes six very different examples, signed by Mah Rana, Benjamin Lignel, Nicolas Cheng/Beatrice Brovia, Mette Saabye, Noon Passama and

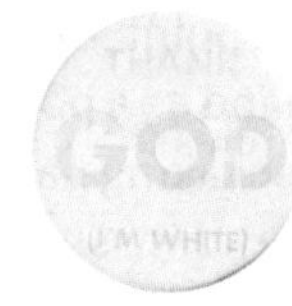

Volker Atrops. Since the early 2000s, Mah Rana has been working on a project called *Meanings and Attachments*. She interviews ordinary people about the jewellery they wear, asking what it means to them. What makes the project valuable is that it considers jewellery of all kinds rather than focusing narrowly on contemporary art jewellery. Through photos and short texts, Mah Rana has documented how people use jewellery to celebrate events both large and small. In brief: "Jewellery is Life" – as the text reads on a badge she had made for an exhibition of the same title in 2001 [**319**]. The badge is in constant production and has become a trademark for Rana.

Benjamin Lignel's design education, which consisted of two years of furniture design and five days of jewellery making, was decisive for the way he first approached jewellery as a medium.[38] His primary interest was to explore ideas about body decoration and the use context while keeping one step back from the actual production. Although over the years he has gradually become more involved in the making, the various "badges" to which he has put his name effectively stand out as a design-driven alternative to craft-based art jewellery.

Lignel is probably best known for his brooch "Manifest (Thank God)". Like other political badges, this "manifesto" consists exclusively of words. The text "Thank God (I'm White)" is printed white on white, while the back is gold plated [**252**]. A provocative work, "Manifest" is one of the few pieces in my collection I can never imagine myself actually wearing. Although the text is meant ironically, there is a real danger the people I encounter wouldn't quite see it that way. The work is from 2008, the year Barack Obama was campaigning to become US president. For many, his skin colour was enough to make them question whether he was suitable for that office. In a catalogue, Lignel printed an excerpt from a *New York Times* article as a way of illustrating the topical background for his "manifesto":

> What is happening, I think, is this: Religious prejudice
> is becoming a proxy for racial prejudice. In public at

least, it's not acceptable to express reservations about a candidate's skin color, so discomfort about race is sublimated into concerns about whether Mr. Obama is sufficiently Christian.[39]

On the badge, Lignel has given greatest prominence to the word "God", thus highlighting the connection between religion and race and, by implication, the way white people claim God for themselves. But whereas he had hoped to stimulate debate about racism, more recent developments in both the US and his native France left him feeling increasingly uncomfortable about the badge. Many find the text shocking, if not downright offensive; when, if ever, is it acceptable to play on such feelings? What signal does it send when a privileged white person deploys a slogan that bolsters the notion of white supremacy, thereby creating a racist object? Consequently, in 2019 Lignel decided he would no longer exhibit this piece.

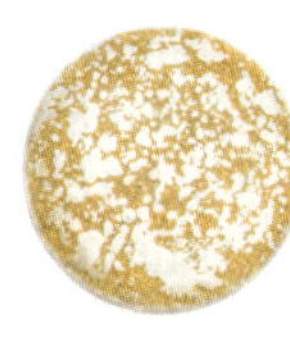

The connotation of a political message was also the reason why Nicolas Cheng and Beatrice Brovia chose the pin badge as a form for their *Gold Rush* series [111]. The grains of gold that sparkle in these brooches are taken from electronic waste. A regular mobile phone, for example, contains around 50 mg of gold, so our current enormous consumption of phones and other electronic gadgets results in large amounts of the precious metal eventually finding its way onto the scrap heap. About ten per cent of all the gold that is mined ends up in electronic products. Very little of it is recycled. Consequently, anyone who fancies themselves as a modern-day gold digger should head for the places where this kind of waste is stored. By conducting what they call "domestic mining", Cheng and Brovia draw attention to the environmental problem that our over-consumption of electronics represents.

Mette Saabye has covered a large pin badge with gold leaf, thus creating for her customers an eye-catching and cheap gold brooch [506]. In principle the number she could produce is endless, because this is a work that effectively democratises the genre of gold jewellery and the aura that

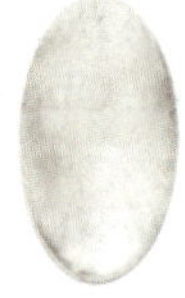

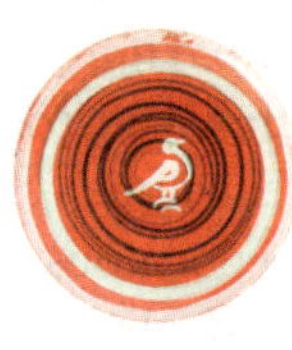

goes with it. The use of gold leaf also raises the question of whether this "gold jewellery" should be regarded as genuine or counterfeit, copy or original.

Another artist who has used the badge as a conceptual starting point for affordable brooches is Noon Passama. Admittedly, her "Extra Buttons", as she calls them, are neither flat nor circular but plump, oval – and lightweight [304]. The connection to pin badges is only apparent on the back, which is fitted with a plastic disc and pin clasps that resemble safety pins. The form was first modelled in wax using computer technology. Like many 21st-century jewellery artists, Passama uses methods such as rapid prototyping and 3D printing. The prototype is then reproduced in copper by means of electroforming and finally spray-painted. The use of industrial techniques allows rapid and numerous reproductions. At its exhibition stand in Munich in 2012, Galerie Ra had an entire wall covered with "Extra Buttons" in various shapes and colours.

As a young man, Volker Atrops made his own punk-inspired badges, which he has since followed up with several series that resemble neither mass-produced political statements nor exclusive art objects, despite often being described as brooches in exhibition catalogues. My own brooch has the title "Hiesiger" (2016), a German word meaning "a local" or "someone from hereabouts" [16]. Three or four centuries ago, Atrops's home region was famous for a type of ceramic with a fixed colour scheme and decorative style that was central to the local identity. Although Atrops has pointed out the absurdity of drawing a bird on a plate and surrounding it with circles, the act of highlighting the local in a world dominated by international, standardised and mass-produced goods is in itself a political gesture.[40] Atrops received the Herbert Hofmann Prize at the *Schmuck 2017* exhibition in Munich for the series to which "Hiesiger" belongs. In its justification, the jury drew attention to the friction these pieces produce in relation to tradition:

At first glance, they are reminiscent of domestic artefacts painted in some European folk art style. Yet there is something incongruous about them: for the underlying material is not pottery or glass, as we might expect, but plastic. A further anomaly is their colourfulness and the layering of drawings. Blotches, stars and dashes subvert the folkloristic reverie and transform the brooches into badges of street culture.[41] These are brooches that invite us to question cultural codes, the jury maintains, adding: "At the same time they offer a reflection on tradition, identity and contemporary making."[42]

An item similar to the pin badge is the name tag, which identifies a person by name or professional function. The Swedish jewellery artist Auli Laitinen plays on this type of object in brooches with texts such as "I Am Swedish" [244] and "I Am Human" [521–523]. With these, she seeks to prompt conversations about identity and nationality, not least with regard to who has the right to call themselves Swedish. "Is it possible to question prejudice and xenophobia through jewellery?" was one of the questions she and twenty-eight other artists explored in the exhibition *Alla*, which toured Sweden in 2012 and 2013. Taking the brooch as their shared medium, they "wanted to stimulate debates about identity, xenophobia and notions of Swedishness".[43]

As mentioned, Laitinen's brooches resemble the typical name tags worn by people in public institutions. When used as jewellery, the effect is ironical. For these are not handmade brooches but rather mass-produced items ordered by the artist. But the technique underlines the content. The choice of an impersonal, institutional device can be interpreted, on the one hand, as a "critique" of the fact that decisions with momentous consequences, such as whether or not to issue a residence permit or citizenship, are taken by anonymous bureaucrats and, on the other, as an indictment of a society characterised by too much conformity. Questions about identity are closely related to investigations of concepts such as "authentic" and "genuine", and consequently they produce a tension between the text and the technique. As Walter Benjamin pointed out,

the essence of the work of art changed when the possibility
of reproduction and duplication became commonplace.
Reproduction deprives the artwork of its "aura", he
claimed.[44] We can only speak of an artwork as genuine and
authentic when it is truly unique. Laitinen challenges this
way of thinking because in principle her brooches could
be reproduced endlessly. Paradoxically, one of the reasons
I like to wear this "I Am Human" tag is the very fact that it
does not blatantly proclaim, "This is a brooch!" And perhaps the same characteristic explains the popularity of the
pin badge as a medium among jewellery artists. For many,
it conveys the message that jewellery is not about decoration so much as communication. It is a means to "make a
statement". In addition, this type of jewellery asks to be read
as a broader cultural phenomenon rather than a personal
artistic statement. Since they are usually produced in multiple copies, they tend to be easily affordable and, at the
same time, easy to wear.

Art jewelry is a subculture.
It's jewelry done with
consciousness and is
designated by its value, not as
commodity, but as content.

—Susan Cummins[45]

Jewellery as art

In the early 1970s, crafts were often associated with counterculture. Many craftspeople saw it as their task "to shout out a warning", as art historian Jan-Lauritz Opstad put it in a book about crafts in Norway.[46] Environmental pollution and the nuclear arms race were two key concerns on people's minds, while the dream of a life in greater harmony with nature found expression in rustic pottery mugs and hand-woven textiles.[47] Increasing the volume of consumable goods was seen as problematic. As jewellery artist Konrad Mehus stated in an interview on the occasion of the exhibition *Kunsthåndverk 70*: "Seeing, on the one hand, a world full of poverty, misery and insoluble problems while developing various products or things on the other. For whom? What for? It's a contradiction that causes doubt and makes the desire to do something 'socially beneficial' more urgent."[48]

This was very much my own way of thinking, and I was excited about the changes it led to in the crafts field. No longer happy to produce beautiful objects for the wealthy, craftspeople began to base their work on new principles. A clear sign of this new orientation was the founding of Norske Kunsthåndverkere (the Norwegian Association for Arts and Crafts) in 1975. Under this new identity, the emphasis was on creating non-material value, i.e. art.[49] In other words, concept and expression now took priority over utility and function. Another major development was the introduction of state grants and bursaries, which made it possible for a larger number of craftspeople to work without having to submit entirely to commercial considerations.

In Norway, jewellery artists contributed actively to this new orientation, and ever since they have preferred to see themselves as craftspeople (and jewellery artists) rather than gold- or silversmiths. Since the 1970s, few jewellery artists in Norway have a classical goldsmith's training. Most have their education from the Oslo National Academy of the Arts, the only college in Norway with a department of metal and jewellery. As an institution, it has been highly receptive to new ideas in the field.

Norway's reorientation in the field of crafts reflected a similar trend in the wider world. As far as jewellery was concerned, this led to what became known as "the new jewelry".[50] The keyword for this movement was freedom. The prevailing attitude was that anything was allowed, in contrast to the mindset in the goldsmith profession, which was steeped in rules about right and wrong and highly conservative in its notions of form and function. The emphasis in traditional craft circles on technical excellence as a prerequisite for quality was no longer considered a valid criterion. Similarly, normative ideas of what counts as beautiful were also rejected.

The emancipation of art jewellery was particularly evident in the approach to materials. Critical questions were asked about the social implications of gold and diamonds, and many practitioners stopped using such materials entirely.[51] Not only is the extraction and sale of gemstones associated with war and crime, but jewellery made of precious substances has always been used to signal wealth and social status. One artist who addressed this issue in many pieces was Konrad Mehus, now a central name in my collection. Other artists combined precious and non-precious metals in surprising ways and demonstrated a new

boldness in their use of large formats. This is true of two of
the other jewellery artists associated with the new orientation in Norwegian crafts, Tone Vigeland and Toril Bjorg.
Both have been important for my understanding of what
jewellery is and can be.

Samtidssmykker – an exhibition (1986)
It wasn't until Hordaland Kunstnersentrum (today Hordaland Kunstsenter) opened its new gallery for crafts and
fine art at Klosteret in Bergen in 1985 that I truly began to
appreciate the new art jewellery. I had joined the centre a
couple of years before and shared the position of exhibition
director with Lise Jonette Gjertsen. Lise was responsible for
crafts, while I was in charge of fine art.

In January 1986, we showed an exhibition with almost
a hundred pieces of jewellery from the collection of the
Nordenfjeldske Kunstindustrimuseum in Trondheim under
the title *Samtidssmykker* (Contemporary Jewellery). Many
of these works had been shown the previous year at the
museum's own exhibition *Smykker-85* (Jewellery '85), the
first international exhibition in Scandinavia of the new art
jewellery.[52] The selection the museum offered to us emphasised developments in the 1980s and "the massive upheaval
in the concept of jewellery, which has, for one thing, utterly
turned the aspects of value and investment on their head".[53]
The exhibition claimed to be international, but that was
a bit of an exaggeration. Apart from a few Danish artists
and well-known European names such as Otto Künzli, Paul
Derrez and Emmy van Leersum, the rest were from the USA,
Canada and Norway. This is interesting in itself because
it confirms the orientation towards North America that
has characterised Norwegian cultural life throughout the
post-war period. In his opening address at the exhibition,
Jan-Lauritz Opstad, director of Nordenfjeldske, declared:
"It is typical of the Norwegian artists that they make
experimental but thoroughly usable jewellery, while the
Americans are the ones who stretch the 'rules' furthest

and seem the most free and easy."[54] The journalists clearly echoed his enthusiasm, with one boldly opening her review with the words: "Art jewellery is one of the most experimental, advanced and exciting fields in contemporary international art!"[55]

The qualities of the jewellery in the *Samtidssmykker* exhibition that were highlighted as distinctive were the colourfulness, rejection of tradition, use of a multiplicity of cheap materials and the fact that it could "be hung up as decoration when not in use".[56] While there was some gold and silver to be seen, the more abundant metals were steel, brass, aluminium, niobium and titanium. Other materials included Plexiglas, plastic, nylon, wood, ebony, feathers, horsehair and paper. On top of which there were items made of familiar objects such as knitting needles, pipe cleaners, toothbrushes, gramophone records, postage stamps, bits of rubber tubing and chopsticks.

The newspaper *Bergens Tidende* focused on a brooch by the American Marjorie Schick and a bracelet by the Dane Mikala Naur to illustrate its review of the exhibition. Few have broken with conventional notions of jewellery as radically as Schick (1941–2017). Using painted wooden sticks, she built large constructions that were anything but practical to wear. But as she herself put it: "I cannot imagine any artist self-consciously producing art who doesn't think of the work surpassing boundaries."[57] This artistic ambition and determination to innovate was evident in many of the works in the exhibition. In short, it thoroughly undermined conventional ideas of jewellery. As the then young and highly promising artist Gry Eide from Bergen had already said: "The concept of jewellery is taking on an expanded meaning. A piece of jewellery today is a piece of art associated with a person and which that person can carry around with them! It's hard to give a more precise definition of the word 'jewellery'."[58]

For me, as someone who worked with contemporary art on a daily basis, the exhibition and the buzz surrounding it intensified my curiosity for jewellery of this kind. In my work at the time, I was fascinated on the one hand by avant-garde genres that few Norwegian museums had yet shown an interest in, such as photography, video and performance art and on the other by popular imagery: advertising, photography, posters and other types of mass-produced pictures. In art jewellery I discovered an avant-garde art form with the potential to become part of people's everyday lives. Through its very use, jewellery permeated different social settings in ways that often crossed the public-private boundary. And it wasn't fixed to one static place. The most succinct definition of art jewellery was "wearable art", a term coined by Susanna Heron in the early 1980s.[59]

Samtidssmykker was not a sales exhibition, but the quantity and diversity of materials employed and the range of expressive strategies gave me a good insight into what was happening in the field. It introduced me to what has been called the standard narrative of contemporary art jewellery. In the words of art historian Damian Skinner, it is a narrative that revolves around "the critique of preciousness".[60] If there is one thing that has been a consistent feature of art jewellery since the 1970s it is precisely this insistence on the idea that what makes a piece of jewellery valuable is something other than the value of its materials.

Changed values

A classic example of a piece of jewellery that thematises different types of value is the bracelet "Gold Makes You Blind" by the Swiss-German artist Otto Künzli [235]. For various reasons, Künzli decided to stop using gold around 1980. On the one hand, he found it frustrating that customers often seemed more interested in the investment value of his work than in its content, and, on the other, he disliked the goldsmith's maxim, "If you can't think of anything sensible, at least make it from gold." Concerning his decision, he has said:

235

A "final work with gold" was created as a manifestation of this decision: a bangle of black rubber, the interior consisting of a golden ball – like a snake with a small elephant in the belly. It was time for gold to return to the darkness.[61]

I can well understand the artist's desire to shift attention away from the value of gold, but what I find most interesting about this work is its appeal to trust. We are told that the rubber conceals a little ball of gold, but to prove this claim we would have to destroy the bracelet. Thus we have to trust the artist is telling the truth.

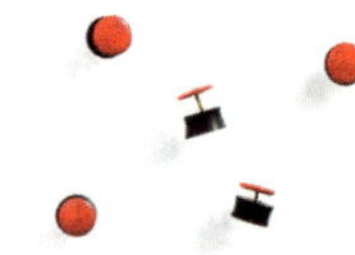

241

Another iconic work by Otto Künzli from 1980 is the miniature brooch "The Red Dot", which consists of a drawing pin and a piece of rubber [241]. In exhibitions, a red dot is used to indicate that a work has been sold. It is the very symbol of art's commercial aspect; the presence of a red dot makes it clear to all that a transaction has taken place. Künzli calls it "a badge of power".[62] During this period, he was particularly interested in making jewellery that his own generation could afford to buy, which is part of the background for "The Red Dot". The idea came to him when he was invited to exhibit in a fine art gallery in Basel. During the preparations, he was repeatedly reminded that this was a gallery not for jewellery but for serious art, a circumstance his own exhibition should reflect. Annoyed by this scepticism towards jewellery art, Künzli ended up proposing that they mount an exhibition where nothing would be sold. They would leave the gallery empty, except that he himself would be there in person to mark each visitor with a red dot.[63] Thus the guests would be transformed from potential buyers into purchased works. But the action would also turn each and every visitor into an owner of a work by Künzli – for free. This ironic proposal was not to the gallery's liking, and the exhibition was cancelled. But the idea for the "The Red Dot" had been born, and in the years that followed it would become something of a trademark for Künzli. It has sold in the thousands. Ten kroner was the price when I bought a copy at RAM galleri in Oslo in 1996.

Jewellery that questions what is valuable has since become a leitmotif of my collection. Over the years I have also sought to buy works by several of the international artists who helped to define the new art jewellery in the 1970s and 1980s. Major names besides Künzli are Gijs Bakker, Onno Boekhoudt, Caroline Broadhead, Johanna Dahm, Paul Derrez, Winfried Krüger, Ruudt Peters, Bernhard Schobinger and Tore Svensson. But in the 1980s my interest was still primarily fixed on what was going on in my native Norway.

A change of style: postmodernism
In the 1980s art changed. For Øystein Loge, a critic with *Bergens Tidende*, the *Samtidssmykker* exhibition was a clear indication of this: "The exhibition's insightful selection reflects an evolution in taste that can only be described as a *stylistic shift* in our current age. What we see here in the miniature format of jewellery is possibly nothing less than a cultural reorientation."[64] This reorientation he characterised as a rejection of the back-to-nature values of the hippie culture and "an affirmation of a dynamic, urban present, a yes to space travel and computers, to the city".[65]

The change of style soon had a name: postmodernism. In the Norwegian context, the first use of the term can be traced to an architecture magazine in 1979.[66] I myself subscribed to the former Marxist culture magazine *Profil*, which in 1984 relaunched itself as a platform for postmodern ideas. According to its editors, Arne Stav and Morten Søby, politics were no longer the in thing. What counted were fashion and trends. Another thing that was "in" was "using tradition as a convenient collection of props, a junk room full of stuff to discover, collect, quote and combine", or as they put it in their first editorial: "In other words, it's all about a freer disposition of styles, materials and experiences."[67] The dogmas of modernism were thrown on the scrap heap and with them the belief in the good and the true. For the proponents of modernism, postmodernism represented first and foremost bad taste and decline. Consumerism and the spread of television and pop culture had given the burgeoning middle class tastes that were rather different from those hitherto associated with the cultural elite. Postmodernism was therefore very much about questioning who had the right to define what counts as good taste and hence also good art and design. The result was a better understanding of culture's many intangible aspects, including the concept of art, and a greater respect for differences, whether a product of culture, class, generational affiliation, geography or gender.

While my political views remained unchanged, I fully embraced postmodernism as it found expression in art. Not the neo-expressionist trend in painting, which also enjoyed a renaissance in the 1980s; that didn't interest me so much. But art that questioned the concept of art and the role of the artist, or that problematised words such as ugly and beautiful, high and low, or which explored new media and materials – all this I found fascinating. One exhibition that has stuck in my mind is *Post-Painting* by the Danish-Icelandic duo Elmer and Bergljot R. In 1984 the pair filled Bergens Kunstforening with expanses of hanging plastic on which they had painted full-size copies of famous artworks in crude brushstrokes. "Post-painting does not presuppose particular conditions or personality," they wrote in their manifesto.[68] For them, art was devoid of meaning; the only option that remained was eternal repetition. Original and reproduction had become one and the same thing.

I was often in Copenhagen, where postmodern philosophy was held in high regard at the Academy of Fine Arts. In the early weeks of 1987, I invited the rector of the academy, Else Marie Bukdahl, and the young art historian Ane Hejlskov Larsen to Bergen to present these new ideas at a seminar at Bergens Kunstforening. This coincided with the exhibition *Nybrott* (Breaking Ground), which I had curated. Filling both the Kunstforening and Hordaland Kunstnersentrum, the exhibition included work by six recently graduated sculptors: Lone Høyer Hansen, Henrik B. Andersen, Søren Jensen, Marianne Hesselbjerg, Pontus Kjerrman and Karin Westerlund.

It was also in the mid-1980s that I made my first art investment. By investment I mean that I went to the bank and took out an expensive consumer loan. With a large student debt and only a part-time job, there was no other way. In this case it was not jewellery that I bought but a cabinet made by Liv Mildrid Gjernes. I made the purchase just before Christmas 1985, but for several months the cabinet had been hanging on the wall of Hordaland Kunstnersentrum for all to enjoy. When a visitor began to show interest, I had to act. I rushed off to Sunnmørsbanken, the quintessential yuppie bank, which approved a loan of 5,000 kroner on the spot, and with that the cabinet was mine.

Gjernes was one of the artists I found most interesting in the 1980s. That probably says a lot about my tastes. Her furniture designs represented an alternative to rational, functionalist thinking. Gjernes's process in making this cabinet was to work directly with the wood without doing preparatory drawings. It is a crafted object that should be judged not in terms of the technical skills involved but on the basis of its originality and ability to arouse thoughts and feelings in the viewer. Museum colleagues in Sweden and Denmark were inclined to dismiss Gjernes's colourful and expressive furniture as barbaric and riddled with "faults".[69] They didn't understand that she drew greater inspiration from Norwegian folk art than from Scandinavian Design.

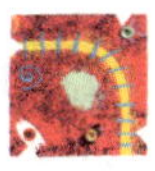
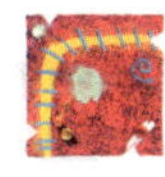

352

The first art jewellery that I bought was also an example of postmodernist aesthetics: a bracelet (now broken) and a pair of colourful earrings [352] by the English artist Annie Sherburne. The basic material was veneer, which, together with the expressively applied paint and glued-on glass stones, gave the earrings a playful, urban look. Sherburne is known primarily as a textile artist, and her exhibition in Bergen in early 1987 consisted of monumental

woollen rugs and accessories. It was she who described
her hats and jewellery as accessories, so the level of artistic ambition behind these works is perhaps debatable.

The year 1987 was important for me in several
respects. I moved from Bergen to Moss, where, on Sunday,
1 March, I took up a new position as curator and editor at
Galleri F 15. The job involved closer contact with Nordic
art circles, reflecting the profile of the institution. In the
autumn I travelled to Stockholm to see the exhibition
Implosion. A Postmodern Perspective, curated by Lars
Nittve for the Moderna Museet. In my review of the exhibition in the magazine *F 15 Kontakt*, I noted that here again
it was a matter of traditional value hierarchies being
overturned. For "what is original and what is copy when
you can create synthetic 'reality' on a computer screen or
in a gene laboratory? What is authentic when first-hand
experience of the world increasingly comes from the
television or other media?"[70] With so much razzle-dazzle,
the world can only be grasped in fragments. The preferred
medium was assemblage and collage, and anything damaged or deformed became important.[71]

The punk movement also had an aesthetic impact on
fashion and the broader youth culture. Punk challenged
the basic norms of conventional clothing and forever
changed our ideas of what body decoration can be. Safety
pins were used as piercings and also found their way into
the field of art jewellery. Another aesthetic legacy of punk
was a taste for the colour black and for spikes [327, 158]. The
1980s urban "look" was in many ways dark and aggressive.

Punk also helped to spread the popularity of the
do-it-yourself aesthetic. Bracelets made from torn up bin
liners and paper clips combined with plastic beads were
typical of the period and illustrate just how far Norwegian jewellery artists had distanced themselves from the
values of traditional goldsmithing by the 1980s [358–359].
The most radical work in my collection in this respect
is a piece by the artist Kjartan Slettemark (1932–2008).
He is often spoken of as one of the artists who helped to

327

158

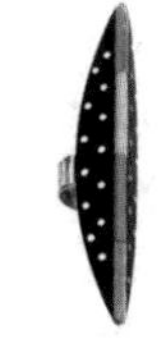

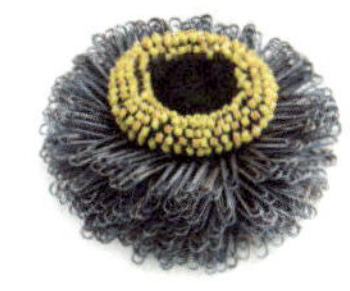

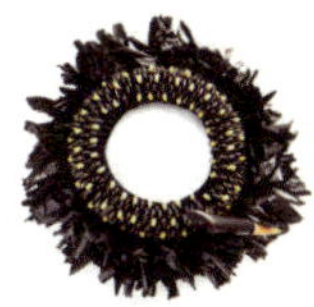

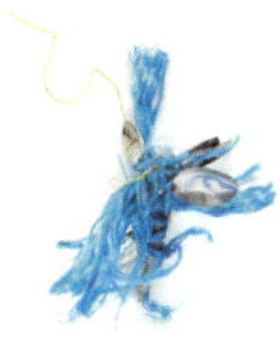

define a new postmodern visual culture in Norway.[72] In 1988 I invited him to Galleri F 15 to do a live video performance. He arrived wearing in his jacket buttonhole an item of jewellery he himself had made from teaspoons, scraps of rope and telephone wire [355]. My enthusiasm for this unusual adornment eventually persuaded him to give it to me as a gift. Slettemark hailed from Sunnfjord, which is also where my father came from. That meant we had a lot to talk about, and I told him that, according to my father, I was descended from Jostedalsrypa. Local legend has it that Jostedalsrypa, which means "the maid of Jostedal", was the only girl in Jostedal to survive the Black Death. The legend should not be taken too literally, but it does explain why Slettemark later depicted me as a ptarmigan in a series of portraits made from scrap materials (the Norwegian word *rypa* or *rype* means grouse or ptarmigan but is also slang for a sexy or pretty young woman).[73]

It is impossible to talk about postmodernism in the 1980s without mentioning the Italian design group Memphis. The group was founded in Milan in 1981, and in 1984 Galleri F 15 mounted the first comprehensive review of their production. At that point, the V&A in London was the only other institution to have honoured Memphis with an exhibition. During the sixteen days that it ran, the F 15 show attracted some 30,000 visitors. That's a massive number. A few years later, the gallery repeated this success with an exhibition of Memphis's more recent collections. That was the occasion when I bought the cabinet I describe in the preface. With its colourful but not always entirely practical furniture, the Memphis group challenged prevailing notions of "good form" and "good taste". They made frequent use of pastel colours and laminated wood but also knew how to instrumentalise humour. Ornamentation and decoration, two of the bugbears of modernism, had now become positive qualities. In the 1980s Memphis was widely reviewed – and copied. The design historian Fredrik Wildhagen, an important theorist in 1980s Norway, kept a close eye on the new trends. "Freestyle classicism" were the

words he used to characterise the new, urbane movement
he saw unfolding – including among jewellery artists.[74]

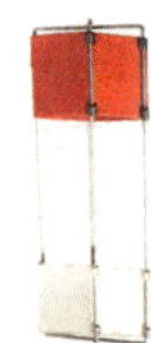

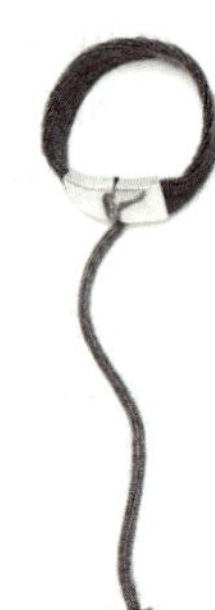

My first art jewellery

I focus on postmodernism because it provided the conditions for a new vitality in Norwegian crafts. For one thing,
Norwegian art jewellery underwent a breakneck evolution, leading to greater international activity. In 1986 the
exhibition *Designs for the Body. New Norwegian Jewellery*
toured to four American institutions. Tone Vigeland had
already blazed a trail and was thus an obvious choice for
inclusion among the thirteen exhibitors. The following
year, a new exhibition, *Norwegian Jewellery*, this time with
nineteen participants and more than a hundred pieces,
was shown in the Netherlands and Japan. "A milestone"
is how Paul Derrez described this show, which in his view
documented that Norway's jewellery artists could now be
judged by the highest international standards.[75]

Depicted in the catalogue is a brooch by Sigurd
Bronger, the first example of his work that I bought [70].
Toril Bjorg was represented by a piece of silver jewellery
with a knitted part and a smooth, shiny clasp. I bought a
closely related piece from her around the same time [43].
It was the same with the rings I own by Toril Glenne [159].
In the catalogue, Derrez writes about her:

> Toril Glenne has no less than four different knives
> to hand at her goldsmith workbench. She works
> directly in ebony, cutting out organic or more archi-
> tectural forms which she then inlays with silver or
> synthetic material. One piece gives rise to the next,
> sometimes quite literally when a new piece is assem-
> bled from others which have been scrapped. Toril
> has a technique which is charming in its directness
> and the energy it emanates.[76]

The new energy that Derrez identified in the Norwegian
jewellery scene was evident in these freer ways of working, such as knitting with silver wire or working without

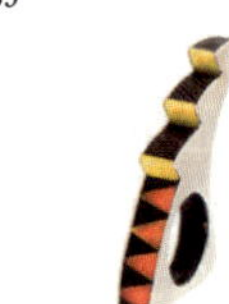

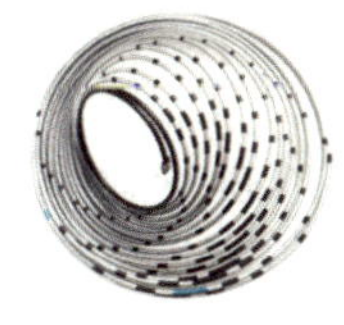

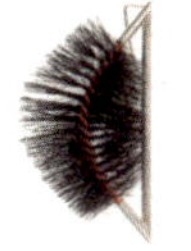

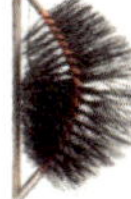

preliminary sketches, but it also found expression in the choice of materials. Ingjerd Hanevold's bracelet made from anodised aluminium is an example of both [172], while Inger Marie Berg was represented with earrings made from nylon fibre from the Jordan brush factory, secured by the twisting technique used to make bottle brushes. I bought a version of these items in 1989, and for many years they were some of my favourite earrings [28].

Postmodernism encompassed many contradictions, as is evident from the purchases I made in the 1980s. Memphis had to compete with pre-modern impulses, one manifestation of which was the Danish goldsmith Torben Hardenberg's tribute to Christian IV. The year 1988 was the 400th anniversary of the coronation of Christian IV as King of Denmark and Norway, an event celebrated in a number of exhibitions and events, not least in Denmark. When the Copenhagen department store Magasin invited Hardenberg to design a display to mark the occasion, he came up with a series of theatrical tableaux full of deliberate baroque pastiche. Visitors were enchanted by gushing fountains, columns, music, mourning crape, jewellery and goblets. Feeling much the same excitement at Galleri F 15, we were able to bring the exhibition to Moss. In his review for *Dagbladet*, the critic Harald Flor wrote: "Hardenberg has captured the baroque king in the postmodern spirit. He deploys an opulence like that of Benvenuto Cellini. And a sauciness worthy of Jean Paul Gaultier when it comes to mixing the genuine and the fake."[77] The dramatic story of Kirsten Munk, one of the wives of Christian IV, provided the inspiration for a number objects, one of which was "Kirsten Munk's Confectionery Bowl", which I was able to acquire [179]. This soon had the company of a pair of earrings by the same artist, after I visited him in his equally baroque home [180].

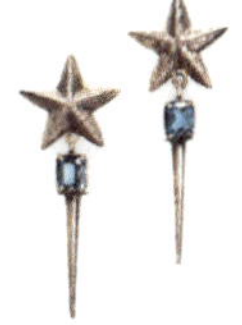

The mix of old and new, high and low made postmodern art accessible on a variety of levels. As a method, it encouraged an eclectic approach: "The Post-Modern Age is a time of incessant choosing," as the architectural

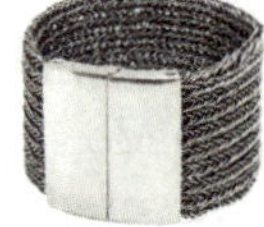

theorist Charles Jencks put it.[78] The result was a practice characterised by eclecticism and pluralism, two words with a positive ring in the 1980s.

For a variety of reasons, as the decade progressed, I began buying steadily more pieces, also of larger and more expensive kinds, by artists such as Toril Bjorg [40] and Liv Blåvarp. I lived alone and had no one else to consider when deciding financial priorities. I had a full-time position and earned extra income from my work as a picture editor and consultant for publishers. And the arrangement I had with Galleri F 15 that allowed me to pay for purchases in instalments was crucial. Each month, a fixed amount was deducted from my salary. The fact that, by the time I ended my contract there two years later, I had run up a debt of 80,000 kroner is a different story.

In the winter of 1989/90, when NRK, the Norwegian broadcasting corporation, still enjoyed a monopoly as the national television channel, I took part in a series of Friday night film programmes. My role was to select the "Commercial of the Month". It was an opportunity to display eye-catching jewellery by artists such as Toril Bjorg, Tone Vigeland and Liv Blåvarp. On several occasions, the programme's presenter, Pål Bang-Hansen, caught me off-guard by commenting on the jewellery I was wearing rather than asking about the relevant film: "What kind of woodcarving is it you have around your neck?" was his question about a necklace by Blåvarp [50]. It helped to define me as a collector of jewellery. At the same time, the platform made me an ambassador for the art form. It was a role I was acutely aware of. To wear art jewellery is to introduce art into various social contexts but without the security provided by a gallery or museum.

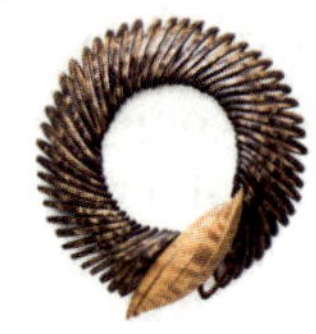

Several writers have identified a tendency in Norwegian crafts that has to do with the awareness of being a bearer of tradition.[79] For Derrez, for example, Toril Bjorg's use of knitting indicated something "typically Norwegian",[80] while Wildhagen interpreted Liv Blåvarp's wooden necklaces as an expression of "critical regionalism", a tendency that highlights traditional rural crafts but which "has an independent starting point in the 1980s".[81] The crucial characteristic of critical regionalism, he explained, was "that it points to local, often historical, precedents. Thus it allows one to maintain one's sense of belonging to local culture and history and to manifest one's roots and the locally idiosyncratic".[82]

At an exhibition in 1988 at Nordenfjeldske Kunstindustrimuseum in Trondheim, this practice was referred to as "neo-tradition". The exhibition attracted a lot of attention, and I took part in a seminar held in conjunction with the event. Here it was noted just how firmly postmodernism had taken hold in Norwegian crafts. The exhibited works contained many borrowings from and references to the design culture of earlier periods. As was explained: "Neo-tradition [addresses] a culture one has lived in and with for generations. Accordingly, techniques, materials and modes of expression are all familiar. One knows them from the inside."[83]

368

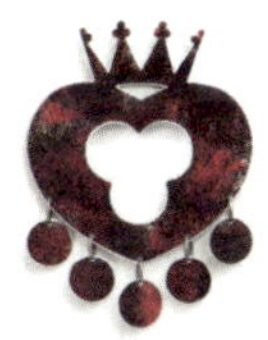

264

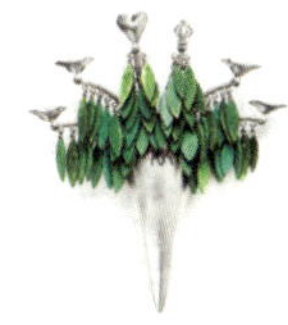

Among the pieces in my collection, this neo-tradition category would apply in particular to a number of *søljer*. These brooches are an integral feature of Norway's traditional folk costumes, and both Lars Sture and Konrad Mehus have made modern variants of them. Sture had his breakthrough with a series of *søljer* made from anodised aluminium [368]. The material was new and unfamiliar, but the motifs were recognisable: hearts, crowns and dangling elements all referred clearly to the tradition. "Carrot *sølje*" from 1991 was Mehus's first excursion into the genre, in which he successfully created a strikingly new *bolesølje*, or "branching brooch" [264]. The distinctive feature of this type of brooch is its six tubular protrusions, each embellished with an animal or bird.[84] "Carrot *sølje*" also has six "out-

growths", but they are treated like fronds sprouting from
a carrot-shaped stem of silver. At the end of each branch
sits a bird, a heart or a crown. The heart and pairs of birds
are classic love symbols, while the crown is an ancient
symbol of dignity. Discreetly concealed among the green-
painted leaves that dangle from the branches is an elk, with
the same silhouette as the one on Norwegian traffic signs.
The erotic mystique associated with the forest and the big
animal is further underlined by the carrot shape, a familiar
phallic symbol in much folklore. With this renewal of the
sølje genre, Mehus added a lusty, saucy celebration of love
and fertility to the Norwegian *bunad* tradition.

I bought my edition of "Carrot *sølje*" at Galleri Format in 1992, but Mehus has produced several versions
since unveiling the prototype in his 1991 solo exhibition at
Kunstnerforbundet. It was an exhibition that had *søljer* as
its theme, but his objective was critical: "The *sølje* project
[…] is a rebellion against established norms and everything
they symbolise."[85] This was especially apparent in the *Poor
Man's Søljer* series. In the past, *søljer* were used to reflect
status. The larger the *sølje* and quantity of gold and silver,
the more powerful the wearer would seem. Not wanting to
play a part in this social game, Mehus designed alternative
forms of *søljer* that signal who one is and what one stands
for. The items in his *Temporary Brooches* series consisted
of cardboard cough-sweet boxes with dangling elements
in the form of painted wooden hearts or bottle caps [272]. At
the exhibition, these were priced at 349.50 kroner, although,
as the title suggested, they would hardly last forever. "Poor
Man's Sølje with Golden Hearts" was also based on a cough-
sweet box (of the Dent brand) but this time made from
patinated copper [271]. Here again we find the crowns, birds
and coins, while the baubles take the form of gilded hearts.

The materials used in the six *søljer* by Mehus in my
collection range from precious to non-precious, formal
to informal, rich to poor. The boxes and buttons have no
material value but indicate a practice in which nothing goes
to waste and where ordinary, worthless items can be trans-

272

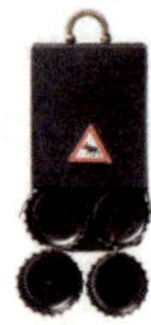

271

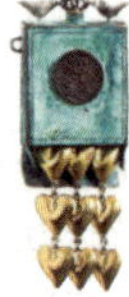

formed into adornments. These small objects also function as carriers of coded significance and as such are central to the cultural grammar Mehus has developed over the years.

Seen from outside, the inspiration of folk art is a characteristic feature of Norwegian crafts in general. To quote from a 1994 catalogue text by the Danish art historian Jørgen Schou-Christensen: "The scepticism that artists and craftspeople have sometimes expressed towards folk art has never really taken root in the Norwegian context, and for those of us looking on from the outside, this is something we must accept if we wish to understand and appreciate Norwegian crafts today."[86] Other foreign colleagues have also been somewhat perplexed by this element of historic folk culture. When I contributed an article about the history of Norwegian jewellery art to a Nordic anthology, the Danish editors could not understand why I wanted to include a photo of a 19th-century provincial bridal crown.[87] As far as they were concerned, folk art had nothing to do with art jewellery. In their own country, the history of the medium began with the workshop of Georg Jensen, founded in 1904, and other representatives from the applied arts movement. But when shown the hairband by Lars Sture and pieces by Liv Blåvarp and Elsie-Ann Hochlin [188], and on hearing how popular the making of knives has remained in Norway [280], they had to acknowledge that the history of art and design in Norway is in many respects a very different narrative from its counterpart in their own country.

Blåvarp, Sture and Mehus have all spoken of folk art as a source of inspiration, but they also mention the need to be wary: "You're balancing on a knife-edge when you use traditional materials in art," Mehus claims.[88] The balancing act he is referring to concerns living in the present rather than the past; it's about maintaining an international perspective, rather than one that is national, narrow and romanticised, and a critical gaze. As he says in the same interview: "When tradition blocks your view, it becomes scary. But as a vantage point from which to enjoy the view, tradition is great."[89]

188

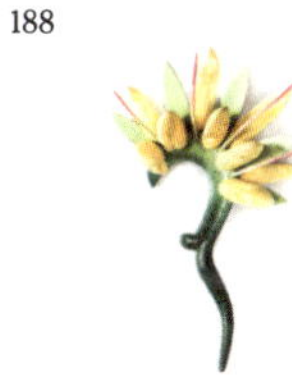

280

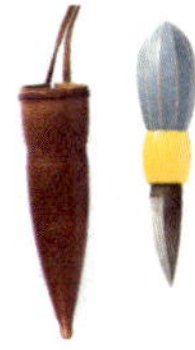

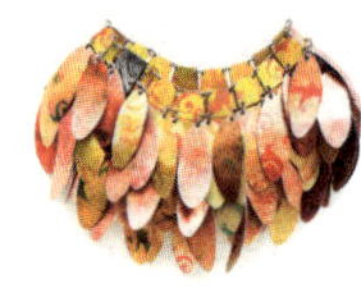

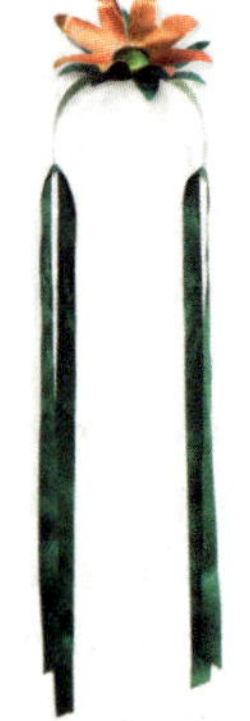

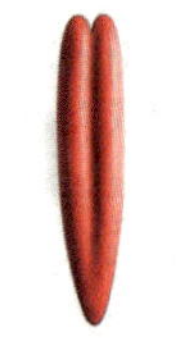

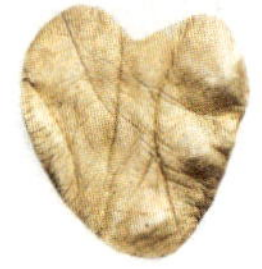

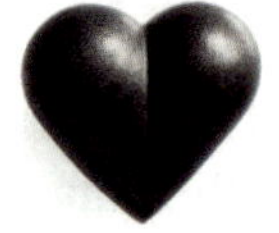

It was that kind of view that Sture's 1992 solo exhibition at RAM galleri in Oslo represented. It was a success in terms of museum purchases but was thoroughly disparaged by the critic Karin Blehr in the magazine *Kunsthåndverk*. In her view, his jewellery was neither kitsch nor camp enough, just boring and bad.[90] For my own part, I had long since become a Sture fan and had by that point already acquired a necklace that is still one of the most voluminous in my collection [369]. The exhibition at RAM included bags and hairbands in anodised aluminium. I secured myself a hairband topped with a large tulip form [371]. Working with large formats at the intersection between jewellery and clothing, Sture has been described as a representative of "the scenographic direction in modern Norwegian jewellery art".[91] His hairband is certainly made to impress, and I immediately promised the artist that I would wear the piece the next time I got married. At the time, I lacked a prospective groom, but three years later, that problem was solved. When Mogens and I welcomed our wedding guests on the island of Funen on 22 July 1995, the hairband was put to use at last.

Being in love probably explains why hearts figure so frequently among the jewellery I bought in the mid-1990s. A bestseller in jewellery shops around the world, the heart motif has been thoroughly trivialised both as jewellery and as a symbol. Even so, it remains a beautiful form with universal currency as a symbol of love and unity. For many jewellery artists, the challenge is to design jewellery that incorporates the heart motif in ways that look genuinely fresh and unfamiliar. I have some examples where they have succeeded. Synnøve Korssjøen's enamelled heart brooch is a conventional red but has an unconventional elongated shape [219]. In Carolina Vallejo's brooch the heart is asymmetrical, and its surface bears the imprint of the palm of an open hand. In this way she combines the symbols of love and trust [394]. By contrast, Kim Buck's heart brooch would seem to symbolise emotional indifference – thanks to its covering of Teflon [96].

Bourgeois culture has never been much of a force in Norway. The middle class was always too thin on the ground. The upper class was even smaller, and the country has never had a nobility. If there is anything truly fundamental and essential to the Norwegian mindset, it is "huts and houses, and no castle", as it says in a poem by Bjørnstjerne Bjørnson.[92] Consequently, the Norwegian peasant was for the most part free. In fishing and agriculture, the contribution of women to the survival and well-being of the family has always been as important as the exertions of the men, and this has given women a strong social position. But living conditions so far north have always been harsh. At least until the discovery of oil in the 1970s, thrift was a cardinal virtue for almost everyone. Many in Norway will recognise the sentiment expressed by Emily Lowe, an Englishwoman who wrote an account of a lengthy trip to Norway in 1856. In this she advises other travellers to take just one complete change of clothes: "What is the use of more in a country where dress and finery would be in the worst taste?"[93] At the same time, this free peasantry possessed a solid foundation for a rich cultural development in its wealth of crafts, music and storytelling traditions, and many rural artists have found a place in Norwegian art history as well-known names. What Norway lacks in aristocratic splendour it makes up for in so-called folk art. To this day, there are artisans who carry on the traditions, especially in woodcarving, silversmithing, knife making and Sami *duodji* (handicraft).

One can of course ask what all this has to do with Norway as it is today, a prosperous, post-industrial society with high standards of living. But there is a lot to suggest that aspects of an older, rural mentality still survive today.[94] It is the structures of the rural community that provide the model for the modern state, and the mentality of the peasant farmer lives on in many Norwegian towns. Within their respective families, my father was of the first generation to leave the land, my mother of the second, and this cultural heritage still played a part in my own upbringing. One aspect of this legacy is a mistrust of institutionalised elites and privilege, as well as the received doctrines of good taste that go with them. All this may explain why Norway lacks certain traditions relating to taste and culture, not least in the fields of crafts and design, that are common in other countries.

The outside world's perception of what is typically Norwegian sometimes differs from that of Norwegians themselves. For example, to my mind, Tone Vigeland's jewellery has more in common with international minimalist sculpture than Norwegian silversmithing, but in the international literature, her work tends to be viewed in relation to her geographical roots. Either way, her use of nails as a basis for jewellery represented a radical renewal of Norwegian art jewellery in the early 1980s. For one of her rings, now in my collection, she hammered flat a bunch of steel nails [403]. After boiling them in linseed oil, they became black and glossy. A thin strip of gold was added as an effective contrast. The sharp tips of the nails give an aggressive touch, while the gold references its ancient function as a symbol of eternity and light. In a text I wrote in 1989, I suggested that this nail jewellery "epitomises the beauty and defiance of modern, independent woman".[95]

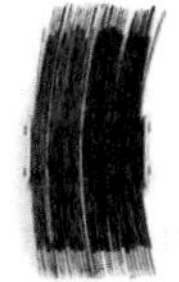

In a bracelet she made a decade later, Vigeland used another technique she has become famous for, namely a metal mesh to which she attaches further pieces of metal [404]. The method of construction makes the bracelet highly responsive and flexible while conveying associations to armour. For Robert Lee Morris, who ran the Art Wear gallery in New York, where Vigeland exhibited in the 1980s, this type of jewellery reflected "the spirit and angst of the Viking culture".[96] It would seem that similar associations prompted the American gallery owner and jewellery collector Helen W. Drutt to characterise Vigeland's jewellery as "barbaric designs".[97]

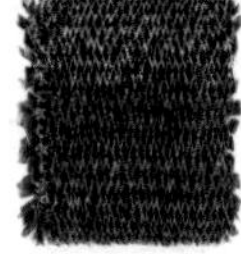

According to my trusty old Danish encyclopaedia, the words "barbarian" and "barbaric" imply conduct that is "raw", "cruel" and not in conformity "with the general rules of cultivated society".[98] For the ancient Greeks, the barbarians were "the others". Barbarians are the foreigners whose customs and forms of expression seem less refined than our own. Not surprisingly, the Norwegians do not see themselves in this way, which probably explains why few Norwegian writers have noted anything barbaric in Vigeland's jewellery. But perhaps we should choose to regard the label as a compliment. Taking a broader view, barbarism can be taken to imply power, strength and, when seen from the outside, something different from the already familiar. It is in this sense that Drutt uses the word. Vigeland's work, she believes, would not have been possible in any other country.[99]

Vigeland herself has also chosen to see the link to the Viking era as something positive, because it means that she is not automatically equated with everything that is "international". As has been said of her "body ornament" in another book: "Vigeland does not follow trends in contemporary art in her work."[100] This quality of Vigeland's work has also been noted by the Danish artist Per Kirkeby:

> Today, most ambitious jewellery making is individualistic and contrived in its originality. It uses a trick or twist to ensure it looks like "art". But that is not the case with Tone Vigeland's work. Her pieces radiate patience, are slow and at peace with themselves. And if they show few affinities to the current zeitgeist and more general rules of craftsmanship, at least they establish rules of their own, rules that require great fortitude to be applied with such calm and self-evident rigour.[101]

It is unclear whether Kirkeby recognises Vigeland's jewellery as art, but at least he affirms their autonomous value.

For me, the most important thing about Vigeland's work is its sculptural quality. In my bracelet, this is evident in the singular unified form and the absence of a clasp. The grey-black tone produced by the oxidation of the silver also distances the work from the category of "silver jewellery". In many cultures, jewellery is credited with talismanic properties. Certain stones and materials are assumed to possess magical powers that protect the wearer from the various dangers of the world. With its bold idiom, Vigeland's bracelet is reminiscent of such beliefs. Here the protective magic is the result of the sharp edges and the armour-like construction to which the metal elements are attached. But the aggressive, austere appearance is misleading. On the arm, the bracelet feels soft and is as elastic as a sock. In other words, it is full of contradictions.

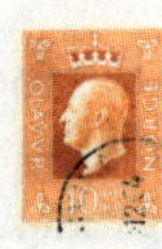

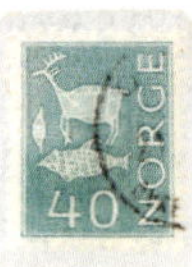

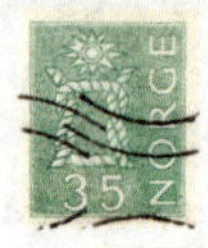

The question of what constitutes "Norwegianness" is a recurrent theme in my collection. But I am wary of attempts to fetishise Norwegianness. What interests me more are visual expressions of belonging, of cultural anchorage, that simultaneously avoid the dogma trap. These might occur in references to the *sølje* genre or in the choice of symbolism. Postage stamps, for example, which some jewellery artists have used, could be considered a national symbol [189–191]. Food is also an essential part of a national culture. One of the Mehus brooches resembles a flattened screw-top tube with the inscription "kaviar" [266]. Norwegian caviar does not carry the connotations of luxury life that we associate with genuine Russian caviar. Quite the contrary, it is a cheap and thoroughly common spread made from cod roe. For Mehus, Mills caviar has always been a part of life. When he made this brooch in 1993, this popular brand had been an enduring presence on Norwegian dining tables for over forty years.

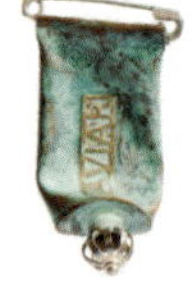

The caviar tube brooch, or "Food Container", to use its official title, was Mehus's answer to a task set during the Åkersvika Addenda, an international workshop held in August 1993. The workshop was part of the cultural programme ahead of the 1994 Winter Olympics in Lillehammer. The participants were Manfred Bischoff, Rian de Jong, Esther Helén Slagsvold (organiser), Ingjerd Hanevold, Hazel Jones, Marilia Maria Mira, Marjorie Schick, Lars

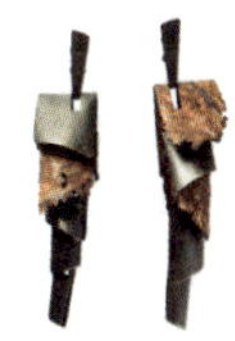

175

Sture and Per Suntum. All were asked to develop works based on, firstly, found objects and, secondly, techniques related to those used in the many items of Viking jewellery found in the Åkersvika area. This was in tune with the thematic emphasis for the Lillehammer Olympics, which was "people and environment seen in an ecological, future-oriented perspective".[102] The results were shown at Lillehammer Art Museum. There I bought a pair of earrings made of oxidised silver and iron by Ingjerd Hanevold [175] and later a version of Mehus's tube brooch, which he imagined as a future archaeological find. The half-empty packaging is reminiscent first and foremost of waste, but for anyone interested in archaeology, the questions to ask would be: What is this? What was the tube used for, and what does it tell us about life and values in Norway at the time it was created?

I myself was in Lillehammer for most of the month of February 1994. As head of arts coverage at NRK television, I was responsible for fifteen minutes of cultural content per day in the broadcasts from the Olympic town. One of our guests during this period was the jewellery artist Elsie-Ann Hochlin, a contributor to the international exhibition *In Touch* at Maihaugen in Lillehammer. In this exhibition, jewellery artists such as Ramón Puig Cuyàs, Thomas Gentille, Nel Linssen, Wilhelm Tasso Mattar and Bruce Metcalf were shown for the first time in Norway. The previous year, I had invited Rian de Jong to talk about the *Addenda* project in a summer TV programme. For her appearance, she wore a large red pendant made of wood that thoroughly captivated me. I was later able to buy it [207].

One of the valuable things about Addenda was its international aspect. Many of the artists later returned to Norway with exhibitions, and as the 1990s progressed, contacts between Norwegian and foreign jewellery artists steadily increased. I too began to adopt a more international perspective. I visited Galerie Ra in Amsterdam for the first time in 1988, and again in 1990. This resulted in the purchase of zeitgeisty works by Lia de Sain (now lost)

207

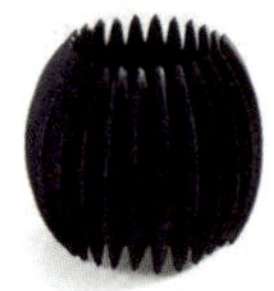

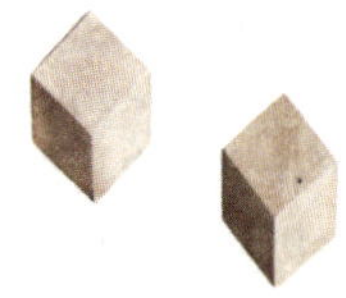

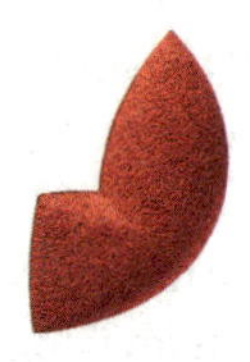

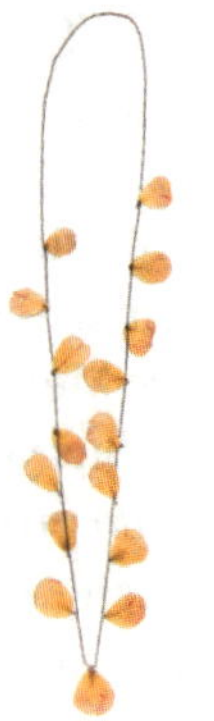

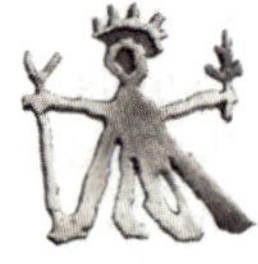

and Janke Ijff [195]. Plastic and rubber jewellery was all my budget would stretch to at the time, and it was immensely gratifying that Galerie Ra carried (un)limited edition jewellery that I could actually afford. After that, the gallery was a regular destination on subsequent trips to the Netherlands [123, 385]. Of all the works I have bought at Ra, the one I have probably worn more than any other is a necklace of laminated rose petals by Esther Knobel [216].

In retrospect, it may seem surprising that I remained oriented primarily towards the Norwegian scene for so long. But for my generation of writers and artists, the most widely held ambition was a career on the national level, and this influenced what we worked on and who we worked with. In the international exhibition *Ornamenta 1* at the Schmuckmuseum Pforzheim (Pforzheim Jewellery Museum) in 1989, only three Scandinavian artists were represented, all from Norway: Tone Vigeland, Gry Eide and Morten Kleppan. Of these, only Vigeland continued working as a jewellery artist into the 1990s. But international participation gradually became more common, with the result that the national theme became less accentuated yet more problematic. As the logo, or pictogram, for the cultural programme of the 1994 Lillehammer Winter Olympics reminded us, there is not just one Norwegian culture or identity but many [456]. This logo represented the Sami mother-earth goddess Máhttaráhkku, who is considered the source of all life. Inspired by an illustration by the North Sami multimedia artist Nils-Aslak Valkeapää/Áillohaš (1943–2001), the pictogram featured conspicuously in the many exhibitions and other cultural events during the games.

In due course it seemed only natural that I too should expand my collecting interests to artists from other countries. This soon included several from Denmark. As a result of meeting Mogens, I myself moved to Denmark in the autumn of 1994, first to Funen and later to Copenhagen, since when I have concentrated on a career as a freelance writer and curator.

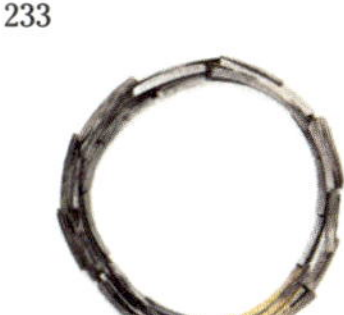

233

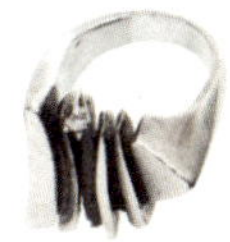

234

Denmark and diamonds

The foremost jewellery artist on Funen is Anette Kræn. She is known for jewellery that combines soft horsehair with hard metal [233]. She is also the woman behind my first ring with a diamond [234]. I received it as a morning gift from Mogens the day after our wedding, which was also my fortieth birthday. The choice of material plays on the contrast between the raw and the refined. The smooth, angular, oxidised silver surfaces are suggestive of rocks and mountains, and sitting on top of them is the diamond. In its idiom it reminds me of a decisive moment on Galdhøpiggen, Norway's highest mountain. One summer evening in 1993, we stood alone, just the two of us, on the peak and watched as the mist dispersed, revealing the landscape beneath. At that point, Mogens pulled out a couple of miniature bottles of sloe schnapps, and we began to discuss whether we might have a future together.

The diamond is simultaneously complex and easy to read. Diamonds are the hardest of all minerals, and, when cut, they have a wondrous sparkle. Things that glitter and shine are natural eye-catchers. If ever jewellery is meant to attract attention or evoke a festive spirit, then nothing is more suitable than diamonds – for those who can afford them. For most people, their appeal is probably captured by the words "A diamond is forever". It was the advertising agency N.W. Ayers that came up with the phrase as a slogan for the world's leading diamond company, De Beers, in 1947. Another marketing strategy that has proved highly successful is to link the value of the diamond to the "four Cs": cut, clarity, colour and carat (1 carat = 0.2 grams). This gave the purchaser a frame of reference with quantifiable values that made them feel more confident when making an investment.

Diamonds are a popular love gift. Not only does a diamond symbolise the desire for a bond that is eternal, it is also conspicuous evidence of a willingness to invest in the relationship. The bigger the diamond, the deeper the love. Material value and desire are therefore inseparable in the

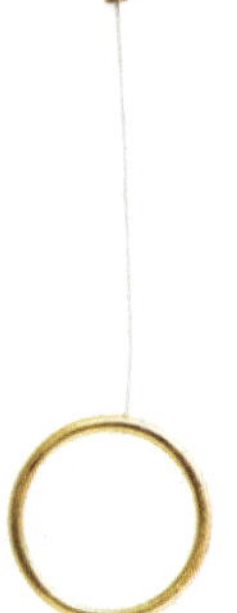

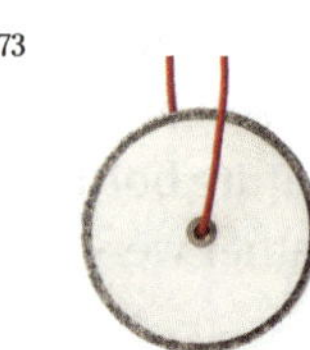

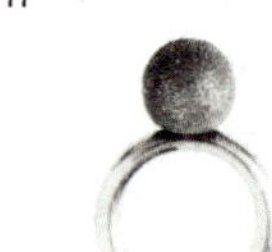

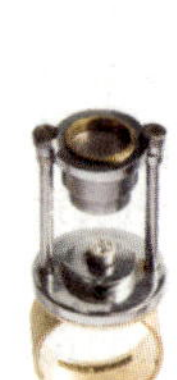

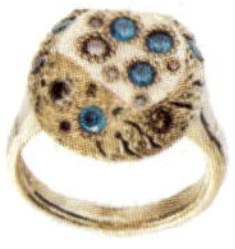

context of the enchantment we associate with diamonds. As Marilyn Monroe sings in the film *Gentlemen Prefer Blondes*: "A kiss on the hand might be quite continental, but diamonds are a girl's best friend." I too have a soft spot for the romantic clichés relating to diamonds, albeit with some ambivalence. For a long time I rejected diamonds as a bourgeois excess; if I were to own a diamond, I would have to receive it as a love gift from a man. Its size would be immaterial.

It was also Mogens who gave me my second diamond. On receiving a doctorate from a Norwegian university, one is also entitled to a doctoral ring. It was not something that interested me when I did my Dr. Philos. at the University of Bergen in 2000, but to make up for it, Mogens gave me a ring by Margaret Bridgwater. Attached to this ring is a tiny diamond at the end of a thin nylon thread [62]. When the ring is worn, the diamond bobs about like an insect's antenna.

The Norwegian jewellery artist Sigurd Bronger gave me my third diamond when I turned fifty, although it is perhaps an exaggeration to call it a diamond. A grinding wheel encrusted with powdered diamonds, mounted between two smaller plastic discs, gives this circular pendant a sparkling outer edge [73]. Thanks to their hardness, durability and ability to resist chemicals, diamonds are widely used in various industrial contexts, although the tools in which they figure generally use residues from other production processes, putting them in a much lower price range than solid gemstones. Consequently, the quality of Bronger's diamond jewellery has to be assessed by measures other than the four Cs.

After that I started buying diamonds myself, first in the form of further pieces by Bronger [77]. Diamonds are the only gems he uses, but he always does so with a critical approach. In "Big Diamond Ring" a small but perfectly cut diamond is set beneath a magnifying glass, so that the wearer always sees it larger than it really is [74]. Thus the illusion of a large diamond is maintained. This could be

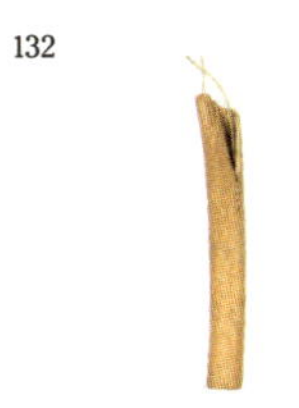

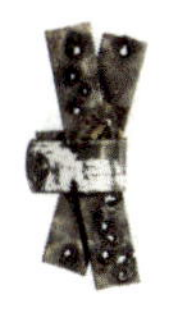

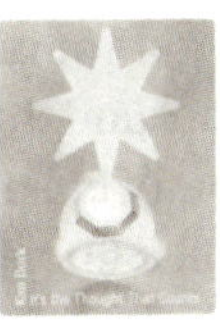

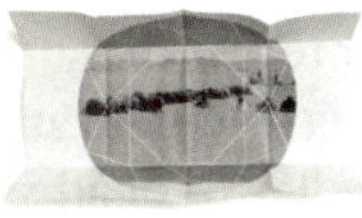

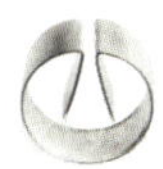
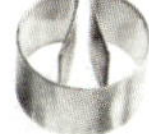

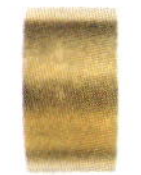
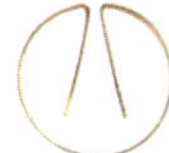

a solution for the penurious lover, but at the same time it comments ironically on the idea that love is proportional to the size of the diamond. When using diamonds, jewellery artists typically seek to undermine the commercial clichés by mixing them with imitations [144], combining exclusive and cheap materials [132], preferring rough diamonds to ones that are cut [344] or doing as Kim Buck has done: symbolising the diamond by means of a ring of sheet metal [102].

Thanks to its role as an expression of both economic and social capital, the diamond is "supra-individual", to use a term coined by Georg Simmel.[103] Its symbolism is not just personal but is rooted in the value system and concepts of society as a whole. This makes it a challenging subject for the critically minded jewellery artist. Lurking in the background are stories of brutal and exploitative working conditions among those who extract and trade these coveted items. This is the theme of Suska Mackert's work "Diamond" [470] and the reason why many jewellery artists choose not to work with diamonds.

Of all the jewellery artists I have met, the one I have collaborated with most is Kim Buck. Kim was also the first Danish jewellery artist of my acquaintance and one of the artists I have written about most often, and from whom I have either purchased or received the greatest number of works. It was he who made the earrings I wear most frequently [94] [95]. Over the years, we have become close friends.

I had been aware of Kim for a long time, ever since his solo exhibition at Galerie Perspective in Oslo in 1988. "Kim Buck is a master of form," wrote Alf Hammervold in the specialist Norwegian journal *Gullsmedkunst* on that occasion.[104] Hammervold highlighted Buck's clear, strict and simple forms animated by elements of vibrant colour. Aluminium was a dominant material, whose unpretentious, industrial associations are particularly apparent in a ring with a replaceable aluminium component that mimics cheap corrugated iron. But if the value of the materials is low, the value of the invested work is high [81]. "Labour is the most expensive part of my jewellery," Kim claimed in a 1991 newspaper interview: "I would prefer them to have value because of the work I have put into them rather than the materials from which I made them."[105] This is why he always places such emphasis on perfect and precise workmanship. The materials might be non-precious, but their value is greatly enhanced by the work process.

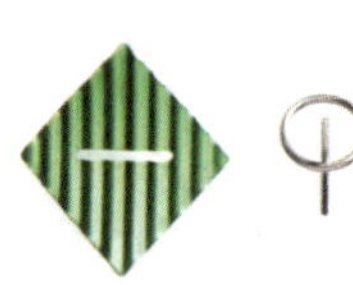

The article in *Gullsmedkunst* also praised Kim's ability to find new solutions to classical problems. The form often represents an answer to a practical problem, or the construction becomes the content [85]. One of Kim's central concerns at that time was finding logical ways to fasten things and materials without the use of solder, glue or pins. One such problem is that of fastening clothes around the body. One of the oldest jewellery items we know of is a pin that was used to hold textiles together, a so-called fibula, which comes from the Latin *figere*, meaning "to attach". Kim has developed his own twist on this classic theme. The fibula in my collection consists of a silver disc with a round hole in the middle and a rectangular recess that holds the head of a loose needle [84]. Pinching some fabric through the hole, one pierces it with the needle, the head of which slots into the recess in the disc, thus holding everything in place. It is a useful, self-explanatory object that neatly references its historical ancestors.

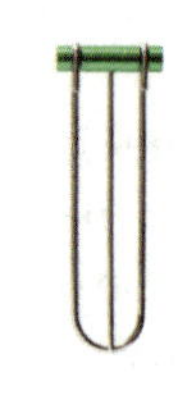

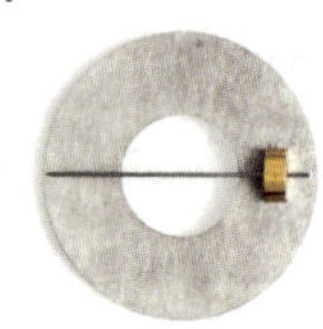

Kim and I share an interest in jewellery as a cultural signifier. Over the years, his work has developed in an increasingly conceptual direction, which means that the aspect of functionality has become less relevant. In 2002, when Aarhus Kunstbygning invited me to propose an artist for the exhibition *De utvalgte* (The Chosen), my choice fell on Kim. The other contributors were all fine artists. Mixing crafts with fine arts is not always a popular strategy, and at a reception for the nominators and nominees, one of my colleagues from the fine arts field demonstratively refrained from greeting either Kim or myself. But the institution was clearly in favour of Kim's participation, and he responded superbly to the task he was set: to explore what jewellery and jewellery art are and can be. One of his starting points was the advertising slogan "Real gold, real joy".

The ad tries to convince us that joy can be bought. The goldsmithing sector lives from the symbolic function of jewellery in various rites of passage. Not least, jewellery plays a crucial role as an expression of love. Real gold connotes real emotions. Durability conveys promises such as "yours forever", while the material value serves as both a visible and a symbolic expression of the investment one person is willing to make in their relationship to another. For people like Kim, who pursue an artistic goal in their work, industrially mass-produced and standardised goods represent a major challenge. For the artist, it is not enough to replicate clichés, even though he too wants his work to convey understandable codes within the social game. Accordingly, Kim devised a variety of interpretations of the standard repertoire, one of which took another cliché as its title: "It's the Thought That Counts". As one of the central works in Kim's production, this was later selected for the European touring exhibition *Gifts*.[106] Sadly, it is not in my collection.

"It's the Thought That Counts" consists of two small boxes. One contains a red heart, the other a number of loose diamonds arranged in a ring. It is an ambiguous work that mocks the common focus in the jewellery sector on monetary value and carats while simultaneously emphasising jewellery's function as a symbolic expression of emotion. In the artist's own experience, potential buyers and gift-givers frequently rank investment value above his personal creative input, to a disturbing extent even. What these boxes contain is, therefore, not wearable jewellery but "the pure commodity". "It might seem almost absurd to be concerned with matters in which we play no part and that we seemingly cannot influence, but it fascinates me to describe these values and demonstrate them visually through the medium of jewellery from which they spring," Kim noted at the time.[107] And he added:

In my work with jewelry in recent years, I have endeavored to focus on and illustrate the mechanisms at work in our dealings with jewelry, for the wearer himself and between the wearer and the world around him. As a goldsmith, I have no part in creating these values for a piece of jewelry and the values are just as great or 'genuine' in a mass-manufactured piece from a jewelry-store chain as they are in a ring that was created as a result of an artistic and craftsmanly process on a high level.[108]

The following year, in 2003, he made a jewellery vending machine. When I fed it with three twenty-krone coins, it spat out a box containing a folded "gold bracelet". The purchase was as straightforward and mundane as buying a packet of cigarettes or condoms. Admittedly, the material used was not genuine gold but rather gold-coloured plastic foil. The package also included a straw, which was needed to inflate the bracelet, and the printed warning "Gold can damage your morals". The typography and layout matched the health warnings on cigarette packets [105]. The irony is directed at each and every one of us, susceptible as we are to the tricks and conventions of advertising. As the decade progressed, this kind of meta-jewellery, i.e. jewellery about jewellery, became a central element of Kim's practice [87].

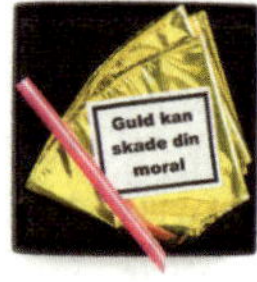

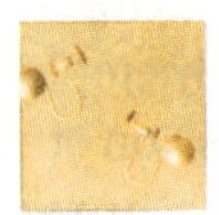

Three Nordic exhibitions
Shortly after moving to Denmark, I was contacted by the jewellery artist Jan Lohmann, the driving force behind efforts to establish a Nordic jewellery triennial. By that point, Lohmann had been running Galerie Metal in Copenhagen for some twenty-odd years, an establishment that had become the go-to venue for new jewellery art in Scandinavia. Lohmann succeeded with his plan. When Copenhagen took its turn as European Capital of Culture in 1996, one of the items on the programme was the first Nordic Jewellery Triennial, which opened in January at the Danish Museum of Decorative Art (now Designmuseum

Danmark). The queue of people wanting to attend the opening stretched far down Bredegade, and the exhibition duly received considerable media coverage. Together with the art historian Lise Funder, Lohmann also edited an extensive book with historical articles about the development of art jewellery in the Nordic countries and presentations of the participating artists. Although I was the one who contributed the text on Norwegian jewellery,[109] I was unable to buy physical mementoes of the event in the form of jewellery. Nonetheless, the exhibition was important for me in so far as it heightened my interest for jewellery artists from elsewhere in the Nordic region. One set of works I found particularly fascinating comprised Janna Syvänoja's brooches made from the pages of telephone directories [383].

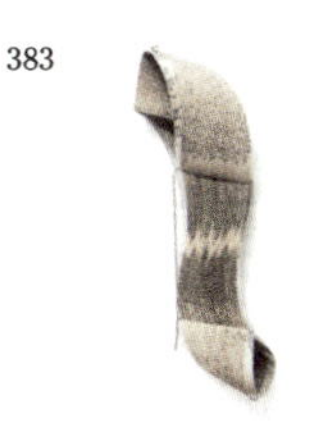

The aim of establishing a regular triennial in the Nordic region has proved difficult to achieve. Six years would pass before the second event at the Röhsska Museum in Gothenburg, where again it was artists who were the driving force. This time, most of the twenty-six invited artists had made their debut in the 1990s, thus representing a younger generation than those who took part in 1996. In addition, there were participants from Estonia and a contribution by Vivianna Torun Bülow-Hübe as a "smith of honour". I wrote the main article for the accompanying catalogue,[110] and this time I managed to buy three works as mementoes of the project: a brooch by Castello Hansen [177], another by Per Suntum [374] and a necklace by Hilde Dramstad [125].

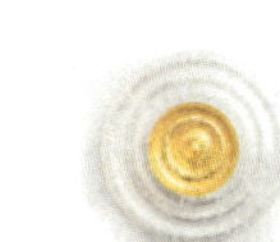

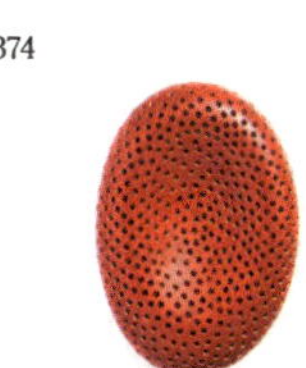

Writing brings insight, and it is often the act of writing about a work or an artist's production that triggers in me the desire to own. Hansen and Dramstad represented the outer poles in a debate that preoccupied me around the year 2000. This is best summed up by the Belgian theorist Thierry de Duve, who points out that the classical values make little sense in the context of fine art post Duchamp. The statement "this is beautiful" has been replaced, he claims, by "this is art" in modern evaluations of art.[111] I could not accept this either-or attitude. To my mind, both statements deserved consideration, not least because

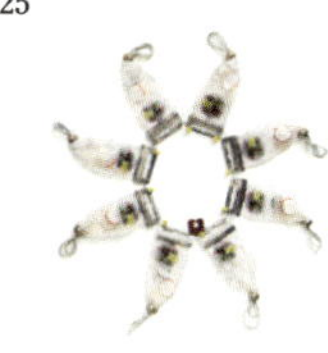

beauty and art are both very fluid concepts in Western thought. In an article in the magazine *Kunsthåndverk* in 1999, I wrote:

> We have dutifully packed away terms such as beauty, beautiful and attractive as words that are taboo in professional jargon. Instead, the beautiful has been allowed to flourish unconstrained in other arenas: in fashion, advertising, interior design magazines. Such media continue to serve a longing for beauty, which I for one am convinced exists in us all. Not as a need for certain rules of harmony and balance, or as something that transcends time and class. What we perceive as beautiful is highly variable and culturally dependant, yet our need for it remains.[112]

On returning to this discussion a few years later in the book *Craft in Transition*, it was precisely as a tribute to beauty that I interpreted Hansen's brooch.[113] With its combination of gold, silver and transparent acrylic, it is an object that *shines*. In Norwegian, the word for beautiful is *skjønn* (pronounced roughly like the German *schön*), a word with the same etymological root as English "shine". *Skjønn* comes from Low German *schōne*, meaning "beautiful", "light", "clear", and can be traced even further back to a root meaning "conspicuous" and "brilliant". Thus "the beautiful" is something that shines. The type of beauty that relates to brilliance and light is central to the art of jewellery. The use of sparkling gemstones and shiny materials such as silver and gold is hard to interpret without assuming a desire to create something beautiful that serves as a tribute to beauty as a value.

In the early 2000s, the concept of beauty found its way back into art discourse. To quote the Danish writer Inga R. Gammel: "As a phenomenon, beauty is the salt of life. Without it one might exist, but one doesn't live."[114] The American philosopher Arthur C. Danto puts it like this: "Beauty is an option for art and not a necessary condition. But it is not an option for life. It is a necessary condition for life as we would want to live it. That is why beauty, unlike the other

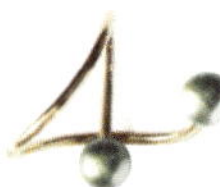

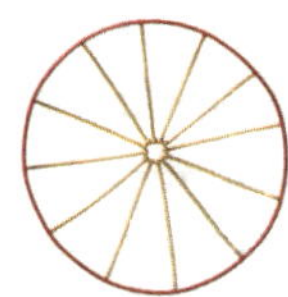

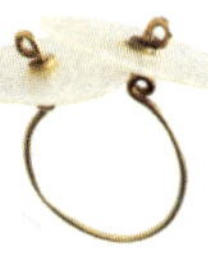

aesthetic qualities, the sublime included, is a value."[115] This attitude was also becoming evident in the field of art jewellery. Precious metal began to make a comeback and ornament and concept were no longer viewed as mutual contradictions.[116] Some of my jewellery was bought for the simple reason that I found it beautiful. These are pieces that triggered all the physical responses we associate with beauty: gasps, goose bumps, a twinge in the diaphragm. Stendahl syndrome is something I can easily identify with. In Denmark, where many jewellery artists are still trained as goldsmiths and craftsmanship still holds prestige, there is a greater acceptance of beauty as value, and hence also of the kind of aesthetic that features gold, pearls and mother-of-pearl [215, 150, 323].

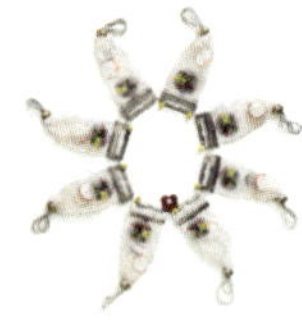

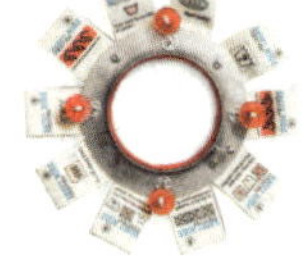

At the same time, I am equally interested in jewellery that is critical, makes a statement or has a story to tell. In the late 1990s, narrative jewellery was one of the principal new directions in international art jewellery. As a category that was well represented at the second Nordic Jewellery Triennial, it was here that Dramstad's work belonged. One of the works she presented at the show was the necklace "White Wedding" [125]. This consists of several small wash bags containing antacid tablets. Each bag also carries a label with the advertising slogan "My mammy always washes with Ivory Snow" and a picture of an archetypical 1950s housewife. With its "pictures and banalities from everyday life", "White Wedding" is typical of Dramstad's work from this period.[117] Her first solo exhibition at Kunstnerforbundet in Oslo in the spring of 2000 was a roaring success. Of the eighteen works on display – necklaces, brooches and rings – she sold virtually everything, including the brooch "Good Advice 2" to me [124]. The title of the exhibition was *Dry Clean Only*, a phrase that suggested objects made from fragile materials that need careful handling. In other words, Dramstad does not make durable jewellery for everyday use. At the same time, the title alluded to the labels and messages that are usually hidden within our clothes. In today's welter of consumer goods,

such labels play an ever more obtrusive role. Dramstad's
jewellery plays on the design language of these labels, to
which she invariably adds a twist. The labels Dramstad
uses in "Good Advice 2", for example, are not from items
bought in shops; instead she has designed them herself.
The texts are of her own formulation, while the fonts and
symbols reflect the graphic styles of labels she has "sam-
pled" and manipulated on the computer. She then prints
her designs directly onto textiles and plastics, thus putting
her personal imprint on these materials. Despite its socially
critical aspect, what we register in Dramstad's jewellery is
humour rather than chastisement.

The public had to wait even longer for the triennial's
third incarnation, but when at last it came, it enjoyed the
heavyweight institutional backing of the National Museum
in Oslo and was accompanied by an extensive publication.[118] *From the Coolest Corner. Nordic Jewellery* opened in
Oslo on 19 January 2013. It was preceded by a two-day international symposium at the Oslo National Academy of the
Arts. This included many artist presentations: Sofia Björkman, Kim Buck, Jantje Fleischhut, Stefan Heuser, Helena
Lehtinen, Yuka Oyama, Karen Pontoppidan and Manuel
Vilhena. In addition, there were lectures by theorists,
including Liesbeth den Besten, Marjan Unger and myself.
Artists from all Nordic countries, again including Estonia,
had been encouraged to submit material. I was a member of
the jury, which selected a total of 156 works by sixty-one art-
ists. And finally, we invited a guest artist from each country:
Kim Buck, Helena Lehtinen, Konrad Mehus, Kadri Mälk and
Tore Svensson.

At the time, I was heading a research project at the
Bergen National Academy of the Arts: *Creating Art Value.
A Research Project on Rubbish and Ready-mades, Art and
Ceramics.* The ability of artists to transform found objects
and other bric-a-brac into new art has always fascinated me,
and, as both a theme and a material, "rubbish" is a common
denominator in many of the pieces in my collection. One of
them was shown in *From the Coolest Corner.* Marie-Louise

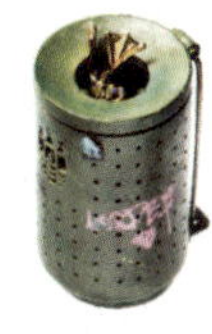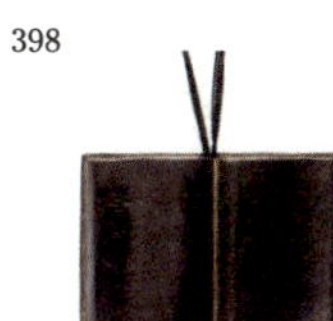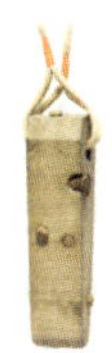

Kristensen's brooch "Cph: Faire la féte – et après" [226]. The motif is an exact miniature model of a municipal rubbish bin of the kind found in Copenhagen. An object familiar to every resident of the Danish capital, they are often filled to the brim with debris from outdoor parties.

Tanel Veenre's neckpiece "In the Beginning Was the Word", the second work I bought from the exhibition [398], conveys a very different mood. The pendant is shaped like an open book but without text, while the cord that goes around the neck resembles a bookmark ribbon. This is not a book but the image of a book. As one of the other jury members, Liesbeth den Besten, wrote in the catalogue: "To wear a book as a necklace is like a subversion of the object."[119] The material is jet, sometimes referred to as black amber due to its many similarities to the latter. Some of the jewellery that has survived from the Viking era was made from jet, but today the material is rarely used. Some people believe the stone has healing properties, or that it protects against evil spirits and negative energies. Accordingly, my first associations on seeing the material and the motif were grimoires, ancient volumes of arcane knowledge and witchcraft, which are known in the Scandinavian languages as "black books". Many of these circulated widely in Europe from the Middle Ages on. But by choosing the opening words of the Gospel of John for his title, it is more likely the artist had the Bible in mind.

My own contribution to the catalogue addressed a very different topic, namely the use of wood.[120] Two years before, I had bought a necklace by Tobias Alm, "Traces of Function 11.19" [8]. Alm participated in the triennial with several works from the same series. The choice of wood as a material is often seen as "typically Scandinavian". It is a perception that can be traced back to the aesthetic ideals of Scandinavian Design, a label conferred by various American commentators in the 1950s. With its respect for functionality and natural materials, this type of design made plentiful use of unpainted wood. As early as the first Nordic Jewellery Triennial, several reviews remarked on the prevalence of natural motifs and materials. This, it was

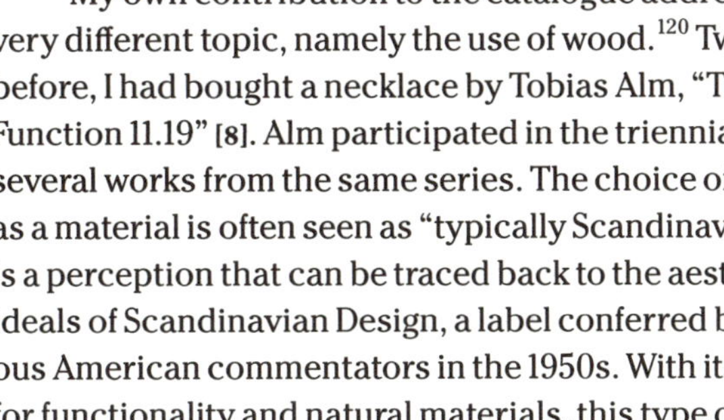

claimed, reflected the close relationship Scandinavians enjoy with nature. It is a view that Alm plays on. The components in "Traces of Function" are various pieces of wood that are either connected by joints or tied together with cotton thread. In the world of carpentry, chiselled grooves and recesses are common features of construction that need no explanation – their function is obvious. The same cannot be said when they appear in jewellery. But as so often when artists adopt materials or elements from other fields of activity and treat them as raw material for their creative pursuits, the aim is to draw attention to practices external to art. Effectively, Alm is creating a visual idiom from elements that were not intended for artistic use. Things from everyday life that usually pass unnoticed are brought into sharper focus and invested with new value. "Traces of Function" is a piece that confronts the carpenter with the artist, the useful and the practical with the "superfluous" and the aesthetic. It addresses the various purposes of work as such. This, far more than the relationship to nature, is the discourse that underlies Alm's use of wood.

Coolest Corner featured so much jewellery using various types of wood that it seemed almost like a renaissance. There were probably several reasons for this. In a period of economic crisis when the price of gold, other precious metals and gemstones are at record highs, wood is a cheap alternative. It is also easy to get hold of in most places. Recent decades have seen an increased focus on where materials come from, and whether production and further processing have been achieved in an environmentally responsible and sustainable manner. Here again, wood ticks the boxes. Summarising the connotations of wood as a choice of material, we end up with a list of terms such as tradition, commonplace, affordable, readily available, sustainable and organic. These are values that matter to me too, and my collection contains wooden jewellery signed by several of the contributors to *Coolest Corner*, from Liv Blåvarp [52] and Helena Lehtinen [250] to Tanel Veenre [397] and the aforementioned Tobias Alm.

52

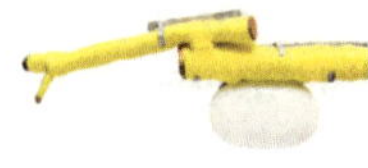

250

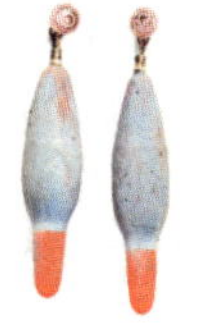

397

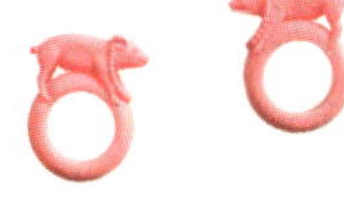

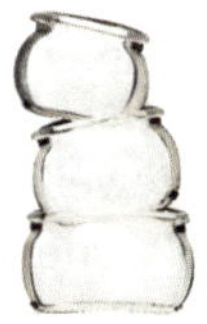

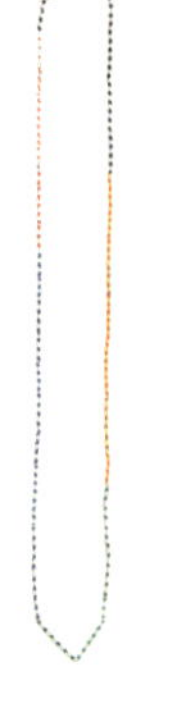

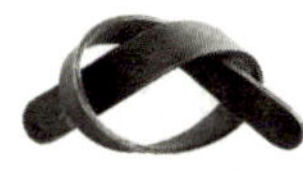

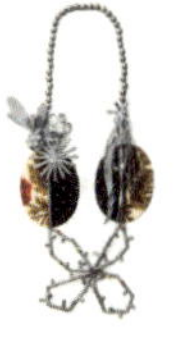

The world is opening up

In parallel with *From the Coolest Corner*, a number of galleries and museums in Oslo mounted jewellery exhibitions of their own, some with an international profile, such as *Aftermath of Art Jewellery* at the Vigeland Museum, initiated by Sigurd Bronger,[121] and *Below Sea Level – Jewellery from the Netherlands*, curated by Liesbeth den Besten at Galleri Format. At the latter, many, including myself, took the opportunity to acquire one of Ted Noten's "Miss Piggy" rings through a process of exchange [297]. Here, five hundred pink rings were mounted on the wall in an arrangement resembling a handgun. Visitors were invited to take one of them by swapping it for a ring they had brought with them. What mattered here was not whether the contributed item was cheap or expensive but the fact that people were swapping old stories for new ones. After a while, the image of the gun, a symbol of aggression, evolved into something more diffuse and varied in content. The portrait that emerged of Oslo's inhabitants was, however, somewhat less than flattering. The trust and generosity that the artist showed with the invitation "Wanna Swap Your Ring", as the work was called, were reciprocated with rings made from steel wire, straw, hair ties and one-krone coins (which have a central hole). One was left with an impression of greed and miserliness. And this was precisely what the project aimed to achieve: to discover what it would reveal about a city when its residents arranged their rings side by side.

Below Sea Level contained many temptations, such as the brooch "Kitchen Glass no. 26" by Gésine Hackenberg [163] and the necklace "Out of the Office" by Manon van Kouswijk. The latter is made from the plastic sheaths of industrially produced paperclips [224]. Lucy Sarneel's pin brooch "Knot" should perhaps be regarded more as a souvenir and was bought as a gift for Mogens from this outing [332]. But at the stand set up by Galerie Marzee during the conference, I bought a seminal piece by the same artist, the necklace "La Double Vie" [337]. The combination of textile and zinc is typical of Sarneel's work. What all these purchases have in

common is that their materials reference everyday objects
such as storage jars, office supplies and consumer textiles.

I have often bought work by international artists at
exhibitions they have held in Norway, ranging from Annie
Sherburne and Rian de Jong to Otto Künzli and, again, Lucy
Sarneel. Meetings with artists in various contexts have often
prompted an interest in their work that led to a purchase. In
the year 2000, Onno Boekhoudt and I were examiners at the
Academy of Art and Design (HDK) in Gothenburg [54]. This
was the first college in Scandinavia to define art jewellery as
its primary focus. The decision was taken in 1992, when Tore
Svensson and Christer Johnsson were working in the Metal
Department. Svensson was also one of the driving forces
behind Galleri Hnoss, where Boekhoudt had an exhibition
during the days I was there in the role of examiner. One of
the important themes of his work is holes. "The hole, being
busy with nothing, that's liberating," he has said. It is quite
simply the essence of jewellery: "The hole is inside of the
piece, it touches the body, is intimate and personal."[122] In
the ring of his in my collection, the hole has the shape of a
house. When not in use as "room for a finger", it can be filled
with a tiny wooden house of the same shape and dimensions as the hole. He has made a hundred versions of this
ring, with the houses painted in different colours. Since
I was living in a yellow house at the time, that was the colour
I chose. In use, the ring provides an architectural space for
the finger, but it is also an anti-ring. It is an uncomfortable
item to wear, as Boekhoudt himself readily admitted.

Meeting artists or hearing them talk about their work
has often made me want to learn more. The group behind
Galleri Hnoss were skilful in persuading international artists
to exhibit and, in many cases, to accompany their shows
with lectures or workshops. In 2004, for example, I met Nel
Linssen for the first time during an exhibition of her work in
Gothenburg. Mogens had already bought a bracelet of hers
at Galerie Ra several years earlier [259], and at Hnoss I bought
myself a necklace [260]. With paper as her main material, Linssen was a master at producing finely tuned colour schemes.

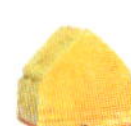
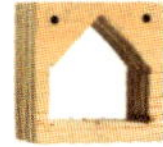

54

259

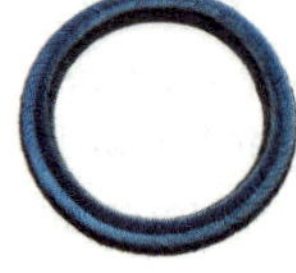

260

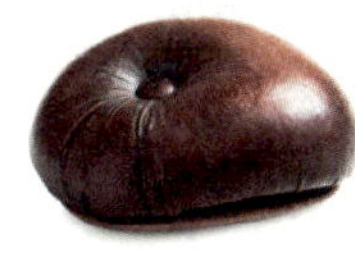

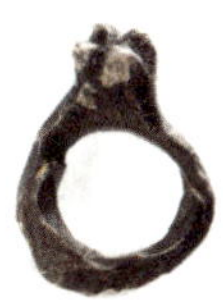

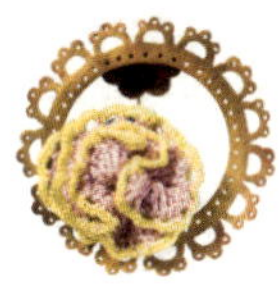

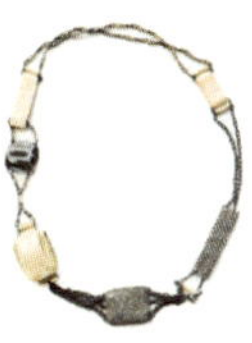

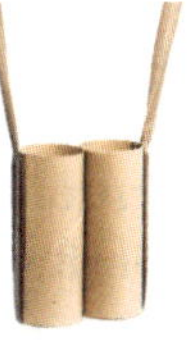

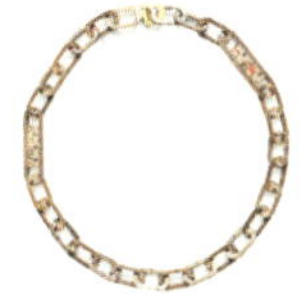

My work as an examiner of art jewellery students – at HDK in Gothenburg under Kim Buck, the Oslo National Academy of the Arts under Ingjerd Hanevold, Ädellab/Konstfack under Ruudt Peters and later Karen Pontoppidan, the School of Jewellery at Birmingham City University under Jivan Astfalck, the Royal College of Art under Hans Stofer and Alchimia Contemporary Jewellery School in Florence under Ruudt Peters – has been a source of valuable experience. Working as an examiner has introduced me to new generations of artists, their work and thought, and it has left its mark on my collection. Many if not most collectors do not buy from graduation exhibitions. They generally wait to see whether the artist is able to establish a professional career and the contours of an enduring reputation have started to emerge. That's not my approach. On the contrary, I consider it important to support promising talent no matter what the prospects for their future.

I have therefore bought many works from MA graduation exhibitions. Pia Aleborg from Sweden made a collection based on fragments of a Chesterfield sofa. My own brooch from this series raises questions about luxury, tradition and class [6]. The Norwegian Margit Flaa impressed me with rings of forged iron [138] and Sally Collins from England with brooches that incorporated crocheted elements [115]. For her necklace "My Four Guardian Angels", Dana Hakim from Israel used elements of found metal and plastic. Her materials evoke associations with fences, barriers and protective devices, which I interpret as a topical reference to conditions in a conflict zone [166]. By contrast, Swede Kajsa Lindberg's necklace "Every Day – Binoculars" made me smile [258]. At first glance one immediately thinks these "binoculars" are made of empty loo paper tubes, which they certainly resemble, whereas the material used is in fact copper. Such transformations of familiar, banal items into wearable jewellery are a hallmark of Lindberg's work. A few years later, she was making delicate necklaces from folding rulers [257]. In 2019, while still an MA student at the Oslo National Academy of the Arts, the Norwegian Olaf

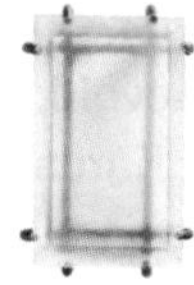

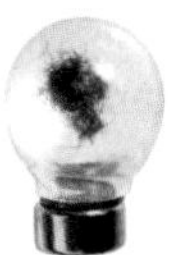

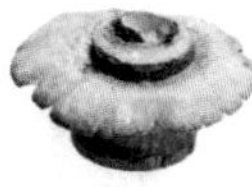

Tønnesland Hodne contributed to the *Talente* exhibition in Munich. One of the brooches he showed there, "Window (rectangle)", is now mine [547]. The material is industrially produced quartz cut in a classic style.

Some of the smallest works I own are also the products of memorable MA projects. Titti Bjernér at Konstfack collected the nap from a sweater and sealed a tuft of it inside a tiny glass bulb, thus turning a superfluous substance into a treasure that could even be worn on the sweater from which it came [39]. Stone setting is an art in its own right. Consequently, the way David Roux-Fouillet chose to do it attracted attention at his 2011 graduation show at the Royal College of Art in London. He used a rifle to shoot the stone into place. As he himself put it: "Like the tools traditionally used in jewellery making, a rifle is a tool of precision, I have modified it from a tool of destruction to a tool of creation."[123] I don't have a finished work of his, only a jewel that was created in the split second when I pulled the trigger: a blue synthetic corundum in a lead mount [519].

Things and thoughts

In the course of my work as a curator and writer, I have made the acquaintance of many artists, but for a long time I had almost no colleagues in Norway who wrote about contemporary crafts. On becoming editor of the Norwegian magazine *Kunsthåndverk* in 1998, I took charge of a platform with a broader reach. My immediate priorities were to improve international visibility and networking, and for the first time I had an academic paper accepted in English. This was presented on 25 April 1998 at the conference *Ideas in the Making. Practice in Theory*, organised by Pamela Johnson at the University of East Anglia. My subject was recycling as a strategy in Norwegian crafts. During the 1990s, it became increasingly common to use ready-made objects as a starting point for new works. In the crafts field as a whole, this was initially a controversial approach to materials, because most people associated it with fine art. But in art jewellery, the strategy was already widespread, and in my paper I focused on Konrad Mehus as an example.[124] At the conference, I met Martina Margetts, Edmund de Waal and Caroline Broadhead, all of whom I have since worked closely with.

Some parts of the art world have long harboured the fear that (too much) theory can be harmful to practice, but as of the year 2000, following the Bologna Process, the need to strengthen theoretical teaching at art colleges became urgent in both Norway and the rest of Europe. It was an effort to which I contributed as a part-time professor of crafts history and theory in Oslo, Bergen and Gothenburg in the 2000s.[125] Today, educational institutions in Scandinavia see more of their teaching done in English than in Norwegian, Swedish or Danish, and international exchanges and collaborations have become commonplace. At the turn of the millennium, the situation was very different. There were no international craft fairs, few international conferences and few biennials or the like where people interested in crafts could congregate. Neither were there any academic journals for the field, with the exception of the *Journal of Design History*, which occasionally published a special issue on crafts.

Living over in Germany, however, was Gabi Dewald, then the editor of *KeramikMagazin*, and someone who was feeling the same professional loneliness as I was. It was she who promoted the idea of a European think tank for writers in the field. With characteristic energy, she persuaded the small town of Gmunden in Austria to host an annual four-day gathering. At the founding meeting in 2004, we were a modest group of just six people: Peter Assmann from Austria, Tanya Harrod and Edmund de Waal from Great Britain, Love Jönsson from Sweden, Gabi Dewald and myself. Two further co-founders, Liesbeth den Besten from the Netherlands and Louise Mazanti from Denmark, were unable to attend. The following year, the group was enlarged by Mònica Gaspar from Spain and, following her, Benjamin

Lignel from France and Glenn Adamson from Great Britain/
USA also joined. This network has been very important to
me both personally and professionally – and it too has left
traces in my jewellery box. In our first manifesto, we formu-
lated our objectives thus:

> Historically the applied arts have suffered both from
> a lack of critical attention and from the absence of an
> international perspective. The Think Tank, in pro-
> viding a European platform for leading thinkers, will
> encourage engaged discourse of the rapidly changing
> identity of the applied arts. The challenge is to articu-
> late the significance of our field.[126]

What bound us together was a rejection of fixed definitions
of crafts. As Gabi Dewald succinctly put it:

> We are not concerned with preserving the estab-
> lished order. We are concerned with the relevance
> and validity of a form of art that is subject to a radical
> change in the wake of completely new production
> and communication processes, a form of art that is
> gaining in importance in an increasingly virtualised
> world, thus begging the question: what form does
> applied art take in the third millennium?[127]

This applies also to art jewellery, as one discipline in the
broader crafts field.

For each meeting of Think Tank, we agreed on a
one-word theme. In addition to preparing a paper, each
participant brought along two objects relevant to the
theme. These should be of a size that could easily be carried in a pocket or hand luggage. In addition to providing
a basis for our own discussions, these objects should be
suitable as exhibits with the potential to inspire conversations with a broader audience. For the first meeting,
which had *Languages* as its theme, I took along a textile
by Bente Sætrang and a ceramic object by Caroline Slotte.
The following year, when the keyword was *Places*, the
objects I had with me were a brooch by Sigurd Bronger and
a lamp by Lagombra (Anders Jakobsen). Although Think
Tank addressed the full breadth of the crafts field, jewel-

lery received plenty of attention. Jewellery was a central professional concern for Liesbeth den Besten, Mònica Gaspar and Benjamin Lignel, while for me it was certainly more than a secondary interest. But the objects that had the deepest impact on my jewellery collection were those that Gabi Dewald chose to share. The works she brought with her by Christoph Zellweger and Hilde De Decker fascinated me so much that I later bought pieces from the same series.

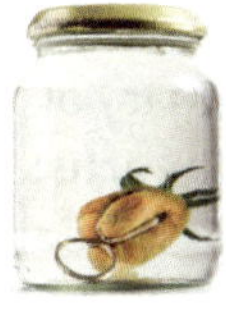

We usually associate bones with grave finds and archaeological excavations. They symbolise death and decay and are somehow repellent. In his *Relic Ossarium* series, Zellweger has covered bone-like forms in pink flock, giving them a soft velvety surface that one immediately wants to stroke with the fingers [419]. Thus we find them attractive and repellent at the same time. The covering also makes it unclear whether the bone fragments with their strange outgrowths are real or manipulated, natural or artificial. Although bones might seem fairly anonymous, they are one of the most recognisable and informative things to remain after death. Accordingly, bones have always been important as religious relics from which the devout draw spiritual sustenance. In a secularised society, it is unclear whether anything could serve as a substitute. But perhaps jewellery has a role to play here. Could we view Zellweger's pink bone as a modern relic or a symbolic prosthesis?[128] These were questions that were asked when this series was presented at the Gmunden meeting in 2006, which had chosen *Gift* as its theme.

Hilde De Decker is the author of a ring that is condemned to an existence in a jar full of clear vinegar [120]. The reason for this is that where we expect a stone we find organic material instead, namely a tomato. It takes time for a tomato to grow into a fully ripe fruit, but how can we judge whether in this case that time was long or short? In 2009, our subject was *Speed*, the relational nature of which De Decker's ring helped to illustrate. What we experience as fast or slow depends on what we measure it in relation to. The time it takes to produce a tomato depends on the processes of growth and ripening. And this is how it is with many craft processes as well. They demand the time it takes, although De Decker's "tomato ring" can also be interpreted as "a humorous, strong-willed and ambivalent ode in praise of slowness".[129] The lid of the jar containing the ring mimics the labelling on the lids of commercially produced preserves. As a trademark the artist has used her surname, De Decker, while the title is in Flemish, "Voor Boer en Tuinder" (For the Farmer and the Market Gardener), below which are the words "contains silver".

In 2010, Think Tank's subject was *Currency*. Here the main questions were: What are the values of craft, and is craft a "valid currency" in contemporary art? Benjamin Lignel brought along some brooches from Lin Cheung's series *Wear Again, Again*. A few years later I bought a brooch from this series at Micheko Galerie in Munich [113]. As Lignel pointed out, jewellery can fall into disfavour and be condemned to early retirement in the burial chamber that a jewellery box sometimes becomes.[130] But in *Wear Again, Again*, Cheung has found a twist that promises redundant pieces a second life. Her brooches resemble the type of boxes in which cut gems are kept, a receptacle familiar to anyone in the jewellery trade. The boxes are covered in coloured flock and lined with a little leather cushion. As brooches, they frame an absence, although as Lignel writes: "These are not blanks, but hosts: ready to promote your unused jewellery, and give it a site to stage a tentative come-back."[131] If you want, you can attach a brooch to the leather.

My own contribution to *Currency* was an item specially bought for the occasion: "Change" by Otto Künzli [237]. The pendant consists of a commemorative Norwegian ten-krone coin from 1964, issued to mark the 150th anniversary of the Norwegian constitution. A rubbing of the coin the artist made before reworking it shows that it originally bore an image of the Eidsvoll building, where the constitution was signed, on one face and Norway's national coat of arms on the other.[132] Künzli's *Change* series brought together

113

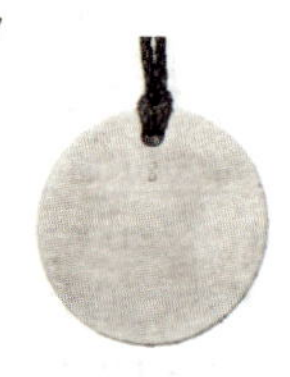

237

coins from thirty-eight countries. From each he erased the portrait of the regent and any other national symbols. He then polished the resulting disc, making it into a mirror in which the owner could view her own face – "a frame for your fame", as Künzli put it in a text that accompanied the purchase. With its empty polished surface, the only qualities that indicate that this was once a coin with a fixed monetary value are its size, weight and the markings around the edge. In many cultures, coins are often worn conspicuously on clothes or chains as a symbol of prosperity. But what value do they really have once the symbols have been removed and the coin is no longer in circulation as a means of payment? Künzli's modifications deprive the coins of their value as currency while investing them with new value as art jewellery. Not only does this displacement from one sphere of circulation to another increase their material value, it also extends their life expectancy. As does the artist's signature – a figure of eight (*otto* in Italian), which, turned on its side, is the mathematical symbol of infinity. There is no danger of this coin being withdrawn from circulation when a new monarch takes the throne or if the euro were to replace the national currency. Chosen and upgraded, it shows the power of art to influence the life cycle of things.

Think Tank issued its final publication in 2011. This took the form of a folded sheet of paper to which each participant had contributed two brief statements about the same two jewellery series: Kiko Gianocca's brooches with the collective title *With Other Eyes*, and the installation *Aeon Profit – Piano Forte* by the artist trio A5 (Romina Fuentes, Adam Grinovich and Annika Pettersson). In addition to owning a piece of the latter installation, I have a brooch by Gianocca, "Never Been There 3", which is similar to those that Think Tank contemplated.

Like the brooches in *With Other Eyes*, the surface of "Never Been There 3" is a black rectangle, an empty surface or, if you will, an absolute zero [154]. Mounted on the back, however, is a digitised print of a photograph the artist bought on eBay. The person in the photograph is unknown,

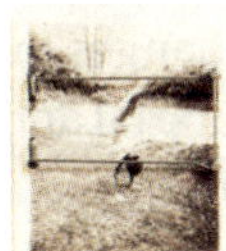

as is the situation and the location. The choice of precisely this photograph does not carry a particular meaning or emotion, but the idea of wearing the image of an unknown person to one's chest is what I find appealing about this brooch. At the same time, the anonymity makes the photo a symbol of forgetting and loss. All photography is a memento mori (a reminder of the inevitability of death), Susan Sontag claims in her essay "On Photography", a message that "Never Been There 3" vividly conveys through its juxtaposition of a photograph and its empty black front.

I have seen the installation *Aeon Profit – Piano Forte* in both Stockholm and Munich, where, in each case, it filled a large wall. For this, the group A5 chopped up an entire piano and grouped or bundled the parts together to form an array of necklaces. In total they created 145 kilos of jewellery. My own item consists of two keys, one black, one white [4]. It is a pairing that probably owes its existence to chance, because the combinations of components all seemed rather random. At the 2011 Think Tank, where the keyword was *Show*, there was a lot of discussion about what the individual necklaces represent. Was this work "display-dependent"?[133] Does the jewellery function primarily as a souvenir for those of us who know the story?

For the three artists who make up A5, the aim of the project was to explore concepts such as authorship, originality and value. The piano is an icon of bourgeois culture, but here it has been destroyed and turned into wearable symbols. Classic bourgeois conceptions of beauty as something harmonious and unified have been replaced by fragmentation and randomness. The once glossy, perfectly lacquered surface is now only present as small patches on otherwise rough-hewn parts. Whether these changes in use and aesthetic idiom have enhanced the material and cultural value is open to debate. But the title promises "aeon profit", and aeon can mean both an indefinitely long time and something that persists through eternity. It is a title that puts the transformation of the piano into jewellery into perspective. Even so, the value here depends on our willing-

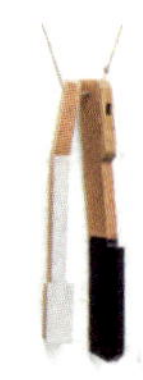

4

ness to accept this as jewellery art. As Liesbeth den Besten concluded at our meeting: "In all its ambiguity, it is a typical 21st century piece of craft in need of a context, a narrative and involvement by the wearer."[134]

Think Tank met for the last time in 2012. The factors that brought it to an end were part personal, part financial. But during the nine years it existed, the field as a whole had changed dramatically. New magazines and websites had been launched, providing multiple arenas for discussion and publication. Artistic research had become a centre of focus at art schools and academies, and the development of theory was also being treated as a matter of priority. New craft fairs, including Collect in London, invited us onto the panel debates of their supplementary programmes. Increasingly, we would meet at other seminars and conferences around Europe. I myself was able to invite Mònica, Love and Gabi to Norway when the Think Tank exhibition *Speed* was shown at Galleri Format in Bergen. All of them contributed to the seminar *Fartsfylt kunsthandverk* (Speedy Crafts) at Vestlandske Kunstindustrimuseum on 3 June 2010. The questions we discussed were of relevance to many of the works in my collection. As I put it in the invitation:

> The "slow" movement has the wind in its sails. Ever more frequently we hear terms like "slow food" and "slow cities". The desire to slow down is spreading. Craft production plays a central role in this movement, but is this ideological framework a natural home for crafts? Do crafts represent first and foremost the "aesthetic of slowness"? We also ask: Is slow better than fast? Do handmade objects carry greater emotional and cultural value than industrially made goods?

As always, we were better at asking questions than finding answers, but it was clear that we all wanted the craft field to retain its contradictory potential.

On 7 April 2011, I was able to invite Gabi and Liesbeth to take part in the seminar *Valuable or Worthless? Crafts in Transition* at the Oslo National Academy of the Arts. In the invitation, I referred directly to the work of Think Tank:

What kind of values do the crafts/applied arts represent? How do makers, theorists and the market contribute in creating these values and give significance to objects? This seminar does not aim to give exhaustive answers, but the questions are examples of issues addressed by Think Tank. A European Initiative for the Applied Arts.

Others who I invited to speak at this seminar included a couple of artists who had contributed to our exhibitions: the jewellery artist Ted Noten and the ceramicist Caroline Slotte. The latter was taking part in Think Tank's *Currency* exhibition, which opened on the same day at Galleri Format in Oslo. Both artists represent a conceptual approach to materials and media, and it is striking just how frequently we turned our attention to crafts with a clear conceptual focus. It has to be said that conceptual art is easier to talk and write about than the kind of crafts that spring from "tacit knowledge" and whose primary justification is their aesthetic qualities. In my collection, however, there is room for both.

A piece of jewellery can symbolise the happiness of a moment or the memory of a whole life.

— Marjan Unger [135]

My jewellery hot spots

327

360

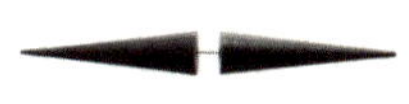

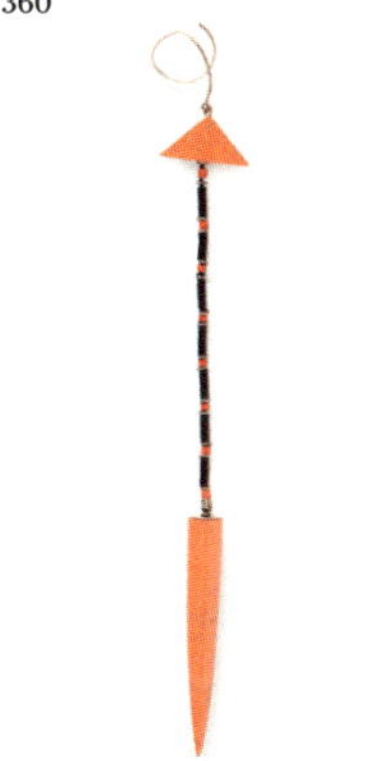

A collection needs a home, but, for my part, I associate collecting with travelling. Visiting a new city, a museum or arts fair, or chancing upon a new gallery, often leads to the discovery of a new artist, which results, in turn, in new purchases. Thanks to my interest in jewellery, I have made contacts in many countries, and among them gallery owners have been especially important. But the places I have actually visited have largely been a result of where I happened to be living and where my work took me. Consequently, my jewellery hot spots don't always coincide with what the literature identifies as major centres of art jewellery. They also strongly reflect the geographical range of my professional work, which has been confined largely to Northern and Central Europe.

203

372

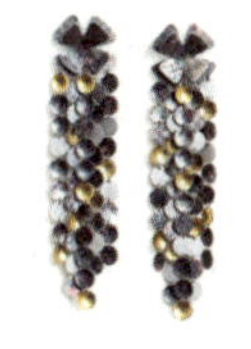

Oslo

Oslo lacks a dedicated art jewellery gallery. For a few years in the late 1980s, Galerie Perspective, run by the goldsmith Nicolai Marcussen, filled that gap. As a frequent visitor, I bought jewellery by Heidi Sand [327], Anne-Karine Solgaard [360], Grethe Jilsøy [203], Lars Sture [372] and Inger Marie Berg [28]. The exhibition *Øret i fokus* (The Ear in Focus) (1989)

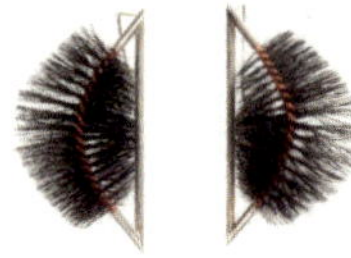

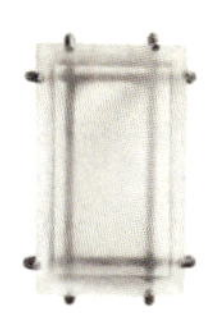

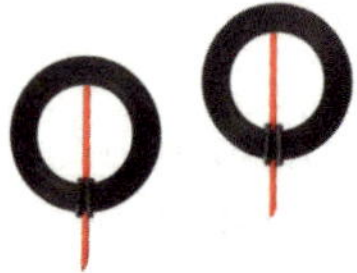

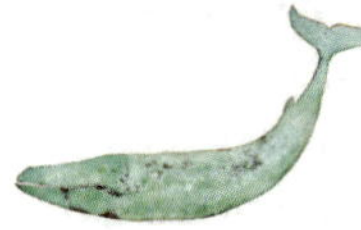

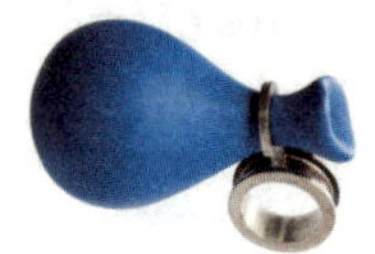

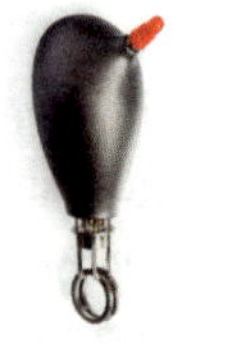

is especially memorable. In 2019, jewellery artist Camilla Luihn took up the tradition of combining a gallery with her own workshop. Part of the space she occupies in Basarhallene in Oslo is given over to the gallery Portabel, where presentations of newly graduated artists form an important part of the profile. My first purchase there was a brooch by Olaf Tønnesland Hodne [547].

In Oslo, the central venues for art jewellery have not been privately owned galleries but artist-run exhibition spaces that promote the full spectrum of craft disciplines. The most important are Galleri Format, Kunstnerforbundet and RAM galleri. In 1991, I went to the opening of Galleri Format, owned by the Norwegian Association for Arts and Crafts. In its first year of existence Format was my source for a number of affordable and wearable items [228, 353]. In addition, there are several sales outlets run by crafts collectives. Kunsthåndverkerne i Kongensgate was launched in 1979, Brudd in 1985.

RAM galleri

In the 1990s, my priority destination was RAM galleri, particularly in the years when it was run by jewellery artist Heidi Sand. Sigurd Bronger had two major solo exhibitions there, and I bought pieces from both. Two rings are typical of Bronger's style at the time. Where an ordinary ring would have a mounted stone, these have "unnaturally" large outgrowths made from Cibatool that resemble bladders or balloons [75, 76]. One of them is also embellished with a red-capped bicycle valve. This reinforces the illusion that the form is "inflated", adding an aspect of absurdity and humour. Due to its size, it is a difficult piece to wear. But there is a difference between difficult and impossible. The distinction between what is and is not wearable is always shifting. As Jay-Z rapped to his then girlfriend Beyoncé: "That rock on ya finger is like a tumor."[136] It is largely a question of habits and conventions, but I have to admit I have never worn either of these rings for more than a couple of minutes at a time.

At the exhibition *Bæreinstrumenter* (Wearable Devices) in 1998, Bronger's jewellery was presented like scientific instruments in a technical museum. Some of the displays were more suggestive of 18th-century cabinets of curiosities, an aspect that was further emphasised when the same objects were shown the following year at Galerie Ra under the title *The Weird and the Wonderful*. Cabinets of curiosities always had space for a little of everything. Oddities of the natural world were displayed side by side with exotic trophies and exquisite man-made objets d'art. Bronger's collection mixed the worthless with the valuable, trivial items with design icons. This was also true of the brooch I later acquired [68]. For this he used a component from an old telephone, but not just any old phone. It came from one of the preeminent symbols of modern industrial production in Norway, a 1931 telephone made from Bakelite. By adopting this new synthetic material, the time it took to manufacture a telephone was reduced from seven days to seven minutes. The telephone was developed by the engineer Johan Christian Bjerknes, while the external design was the work of the artist Jean Heiberg. "Logical, cubist and practical, the telephone stands out as an industrial gateway project for Norwegian functionalism" – such was the verdict of the design historian Fredrik Wildhagen.[137] The model became an international success and was for several decades the benchmark for modern telephone design. Bronger's interest in new synthetic materials, as evidenced by the aforementioned rings, echoes the introduction of Bakelite in the 1930s. The telephone's hollow case once had a practical function, but emptied of its utility it becomes a purely decorative ornament; something useful has become an object of useless beauty. At the same time, the phone symbolises a medium of communication. As a ready-made in a piece of jewellery, it serves as a literal reminder that art too is about communication.

RAM galleri also introduced international artists to a Norwegian audience. The exhibition I remember best was Rian de Jong's *Bei Mir Bist Du Schön*, in 1995. It has prob-

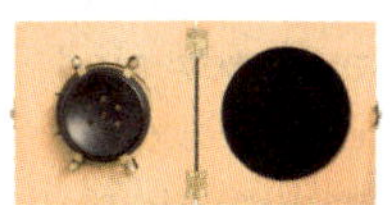

68

ably stuck in my mind because of the song that filled the room – and because I was allowed to handle the jewellery. The title of the exhibition was taken from the hit song that provided the acoustic background. As I entered the room I was regaled by the words, "I could say 'bella, bella' even 'sehr wunderbar'. Each language only helps me tell you how grand you are." And then came the famous Yiddish refrain, "Bei mir bist du sjejn", which translates as, "To me you are beautiful". The song created a warm, positive atmosphere. Otherwise, the exhibition consisted of ten tables with chairs. There was a hand mirror on every table, and beneath the tabletop was a drawer illuminated from within. The light was important. It seeped out through the cracks when the drawer was closed, acting as a magnet to the inquisitive visitor. When opened, the drawer revealed the jewellery, laid out on a bed of paper, wood or sand. The fact that as visitors we were invited to explore – to sit down, open a drawer, take out the jewellery, try it on and then pick up the mirror and study the effect – heightened our awareness of actions which, for many people, are part of jewellery's enchantment. Each drawer was a jewellery box, or treasure chest, each table a dressing table. Thus the exhibition encouraged a ritual that many people are familiar with from their own lives. That ritual also included taking the jewellery off again, returning it to its place of storage and gently closing the drawer. One went from one table to the next, where the ritual was repeated to the constant accompaniment of the song: "You're really swell, I have to admit you deserve expressions that really fit you."

RAM galleri's press release for the show pointed out how unusual it is to be allowed to handle jewellery at an exhibition in the way Rian de Jong invited us to do: "Jewellery is usually exhibited in locked display cases that tend to create a distance between it and the visitor. For works that are already torn between the outer poles of the functional and the autonomous, this almost inevitably forces us to judge them emotively as 'non-wearable art objects'."[138] It was precisely this barrier Jong wanted to

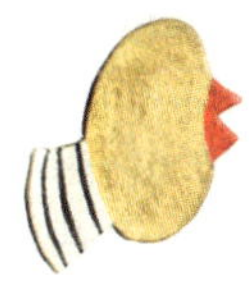

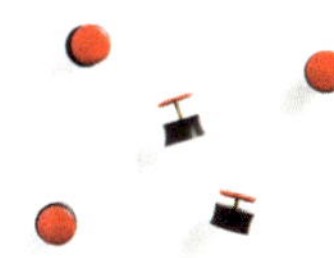

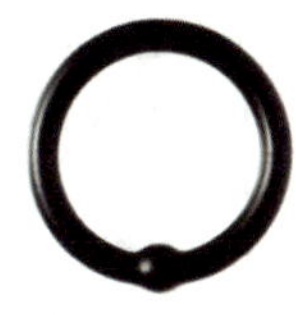

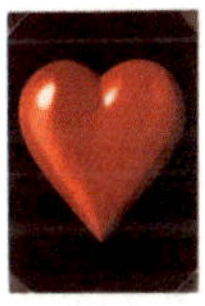

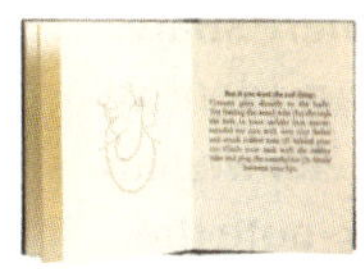

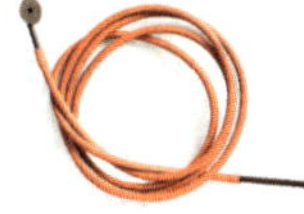

break down by encouraging a familiar ritual to illustrate that also this type of jewellery exists to be used.

Nothing enflames my desire to buy more than the opportunity to try jewellery on my own body, but in 1995 my finances were extremely tight. At *Bei Mir Bist Du Schön*, I had just enough for a small gift for Mogens, a plywood brooch with an incision that lets you slot it onto the edge of a pocket or a neckline [206].

Another important exhibition at RAM galleri by an international guest was Otto Künzli's solo show in 1996. That served as the excuse for a seminar at the Museum of Decorative Arts and Design in Oslo, which featured talks by both Künzli and myself and ended with a boat trip on the Oslo Fjord for the entire Norwegian jewellery community. This was my first meeting with Künzli. The building in Kongens gate where RAM galleri was based at the time still bears a trace of his visit. Adorning the façade is a large red dot, a miniature version of which I purchased [241]. In addition, I bought a bracelet [235], a brooch [236] and "The Manhattan Piece" [239], a work that Mogens loved to demonstrate at festive gatherings over the ensuing years.

"The Manhattan Piece" undermines all conventional notions of the function of jewellery. Künzli got the idea for the piece during a visit to New York in the 1980s. The sight of steam rising through grates in the streets inspired him to view the metropolis as both a body and a wearable object. Elsewhere in the same city, he was confronted by an active anti-smoking campaign. "The Manhattan Piece" can be interpreted as a critical commentary on the fanaticism of some of the anti-smoking campaigners, in that it plays on the magical and ritual aspects of smoking. As an actual object, the "jewellery" is contained in a tin identical in size and shape to that of Dannemann cigarillos. Inside, one finds a manual that explains in text and drawings how the item is used. You conceal the long rubber tube inside your clothes, keeping the end with the mouthpiece in the palm of your hand. The other end you push through an

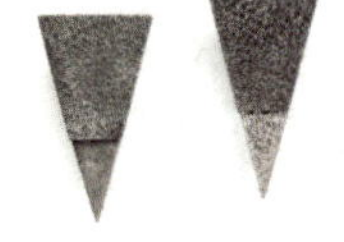

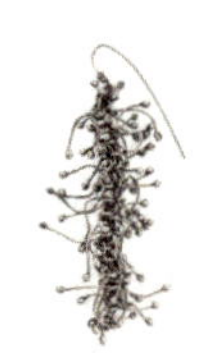

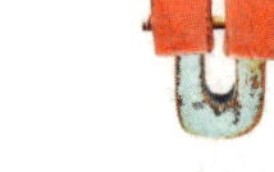

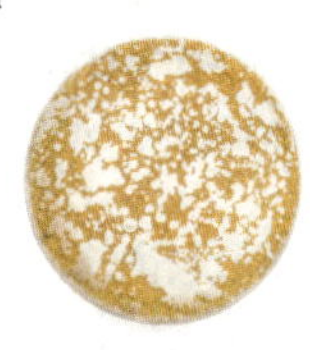

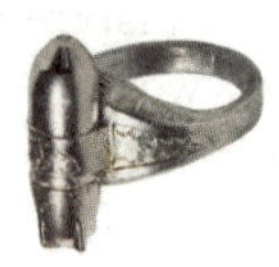

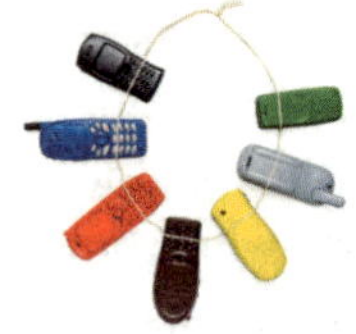

ear piercing or through the fabric of the garment on your upper back. Having inhaled from a cigarette, you can then blow into the hose and enjoy the surprise of onlookers when they see a wisp of white smoke emerging from your back or from behind your ear.

Kunstnerforbundet

Kunstnerforbundet is the largest and oldest of Oslo's artist-run institutions. My first purchases from there, in 1988 and 1989, were earrings by Tone Vigeland [406, 407]. One of the most recent is a brooch by Canadian Jamie R. Kroeger [548], who graduated from the Oslo National Academy of the Arts in the spring of 2019. For a long time, Kunstnerforbundet showed fine art and crafts on separate floors. It was therefore a historic gesture when they started 2019 with all their rooms devoted to jewellery. This show, entitled *Everyone Says Hello*, was curated by Lars Sture. On display were roughly a hundred works by twenty artists from different countries, and it was Kunstnerforbundet's most visited exhibition of the year.

Crafts are often said to have a close connection to everyday life. Sture wanted to query this conception by showing how the everyday life of, say, a Sami in the wilds of Finnmark differs from that of a Jew in Israel or a resident of London. At the same time, people everywhere share aspects of experience in the form of alienation, identity issues and environmental problems. From a Norwegian point of view, it was particularly refreshing to note the parallels between the contributors from Norway/Samiland and New Zealand/Aotearoa. I already owned earlier versions of several of the works on show: Nicolas Cheng and Beatrice Brovia's brooches using gold from electronic waste [111], Nanna Melland's "Ring of Ignorance" [518] and finally Lisa Walker's chain of mobile phones painted in different colours [412]. The phones are strung together on a braided cord, echoing a Maori technique for making jewellery. This focus on the kind of consumer items that people

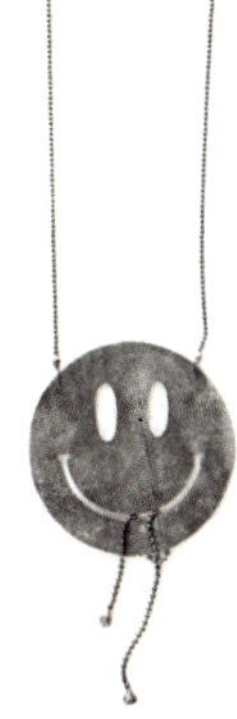

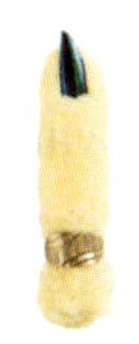

replace frequently despite a sense of strong attachment is typical of Walker's work.

Everyone Says Hello also provided a couple of new purchases: a necklace from the series *Places I've Been, Things I've Seen* by Camilla Luihn, made from recycled zinc and presented as a picture in a found frame [205], and a brooch by Helene Duckert in the form of a finger adorned with a ring. The finger is made from foam rubber while the element that looks like a dark blue nail is a wing cover from a beetle. Encircling the finger is a signet ring that was marketed as gold but is in fact made of brass [528]. The brooch was part of a larger installation that one critic described as a "manic-depressive accumulation of miscellaneous objects from a mundane existence in high gear: cigarette packets, coffee mugs, toys, beer mats, promotional items".[139] All the materials in the installation were things Duckert had either pilfered, found or been given. Referencing brands, consumerism, globalisation and body attributes, they expose the hierarchies that dictate whether materials are of high or low value. The anti-aesthetic appealed to me, as did Duckert's playful, cheeky approach to art in general and jewellery in particular. A remark made by Lisa Walker in another context is well suited to Duckert's installation: "The strange world of contemporary jewellery would fit perfectly into contemporary art, some day they'll finally realise that."[140]

Amsterdam

The Netherlands has been a centre for the development of jewellery as an independent art form since the 1960s. The country has long been home to some of the most important galleries in the field. In addition to Galerie Ra, these include Galerie Marzee (1979–), Galerie Louise Smit (1986–2012), Galerie Rob Koudijs (2007–) and, since 2019, Galerie Door. Many of the artists I hold in high regard are represented by one or other of these galleries: Lisa Walker, Karl Fritsch and Sigurd Bronger by Ra, Dorothea Prühl and

Lucy Sarneel by Marzee, and Helen Britton, David Bielander, Daniel Kruger and Kiko Gianocca by Rob Koudijs. I have bought jewellery from all of them, even if more often from their stands at art fairs in London and Munich than from their respective headquarters in the Netherlands.

One brooch that always reminds me of a trip to Amsterdam together with Mogens, and which included a visit to Galerie Rob Koudijs, consists of a piece of metal from a Mercedes-Benz [292]. Ted Noten has used a variety of strategies to reach new target groups. In 2001 he cut a hundred pieces from a white Mercedes-Benz by hand and turned them into brooches. Could people's interest in such cars be transferred onto jewellery? After all, the car has been called "a large piece of masculine jewellery".[141] Noten's interest in deconstructing status symbols, whether a car or jewellery, is a further aspect of this work. In addition, it satisfies one of the conditions he sets out in his jewellery manifesto: "Jewellery must be shamelessly curious."[142] For Mogens, this fragment was the closest he ever came to owning such an expensive and classy car, and it is probably the brooch he used most often.

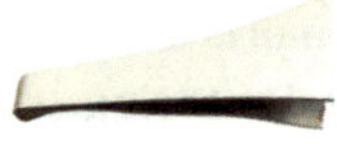

Gallery Ra

I have already mentioned Galerie Ra more than once. It was launched in Amsterdam in 1976 by Paul Derrez, who ran it until the end of 2019. Over the course of some four hundred exhibitions, the gallery demonstrated an immense breadth of interest, but if there is one thing that has defined its profile, it is a liberal attitude towards sex: "More than other jewellery galleries, Ra is a platform for work in which homo and hetero eroticism as well as sex plays an emphatic role."[143] A necklace by Peter Hoogeboom illustrates the point [193]. It was created for the exhibition *Erotic Toys for Girls and Boys*, which Ra arranged as part of the cultural programme during the Gay Games in Amsterdam in 1998. The work is called "Bouncing Balls", and to give its titular objects their bulge and bounce, they can be filled with

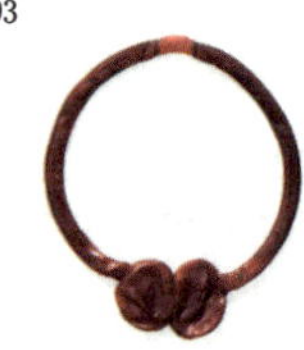

lubricant (or water) through an opening equipped with a stopper. Or rather, they could. For the work is made from the same type of rubber as condoms, a material that does not last forever and which, over the years, has lost its elasticity. But it was fun while it lasted!

Derrez is himself a jewellery artist, and together with his husband, Willem Hoogstede, he too has built up an extensive collection. The interesting thing about this collection is that it also chronicles the gallery's exhibitions, from each of which the couple always bought at least one work. In 2013, when their collection was shown at CODA Museum in Apeldoorn under the title *Dare to Wear*, I was invited to give a lecture. The title I chose was "Why Wear?" One of the answers I gave to my own question was the joy it gives to others. As long-standing ambassadors for the wearing of jewellery, Hoogstede and Derrez have never been afraid of bold colours or large forms. The brooch I possess by Derrez is from a series he called *Dot-brooch* [121]. It is made of white acrylic plastic, with inlaid dots of various colours and sizes. Some of the dots are transparent and change tone depending on the underlying garment. It is a piece that immediately makes one think of a painter's palette. In 2015, Derrez received the Herbert Hofmann Prize for two brooches in this series. I myself was on the jury, together with Andi Gut, Karl Rothmüller and Marjan Unger, but didn't buy my own brooch until a couple of years later. In our justification, we stated that if there is one thing we all need in the current day and age it is "optimism, cheerfulness and happiness", qualities we felt were manifest in *Dot-brooch*.[144]

During my visit to the Netherlands for the *Dare to Wear* show, I stayed a few days with Paul and Willem, and one evening they invited two up-and-coming jewellery artists to dinner. Thus I got to know Réka Fekete and Jie Sun, both of whom soon found their way into my collection. Fekete borrowed the opening words of Nina Simone's song "Feeling Good" as the title for her necklace "Birds Flying High" [135]. It's a happy, optimistic song, which also contains the lines

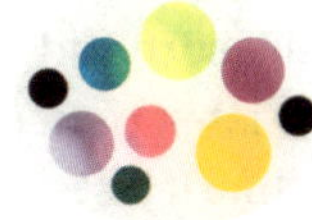

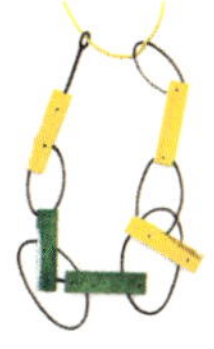

It's a new dawn
It's a new day
It's a new life
For me
And I'm feeling good

This was therefore the obvious piece of jewellery to wear when in 2015 I received an award as the "New Norwegian Language User of the Year" during a festival devoted to Nynorsk, the New Norwegian language.

The connotations of Sun's brooch are more ambivalent. With the title "Young and Beautiful", the work resembles a soft-serve ice-cream cone covered with glass crystals shaped like lucky four-leaf clovers [373]. It alludes to youth and falling in love, but here the experience is compared to ice cream. It brings short-term pleasure and happiness but cannot be preserved or kept for later. Hence the underlying message: Make the most of it while it lasts!

Halle

Most of the Think Tank exhibitions were held in mainland Europe. When *Places* opened at Galerie im Volkspark, the exhibition venue of Burg Giebichenstein Hochschule für Kunst und Design (Burg Giebichenstein University of Art and Design), in Halle on 25 April 2007, Gabi Dewald and I were invited to attend. Our contact person was the art historian Renate Luckner-Bien, a close friend of Dorothea Prühl, to whom Renate introduced us. Prühl has been described as both a beacon of contemporary jewellery[145] and "a jeweller's jeweller".[146] Before 1989 and the fall of the Berlin Wall, few in the West knew of her, and she was nearly sixty by the time she had her first solo exhibition outside Germany. When asked in 2011 what it was like to be an artist and teacher in the former GDR, she replied that one's main concern was to avoid, as far as possible, being drawn into some kind of programme: "Because a programme would mean definition, and every definition made one vulnerable to attack."[147] Working with jewellery, one was, however, freer

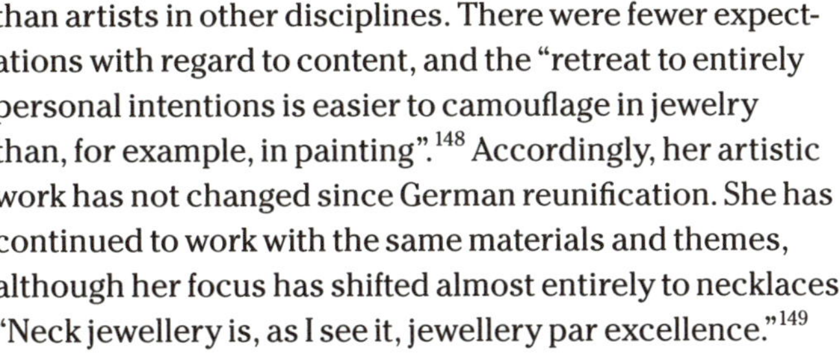

316

than artists in other disciplines. There were fewer expectations with regard to content, and the "retreat to entirely personal intentions is easier to camouflage in jewelry than, for example, in painting".[148] Accordingly, her artistic work has not changed since German reunification. She has continued to work with the same materials and themes, although her focus has shifted almost entirely to necklaces. "Neck jewellery is, as I see it, jewellery par excellence."[149]

It was with a sense of awe that I sat on the bench in Prühl's simple kitchen in Halle as she fetched box after box of jewellery. The moment I hung "Swans" around my neck, I knew I had to have it [316]. The simplicity with which she evoked life and movement was bewitching. Given the level of abstraction, one probably wouldn't think of swans without knowing the title, but having heard that keyword, one immediately starts to discern the necks and wings of swans in the meandering lines.

317

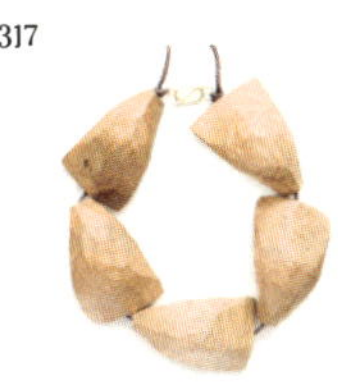

For Prühl, form, technique and materials are inseparable.[150] In the winter months, she prefers to work with hard metals, such as titanium and steel, which require planning and precision. These she neither polishes nor colours, because she wants their surfaces to reflect the character of the material itself. During the summer, she collects and dries wood she finds in her surroundings, such as cherry, elm, alder and birch. A good saw and a sharp knife are the only tools she needs to transform these pieces into "jewels". The marks of the paring knife are left conspicuous. Regardless of the material, Prühl's necklaces are invariably large and sculptural but not heavy. They are constructed like classic jewellery: pieces of wood are arranged like pearls on a string [317] and metal elements are linked together to form a chain [483], while her most recent work reinterprets the theme of the pendant on a gold chain [484].

483

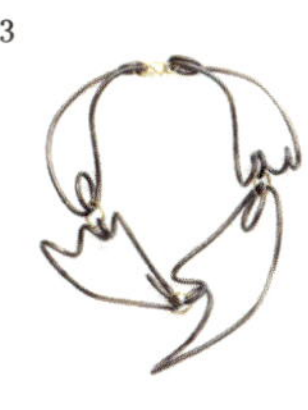

484

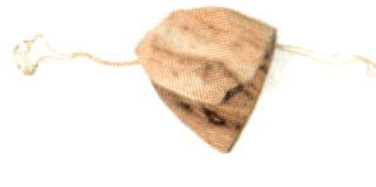

In her forms, she draws inspiration from nature, frequently alluding to birds and insects. To me, this symbolises a free spirit, but Prühl herself denies any deeper significance behind her choice of themes. Luckner-Bien is also clear on this point: "The more or less recognisable motif conceals no recondite messages; hence it permits no interpretations which might refer to anything extrinsic. These are things that need no mediation. They are not ambivalent. There is no narrative anywhere."[151] Nature provides the starting point, but it is transformed into ornament. Even so, this link to nature reflects a value choice. It serves to remind us that as humans we are part of nature and affirms what Prühl sees as the basis for both making and wearing jewellery, namely "to retain a connection to the earth".[152]

As a long-time teacher and professor of jewellery at Burg Giebichenstein, Prühl helped to define what is now recognised as the "Halle school". A focus on the making of one-off works is now a hallmark of the education at Burg Giebichenstein. As Liesbeth den Besten puts it: "In contrast to the fast assemblage trend in jewellery, jewellery from Halle is the result of a process of making."[153] Central objectives include refining the student's sense for materials and form, and a greater emphasis on sensual qualities than on conceptual approaches.

My first visit to Halle came several years after Prühl had retired as professor. By that time, the Jewellery Department was under the direction of Daniel Kruger. It was he who showed me around the school, and he too has since become an artist I follow closely. One of the first things I bought at Galerie Biró in Munich in 2011 was a pendant by Kruger that resembles a pastel version of the colour circle, in which yellow, orange and pink are contrasted with purple, blue and green [229]. Each colour is contained in a separate oval within the main circle, so that collectively they suggest associations to a flower. Organic and geometric shapes that interact and counteract are a recurring feature of Kruger's work, together with the use of contrasting but mutually reinforcing colours [230].

Kruger grew up on a farm in Namibia far from shops and entertainment. It was a situation that taught him to improvise, and he became acquainted with handicrafts at an early age. Crocheting and knitting are techniques

229
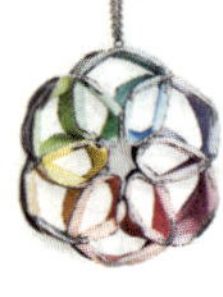

230
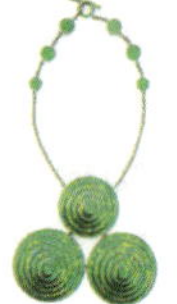

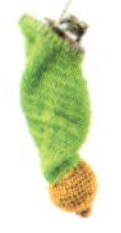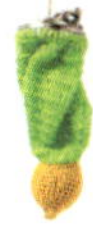

he mastered as a boy and which he has continued to use throughout his artistic career. The earrings he crocheted for me are an example of this [231]. As one of the few craft techniques that has never been fully mechanised, crocheting has retained homely associations of potholders and doilies, bed rugs and kitchen curtains. Kruger is one of the first jewellery artists I encountered to use the technique in their work.

One quality of Kruger's art that has been widely remarked upon is his anti-hierarchical approach to materials. But what is unique to him is that this also applies to materials, techniques and effects that have been regarded, historically and culturally, as feminine.[154] When a male artist rises above gender stereotypes by using glass beads, lace or crochet work, he creates a broader space for all of us to move in.

Munich

If there is one international centre for jewellery, it must be Munich, in Germany.[155] This can be explained in part by the existence of the Department of Jewellery and Hollowware at the Academy of Fine Arts, and in part by Schmuckschau, an exhibition that has been held annually since 1959. In addition, there are many galleries with a focus on art jewellery. When in Munich, my shopping itinerary takes me to Galerie Biró, Galerie Spektrum, Galerie Wittenbrink, Micheko Galerie and Maurer Zilioli – Contemporary Arts.

Akademie der Künste

The jewellery class at the Akademie der Künste (Academy of Fine Arts) is unlike any other I know of. They have no degree system, exams or divisions according to annual intakes. Instead, students spend five years immersing themselves in their own work in a class of around twenty. In order to be accepted, applicants must already have completed a foundation course, thus dispensing with the need for an

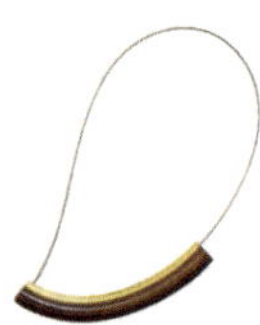

introduction to basic techniques. Five new students are admitted each year, with applicants coming from around the world. Otto Künzli was professor from 1991 until 2014, when he was succeeded by Karen Pontoppidan.

Both Künzli and Pontoppidan are firmly committed to what can be called a conceptual approach, which thematises every aspect of jewellery in terms of its cultural status and significance. In the series *Fragment*, from the 1980s, for example, Künzli created necklaces from sections of picture frames [242]. As a surround for a painting, the frame plays a subordinate role and often passes unnoticed, but that's not how it is here. Indeed, one commentator has claimed that the opposite is true; here the picture frame reduces the user to a supportive background.[156] I for my part would offer a rather different interpretation. For me, this is jewellery that questions the function and status of its own medium: Is it the function of neck jewellery to serve as a decorative frame for the face? Does the frame symbolise the difficulty jewellery has in being accepted as an autonomous art form? This is an aspect of jewellery that art historian Glenn Adamson discusses in his book *Thinking Through Craft*, with reference to Jacques Derrida's concept of *supplément*. For Derrida, the *supplément* is an ambiguous concept. It can refer either to an add-on that *expands* something that is already complete, or to an addition that *complements* something incomplete and which consequently functions as a corrective. In either case, the supplement highlights a deficiency while simultaneously being superfluous.[157] It is easy to see how this can be applied to jewellery. According to Adamson: "Like any good supplement, a piece of jewellery both compensates for and exposes a lack in the thing that is adorned. To wear a piece of jewellery is to tacitly admit a need for ornamentation as a means of expressing character."[158] Whether this is how Künzli sees it, we don't know. Even so, it is a question the series *Fragment* raises with ironic ingenuity.

Two factors that make it difficult for jewellery to be accepted as art on a level with, say, painting are, firstly, that

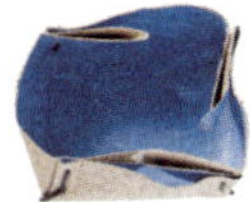

jewellery can be used and, secondly, that it has a foundation in crafts. By using a ready-made, Künzli has distanced himself from jewellery's craft aspect while retaining its function as a wearable object. For her *Context* series, from 2013, Karen Pontoppidan chose a different strategy to address the relationship between arts and crafts. The series consists of a total of one hundred brooches made of pieces of canvas painted in different colours and folded into box-like shapes. At Galerie Rob Koudijs's stand at the Collect fair in London in May 2013, I purchased a blue one for the tidy sum of 160 euros [308]. The sale price was part of the concept: the fact that there were many versions allowed the artist to ask a lower price than would be usual for an original, handmade work.

Pontoppidan delegated the production of these brooches to other people. The canvases were painted by artist friends; goldsmith colleagues and students made the metal frames and clasps; and the components were assembled by designers. Thus the series represents a lot of manual work, with the artist herself contributing nothing but the concept. The production imitates the work process of many successful fine artists and designers who run workshops with teams of assistants. The process shows a considerable element of irony, but there is also a serious intent. "Important for me is a general change in perspective," Pontoppidan has said in an interview. "Instead of evaluating contemporary jewelry as a matter of personal artistic expression, I prefer to view contemporary jewelry as an important cultural phenomenon, and therefore cooperation is as valid as individual work."[159] The question is whether this production process invites other interpretations. Is *Context* sculpture or jewellery, painting or decoration?

Pontoppidan was herself a student of Künzli's and participated in one of the most stimulating jewellery exhibitions I have ever seen, namely the one Künzli curated in 2008 to mark the 200th anniversary of the Academy of Fine Arts. With the eccentric title *Des Wahnsinns fette Beute* (The

Fat Booty of Madness), the show featured all the eighty-odd
students who had studied under Künzli thus far. In total,
they presented around a thousand works. Each contributor
had his or her own display case or cabinet, each different
from the next and all of them scattered higgledy-piggledy
around the room in a way that emphasised the diversity
of personalities and styles of expression. It was here I first
became acquainted with the concept of auteur jewellery.[160]
In Germany, this term is more commonly used than "new
jewellery", but they denote roughly the same thing: jewellery that has liberated itself from the goldsmith profession
to become an autonomous artistic discipline. The exhibitors also had something else in common:

> Künzli's class is driven by questions, perhaps doubts
> – as the engine of its urge to create: where does jewel-
> lery happen, where does jewellery occur – in everyday
> living, in rituals, ceremony, tradition, the present –
> what is jewellery, how is jewellery shown, where are
> the loci of jewellery and so forth. The answer – often
> cryptic and metaphorical – is provided by jewellery
> itself and the way it is presented and communicated.[161]

Over the years, many of the artists who trained at the
Academy in Munich have helped to augment my collection:
Volker Atrops, Peter Bauhuis, David Bielander, Alexander
Blank, Helen Britton, Karl Fritsch, Mari Ishikawa, Junwon
Jung, Sally Marsland, Nanna Melland, Karen Pontoppidan,
Gisbert Stach, Lisa Walker and Jing Yang.

Schmuck

As just one part of the International Craft Fair in Munich,
Schmuck is a week-long exhibition within the framework of
a massive trade fair. In the same hall, one finds two further
exhibitions: *Talente*, a platform for young craftspeople, and
Meister der Moderne, which features the already established.
These too generally include a number of jewellery artists. In
the 2000s, a number of art jewellery galleries from different countries set up *Frame*, in which each is represented

by a stand, forming a frame around *Schmuck*. The number
of shows and events elsewhere in Munich has also risen
each year. Central to these activities is the exhibition at the
Pinakothek der Moderne – Die Neue Sammlung, Munich's
primary municipal museum of arts and crafts, which has
often taken the form of a retrospective show for a single
jewellery artist. Thus today, *Schmuck* is just one small part
of what is known internationally as Munich Jewellery Week.

I visited Jewellery Week for the first time in 2004 and
have attended almost every year since. What drew me there
initially was the fact that Sigurd Bronger was participating
in *Schmuck*. Any artist can apply to take part, with the selection being made by a one-person jury. In 2004 the juror was
Hermann Jünger (1928–2005), the grand old man of German
art jewellery. When it came to Bronger, the works chosen
were a series of vibrantly coloured brooches. A close exam-
ination of these pieces revealed that framed within each was
an eraser. Printed on the back of the example in my collection is the name TATE. What Bronger is doing in this series is
highlighting a particular kind of museum object [71].

Since the start of the millennium, interest in *Schmuck*
has increased year by year. In 2004, 330 artists from twenty-
four countries applied to take part. When I was invited to
select the works for *Schmuck 2014*, there were 552 applicants from forty-three countries to choose from. By 2019,
the number had risen to 762 artists from fifty-two countries.
The number of contributors who are ultimately selected
has, however, remained fairly constant at around sixty-five
each year. Being a juror meant that, in the autumn of 2013,
I had to sift through several thousand photos over the
course of two days. Consequently, the initial selection was
determined largely by gut feeling. My focal concerns were
to choose works that would form an interesting exhibition,
both visually and thematically. One of those who made an
immediate impression was Réka Fekete. At that point, her
name was entirely new to me, and when, later in the autumn,
I saw her necklace "Birds Flying High" [135] at Galerie Ra
in Amsterdam, I bought it with the promise of lending it to

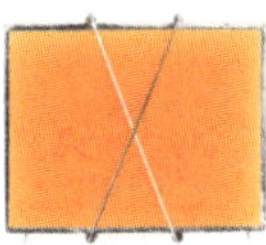

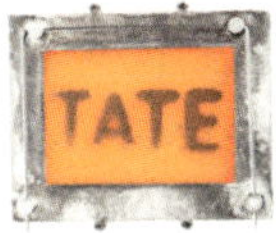

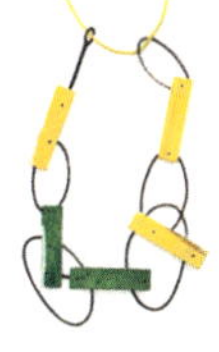

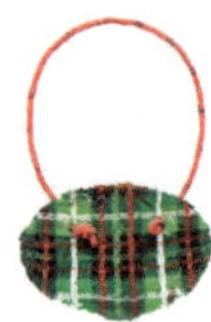

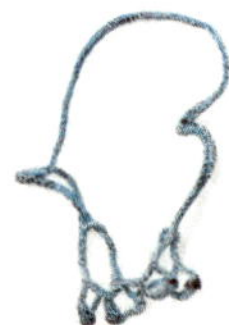

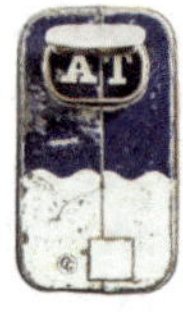

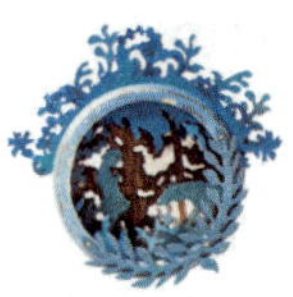

Schmuck. This was the work she was represented by in the catalogue, but the necklace was not shown at the exhibition because it got stuck in the customs of Norway.

I secured a few works from *Schmuck 2014* as a memento of my jury assignment: a breastplate by Shelley Norton, made from melted plastic bags painted with a tartan pattern [290], a necklace by Mikiko Minewaki, in which she has morphed a soft-toy dinosaur beyond all recognition [285], and a brooch by Jo Pond from the series *Made in Great Britain*, based on old metal [307]. The material bears the scars of heavy handling, and on top of the main corpus is a smaller tin-upon-a-tin. Both the decoration and material symbolise modernism and mass production. It is a brooch that helps us to notice beauty in the commercial, urban landscape of signs and product packaging. Another artist in the exhibition with brooches based on old metal was Anna Talbot. The year before, I had bought a similar brooch from her [384].

It is probably no coincidence that the materials used in many of the works I selected for *Schmuck* bore the marks of rust and wear and tear or illustrated the reuse of plastics, lolly sticks, toys and other everyday items. One of the subjects that have preoccupied me most as an art historian has been the use of ready-mades and found things in art. The value of such materials lies in the lives they have already led. They carry a story of other types of knowledge, other modes of production, and often show traces of human use. In reusing them, one also recycles their individual histories. It is a choice of materials that can also be viewed as a democratisation of the art of jewellery. Rare and expensive materials are replaced by others that are cheap and readily available and to which most people already have a relationship as consumers. At the same time, their reworking by artists invests them with new histories and functions. Thus I would claim that the thematic thread running through my selection for *Schmuck* was disenchantment combined with re-enchantment.[162] It was the sociologist Max Weber who first described the modern world as disenchanted. He proposed that the rational had triumphed over the irrational, a shift that entailed, among other things, the replacement of magic and superstition with scientific explanations. But in the 2000s, re-enchantment became a keyword in parts of the contemporary art world. It was all about enhancing the scope for emotions, dreams, desires and mystery.

Apart from Bronger's eraser brooch, I didn't buy anything on my first visits to *Schmuck*, neither at the fair nor at any of the other exhibitions in Munich. But in 2008, I was simply blown away by the work of Lisa Walker. At the same time as she participated in *Des Wahnsinns fette Beute*, she also had an extensive solo exhibition, *Gold and Bones*, at Galerie Goethe. Like all of Walker's shows, it was a colourful affair: a forest of pedestals in various sizes in a range of colours – yellow, green, orange, blue, red, brown and white – formed the setting for an array of equally eye-catching necklaces and brooches. But as Liesbeth den Besten wrote of Walker's work at this time: "They may look cheerful, but they are not easy." To which she added: "She constantly violates the rules of good taste, not as a rebellion but as a heartfelt freethinker, a liberal at any price."[163] Paul Derrez, one of Walker's gallerists, was of a similar mind: "Lisa's work is not charming but confrontational," he claimed.[164] What I for my part found particularly fascinating was the fact that everything she makes can be interpreted as an answer to the question many of us still struggle with: What can jewellery be?[165]

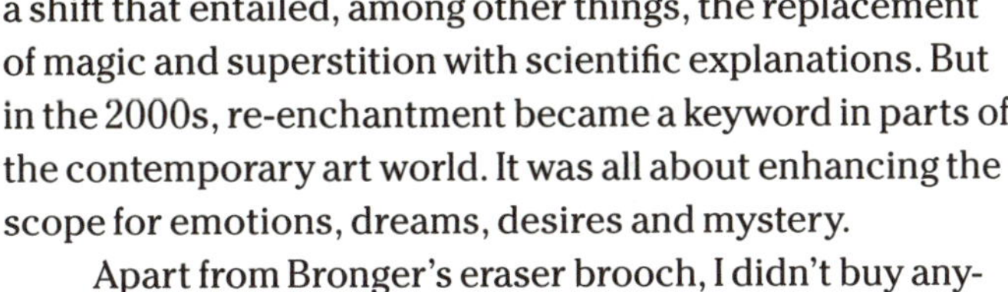

The necklace I fell in love with most could well be described as festive. It consists of a quantity of pearls and heavy, bright yellow plaited wool [411]. The way the pearls are mounted is highly unconventional: they are pressed into a generous coating of glue, a substance trained jewellers usually avoid. As Walker herself says: "It's pretty much a goldsmith's cheat material, you're not really meant to use it, and if you do then very secretly."[166] But that's not how Walker does things. On moving to Munich from New Zealand in 1995, she felt she had to rid herself of many of the classical values she had acquired in her earlier training as a jewellery artist. Glue became a catalyst in this process, in that she adopted it as a material in its own right. As something that presupposes neither practice nor a master's certificate, the conspicuous use of glue represents an act of deskilling and a forthright "statement". One thing I always find interesting are methods that challenge our notions of "good craftsmanship". Just as one speaks of "deskilling" in relation to contemporary art jewellery, one can also speak of "reskilling". Walker's jewellery is challenging in different ways: "The work is about definitions. Lisa pushes hard on the physical and conceptual limits of jewellery. It is integral to her practice to test the definitions of beauty and challenge physical portability."[167] Or as fellow jeweller Warwick Freeman sees it: "You will see only violence to material, to craft and ultimately to your aesthetic sensibilities,"[168] but at the same time, he feels, it is precisely this that gives her jewellery its "nerve".[169]

A few months later, a part of Walker's exhibition was shown under the title *Sometimes* at Platina in Stockholm, and it was there I took the opportunity to lay hands on both the "pearl necklace" and a brooch made of fur and gold leaf [**410**]. In the latter, the gold leaf is attached with glue: "I discovered a technique of covering the drying glue from a hot glue gun with gold leaf, then gently kneading it till the glue hardened completely, creating globule type gold shapes that could be used for all sorts of purposes," she said in an interview with *Klimt02*, one of the principal online magazines for art jewellery.[170] Like so many jewellery artists, she is enthusiastic about gold as a material:

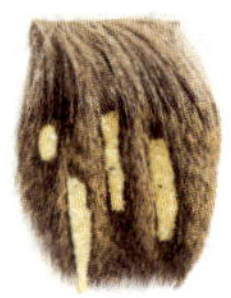

> I've always wanted to use more of it but couldn't afford it. It's a gorgeous, beautiful, flexible material that has this unbelievable history attached to it, you can't escape it. Gold can transform the preciousness of a piece (though preciousness can certainly exist without gold), I like this and try to play with it sometimes.[171]

But fur is also a material with strong connotations of luxury and eroticism. The brooch refers straight back to the versatile artist Meret Oppenheim (1913–1985), who in the 1930s covered a bracelet in fur, as she also did with a cup, saucer and spoon, creating her iconic *Breakfast in Fur*. I see Walker

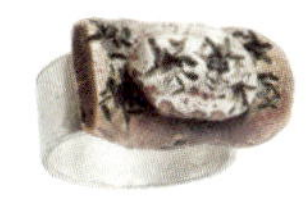

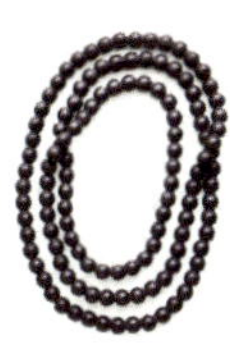

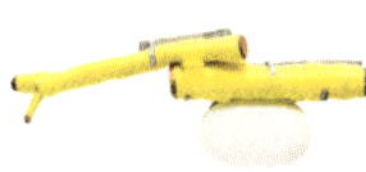

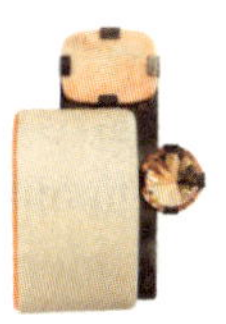

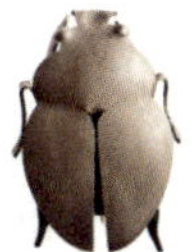

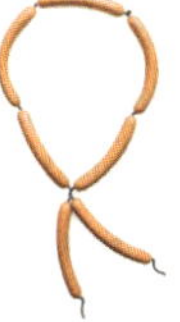

as a successor to Oppenheim. Both cultivate assemblage as a method and are fearless in terms of the materials they combine and their ways of doing it. Neither adheres to the rules of feminine adornment, and despite the humour they use in undermining those conventions, their intention is serious.

It wasn't until 2011 that I undertook my first proper buying spree at *Schmuck*. By then, I had had a few years of full-time engagement as a researcher and professor at the Bergen Academy of Art and Design. This gave me a bit of financial breathing space, as our bank adviser put it. Air pockets of this kind always stimulate my urge to buy. During Jewellery Week, I acquired a ring by Karl Fritsch [143], a necklace by Susanne Klemm [212], brooches by Helena Lehtinen [250] and Ute Eitzenhöfer [131] and two pieces by David Bielander: a brooch in in the form of a beetle [33] and a necklace resembling a string of sausages [37].

Bielander's exhibition at Galerie Biró that year had the title *A Theatre of Appearance*. The reference to theatre is well chosen because theatrical effects such as sudden transformations and optical illusions are a mainstay of Bielander's work. This is also true of the two works I acquired. The brooch is made from a simple steel teaspoon, which has been bent, cut and sandblasted to resemble a beetle, and fitted with a gold clasp. Every detail of the spoon is used, including the embellishment on the handle, which is visible on the beetle's legs. But if you didn't know it, you would never think of a spoon on seeing the brooch. Unlike many who recycle things, Bielander does not make it clear what he took as his starting point. This is an important point for him, as is the goal of making the end result look self-evident and simple, regardless of how long it has taken to arrive at the final solution.

Bielander had long wanted to use sausages as a jewellery motif, ever since he dicovered several of them lurking in the bentwood back of the classic No. 14 café chair designed by Michael Thonet in 1859. Having bought twelve of the chairs, all he had to do was cut them into sections, which he then painted. This was a different process than if he had designed a sausage himself. He produced the work in three versions, "Weisswurst", "Frankfurter" and "Wienerle", all of which use the shapes as found: "The sausages have always been in these chairs! I only had to set them free."[172]

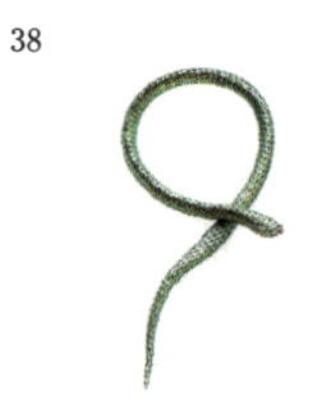

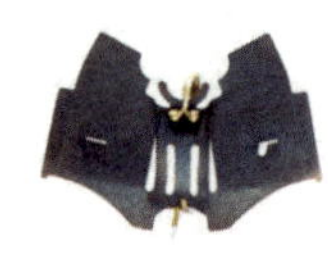

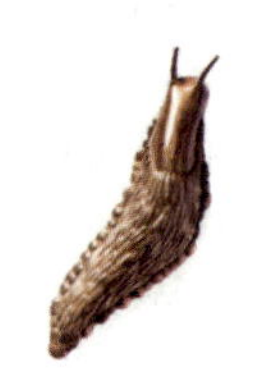

With jewellery, the material is often the first thing one notices. But not so with Bielander's work. Here it is the motifs that catch the attention, whether they be sausages, snakes [38], moths [34] or slugs [35]. It is only on closer inspection that one begins to appreciate the art of transformation involved in making a beetle from a spoon, or sausages from a chair or a moth from part of a disposable lighter. The visual illusion helps to sharpen our perception. It is a trick he used to the full in his retrospective show *Demiurg*, which took place in Munich during *Schmuck 2014*. The exhibition was initially created for the Museum voor Moderne Kunst Arnhem in the Netherlands the previous year to mark Bielander's winning of the 2012 Françoise van den Bosch Prize. For this he created five dioramas, some representing landscapes, others interiors. The jewellery featured as true to life props in these enchanting fairy-tale worlds. The exhibition was fascinating for the originality of its displays and as an opportunity to trace Bielander's development over a twenty-year period. When KRAFT, a gallery in Bergen, asked if I could curate their opening exhibition, I suggested *Demiurg*. The Oxford English Dictionary defines the word "demiurge" as "a being responsible for the creation of the universe". The term derives from the Greek words for "public" (*demios*) and "working" (*-ergos*). The earliest known use of the word is in a Homeric hymn to the god of craftsmen, Hephaestus.[173] I thought it a nice idea for a gallery devoted to crafts to signal a link between antiquity and the present when establishing a perspective on craft-based work. Moreover, *Demiurg* was notable for the originality of its exhibition format, which succeeded in presenting numerous small objects as elements in a total installation. So that's what we chose to do. In May 2014, the exhibition was shown at KRAFT in Bergen, with the demi-

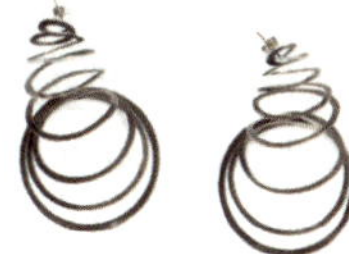

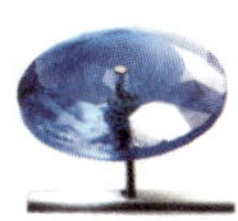

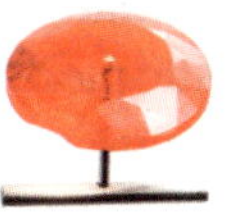

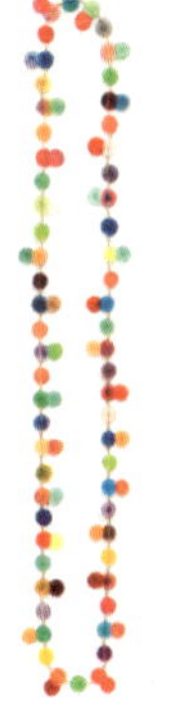

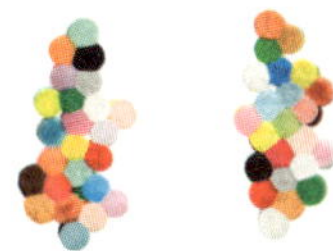

urge Bielander attending in person to present his work and to demonstrate his smoke-ring machine.

London

The city I have visited most often is London. Although it has several art and design schools that offer training for jewellery artists, it has surprisingly few galleries for contemporary art jewellery. The first was Electrum, founded in 1971 by curator Ralph Turner and jeweller Barbara Cartlidge. Turner, who died in 2017 at the age of eighty-one, was an elderly gentleman when I got to know him as a fellow member of the jury for the exhibition *Talente* in Munich. Admittedly, we did not agree on who should receive prizes, but he has been important to me as the author of books on art jewellery.[174] Tone Vigeland's first solo exhibition outside Norway was at Electrum in 1981. The gallery has also presented Toril Bjorg. For many years, Electrum was a regular item on my itinerary when visiting London, even if I generally went there just to look rather than buy. An exception is one of my favourite pairs of earrings, which are made by Reiko Ishiyama [201]. Turner withdrew from the management of Electrum at an early stage, and in the course of the 1990s the gallery gradually became less interesting.

Lesley Craze ran a gallery in her own name from 1984 until it closed in 2015. There I picked up several pieces that were not too demanding to wear, including a couple of rings by Herman Hermsen [183, 184] and earrings and a necklace by Karola Torkos [386, 389]. When friends with young children see the colourful round blobs of plastic that Torkos has used, they are reminded of the hours they have spent making designs with Hama Beads, and for my own part, these are pieces that always put me in a good mood.

My jewellery shopping in London gained momentum with the launch of Collect in 2004, a craft fair organised by the Crafts Council. In the first years, Dutch jewellery galleries were given a high profile, and it was at the stand of Galerie Louise Smit that I first discovered Felieke van der

Leest, who has since moved to Norway. Van der Leest's jewellery is figurative and narrative, and one of the works I took home with me was the crocheted ring "Target Rabbit" [248]. The motif is a rabbit standing upright and alert. The target on his face explains why.

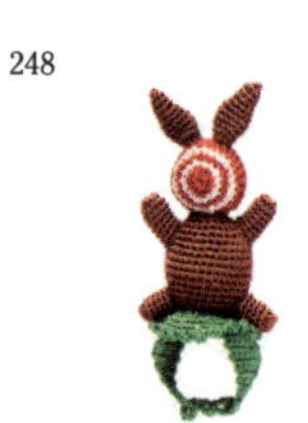

The following year, the rabbit was joined by a new animal figure, "Pregnant Polar Bear" [246]. This consists of a tiny swaddled bear cub that can be worn as a brooch. Only the artist and the owner know that when the cub is taken out on an excursion, the soft body of its mother is waiting at home to receive it back when it returns. Animals have always played a central role in van der Leest's art. She grew up close to a zoo, where giraffes, elephants and other exotic animals were an everyday sight. As in "Pregnant Polar Bear", she starts out with a mass-produced plastic model animal, which she gives a new identity by adorning it with crocheted clothes and accessories. I am always filled with amazement when I see van der Leest's meticulous crochet work, which requires the use of the finest threads and needles. The format, the fact that these figures are so small, is also part of their appeal.

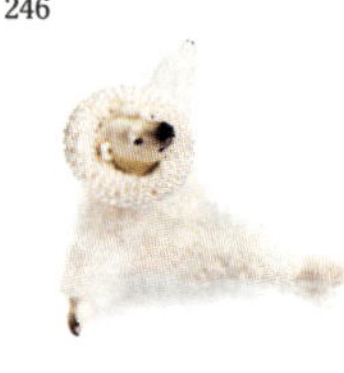

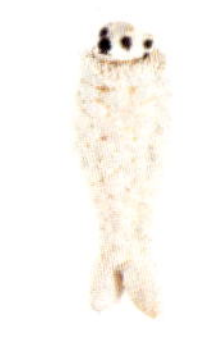

My second purchase at Collect in 2005 was from the stand of Galerie Marzee. Ute Eitzenhöfer had taken a piece of driftwood as the setting for five small diamonds. Both elements could be described as natural materials, but whereas the wood has been shaped and smoothed by wind and water, the diamonds have been cut by human hand [132].

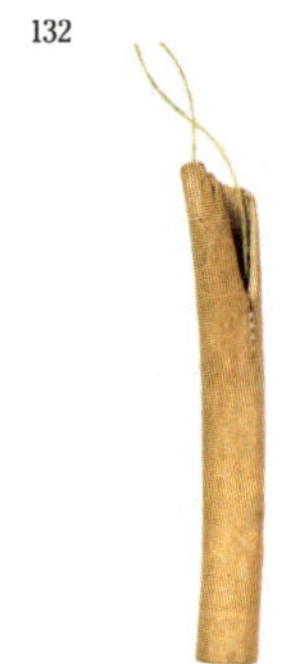

Gallery SO

I discovered Gallery SO through their participation in Collect. They stood out for their strong conceptual orientation. The gallery was launched in 2003 in Solothurn, Switzerland, and six years later they opened a branch in London. The owner, Felix Flury, is himself a trained gold- and silversmith.

There are two artists in particular whose work I have bought at SO, namely Bernhard Schobinger and Hans

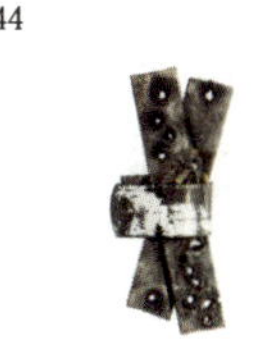

344

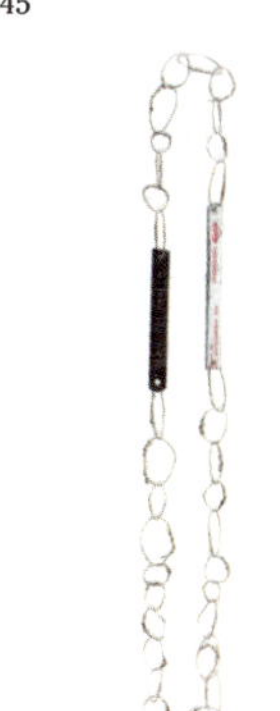

345

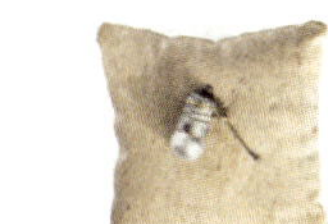

346

Stofer. Both are Swiss, and both make frequent use of ready-mades and found materials as their starting point. But whereas Stofer's objects and jewellery often have a humorous edge, the edges in Schobinger's works are quite literally sharper. For example, the ring and necklace in my collection incorporate bits of old saw blades [344, 345]. Despite the sharp teeth that make them look so aggressive, I have, however, never sustained any injury when wearing them. The first work I bought by Schobinger was rather different. Stuck through a well-used and somewhat grubby pin cushion he inherited from his mother is a needle, from which a small light bulb hangs [346]. On closer inspection, this turns out to be an optical illusion: the light bulb is in fact a genuine pearl, and wound around the screw fitting is a thin gold wire.

There is certainly no shortage of playful illusion and so-called trompe l'oeil in Stofer's "Off My Trolley", a work Gallery SO presented at Collect in 2009. The work consists of a trolley loaded with objects that allude to an active painter's studio: tins with brushes, fag ends, plastic cups and used paint tubes. Every item in this assemblage of junk and useful stuff is made by hand: the cigarette butts are not real but illusions made from metal; admittedly, the wooden handles of the paint brushes in the old tins are the real thing, but instead of bristles they are tipped with the bowls of spoons and the like. Scattered among this paraphernalia are examples of Stofer's jewellery. Like his objects, they evade the normal categories of design and crafts.

As a skilful craftsman, Stofer can transform found objects into either non-functional art objects and jewellery or new and functional tools. There's a profound irony in the fact that "Off My Trolley" comes across as a collection of ready-mades (read: fine art), whereas what Stofer has done is to make things that merely resemble ready-mades (read: crafts). In today's art world, the ability to perform this kind of magic is vastly underappreciated – as the title clearly suggests. Because someone who is "off his trolley" is inclined to behave in unusual ways or to do things that

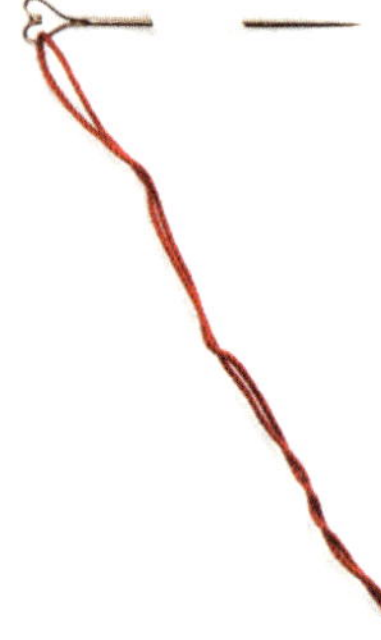

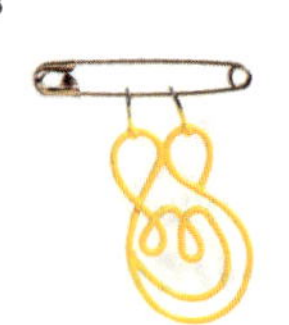

appear rather stupid. "In polite *Collect*, Hans Stofer's *Off My Trolley* stood out with an imagined soundtrack of The Clash. His piece of resistance was 'in your face', using punk and scatter-art strategies, a piece of work where nothing more needed to be said – the piece was the message," wrote jewellery artist Jivan Astfalck in a review.[175]

"Off My Trolley" also featured in Stofer's solo exhibition *Walk the Line*, at Gallery SO in London in 2010. There I bought a sewing needle with a heart-shaped eye and red thread [364]. One attaches the needle directly to a sweater, while the thread is slung around the neck like a necklace. I also brought a brooch made of wire [363]. This is attached to a garment by means of a safety pin that always remains visible – in stark contrast to the way we usually use safety pins. As cultural theorist Gitte Duemose Hansen points out, the safety pin belongs to a category of useful things "that should be neither seen nor mentioned".[176] This is because it represents a temporary emergency measure intended to prevent an embarrassing episode and to ensure a decent appearance. Accordingly, the safety pin is the opposite of jewellery: "The proper place for this little device is therefore on the inside of the garment, close to the zone of modesty and demureness. Our conception of this zone has a contagious effect on our conception of the thing, and thus conceptually the safety pin subsists far removed from the category of jewellery."[177] It is therefore a provocative gesture to use a safety pin as a permanent solution to the problem of finding a good fastening mechanism.

Stockholm

The exhibition *New Jewellery. International Art Jewellery*, presented at Kulturhuset in Stockholm in 1986, is considered a historical turning point in Sweden.[178] Although at the time, I had to make do with the thinner catalogue with black-and-white illustrations, it was sufficient to convince me of something new and exciting in the field of art jewellery. Even so, I would argue it wasn't until the early 2000s that

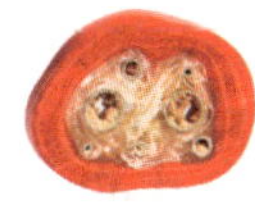

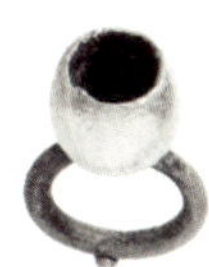

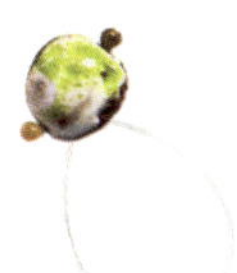

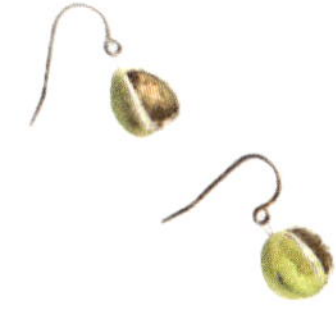

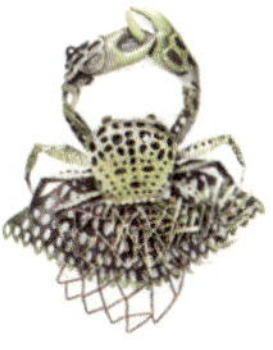

Stockholm really became a centre for art jewellery. Between 2003 and 2006, the project *Craft in Dialogue*, the brainchild of Päivi Ernkvist and Zandra Ahl, aimed to internationalise Swedish crafts by promoting exhibitions, seminars, visitor programmes and publications. So when jewellery artists Auli Laitinen and Agnieszka Knap decided to initiate an international seminar on beauty, *Craft in Dialogue* stepped in as host. In November 2004, twenty-one crafters and designers were invited to a three-day workshop to immerse themselves in "Thoughts on Beauty". They were divided into three groups, headed by Mònica Gaspar, Jivan Astfalck and myself. It was here I met Liesbeth den Besten for the first time, along with jewellery artists Jenny Edlund, Hilde De Decker, Karl Fritsch and Christoph Zellweger.

Stockholm has several artist-run exhibition venues, but the most important gallery for international art jewellery is without doubt Platina. Sofia Björkman has run Platina as a gallery-cum-studio since 1999, for the first ten years in association with fellow jeweller Åsa Skogberg. I visited the gallery for the first time in 2002. In the years that followed, I bought a number of small works by well-known international names such as Ruudt Peters [305] and Peter Bauhuis [20]. In 2004, I fell in love with a ring plus matching earrings by Sam-Tho Duong [127, 128]. The forms were moulded around cherry stones, then enamelled in shades of pale green and white suggestive of spring and budding plants. New ways of using enamel have always fascinated me.

Platina has also been my source for jewellery by major Swedish artists such as Hanna Hedman and Karin Johansson. Hedman addresses the threat to species diversity in nature [181]. The brooch "Potamonautes lividus" refers to an African freshwater crab that is on the red list of endangered species. For the composition of her necklace "Shortcut" [204], Karin Johansson has drawn inspiration from city maps.

Björkman herself is responsible for a brooch with the humorous title "Wanna Be Precious" [47], which I have often

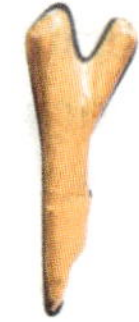

47

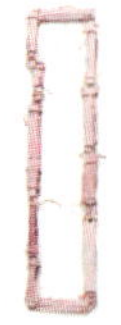

56

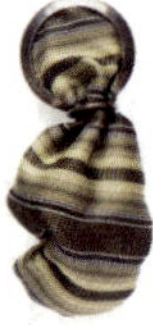

243

worn. This piece resembles a wooden stick but turns out on closer inspection to be an imitation of wood made of laminated plastic. In other words, the material is counterfeit and cheap. By contrast, a necklace by Sara Borgegård Älgå, which I bought in 2009, is made from real pinewood, albeit it camouflaged by pink paint [56]. Another important jewellery artist in Sweden is Auli Laitinen. Her series *Out of the Closet* consists of brooches made from ties. I bought one of them at Platina in 2005 [243]. Its shape alludes to a well-filled scrotum and hence also to the expression "to have balls". Someone with the balls for something has the courage to do it. With this reference to testicles and testosterone, the work could be seen as a celebration of masculinity, but when I as a woman wear the brooch, that message acquires an ironical twist. The motif also becomes a distraction from all those feminine attributes that tend to get exposed in public spaces.

Thirty years after its 1986 review of international art jewellery, Kulturhuset presented a new survey of the field: *Open Space – Mind Maps. Positions in Contemporary Jewellery*, curated by art historian and gallery owner Ellen Maurer Zilioli. Various perspectives were indicated by loose keywords such as Sign, Icons, Secret Beauty, Limits, Nomadism, Storytelling and Image and Poetry. Many of the artists who interest me were represented. Suska Mackert and Maisie Broadhead, for example, both contributed works that were not jewellery as such but rather about jewellery. One of the people who impressed me deeply at *Open Space – Mind Maps*, and from whom I later bought a necklace, was Beatrice Brovia. Many of Brovia's works address the issue of different value systems. As we've already seen, the question of what makes a piece of jewellery valuable has been a central theme for jewellery artists since the 1970s. In the 2000s, this discussion took on a different tone. In our current consumer culture, brands have become omnipresent as markers of group identity. With powerful support in Naomi Klein's international bestseller *No Logo* from 1999, the critique of brands, their dominance and promotion of pre-packaged lifestyles grew louder. Brovia has focused in particular on the prominent role of branding in sports, and at one point she even noted parallels between sports and art production: "I started to see similarities between athleticism and the artistic process that is at the core of my making: both practices entail a 'competitive' type of expenditure that isn't really economic or logical or based on an actual need or on an expectation of profit."[179] "Cre\$t", a piece from her *Exonumia* series, is about the symbolic value of emblems and the way we gain status by flaunting them [80]. This jewellery is both a "marker of the body" and a "surface through which communication is made possible".[180]

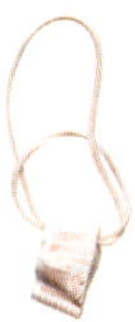

Copenhagen

In Denmark, the average jewellery artist is a trained goldsmith who combines her workshop with a sales outlet. The most important to me have been Kim Buck, who has been operating since 1990, Kasia Gasparski, who started Guldkompagniet in 1998, and Mette Saabye, who launched her own gallery-cum-workshop in 2005.

What Copenhagen has always been short of is dedicated jewellery galleries. When I moved to Denmark in the mid-1990s, Galerie Metal was the principal exhibition venue for international jewellery art. But Jan Lohmann, who ran the gallery at the time, subsequently moved away, and ever since the venue has never been the powerhouse it once was. One significant venture since then has been The Most Secret Gallery, an initiative of Kim Buck. This sprang from a joint exhibition Buck organised together with Karin Seufert and Tore Svensson in 2013. They called their exhibition *KGB*, after the initial letters of the respective cities where the artists live and work, and where the exhibition was shown: Copenhagen (spelt with a K in Danish and German), Gothenburg and Berlin. Echoing the acronym for the secretive Soviet intelligence agency, it was an easy name to remember. But might there be similarities other than just the name, I wondered in my opening speech, even if only in a figurative sense: the three artists could be viewed as agents whose mission is to spread an interest in art jewellery among the wider population, although they do so with complete openness and without hidden agendas.

The exhibition *KGB* opened on 29 June, the same day as the 2013 Biennale for Crafts and Design opened in Rundetårn. In conjunction with the latter, a seminar was arranged in Copenhagen, which was led by Jivan Astfalck, Dennis Dahlqvist and Jessica Hemmings. I had been a member of the biennial's jury, together with Dahlqvist, and knew Astfalck well from my work as an examiner at the MA class at the School of Jewellery at Birmingham University in England, which she headed. I had also met Hemmings, one of the foremost theorists on textile art, on several earlier occasions. Inviting them home for drinks on the roof terrace of Bordings Friskole, where I and Mogens lived at the time, was therefore an obvious thing to do. Since the Nordic touring exhibition *From the Coolest Corner* had opened at Designmuseum Danmark the day before, the city was full of visiting jewellery artists. Kim Buck was represented in the exhibition as an honorary artist from Denmark and Tore Svensson as the same from Sweden. They too came over to join our gathering, which ended up with Mogens improvising a dinner for some twenty people. I mention this because it was at that dinner that Svensson asked if he could incorporate me into his portrait gallery [378]. He was creating a series of portraits of significant figures from his personal jewellery network. I readily admit that the prospect of being portrayed appealed to my vanity. In the era prior to the smartphone and social media, which have allowed everyone to gain maximum exposure, having your portrait done was a sign of prestige: one had joined the elect and was worthy of being remembered. The art portrait still carries some of this nimbus. At the same time, I know that the immortalisation we associate with portraits is mere illusion. I have often studied medallions with images of long-dead and unknown people and thought just how little they tell us about their human subjects. What commemorative jewellery of this kind conveys to posterity is primarily an impossible desire to remember and be remem-

378

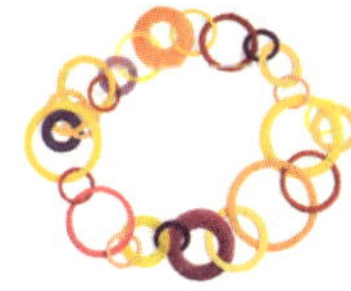

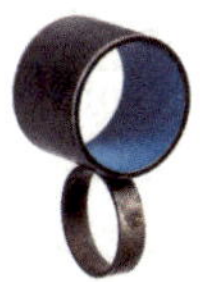

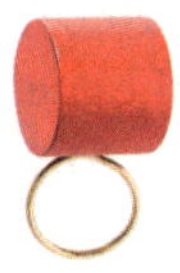

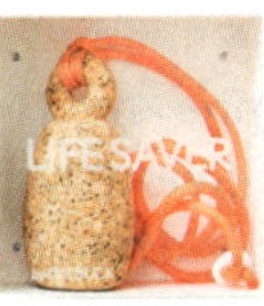

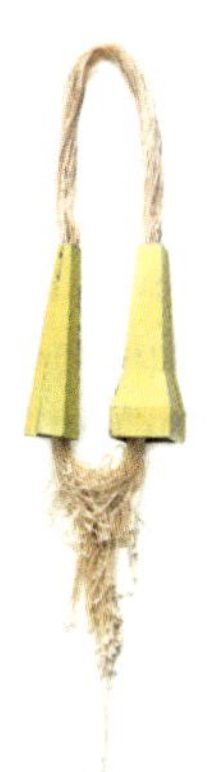

bered. Impossible because the problem with portraits is that it isn't the model who ensures their long-term survival but rather the artistic and conceptual qualities of their execution.

The *KGB* exhibition has also left lasting traces in my jewellery box. A necklace by Seufert is made from plastic corks of various sizes and colours, which she melted using an iron or hot-air gun to the point where they could be linked together to form a chain [350]. From Svensson I bought a ring whose ornament is a short section of black steel tubing painted vibrant blue on the inside [380]. Another ring of his features a cylinder of red painted wood that roughly corresponds to the internal space of the former ring [379]. Plastic, steel and wood are not precious or valuable materials in the conventional sense. How jewellery gets invested with value independently of its constituent materials was a question this exhibition addressed head on. One of the answers was that the ways artists transform materials involves both a transfer from their original more mundane contexts and an enhancement that results from the craftsmanship to which they are subjected. Thus they acquire artistic value. A desire, on the one hand, to promote the appreciation of contemporary art jewellery among Danish audiences and, on the other, for opportunities to collaborate and exhibit with foreign colleagues was what motivated Buck to set up The Most Secret Gallery when in 2014 the neighbouring premises became available to rent. So far, he has managed one exhibition a year.

The guests in the first exhibition at The Most Secret Gallery were Swede Sara Borgegård Älgå and Japanese-German Mari Ishikawa. Kim himself showed the series *Life Saver* [109]. Works by all three ended up in my collection. Borgegård's materials are iron and steel, which she paints and then sands down in places to allow the underlying metal to shine through, thus creating a patina. It is as if time has already left its mark. Her forms are inspired by industrial architecture [57]. The bundle of numerous separate threads on which these elements are suspended makes a soft contrast to the angular industrial style of the metal-

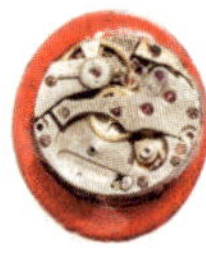

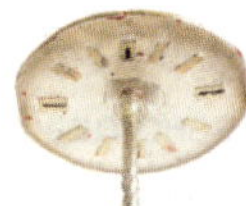

work. The yarn is of the kind weavers use as warp thread. Thus she establishes a link to the culture of textile crafts and combines references to two distinct spheres, one with masculine, the other with feminine connotations. Ishikawa works with the themes of time and memory in her series *Memory*, which features pieces of old watches. When used in jewellery, these clockwork mechanisms are subject to very different laws than the ones that applied when they served as timepieces [198, 200]. To me they suggest our ability to travel freely through time in our memories and dreams, but given the title, *Memory*, the watch elements may well be a melancholy reminder that all memories fade in time.

For Ramón Puig Cuyàs and Silvia Walz as well, Kim's invitation to exhibit at The Most Secret Gallery in 2016 represented their first exposure in Copenhagen. As the guest speaker at their opening, I was particularly intrigued by the fine use of enamel that both artists show in their work [415, 116].

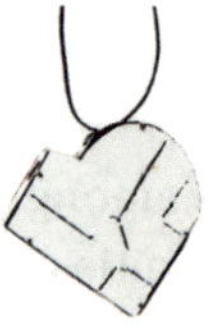

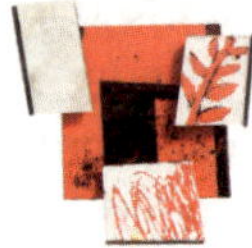

Aotearoa New Zealand

Ten artists from Aotearoa New Zealand are represented in my collection. With a population of just over three million, this is a country with a surprising number of good jewellery artists and galleries. I visited New Zealand in September 2015, in response to an invitation from Objectspace, the country's leading crafts organisation. The main purpose of my trip was to get to know the crafts scene and to deliver some lectures.

On landing in Auckland, I went straight to the Auckland Art Gallery, which was showing the exhibition *Wunder-rūma*. I had seen an earlier version of this show in Munich the previous year, but the presentation in Auckland was different. The jewellery by the seventy-five selected artists was exhibited in dialogue with fine art from the museum's own collection. The works were also grouped in clusters based on various types of kinship, which were announced by keywords. One of the largest groups was *Tools*. The notion that jewellery and tools are related struck a chord

with me. It's a focus that highlights jewellery's connections
to everyday life and practical objectives rather than to
luxury and festivities. It represents something of the same
down-to-earth approach to culture and daily routines that
runs through Norwegian art and culture. The literature
on Norwegian design is full of stories about ski bindings,
rubber boots, Leca blocks, paper clips, cheese slicers and
the successful Mustad's fishing hooks.[181] I was therefore
surprised that the two curators, Warwick Freeman and Karl
Fritsch, used a jointly made work consisting of a lead sinker
and a gold fishing hook as a signature for the exhibition. In
the catalogue, Freeman explains the powerful symbolism of
the fishing hook in the mythology of the Maori, and how in
their art they transformed it from a functional to a wearable
object, the *hei matau*, or fishhook pendant.[182]

Freeman himself has created a group of six different
hooks, *Story of the Hook*, which is among the favourites in
my collection [142]. The ensemble includes a fishing hook,
one of the oldest tools we know of, although in modern life
we do of course have hooks for other purposes as well.
Freeman reproduces both curtain hooks and the hooks of
coat hangers but has made them of materials that have frequently been used in jewellery over the years, such as bone,
jade, silver and gold. I interpret this ensemble as a critical
comment on our understanding of what constitutes the contemporary in contemporary art jewellery. We carry the past
with us in the present. It is inscribed into our traditions and
rituals, and as a layer of meaning in the materials and motifs
that artists work with.

A nation of two cultures

At the National Museum Te Papa, the curator of Maori art,
Nigel Borell, demonstrated the wealth of Maori jewellery
heritage. The main material in these works is pounamu,
a dark green nephrite jade. It was thought-provoking to
note the conspicuous presence of Maori culture in New
Zealand's art and cultural life compared to the obscurity

142

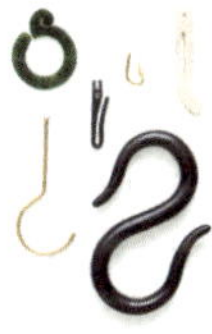

of Sami art and culture in Norwegian national contexts. In
Aotearoa New Zealand, one is aware of an ongoing reassess-
ment of the colonial past and the bicultural present.

One of the central Maori artists is Areta Wilkinson.
I had the good fortune to see her exhibition *Whakapaipai
– Jewellery as Pepeha* at the Dowse Art Museum in Wellington. *Whakapaipai* means to "make beautiful, to adorn"
and *whakapai* "to revise", "improve", "bless" or "set", as in
setting a table, while the term *pepeha* means "to announce",
"distinguish", "identify" or "locate". In other words, the
exhibition title encompassed an entire programme. Wilkinson's jewellery was presented on life-size silhouette figures
based on her own Maori relatives. This installation was
surrounded by a series of photograms and cyanotypes
(blueprints) with impressions of jewellery. Resembling
shadows, these images seemed to suggest the memories
we carry around within us. They served as reminders of the
value of continuity and belonging, and of having something
to pass on to the next generation.

Jewellers of European descent (*pakeha*) have been
accused of cultural appropriation for their use of Maori
materials and motifs. Pounamu in particular has been
described as a culturally and historically charged material.
But where does one draw the line between inspiration,
exchange and appropriation? There is no evidence to
suggest the Maoris ever made rings, so when the European
immigrant Karl Fritsch makes a ring of pounamu, he is creating a type of object that didn't previously exist [145]. Is it fair
to speak of appropriation here? If anything, the significance
of the material is that it helps him to position himself in his
new homeland.

The now-retired director of Objectspace, Philip
Clarke, drove me around both the North and South Islands.
During the trip I met three generations of jewellery artists
in the cities of Auckland, Wellington and Dunedin. We also
spent a night in Middlemarch in Central Otago, as guests of
Patricia Bosshard-Browne and her husband, Kobi Bosshard,
"the grandfather of contemporary New Zealand jewel-

145

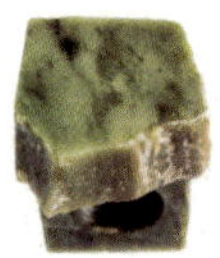

lery". The route to their house took us through a mountain landscape with numerous traces of gold mining. Originally from Switzerland, where he studied goldsmithing, Bosshard came to New Zealand in 1961, at the age of twenty-one. A classic craftsman, he focuses on materials and processes, working for the most part in silver. The pieces of his that I have are a set of earrings and a finger ring, made according to rules he defined for himself in the 1980s [59]. These dictate that he should never subject a piece of silver to more than one rolling. Neither does he allow himself to correct the edges. Anything left over in making one work is to be used in the next. Thus, when he made my ring, the piece that was cut from the centre became one of the hanging elements in the earrings. As a method that leaves all the operations visible in the result, his jewellery appears raw and powerful.

We also called in on Alan Preston and Warwick Freeman. Both were major figures in the so-called Shell, Stone, Bone movement. In the 1980s, this movement sought a contemporary language to express national identity in full recognition of the country's bicultural heritage. Practitioners adopted and revitalised traditions known from the Maori and Pacific islands, in which the defining characteristic of their work was the use of natural materials [140]. As Damian Skinner has written: "The new movement established the prestige of bone, stone and shell as signifiers of living in Aotearoa."[183]

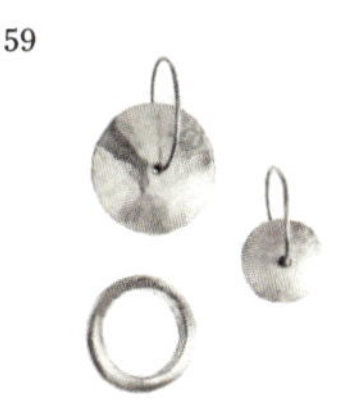

59

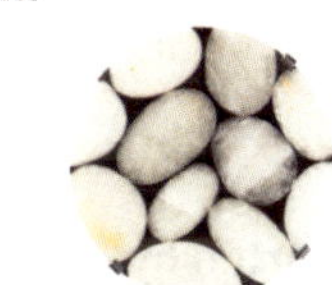

140

Galleries

When the Jewellers Guild of Greater Sandringham (Sharon Fitness, Renee Bevan and Raewyn Walsh) interviewed me about similarities and differences between Scandinavia and New Zealand, one major difference I focused on was New Zealand's relatively high number of galleries, both private and artist-run, that exhibit art jewellery.[184] The oldest of these is Fingers in Auckland, which was started by a group of young jewellery artists as far back as 1974. Today, it represents over fifty artists. Another venue in Auckland is

Masterworks Gallery, where I discovered Moniek Schrijer. She had recently returned from a study trip to Amsterdam, where Johannes Vermeer's painting *Girl with a Pearl Earring* inspired her to make earrings that quoted Vermeer in their form but with pieces of mother-of-pearl shell instead of pearls [349]. Thus she combined impressions from the Netherlands with her New Zealand heritage.

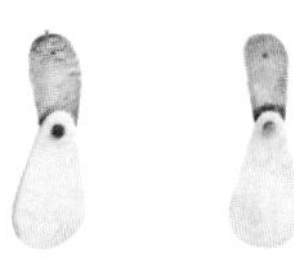

Avid Gallery in Wellington was showing the exhibition *Handshake 2* when I visited. *Handshake* is a mentor and exhibition project started by jewellery artist and teacher Peter Deckers. Its purpose is to link up newly established jewellery artists in New Zealand with international mentors whom they look up to. Simultaneous with the presentation of this project, Peter Deckers's own work was on show in the window gallery The See Here, also an artist-run project. I have rarely encountered such an inclusive and generous art community as the one I found in New Zealand, and I wonder whether there is a connection between the solidarity among the artists and the strength of their work.

The National

The National, a gallery in Christchurch, was started by Caroline Billing in 2004. When I visited, they were showing a solo exhibition by Lisa Walker. It is Walker who has shown the greatest resistance to the use of natural materials such as stones and shells as an expression of her national identity. "Perhaps there is more to say than just respect for nature," as she puts it.[185] Even so, she shares the collector's instinct. Finding one's materials in nature means one is always on the look out for something suitable for use in one's work. But rather than depend on nature, Walker picks up things that are broken, discarded or cheap – in short, remnants from spheres of life other than the beach or the forest. Liesbeth den Besten has described Walker and her partner, Karl Fritsch, as "champions of a new brutalism".[186] "Whether using precious metals and stones or discarded materials and wool", den Besten writes, "their aim was not

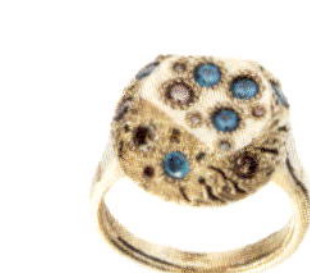

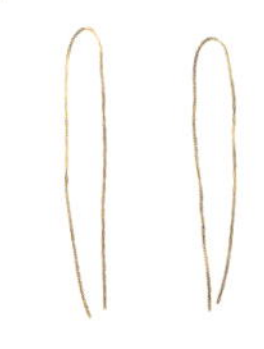

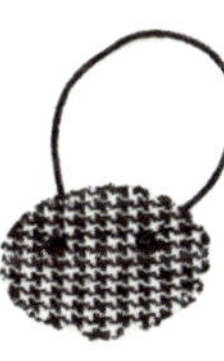

to make graceful, pleasing ornaments but to challenge our ideas about beauty."[187] This is true for some of the works I own by these two artists, but the purchases I made at The National do not quite match this characterisation. The brutalist aspect can be overlooked, and beauty is in the eye of the beholder [144, 413].

I made several purchases at The National. Firstly, I augmented my collection with another breastplate by Shelley Norton [291]. After visiting various museums with Polynesian artefacts, I was better equipped to understand this genre. Breastplates are an adornment used in many Polynesian cultures. Made of metal, they provided physical protection in combat, while in other contexts they served rather as a symbol of power. Norton's breastplates are made of plastic, the most ubiquitous material of our time. The plastic has been melted and smoothed into a hard flat disc, then painted to imitate Scottish textile patterns, in this case dog-tooth check. Thus she combines references to two different cultural traditions in one contemporary jewellery idiom. This is also a work that fits a trend that Kevin Murray has described as "poor craft", which involves the use of cheap materials one finds readily to hand.[188] Preferably, these will be materials that demonstrate resistance to the prevailing economic system in virtue of their being "found". A critical stance towards conventional ideas of what is precious was a common feature in much of the art jewellery I saw in New Zealand. Another good example of this is a gold bar signed by Moniek Schrijer, which I also bought at The National [347]. Big and brash, this particular bar has no trace of real gold. Instead, it is made of cork, plaster, sand, brass and spraypaint.

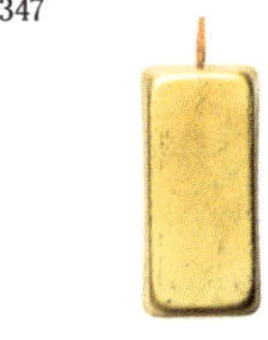

In this chapter, I have sought in particular to highlight those galleries that show art jewellery. Marjan Unger has claimed that the only thing that binds art jewellery together is the galleries that exhibit it.[189] Collectively, they constitute the platform for this type of art. Since museums display art jewellery only sporadically, it is the galleries that define the field and who play the vital role of communicating this type of jewellery to a broader audience. Unger has therefore suggested "gallery jewellery" as a more appropriate term than "studio jewellery", "art jewellery" or "contemporary jewellery".[190] Although her suggestion has not been widely adopted, the significance of galleries cannot be overestimated. It is they who have largely created and educated an audience for this art form.

Jewelry is such a rich medium – inexhaustible.

— Suska Mackert[191]

Jewellery as comment

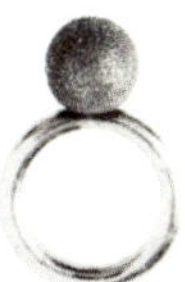

77

19

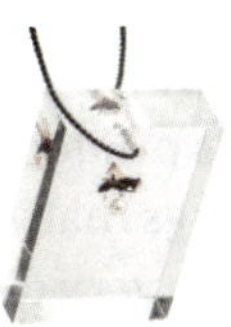

294

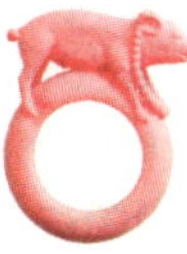

297

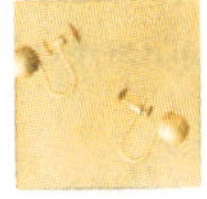

87

The 1990s saw the inflationary use of the word "conceptual". When I searched for "conceptual jewellery/jewelry" while working on this book, Google reported roughly 100,000 images for me to look at. Among the first hundred was a ring I own by Sigurd Bronger [77], a bracelet by Gijs Bakker [19], several works by Ted Noten [294, 297] and a series of brooches by Kim Buck [87]. The differences between these four artists are more striking than their similarities. Evidently, concept art cannot be defined in terms of specific materials or a clear style, so what justifies putting all these works in the category of conceptual jewellery art?

Conceptual art arose in the 1960s. In his famous text "Paragraphs on Conceptual Art", the artist Sol LeWitt declares that this type of art seeks to "engage the mind of the viewer rather than his eye or emotions".[192] Statements of this kind indicate a desire for art to amount to something more than just beautifully composed and exquisitely executed objects. Investigations into the very nature of art, undertaken with the aim of expanding and changing the conceptual content of the term, have therefore been central to conceptual art since its inception. For some, it is also about expanding art's social and political dimension. From this perspective, the idea that, in the context of art, all materials and media are essentially equally worthy was seen as an expression of the democratisation of art. It is a way of thinking that has had a profound impact also on the art of jewellery.

The question of what constitutes a piece of jewellery as a cultural object, and how far the concept of jewellery can be stretched before it becomes meaningless, has been a central preoccupation for many of the artists who interest me. "Everything you don't understand can be contemporary jewellery" proclaims a sticker handed out by the Moving On Collective during Munich Jewellery Week in 2013 [450]. This is meta-art, art that comments on itself, a feature common to a lot of contemporary art.

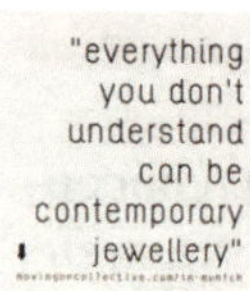

450

549

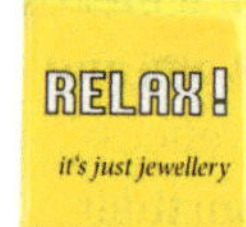

Conceptual art

Mention conceptual jewellery art and for many the first name that comes to mind is Suska Mackert. She is more interested in jewellery as a phenomenon than with making jewellery as such. Accordingly, she collects printed matter, newspaper photos, texts and other things that illustrate how jewellery is used and perceived in very different social contexts. Since 2009, she has compiled her findings in the work *Eine Ordnung des Glanzes* (A Structuring of Lustre). Newspaper cuttings about heads of state adorning each other with medals or people kissing the Pope's ring are just some of the examples of documentation included in the archive. There is no strict order to this two-dimensional museum, as she has called it. The material is sorted into dossiers based on various topics and themes, many of which she has released as printed editions. "The Andy Warhol Collection" [469] is one of several in my collection.

"The Andy Warhol Collection" is based on a 1988 auction catalogue from Sotheby's New York which covered Andy Warhol's collection of expensive jewellery and watches. Mackert has cut all the jewellery items from the

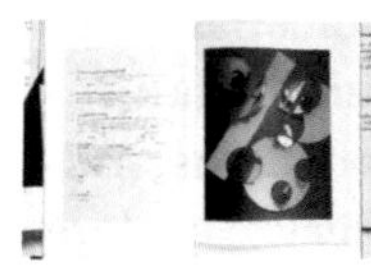

various pictures leaving just their contours. The result is a fragile, fragmented book that she has then photographed and reproduced. As fellow artist Benedikt Fischer has pointed out, Mackert uses "absence as a strategy and reproduction as a tool".[193] This aligns her with the artists of the Pictures Generation, who in the 1970s and 1980s used appropriation and montage to problematise our perceptions of the visual image and what it represents. A piece of jewellery in a catalogue is not the jewellery itself but a reproduction of a photo of a piece of jewellery. The complexity in Mackert's removal of jewellery from the Warhol catalogue is insightfully illuminated by culture theorist Alena Alexandrova:

> Mackert's practice unpacks a conceptual question at the heart of the jewelry object – its status as something added, an accessory. But we know that supplements have a subversive force precisely because of their unstable identity. The jewel's role is to add, to enhance, to indicate status. Yet, at the very moment it adds, it in fact indicates an absence, insufficiency – the wearer is not beautiful or important enough.[194]

Alexandrova also points out that Mackert's manipulations question the equivalence between jewellery and the means used to present it, such as frames, stands and catalogues, which we would also define as supplementary. Thus Mackert's "negative jewellery" highlights the importance of the presentation context while simultaneously portraying the jewellery as a phenomenon that oscillates between materiality and ephemerality.[195] Although Mackert accepts the label of conceptual artist, her practice certainly does not fall under Sol LeWitt's definition: "For me a concept is also emotional. I never think something up. A concept grows and it is hard work to find the precise form," she says.[196] Her way of working requires both patience and precision.

Wearable jewellery can also be conceptual art. In 2007, I saw an exhibition, *Then and Now*, curated by

Caroline Broadhead at the Barrett Marsden Gallery in London, which included several works that illustrate this point. The exhibition identified a current trend in the use of traditional forms, such as cameos and medallions, and the symbolic and sentimental roles of jewellery to explore contemporary issues. This tendency accords with one of the points in Ted Noten's manifesto: "Jewellery must use traditional codes in order to break them."[197]

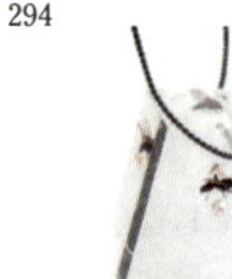

In the piece by Ted Noten that I bought at the exhibition, the appointed representative of tradition and conventional notions of beauty was a pearl [294]. This was cast in acrylic glass together with a fly, which served to symbolise the opposite, namely common notions of the ugly and repulsive. One busy morning I lost this pendant on the way to the train station. Noten made me a replacement, but it was not as nice. It was winter, so the supply of flies was poor. In the new edition, the fly is smaller and skinnier and sits on a similarly diminished pearl. But the idea is just as good.

Kim Buck also contributed to *Then and Now*, showing, among other things, "Loves Me" and "Loves Me Not" [99]. Denmark has its own popular jewellery cliché: the daisy brooch. This was created to celebrate the baptism of Queen Margrethe II, who has the nickname Daisy. In Danish the generic name for the daisy is *margerit*. The brooch represents a daisy and is made from gold-plated silver and white enamel. For over eighty years it has been a bestseller that appeals to all ages. Buck treated this daisy brooch as a ready-made that he could manipulate for his own purposes. On the back one finds the names of both Georg Jensen, the silversmith company that designed the original, and Buck himself. In Buck's adaptation, the flower has lost some of its petals, which can be bought as separate pins. The title words in Danish, "Elsker" and "Elsker ikke", are what young lovesick Danes say when plucking the petals from flowers to discover whether or not their crush loves them in return, the equivalents of the English "(s)he loves me, (s)he loves me

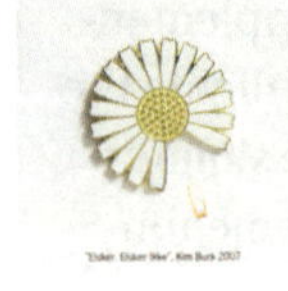
"Elsker/Elsker ikke", Kim Buck 2007

not". But with their simpler grammar ("elsker" and "elsker ikke" mean simply "love" and "love not"), the Danish terms have an ambiguity that also covers Buck's feelings towards the Georg Jensen company.

Many of the works by Noten and Buck display features that make them suitable illustrations of conceptual art. First, they are meta-jewellery: jewellery about jewellery. Second, they are based on things that already exist, a category to which Marcel Duchamp gave the name "ready-mades". In this respect, they contradict both the notion that art must be an expression of personal emotion and the idea that art should bear traces of the artist's hand. In her 1917 defence of Duchamp's famous but now lost urinal sculpture, *Fountain*, Beatrice Wood made three decisive points: First, choosing an object is in itself a creative act. Second, objects become art when emancipated from their utilitarian function. And third, an object acquires a new meaning when given a title.[198] Today, this is an accepted approach to art production. But for jewellery artists it is rarely enough just to transfer a thing from one context of use to another. Generally, the thing is treated as a raw material that is subjected to some form of processing. In this respect, the concept of the ready-made with its "hands off" connotations is misleading.

Caroline Broadhead, the curator behind *Then and Now*, is herself an artist. The work I have of hers, "Dropped Necklace", also satisfies the abovementioned criteria for conceptual art [65]. I saw it for the first time at an exhibition in Munich in 2016. Since it was lying on the floor, I had to bend down to look at it. That affects the way you see a thing. By placing an artwork on the floor, one removes it from the protection provided by the plinth or vitrine. One could easily tread on or trip over something lying on the floor, or simply fail to notice it. Thus the floor represents a loss of status, suggesting in this case that we are dealing with something that isn't really wanted. The materials used in "Dropped Necklace" support this interpretation. The necklace is a second-hand find made of imitation

65

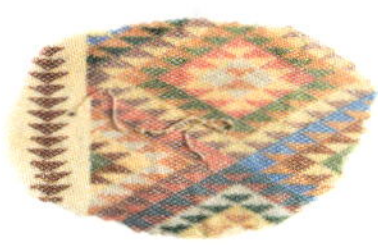

pearls. In other words, a conventional necklace laid out on a surface which, in terms of its colours and patterning, resembles a scrap of Aztec rug. But anyone who tries to pick up the necklace takes the rug with it. For the former is sewn onto the latter, and together they transform into a wearable piece of jewellery. "In my narrative, the necklace has fallen on the floor, and when you go to pick it up, you also pick up the carpet," Broadhead has explained.[199] In this way, she illustrates how things affect each other and how their identities can change.

When we examine "Dropped Necklace" more closely, however, the supposed scrap of rug turns out to be a lattice made from tiny glass beads. In other words, the work plays directly with visual deception. But this visual playfulness, the richness of colour and the laborious work of threading glass beads all constitute a challenge to the more puritanical aspects of the conceptual art tradition, which has been markedly cerebral and has shown little interest in manual work. I would therefore argue that jewellery artists have been central in opening up conceptual art to aesthetic and sensory qualities.

Even when a piece of jewellery is made from a ready-made and has been given a title, it can (generally speaking) also be used. For some in the art world, this is reason enough to relegate jewellery and crafts in general to a subordinate category relative to so-called free or fine art. When I take part in public debates where I expect this to be the prevailing attitude, I often wear a ring by Katja Prins [314]. Embedded in this ring is a white porcelain component with a tiny hole in the middle. This element immediately evokes associations with sanitary porcelain; however, I do not know whether Prins had Marcel Duchamp in mind when she made the ring. Duchamp's celebrated work *Boîte-en-valise*, a kind of portable travel exhibition, consists of a suitcase full of miniature replicas of his works. These include a handmade copy of *Fountain*, which I would find it hard not to classify as art on a level with Prins's ring.

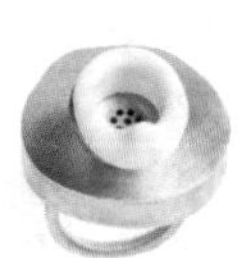

314

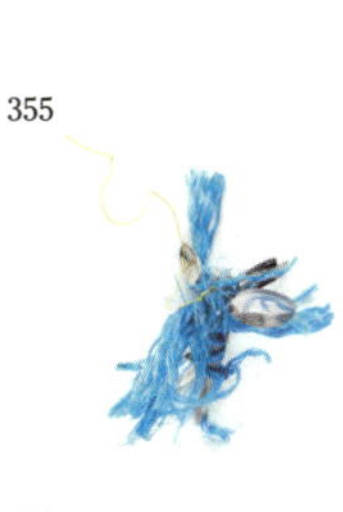

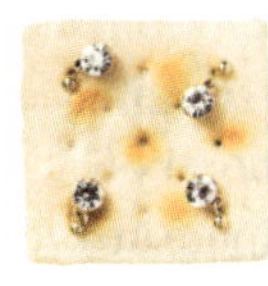

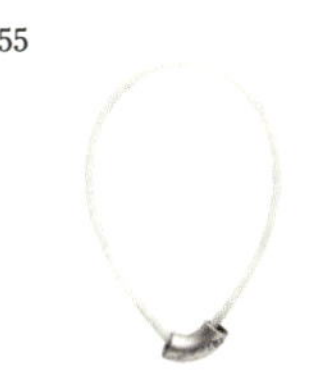

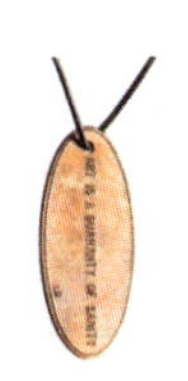

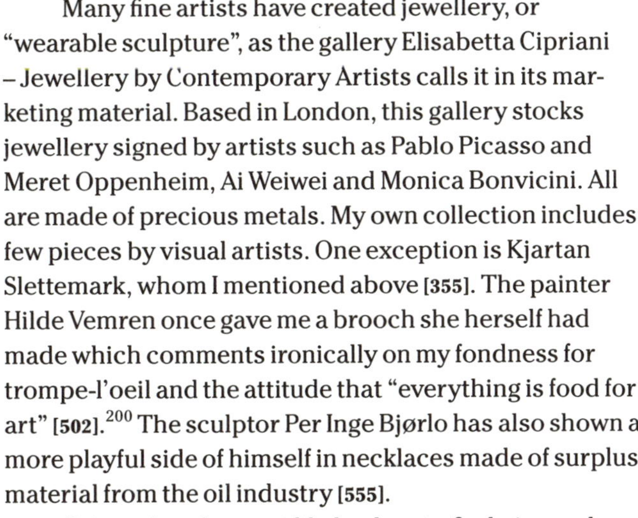

Many fine artists have created jewellery, or "wearable sculpture", as the gallery Elisabetta Cipriani – Jewellery by Contemporary Artists calls it in its marketing material. Based in London, this gallery stocks jewellery signed by artists such as Pablo Picasso and Meret Oppenheim, Ai Weiwei and Monica Bonvicini. All are made of precious metals. My own collection includes few pieces by visual artists. One exception is Kjartan Slettemark, whom I mentioned above [355]. The painter Hilde Vemren once gave me a brooch she herself had made which comments ironically on my fondness for trompe-l'oeil and the attitude that "everything is food for art" [502].[200] The sculptor Per Inge Bjørlo has also shown a more playful side of himself in necklaces made of surplus material from the oil industry [555].

Otherwise, the most likely place to find pins and jewellery by well-known artists is museum shops, where such works are often stocked as spin-offs to accompany a major exhibition by the artist in question. For the most part, jewellery of this kind falls into the category of souvenirs, like the amulet with a quote from Louise Bourgeois: "Art Is a Guaranty of Sanity" [60]. This, Bourgeois once claimed, was the most important statement she ever made. The amulet was sold at Tate Modern in conjunction with the museum's major Bourgeois retrospective in 2008. "Love Is What You Want" was the title of Tracey Emin's retrospective at the Hayward Gallery in 2011, and not surprisingly that sentiment also featured on a badge that visitors could buy [133].

Gendered pearls

It is no coincidence that when jewellery artists reference the theme of traditional jewellery, they often turn to the pearl necklace. The significance accorded to pearls is ambivalent. In nude painting, pearls are often used as an erotic accessory that evokes fantasies about female desire.[201] Pearls are very much about women. "No other gem is so consistently gendered female," declares Melanie Holcomb, the curator behind the exhibition *Jewelry. The Body Transformed.*[202] The foundations for this gendered tradition were laid way back in antiquity, but then with negative connotations. According to certain ancient philosophers, only fools waste time that could be devoted to spiritual matters on such material interests. In their view, women who wore pearls were fools for this reason.[203] In the 19th century, however, the significance of pearls changed. In the West, they came to symbolise respectability and high status and were seen as a sign of virtue or even prudishness. Consequently, in the past century, the pearl necklace was associated primarily with safe conservatism and conformity.

These connotations are central to understanding the more subversive use of pearls by contemporary artists. When Ted Noten was invited to participate in a 1995 exhibition that took the pearl necklace as its theme, he decided to wrap a pearl necklace around the neck of a dead mouse, which he then cast in acrylic. Equipped with a steel wire, this could be worn as a pendant. The question Noten was asking was: Who is wearing the best jewellery – the woman with the pendant, or the mouse adorned with pearls? With the title "Turbo Princess", this was the work that gave Noten his international breakthrough.[204] In 2012, Art Jewelry Forum invited him to design a pin that would serve as a gift to anyone who supported AJF financially that year. The result was "Little Princess", a pin in the shape of a mouse with a pearl necklace made from white Plexiglas [550].

A staged photo portrait I have by Maisie Broadhead, with the title "Chained", shows an elegantly dressed woman wearing a chain with links made from strings of glass beads [66]. It is a kind of scene that seems familiar from historical portraits, but the pearl chain extends beyond the picture frame, out into our reality and time. Thus a connection is established between the past and the present. In the photo, the jewellery passes like a noose

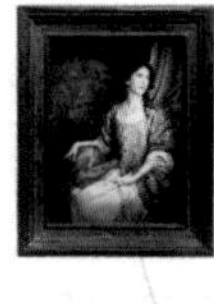

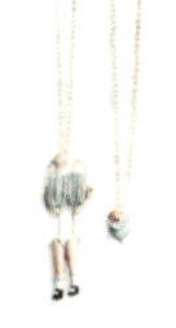

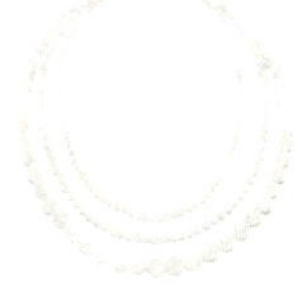

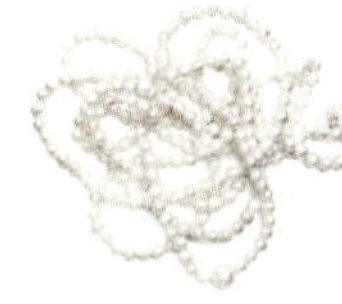

around the woman's neck. The role society assigns to her is strangulating.

The long pearl necklace that Matt Smith's geisha figure holds in her hands is of a more alluring kind [357]. The statuette is a response to a collection of Parian ware in the Fitzwilliam Museum in Cambridge, England. This is a type of porcelain that was developed in England in the early 1840s. It resembles marble and was used to make miniaturised, mass-produced versions of famous sculptures and busts for a broad market. To emphasise the attractiveness of the material and the fine modelling, figures made of Parian porcelain were often left undecorated. From our contemporary vantage point, however, these objects generally strike us as kitsch. By combining a geisha figure with a pearl necklace, Smith prompts a highly pertinent discussion of the ways in which taste, gender, class, eroticism and exoticism have been portrayed in his own field of ceramics and in culture in general.

I have never owned a regular pearl necklace, but several of the pieces in my collection ironically comment on or play with the idea of such an item. Mette Saabye has used an antique pearl necklace to string together the separated parts of a female doll [322]. The facial features of the disembodied head always make me think of snobbish Maggie in the comic strip *Bringing Up Father*. This is Saabye's way of associating pearls with a specific female role. Lise Lefebvre has designed a three-string pearl necklace [249]. This was sold as a piece of flat fabric on which the outline of the necklace was drawn with dotted lines. I had to cut it out myself, and now I find it an ideal piece of jewellery to take on holiday. It takes up no space, weighs nothing and you don't even have to take it off when going through security.

The pearls in the necklace by Julie Usel are made of thin cellophane [392]. Hans Stofer has connected strings of freshwater pearls with lengths of ball chain of the kind used for plugs in sinks and bathtubs [365]. It is an ambiguous combination that could be seen either as trivialising

the aura of pearls or helping us to notice the beauty of the
mundane chain.

What all these necklaces have in common is a
refreshing absence of aristocratic fustiness and bourgeois
conformity.

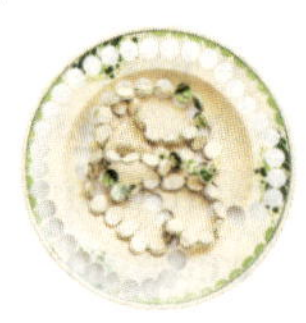

164

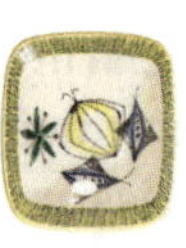

165

Ready-mades and trash
An artefact can acquire a new and unexpected life by
being transformed into something utterly different.
Gésine Hackenberg has made necklaces and rings by
cutting circular pieces from faience crockery and treating
them as if they were pearls or gemstones [164, 165]. What
remains is a bowl or dish with a series of holes. From the
point of view of the jewellery, the perforated crockery is a
residual material. But when the jewellery isn't in use, the
receptacle presents itself as the obvious place to store
it. Jewellery made from such household items carries
a domestic aura as a kind of bonus. The material and
object to which the jewellery refers are associated with
the kitchen, food and the ritual of mealtimes. We become
emotionally attached to artefacts we use on a daily basis.
This is true both of household items and of jewellery.
Some of them become favourite objects that we treasure
for many reasons other than just their material value. It is
this emotional attachment to familiar things that Hackenberg seeks to highlight.

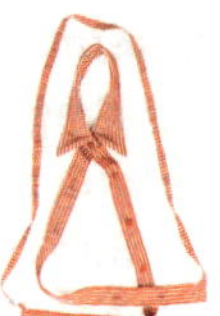

311

"Lady Manhattan" is made from a striped shirt,
which I now wear around my neck as a piece of jewellery [311]. It was originally part of Camilla Prasch's series
Ordnung Lass' Sein (Order, Leave It Be). The title plays
on the familiar German expression "Ordnung muss sein"
(Order, there must be). In this series, Prasch set out to
challenge her inner perfectionist and her German origins
by cultivating things that were damaged or broken and by
stretching the concept of jewellery in her choice of material and methods. She is especially interested in exploring
the boundary between clothes and jewellery.

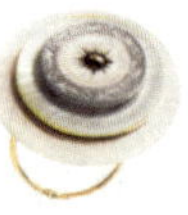

324

277

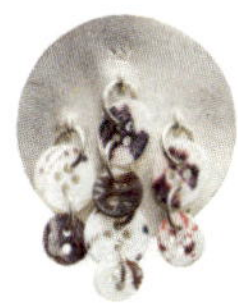

540

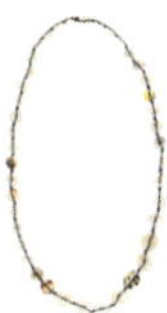

110

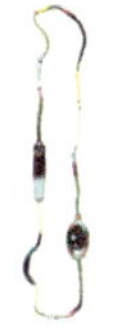

131

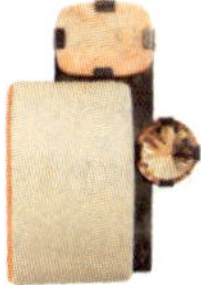

527

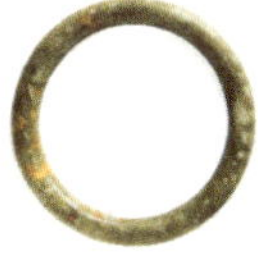

When I visited my grandma in Hallingdal as a child, I always asked to play with her box of buttons. I would spend hours sorting the buttons by colour and size. My favourites were the ones made of mother-of-pearl. It is a taste I share with others. Mette Saabye has made rings from mother-of-pearl buttons [324], and Konrad Mehus has used them as baubles in his *sølje* for a child [277]. When the Norwegian Authors' Union celebrated its 125th anniversary in 2018, the dinner tables were strewn with buttons and glossy pictures. In Norwegian, "to work for buttons and glossy pictures" is a fixed expression that means to work for peanuts, or for chicken feed; in other words, rather than a decent wage one is fobbed off with symbolic gifts. It is a situation familiar to many artists. One of the guests at the anniversary dinner was my friend the author Helga Eriksen. At the end of the event, Helga collected some of the finest mother-of-pearl buttons and had them made into a necklace for me [540].

Many jewellery artists have a soft spot for junk and stuff that lands on the scrap heap. "Today's waste, tomorrow's raw material" is an ever more common refrain.[205] The copper that Nadene Carr has enamelled and transformed into beautiful necklaces is scrap metal taken from a old refrigerator she found in a junk yard [110]. Ute Eitzenhöfer has incorporated part of a shampoo bottle in a brooch [131]. Nicolas Cheng and Beatrice Brovia make bracelets from pulverised computer components [527]. In its colour and shape, this bracelet resembles the traditional jade bangles many Chinese women wear to ward off evil. The similarity is intentional. The artist asks: "Can this material, used for CPU boards, be seen as a new jade, on which the value systems of our contemporaneity are based? Will it eventually become a hybrid rock – a fossil of our world – in a hypothetical future, when archaeologists will dig it up from the depths of the earth?"[206] In jewellery of this kind it is impossible to distinguish the concept from the material, since it is the material that carries the message.

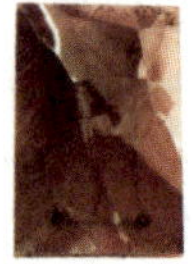

In their project *Kino*, Cheng and Brovia transformed smartphone screens into brooches [112]. These screens represent the interface through which we now interact and communicate with the world. Cracks in the glass had made the phone worthless, but in the brooch the cracks form a beautiful pattern of lines. The tinted foil gives the screen a slight haze, but it is still possible to see one's reflection in it, and to see through it. On the back there is a clasp of gold and tantalum. Both metals are common in mobile phones, and both are notorious conflict minerals. This means that the extraction of and trade in these metals has been linked to slave labour, armed conflicts, money laundering, human rights violations and corruption – things few of us want to be associated with but which we carry round like an albatross in the form of our mobile phones. In *Kino*, Cheng and Brovia seek to highlight this reality by making the materials we generally do not see but which are present in our electronic devices, visible in the form of jewellery worn on the body. The question their work poses is addressed to us as consumers: What are our responsibilities?

Metal has always been used as a hard currency. Jewellery has been melted down or modified throughout history. Sometimes the aim was simply to adapt certain adornments to a new owner or to give them a more modern look. As Julia Manheim has pointed out, however, it is only in recent times that the recycling of materials and artefacts has been motivated by a concern for the environment.[207] But the result is that recycled materials have acquired a new status. "It's what we salvage that must become the new precious," as Susan Cohn has put it.[208]

Upcycling

By the early 2000s, recycling was a well-established concept. In artistic contexts, recycling usually implies an enhancement of a material's status and value. As a process, it is a form of reuse to which William McDonough

and Michael Braungart gave the name "upcycling".[209]
As the foregoing examples show, in the context of art, it
is a question not of a specific aesthetic but of a method.
The material, in the form of artefacts or trash, must have
had an earlier life. Upcycling always involves an element
of recycling. For the result to count as an example of
upcycling, as opposed to downcycling, the reuse must
enhance the value of the relevant material.

A good example of upcycling is Benedikt Fischer's
brooch "Unus Unus" [136]. The material is plastic from an
old safety helmet. Parts of the surface appear to be covered in embroidery, but the tiny lines are engraved with
a scalpel and chisel. Thus the brooch represents the cultures of both industry and crafts. The title is a reference
to Unus the Untouchable, a mutant superhero character
in the American cartoon series *X-Men*. He acquired the
nickname in response to his ability to project an invisible
force field around himself as a protection against harmful
attack. It is an ability that recalls the function of talismans
or amulets. Since time immemorial, people have worn
objects they hope will protect them from evil or harm.
It could be anything from a strangely shaped object to a
part of an animal. It is this tradition that Fischer plays on
in "Unus Unus", which transforms a piece from a safety
helmet into a symbolic talisman.

Monica Cecchi's favourite material is old metal tins.
"It is a very interesting material, it has a huge colour and
pattern palette, even the scratches and bumps have a
story to me," she has said.[210] In addition, it reminds her of
her childhood and her grandmother, who kept buttons
and other things worth hanging on to in old cake tins. But
there is nothing nostalgic about the necklace I fell for at
Galerie Biró in Munich in 2019. In this, Cecchi has combined pieces cut from old metal tins so that remnants of
text and images form the head of a lion giving a menacing
roar: "Grrroowl" [538]. Although I have little interest in
astrology, the fact that Leo is my star sign means the necklace is well suited to me.

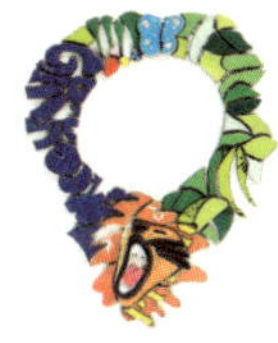

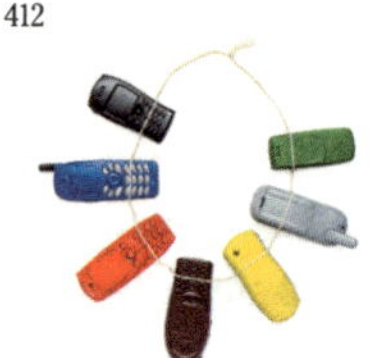

One artist who has embraced junk and discarded items more than most in order to give them new and extended lives is Lisa Walker. For example, she has painted old cell phones and turned them into a necklace [412]. Not so long ago, these devices represented the pinnacle of advanced technology. But with new models being launched all the time, their lifespan is short, both as a status symbol and as consumer goods. It is when they are no longer wanted that Walker steps in to give them a new function and a new value, potentially rendering them immortal by using them to artistic ends. Walker has made several versions of her mobile-phone necklace; mine I bought at the exhibition *Différence et répétition* at NextLevel Galerie in Paris in the summer of 2014. This exhibition explored the concept of repetition in art jewellery and was a collaborative project by Benjamin Lignel, Frédéric F. Martin and myself.[211]

In 2015, I invited Lisa Walker to present her work at a seminar in Gothenburg.[212] There, she stressed that what interested her was not so much recycling as such but rather the limitation of using only objects and materials she found in her immediate surroundings. Whereas her older colleagues in New Zealand have used found shells and stones to signal their local identity, Walker asks whether our contemporary sense of identity and community isn't better expressed by things like mobile phones. At the same time, her choice of materials indicates a shift from a national towards a more global perspective.

In picking up things that others have thrown away, jewellery artists are asking questions about the way we categorise objects as either useful or useless. But at the same time, this kind of jewellery touches on something existential: "Usefulness is transitory, and perhaps the transition from being used to being forgotten is particularly captivating because it reminds us that we are all destined to die one day," writes anthropologist Thomas Hylland Eriksen in a book about waste.[213] Thus art made from discarded things and junk can serve as a memento

mori and as a contemporary equivalent of the vanitas
genre in historical art.

The act of discovering and transforming the surplus of the industrial age into handmade items invested
with new meaning and a new beauty suggests a close
relationship to everyday objects and routines and a
corresponding scepticism towards the pressure to buy
and to over-consume. Like the collage in fine art and the
quotation in literature, reused materials commemorate
their former function and existence even while participating in a new reality. Having crossed a social and economic
boundary, they remind us that art is about questioning
the static and the stable. Metal tins and mobile phones
that have been turned into necklaces, electronic waste
transformed into bracelets, shampoo bottles and safety
helmets that now exist as brooches open a space for
inconsistency and fragmentation where meaning does
not have to be fixed or rational.

Perishable materials
From a sustainability perspective, probably nothing
would be better than to make jewellery that is perishable.
But this presents a conundrum. The idea of spending
money on something that will degrade because it is made
from non-durable materials is easier to accept in theory
than in practice. I can confirm from personal experience
that a piece made from rubber gloves begins to crumble
after a couple of years. In other pieces the plastic has
perished and cracked and yet others have become discoloured. Would I have bought these works if I knew they
would not last? I would like to say yes. If rubber is essential to a certain artistic statement, then rubber it must be.
Time means change, and the idea that art, like life, will
eventually pass away has always appealed to me.

It's a different thing with jewellery that has been
lost for other reasons – pieces that have been broken, left
behind or otherwise mislaid when travelling or on a night

out. I remember every piece I have lost, and when and where it happened.

Nonsense

In a study of the subject, the poet and folklorist Susan Stewart has described nonsense as the activity "by which the world is disorganized and reorganized".[214] Accordingly, we could describe recycling – a typical postmodern art strategy – as a nonsense activity. In order to transform things and materials into something new, one has to override ordinary logic and expectations based on familiarity. Perhaps the foremost nonsense artists in my collection are David Bielander, Sigurd Bronger and Gisbert Stach. All three exploit the humorous potential of the illogical, where we discover that something we perceived as familiar is not what it seems to be.

Bronger's "Condition Measuring Device no. 3", which I gave to Mogens as a Christmas present in 2001, can be worn on the arm like a regular wristwatch [67]. But the internal mechanism includes electronic components of unknown origin and what looks like some kind of pressure gauge. When people asked in a mystified tone what the device measured, Mogens would answer: "Levity!"

For many people, amber is an obsolete, boring and possibly even bourgeois material. Stach has shown that amber can have a very different expressive quality. He pulverises amber and mixes the powder with silicone, producing a compound that can be moulded. It would be wrong to describe this substance as genuine amber, but neither is it fake. What matters here is that the colour can resemble anything from a Wiener schnitzel or a piece of toast to a deep-fried fish finger or a waffle. Thus these are the things Stach takes as motifs for his amber brooches. I have a fish finger [362] and a waffle heart [534], and both are strikingly realistic. But why choose items of fast food? Curator Corinna Rösner has responded by posing questions of her own: "Because these snacks might symbolise

67

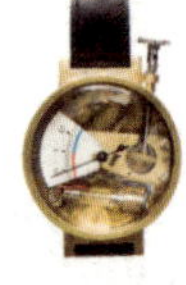

362

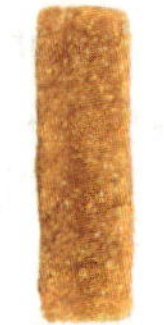

534

modern living? Because they stand for fast consumption and a contradictory statement with a deeper meaning? Because fast food often has a negative connotation of being non-authentic, not genuine?"[215] On the other hand, the result is certainly a genuine Gisbert Stach brooch, even if does seem unusual and illogical to pin a piece of food to your chest.

Like Stach, Bielander has also manipulated materials, and not just things, to achieve deceptive transformations. In 2015 he took the pursuit to a new level in a series of bracelets that resemble corrugated cardboard [32]. The material is in fact silver, while the staple that holds the "cardboard" together is made from white gold. Writing about this series, one commentator points out that camouflage generally employs one of two strategies: either to merge with the background, or to stand out with a false identity.[216] This corrugated cardboard jewellery employs both. On the one hand, the silver is camouflaged by its irregular surface and matt pale-brown colour, and on the other it "acts out a child's rainy afternoon cut-and-paste endeavor proudly worn by a parent".[217] Only its weight, sound and temperature betray its true identity.

Being true to one's materials was a dogma of modernism. This meant one should not attempt to conceal what a thing is made of, for example, by painting woodwork or making plastic look like wood. Manipulations of this kind were perceived as an offence against the real and the natural. It is an ideology that Bielander's illusionism rejects. He demonstrates that most materials can exist in many different forms, each of which has its own characteristic qualities with the potential to be mixed and matched. Accordingly, we should perhaps adopt a different motto: Empathy for material. It is the crafts theorist Ezra Shales who made this suggestion. "'Empathy for material'", he writes, "is a much better rule than 'truth to material'."[218]

When considering the artists mentioned here, it is unwise to separate concept from material. Both are

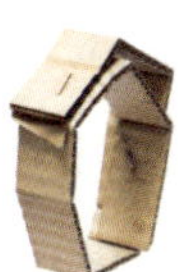

32

aspects of one and the same thing. Perhaps we could even speak of the material having a will of its own. As the textile artist Anni Albers once put it: "Being creative is not so much the desire to do something as the listening to that which wants to be done: the dictation of the materials."[219] It is a sentiment many jewellery artists will recognise, for they often portray their work as a dialogue with the material.

Jewellery is about people.

—Susan Cohn[220]

What jewellery can do

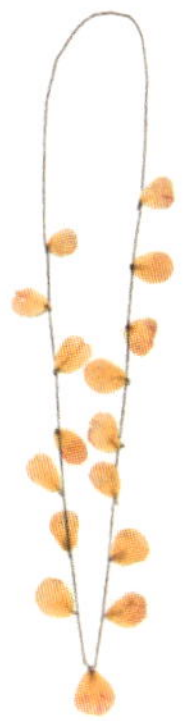

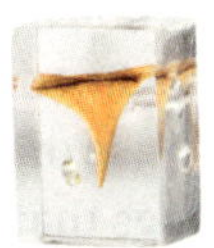

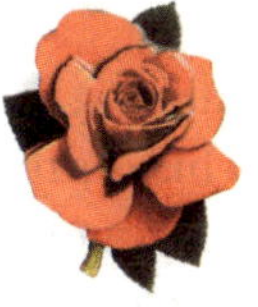

When it comes to clichés about beauty, nothing surpasses flowers, depictions of which will probably never be considered as sublime art. For the modernists, the beauty that flowers represent was despised as kitsch. But in many cultural contexts, flowers figure as potent vehicles of human emotions. They serve as signs of love, friendship, compassion, joy and care. In relation to grief, they can be poetic – albeit perishable – symbols of life and beauty with the power to transform the experience of loss. Flowers retain this capacity to console even when used as a jewellery motif. They can represent extravagance and fragility; they are beautiful yet also banal. We use flowers for decoration and give them as gifts. Jewellery with floral motifs can serve the same function.

The flower that features most in my collection is the rose. I have a necklace made of real rose petals [216] and a pin with a rose thorn [295], but my favourite in this category is a brooch by Renee Bevan, with a photo of a red rose transferred onto walnut wood [31]. A rose is a rose is a rose, said Gertrude Stein. The rose is what it appears to be: a flower, neither more nor less, but for many of us, it is a motif we find it impossible not to interpret, accustomed as we are to its use as a symbol of, for example, love. For Bevan, who lives in New Zealand, the rose is also a cliché associated with Eng-

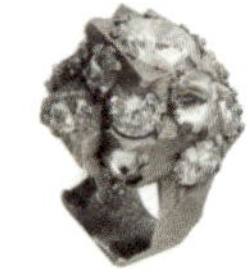

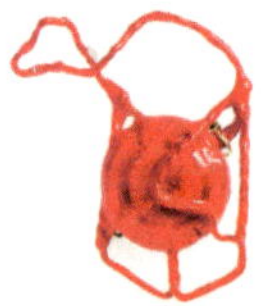

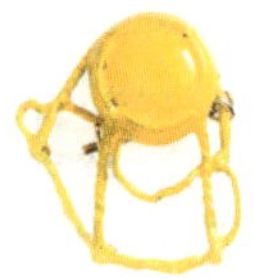

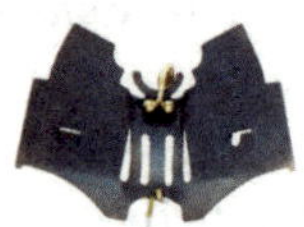

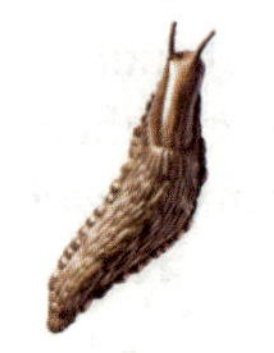

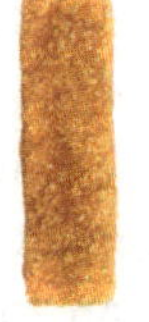

lish taste and style. In this respect, the flower plays a part in the discourse about identity and nationality.

More festive occasions call for the shimmer of gemstones, sparkle and splendour – especially in a woman's attire. Here I have relatively few jewellery items that fit the bill. The most suitable is a ring by Adam Grinovich. The sparkling stones resemble diamonds but are in fact a synthetically produced material, cubic zirconia, which, for ethical and environmental reasons, is becoming increasingly popular [533]. I prefer to signal a festive spirit with a brooch that reminds me of the archetypical celebratory drink, champagne. For the exhibition *Where Does the Parallel World Exist?* at the Bayerischer Kunstgewerbeverein in Munich in 2016, Mari Ishikawa had filled an entire wall with bright yellow brooches made from the metal wires used to hold champagne corks in place. Nothing spells party in quite the way this jewellery does [196, 197].

Humour

If flowers are common as a theme in art jewellery, the diametrical opposite must surely be food; similarly, butterflies abound, while moths and slugs are rarities [34, 35]. It is easy to understand why this is so. When dressing up, we generally prefer things that are decorative and appealing. Consequently, when I turn up wearing a fish finger on my chest or sausages around my neck, people are inclined to point or laugh [362, 37]. It is the element of surprise or incongruity that produces the comic effect. Things that are familiar and ordinary are seldom seen as amusing. As an expression of emotion, laughter is a response to something new and unexpected.

Sometimes one has the impression that humour is perceived as something superficial and easy. This is probably due to the close connection between humour and the joys of play. Tragedy, for example, carries greater artistic weight and status than comedy. But humour amounts to more than just a good laugh. In his novel *The Name of the*

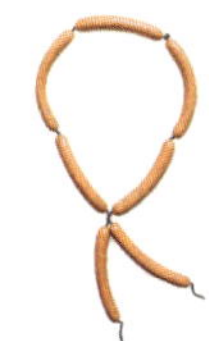

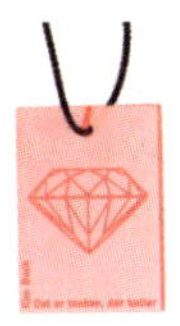

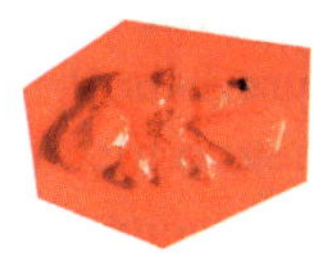

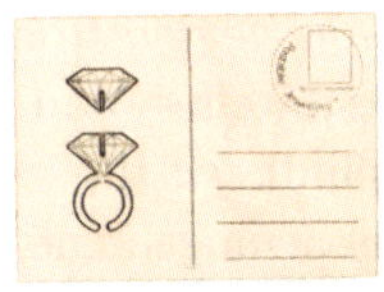

Rose, Umberto Eco describes a number of scholars earnestly discussing whether Jesus could laugh. One elderly participant, the blind Jorge from Burgos, adamantly rejects the idea because, he says, laughter is a source of doubt. In Jorge's world view, faith and doubt are incompatible, and consequently he finds laughter threatening. It is a scene that captures the essence of humour. Humour requires an openness to "double entendre", an ability to see a thing from different angles. I like to use jewellery to tickle people's sense of humour. In addition, it expresses my fundamental attitude to life: when everything seems too much to bear, laughter is the only comfort. Laughter and seriousness do indeed go together, as do laughter and nonsense.

We humans are quick to laugh, according to the philosopher Aristotle. Etymologically, the word jewel comes from the Latin word *jocus*, meaning to play and joke. I have few real jewels in the form of gems but many that play on and ironise their status [88a, 185, 481]. Although this kind of humour may well be somewhat internal, i.e. intended for others within the art jewellery community, its meaning is rarely lost on outsiders.

Unexpected pleasures

One of the most extensive art jewellery exhibitions of the past two decades had the title *Unexpected Pleasures*.[221] An unexpected pleasure is one that wasn't anticipated and could not have been foreseen. Wearing, giving, making or looking at jewellery can all be sources of unexpected pleasure. For the exhibition's curator, Susan Cohn, the aim was to address a design-oriented audience who might not yet be acquainted with the language of contemporary art jewellery. What she hoped was that many people would derive an unexpected pleasure from discovering art jewellery for the first time. And they did. I too encountered a similar enthusiasm when I showed some three hundred jewellery items and objects from my own collection at Nordenfjeldske Kunstindustrimuseum in 2018. "We had no idea jewellery

could be like this," was what many people said. The author
Einar Økland, who gave the opening speech, took his cue
from the song the curator Gjertrud Steinsvåg had chosen
as title for the exhibition, albeit with a change of pronoun
from "my" to "her": *These are a few of her favourite things.*
Økland reminded us of the lyrics of the Richard Rogers's hit,
in which the woman sings about the little things that lift her
spirits: "When the dog bites / When the bee stings / When
I'm feeling sad".[222] I would readily describe the joy I derive
from jewellery as a sense of comfort or well-being.

Sensual appeal

The interplay between jewellery and the body can be compared to the role of the ornament in architecture. In both
contexts, it is all about adding something that serves to
stimulate and enrich the sensual experience. Ornament can
help to focus, frame and attract attention. As the detail that
completes a work, its significance lies first and foremost in
the joy it brings. In his celebrated *Critique of Judgement* from
1790, the philosopher Immanuel Kant places jewellery and
tasteful dressing in the same category as "painting in the
wide sense", along with wall hangings, flower arrangements
and various other things, the "sole function of which *is to
be looked at*".[223] Such things do not pretend to teach history
or science; they are simply there to be seen. That might
sound easy enough, yet seeing involves many overlapping
dimensions – from the joy of recognition and perceptual satisfaction to psychological reward and erotic arousal.

The combining of geometrical forms is one of the
oldest ways to create ornament. Such forms can function
as concrete, abstract figures but are also rich in symbolic
meaning. One example is the circle. As a form without
beginning or end, the circle has symbolised eternity and
perfection, the ultimate and the indivisible since time immemorial. It has been used as a sign of strength and power
but also as a cipher that protects and circumscribes; the
circle can both unify and isolate. Even when not stated or

intended, all these connotations are present in every use of the ring as a form.

The things we choose to adorn ourselves with are influenced by taste, fashion, artistic trends and the time in which we live, but what remains constant in our perception of jewellery as ornamental art is its status as a corporeal rather than an intellectual experience. As a decoration of the body, jewellery touches on central aspects of what it means to exist as a sentient being in the world. It is intimate not just in format but also in virtue of its proximity to the body. The link between jewellery and sensuality is therefore close. Jewellery adds colour and glow to the skin and draws attention to erogenous zones such as the earlobes, neck and throat. But at the same time, our Protestant culture has taught us to regard decoration for decoration's sake with scepticism and, correspondingly, sensual pleasure with shame. To wear jewellery is to challenge such puritanical attitudes.

On the personal level, joy is therefore a keyword in relation to what jewellery adds to life. Jewellery can also enchant in other ways, both as a form of imaginative escape or as a source of pure aesthetic satisfaction. Kevin Murray has illuminated all these aspects in a text about jewellery and pleasure, although he adds a word of warning: "From a critical perspective, the reference to pleasure has potential to consign contemporary jewelry to a frivolous art form."[224] There is a reason why pietistic movements are always inclined to eschew jewellery and ornamentation. Such frivolous pursuits imply an acceptance of the body, of pleasure and laughter, all of which are powerful forces when left unchecked.

Being open to pleasure in all contexts in life was a central issue for the women's lib movement that I became involved in as a young person. This was in reaction to all the corseting and control of women's bodies and their sexuality that had hitherto been the norm. For me, wearing jewellery became a way to demonstrate an acceptance of pleasure and physical presence as aspects of life.

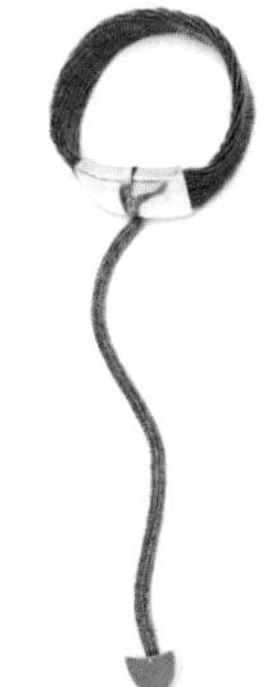

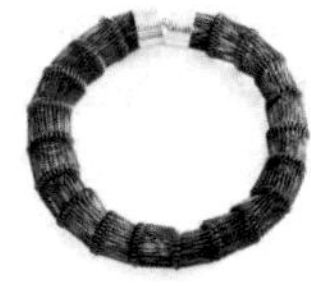

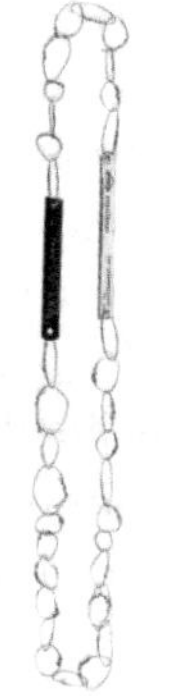

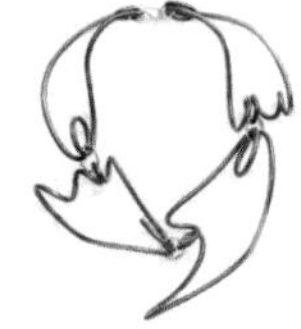

Empowerment

As early as the 1980s, I noticed how jewellery could give me a sense of edge and greater strength. It was a source of mental, if not physical, fortification. This has certainly been my experience when wearing Toril Bjorg's robust, imposing neckpieces [43, 44]. Bjorg has often worked with silver wire using techniques from the field of textiles. The many associations of these pieces range from the rough and the rude to beauty and seduction.[225] Other works that function in a similar way included Bernhard Schobinger's necklace with old saw blades [345], Dorothea Prühl's sculptural neckpieces [483], and Auli Laitinen's brooch with phallic connotations [243]. I am by no means the first to notice the feeling of empowerment that jewellery can give.[226] It is a point that Petra Ahde-Deal discusses in her doctoral dissertation about women's relationship to jewellery. Many of Ahde-Deal's interviewees describe owning or wearing jewellery as a source of strength.[227]

At the exhibition *Women*, arranged by the Swedish gallery Platina in 2017, I bought Jing Yang's work "I Am Not a Vase" [467]. Two years before, Yang had won a prize at the *Talente* exhibition in Munich for the project of which this necklace was a part. As the artist has pointed out, the title can be interpreted in two ways. Firstly, it can mean "I am not a vase, but rather a piece of jewellery". This is literally illustrated by the fact that the metal elements of her necklace, which can be stacked up to resemble a classic vase, fall apart when the jewellery is worn. The second meaning has its roots in China, Jing Yang's home country. In China, the word for a vase can be used to describe an attractive but shallow woman, with the similarity between a vase and the woman being that both are pleasing to look at but effectively empty. In this context, "I am a vase" means "I am beautiful". Jing Yang's work breaks this connection. The vase form is in a constant state of disassembly. Both the woman who made the work and the one who wears it are clearly saying: "I do not want to be a vase; I actually have something to say!"[228]

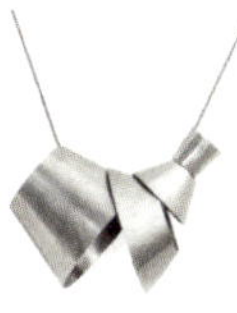

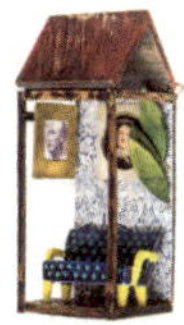

Storytelling

Throughout history, figuration has always been an aspect of jewellery, but European avant-garde art jewellery during the latter half of the 20th century placed a clear emphasis on the geometric and the abstract. As Liesbeth den Besten has written: "Around 2000, figuration was quite unpopular in European contemporary jewelry; practice was based on abstraction and conceptualism."[229] But around the turn of the millennium, this situation began to change, and by 2005 a new book on art jewellery could already devote an entire chapter to "telling stories".[230]

In Scandinavia, two of the foremost representatives of this storytelling trend have been Konrad Mehus and Felieke van der Leest. Both took part in the first international exhibition about the narrative turn in art jewellery, *Maker Wearer Viewer. Contemporary Narrative European Jewellery*. Mounted at the Glasgow School of Art in 2005, this featured work by more than seventy artists from across Europe. The characteristic feature of this kind of jewellery is that, rather than strive to be aesthetic adornment, it seeks to comment on the human condition, based on the personal, social or political experience of the respective artist. According to curator Jack Cunningham, this did not necessarily imply confrontation but could just as much be about having fun.[231]

Many of the artists in my collection were represented in the Glasgow exhibition: David Bielander, Helen Britton, Ramón Puig Cuyàs, Hilde Dramstad, Karl Fritsch, Andi Gut, Sophie Hanagarth, Louise Nippierd, Ruudt Peters, Dorothea Prühl, Mah Rana, Hans Stofer, Ketli Tiitsar, Carolina Vallejo and Silvia Walz. But only Mehus showed a series from which I have a work: *Mark Replies: Two Rooms and a Kitchen* [267].

This is one of Mehus's most important and most personal jewellery series. Each brooch in the series is a three-dimensional room in miniature. In my own example, most of the room is filled by a sofa with polka-dot upholstery. Hanging behind it and on one side are two portraits, which together with a green plant suggest a homely 1950s interior. What Mehus has depicted here is post-war Norway.

In the wake of the Second World War, Norway faced a serious shortage of housing that required many people to live in cramped conditions. In Oslo, where Mehus grew up, the newspapers were full of ads for "two rooms and a kitchen". It was a formulation that encapsulated the dream of owning a home, even if only a small one. It also became a byword for the emergence of the welfare state and for social democratic politics, which focused on housing for all as one of its main goals. In 1953, Mehus and his mother moved into what was at that time a typical apartment – with a living room, bedroom and kitchen. While the sofa in my piece resembles the one they owned, the William Morris wallpaper is a detail that wasn't a part of Mehus's childhood. Neither do the portraits depict his relatives. One, from a bottle of Veuve Clicquot champagne, is of the woman popularly known as the "Yellow Widow", while the other is a postage stamp portrait of King Olav. The use of such found items is typical of Mehus's humour and way of working. The rest of the interior, he claims, is more accurate.[232]

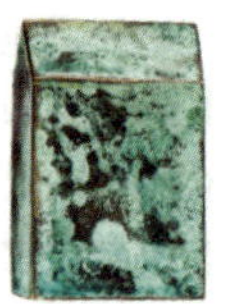

269

In recent years, Mehus has followed up these interiors with a series of archetypical houses. This is a logical consequence of his interest in houses and homes as indicators of social environment [269]. While his depictions of interiors take us into private spaces, his closed houses mark the boundary between the public and private spheres. These jewellery series bring together some of the fundamental questions that Mehus has returned to repeatedly in his art: What does it mean to belong? What is it that shapes us? Not only can jewellery ask such questions, it can also symbolise who we are.

Vehicles of memory

Only very rarely have I taken the step of having jewellery specially made for me. But I do have a couple of pieces that came about in this way and which therefore mean a lot to me.

In 1998, Mogens, his daughter Lise and I spent the month of December travelling across South Africa. On the

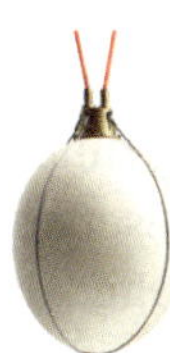

famous Garden Route from Port Elizabeth to Cape Town, we visited an ostrich farm. As a souvenir we bought an ostrich egg. With its thick shell, capable of supporting a weight of up to 150 kilograms, it was no problem to carry it in my backpack. Having brought it safely back to Denmark, it was time to get out the drill, and after a bit of hard work we managed to remove its contents. That we turned into an omelette for twenty people. A few years later, I asked Sigurd Bronger if he could make a work from the still unbroken shell. What he delivered was an enormous pendant [78]. Bronger has made a number of "wearable devices" for eggs. It is easy to understand his fascination. Eggs evoke a mixture of anxiety and delight. When whole we admire them for their beauty and perfection but worry about their fragility – unless it's an ostrich egg. An egg is not a representation of anything; it is what it is. Its form is presented and not *re*presented. I could well appreciate this piece of jewellery for its aesthetic qualities alone – the oval form and the contrast between the white shell and the orange cord – but first and foremost it reminds me of our journey, everything from the experience of riding an ostrich, the landscape we drove through and the people we met through to the meal we prepared for the family on returning home.

In the spring of 2007, I wrote to Lucy Sarneel in Amsterdam. Knowing that she had used textile elements from Dutch folk costumes, I wondered whether she would be willing to do something similar with an equivalent Norwegian material. From my grandmother in Hallingdal I had inherited several fragments of embroidery made for Halling tunics. They had been languishing in a drawer for years, and now I wanted to do something with them. As I wrote to Sarneel: "I hope to be able to express my connection to the area and my family roots through a contemporary necklace." Sarneel's response was positive. In addition to the embroidery, I took with me the *søljer* I had received for my confirmation, to give her an idea of the jewellery tradition associated with Norway's national costumes. Sarneel removed the silver discs from the brooches and replaced them with new

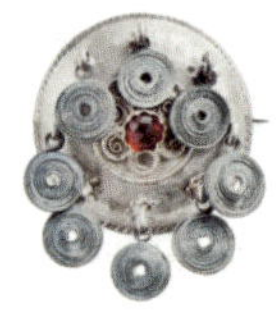

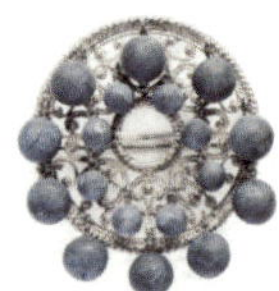

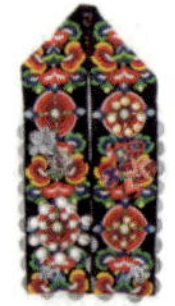

baubles made from zinc [334, 335]. She then attached the discs to the embroidery, which she shaped into a neckpiece to be worn like a collar [336]. To this too she added some elements of zinc, her signature material.

This "collar" encompasses a broad time span. The brooches were almost forty years old, and the embroidery probably much older. In some circles in Norway, this kind of manipulation of cultural heritage is frowned upon. The *bunad* is seen a symbolic garment that should be treated with respect. Yet I have rarely felt my father's presence as forcefully as I did on leaving Sarneel's studio. He had died the previous year, and I was sure he would have appreciated this artistic personalisation of traditional materials. This is a piece of jewellery that tells where I come from, but the reworking constitutes a breach of rules that adds elements of the present and the foreign, and of individuality. At the same time, it represents a bond to my origins and my personal biography. Petra Ahde-Deal writes in her dissertation that the aspect of jewellery that the women she interviewed highlighted as most important was the fact that it "connects them to their own biographies: [jewels] are devices for keeping memories alive".[233] This is also true for me.

Politics and emotions

During a holiday in Laos in the spring of 2012, we passed a sign that read Bomb City. We were on our way to the Plain of Jars, a mountainous area in Xiangkhouang Province where thousands of ancient jars cut from stone lie scattered about in clusters of varying size. If it weren't for all the landmines from the Vietnam War that still remain to be cleared, this would be a major tourist attraction. Laos is the most bombed country in the world. During the Vietnam War, it was here that the Americans dropped plane-loads of bombs, either because they had failed for some reason to drop them on Vietnam or in order to destroy paths the Viet Cong guerrillas used to move between North and South Vietnam. It made a strong impression on us to see that thirty-seven

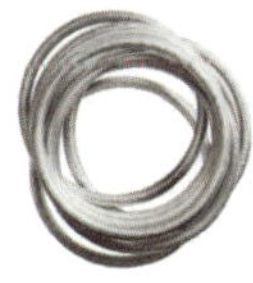

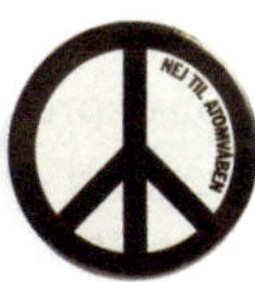

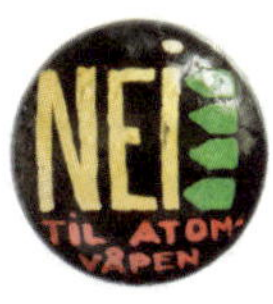

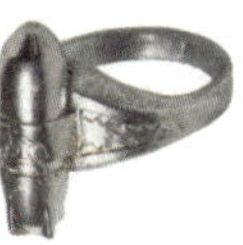

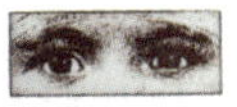

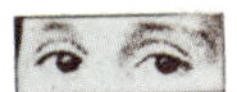

years after the war, bomb disposal teams were still scouring the landscape. Cluster bombs in particular have remained an enduring cause of injuries and a major obstacle to agriculture. On the other hand, unexploded ordnance (UXO) has become a resource. Over small fires in front of their homes in Bomb City, people melt down the aluminium from bomb casings and pour it into moulds to make bangles [12]. It was gripping to witness materials from a destructive killing machine being turned into adornments for the body.

In one way or another, war is a theme that several of the works in my collection have in common. From the No to Nuclear Weapons badges [426, 489] to Nanna Melland's thought-provoking nuclear-warhead ring, which she calls "Ring of Ignorance" [518]. Just two years after the Americans dropped nuclear bombs on Hiroshima and Nagasaki, a company in the United States put a ring shaped like an atomic bomb in millions of cereal boxes. The ring was accompanied by an explanatory leaflet: "You'll see brilliant flashes of light in the inky darkness inside the atom chamber. These frenzied vivid flashes are caused by the released energy of atoms. PERFECTLY SAFE – We guarantee you can wear the KIX Atomic 'Bomb' Ring with complete safety." Having come across one of these rings, Nanna Melland made a cast of it and produced a new version in tin. The question I ask myself is: What on earth possessed someone to make a toy that celebrates something as destructive as an atomic bomb? Or as Melland's title suggests: Is it possible to be so ignorant?

It is our compassion that Camilla Luihn appeals to in her series *The Aleppo Piece*. In this, she has transferred newspaper images of children in Aleppo to small enamel brooches. She limits herself to just their eyes [482]. I have two of these brooches, but the series as a whole consists of a hundred. A hundred pairs of eyes – gazing out at us with everything from fear, despair and helplessness to wonder, smiles and strength – that serve as a constant reminder of the desperate plight of civilians in Syria.

Among the jewellery artists I know, the one who makes the most conscious use of the medium to comment on

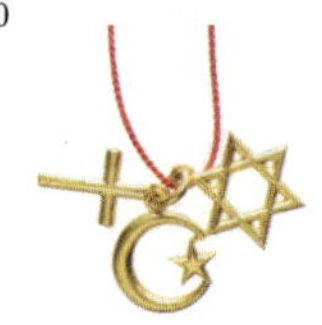

current political issues is Kim Buck. In a number of works, he has addressed the (mis)use of religion to legitimise injustice. Crosses, anchors and hearts are familiar Christian symbols of faith, hope and love. They also frequently figure as charms. Kim Buck has created his own twist on this theme in the work "Faith, Hope and Love" [90]. The cross is still there, but the anchor and the heart have been replaced with the Star of David as a symbol of Judaism and the crescent moon as a symbol of Islam. The juxtaposition expresses a desire for peace and reconciliation between these religions. Benevolence is a central value in the basic texts of all three, meaning that this piece is also a plea for tolerance. But as we know, "In war and love much is unfinished," to quote the Norwegian poet Torgeir Rebolledo Pedersen.[234]

In the autumn of 2019, the Australian jewellery artist Susan Cohn toured Denmark with the performance *meaning(less)ness*, which she developed in collaboration with the director David Pledger. The performance was a reaction to Denmark's "jewellery law", which the country's parliament, the Folketing, had passed in 2016. This law is aimed at asylum seekers and allows the state to seize jewellery and other valuables worth more than 10,000 kroner. The exception is objects of sentimental value, such as engagement and wedding rings. In deciding which objects qualify as such, the police are obliged to base their assessments on the statements of the refugees themselves. The law attracted international attention, with historical parallels being drawn to the treatment of Jews during the Second World War. The news reached all the way to Melbourne, where Cohn lives, and her response was outrage: "This reducing of the value of jewellery to an asset is contemptuous and ignorant of the crucial role jewellery plays in people's lives – especially people fleeing from war and trauma."[235] In her performance, she reflected on the refugee policies of both Australia and Denmark. How should one assess whether jewellery is meaningful or meaningless? Doesn't all jewellery have a sentimental value, whether it's a souvenir ring that reminds you of a place you have visited, an heirloom or a love gift?

As an antidote to the act of depriving people of heir-
looms, or jewellery that symbolises kinship or emotional
ties, over and above any other value it might have, Cohn
suggested giving gifts. "I offer that one of the ways that we
can rewire our society, think more about the hope of what
we might gain instead of the fear of what we might lose, is
through gifting. Because gifting binds us together. And it
acknowledges our belonging. So I open that door by giving
the first gift."[236] She ended her performance by sitting down
at her workbench and making a clover leaf from silver,
which she then attached to a pin and placed in a box that
already contained a three-leaf clover. Thus she turned the
three-leaf clover into a lucky four-leaf clover. Each member of the audience received an identical item as a parting
gift [544].

Denmark's jewellery law is a classic example of symbol
politics. The story would not be complete without saying
that, in the first three years after the law was enacted, it was
applied only ten times, and not a single piece of jewellery
was confiscated.

Wearable communication
When jewellery leaves the artist's hands, it sets out on a
long journey, during which it is constantly gathering and
absorbing input from its new circumstances. As a user,
I introduce the pieces I wear to new and contemporary
contexts over which the artist has no control. Accordingly,
a piece of jewellery that is worn becomes a carrier of meaning in a way that pieces in a gallery or a museum never do.
It is this dimension of jewellery that the artist Lin Cheung
highlights with the term "jewellery-to-be".[237] For her, jewellery is incomplete until it is used. It only achieves its full
meaning by coming into contact with a body. A ring without
a finger is merely an object with a hole in it; a necklace without a neck and shoulders to give it form is generally just an
empty, flat artefact, while earrings are only seen as intended
when the clasp is hidden behind the earlobe. In addition,

there is all the emotion and intellectual thought that the user invests in the jewellery.

The special thing about collecting jewellery is precisely this, that you are dealing with objects you can wear on your own body. In her book *Jewellery Matters*, Marjan Unger claims that very few people who have studied and written about jewellery have confronted the fundamental question of why people wear it.[238] Since it is not something we need in order to survive, there must be some other explanation. This leads on to questions about the meanings and values we attach to jewellery. In the current book, I have tried to provide my own answers. Ruudt Peters has offered a more succinct view. Jewellery, he claims, captures every aspect of life: It is "history and pain, it's religion, suffering, emotions, love, eroticism, sex."[239] Such a passionate approach would seem to be destined for a head-on collision with the "disinterested pleasure" that has been cultivated ever since Immanuel Kant proposed that ideal in 1790. For Kant, aesthetic objects are those that arouse pleasure without evoking sensual desire or a desire to own them. This principle must apply as a necessary precondition for any discussion of aesthetics, he claims. But as the author Siri Hustvedt and others have pointed it, it is absurd to treat aesthetic objects as things that do not stand in some relationship to the viewer's body.[240] I would add that this is particularly true of jewellery. And it is for this reason that I have placed such emphasis on the sensuous appeal of jewellery and on explaining why I wear it, what it communicates and what it means to me. In addition to which I acknowledge collecting as a passion that has afforded me great joy.

In use, jewellery gives us something to look at and to talk about. With jewellery you can comment on a social situation or demonstrate an attitude without having to raise your voice. Jewellery can amuse, surprise, provoke, touch, irritate. Even when jewellery is unique and emphasises the individuality of the wearer, the reason for wearing and owning it can be social: jewellery invites conversation.

Notes

1 Walter Benjamin, "The Collector", in: idem, *The Arcades Project*, transl. Howard Eiland and Kevin McLaughlin, Cambridge, MA: Harvard University Press, 1999, p. 205.
2 Elton John, *Me*, London: Macmillan, 2019.
3 Louise Lee, "Itmar Simonson. What Makes People Collect Things?", 1 April 2015, <https://www.gsb.stanford.edu/insights/itamar-simonson-what-makes-people-collect-things>, accessed 1 March 2020.
4 Werner Muensterberger, *Collecting*, Princeton: Princeton University Press, 2014, p. 11.
5 Ibid.
6 Ibid., p. 3.
7 Fredrik Sjöberg, *The Fly Trap*, transl. Thomas Teal, New York: Pantheon Books, 2015.
8 Erling Kagge, *Kunsten å samle kunst*, Oslo: Kagge forlag, 2015, p. 31.
9 Elizabeth Taylor, *My Love Affair with Jewelry*, New York: Simon & Schuster, 2002, p. 73.
10 Ibid., p. 11.
11 Walter Benjamin, "The Collector", in: idem, *The Arcades Project*, transl. Howard Eiland and Kevin McLaughlin, Cambridge, MA: Harvard University Press, 1999, p. 204.
12 Walter Benjamin, "Unpacking My Library. A Talk about Book Collecting", in: idem, *Illuminations*, transl. Harry Zohn, New York: Schocken Books, 1969, p. 60.
13 Ibid., pp. 59–67.
14 Ibid., p. 67.
15 Orhan Pamuk, *The Museum of Innocence*, transl. Maureen Freely, New York: Alfred A. Knopf, 2009.
16 Ingar Kaldal, "Minna og mytane – og verdien av dei som historisk materiale", *Historisk tidsskrift*, no. 4, 2008, p. 668.
17 Walter Benjamin, "The Collector", in: idem, *The Arcades Project*, transl. Howard Eiland and Kevin McLaughlin, Cambridge, MA: Harvard University Press, 1999, p. 206. Benjamin's original formulation is "Sammler sind Menschen mit taktischem Instinkt" (see idem, *Gesammelte Schriften, Band V.1*, Frankfurt am Main: Suhrkamp Verlag, 1982, p. 274). Literally speaking, the word *taktisch* translates as "tactical", but the context gives ample reason to believe that Benjamin meant the word in the sense of "tactile".
18 Pamela Johnson, "Out of Touch. The Meaning of Making in the Digital Age", in: Tanya Harrod (ed.), *Obscure Objects of Desire*, London: Crafts Council, 1997, pp. 292–293. See also: Jorunn Veiteberg, "Touching Stories", in: Benjamin Lignel (ed.), *Shows and Tales*. Mill Valley: Art Jewelry Forum, 2015, pp. 126–133.
19 David Liston, *Museum Security and Protection. A Handbook for Cultural Heritage Institutions*, 1993; quoted from Fiona Candlin, *Art, Museums and Touch*, Manchester: Manchester University Press, 2010, p. 189.
20 Walter Benjamin, "The Collector", in: idem, *The Arcades Project*, transl. Howard Eiland and Kevin McLaughlin, Cambridge, MA: Harvard University Press, 1999, p. 210.
21 Marjan Unger, *Jewellery in Context*, Stuttgart: arnoldsche, 2019, p. 154.
22 Marjan Unger, "Jewellery in Context", in: idem and Suzanne van Leeuwen, *Jewellery Matters*, Amsterdam: Rijks Museum/Rotterdam: Nai010 Publishers, 2017, p. 57.
23 Ibid., p. 55.
24 Georg Simmel, "Adornment", in: David Frisby and Mike Featherstone (eds.), *Simmel on Culture*, London: Sage Publications, 1997, pp. 206–211 ("Psycholgie des Schmuckes", *Der Morgen. Wochenschrift für deutsche Kultur*, vol. 2, no. 15, 1908, pp. 454–459).
25 Ibid., p. 206.
26 Simone de Beauvoir, *The Second Sex*, transl. H.M. Parshley, London: Jonathan Cape, 1953, p. 29.
27 Ibid., pp. 190–191.
28 Rebecca Ross Russell, *Gender and Jewelry*, s.l.: CreateSpace, 2010, pp. 72–73.
29 Torborg Nedreaas in *Norge*, vol. I, 1954; quoted from Karin Moe, "Torborg Nedreaas og Stord", *Syn og Segn*, no. 2, 1996, p. 182.
30 Petra Ahde-Deal, *Women and Jewelry – A Social Approach to Wearing and Possessing Jewelry*, doctoral dissertation, Department of Design, Aalto University, Helsinki: Aalto Arts Book, 2013, p. 20.
31 Jo Freeman, "Say It with Buttons", *Ms.*, no. 3, 1974, pp. 48–53.
32 <https://en.wikipedia.org/wiki/Pin-back_button>, accessed 26 August 2019.
33 Jo Freeman, "Say It with Buttons", *Ms.*, no. 3, August 1974, pp. 48–53.

34 <https://jongrepstaddotcom.files.wordpress.
com/2018/02/nta_symbolet.pdf>, accessed 7 February
2019.

35 Thor Sørheim, *Stuntpoetenes historie*, Oslo: Flamme
Forlag, 2016, p. 195.

36 The L and E taken from Langslet's name can be used to
form the verb *le*, the Norwegian for "laugh".

37 Thor Sørheim, *Stuntpoetenes historie*, Oslo: Flamme
Forlag, 2016, p. 195.

38 <http://www.nextlevelgalerie.com/en/artistes/
bio/1113/benjamin-lignel>, accessed 18 November 2020.

39 Nicholas D. Kristof, "The Push to 'Otherize' Obama",
The New York Times, 21 September 2008; quoted in *Benjamin Lignel*, auction catalogue for Pierre Bergé & Associés,
Brussels, 20 November 2011, p. 40.

40 Marina Elenskaya, "Out and In-Between with Volker
Atrops", *Current Obsession*, no. 5, 2016, pp. 64–71.

41 "Volker Atrops", in: *Schmuck 2018*, Munich: GHM-
Gesellschaft für Handwerksmessen mbH, 2018, p. 11.

42 Ibid.

43 Quoted from Jorunn Veiteberg, "Avsmak? Nya normer
inom konsthantverket på 2000-talet", in: Christina Zetterlund, Charlotte Hyltén-Cavallius and Johanna Rosenqvist
(eds.), *Konsthantverk i Sverige, del 1*, Stockholm: Mångkulturelt centrum, 2015, p. 136.

44 Walter Benjamin, "The Work of Art in the Age of Mechanical Reproduction" (1936), in: idem, *Illuminations*, transl.
Harry Zohn, New York: Schocken Books, 1969, pp. 217–252.

45 "What Is Art Jewelry to You?" *Art Jewelry Forum*, 10
January 2018, <https://artjewelryforum.org/what-is-art-
jewelry-to-you#inline-content-1>, accessed 21 June 2020.

46 Jan-Lauritz Opstad, *En ny bevissthet*, Oslo: C. Huitfeldt
forlag, 1989, p. 32.

47 Ibid.

48 Konrad Mehus, "I hodet på en kunsthåndverker"
(1970); quoted in *Kunsthåndverk*, no. 1–2, 2001, p. 7.

49 Jan-Lauritz Opstad, *En ny bevissthet*, Oslo: C. Huitfeldt
forlag, 1989, pp. 19, 26.

50 Peter Dormer and Ralph Turner, *The New Jewelry*,
London: Thames and Hudson, 1985.

51 Wilhelm Lindemann, "Thinking Jewellery. A Theory
of Jewellery", in: idem (ed.), *Thinking Jewellery*, Stuttgart:
arnoldsche, 2011, p. 12.

52 *Smykker-85*, Trondheim: Nordenfjeldske
Kunstindustrimuseum, 1985, unpaginated.

53 Letter to Hordaland Kunstnersentrum from director
Jan-Lauritz Opstad, dated Trondheim, 11 December 1985.
In the archive of Nordenfjeldske Kunstindustrimuseum.

54 Quoted from Sissel Hamre Dagsland, "Smykker som
kunst og lek", *Bergens Tidende*, 18 January 1986.

55 Ibid.

56 Ibid.

57 Matt Lambert, "Who's Afraid of Marjorie Schick?",
Art Jewelry Forum, 14 April 2016, <https://artjewelry-
forum.org/who's-afraid-of-marjorie-schick>, accessed
19 December 2017.

58 Odd Johan Holen, "Vi pynter oss med plast", *Bergens
Tidende*, 1984.

59 The term "wearable" first appeared in print in a press
release about Heron's exhibition in the V&A museum shop
in 1982.

60 Damian Skinner, "All the World Over. The Global
Ambitions of Contemporary Jewelry", *Art Jewelry Forum*,
15 June 2012, <https://artjewelryforum.org/articles/all-
world-over-global-ambitions-contemporary-jewelry-0>,
accessed 6 May 2019.

61 *Otto Künzli. The Third Eye*, Amsterdam: Stedelijk
Museum, 1991, p. 20.

62 Ibid., p. 14.

63 Ibid.

64 Øystein Loge, "Vitner om sin tid", *Bergens Tidende*,
29 January 1986.

65 Ibid.

66 Bjarne Riiser Gundersen, *Da postmodernismen kom til
Norge*, Oslo: Flamme Forlag, 2016, p. 11.

67 *Profil*, no. 2/3/4, 1984, unpaginated.

68 *Post-Painting*, exhibition flyer, Bergen Kunstforening,
1984.

69 Jorunn Veiteberg, "Barbariske tendensar", *Syn og Segn*,
no. 1, 2004, pp. 78–79.

70 Jorunn Veiteberg, "Moderna Museet med postmoderne blikk på kunsthistorien", *F 15 Kontakt*, no. 8, 1987,
pp. 8–9.

71 Eivind Røssaak, "Om det postmoderne. Et tilbake-
blikk", in: *Blodig alvor*, Bergen: Bergen Kunstmuseum,
2009, p. 30.

72 Ibid., p. 29.

73 See *Hyperfoto*, no. 2, 1995, p. 46.

74 Fredrik Wildhagen, *Norge i form*, Oslo: J.M. Stenersen
Forlag, 1988, p. 208.

75 Paul Derrez, "New Energy", in: Heidi Sand (ed.), *Norwegian Jewellery*, Oslo: The Royal Ministry of Foreign Affairs,
1987, unpaginated.

76 Ibid.

77 Quoted from Bente Scavenius, *Torben Hardenberg,
Guldsmeden*, Copenhagen: Gyldendal, 2006, p. 24.

78 Charles Jencks, *What Is Post-Modernism?*, London:
Academy Editions, 1986/1989, p. 7.

79 Fredrik Wildhagen, *Norge i form*, Oslo: J.M. Stenersen
Forlag, 1988, pp. 181, 209, 211.

80 Paul Derrez, "New Energy", in: Heidi Sand (ed.), *Norwegian Jewellery*, Oslo: The Royal Ministry of Foreign Affairs, 1987, unpaginated.

81 Fredrik Wildhagen, *Norge i form*, Oslo: J.M. Stenersen Forlag, 1988, p. 209.

82 Ibid., p. 211.

83 Jan-Lauritz Opstad, "Neo-tradisjon – omkring utstillingen og dens tittel", reprinted in: Jorunn Veiteberg (ed.), *Det veltalende objekt*, Oslo: Det Tenkende Øye/Norske Kunsthåndverkere 1997, p. 62.

84 See Jorunn Fossberg, *Draktsølv*, Oslo: Universitetsforlaget, 1991, p. 70, and Laurann Gilbertson, "Norwegian Traditional Brooches", *Ornament*, no. 4, 1996, pp. 36–39.

85 Konrad Mehus, "Søljeprosjektet", in: *Skattekista*, Molde: Møre og Romsdal Kunstnersenter, 1999, p. 12.

86 Jørgen Schou-Christensen, "The Presence of the Past and the Presence of Now", in: Sissel Ree Schjønsby (ed.), *In Touch*, Oslo: De norske bokklubbene/Kulturprogrammet for de XVII Olympiske Vinterleker på Lillehammer, 1994, p. 25.

87 Jorunn Veiteberg, "Norwegian Jewellery 1900–1995", in: Jan Lohmann and Lise Funder (eds.), *Nordisk smykkekunst / Nordic Jewellery*, Copenhagen: Nyt Nordisk Forlag Arnold Busck, 1995, pp. 129–138.

88 Arnhild Skre, "Skrått blikk på tradisjonen", *Dag og Tid*, 19 December 1991, p. 14.

89 Ibid.

90 Karin Blehr, "Ikke dårlig nok", *Kunsthåndverk*, no. 2–3, 1992, p. 67.

91 Jørgen Schou-Christensen, "The Presence of the Past and the Presence of Now", in: Sissel Ree Schjønsby (ed.), *In Touch*, Oslo: De norske bokklubbene/Kulturprogrammet for de XVII Olympiske Vinterleker på Lillehammer, 1994, p. 26.

92 "Norge, Norge!" (1890), in: Bjørnstjerne Bjørnson, *Dikt og Sanger, i utvalg*, ed. Johan Hertzberg, Oslo: Gyldendal Norsk Forlag, 1940, pp. 71–72.

93 Emily Lowe, *Unprotected Females in Norway; or, The Pleasantest Way of Travelling There*, London: Routledge & Co., 1857, p. 2.

94 Nina Witoszek, "Der Kultur møter Natur: Tilfellet Norge", *Samtiden*, no. 4, 1991, pp. 13, 18.

95 Jorunn Veiteberg, "Tone Vigeland", in: idem, *Rooms with a View*, Oslo: The Royal Norwegian Ministry of Foreign Affairs, 1989, p. 36.

96 Quoted from Anniken Thue, "Links. The Jewelry of Tone Vigeland 1958–1995", in: idem (ed.), *Tone Vigeland*, Oslo: Oslo Museum of Applied Art, 1995, p. 48.

97 Quoted from Therese Hauger, *Nyere norsk smykkekunst 1945–1990*, master's dissertation in art history, University of Bergen, 1994, p. 29 (unpublished).

98 *Salmonsens Konservationsleksikon*, vol. II, 2nd edn., ed. Christian Blangstrup, Copenhagen: J.H. Schulz Forlagsboghandel, 1915, p. 647.

99 Helen W. Drutt English, "Reflections", in: Cecilie Malm Brundtland, *Tone Vigeland Jewellery + Sculpture*, Stuttgart: arnoldsche, 2003, p. 13. But to give credit where it is due, Drutt English is one of several commentators who have noted similarities between Vigeland's idiom and the work of Richard Serra and minimalism.

100 Peter Dormer and Ralph Turner, *The New Jewelry*, rev. edn., London: Thames and Hudson, 1994, p. 179.

101 Per Kirkeby, *Munch*, Copenhagen: Edition Bløndal, 1999, p. 11.

102 Esther Helén Slagsvold Hekne, "Åkersvika Addenda '93", in: Ingebjørg Astrup (ed.), *Åkersvika Addenda*, Lillehammer: LOOC, 1993, p. 10.

103 Georg Simmel, "Adornment", in: David Frisby and Mike Featherstone (eds.), *Simmel on Culture*, London: Sage Publications, 1997, p. 208.

104 Alf Hammervold, "Smykkeutstilling. En dansk mester", *Gullsmedkunst*, no. 5, 1988, p. 20.

105 *Jyllandsposten*, 21 February 1991.

106 Jorunn Veiteberg, "Ambigious Gifts", in: Tanya Harrod and Edmund de Waal (eds.), *Gift*, Gmunden: Think Tank. A European Initiative for the Applied Arts, 2007, pp. 41–45, 54–55.

107 Quoted in Jorunn Veiteberg, *Kim Buck. It's the Thought That Counts*, Copenhagen: Nyt Nordisk Forlag Arnold Busck, 2007, p. 83.

108 Ibid.

109 Jorunn Veiteberg, "Norwegian Jewellery 1900–1995", in: Jan Lohmann and Lise Funder (eds.), *Nordisk smykkekunst/Nordic Jewellery*, Copenhagen: Nyt Nordisk Forlag Arnold Busck, 1995, pp. 129–196.

110 Jorunn Veiteberg, "Jewellery. The Art of Small Objects and Large Subjects", in: Lise Funder (ed.), *Nordisk smycke triennal 2 / Nordic Jewellery*, Copenhagen: Nyt Nordisk Forlag Arnold Busck, 2001, pp. 18–25.

111 Thierry de Duve, *Kant after Duchamp*, Cambridge, MA/London: MIT Press, 1996/1999, p. 302.

112 Jorunn Veiteberg, "Det vakre som verdi og vanske", *Kunsthåndverk*, no. 4, 1999, inside cover.

113 Jorunn Veiteberg, *Craft in Transition*, transl. Douglas Ferguson, Bergen: Kunsthøgskolen i Bergen, 2005, p. 45.

114 Inga R. Gammel, "Om skønhed – et teoretisk tabu", *Passepartout*, no. 8, 2000, p. 39.

115 Arthur C. Danto, *The Abuse of Beauty. Aesthetics and the Concept of Art*, Chicago/La Salle, IL: Open Court, 2003, p. 160.

116 Mònica Gaspar, "Jewelry in the Expanded Field.

Between Applied Social Art and Critical Design", in: Damian Skinner (ed.), *Contemporary Jewelry in Perspective*, New York: Lark, 2013, pp. 228–229.

117 Lise Funder (ed.), *Nordisk smycke triennal 2/Nordic Jewellery*, Copenhagen: Nyt Nordisk Forlag Arnold Busck, 2001, p. 70.

118 Widar Halén (ed.), *From the Coolest Corner*, Stuttgart: arnoldsche, 2013.

119 Liesbeth den Besten, "Tanel Veenre", in: ibid., p. 86.

120 Jorunn Veiteberg, "Between Common Craft And Uncommon Art – On Wood in Jewellery", in: ibid., pp. 23–29.

121 André Gali, Petra Hölscher and Hege Henriksen (eds.), *Aftermath of Jewellery*, Stuttgart: arnoldsche, 2013.

122 Liesbeth den Besten, "Onno Boekhoudt. 'It Should Be Something Like Breathing'", in: Carin E.M. Reinders (ed.), *Onno Boekhoudt. Work in Progress*, Apeldoorn: CODA, 2010, p. 105.

123 <http://www.patrickbrillet.co.uk/diamond-shot/>, accessed 20 November 2020.

124 "Report from a Borderland. The Use of Ready-Mades, Recirculation and Other Contemporary Strategies among Norwegian Craft Artists", in: Pamela Johnson (ed.), *Ideas in the Making*, London: Crafts Council, 1998, pp. 69–76.

125 Jorunn Veiteberg, "Teori og kunsthandverk", in: Nina Schjønsby (ed.), *245 år. Kunst- og designutdanningen i Bergen*, Bergen: University of Bergen, 2017, pp. 239–243.

126 "Manifesto", in Gabi Dewald (ed.), *The Foundation*, Gmunden: Think Tank. A European Initiative for the Applied Arts, 2004, p. 5.

127 Ibid., p. 3.

128 Gabi Dewald, "Christoph Zellweger", in: Tanya Harrod and Edmund de Waal (eds.), *Gift*, Gmunden: Think Tank. A European Initiative for the Applied Arts, 2007, p. 84.

129 Gabi Dewald, "Hilde De Decker", in: Benjamin Lignel and Jorunn Veiteberg (eds.), *Speed*, Gmunden: Think Tank. A European Initiative for the Applied Arts, 2009, p. 54.

130 Benjamin Lignel, "Lin Cheung", in: Gabi Dewald and Mònica Gaspar (eds.), *Currency*, Gmunden: Think Tank. A European Initiative for the Applied Arts, 2010, p. 48.

131 Ibid.

132 Jorunn Veiteberg, "Otto Künzli", in: ibid., p. 52.

133 Mònica Gaspar and Benjamin Lignel (eds.), "Foreword", in: idem, *Show*, Gmunden: Think Tank. A European Initiative for the Applied Arts, 2011, unpaginated.

134 Liesbeth den Besten, "About the One and the Whole", in: ibid.

135 Marjan Unger, *Jewellery in Context*, Stuttgart: arnoldsche, 2019, pp. 157–158.

136 *American Craft Magazine*, no. 1, 2010, p. 58.

137 Fredrik Wildhagen, *Norge i form*, Oslo: J.M. Stenersen Forlag, 1988, p. 109.

138 <www.ramgalleri.no/index. php?option=com_k2&view=item&id=99:bei-mir-bist-du-shön&Itemid=131&lang=no>, accessed 3 January 2015.

139 Tommy Olsen, "Samtidsarkeologi for viderekomne", *Kunsthåndverk*, 17 January 2019, <http://www.kunsthandverk.no/anmeldelser?offset=1548239192628>, accessed 19 February 2020.

140 Andy Lim (ed.), *Lisa Walker "Unwearable"*, Cologne/New York: Darling Publications, 2008, p. 30.

141 Einar Økland, *Oss imellom?*, Oslo: Samlaget, 2020, p. 158.

142 Gert Staal, *Ted Noten. CH2=C(CH3)C(=O)OCH3 enclosures and other TN's*, Rotterdam: 010 Publishers, 2006, p. 116.

143 Marjan Boot, "Changes", in: *Radiant*, Amsterdam: Galerie Ra, 2006, p. 173.

144 *Schmuck 2016*, Munich: GHM-Gesellschaft für Handwerksmesses mbH, 2014, p. 11.

145 Florian Hufnagl (ed.), "Foreword", in: idem (ed.), *Dorothea Prühl. Colliers / Necklaces*, Stuttgart: arnoldsche, 2009, p. 7.

146 Susan Cummins, "Collector's Choice", <https://art-jewelryforum.org/susan-cummins>, accessed 4 October 2019.

147 Benjamin B. Walter, "On Frogs and Cars. Dorothea Prühl", *Art Aurea*, no. 2, 2011, p. 32.

148 Ibid.

149 <http://www.dorothea-pruehl.de/about-my-work/>, accessed 5 October 2019.

150 Benjamin B. Walter, "On Frogs and Cars. Dorothea Prühl", *Art Aurea*, no. 2, 2011, p. 32.

151 Renate Luckner-Bien, "Of the Simplicity That Is So Difficult to Attain", in: Florian Hufnagl (ed.), *Dorothea Prühl. Colliers/Necklaces*, Stuttgart: arnoldsche, 2009, p. 87.

152 Reinhold Ziegler, "Syklus tellus", *Kunsthåndverk*, no. 3, 2009, p. 21.

153 Liesbeth den Besten, *On Jewellery*, Stuttgart: arnoldsche, 2011, p. 200.

154 Jorunn Veiteberg, "Visual Pleasures/Augen-Freuden", in: *Daniel Kruger. Zwischen Natur und Künstlichkeit/Between Nature and Artifice*, Stuttgart: arnoldsche, 2014, pp. 196–203.

155 Liesbeth den Besten, "München – smykkehovedstaden", *Kunsthåndverk*, no. 2, 2004, pp. 34–37.

156 <https://collection.cooperhewitt.org/objects/554917379/>, accessed 5 December 2019.

157 Glenn Adamson, *Thinking Through Craft*, Oxford: Berg, 2007, p. 11.

158 Ibid., p. 21.

159 Susan Cummins, "Karen Pontoppidan. Context", *Art Jewelry Forum*, 6 February 2014, <https://artjewelryforum. org/karen-pontoppidan-context-0>, accessed 8 October 2019.

160 Maribel Königer, "A Class of Its Own", in: Florian Hufnagl (ed.), *The Fat Booty of Madness*, Stuttgart: arnoldsche, 2008, p. 31.

161 Ellen Maurer Zilioli, "Construction Site Jewellery", in: ibid., p. 62.

162 Jorunn Veiteberg, "Statement", in: *Schmuck 2014*, Munich: GHM-Gesellschaft für Handwerksmesses mbH, 2014, p. 7.

163 Liesbeth den Besten, "Lisa Walker", in: Andy Lim (ed.), *Lisa Walker "Unwearable"*, Cologne/New York: Darling Publications, 2008, p. 57.

164 Paul Derrez, "Lisa Walker", in: ibid., p. 108.

165 Kate Rhodes and Nella Themelios (eds.), *An Unreliable Guidebook to Jewellery by Lisa Walker*, Melbourne: RMIT Design Hub Gallery, RMIT University, 2019, p. 5.

166 Ibid., p. 37.

167 Kerianne Quick, "Lisa Walker. Put a Cord on It", *Art Jewelry Forum*, 2011, <https://artjewelryforum.org/lisa-walker-put-a-cord-on-it>, accessed 13 December 2013.

168 Warwick Freeman, "The Nature of the Material", in: Andy Lim (ed.), *Lisa Walker "Unwearable"*, Cologne/ New York: Darling Publications, 2008, p. 204.

169 Ibid.

170 Lisa Walker, "Statement", 2008, <https://klimt02.net/ events/exhibitions/gold-and-bones-galerie-goethe-53>, accessed 29 March 2020.

171 Ibid.

172 *David Bielander. Building a Steak of Creativity*, Perth: FORM, 2011, p. 20.

173 See Richard Sennett, *The Craftsman*, New Haven: Yale University Press, 2008, p. 21.

174 *Talente* has been organised annually since 1980 as a special exhibition at the International Craft Fair in Munich. The exhibition is open to young craftspeople and designers. The jury, which meets during the fair, awards a talent prize to some of the participants. I was on the jury with Ralph Turner in 2005 and 2006.

175 Jivan Astfalck, "Embedded Resistance", posted 7 June 2009, <https://journalofmoderncraft.com/author/ jivanastfalck>, accessed 29 February 2020.

176 Gitte Duemose Hansen, "Sikkehedsnålen", in: Christa Lykke Christensen and Carsten Thau (eds.), *Omgang med tingene*, Aarhus: Aarhus Universitetsforlag, 1993, p. 157.

177 Ibid.

178 Inger Westberg, "The Swedish Perspective", in: Ellen Maurer Zilioli (ed.), *Open Space – Mind Maps*, Stuttgart: arnoldsche, 2016, p. 23.

179 "Beatrice Brovia", in: ibid., p. 95.

180 Ibid., p. 96.

181 Nanna Segelcke, *Norsk kvalitet*, Oslo: Dreyer, 1989.

182 Warwick Freeman, "Tales of Wonderland", in: idem (ed.), *Wunderrūma*, Wellington: Hook and Sinker Publications, 2014, pp. 5–6.

183 Damian Skinner, *Kobi Bosshard. Goldsmith*, Auckland: David Bateman Ltd, 2012, p. 79.

184 "Jorunn Veiteberg in NZ", *Overview*, 25 November 2015, <http://www.jewellersguildofgreatersandringham. com/overview-25-november-2015.html>, accessed 3 November 20120.

185 Andy Lim (ed.), *Lisa Walker "Unwearable"*, Cologne/ New York: Darling Publications, 2008, p. 37.

186 Liesbeth den Besten, "Europe", in: Damian Skinner (ed.), *Contemporary Jewelry in Perspective*, New York: Lark, 2013, p. 109.

187 Ibid.

188 Kevin Murray, *Craft Unbound*, Fishermans Bend: Craftsman House, 2005, p. 18.

189 Marjan Unger, *Freedom Has Its Limitations. Jewelry Today, Seen from a Dutch Perspective*, Amsterdam: Premsela, The Netherlands Institute for Design and Fashion, 2012, unpaginated.

190 Ibid.

191 Benedikt Fischer, "The Absent and the Given. In Conversation with Suska Mackert", *Art Jewelry Forum*, 22 March 2015, <https://artjewelryforum.org/artists/the-absent-and-the-given>, accessed 28 April 2020.

192 Sol LeWitt, "Paragraphs on Conceptual Art" (1967), in: Charles Harrison and Paul Wood (eds.), *Art in Theory 1900–1990*, Oxford: Blackwell, 1992–95, p. 836.

193 Benedikt Fischer, "The Absent and the Given. In Conversation with Suska Mackert", *Art Jewelry Forum*, 22 March 2015, <https://artjewelryforum.org/artists/the-absent-and-the-given>, accessed 28 April 2020.

194 Alena Alexandrova, "Around, but Never at the Centre. Weaving an Atlas of Jewels and Gestures", <http://www. suskamackert.com/>, accessed 6 March 2020.

195 Ibid.

196 Liesbeth den Besten, *On Jewellery*, Stuttgart: arnoldsche, 2011, p. 84.

197 Gert Staal, *Ted Noten. CH2=C(CH3)C(=O)OCH3 enclosures and other TN's*, Rotterdam: 010 Publishers, 2006, p. 116.

198 Beatrice Wood, "The Richard Mutt Case", *The Blind Man*, no. 2, 1917, unpaginated, <http://sdrc.lib.uiowa.edu/ dada/blindman/2/05.htm>, accessed 3 November 2020.

199 Kimberley Chandler, "Bibbidi-Bobbidi-Boo", *Art Jewelry Forum*, 26 December 2015, <https://artjewelryforum.org/bibbidi-bobbidi-boo>, accessed 14 May 2017.
200 Lisa Walker quoted in Justine Olsen, *Lisa Walker, New Zealand's Jeweller Provocateur*, Wellington: Te Papa, 2018.
201 Melanie Holcomb, "The Seductive Pearl", in: idem (ed.), *Jewelry*, New York: The Metropolitan Museum of Art/New Haven: Yale University Press, 2018, p. 171.
202 Ibid., p. 174.
203 Silvia Malaguzzi, *The Pearl*, New York: Rizzoli, 2001, pp. 23–25.
204 Marie-Louise Kristensen, "Teds verden", *Kunstuff*, no. 18, 2008, p. 10.
205 Kate Franklin and Caroline Till, *Radical Matter*, London: Thames and Hudson, 2018, p. 13.
206 Nicolas Cheng, *World Wide Workshop*, doctoral dissertation, Academy of Art and Design, University of Gothenburg, 2019, p. 163.
207 Julia Manheim, *Sustainable Jewellery*, London: A & C Black, 2009, p. 17.
208 Susan Cohn (ed.), *Unexpected Pleasures*, New York: Skira Rizzoli, 2012, p. 54.
209 William McDonough and Michael Braungart, *Cradle to Cradle*, New York: North Point Press, 2002.
210 <http://www.test2.travelideas.es/files/files/0/5/7/1750.pdf>, accessed 13 March 2020.
211 The same theme was explored in May 2014 in four week-long exhibitions curated by Benjamin Lignel at KRAFT, a centre for contemporary arts and crafts in Bergen.
212 *About Time*, Academy of Art and Design, University of Gothenburg, 7 November 2015.
213 Thomas Hylland Eriksen, *Søppel*, Oslo: Aschehoug, 2011, p. 161.
214 Quoted from Joanna Cubbs and Eugene W. Metcalf Jr., "Sci-Fi Machines and Bottle-Cap Kings. The Recycling Strategies of Self-Taught Artists and the Imaginary Practice of Contemporary Consumption", in: Charlene Cerny and Suzanne Seriff (eds.), *Recycled Re-Seen*, New York: Harry N. Abrams, 1996, p. 49.
215 Corinna Rösner, "Woodgrouse Pâtés and Other Metamorphoses", in: *Gisbert Stach. Jewellery and Experiment*, Stuttgart: arnoldsche, 2018, pp. 13–14.
216 Rutger Emmelkamp, "David Bielander, Cardboard, One On One No 15", *Art Jewelry Forum*, 31 May 2015, <https://artjewelryforum.org/articles-series/david-bielander-cardboard>, accessed 15 March 2020.
217 Ibid.
218 Ezra Shales, *The Shape of Craft*, London: Reaktion Books, 2017, p. 21.

219 Quoted in Andy Lim (ed.), *Lisa Walker "Unwearable"*, Cologne/New York: Darling Publications, 2008, p. 397.
220 Benjamin Lignel, "On Curating Unexpected Pleasures. Susan Cohn in Conversation", *Art Jewelry Forum*, 1 May 2013, <https://artjewelryforum.org/museum-profiles/on-curating-unexpected-pleasures-the-art-and-design-of-contemporary-jewellery-susan->, accessed 1 May 2013.
221 The exhibition opened at the National Gallery of Victoria, Australia, in 2012 and was subsequently shown at the Design Museum, London.
222 Einar Økland, *Oss imellom?*, Oslo: Samlaget, 2020, p. 156.
223 Immanuel Kant, *Critique of Judgement*, transl. James Creed Meredith, Oxford/New York: Oxford University Press, 2007, p. 152.
224 Kevin Murray, "Pleasure", in: Damian Skinner (ed.), *Contemporary Jewelry in Perspective*, New York: Lark, 2013, p. 69.
225 Jorunn Veiteberg, "Toril Bjorg", in: *Toril Bjorg. Silver Jewellery*, Oslo, 2004, unpaginated.
226 Hanne Loreck, "Time and Again, the Personal is Political", in: Angelika Nollert (ed.), *Schmuckismus*, Stuttgart: arnoldsche, 2019, p. 37.
227 Petra Ahde-Deal, *Women and Jewelry – A Social Approach to Wearing and Possessing Jewelry*, doctoral dissertation, Department of Design, Aalto University, Helsinki: Aalto Arts Book, 2013.
228 Jing Yang, "I Am Not a Vase", 2016, <http://www.kathlibbertjewellery.co.uk/twenty-twenty/jing-yang01.html>, accessed 18 November 2020.
229 Liesbeth den Besten, "David Bielander. Man of Ideas", *Metalsmith*, no. 5, 2014, p. 46.
230 Catherine Grant (ed.), *New Directions in Jewellery*, London: Black Dog Publishing, 2005, pp. 131–147.
231 Jack Cunningham, *Maker Wearer Viewer*, Glasgow: Glasgow School of Art, 2005, p. vi.
232 Jorunn Veiteberg, *Konrad Mehus. Form Follows Fiction*, Stuttgart: arnoldsche, 2012, p. 8.
233 Petra Ahde-Deal, *Women and Jewelry – A Social Approach to Wearing and Possessing Jewelry*, doctoral dissertation, Department of Design, Aalto University, Helsinki: Aalto Arts Book, 2013, p. 33.
234 Torgeir Rebolledo Pedersen, *Dikt i utvalg*, Oslo: Forlaget Oktober, 2019.
235 Marcus Fairs, "Susan Cohn Plans Performance in Response to Denmark's Controversial 'Jewellery Law'", *Dezeen*, 6 April 2018, <https://www.dezeen.com/2018/04/06/susan-cohn-plans-series-of-performances-in-response-to-denmark-jewellery-law/>, accessed 8 April 2020.

236 Tracey Clement, "Susan Cohn on the Personal and
Political Power of Jewellery", 3 September 2019, <https://
artguide.com.au/susan-cohn-on-the-personal-and-politi-
cal-power-of-jewellery>, accessed 2 December 2019.
237 Lin Cheung, "Wear, Wearing, Worn. The Transitions
of Jewels to Jewellery", in: idem et al., *New Directions in
Jewellery II*, London: Black Dog Publishing, 2006, pp. 13–14.
238 Marjan Unger, "Jewellery in Context", in: idem and
Suzanne van Leeuwen, *Jewellery Matters*, Amsterdam:
Rijks Museum/Rotterdam: Nai010 Publishers, 2017, p. 25.
239 <http://www.ruudtpeters.nl/index.php?id=295>,
accessed 16 June 2020.
240 Siri Hustvedt, "Sontag on Smut. Fifty Years Later", in:
idem, *A Woman Looking at Men Looking at Women*, New
York: Simon & Schuster, 2016, pp. 61–78.

Literature

Adamson, Glenn. *Thinking Through Craft.* Oxford: Berg, 2007.

Ahde-Deal, Petra. *Women and Jewelry – A Social Approach to Wearing and Possessing Jewelry.* Doctoral dissertation 1/2013, Department of Design, Aalto University. Helsinki: Aalto Arts Book, 2013.

Astrup, Ingebjørg (ed.). *Åkersvika Addenda.* Lillehammer: LOOC, 1993.

Beauvoir, Simone de. *The Second Sex.* Translated by H.M. Parshley. London: Jonathan Cape, 1953.

Benjamin, Walter. *Illuminations.* Translated by Harry Zohn. New York: Schocken Books, 1969.

Benjamin, Walter. *The Arcades Project.* Translated by Howard Eiland and Kevin McLaughlin. Cambridge, MA: Harvard University Press, 1999.

Bjørnson, Bjørnstjerne. *Dikt og Sanger, i utvalg.* Edited by Johan Hertzberg. Oslo: Gyldendal Norsk Forlag, 1940.

Blodig alvor. Norsk kunst på 80-tallet. Bergen: Bergen Kunstmuseum, 2009.

Brundtland, Cecilie Malm. *Tone Vigeland Jewellery + Sculpture. Movements in Silver.* Stuttgart: arnoldsche, 2003.

Buhrs, Michael, and Zilioli, Ellen Maurer (eds.). *Karen Pontoppidan. The One Woman Group Exhibition.* Berlin: Distanz Verlag, 2019.

Candlin, Fiona. *Art, Museums and Touch.* Manchester: Manchester University Press, 2010.

Cerny, Charlene, and Seriff, Suzanne (eds.). *Recycled Re-Seen. Folk Art from the Global Scrap Heap.* New York: Harry N. Abrams, 1996.

Cheng, Nicolas. *World Wide Workshop. The Craft of Noticing.* Doctoral dissertation, Academy of Art and Design, University of Gothenburg, 2019.

Cheung, Lin, Clarke, Beccy, and Clarke, Indigo. *New Directions in Jewellery II.* London: Black Dog Publishing, 2006.

Christensen, Christa Lykke, and Thau, Carsten (eds.). *Omgang med tingene.* Aarhus: Aarhus Universitetsforlag, 1993.

Classen, Constance (ed.). *The Book of Touch.* Oxford/ New York: Berg, 2005.

Cohn, Susan (ed.). *Unexpected Pleasures. The Art and Design of Contemporary Jewellery.* New York: Skira Rizzoli, 2012.

Cunningham, Jack. *Maker Wearer Viewer. Contemporary Narrative European Jewellery.* Glasgow: Glasgow School of Art, 2005.

Daniel Kruger. *Between Nature and Artifice. Jewellery 1974–2014.* Stuttgart: arnoldsche, 2014.

Danto, Arthur C. *The Abuse of Beauty. Aesthetics and the Concept of Art.* Chicago/La Salle, IL: Open Court, 2003.

David Bielander. *Building a Steak of Creativity.* Perth: FORM, 2011.

David Bielander. Twenty Years 2016–1996. Stuttgart: arnoldsche, 2017.

Den Besten, Liesbeth. *On Jewellery. A Compendium of International Contemporary Art Jewellery.* Stuttgart: arnoldsche, 2011.

Den Besten, Liesbeth, and Veiteberg, Jorunn. *Caroline Broadhead.* Stuttgart: arnoldsche, 2017.

Dewald, Gabi (ed.). *The Foundation.* Gmunden: Think Tank. A European Initiative for the Applied Arts, 2004.

Dormer, Peter, and Turner, Ralph. *The New Jewelry. Trends + Traditions.* London: Thames and Hudson, 1985.

Dresden, Anne, Heuzé, Michèle, and Lignel, Benjamin (eds.). *Medusa. Jewellery & Taboos.* Paris: Paris Musées, 2017.

Duve, Thierry de. *Kant after Duchamp.* Cambridge, MA/ London: MIT Press, 1996/1999.

Elsner, John, and Cardinal, Roger (eds.). *The Cultures of Collecting.* London: Reaktions Books, 1994.

Eriksen, Thomas Hylland. *Søppel. Avfall i en verden av bivirkninger.* Oslo: Aschehoug, 2011.

Erlhoff, Michael (ed.). *Ornamenta 1. Internationale Schmuckkunst.* Munich: Prestel-Verlag, 1989.

Felieke van der Leest. The Zoo of Life. Jewellery and Objects 1996–2014. Stuttgart: arnoldsche, 2014.

Fossberg, Jorunn. *Draktsølv.* Oslo: Universitetsforlaget, 1991.

Franklin, Kate, and Till, Caroline. *Radical Matter. Rethinking Materials for a Sustainable Future.* London: Thames and Hudson, 2018.

Freeman, Warwick (ed.). *Wunderrūma.* Wellington: Hook and Sinker Publications, 2014.

Frisby, David, and Featherstone, Mike (eds.). *Simmel on Culture.* London: Sage Publications, 1997.

Funder, Lise (ed.). *Nordisk smycke triennal*. Copenhagen: Nyt Nordisk Forlag Arnold Busck, 2001.

Gali, André, Hölscher, Petra, and Henriksen, Hege (eds.). *Aftermath of Jewellery*. Stuttgart: arnoldsche, 2013.

Gaspar, Mònica, and Dewald, Gabi (eds.). *Currency*. Gmunden: Think Tank. A European Initiative for the Applied Arts, 2010.

Gaspar, Mònica, and Lignel, Benjamin (eds.). *Show*. Gmunden: Think Tank. A European Initiative for the Applied Arts, 2011.

Gisbert Stach. Jewellery and Experiment. Stuttgart: arnoldsche, 2018.

Grant, Catherine (ed.). *New Directions in Jewellery*. London: Black Dog Publishing, 2005.

Gundersen, Bjarne Riiser. *Da postmodernismen kom til Norge*. Oslo: Flamme Forlag, 2016.

Halén, Widar (ed.). *From the Coolest Corner. Nordic Jewellery*. Stuttgart: arnoldsche, 2013.

Handshake: 12 Contemporary Jewelers Connect with their Heroes. Wellington: JEMbooks, 2013.

Harrison, Charles, and Wood, Paul (eds.). *Art in Theory 1900–1990*. Oxford: Blackwell, 1992/95.

Harrod, Tanya (ed.). *Obscure Objects of Desire*. London: Crafts Council, 1997.

Harrod, Tanya, and Waal, Edmund de (eds.). *Gift*. Gmunden: Think Tank. A European Initiative for the Applied Arts, 2007.

Hauger, Therese. *Nyere norsk smykkekunst 1945–1990*. Unpublished master's dissertation in art history, University of Bergen, 1994.

Holcomb, Melanie (ed.). *Jewelry. The Body Transformed*. New York: The Metropolitan Museum of Art/New Haven: Yale University Press, 2018.

Hufnagl, Florian (ed.). *The Fat Booty of Madness*. Stuttgart: arnoldsche, 2008.

Hufnagl, Florian (ed.). *Dorothea Prühl. Colliers/Necklaces*. Stuttgart: arnoldsche, 2009.

Hufnagl, Florian (ed.). *Otto Künzli. The Book*. Stuttgart: arnoldsche, 2013.

Hustvedt, Siri. *A Woman Looking at Men Looking at Women. Essays on Art, Sex, and the Mind*. New York: Simon & Schuster, 2016.

Ilse-Neumann, Ursula. *Jewelry of Ideas. The Susan Grant Lewin Collection*. New York: Cooper Hewitt, Smithsonian Design Museum/Stuttgart: arnoldsche, 2017.

Jarvis, Cheryl. *The Necklace*. London: Harper Collins, 2009.

Jencks, Charles. *What Is Post-Modernism?* New York: Academy Editions/St. Martin's Press, 1986/1989.

John, Elton. *Me*. London: Macmillan, 2019.

Johnson, Pamela (ed.). *Ideas in the Making. Practice in Theory*. London: Crafts Council, 1998.

Kagge, Erling. *Kunsten å samle kunst*. Oslo: Kagge forlag, 2015.

Kant, Immanuel. *Critique of Judgement*. Translated by James Creed Meredith. Oxford/New York: Oxford University Press, 2007.

Kirkeby, Per. *Munch*. Copenhagen: Edition Bløndal, 1999.

Lambert, Sylvie. *The Ring. Design. Past and Present*. Crans-Près-Céligny: RotoVision SA, 1998.

Benjamin Lignel. Auction catalogue for Pierre Bergé & Associés, Brussels. 20 November 2011.

Lignel, Benjamin (ed.). *Shows and Tales. On Jewelry Exhibition-Making*. Mill Valley: Art Jewelry Forum, 2015.

Lignel, Benjamin, and Veiteberg, Jorunn (eds.). *Speed*. Gmunden: Think Tank. A European Initiative for the Applied Arts, 2009.

Lignel, Benjamin, Martin, Frédéric F., and Veiteberg, Jorunn. *Différence et répétition*. Paris: la garantie, 2014.

Lim, Andy (ed.). *Lisa Walker "Unwearable"*. Cologne/New York: Darling Publications, 2008.

Lindemann, Wilhelm (ed.). *Thinking Jewellery. On the Way towards a Theory of Jewellery*. Stuttgart: arnoldsche, 2011.

Lohmann, Jan, and Funder, Lise (eds.). *Nordisk smykkekunst / Nordic Jewellery*. Copenhagen: Nyt Nordisk Forlag Arnold Busck, 1995.

Lowe, Emily. *Unprotected Females in Norway; or, The Pleasantest Way of Travelling There*. London: Routledge & Co., 1857.

Malaguzzi, Silvia. *The Pearl*. New York: Rizzoli, 2001.

Manheim, Julia. *Sustainable Jewellery*. London: A & C Black, 2009.

McDonough, William, and Braungart, Michael. *Cradle to Cradle. Remaking the Way We Make Things*. New York: North Point Press, 2002.

Muensterberger, Werner. *Collecting. An Unruly Passion*. Princeton: Princeton University Press, 1994.

Murray, Kevin. *Craft Unbound. Make the Common Precious*. Fishermans Bend: Craftsman House, 2005.

Murray, Kevin, and Skinner, Damian. *Place and Adornment. A History of Contemporary Jewellery in Australia and New Zealand*. Honolulu: University of Hawai'i Press, 2014.

Nollert, Angelika (ed.). *Schmuckismus*. Stuttgart: arnoldsche, 2019.

Økland, Einar. *Oss imellom?* Oslo: Samlaget, 2020.

Olsen, Justine. *Lisa Walker, New Zealand's Jeweller Provocateur*. Wellington: Te Papa, 2018.

Opstad, Jan-Lauritz. *En ny bevissthet. Norsk kunsthåndverk 1970–1990*. Oslo: C. Huitfeldt forlag, 1989.

Otto Künzli. The Third Eye. Amsterdam: Stedelijk Museum, 1991.

Pamuk, Orhan. *The Museum of Innocence.* Translated by Maureen Freely. New York: Alfred A. Knopf, 2009.

Pamuk, Orhan. *The Innocence of Objects.* New York: Abrams, 2012.

Pearce, Susan M. (ed.). *Interpreting Objects and Collections.* London: Routledge, 1994.

Pedersen, Torgeir Rebolledo. *Dikt i utvalg. I krig og kjærlighet er mye ugjort.* Oslo: Forlaget Oktober, 2019.

Pointon, Marcia. *Brilliant Effects. A Cultural History of Gem Stones and Jewellery.* New Haven/London: Yale University Press, 2009.

Radiant. 30 Years Ra. Amsterdam: Galerie Ra, 2006.

Reinders, Carin E.M. (ed.). *Onno Boekhoudt. Work in Progress.* Apeldoorn: CODA, 2010.

Rhodes, Kate, and Themelios, Nella (eds.). *An Unreliable Guidebook to Jewellery by Lisa Walker.* Melbourne: RMIT Design Hub Gallery, RMIT University, 2019.

Russell, Rebecca Ross. *Gender and Jewelry. A Feminist Analysis.* Self-published with CreateSpace, 2010.

Salmonsens Konservationsleksikon, vol. II, 2nd edn. Edited by Christian Blangstrup. Copenhagen: J.H. Schulz Forlagsboghandel, 1915.

Sand, Heidi (ed.). *Norwegian Jewellery.* Oslo: The Royal Ministry of Foreign Affairs, 1987.

Scavenius, Bente. *Torben Hardenberg, Guldsmeden.* Copenhagen: Gyldendal, 2006.

Schjønsby, Nina (ed.). *245 år. Kunst- og designutdanningen i Bergen.* Bergen: University of Bergen, 2017.

Schjønsby, Sissel Ree (ed.). *In Touch.* Oslo: De norske bokklubbene/Kulturprogrammet for de XVII Olympiske Vinterleker på Lillehammer, 1994.

Schmuck 2014. Munich: GHM-Gesellschaft für Handwerksmessen mbH, 2014.

Schmuck 2016. Munich: GHM-Gesellschaft für Handwerksmessen mbH, 2016.

Schmuck 2018. Munich: GHM-Gesellschaft für Handwerksmessen mbH, 2018.

Segelcke, Nanna. *Norsk kvalitet.* Oslo: Dreyer, 1989.

Sennett, Richard. *The Craftsman.* New Haven: Yale University Press, 2008.

Shales, Ezra. *The Shape of Craft.* London: Reaktion Books, 2017.

Sjöberg, Fredrik. *The Fly Trap.* Translated by Thomas Teal. New York: Panthenon Books, 2015.

Skinner, Damian. *Kobi Bosshard. Goldsmith.* Auckland: David Bateman Ltd, 2012.

Skinner, Damian (ed.). *Contemporary Jewelry in Perspective.* New York: Lark, 2013.

Smykker ·85. Trondheim: Nordenfjeldske Kunstindustrimuseum, 1985.

Sørheim, Thor. *Stuntpoetenes historie.* Oslo: Flamme Forlag, 2016.

Staal, Gert. *Ted Noten. CH2=C(CH3)C(=O)OCH3 enclosures and other TN's.* Rotterdam: 010 Publishers, 2006.

Strauss, Cindy. *Ornament as Art. Avant-garde Jewelry from the Helen Williams Drutt Collection.* Stuttgart: arnoldsche, 2007.

Taylor, Elisabeth. *My Love Affair with Jewelry.* New York: Simon & Schuster, 2002.

Thomsen, Dorthe Kirkegaard. *Livshistorien.* Aarhus: Aarhus Universitet, 2013.

Thue, Anniken (ed.). *Tone Vigeland.* Oslo: Oslo Museum of Applied Art, 1995.

Turner, Ralph. *Jewelry in Europe and America. New Times, New Thinking.* London: Thames and Hudson, 1996.

Unger, Marjan. *Freedom Has Its Limitations. Jewelry Today, Seen from a Dutch Perspective.* Amsterdam: Premsela, The Netherlands Institute for Design and Fashion, 2012.

Unger, Marjan. *Jewellery in Context. A Multidisciplinary Framework for the Study of Jewellery.* Stuttgart: arnoldsche, 2019.

Unger, Marjan, and Leeuwen, Suzanne van. *Jewellery Matters.* Amsterdam: Rijks Museum/Rotterdam: Nai010 Publishers, 2017.

Veiteberg, Jorunn (ed.). *Rooms with a View. Women's Art in Norway 1880–1990.* Oslo: The Royal Norwegian Ministry of Foreign Affairs, 1989.

Veiteberg, Jorunn (ed.). *Det veltalende objekt.* Oslo: Det Tenkende Øye/Norske Kunsthåndverkere, 1997.

Veiteberg, Jorunn. *Craft in Transition.* Bergen: Bergen National Academy of the Arts, 2005.

Veiteberg, Jorunn. *Kim Buck. It's the Thought That Counts.* Copenhagen: Nyt Nordisk Forlag Arnold Busck, 2007.

Veiteberg, Jorunn. *Sigurd Bronger. Laboratorium Mechanum.* Stuttgart: arnoldsche, 2011.

Veiteberg, Jorunn. *Konrad Mehus. Form Follows Fiction. Jewellery and Objects.* Stuttgart: arnoldsche, 2012.

Wildhagen, Fredrik. *Norge i form. Kunsthåndverk og design under industrikulturen.* Oslo: J.M. Stenersen Forlag, 1988.

Zetterlund, Christina, Hyltén-Cavallius, Charlotte, and Rosenqvist, Johanna (eds.). *Konsthantverk i Sverige, del 1.* Stockholm: Mångkulturelt centrum, 2015.

Zilioli, Ellen Maurer (ed.). *Open Space – Mind Maps. Positions in Contemporary Jewellery.* Stockholm: Nationalmuseum/Stuttgart: arnoldsche, 2016.

Portraits

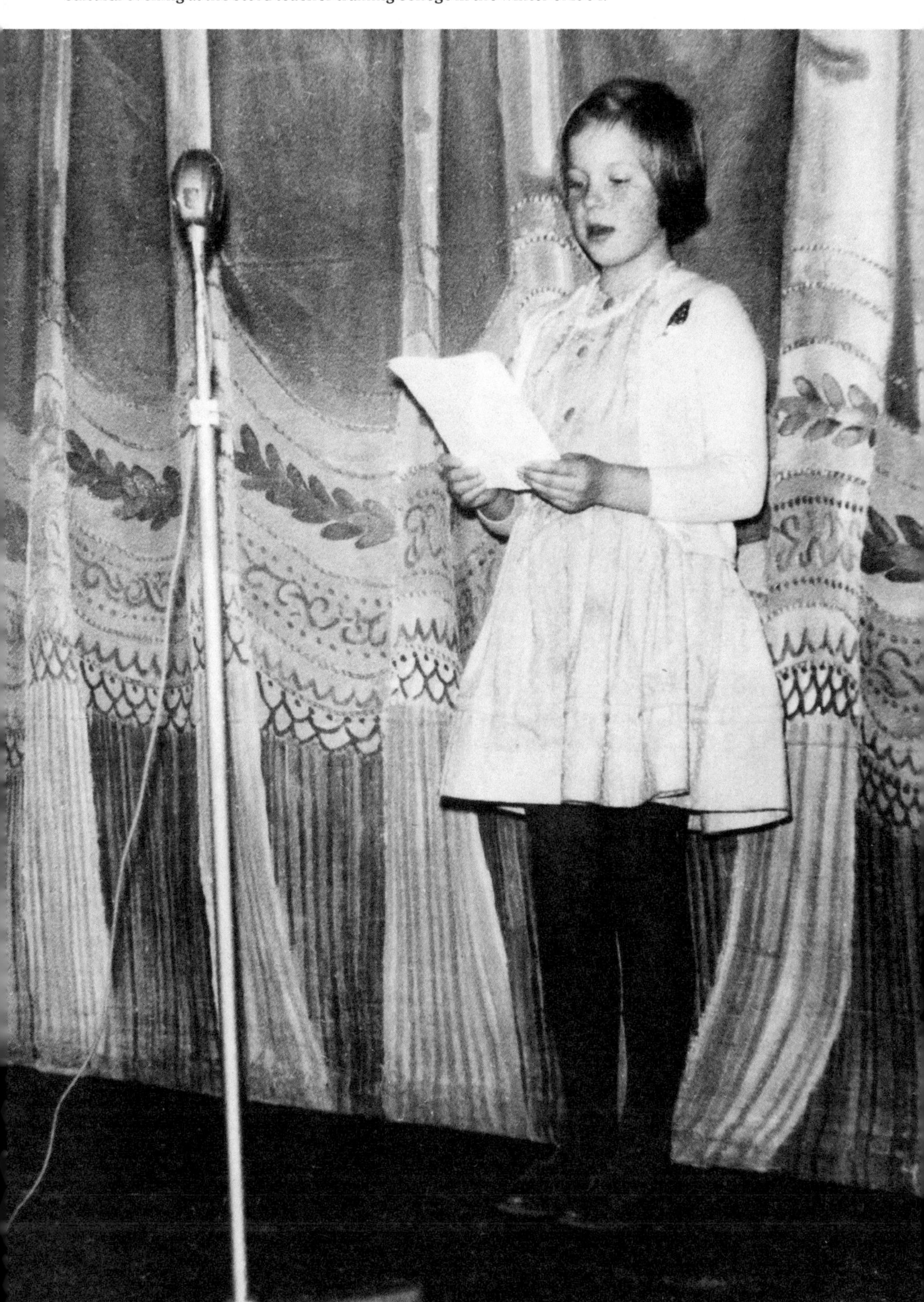

Eight years old, wearing a plastic necklace and "gold" brooch. I am reading a poem by Per Sivle during a cultural evening at the Stord teacher training college in the winter of 1964.

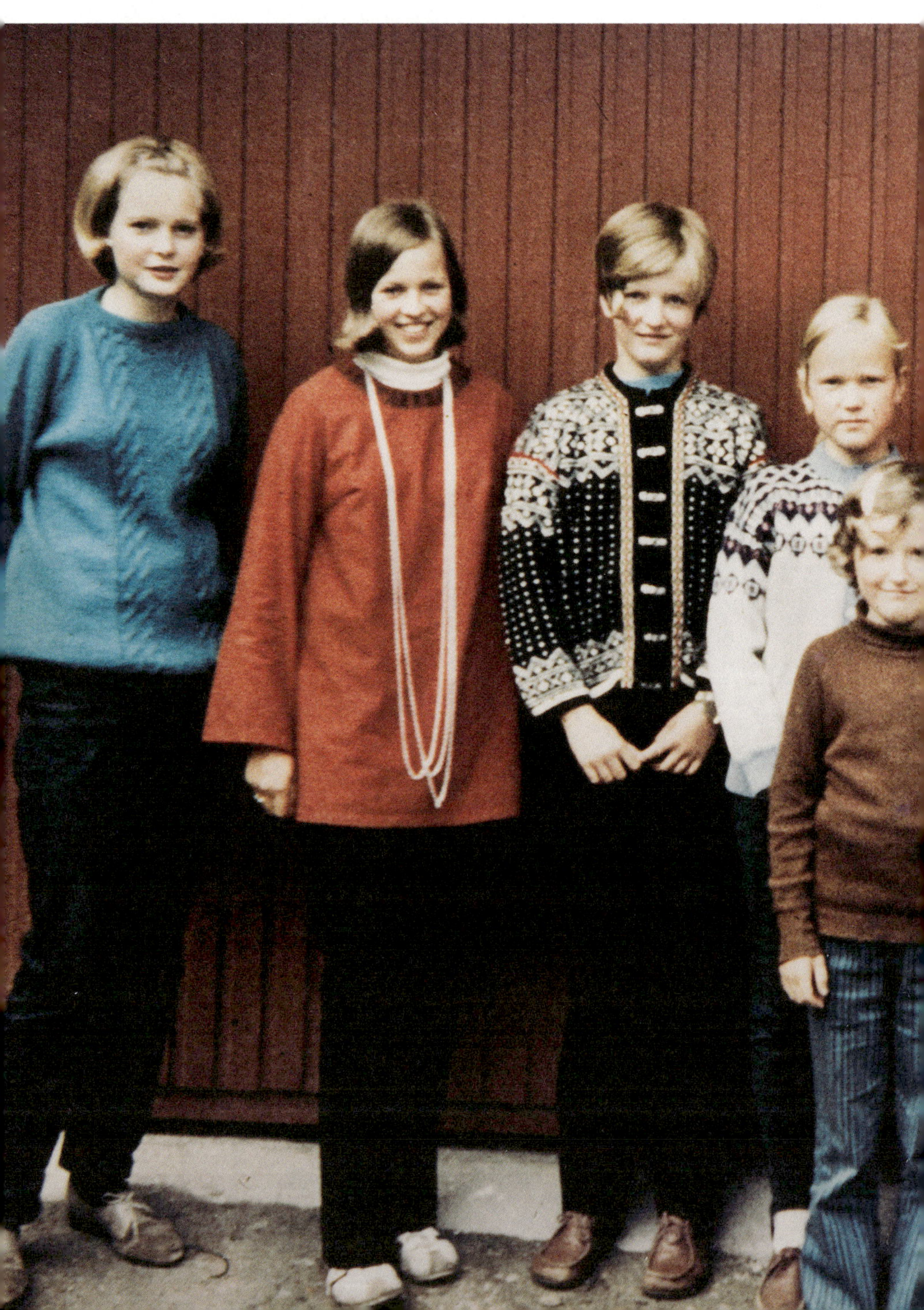

With sisters and cousins in the summer of 1969; I am the only one wearing jewellery. I had made the tunic myself, decorating it around the neck with potato prints.

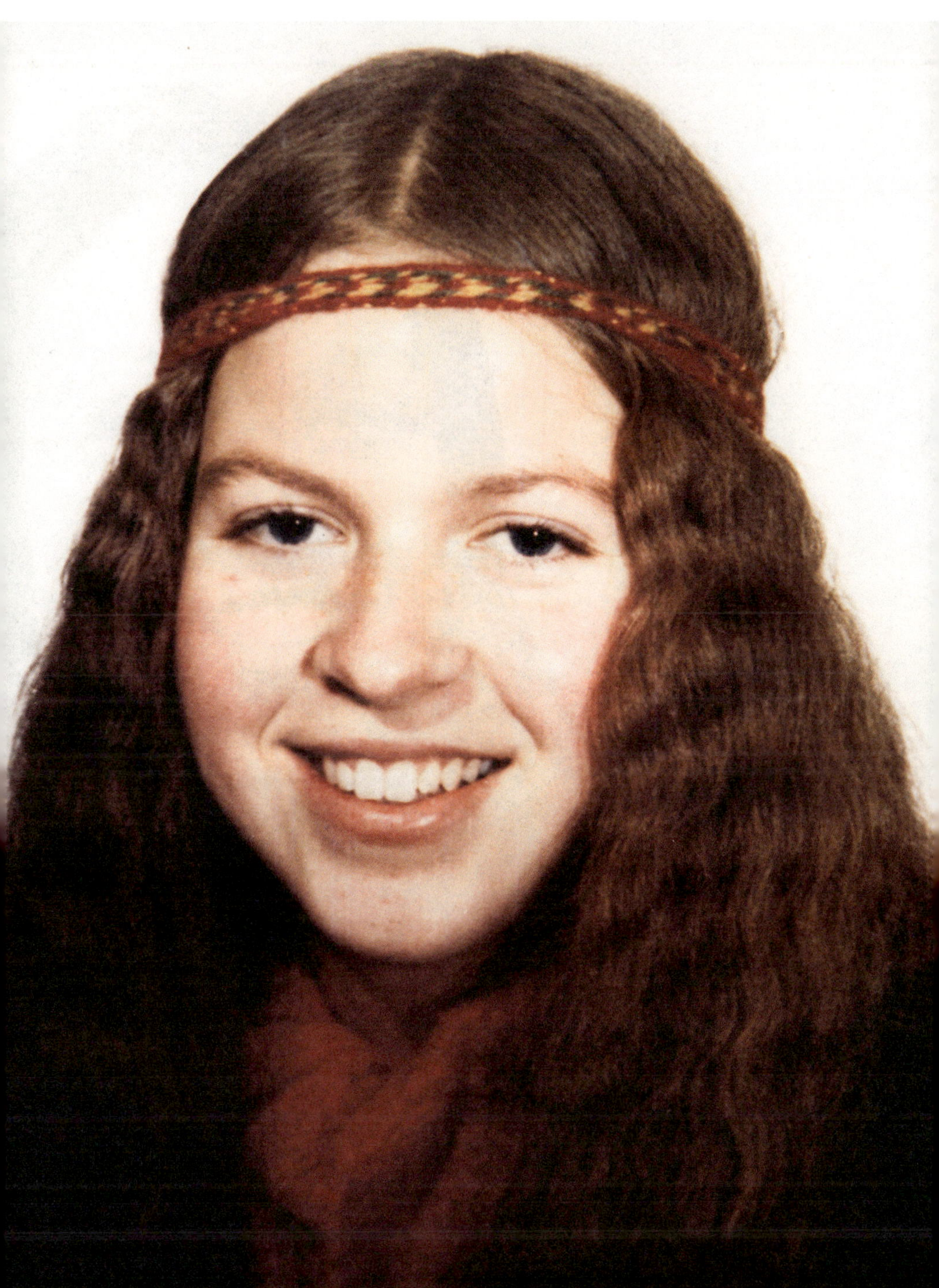

The official ninth-year school portrait at Stord ungdomsskule in the spring of 1971 shows an aspiring fifteen-year-old hippie. I had woven the headband myself.

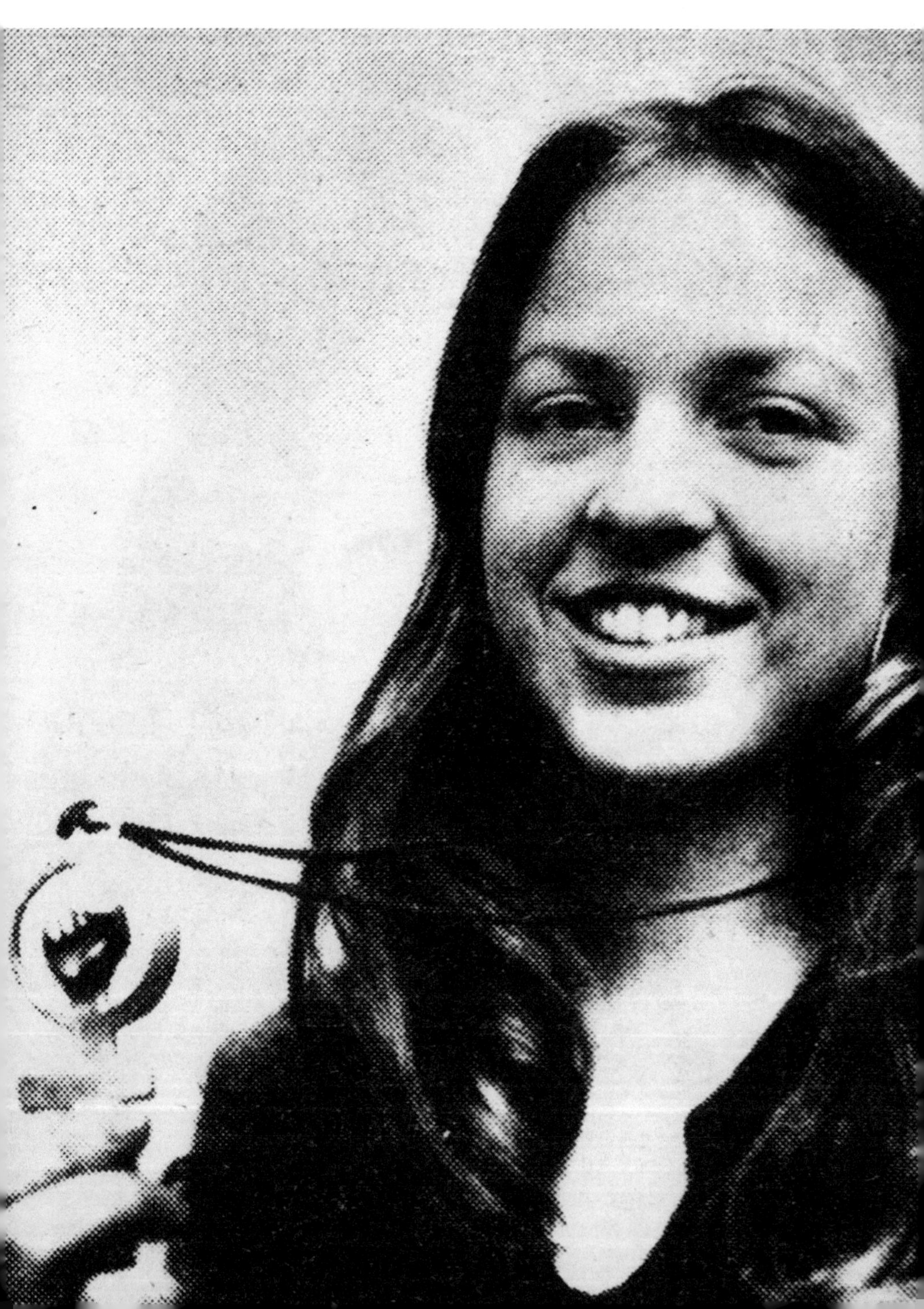

With the women's lib symbol [286] in *Morgenavisen*, in Bergen on 6 March 1976, to mobilise participation for International Women's Day on 8 March.

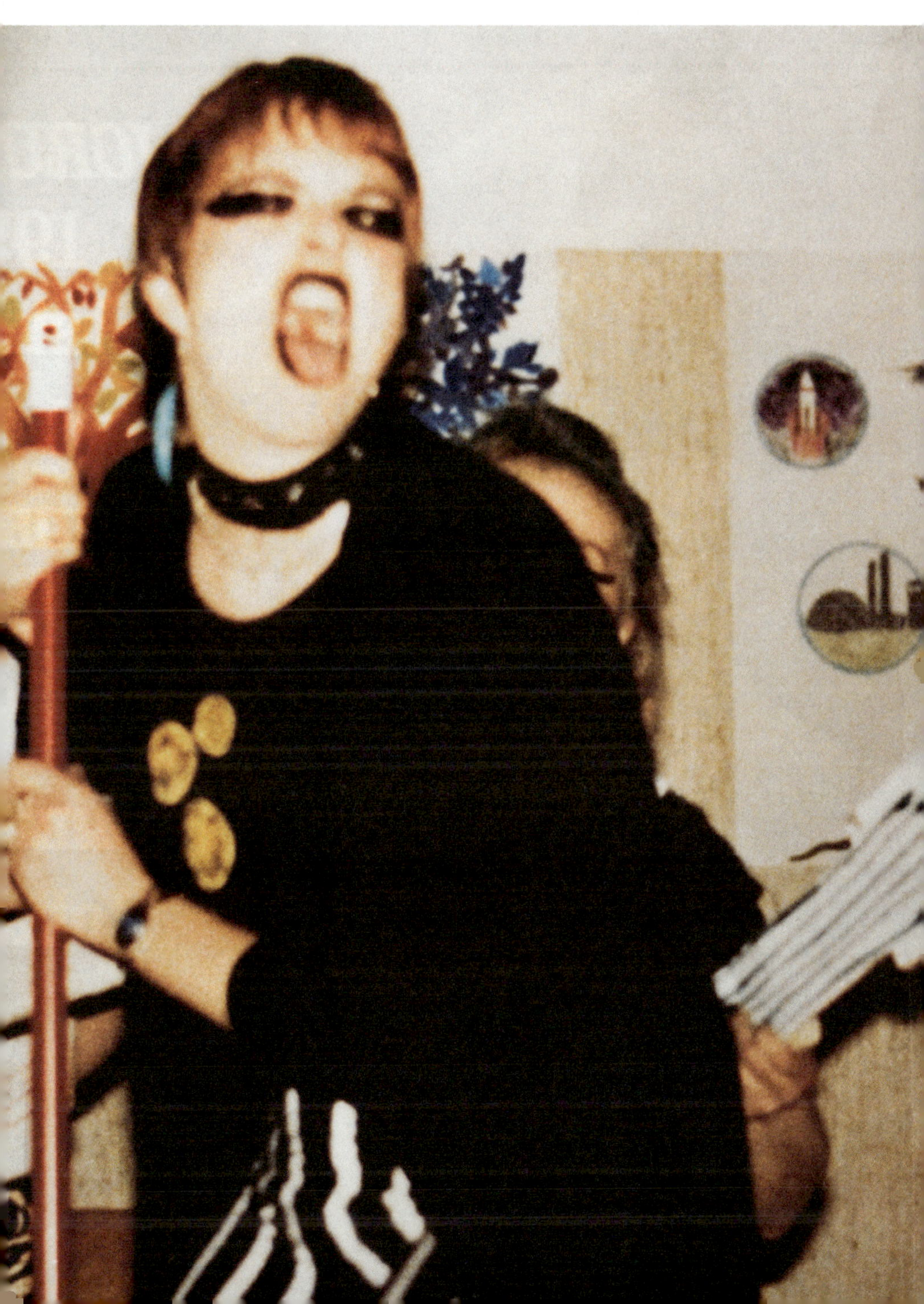

In the role of the German punk singer Nina Hagen at Snoghøj Nordisk Folkehøjskole in Denmark in February 1983.

From the literary programme *Bokstavelig talt* on NRK television on 14 November 1986. I was there to discuss the book *Reklamebildet*, which I had written together with Einar Økland.

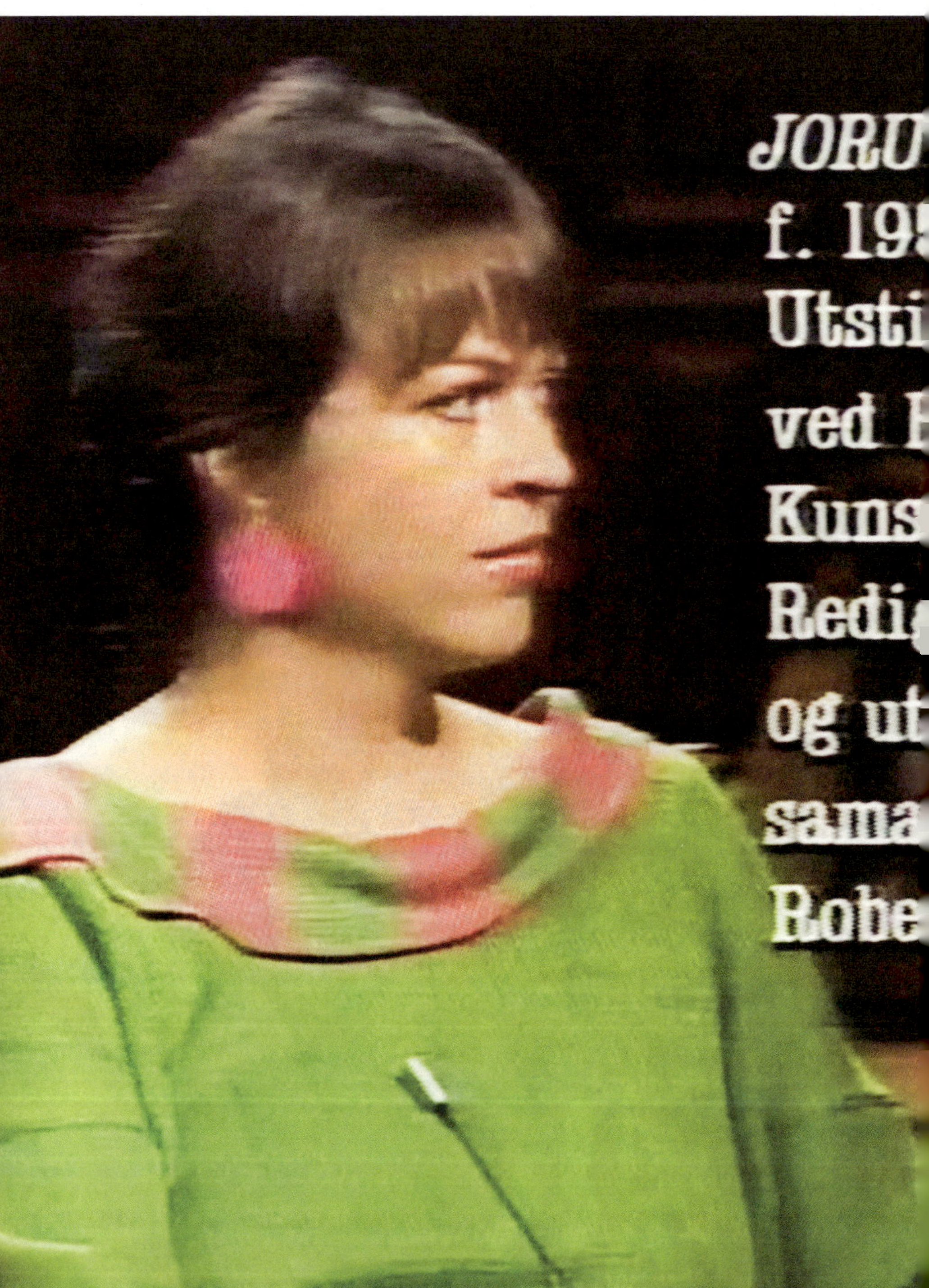

From *Midt i smørøyet*, a programme for young people, on NRK television, on 26 January 1989, where I talked about advertising. I wore these earrings regularly in the years around 1990 **[557]**.

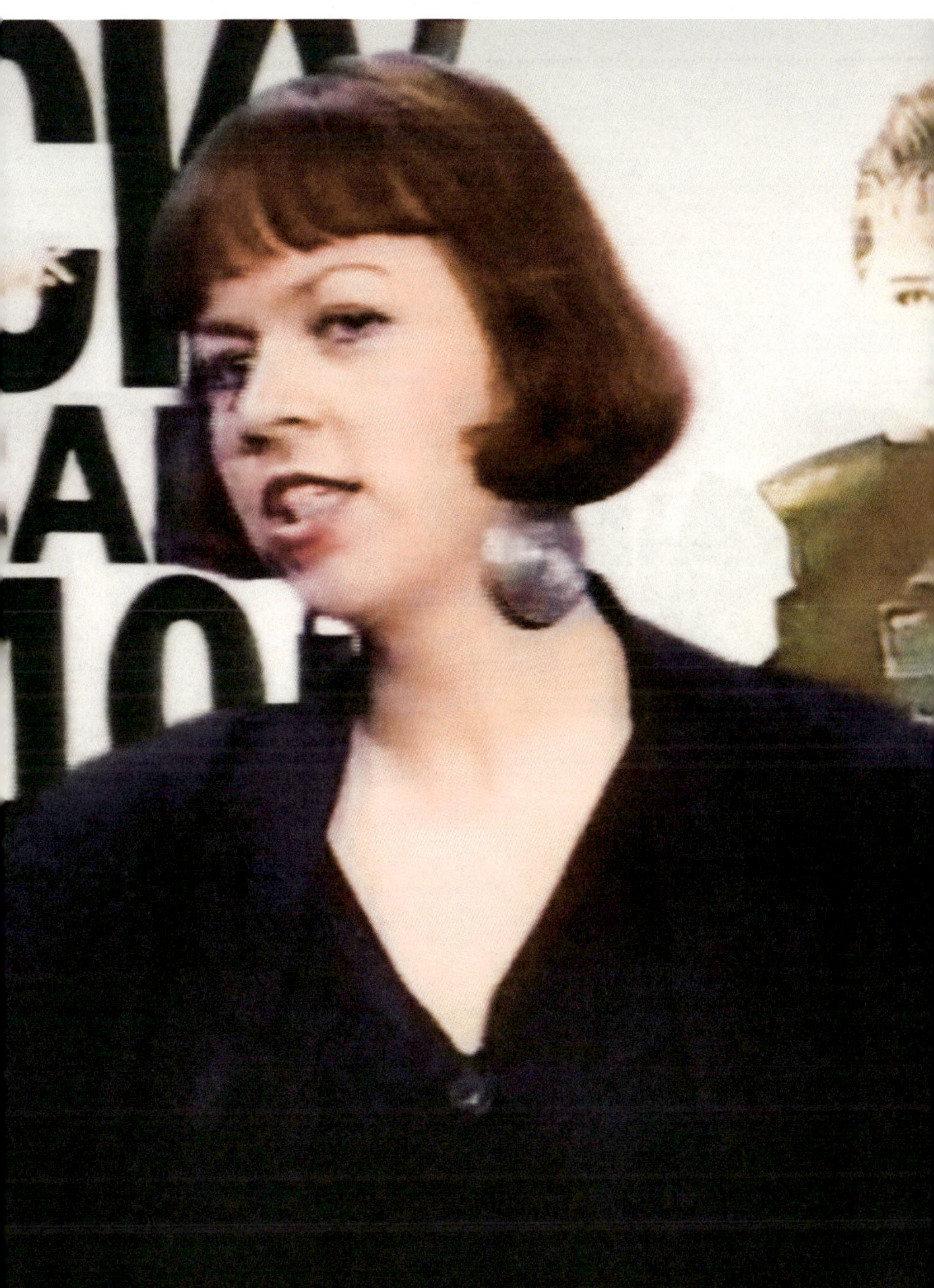

From the opening of the exhibition *Rooms with a View. Women's Art in Norway 1880–1990*, at Rotonda della Besana, Milan, in November 1989. I was commissioner for the exhibition, and I am seen here together with the Norwegian Crown Prince couple and the artist Hilde Vemren. I am wearing a bracelet by Ingjerd Hanevold [172].

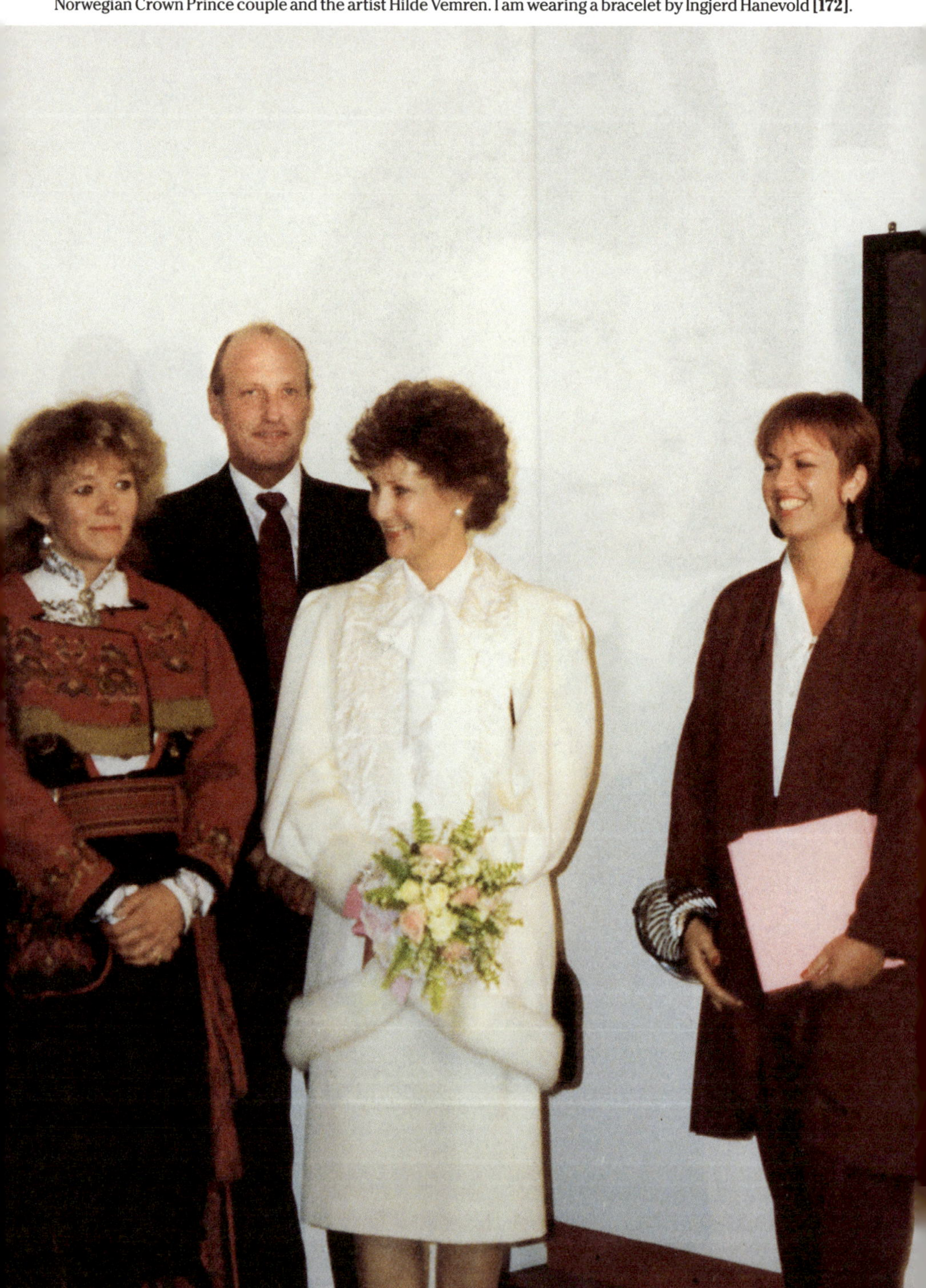

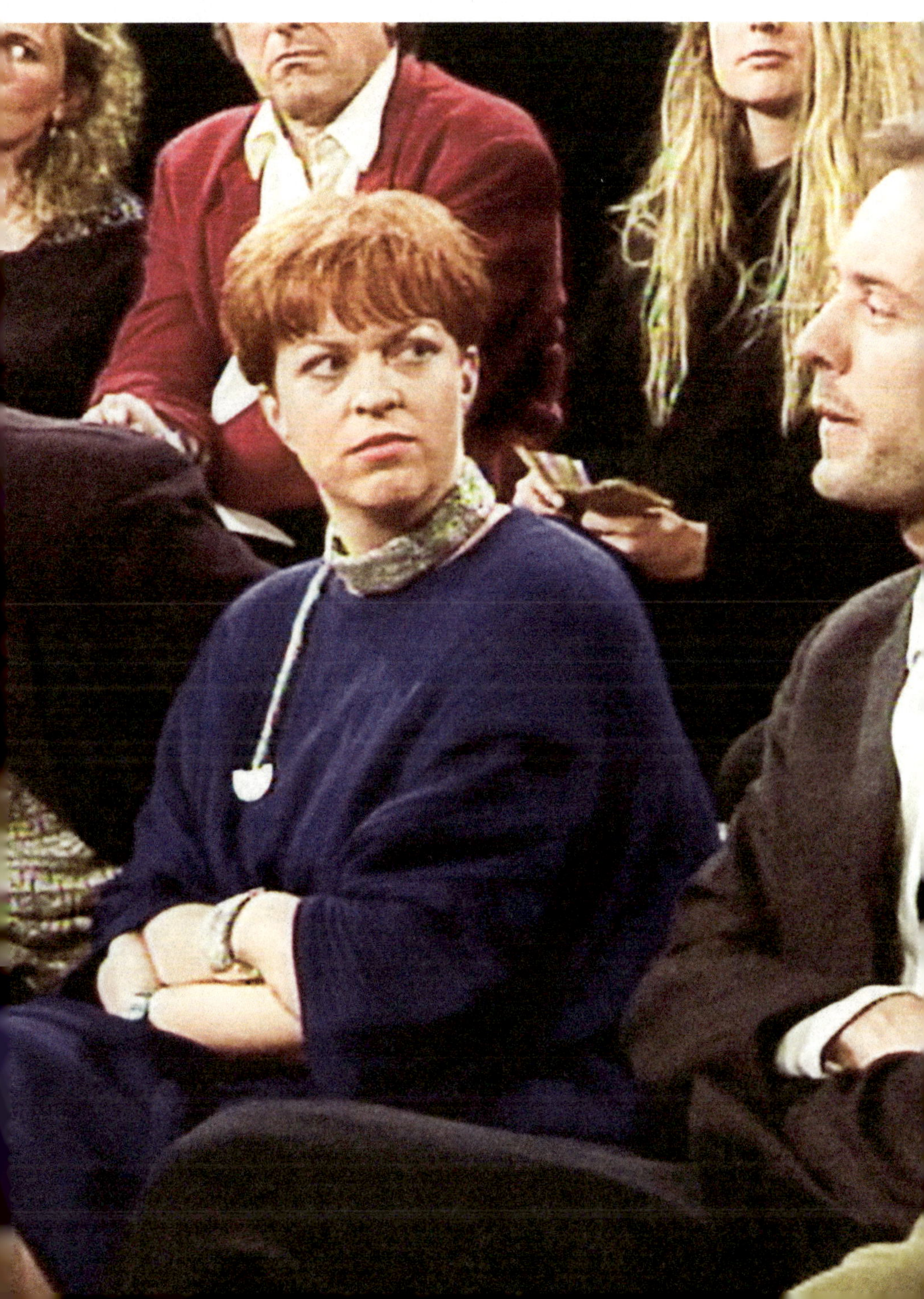

From the debate programme *Antenne 10* on NRK television, on 12 March 1991. The subject was the (lack of) time devoted to figurative art in art education. Necklace and bracelet by Toril Bjorg **[43] [40]**.

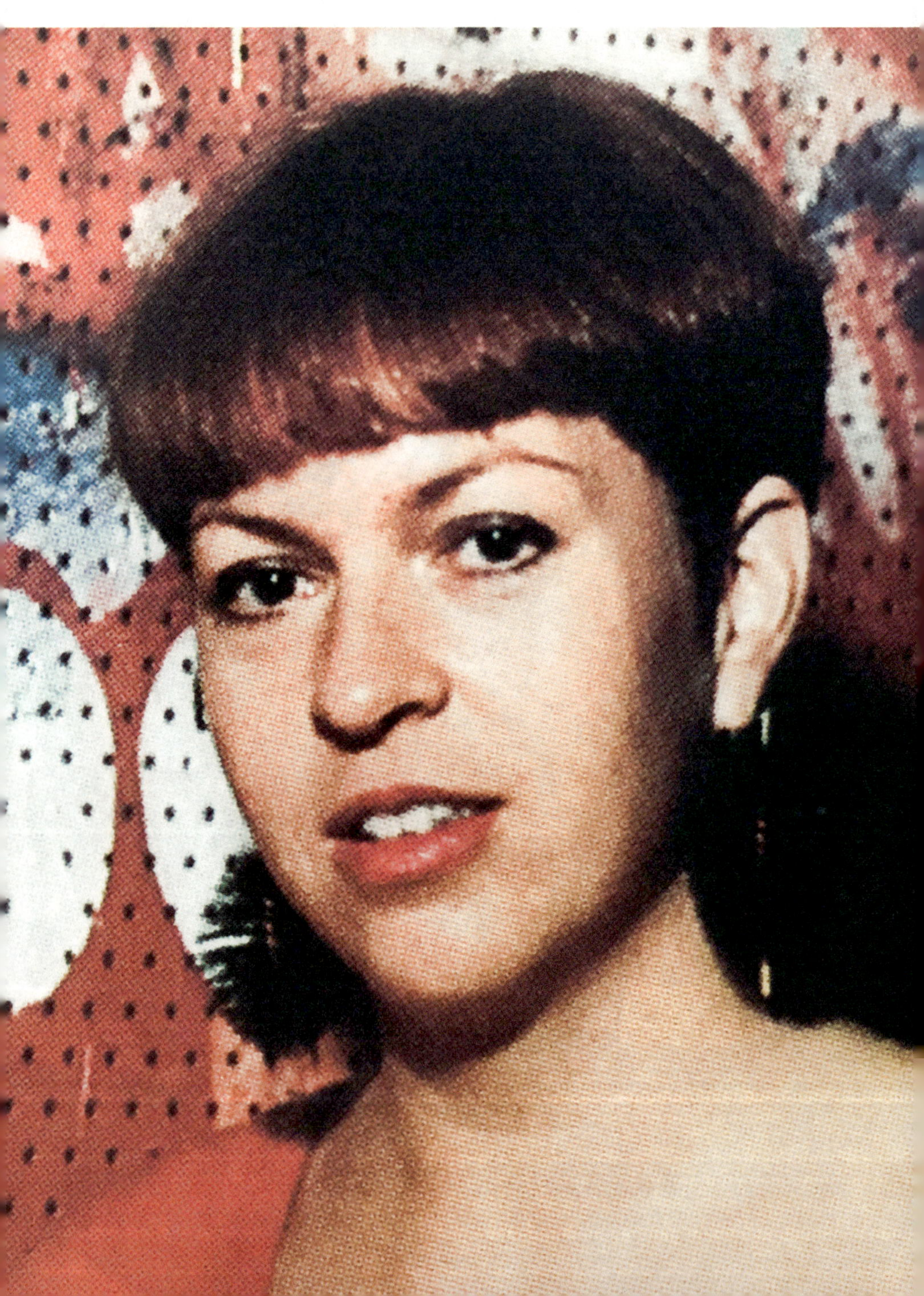

Presentation in *Programbladet* in the spring of 1991 in connection with my appointment as editor-in-chief of art and culture at NRK television. Earrings by Inger Marie Berg [28].

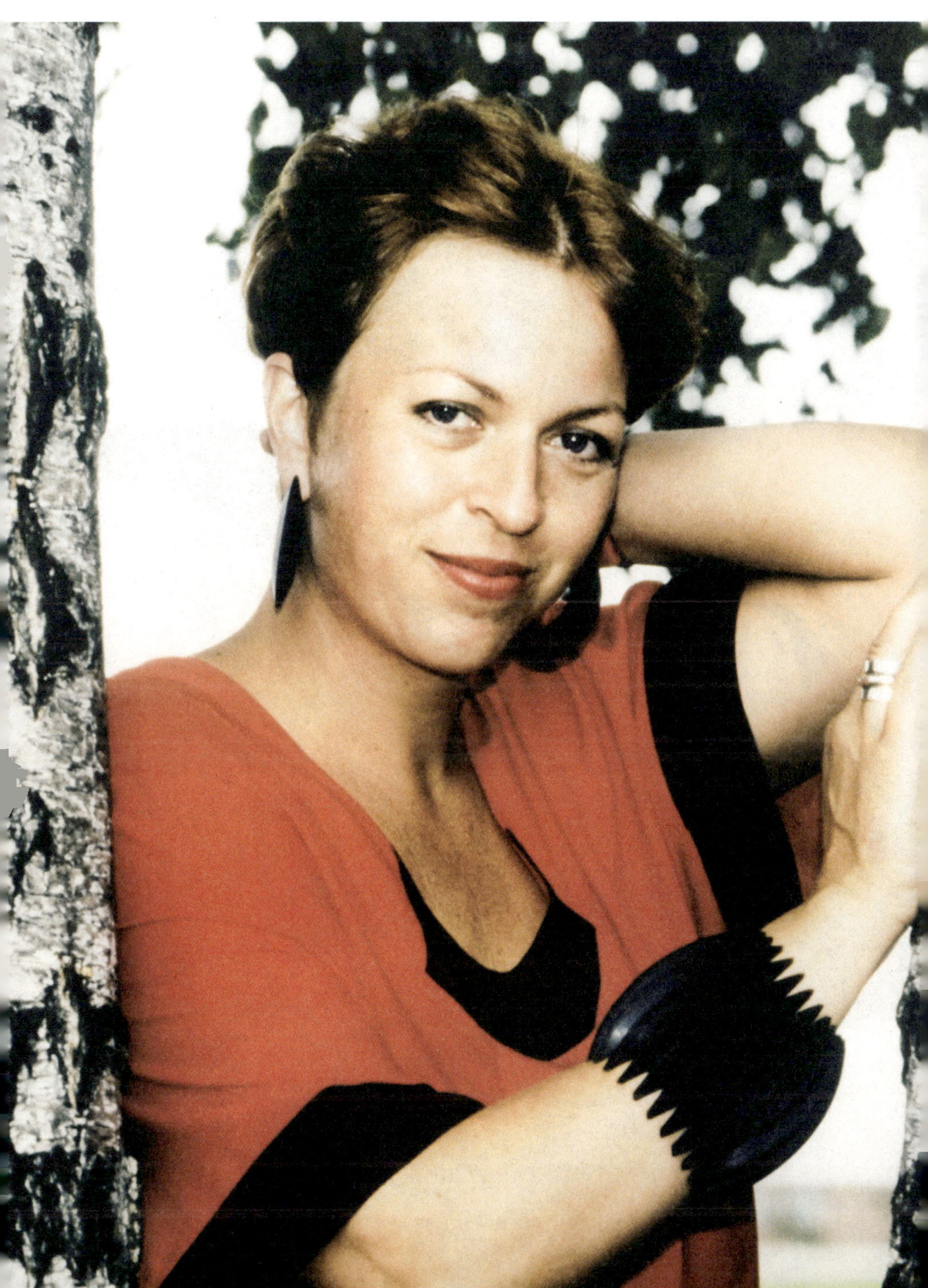

Posing for a press photo wearing a rubber bracelet by Janke Ijff [195], my first purchase at Galerie Ra in Amsterdam, and wooden earrings of unknown origin. Ring by Tone Vigeland [405].

Lunch break at Holbæk station after a visit to the Lousiana art museum in Denmark in the winter of 1992.
Ring by Toril Glenne [158] and earring by Anne-Karine Solgaard [358].

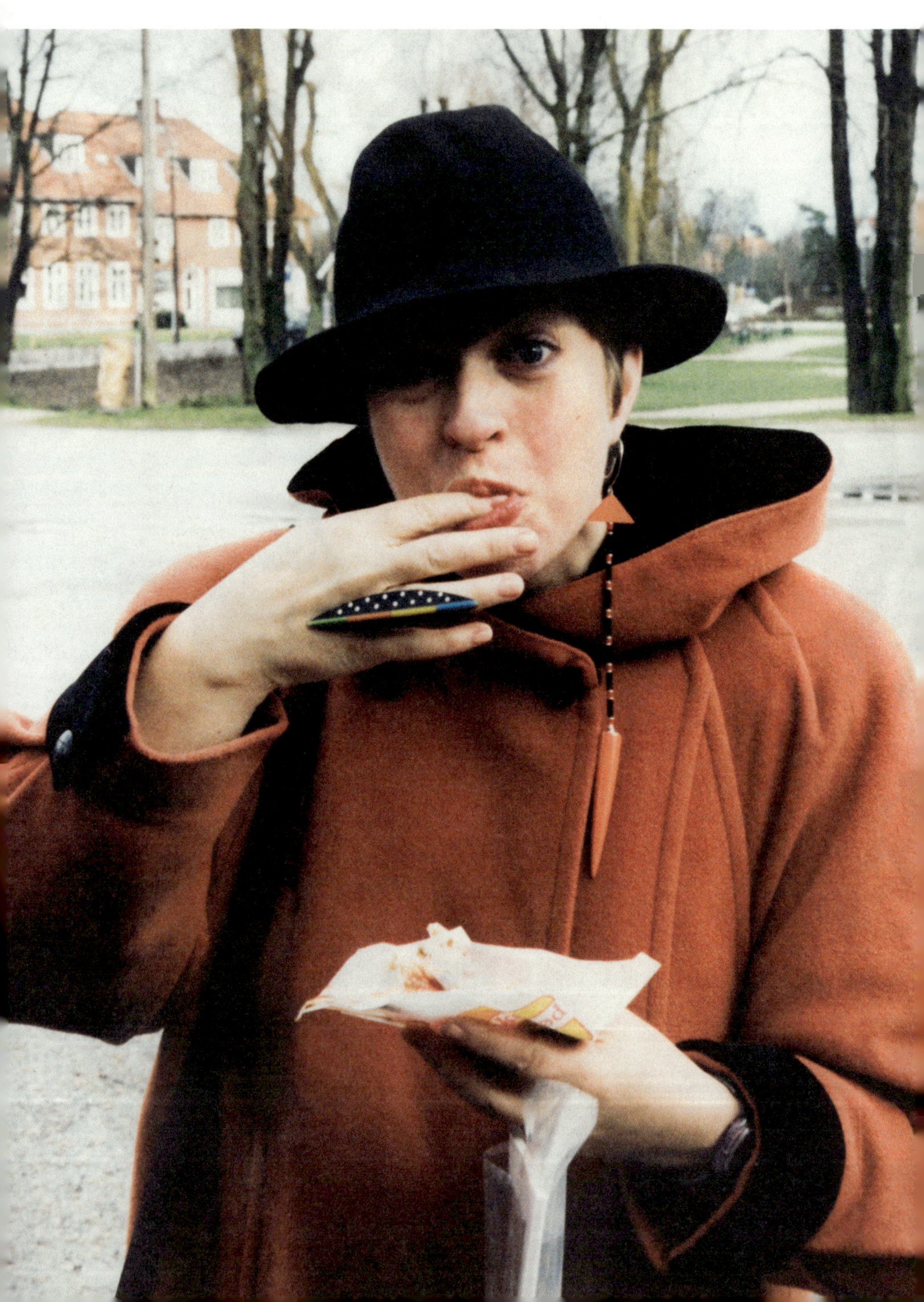

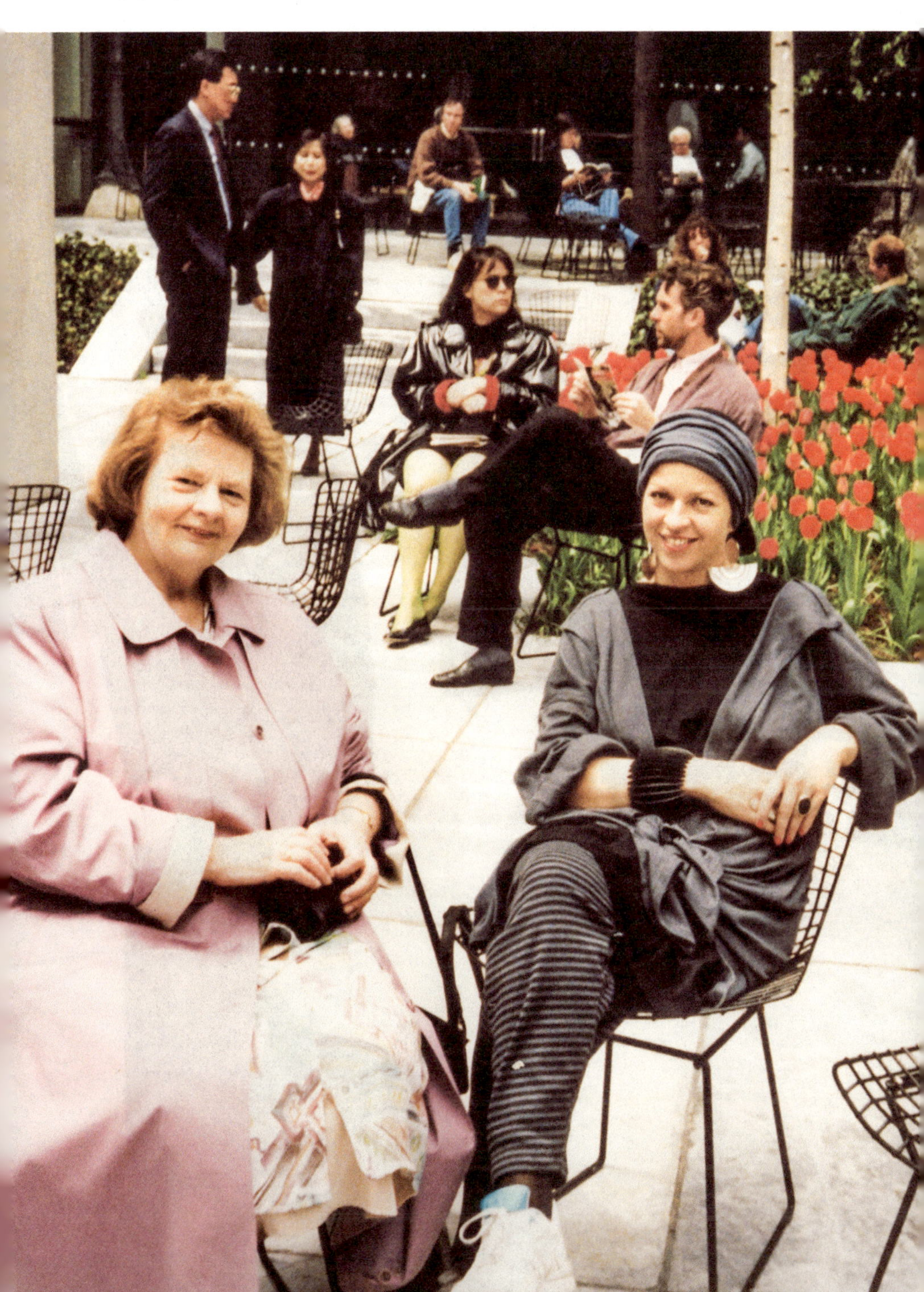

With my mother in New York in May 1992. The earrings were a cheap find in London **[480]**. Bracelet by Janke Ijff **[195]**.

New Year's Eve 1992. Necklace by Lars Sture **[369]**.

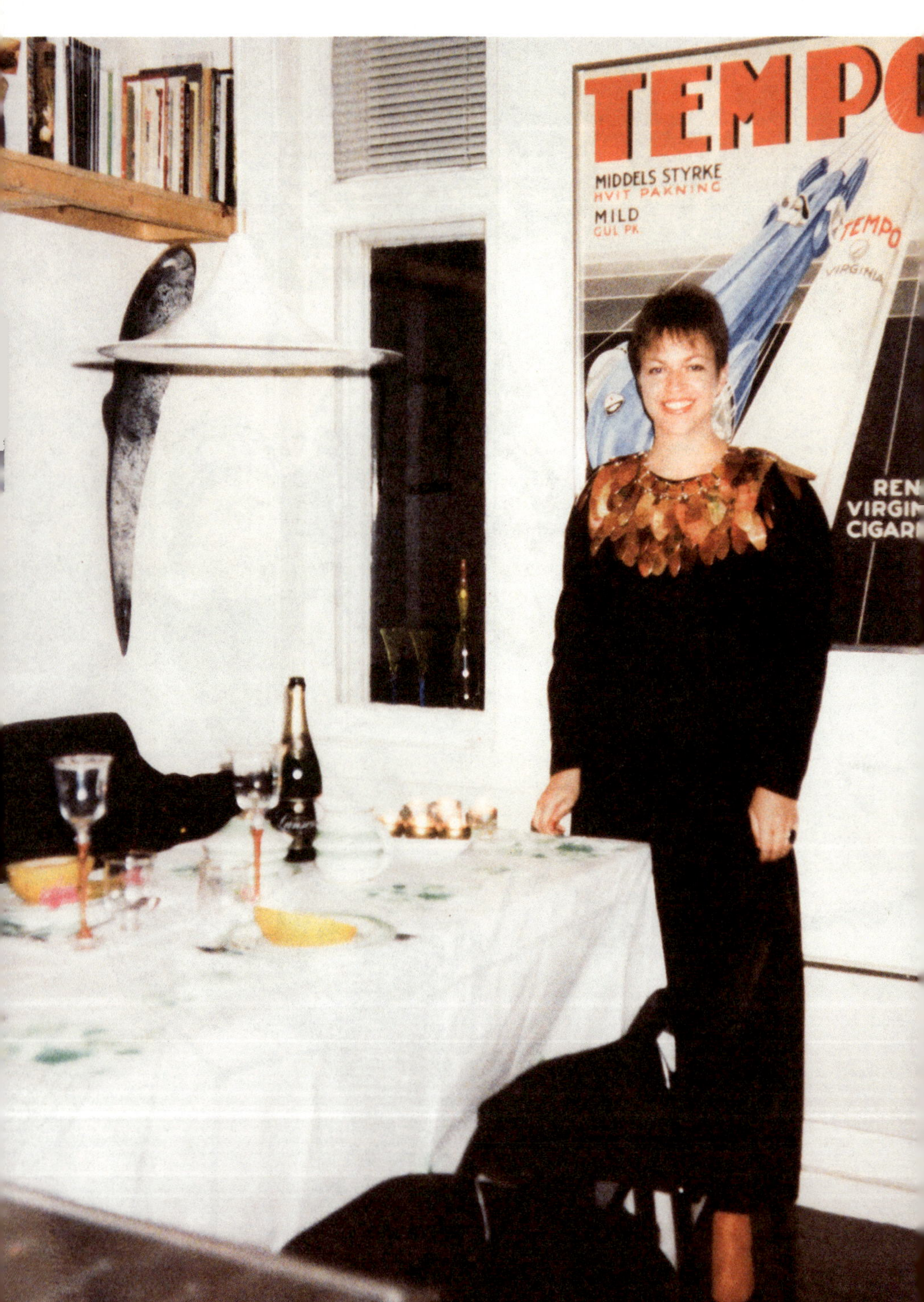

A photo-booth snapshot from 1993. Earrings by Fie von Krogh [228].

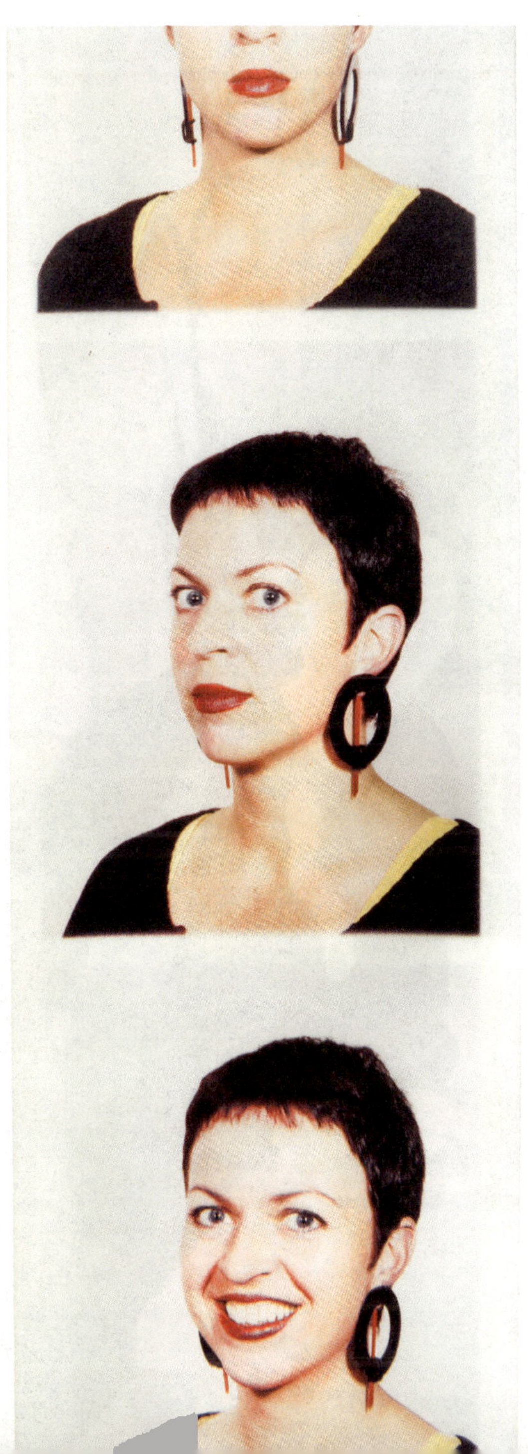

At work for NRK television during the Winter Olympics in Lillehammer, in February 1994. Brooch by Janna Syvänoja [383].

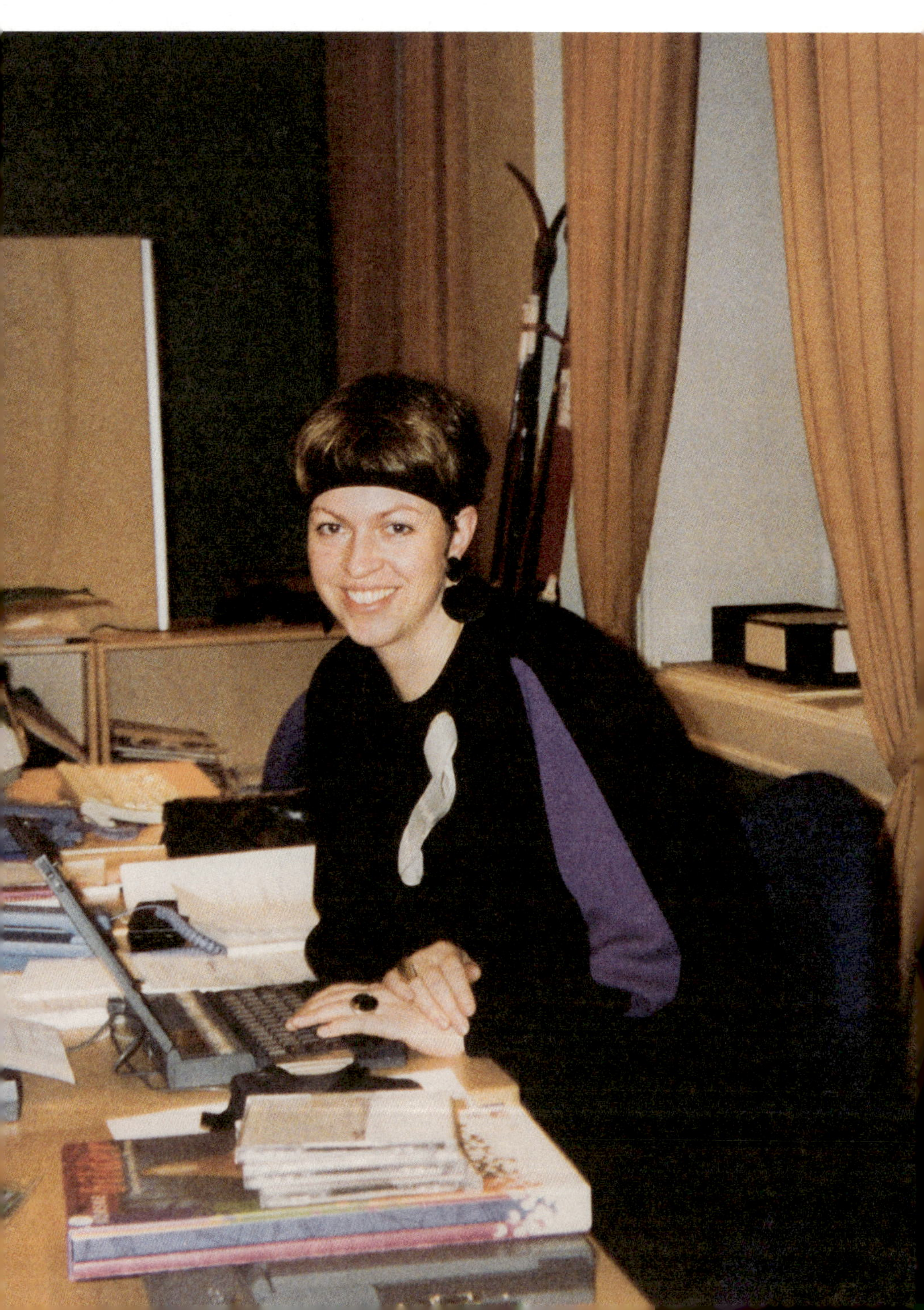

With Mogens on Stord in the summer of 1994. Earrings of unknown origin [202].

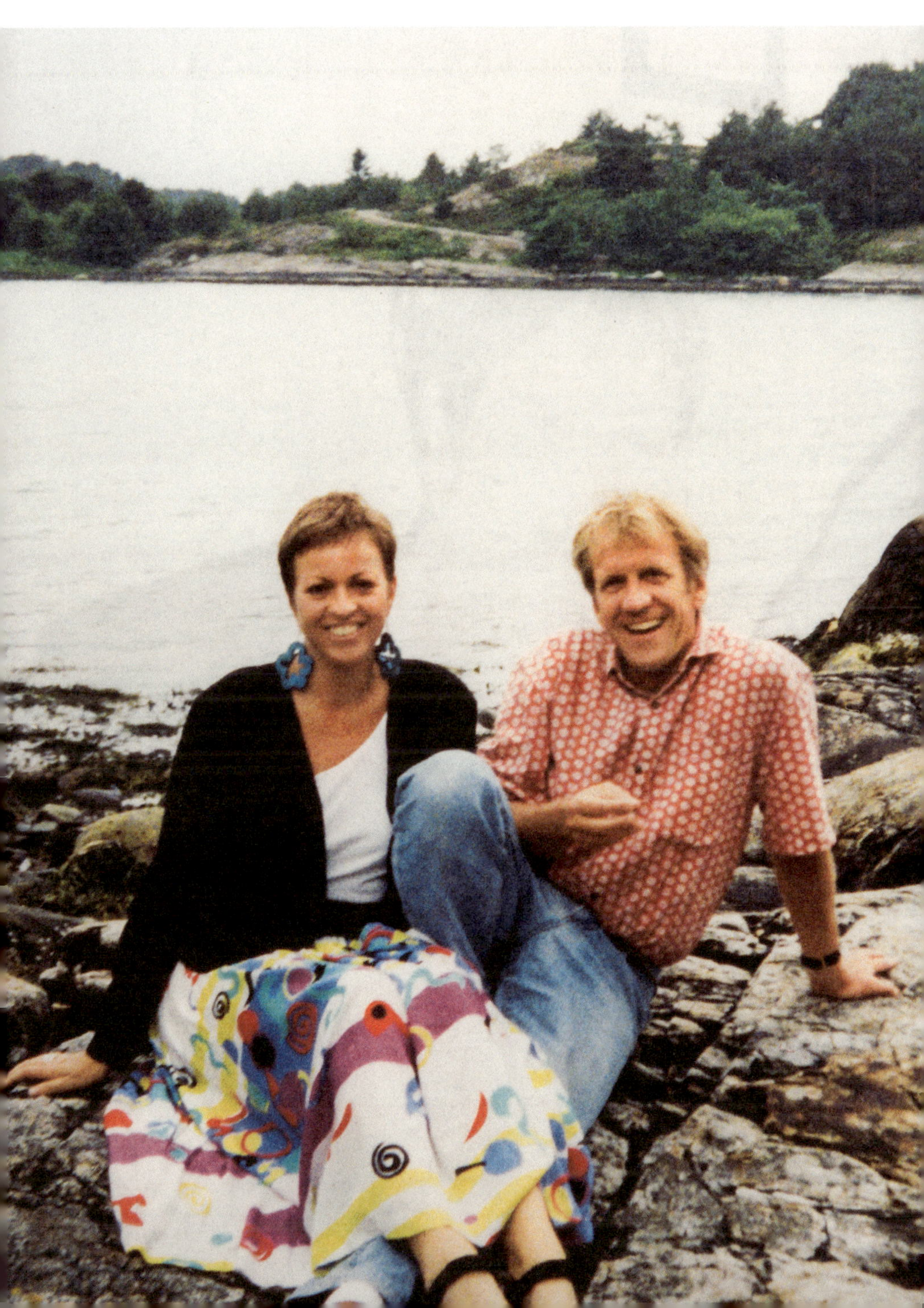

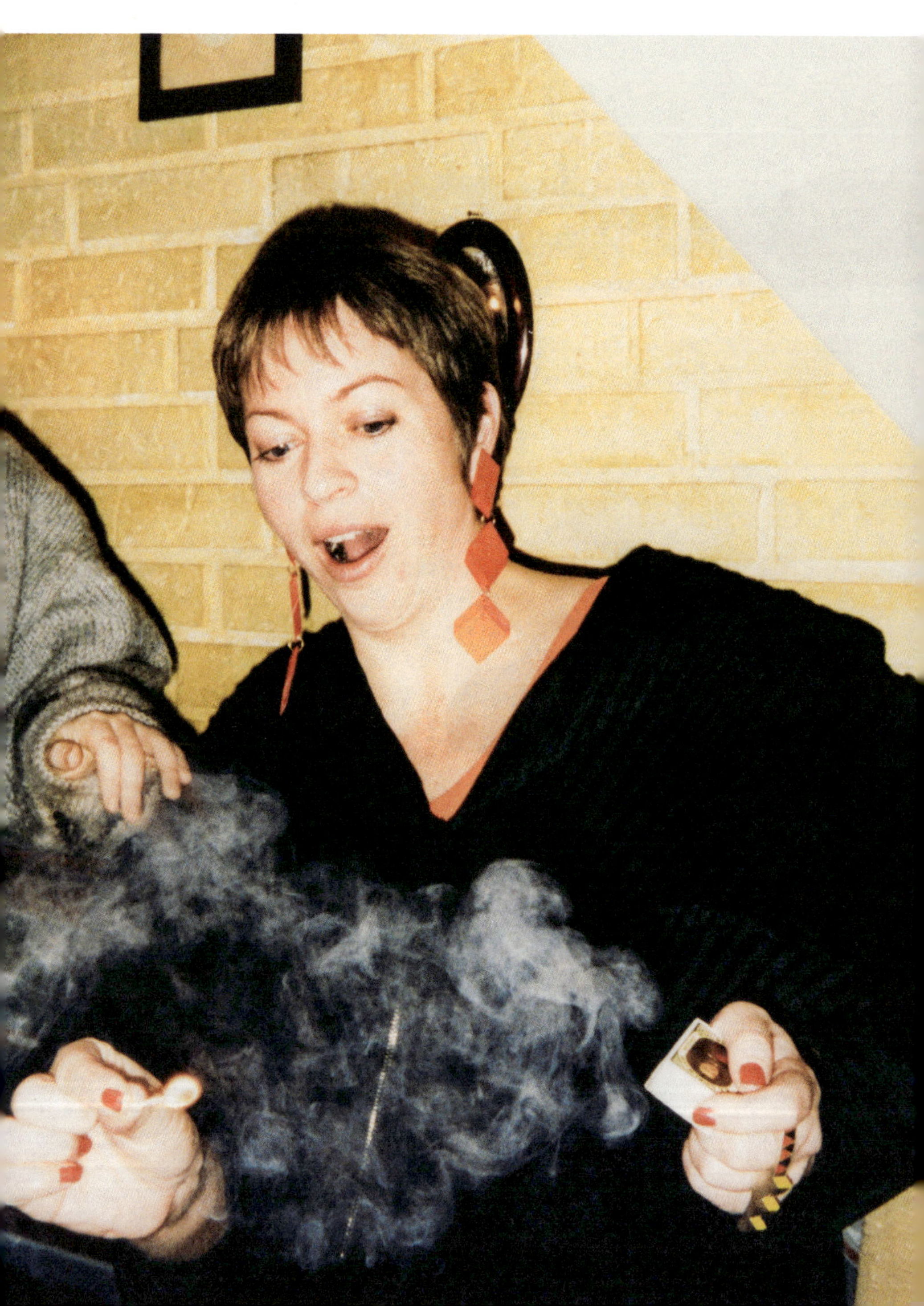

Setting off a table bomb on New Year's Eve 1994. Earrings unidentified, ring by Toril Glenne [159].

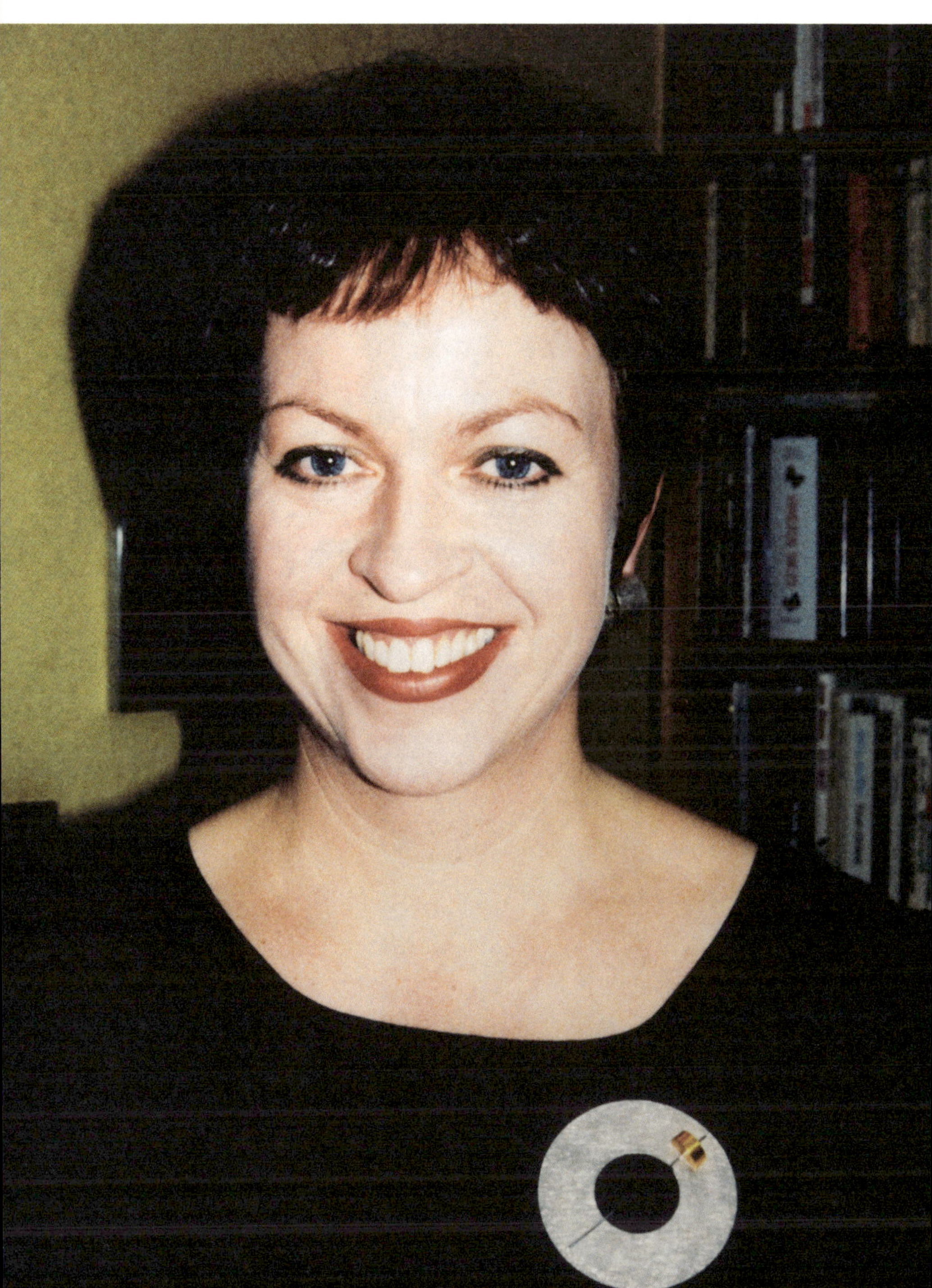

With a brooch and earrings by Kim Buck **[84] [94]** in 1994.

Ready for our wedding on 22 July 1995. Mogens is wearing a propeller bow tie by Konrad Mehus [274]. Headband and earrings by Lars Sture [371] [370].

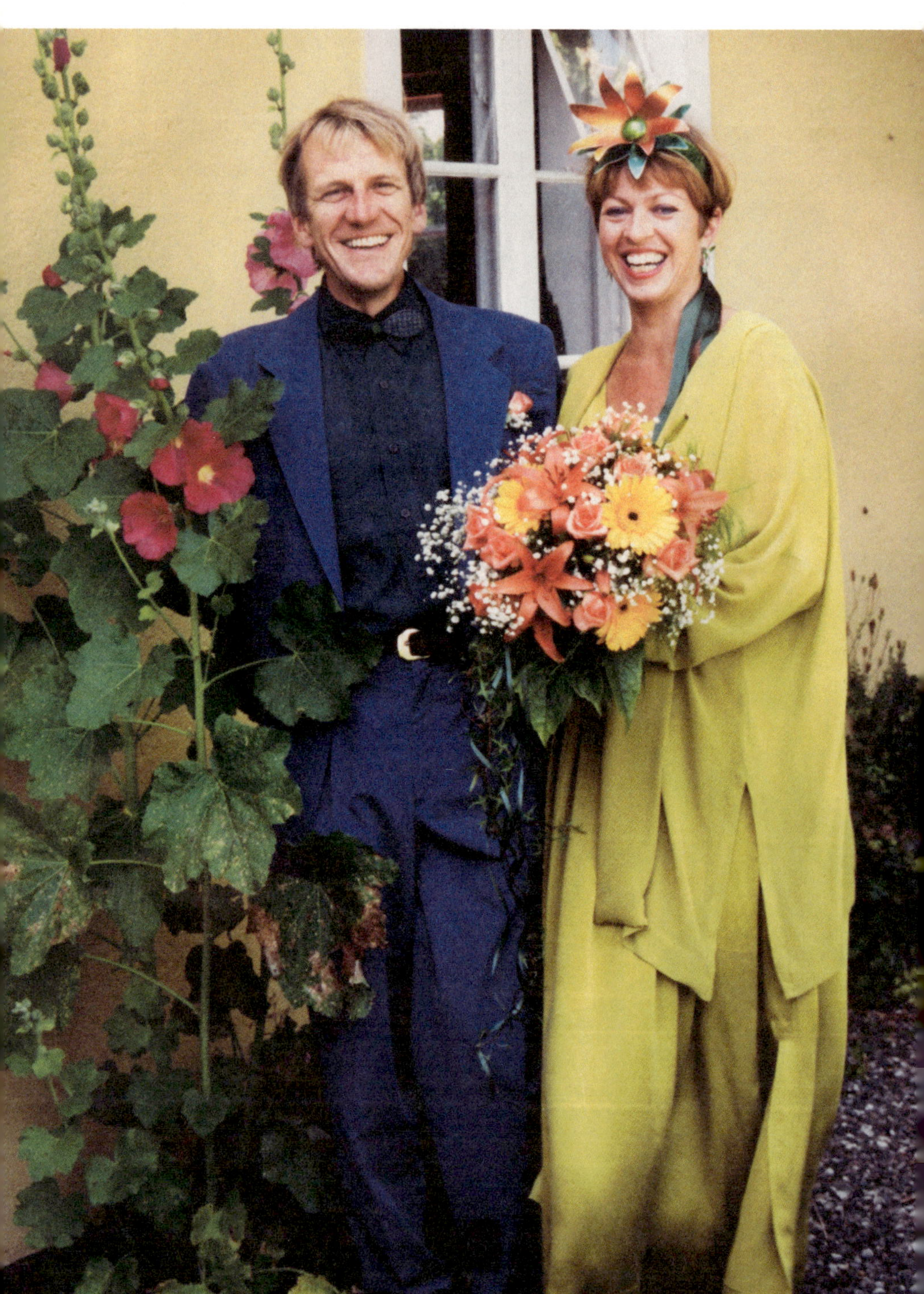

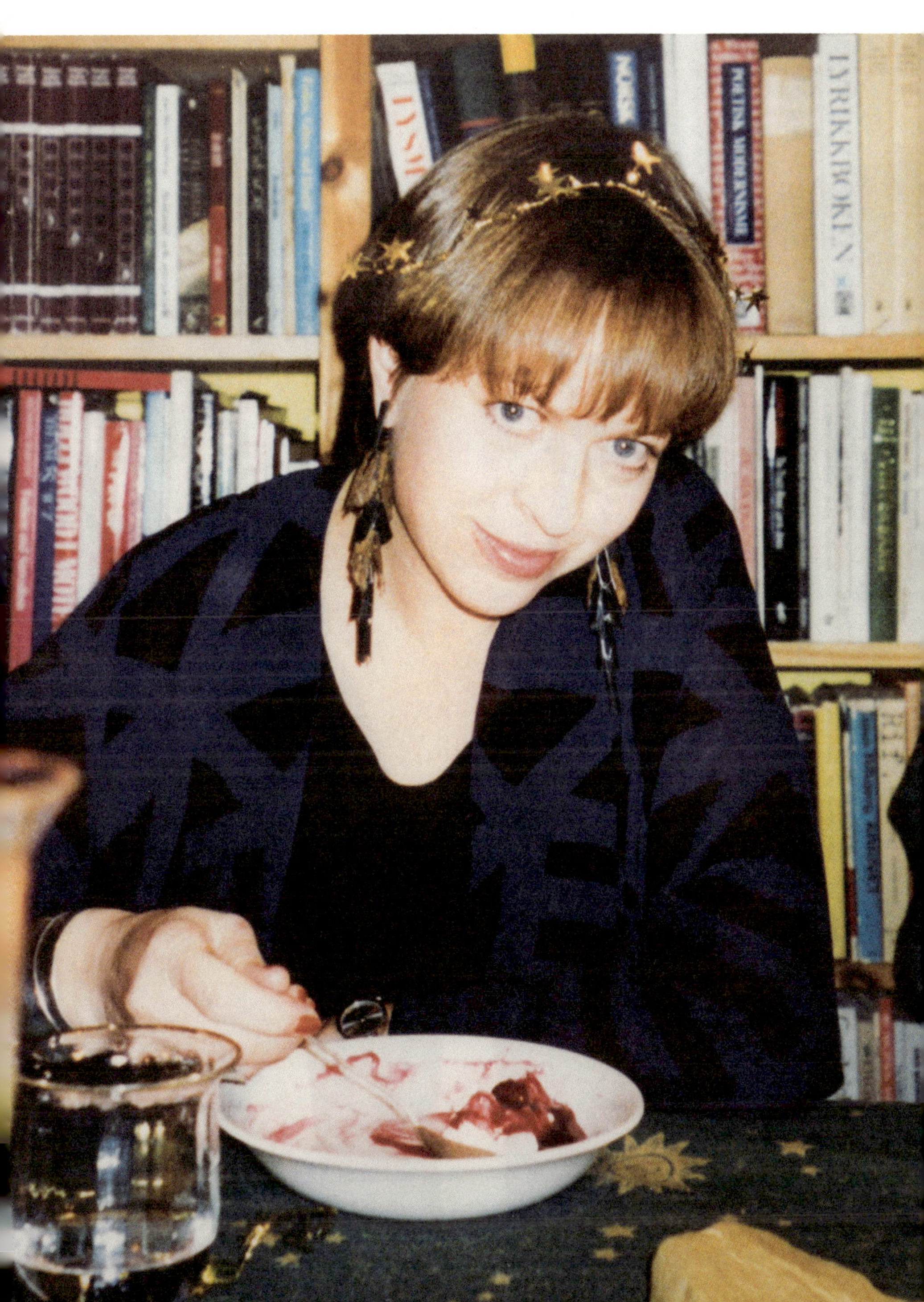
Dressed up for Christmas 1995 with earrings by Ingjerd Hanevold [175].

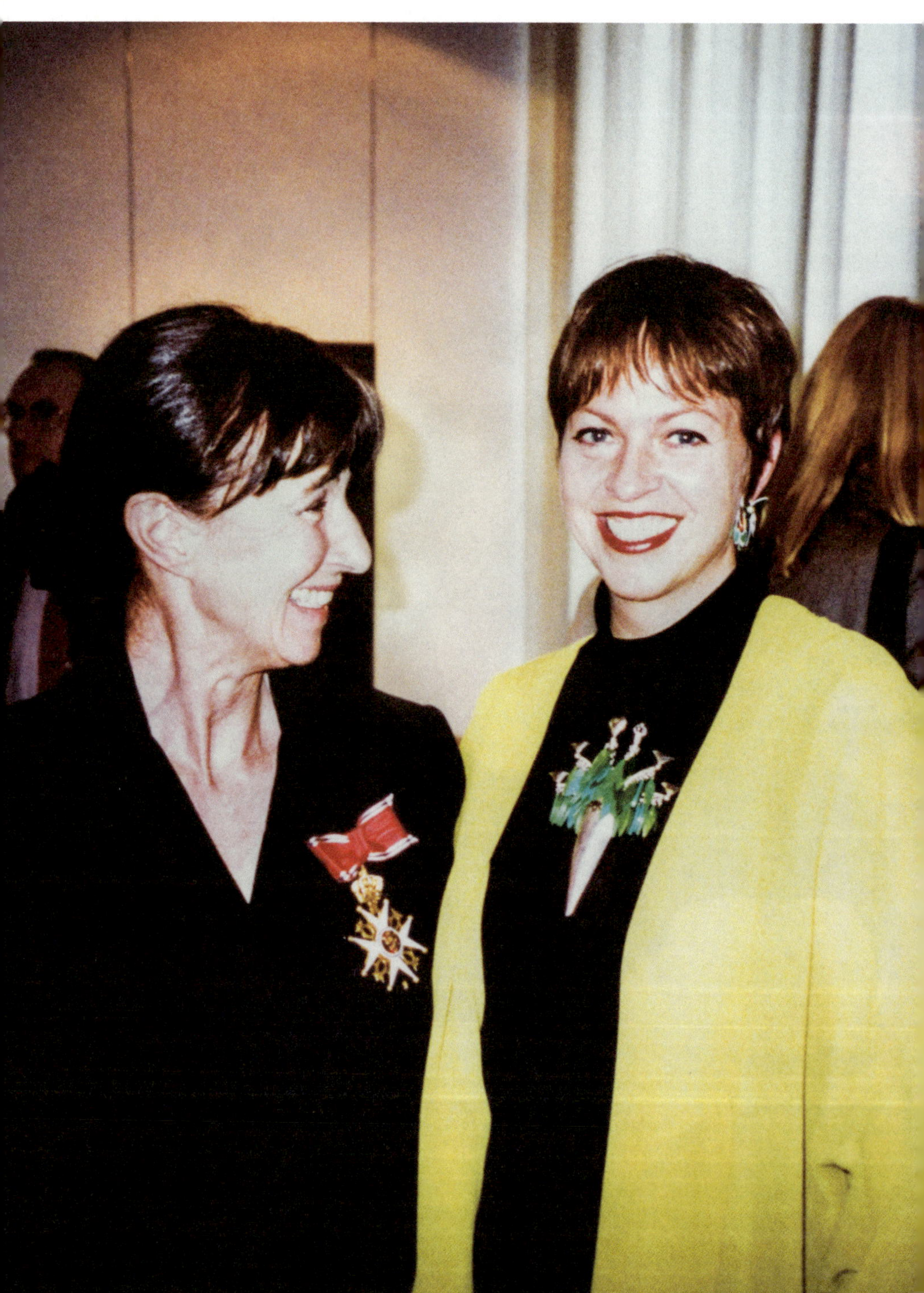

With the jewellery artist Tone Vigeland on the occasion of her appointment as Commander of the Order of St. Olav in Oslo, in 1996. I am wearing a brooch by Konrad Mehus [264].

Earrings by Reiko Ishiyama [201], bought at Electrum in London in 1998.

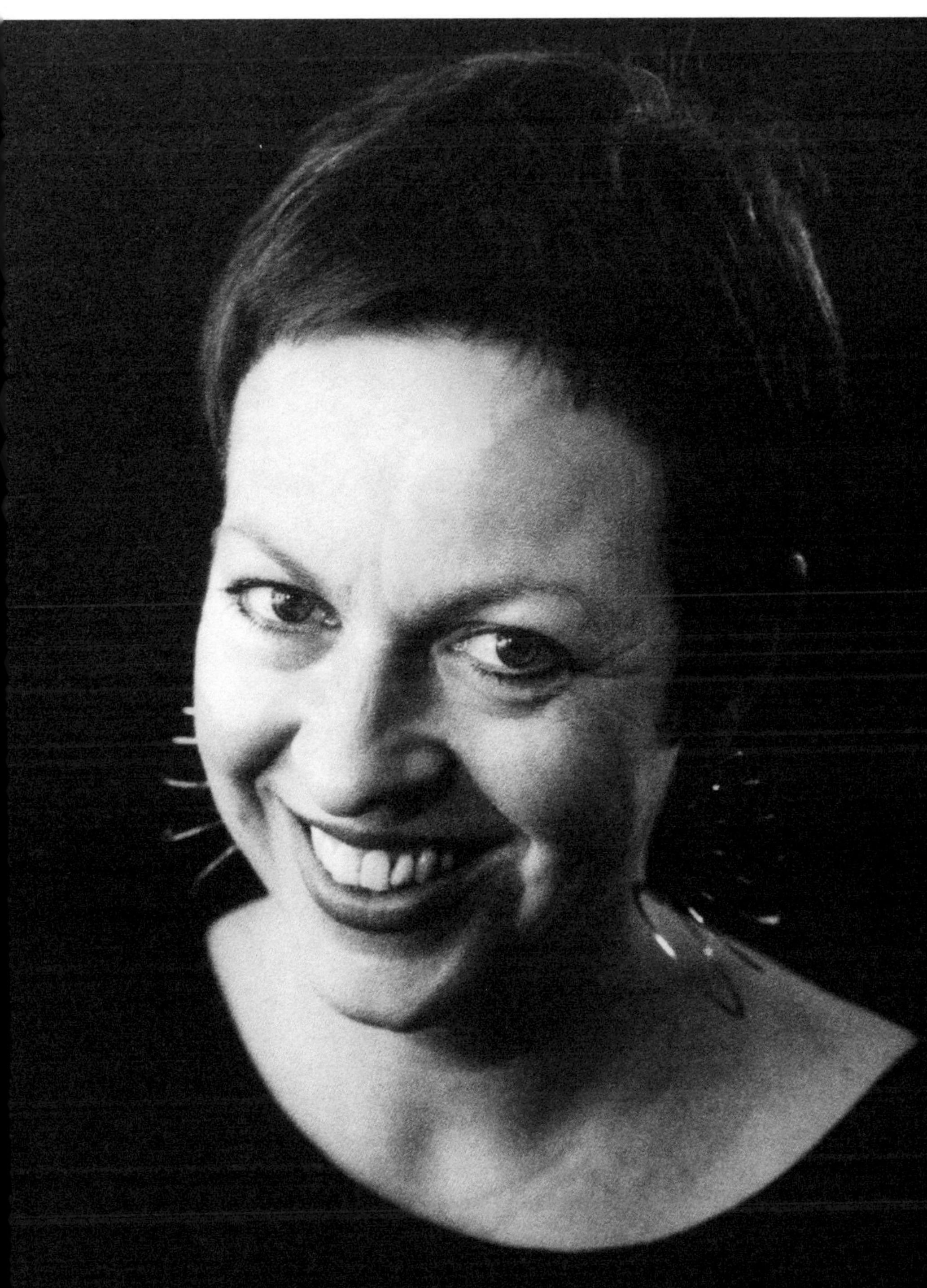

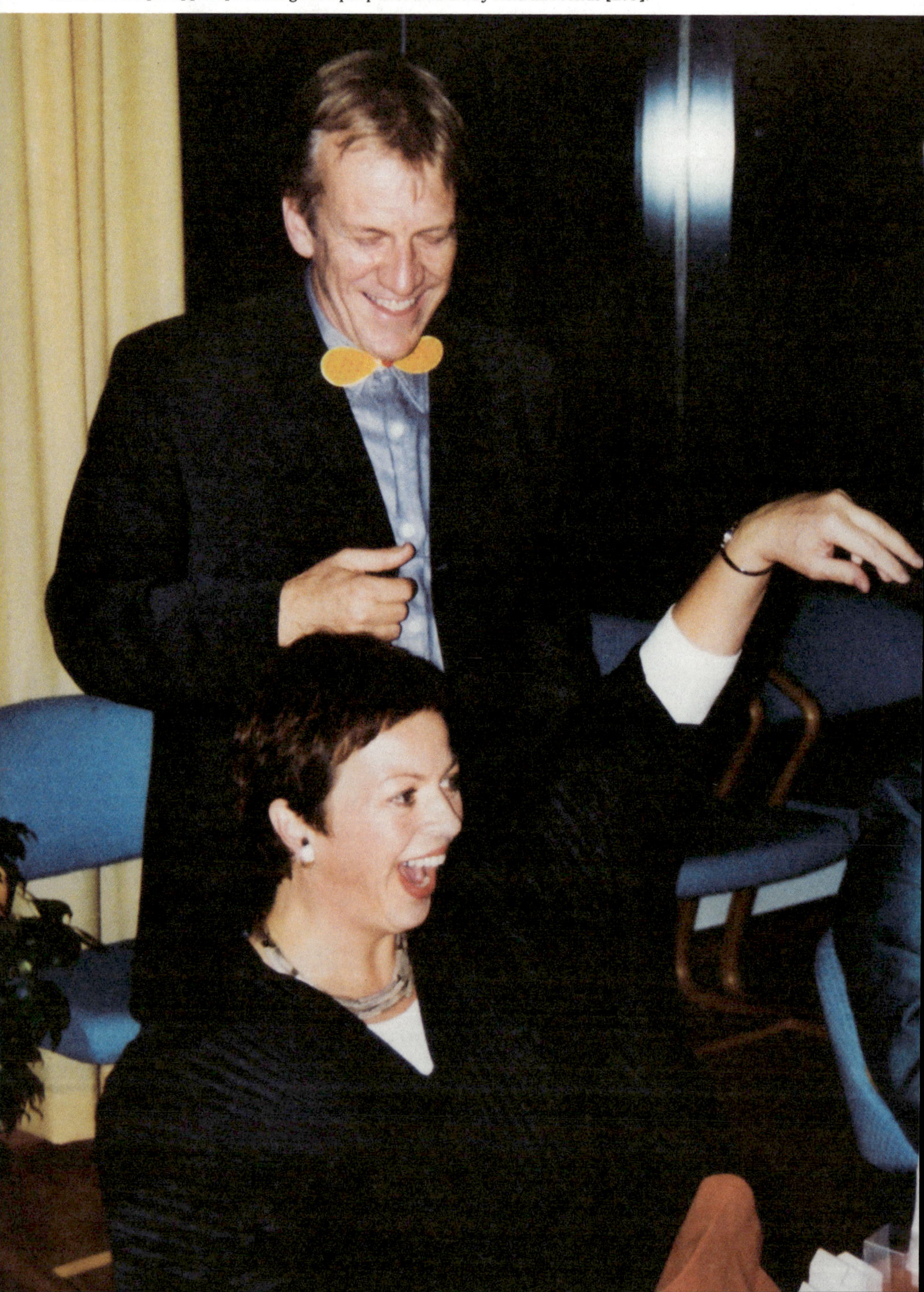

At dinner after the defence of my doctoral thesis in Bergen, in September 2000. I am proudly showing off the "doctoral ring" by Margaret Bridgwater [62], a gift from Mogens. I am wearing a necklace and earrings by Anette Kræn [233] [505] and Mogens a propeller bow tie by Konrad Mehus [275].

Summer 2005 with jewellery by Carolina Vallejo [394].

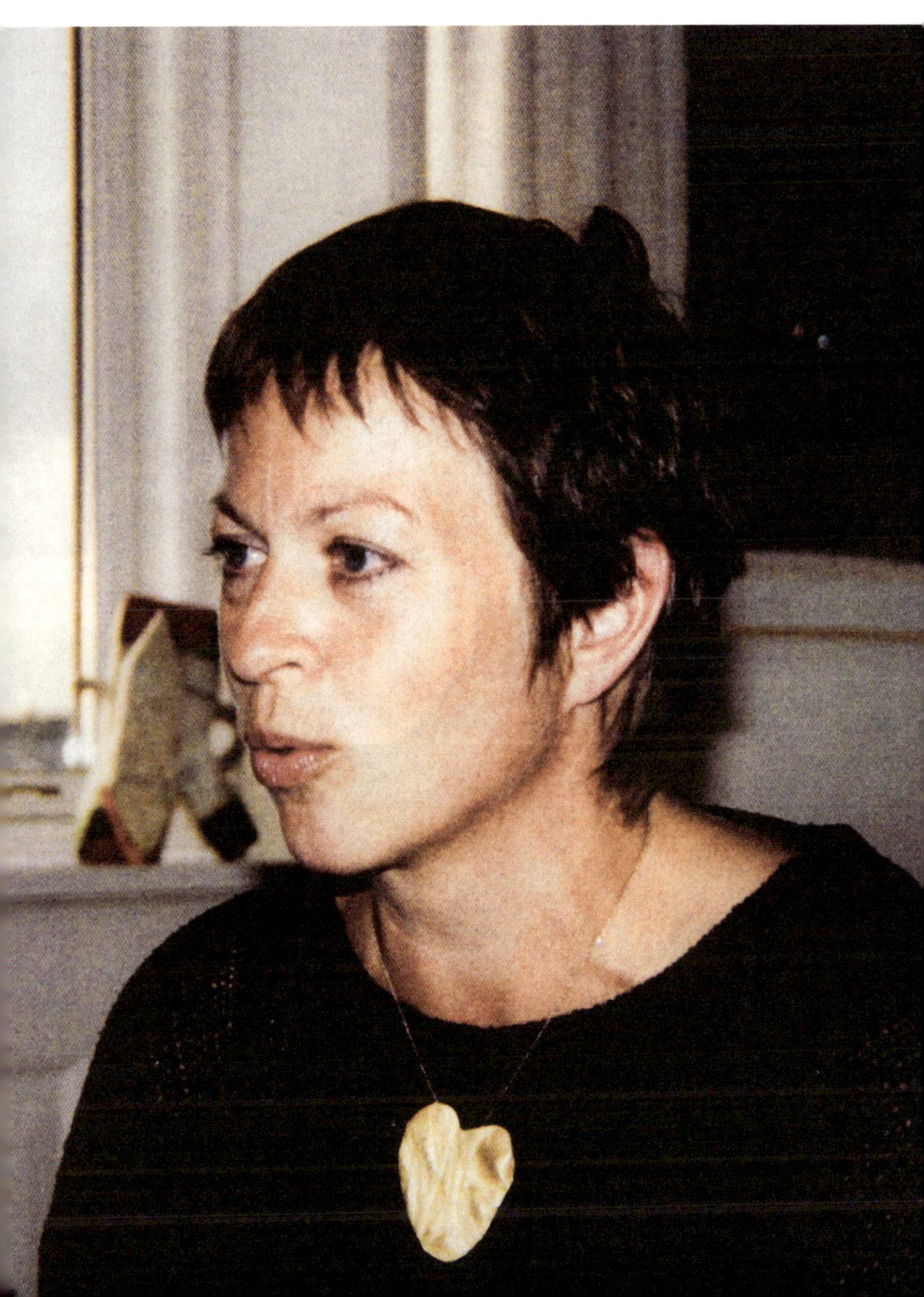

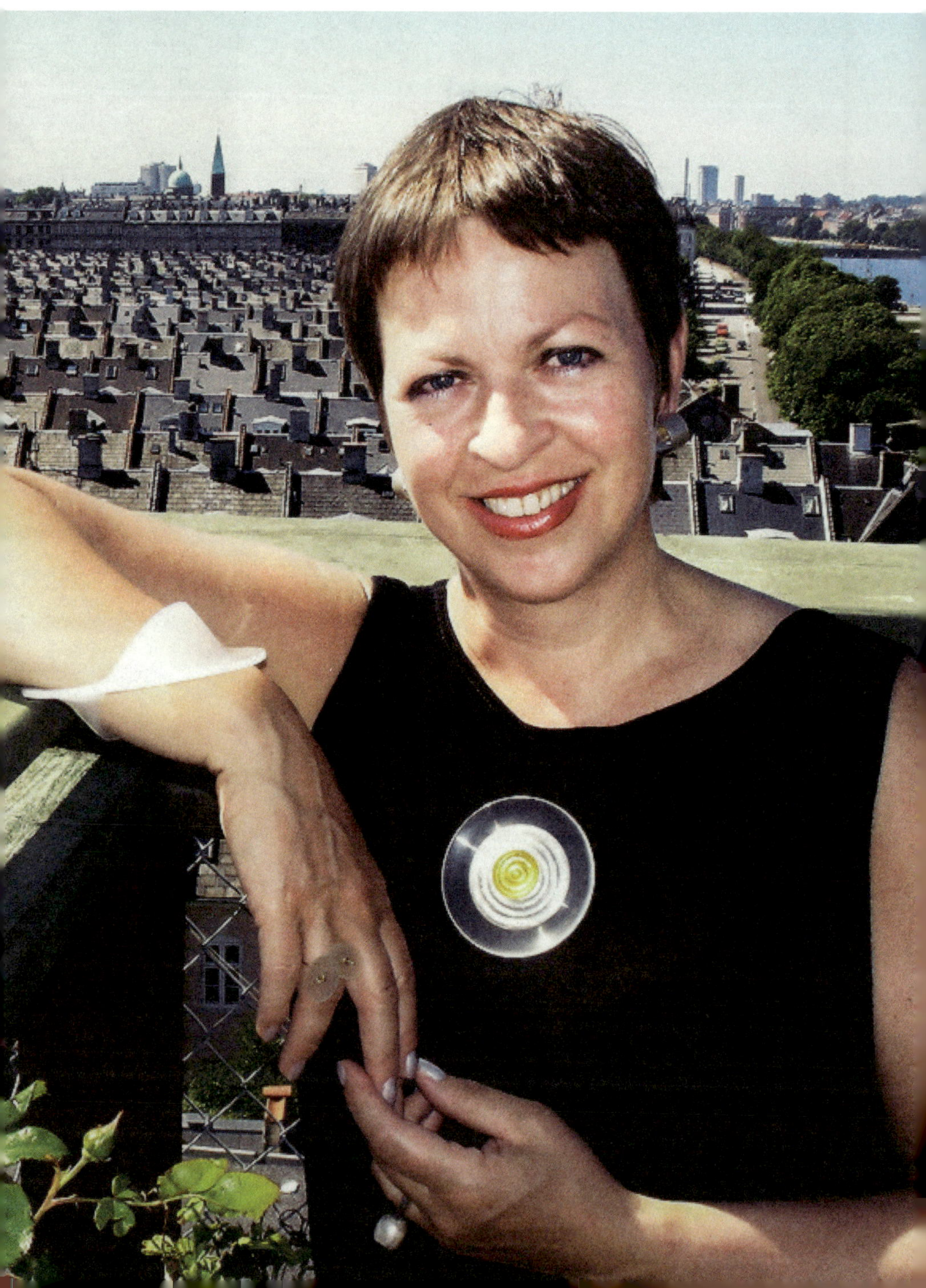

From a portrait interview in *Bergens Tidende* to mark my fiftieth birthday, in 2005. Brooch by Castello Hansen [177], bracelet by Gijs Bakker [19], rings by Peter Bauhuis [20] and Mette Saabye [323] and earrings by Kim Buck [94].

Ready to party with two of my sisters, Anne and Kari, in March 2009. Necklace by Lisa Walker [411].

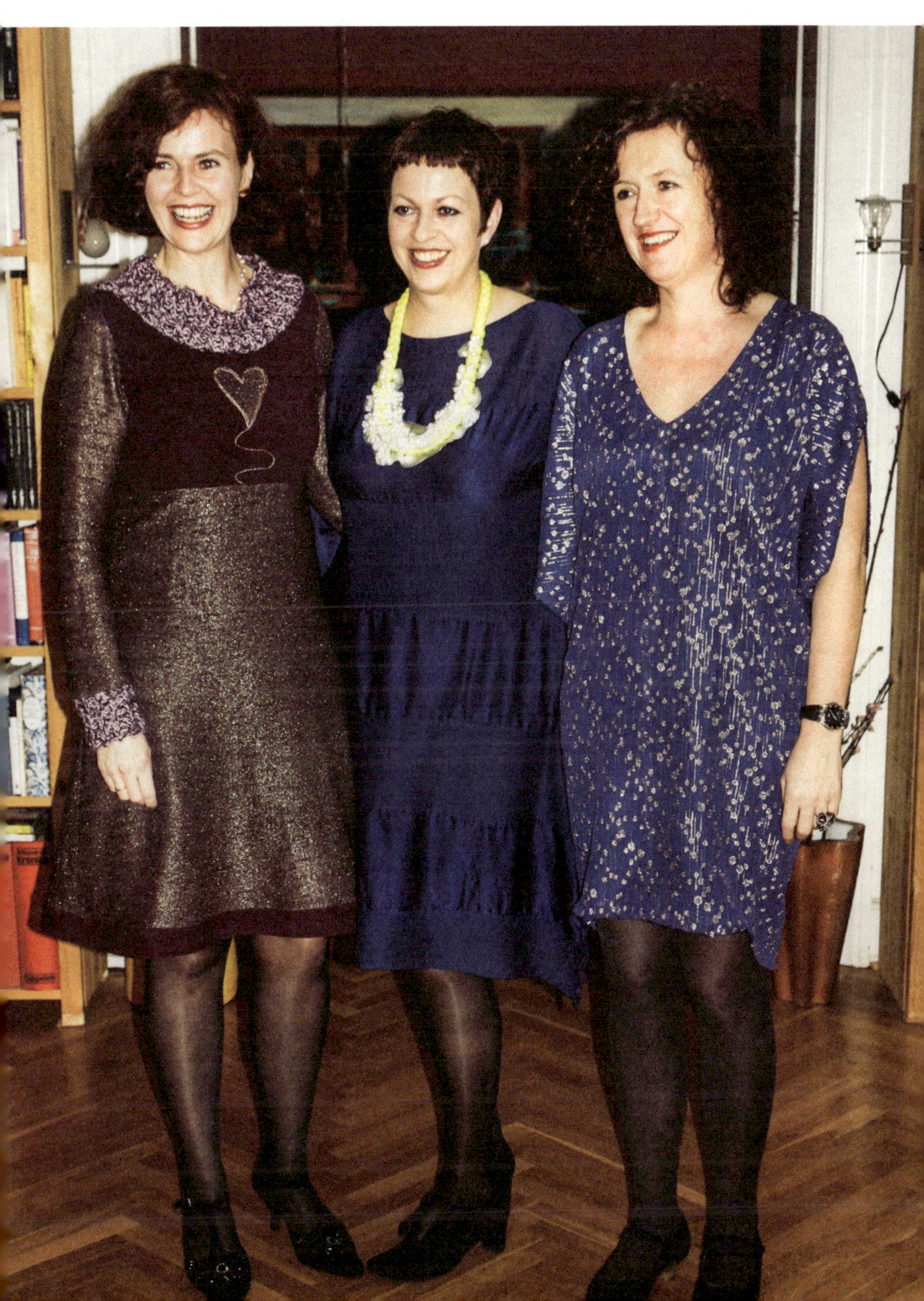

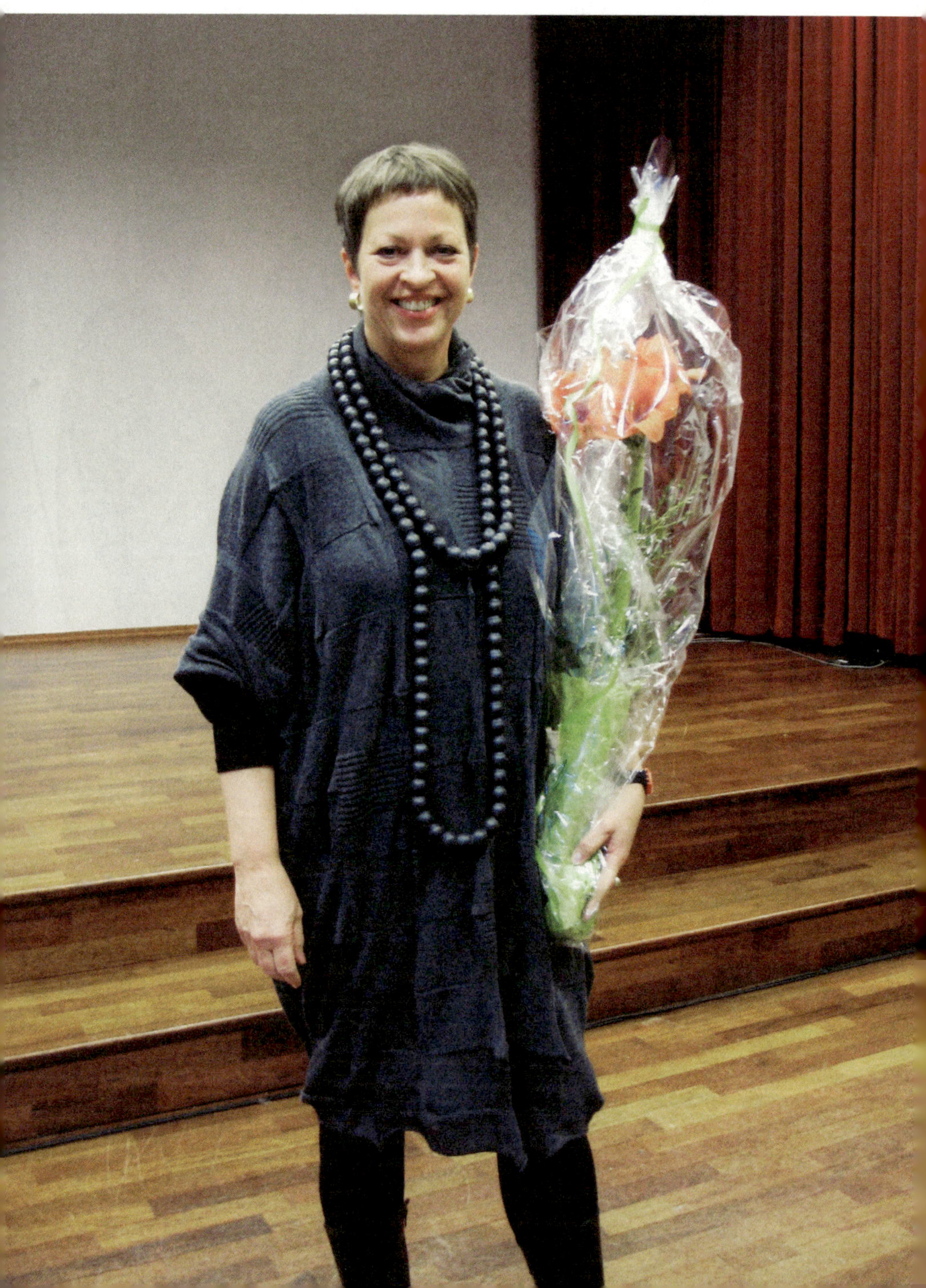

At the closing event of the international conference *Making or Unmaking? The Contexts of Contemporary Ceramics* in Bergen, on 29 October 2011. Necklace by Susanne Klemm [212] and earrings by Kim Buck [94].

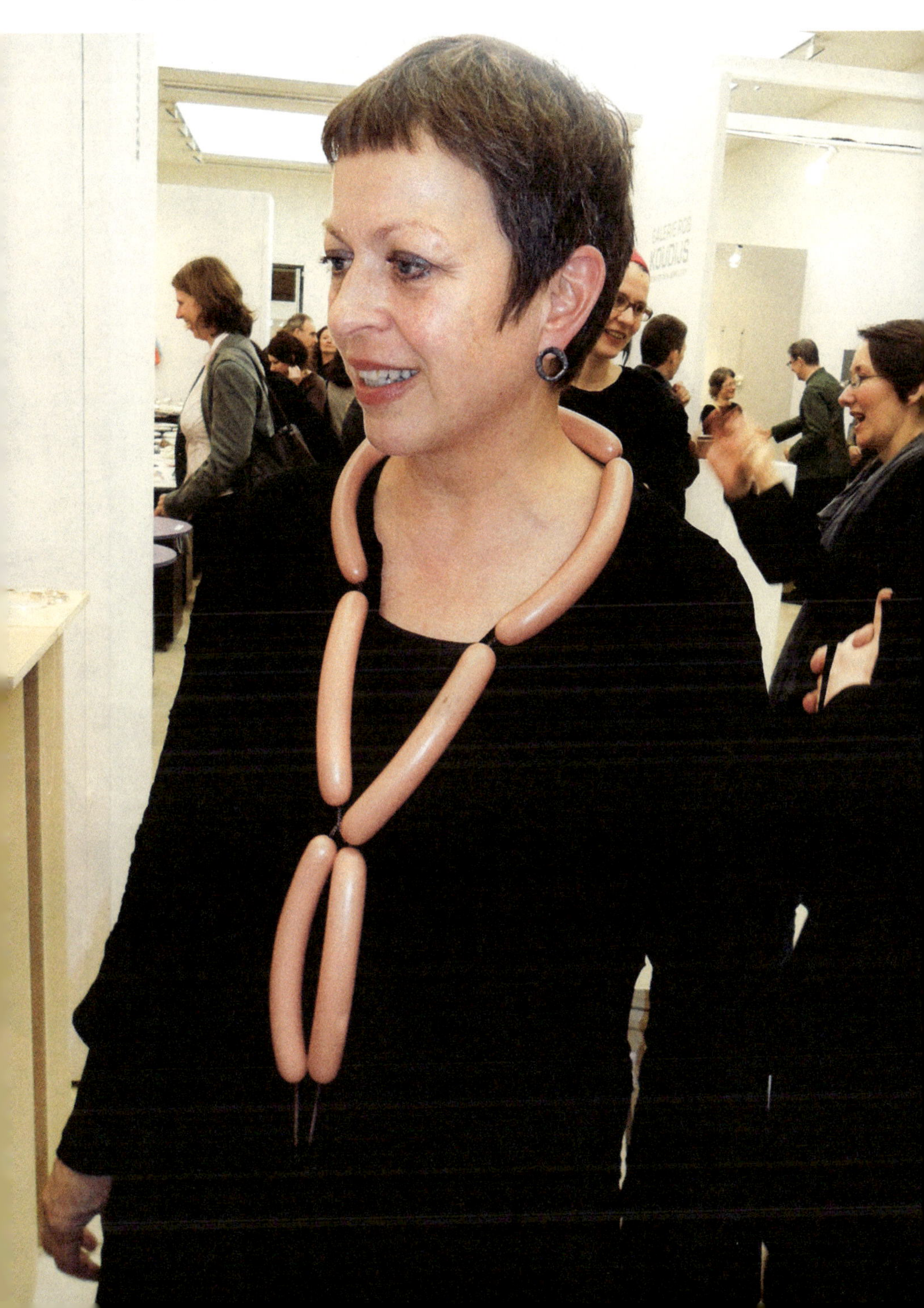

At the arts and crafts fair Collect in London in May 2012. Necklace by David Bielander [37] and earrings by Heeseung Koh [218].

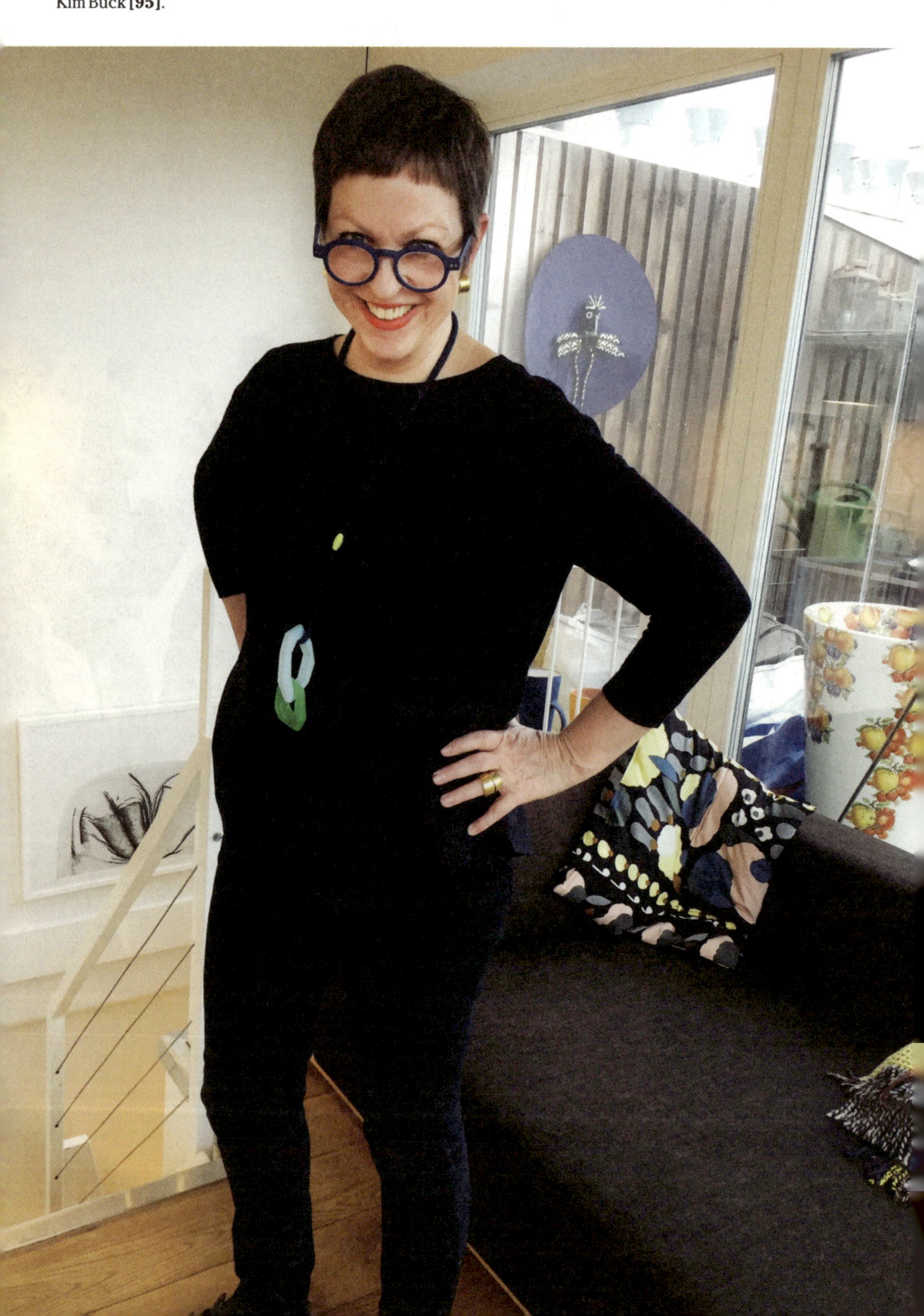

March 2018. Necklace by Macarena Bernal [494], ring by Karin Roy Andersson [11] and earrings by Kim Buck [95].

From the opening of the exhibition *These are a few of her favourite things. Jorunn Veiteberg's jewellery collection* at Nordenfjeldske Kunstindustrimuseum in Trondheim, on 22 September 2018. Necklace by Beatrice Brovia [80].

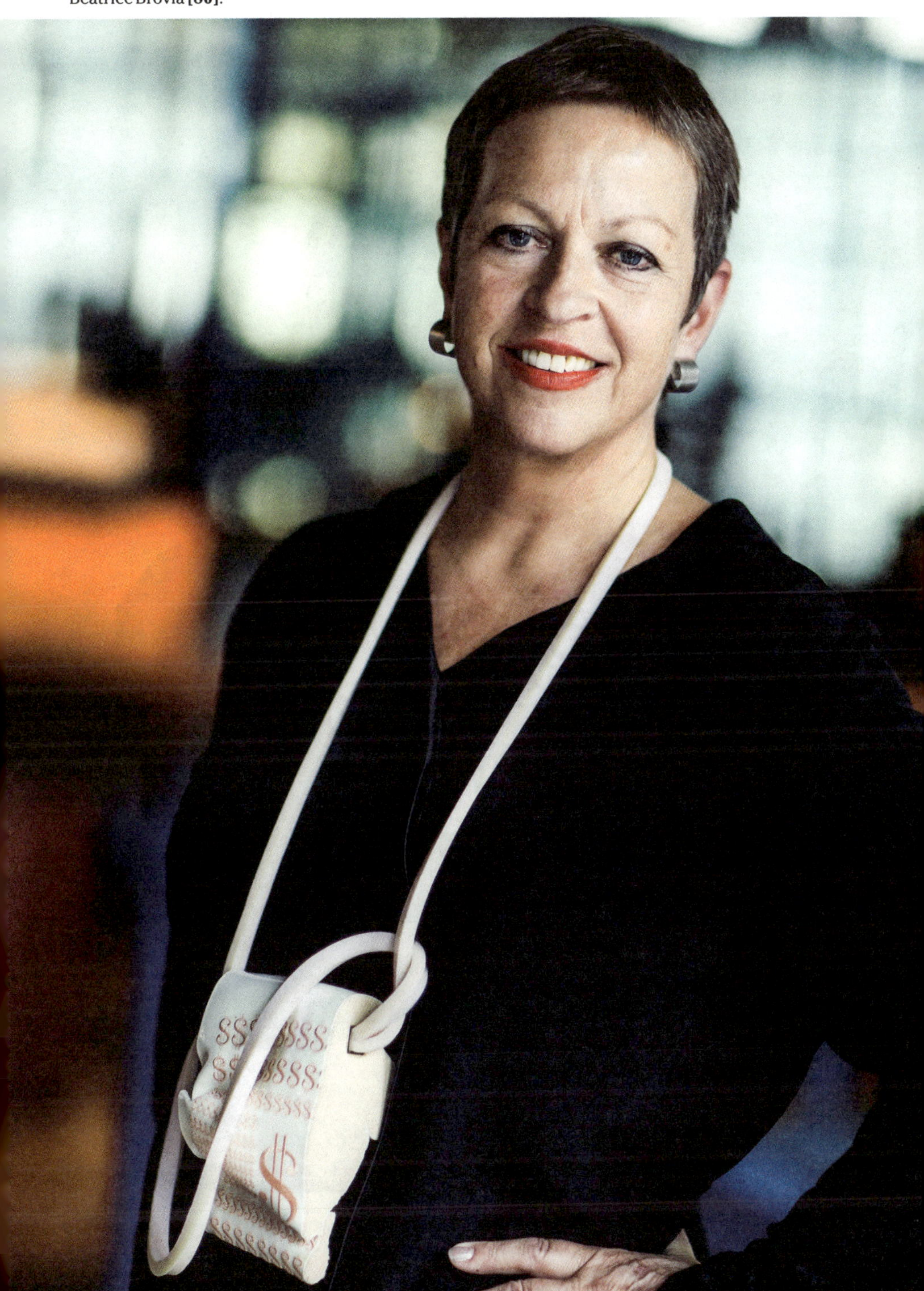

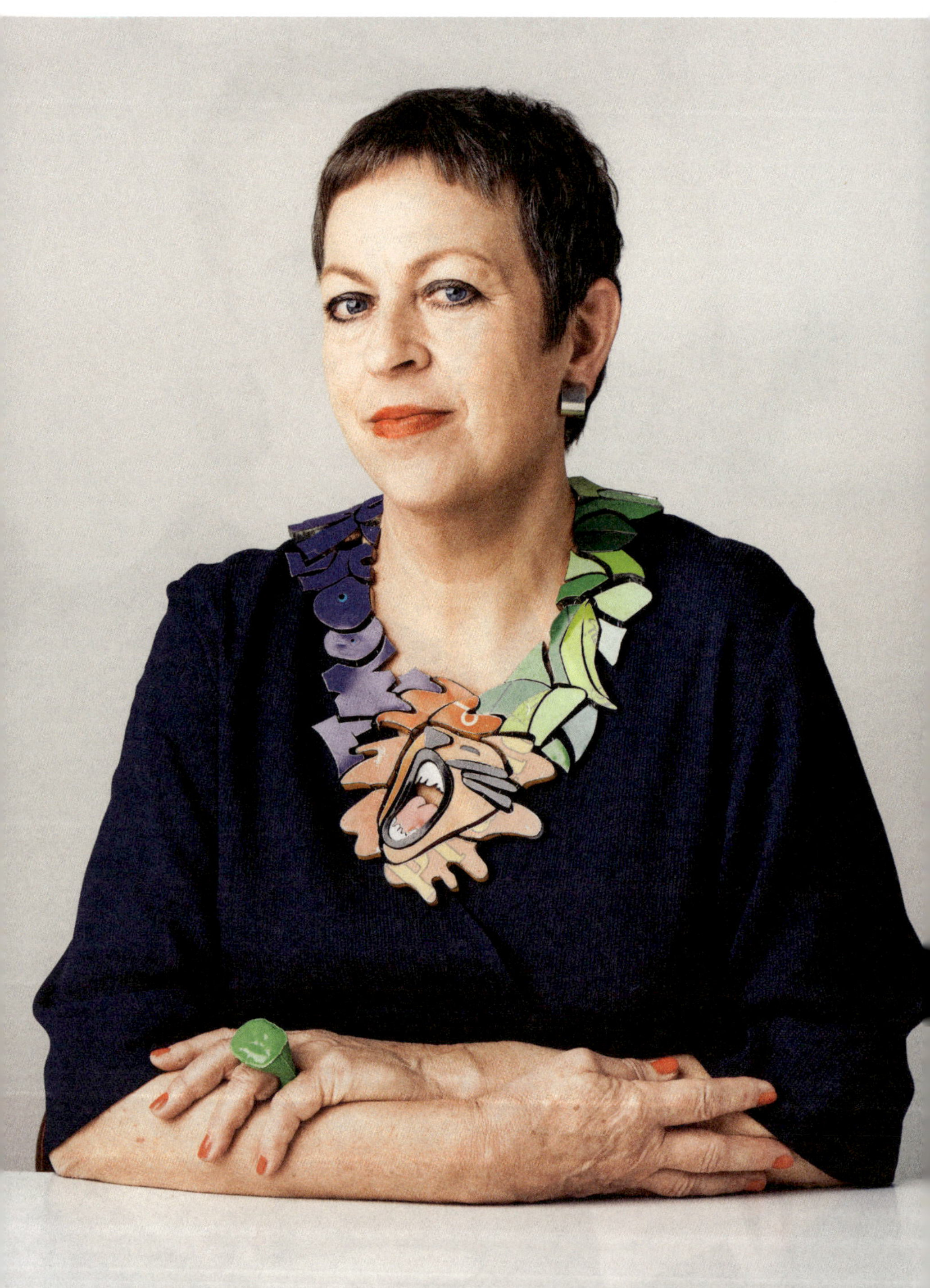

December 2019. Necklace by Monica Cecchi [538], ring and earrings by Kim Buck [92] [94].

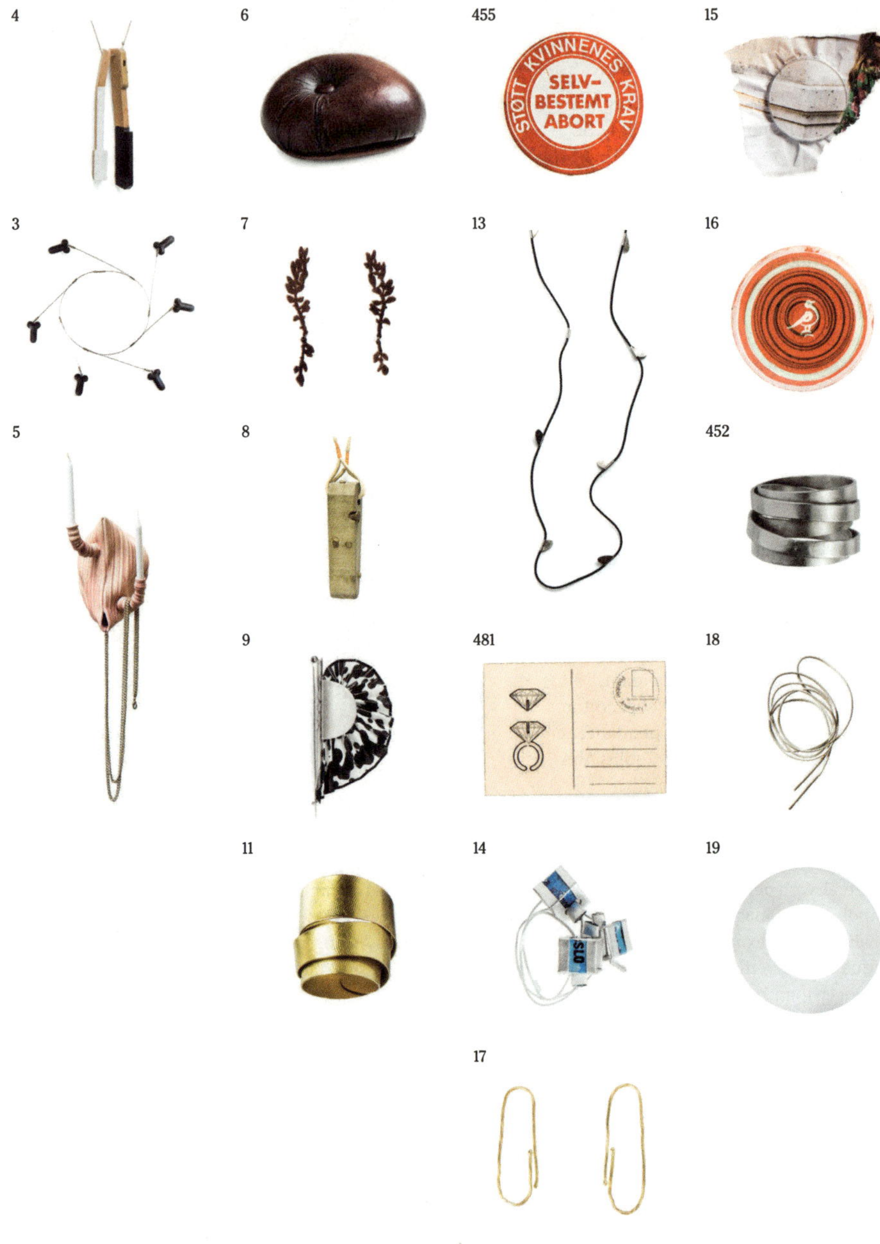

4
6
455
STØTT KVINNENES KRAV
SELV-
BESTEMT
ABORT
15
3
7
13
16
5
8
452
9
481
18
11
14
19
SLO
17

4
A5, SE
"Aeon Profit, Piano
Forte"
Pendant, 2010
Piano keyboards, wood.
L 23 cm
© Adam Grinovich,
Annika Pettersson,
Romina Fuentes
The members of A5
are Adam Grinovich
(b. 1981), Annika
Pettersson (b. 1981)
and Romina Fuentes
(b. 1978).

3
Adsen, Åshild
(b. 1972), NO
"Modern Girl"
Necklace, 1997
Oxidised silver, stain-
less steel. Ø 27 cm
© Åshild Adsen
"Modern Girl" was part
of Adsen's MA project
at Sheffield Hallam
University, in which she
was playing with sexual
stereotypes. By adorn-
ing herself with phallus
symbols, the woman is
showing off her sexual
conquests – something
that Adsen found was
okay for the guys but
not for the girls.

5
Ahl, Zandra
(b. 1975), SE
"Ceramic Lamp", 2004
Raw glazed earthen-
ware, metal chain.
19 × 14 × 14.5 cm,
L chain 77 cm
© Zandra Ahl

6
Aleborg, Pia
(b. 1974), SE
"Take Your Seat!"
Brooch, 2001
Leather, horsehair,
rivets, plywood.
15 × 10 cm
© Pia Aleborg

7
Aleborg, Pia
(b. 1974), SE
"Brown Branches"
Earrings, 2005
Nylon-flocked silver.
L 9.5 cm
© Pia Aleborg

8
Alm, Tobias (b. 1985), SE
"Traces of
Function 11.19"
Pendant, 2011
Wood, cotton.
L pendant 12 cm
© Tobias Alm

9
Andersen, Ingema
(b. 1944), NO
Brooch, 1994
Silver, paper, laquer.
8.5 × 4.3 × 1 cm
© Ingema Andersen

11
Andersson, Karin Roy
(b. 1983), SE
"Catching Big Fish"
Ring, 2014
18 ct gold, 13.3 g.
H 2.8 cm
© Karin Roy Andersson

455
Andreassen, Aase
Rønnaug Dørumsgaard
(f. 1946), NO
«Støtt kvinnenes krav.
Selvbestemt abort»
Badge, 1970s
Ø 4 cm

13
Appel, Nicolai
(b. 1966), DK
"Spots in the Air"
Necklace, 1998
Neoprene, rubber cord,
silver. L 88 cm
© Nicolai Appel

481
Arayavanish, Nutre
(b. 1981), TH
"Postable Jewellery"
DIY ring, 2007
Wood. 10 × 14 cm
© Nutre Arayavanish

14
Asbjørnsen, Marie
(b. 1973), NO
"Another Life"
Ring, 2003
Recycled aluminium
cans, steel wire. H 2 cm
© Marie Asbjørnsen/
BONO, Oslo 2021

17
Atrops, Volker
(b. 1965), DE
Earrings, 2015
Gold. L 4.3 cm
© Volker Atrops

15
Atrops, Volker
(b. 1965), DE
"Piece by Piece"
Badge, 2016
Laminated magazine
clipping. 11.5 × 11 cm
Edition 10 of 25
© Volker Atrops
Made for *Current
Obsession*, the
Vernacular issue 2016.

16
Atrops, Volker
(b. 1965), DE
"Hiesiger"
Brooch, 2016
Reverse glass painting,
plastic, stainless steel.
6.5 × 6.5 × 1 cm
© Volker Atrops

452
Aune, Sigrun
(b. 1946), NO
Ring, 2017
Silver. H 1.9 cm
© Sigrun Aune

18
Bak, Kirsten
(b. 1977), DK
"Baks Jewellery"
Neckpiece, 2007
Leather, 925 silver from
sustainable mining.
L 110 cm
© Kirsten Bak

19
Bakker, Gijs
(b. 1942), NL
"Circle in Circle"
Bracelet, 1967–89
Acrylic. Ø 11.5 × H 4.5 cm
© Gijs Bakker/BONO,
Oslo 2021

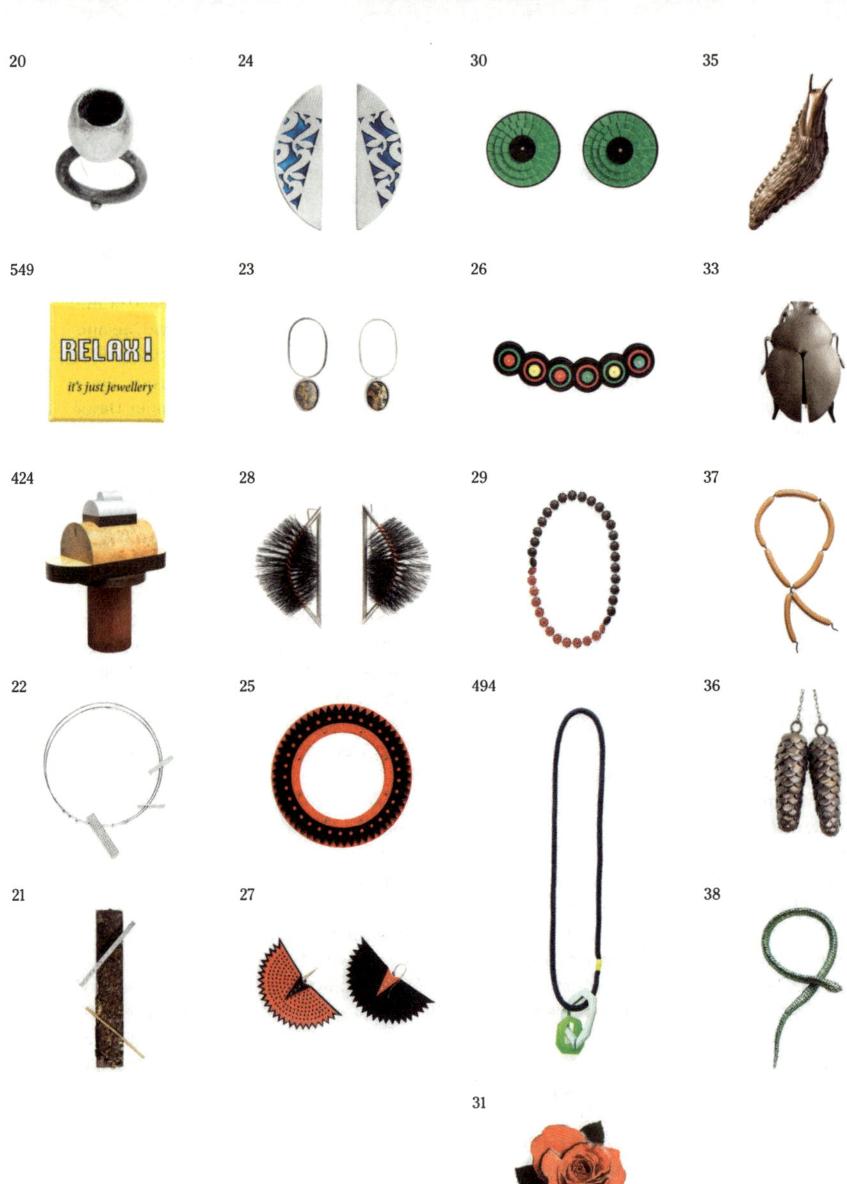

20
24
30
35
549
23
26
33
424
28
29
37
22
25
494
36
21
27
38
31
494

20
Bauhuis, Peter
(b. 1965), DE
Ring, 2004
Silver. 4 × 2 × 2 cm
© Peter Bauhuis

549
Bauhuis, Peter
(b. 1965), DE
"RELAX! it's just
jewellery"
Badge, 2016. 4 × 4 cm
© Peter Bauhuis

424
Bedin, Martine
(b. 1957), FR/IT
"Charlotte"
Cabinet, 1987
Birdseye maple
veneer, maple veneer,
stained maple veneer,
lacquered wood.
134.6 × 119.4 × 65.4 cm
Produced by Memphis
© Martine Bedin/
BONO, Oslo 2021
The cabinet features
one flip-top compart-
ment, five drawers and
two drop-down doors
concealing storage.

22
Behrens, Millie
(b. 1958), NO
Neckpiece, 1990
Silver, gold, copper,
steel wire. 26 × 22.5 cm
© Millie Behrens

21
Behrens, Millie
(b. 1958), NO
Brooch, 1991
Silver, gold, iron,
copper. 9.5 × 3.3 cm
© Millie Behrens

24
Behrens, Millie
(b. 1958), NO
"Blonde"
Earrings, 1993
Silver, enamel. L 5.8 cm
© Millie Behrens
Designed for David-
Andersen, Oslo. In
production until the
company closed in
2001.

23
Behrens, Millie
(b. 1958), NO
"Pebble Stories"
Earrings, 2016
Silver, pebbles. L 5 cm
© Millie Behrens

28
Berg, Inger Marie
(b. 1955), NO
Earrings, 1987
Nylon bristles, silver.
7 × 4 × 4.5 cm
© Inger Marie Berg/
BONO, Oslo 2021

25
Berg, Inger Marie
(b. 1955), NO
Bracelet, 1988
PVC sheet, silver rivets.
Ø 11 cm
© Inger Marie Berg/
BONO, Oslo 2021

27
Berg, Inger Marie
(b. 1955), NO
Earrings, 1988
PVC, silver. 4.5 × 8 cm
© Inger Marie Berg/
BONO, Oslo 2021

30
Berg, Inger Marie
(b. 1955), NO
Earrings, 1988
PVC, silver. Ø 4 cm
© Inger Marie Berg/
BONO, Oslo 2021

26
Berg, Inger Marie
(b. 1955), NO
Brooch, 1992
PVC, silver.
10 × 2.5 × 0.9 cm
© Inger Marie Berg/
BONO, Oslo 2021

29
Berg, Inger Marie
(b. 1955), NO
Necklace, 1997
PVC, silver. L 48 cm
© Inger Marie Berg/
BONO, Oslo 2021

494
Bernal, Macarena
(b. 1982), CL/NZ
"Two Links on a Cord"
Necklace, 2017
Polymer resin, pigment,
textile. L 53 cm
© Macarena Bernal

31
Bevan, Renee
(b. 1980), NZ
"Blush Rose"
Brooch, 2009/2017
Walnut wood, oxidised
silver, paper, polyure-
thane, stainless-steel
wire. 10 × 9 × 3.5 cm
© Renee Bevan

35
Bielander, David
(b. 1966), CH/DE
"Slug"
Brooch, 2004–
Patinated silver
repoussé. L 9.5 cm
Unlimited edition
© David Bielander

33
Bielander, David
(b. 1966), CH/DE
"Scarab/Dung Beetle"
Brooch, 2007
Steel (teaspoon), gold
pin. 4.3 × 3 × 2.5 cm
Edition of 50
© David Bielander

37
Bielander, David
(b. 1966), CH/DE
"Thonet_01
('Wienerle')"
Necklace, 2009/2011
Wood from the chair
Thonet no. 14 (1859/
Bugholz), paint. L 54 cm
© David Bielander

36
Bielander, David
(b. 1966), CH/DE
"Black Forest"
Necklace, 2011
Anodised titanium,
silver chain. L 15 cm
Edition of 12
© David Bielander

38
Bielander, David
(b. 1966), CH/DE
"Mamba"
Necklace, 2012
Anodised titanium,
gold. L 100 cm
Edition of 12
© David Bielander

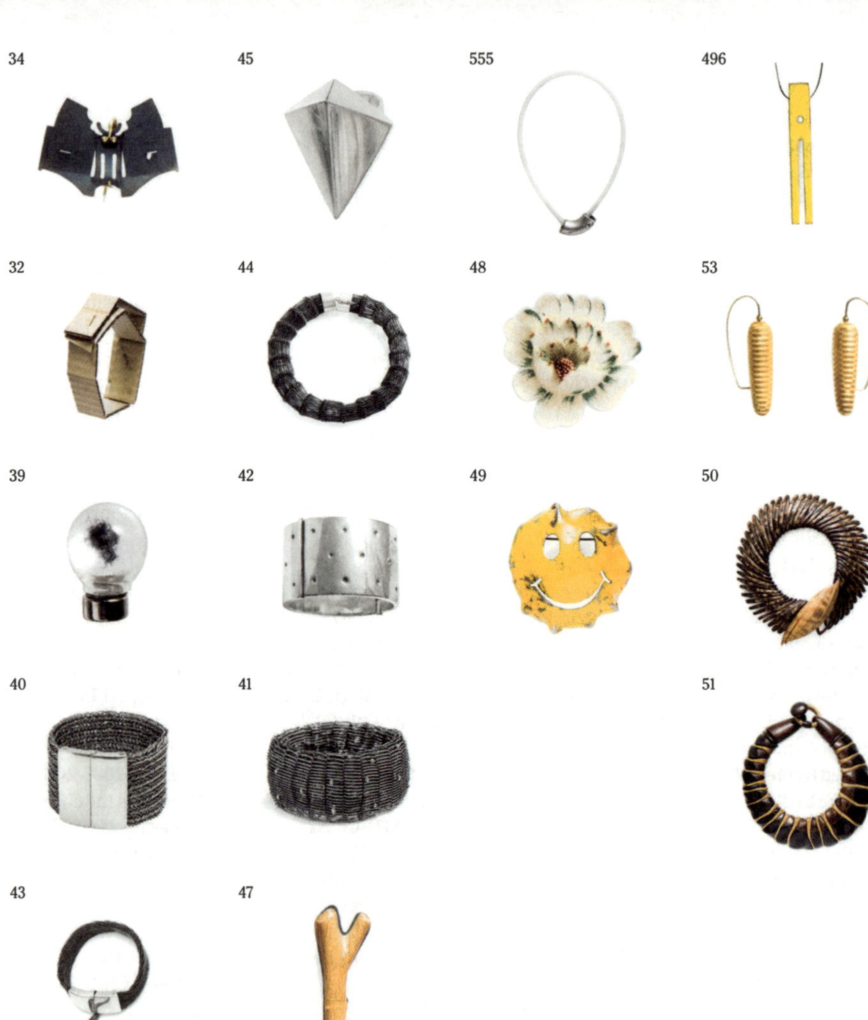

34
45
555
496
32
44
48
53
39
42
49
50
40
41
51
43
47

34
Bielander, David
(b. 1966), CH/DE
"Moth"
Brooch, 2014
Steel (from disposable
lighter), gold. L 3 cm
Unlimited edition
© David Bielander

32
Bielander, David
(b. 1966), CH/DE
"Cardboard"
Bracelet, 2015
Patinated silver, white
gold staples. L 9 cm
© David Bielander

39
Bjernér, Titti
(b. 1974), SE
Pin, 2006
Miniature glass bulb,
wool, magnet. L 1.4 cm
© Titti Bjernér/BONO,
Oslo 2021

40
Bjorg, Toril
(b. 1944), NO
Bracelet, 1987
Silver. H 4.2 cm
© Toril Bjorg/BONO,
Oslo 2021

43
Bjorg, Toril
(b. 1944), NO
Necklace, 1987
Silver. Ø 13.5 cm,
L "tail" 33 cm
© Toril Bjorg/BONO,
Oslo 2021

45
Bjorg, Toril
(b. 1944), NO
Ring, 1987
Silver. 6.7 × 4.3 × 3.5 cm
© Toril Bjorg/BONO,
Oslo 2021

44
Bjorg, Toril
(b. 1944), NO
"Cage"
Necklace, 1998
Oxidised silver. Ø 17 cm
© Toril Bjorg/
BONO, Oslo 2021

42
Bjorg, Toril
(b. 1944), NO
Bracelet, 1998/2000
Silver. H 4.3 cm
© Toril Bjorg/
BONO, Oslo 2021

41
Bjorg, Toril
(b. 1944), NO
"Nest with Dew"
Bracelet, 2004
Silver. H 4 cm
© Toril Bjorg/BONO,
Oslo 2021

47
Björkman, Sofia
(b. 1970), SE
"Wanna Be Precious"
Brooch, 2005
Vacuum-formed plastic
flooring (oak-imitation),
Ureol, silver, steel.
L 12.6 cm
© Sofia Björkman/
BONO, Oslo 2021

555
Bjørlo, Per Inge
(b. 1952), NO
Neckpiece, 2020
Plastic, stainless steel.
32 × 21 cm
© Per Inge Bjørlo/
BONO, Oslo 2021
The materials are
found: the pipe bend
is residual material
from the Norwegian oil
industry and the tube a
hydraulic hose.

48
Bjørnsen, Mona
(b. 1984), NO
Brooch, ca. 2005
Plastic-laminated textile
fragment of a curtain.
Ø 11 cm
© Mona Bjørnsen/
BONO, Oslo 2021

49
Blank, Alexander
(b. 1975), DE
"Smiley"
Brooch, 2013 (in pro-
duction from 2007)
Iron, lacquer, steel.
5 × 5 cm
© Alexander Blank/
BONO, Oslo 2021

496
Bliss, Becky
(b. 1956), NZ
"Peg"
Pendant, 2017
Recycled wood (rimu),
silver, thread. L 12.5 cm
© Becky Bliss/
BONO, Oslo 2021
The humble clothes
peg has been a part
of washing routines
since the 1760s. The
work symbolises that,
despite technological
advances, many ideas
and practices remain
the same and women
still carry out the
majority of cleaning
chores.

53
Blåvarp, Liv
(b. 1956), NO
Earrings, 1985
Birch. L 5.5 cm
© Liv Blåvarp/
BONO, Oslo 2021

50
Blåvarp, Liv
(b. 1956), NO
Necklace, 1990
Norwegian flame birch.
Ø 26 cm
© Liv Blåvarp/
BONO, Oslo 2021

51
Blåvarp, Liv
(b. 1956), NO
Necklace, 1996
Ebony, cocobolo,
lemon tree. Ø 25 cm
© Liv Blåvarp/
BONO, Oslo 2021

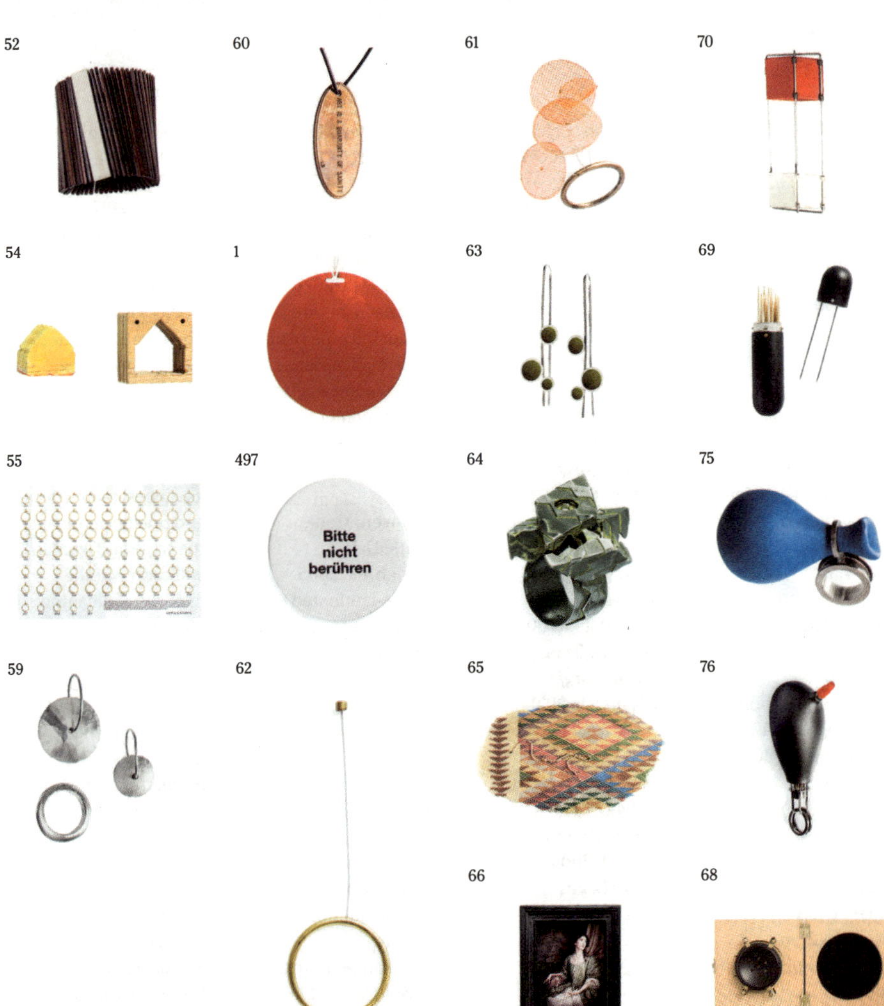

52
60
61
70
54
1
63
69
55
497
Bitte
nicht
berühren
64
75
59
62
65
76
66
68

52
Blåvarp, Liv
(b. 1956), NO
Bracelet, 2003/2017
Whale tooth, wood.
H 7.5 cm
© Liv Blåvarp/
BONO, Oslo 2021

54
Boekhoudt, Onno
(1944–2002), NL
"Room for a Finger"
Ring, 2000
Wood, paint. H 2.9 cm,
D 2.9 cm
Edition of 100
© Heirs of
Onno Boekhoudt/
BONO, Oslo 2021

55
Boons, Sofie
(b. 1989), BE/UK
"The Gold Price"
Poster, 2011. 31.5 × 44 cm
© Sofie Boons
A visualisation of the
change in the gold price
during the past seventy
years. The rings are,
despite their different
sizes, worth the same
amount of money as the
full size ring one could
have bought in 1941.

59
Bosshard, Kobi
(b. 1939), CH/NZ
Set with ring and
earrings, 1988/89–
Sterling silver. Ø large
disc 3.7 cm, Ø small disc
1.7 cm, Ø ring 3.5 cm
© Kobi Bosshard

60
Bourgeois, Louise
(1911–2010), FR/US
"100% Amulet, Art Is a
Guaranty of Sanity"
Pendant, 2007
Engraved copper.
5.5 × 2.5 cm
Limited edition of 1,000
© The Easton Founda-
tion/BONO, Oslo 2021
The necklace is
produced by Third
Drawer Down. The
company was founded
in Melbourne, Australia,
in 2003, and according
to their website they
have "collaborated
with some of the most
influential artists of
our time, translating
their works into gift and
homeware collections".

1
Brand, Zoe
(b. 1984), AU
"Sell Out"
Pendant, 2016
Powder-coated alumin-
ium, cord. Ø 14 cm
© Zoe Brand

497
Brand, Zoe
(b. 1984), AU
"Bitte nicht berühren"
Badge, 2018
Metal, plastic. Ø 6 cm
Edition 15/25
© Zoe Brand

62
Bridgwater, Margaret
(1970–2005), DK
Ring, 2000
Nylon, 18 ct gold,
diamond. H 6.5 cm
© Heirs of Margaret
Bridgwater

61
Bridgwater, Margaret
(1970–2005), DK
"Floating"
Ring, 2001
Silver, silk chiffon,
nylon. H 6 cm
© Heirs of Margaret
Bridgwater

63
Bridgwater, Margaret
(1970–2005), DK
"Dots"
Earrings, 2004
Silver. H 5.2 cm
© Heirs of Margaret
Bridgwater

64
Britton, Helen
(b. 1966), AU/DE
Ring, 2009
Diamonds, silver, paint.
5 × 3.5 × 4 cm
© Helen Britton

65
Broadhead, Caroline
(b. 1950), UK
"Dropped Necklace 1"
Necklace/object, 2015
Second-hand pearl
necklace, glass beads.
65 × 37 cm
© Caroline Broadhead

66
Broadhead, Maisie
(b. 1980), UK
"Chained", 2016
Digital C-type
print, glass beads
(CH00028-2).
37 × 30.5 cm,
L chain 51 cm
© Maisie Broadhead

70
Bronger, Sigurd
(b. 1957), NO
Brooch, 1987
Brass, steel, silver,
enamel paint. 7 × 2.2 cm
© Sigurd Bronger/
BONO, Oslo 2021

69
Bronger, Sigurd
(b. 1957), NO
"Souvenir from
Amsterdam"
Brooch, 1992
Steel, lacquer. 5 × 2.5 cm
© Sigurd Bronger/
BONO, Oslo 2021

75
Bronger, Sigurd
(b. 1957), NO
"Ring no. 2", 1993/94
Cibatool, lacquer, silver.
6 × 6 × 3.7 cm
© Sigurd Bronger/
BONO, Oslo 2021

76
Bronger, Sigurd
(b. 1957), NO
Ring, 1996
Hard foam, silver,
bicycle valve with
red plastic cap.
12 × 6.5 × 4.5 cm
© Sigurd Bronger/
BONO, Oslo 2021

68
Bronger, Sigurd
(b. 1957), NO
"Wearable Device for a
Telephone Receiver"
Brooch, 1997
Gold-plated brass, steel,
Bakelite telephone
speaker. 6 × 6.7 × 2 cm
© Sigurd Bronger/
BONO, Oslo 2021

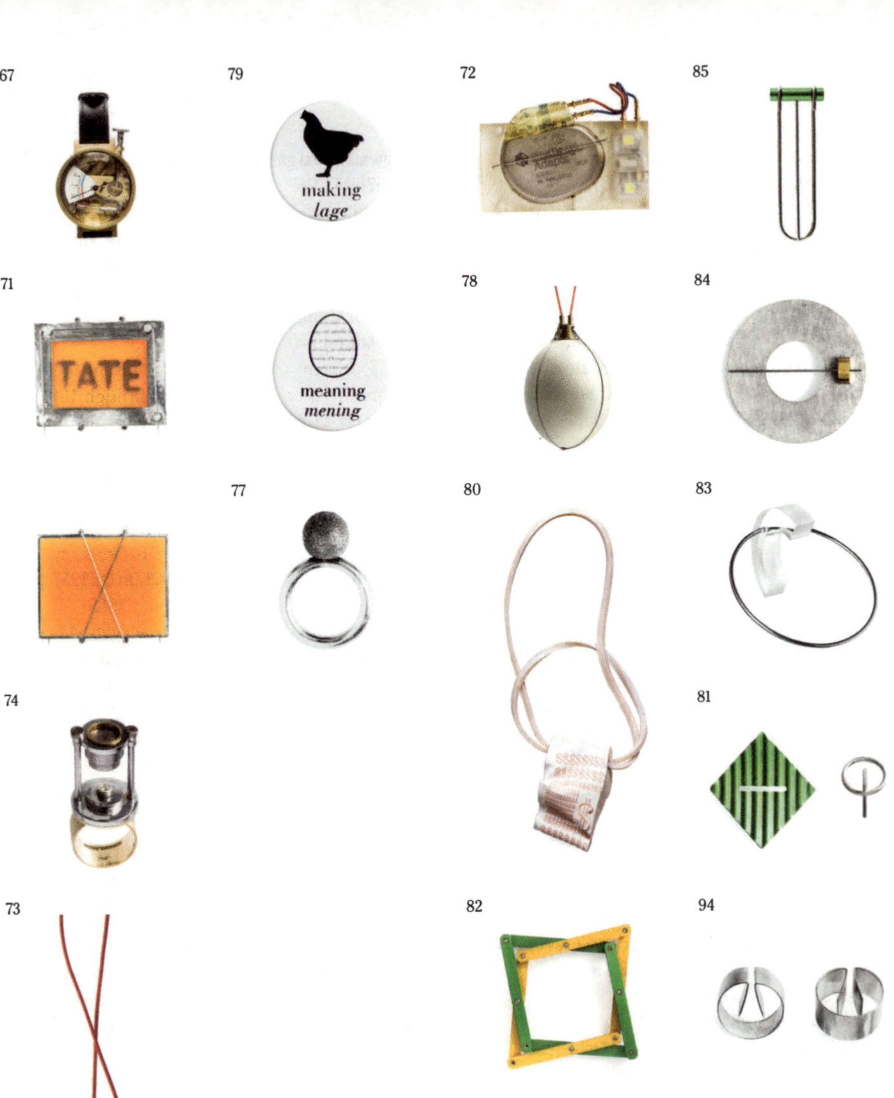

67
79
making
lage
72
85
71
TATE
78
84
77
80
83
74
81
73
82
94
95

67
Bronger, Sigurd
(b. 1957), NO
"Condition Measuring
Device No. 3"
Bracelet, 2000
Gold-plated brass,
leather strap, mixed
media. 25 × 4.6 × 1.5 cm
© Sigurd Bronger/
BONO, Oslo 2021

71
Bronger, Sigurd
(b. 1957), NO
"Eraser brooch", 2003
Eraser from Tate
Gallery, silver, steel.
4 × 4.7 × 1.7 cm
© Sigurd Bronger/
BONO, Oslo 2021

74
Bronger, Sigurd
(b. 1957), NO
"Big Diamond Ring"
Ring, 2005
Brass, chrome-plated
silver, 18 ct gold,
diamond, enlarging lens
(10×). H 4.7 cm
© Sigurd Bronger/
BONO, Oslo 2021

73
Bronger, Sigurd
(b. 1957), NO
"Diamond Necklace",
2005
Diamond dust, acrylic,
silver. Ø 6.5 cm
© Sigurd Bronger/
BONO, Oslo 2021

79
Bronger, Sigurd
(b. 1957), NO,
and James Evans
(b. 1952), CA
"Making/Meaning"
Badges/object, 2006
11 × 16 cm
Edition 19/20
© Sigurd Bronger/
BONO, Oslo 2021
During 6–8 July 2006,
Sigurd Bronger made a
collaborative exhibition
with the writer and
critic James Evans
(originally trained as
a jeweller) at Unit 2
Gallery, London Metro-
politan University.
It was an exhibition
developed on the spot,
and it involved the con-
struction of both visual
and literary texts.

77
Bronger, Sigurd
(b. 1957), NO
Diamond ring, 2011
Diamond-drill,
chrome-plated silver.
3.3 × 2.4 × 1.2 cm
Edition of 10
© Sigurd Bronger/
BONO, Oslo 2021
Made for Galerie Ra's
thirty-fifth anniversary.
The artists of the gallery
were invited to create a
piece of jewellery in a
limited edition.

72
Bronger, Sigurd
(b. 1957), NO
"Wearable Device for a
Pacemaker"
Brooch, 2015
Acrylic, silver, steel,
electronics, pace-
maker (titanium).
5.5 × 7.7 × 1.3 cm
© Sigurd Bronger/
BONO, Oslo 2021

78
Bronger, Sigurd
(b. 1957), NO
Necklace, 2017
Ostrich egg, rubber
cord. L 70 cm,
H egg 19 cm
© Sigurd Bronger/
BONO, Oslo 2021

80
Brovia, Beatrice
(b. 1985), IT/SE
"Cre$t" From the series
Exonumia
Necklace, 2016
Embroidered textile,
foam, rubber, silver.
50 × 20 × 7 cm
© Beatrice Brovia

82
Buck, Kim (b. 1957), DK
Bracelet, 1987
Anodised aluminium,
silver, nylon. Ø 11.5 cm
© Kim Buck/
BONO, Oslo 2021
With a single grip,
the bracelet can be
unfolded or folded. The
inspiration came from
the scissor mechanism
in decorator pliers.

85
Buck, Kim (b. 1957), DK
Brooch, 1987
Steel, aluminium.
7.5 × 2.7 cm
© Kim Buck/
BONO, Oslo 2021

84
Buck, Kim (b. 1957), DK
Fibula brooch, 1987
Silver, steel, aluminium.
Ø 6.5 cm
© Kim Buck/
BONO, Oslo 2021

83
Buck, Kim (b. 1957), DK
Bracelet, 1989
Silver, acrylic. Ø 7 cm
© Kim Buck/
BONO, Oslo 2021

81
Buck, Kim (b. 1957), DK
Ring, 1990
Silver, anodised alumin-
ium (green). 5.5 × 5 cm
© Kim Buck/
BONO, Oslo 2021
The aluminium disc is
interchangeable. The
disc is kept in place
when the ring is on the
finger.

94
Buck, Kim (b. 1957), DK
Earrings, 1991
Silver. 2 × 2 × 1.8 cm
© Kim Buck/
BONO, Oslo 2021

95
Buck, Kim (b. 1957), DK
Earrings, 1991
18 ct gold. 2 × 2 × 1 cm
© Kim Buck/
BONO, Oslo 2021

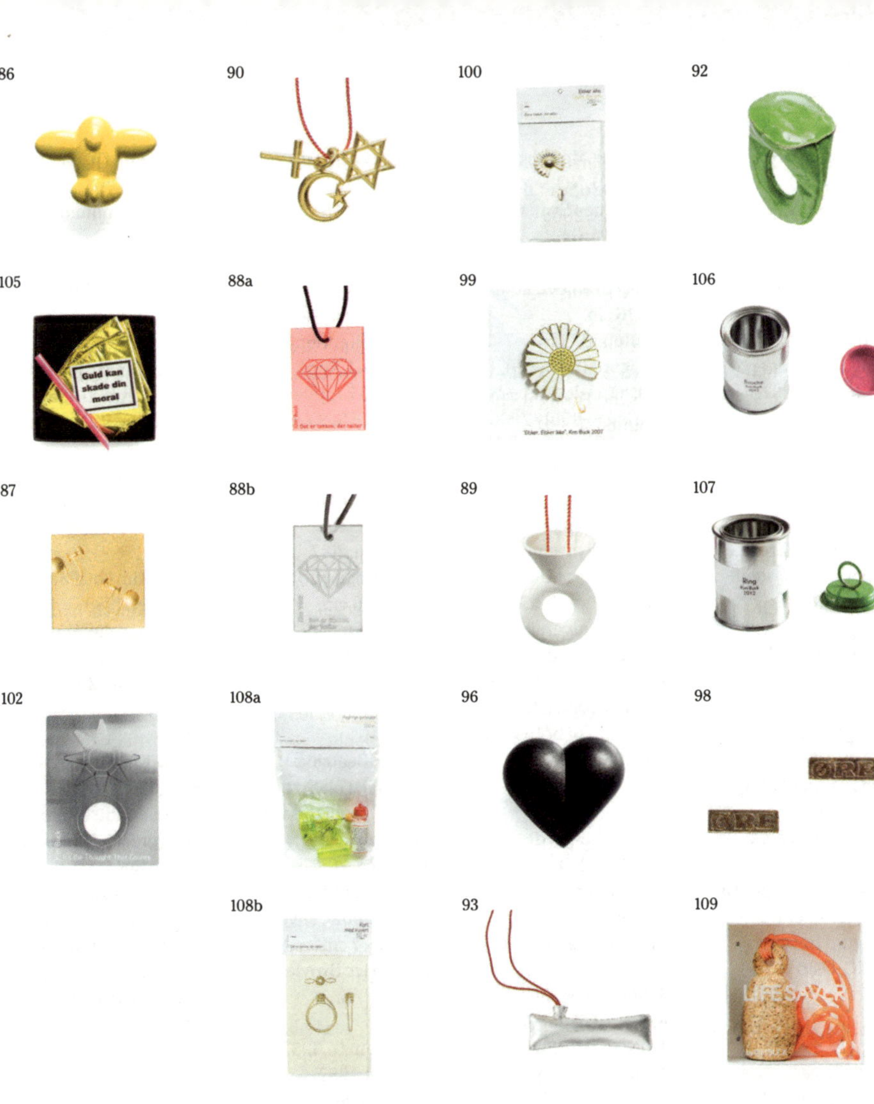

86
Buck, Kim (b. 1957), DK
Pin, 1996
Cibatool, lacquer.
3 × 2.5 cm
© Kim Buck/
BONO, Oslo 2021

105
Buck, Kim (b. 1957), DK
"Gold Bracelet", 2003
Inflatable, metallic-
effect plastic foil.
19.5 × 17 cm
© Kim Buck/
BONO, Oslo 2021

87
Buck, Kim (b. 1957), DK
"Pearl Earrings"
Brooch, 2003
Gold. 4 × 4 × 0.4 cm
© Kim Buck/
BONO, Oslo 2021
In 2003 Kim Buck was
invited to participate
in an exhibition called
The Jewellery Box. The
title made him reflect
on what is often found
in a jewellery box,
and the result was a
series of brooches with
conventional jewellery
as negative prints. The
imprint symbolises the
memory of something
that once was there.

102
Buck, Kim (b. 1957), DK
"Diamond Ring", 2005
Sheet metal. 9 × 7 cm
© Kim Buck/
BONO, Oslo 2021

90
Buck, Kim (b. 1957), DK
"Faith, Hope and Love"
Pendant, 2005
18 ct gold. 2.5 × 3 cm
© Kim Buck/
BONO, Oslo 2021

88a, 88b
Buck, Kim (b. 1957), DK
"It's the Thought That
Counts"
Pendant, 2007
Acrylic. Red 3 × 2.8 cm,
transparent 2.8 × 2 cm
© Kim Buck/
BONO, Oslo 2021

108a
Buck, Kim (b. 1957), DK
"It's the Thought
That Counts"
Vapour ring generator,
2007
8.5 × 9.5 × 4 cm

108b
Buck, Kim (b. 1957), DK
Card with envelope,
2007
Mixed media.
15 × 10.5 cm
© Kim Buck/
BONO, Oslo 2021

101
Buck, Kim (b. 1957), DK
"Little Mirror"
Brooch, 2007
Stainless steel. Ø 4.2 cm
© Kim Buck/
BONO, Oslo 2021

100
Buck, Kim (b. 1957), DK
"Loves Me Not"
Pin, 2007
Gold-plated silver,
enamel. L 2 cm
© Kim Buck/
BONO, Oslo 2021
Manipulated Georg
Jensen brooch.

99
Buck, Kim (b. 1957), DK
"Loves Me.
Loves Me Not"
Brooch, 2007
Gold-plated copper,
enamel. Ø 4.5 cm
© Kim Buck/
BONO, Oslo 2021

89
Buck, Kim (b. 1957), DK
"Receptacle"
Pendant, 2007
Porcelain, cord.
5 × 3.5 cm
© Kim Buck/
BONO, Oslo 2021

96
Buck, Kim (b. 1957), DK
"Teflon Heart"
Brooch, 2009
Teflon-coated silver.
3.5 × 3.5 × 1.1 cm
© Kim Buck/
BONO, Oslo 2021

93
Buck, Kim (b. 1957), DK
"Puffed Up"
Pendant, 2010
Silver. 2 × 6 × 1.7 cm
© Kim Buck/
BONO, Oslo 2021

92
Buck, Kim (b. 1957), DK
"Puffed Up Ring", 2011
Silver, paint.
4.6 × 4 × 3 cm
© Kim Buck/
BONO, Oslo 2021

106
Buck, Kim (b. 1957), DK
Brooch, 2012
Canned box where the
lid can be used as a pin.
Ø pin 4.5 cm
© Kim Buck/
BONO, Oslo 2021

107
Buck, Kim (b. 1957), DK
Ring, 2012
Canned box where the
lid can be used as a ring.
Ø ring 4.8 cm
© Kim Buck/
BONO, Oslo 2021

98
Buck, Kim (b. 1957), DK
"Øre" (Ear)
Earrings, 2014
Copper from a
Danish 25-øre coin.
0.8 × 0.2 × 0.1 cm
© Kim Buck/
BONO, Oslo 2021
The Danish word *øre* is
the word for the coins
that subdivide the
krone and for ear.

109
Buck, Kim (b. 1957), DK
"Life Saver"
Pendant/object, 2014
Cork, nylon cord,
steel, acrylic.
10.9 × 10.9 × 4.6 cm
© Kim Buck/
BONO, Oslo 2021

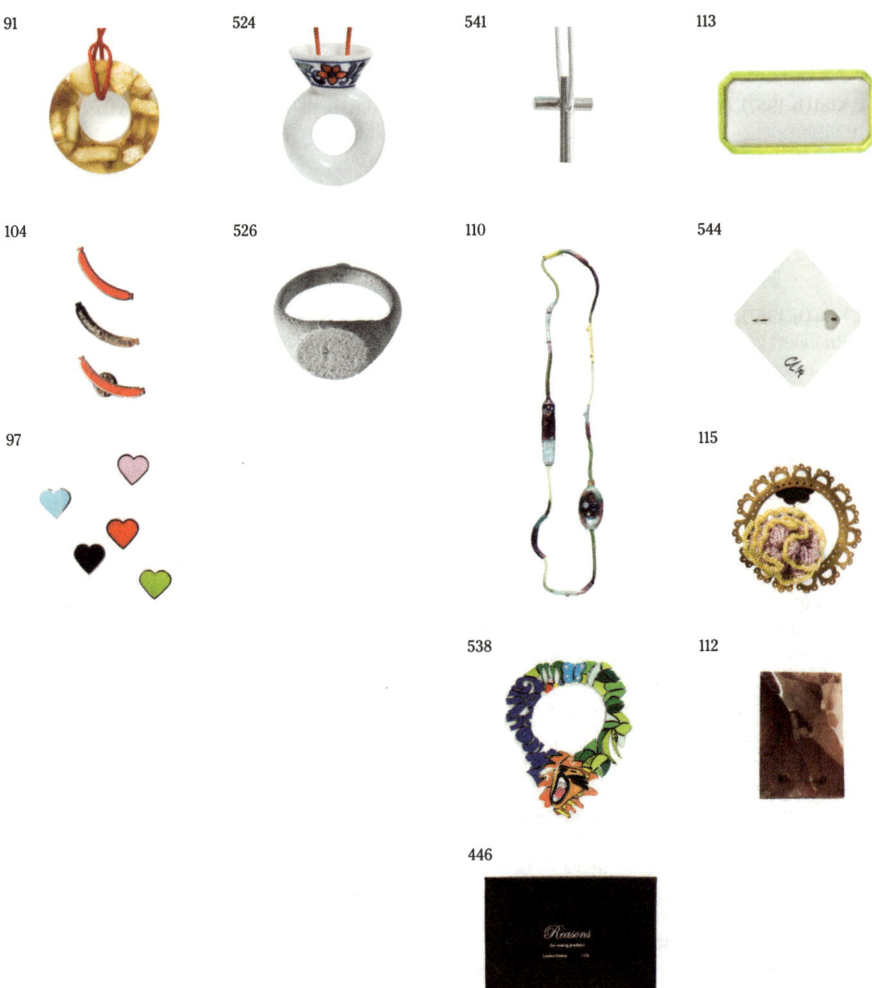

91

524

541

113

104

526

110

544

97

115

538

112

446

504

91
Buck, Kim (b. 1957), DK
"Amber Tube"
Pendant, 2015
Amber, acrylic. Ø 4.3 cm
© Kim Buck/
BONO, Oslo 2021

104
Buck, Kim (b. 1957), DK
"Made in Denmark"
Pin, 2016
Nickel-plated copper,
plastic enamel. L 3.5 cm
© Kim Buck/
BONO, Oslo 2021

97
Buck, Kim (b. 1957), DK
"They Come in
All Colours"
Pin, 2016
Nickel-plated copper,
enamel. 1.5 × 1.5 cm
© Kim Buck/
BONO, Oslo 2021

524
Buck, Kim (b. 1957), DK
"Made in China"
Pendant, 2017
Porcelain.
4.8 × 3.3 × 2.9 cm
© Kim Buck/
BONO, Oslo 2021
Kim Buck made a series
of these pendants
during a residency in
Jingdezhen, the porce-
lain capital of the world.
He asked seven different
porcelain painters to
decorate the pendants
with patterns of their
own choice. This one
has been painted by
彭东 Pong Dong (b. 1988
in Jiangxi Province),
who is a specialist in
antique painting. The
motive is from the Ming
dynasty.

526
Buck, Kim (b. 1957), DK
"Out of Focus"
Signet ring, 2018
Silver. 1.3 × 2 × 2 cm
© Kim Buck/
BONO, Oslo 2021
The title refers to the
effect on the surface of
a ring that occurs when
a casting fails, but it is
also an ironic hint to
how we usually per-
ceive people who wear
signet rings as very
focused and successful
people. The aim of the
artist is to control the
technique so that the
casting fails every time
and thus succeeds.

541
Buck, Kim (b. 1957), DK
"On, Off"
Pendant, 2019
Silver. L long 2 cm,
L short 1.5 cm
© Kim Buck/
BONO, Oslo 2021
In each rod there is a
notch so, when lifted,
the two rods will fall
into each other and
form a cross.

110
Carr, Nadene
(b. 1970), NZ
Necklace, 2016
Copper, enamel, stones,
textile cord. L 56 cm
© Nadene Carr

538
Cecchi, Monica
(b. 1964), IT
"Grrroowl"
Neckpiece, 2019
Antique tin boxes.
26 × 25 × 1 cm
© Monica Cecchi

446
Cheung, Lin
(b. 1971), UK
"Reasons (for Wearing
Jewellery)"
Box with cards,
1998–2008
11 × 15.8 cm
Edition 90/170
© Lin Cheung

113
Cheung, Lin
(b. 1971), UK
"Wear Again, Again"
Brooch, 2010
Nylon-flocked acrylic
and brass, faux leather.
6.7 × 3.5 × 1.6 cm
© Lin Cheung

544
Cohn, Susan
(b. 1952), AU
"meaninglessness"
Fourth leaf pin, 2019
Silver. L 5 cm
© Susan Cohn

115
Collins, Sally
(b. 1983), UK
Brooch, 2008
Patinated copper,
cotton, stainless-steel
pin. Ø 5 cm
© Sally Collins

112
Conversation Piece
(Nicolas Cheng
(b. 1982), HK/SE,
and Beatrice Brovia
(b. 1985), IT/SE)
"Kino"
Brooch, 2014
Quartz crystal, gold,
tantalum, optical film.
7.7 × 5 cm
© Beatrice Brovia,
Nicolas Cheng

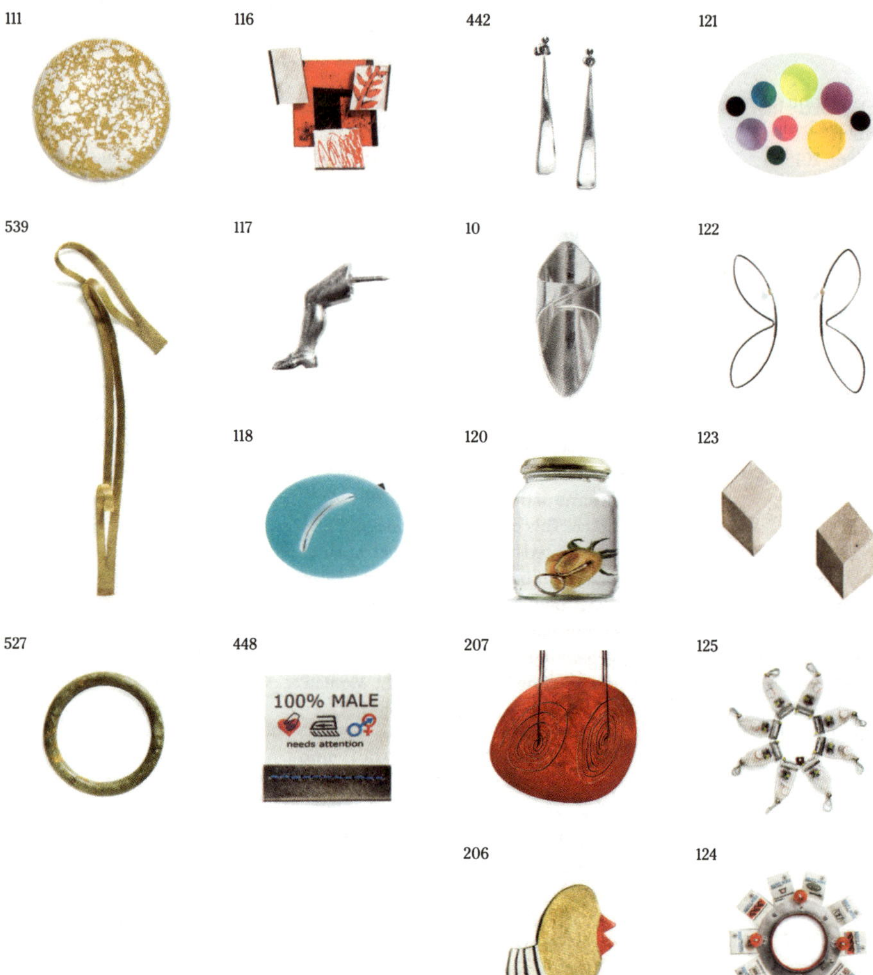

111
Conversation Piece
(Nicolas Cheng
(b. 1982), HK/SE,
and Beatrice Brovia
(b. 1985), IT/SE)
"Gold Rush"
Brooch, 2017
Gold, e-waste, optical
film. Ø 5.8 cm
© Beatrice Brovia,
Nicolas Cheng

539
Conversation Piece
(Nicolas Cheng
(b. 1982), HK/SE,
and Beatrice Brovia
(b. 1985), IT/SE)
"In The Cut"
Neckpiece, 2017
Gold-plated brass,
14 ct gold. 66 × 2 × 0.2 cm
© Beatrice Brovia,
Nicolas Cheng

527
Conversation Piece
(Nicolas Cheng
(b. 1982), HK/SE,
and Beatrice Brovia
(b. 1985), IT/SE)
"Nu Jade"
Bracelet, 2018
E-waste (shredded
plastic, copper and gold
recovered from CPU
boards). 8.2 × 0.9 cm,
inner Ø 6.5 cm
© Beatrice Brovia,
Nicolas Cheng

116
Cuyàs, Ramon Puig
(b. 1953), ES
"Suite Pompeyana
no. 1641"
Brooch, 2016
Oxidised nickel silver,
enamel on steel, ala-
baster, plastic, acrylic
paint. 8 × 8 × 1.5 cm
© Ramon Puig Cuyàs

117
Dada's Diamonds, SE
"Kick It"
Brooch/pin, 2005
Silver. L 2 cm
© Dada's Diamonds
Ida Forss (b. 1971)
and Kajsa Öberg
Avila (b. 1972) are the
women behind Dada's
Diamonds. "Kick It" is
from their first collec-
tion, *Wonderland*, with
inspiration from Lewis
Carroll's *Alice's Adven-
tures in Wonderland*.

118
Dahm, Johanna
(b. 1947), CH
Brooch, 1983
Perspex, steel.
7.3 × 10 cm
© Johanna Dahm

448
Dam, Annette
(b. 1972), DK
"100% Male"
Brooch, 2008
Silver, textile.
3.6 × 3.6 cm
© Annette Dam

442
David-Andersen, Uni
(b. 1930), NO
Earrings, 1970s
925 silver. L 5.5 cm
Produced by the
company David-
Andersen, Oslo

10
David-Andersen, Uni
(b. 1930), NO
Ring, 1980s
Silver. H 5 cm
Produced by the
company David-
Andersen, Oslo

120
De Decker, Hilde
(b. 1965), BE
"Voor Boer en Tuinder"
(For the Farmer and the
Market Gardener)
Object, 2004
Silver, tomato, canning
glass with vinegar.
H 10, Ø 8 cm
© Hilde De Decker

207
de Jong, Rian
(b. 1951), NL
Necklace, 1993
Painted wood. 12 × 14 cm
© Rian de Jong

206
de Jong, Rian
(b. 1951), NL
Brooch, 1995
Wood. 5.8 × 5 × 1.3 cm
© Rian de Jong

121
Derrez, Paul
(b. 1950), NL
"Dot-brooch"
Brooch, 2014
Acrylic, steel needle.
12 × 10 cm
© Paul Derrez

122
Disen, Karen
(b. 1961), NO
Earrings, 2005
Surgical steel, silver,
pearls. 10 × 3 × 3 cm
© Karen Diesen

123
Dobler, Georg
(b. 1952), DE
Earrings, 1988–
Silver. 3 × 2 cm
Unlimited edition
© Georg Dobler

125
Dramstad, Hilde
(b. 1965), NO
"White Wedding"
Necklace, 1999
Silver, textile,
stomach-acid tablets,
plastic. Ø 50 cm
© Hilde Dramstad/
BONO, Oslo 2021

124
Dramstad, Hilde
(b. 1965), NO
"Good Advice 2"
Brooch, 2000
Textile, silver. Ø 12 cm
© Hilde Dramstad/
BONO, Oslo 2021

516
493
131
135
528
133
554
126
129
540
136
128
354
137
127
130
134
488
132

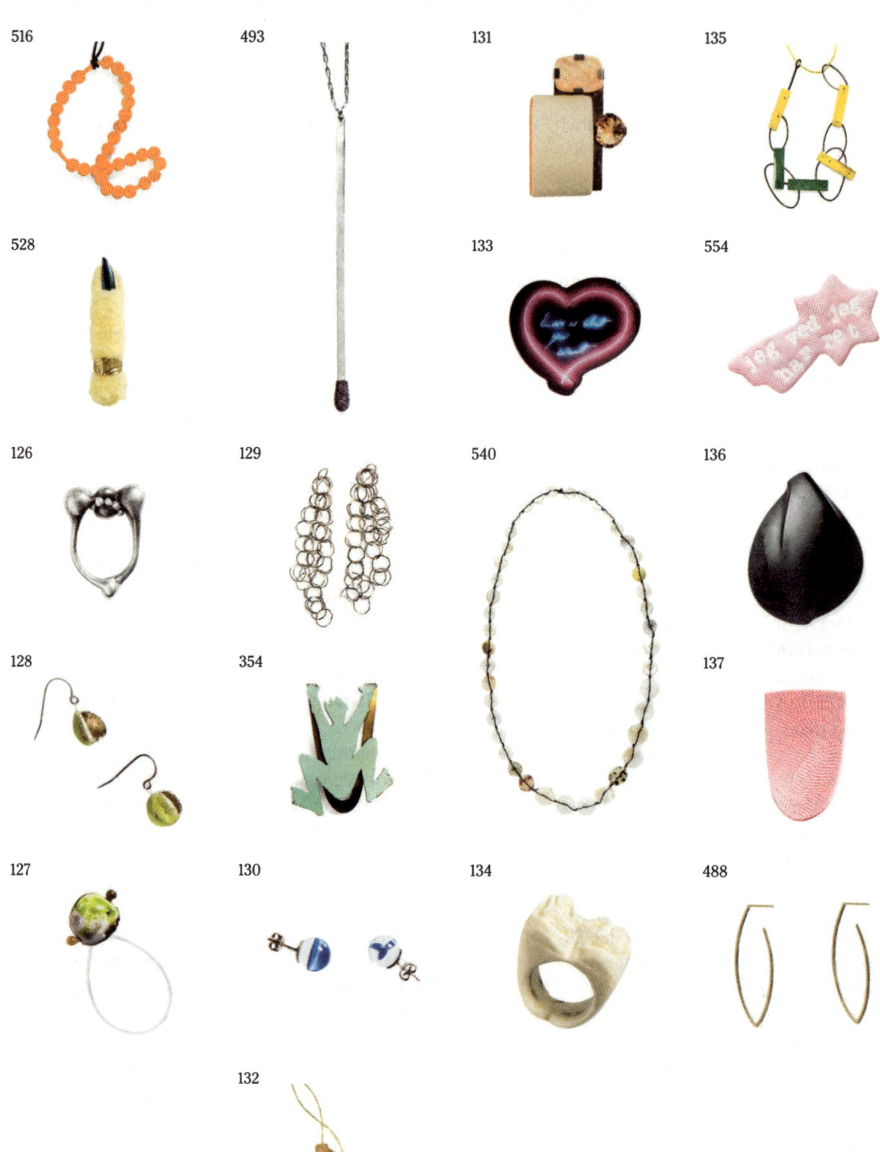

516
Dramstad, Hilde
(b. 1965), NO
Pendant, 2015
Laser-cut steel, spray
paint. 5 × 4.5 cm
© Hilde Dramstad/
BONO, Oslo 2021

528
Duckert, Helene
(b. 1988), NO
"Finger"
Brooch, 2018
Foam rubber, brass,
back shell from beetle.
L 11.5 cm
© Helene Duckert

126
Duong, Sam-Tho
(b. 1969), VN/DE
From the series *Palate*
Ring, 2003
Oxidised silver, pearls.
3 × 2.5 cm
© Sam-Tho Duong

128
Duong, Sam-Tho
(b. 1969), VN/DE
"Cherrypit"
Earrings, 2007
Silver, enamel. L 2.5 cm
© Sam-Tho Duong
The earrings are based
on castings of cherry
stones.

127
Duong, Sam-Tho
(b. 1969), VN/DE
"Cherrypit"
Ring, 2007
Silver, enamel, nylon.
L 3.2 cm
© Sam-Tho Duong

493
Dziuba, Gabi
(b. 1951), DE
"Match"
Pendant, 2017
Silver, zirconia.
L 57.5 cm, pendant
18.6 cm
© Gabi Dziuba

129
Edlund, Jenny
(b. 1959), SE
Earrings, 2014
Silver. L 18 cm
© Jenny Edlund/
BONO, Oslo 2021

354
Eliassen, Lillan
(b. 1961), NO
"Kravlemann"
(Crawling Man)
Brooch, 1993
Copper. 7 × 6.6 cm
© Lillan Eliassen/
BONO, Oslo 2021

130
Eliassen, Lillan
(b. 1961), NO
Earrings, 2002
Silver, glass.
1 × 1 × 2.2 cm
© Lillan Eliassen/
BONO, Oslo 2021

132
Eitzenhöfer, Ute
(b. 1969), DE
Pendant, 2001
Found wood, five
diamonds (0.012 ct,
0.016 ct, 0.017 ct,
0.023 ct, 0.025 ct),
white gold, Kevlar
thread. L 93 cm,
pendant 13 cm
© Ute Eitzenhöfer

131
Eitzenhöfer, Ute
(b. 1969), DE
Brooch, 2010
Plastic (from a sham-
poo bottle), oxidised
925 silver, coral agate,
cubic zirconia, tiger's
eye. 9 × 6 × 3.3 cm
© Ute Eitzenhöfer

133
Emin, Tracey
(b. 1963), UK
"Love Is What
You Want"
Pin, 2011
2.8 × 3 cm
© Tracey Emin.
All rights reserved,
DACS/BONO, Oslo 2020

540
Eriksen, Helga
(b. 1950), NO
Necklace, 2019.
Mother-of-pearl
buttons, thread. L 50 cm
© Helga Eriksen
Made with the help of
Gerd Tinglum.

134
Erland, Jens
(b. 1945), NO
Ring, 2005
Horse tooth.
2.7 × 2.8 × 3 cm
© Jens Erland/
BONO, Oslo 2021

135
Fekete, Réka
(b. 1982), HU/NL
"Birds Flying High"
Necklace, 2013
Steel, wood, aluminium,
paper rope, paint,
silver, sealing wax.
L 44 cm
© Réka Fekete

554
Ferreira, Sara (b. 1971)/
Kritisk pynt (Critical
Decoration), DK
"Jeg ved jeg har ret"
(I Know I'm Right)
Brooch, 2018
Painted polymer clay.
8 × 4 × 0.5 cm
© Sara Ferreira

136
Fischer, Benedikt
(b. 1984), AT
"Unus Unus"
Brooch, 2012
Plastic, remanium.
16.7 × 12.5 × 1.3 cm
© Benedikt Fischer

137
Fischer, Benedikt
(b. 1984), AT
"Sweetness"
Brooch, 2013
Plastic, remanium.
6.5 × 4 × 1.2 cm
© Benedikt Fischer

488
Fischer, Ditte
(b. 1966), DK
"Boat"
Earrings, 2017
24 ct gilded sterling
silver. L 4.8 cm
© Ditte Fischer

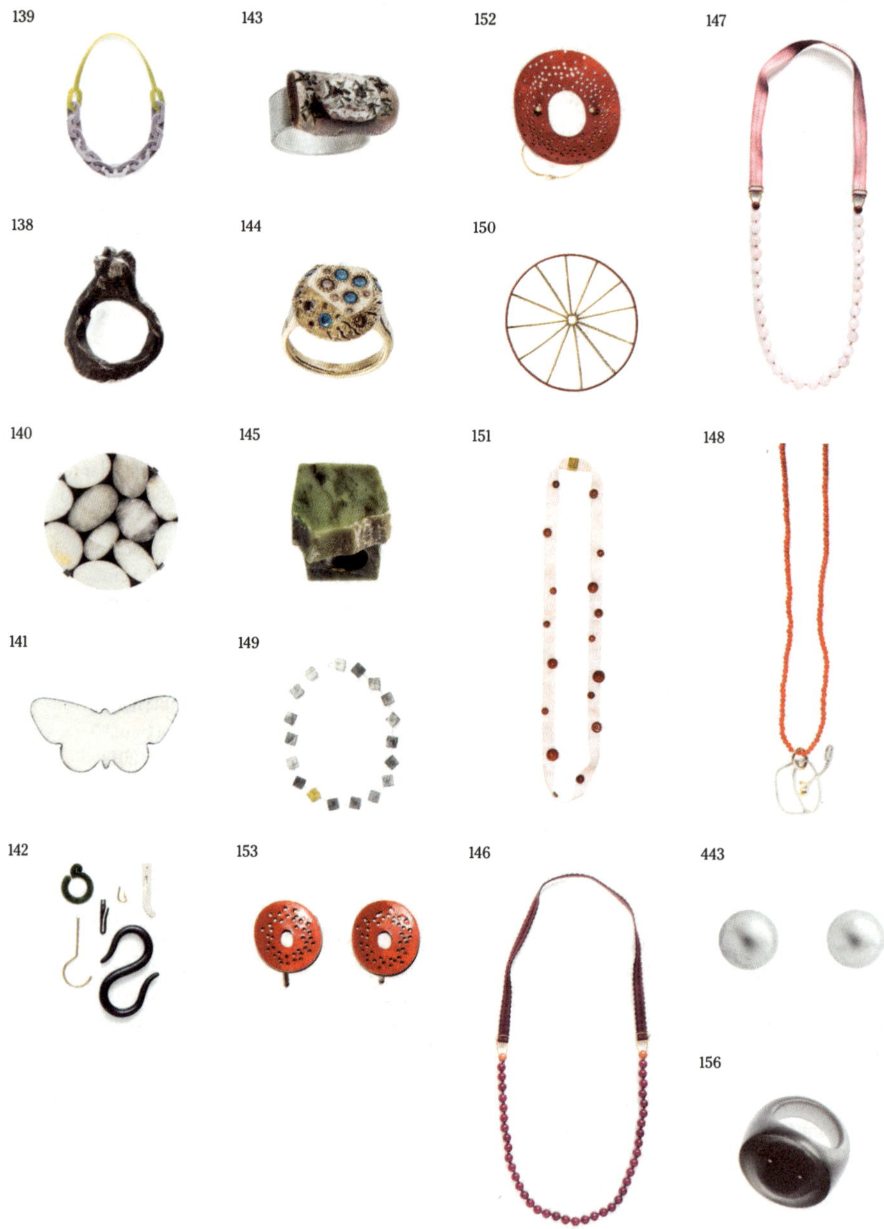

139
143
152
147
138
144
150
140
145
151
148
141
149
142
153
146
443
156

139
Fleischhut, Jantje
(b. 1972), DE/NL
"Precious Plastic_Link"
Necklace, 2012
Rubber, resin. L 36 cm
© Jantje Fleischhut

138
Flaa, Margit
(b. 1979), NO
Ring, 2006
Iron. 4 × 3 × 1 cm
© Margit Flaa

140
Freeman, Warwick
(b. 1953), NZ
"Pebble Brooch"
Brooch, 1998
Resin, silver, quartz
pebbles. Ø 5.7 cm
© Warwick Freeman

141
Freeman, Warwick
(b. 1953), NZ
"White Butterfly"
Brooch, 1999–
Painted silver. 1 × 2.2 cm
© Warwick Freeman

142
Freeman, Warwick
(b. 1953), NZ
"Story of the hook"
Pendants, 2013/2016
6 parts: "Fat Hook" (925
silver), "Gold Hanger"
(750 gold), "Curtain
Hook" (nephrite jade),
"Apron Hook" (925
silver), "Hanger Hook"
(whalebone), "Small
Gold Hook" (fine gold).
L 2.8–14 cm
Edition of 3
© Warwick Freeman

143
Fritsch, Karl
(b. 1963), DE/NZ
Ring, 2011
Silver, rubies,
sapphires, green
garnet. 1.3 × 2.5 × 3.9 cm
© Karl Fritsch

144
Fritsch, Karl
(b. 1963), DE/NZ
Ring, 2013
Blue cubic zirconia,
diamonds, 9 ct gold.
1.7 × 1.7 × 2.6 cm
© Karl Fritsch

145
Fritsch, Karl
(b. 1963), DE/NZ
Ring, 2013
Pounamu (New
Zealand nephrite jade).
3.5 × 3.7 × 4.5 cm
© Karl Fritsch

149
Gasparski, Kasia
(b. 1966), DK
"Square"
Necklace, 1994–/2006
Nylon thread, silver,
gold. Ø 16 cm
© Kasia Gasparski/
BONO, Oslo 2021

153
Gasparski, Kasia
(b. 1966), DK
Earrings, 2002
From the series
About Earrings
Silver, lacquer.
1.5 × 1.2 × 1.4 cm
© Kasia Gasparski/
BONO, Oslo 2021

152
Gasparski, Kasia
(b. 1966), DK
Ring, 2002
From the series
About Rings
Silver, 14 ct gold,
lacquer. 3 × 2.5 × 2.4 cm
© Kasia Gasparski/
BONO, Oslo 2021

150
Gasparski, Kasia
(b. 1966), DK
"Focus"
Brooch, 2003
Gold, lacquer. Ø 7.2 cm
© Kasia Gasparski/
BONO, Oslo 2021

151
Gasparski, Kasia
(b. 1966), DK
Necklace, 2003
Silver, lacquer, 24 ct
gold, silk ribbon.
L 40 cm
© Kasia Gasparski/
BONO, Oslo 2021

146
Gasparski, Kasia
(b. 1966), DK
"Pippi's Choice"
Necklace, 2008
18 ct gold, serpentine
stones, Italian coral,
bra band. L 46 cm
© Kasia Gasparski/
BONO, Oslo 2021

147
Gasparski, Kasia
(b. 1966), DK
"Pippi's Choice"
Necklace, 2008
18 ct gold, serpentine
stones, Italian coral,
bra band. L 45 cm
© Kasia Gasparski/
BONO, Oslo 2021

148
Gasparski, Kasia
(b. 1966), DK
Necklace, 2009
Coral, silver. L 22.5 cm
© Kasia Gasparski/
BONO, Oslo 2021

443
Georg Jensen Company,
DK
"Grape 551D"
Earrings, 2018
Thai sterling silver.
Ø 1 cm
From the *Moonlight
Grapes* collection
designed by Georg
Jensen Design Team.
Inspired by Harald
Nielsen's "Grape" motif
from the 1920s.

156
Gianocca, Kiko
(b. 1974), CH
"Who Am I?"
Ring, 2010
Polyurethane, silver.
2.6 × 2.6 × 3 cm
© Kiko Gianocca

154

157

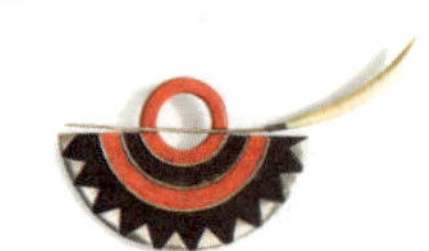

161

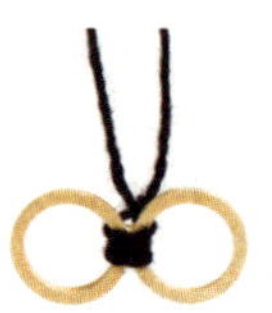

163

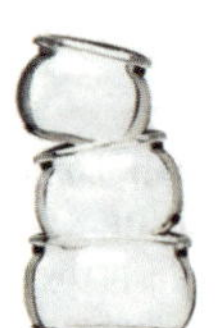

158

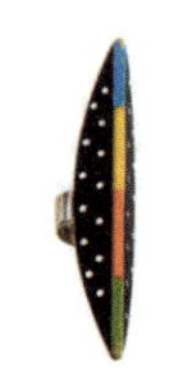

162

166

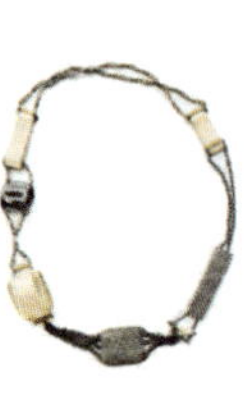

155

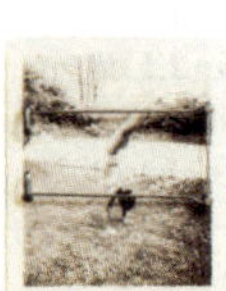

476

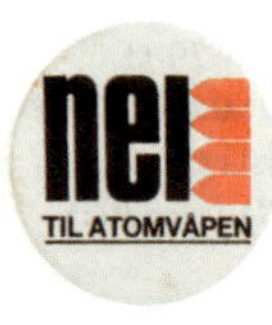

164

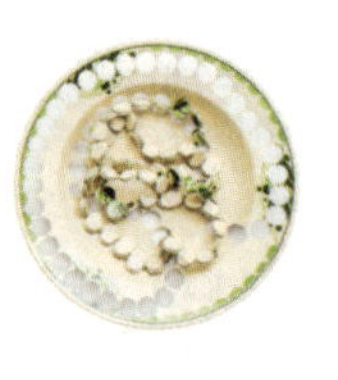

167

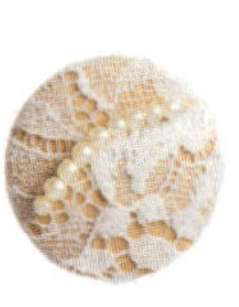

504

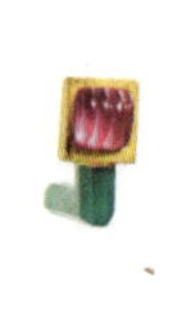

533

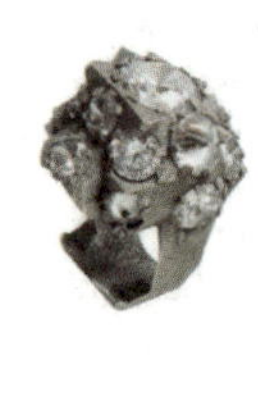

165

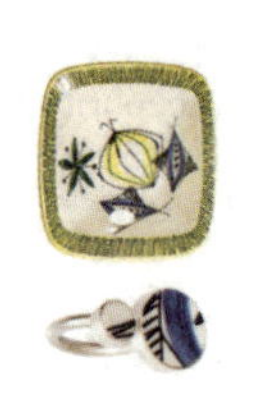

168

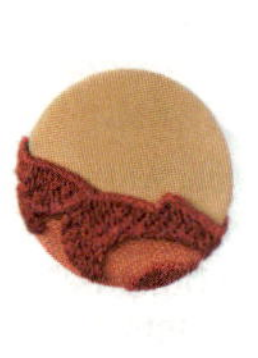

2

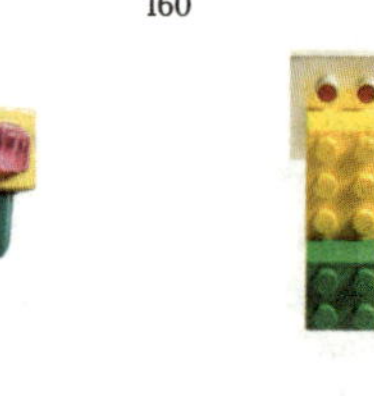

160

169

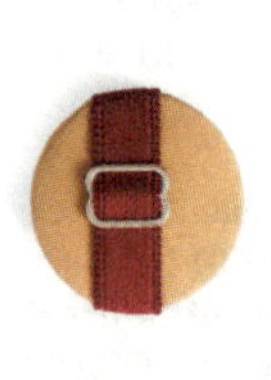

159

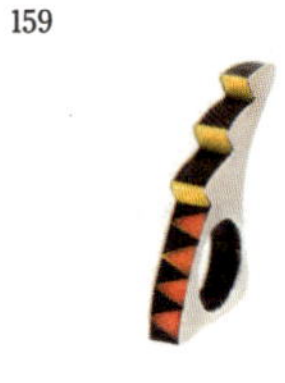

170

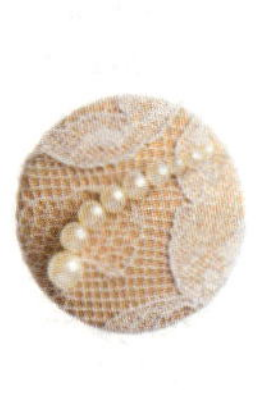

430

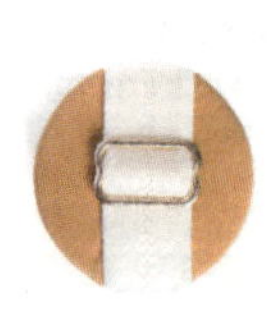

512

154
Gianocca, Kiko
(b. 1974), CH
"Never Been There 3"
Brooch, 2014
Found image,
silver, resin, lacquer.
8.8 × 7.8 × 0.8 cm
© Kiko Gianocca

155
Gianocca, Kiko
(b. 1974), CH
"I Tangled Up the Wool
to Annoy My Mother"
Necklace, 2015
Nylon thread. Length
variable
© Kiko Gianocca

504
Gianocca, Kiko
(b. 1974), CH
"Onward Backward"
Earrings, 2016
Nitinol. L 9.7 cm
© Kiko Gianocca
The earrings can be
shaped in different
ways. They return back
to their original shape
in hot water at >55 °C.

2
Giorgadse, Tatjana
(b. 1987), GE/DE
Earrings, 2018
Synthetic spinel,
wood, agate, silver.
2 × 4 × 5.7 cm
© Tatjana Giorgadse

159
Glenne, Toril
(b. 1946), NO
Ring, 1987
Sterling silver, ebony,
paint, acrylic
6.5 × 3 × 0.7 cm
© Toril Glenne/
BONO, Oslo 2021

157
Glenne, Toril
(b. 1946), NO
Brooch, 1988
Wood, silver, ivory.
11.5 × 7 cm
© Toril Glenne/
BONO, Oslo 2021

158
Glenne, Toril
(b. 1946), NO
Ring, 1990
Ebony, silver, paint,
acrylic. H 9 cm
© Toril Glenne/
BONO, Oslo 2021

476
Grepstad, Jon
(b. 1944), NO
"Nei til atomvåpen"
(No to nuclear
weapons)
Badge, 1979
Ø 3.2 cm

533
Grinovich, Adam
(b. 1981), US/SE
"Settings"
Ring, 2017
Steel, cubic zirconia.
3 × 2.5 × 3.5 cm
© Adam Grinovich

160
Grov, Kirsti Reinsborg
(b. 1967), NO
"Lego"
Brooch, 2001
Silver, enamel.
2.3 × 2.3 × 0.4 cm
© Kirsti Reinsborg Grov/
BONO, Oslo 2021

161
Grov, Kirsti Reinsborg
(b. 1967), NO
"Buttonholes"
Necklace, 2005
Gold, thread.
Pendant 1 × 1.7 cm
© Kirsti Reinsborg Grov/
BONO, Oslo 2021

162
Gut, Andi
(b. 1971), CH/UK
"La Vache"
(Horny Cows)
Ring, 2010
Cow horn, nail polish.
1.8 × 3 × 3 cm
© Andi Gut

164
Hackenberg, Gésine
(b. 1972), DE/NL
"Dressed for
Christmas Dinner"
Necklace, 2008
Ceramics, thread.
Bowl Ø 24 cm,
necklace L 45 cm
© Gésine Hackenberg

165
Hackenberg, Gésine
(b. 1972), DE/NL
"Ring out of a Bowl"
Ring, 2011
Ceramics, silver.
Bowl 15 × 14 × 5.5 cm,
ring 2 × 3 × 3 cm
© Gésine Hackenberg
The bowl "Flamingo"
was designed by Inger
Waage (1923–1995) for
Stavangerflint in 1955.
In production from 1958
to 1967.

163
Hackenberg, Gésine
(b. 1972), DE/NL.
"Kitchen Glass no. 26"
Brooch, 2012
Glass, ruthenium-
plated nickel silver.
11 × 6.5 × 2.5 cm
© Gésine Hackenberg

166
Hakim, Dana
(b. 1977), IL
"My Four
Guardian Angels"
Necklace, 2010
Found materials, metal,
textile, plastic. L 55 cm
© Dana Hakim

167, 168, 169, 170, 430
Hald, Lene (b. 1975), DK
"Illusion"
Brooch, 2008
Textile, rubber, pearls,
metal. Ø 3.7 cm
© Lene Hald

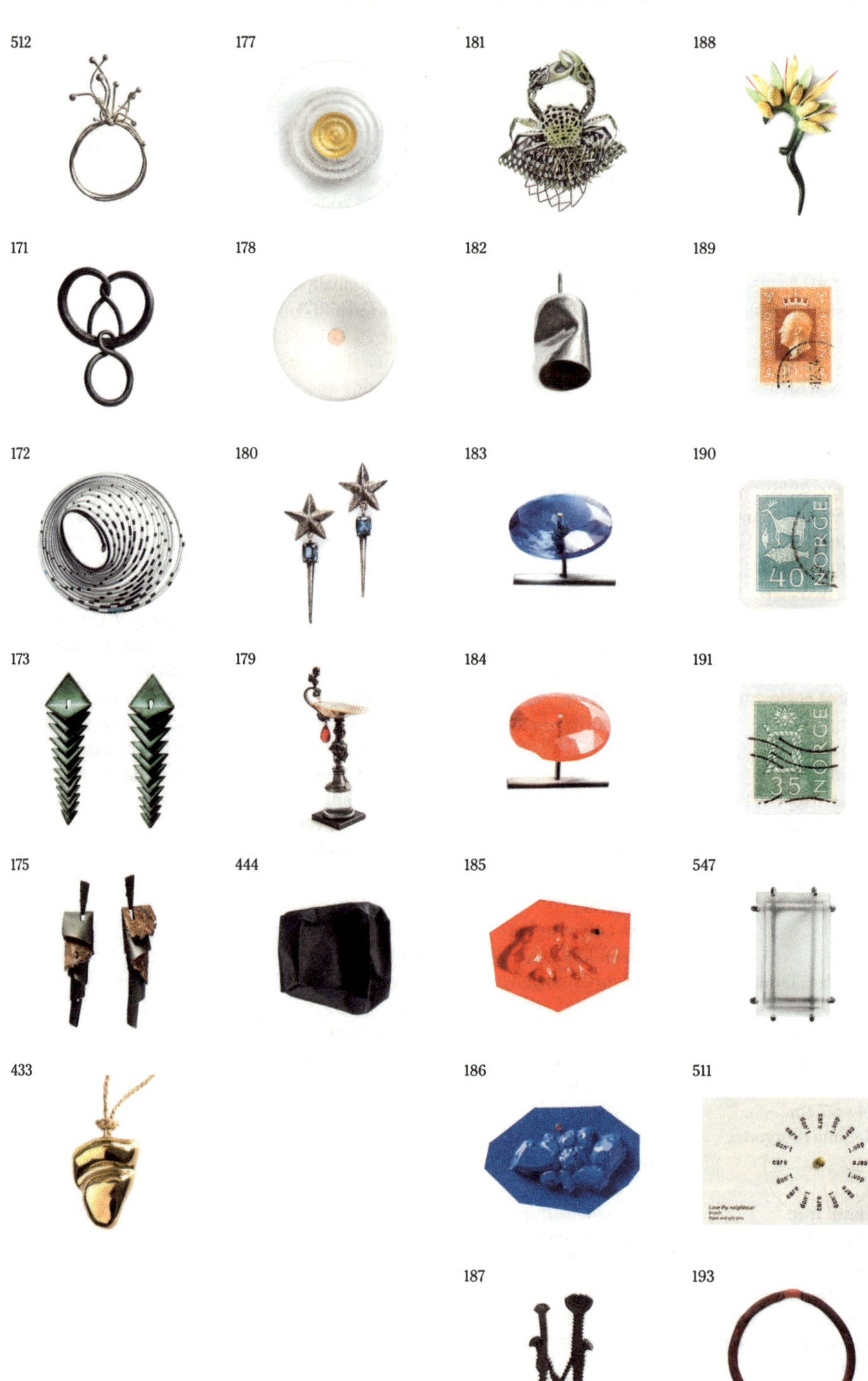

512

177

181

188

171

178

182

189

172

180

183

190

173

179

184

191

175

444

185

547

433

186

511

187

193

514

512
Hald, Lene (b. 1975), DK
"A Sketch Model"
Ring, 2010
Silver. L 3.5 cm
© Lene Hald

171
Hanagarth, Sophie
(b. 1968), CH/FR
"Pretzel Ring" from the
series *Serie-B*
Ring, 2007
Iron. 6 × 4 cm
© Sophie Hanagarth

172
Hanevold, Ingjerd
(b. 1955), NO
"Spiral Bracelet"
Bracelet, 1987
Anodised aluminium.
Ø 17 cm
© Ingjerd Hanevold

173
Hanevold, Ingjerd
(b. 1955), NO
Earrings, 1989
Patinated bronze.
8.6 × 3 × 3 cm
© Ingjerd Hanevold

175
Hanevold, Ingjerd
(b. 1955), NO
Earrings, 1993
Iron, oxidised silver.
13.3 × 2.9 × 2.7 cm
© Ingjerd Hanevold

433
Hangaard, Susanne
(b. 1972), DK
"Golden Shame"
Necklace, 2017
Glazed porcelain with
lustre, Japanese cotton
string. L 44 cm, pendant
3.5 × 3 × 1.5 cm
© Susanne Hangaard

177
Hansen, Castello
(b. 1965), DK/SE
Brooch, 2001
Acrylic, silver leaf,
gold leaf. Ø 6.8 cm
© Castello Hansen

178
Hansen, Castello
(b. 1965), DK/SE
Brooch, 2008
Cibatool, paint, recon-
structed pink coral.
Ø 8 cm
© Castello Hansen

180
Hardenberg, Torben
(b. 1949), DK
Earrings, 1988
Silver-plated copper,
synthetic sapphires.
9 × 3.5 × 1 cm
© Torben Hardenberg

179
Hardenberg, Torben
(b. 1949), DK
"Kirsten Munk's
Confectionery Bowl"
Object, 1988
Silver-plated and
patinated bronze,
baroque pearl, Plexi-
glass base, synthetic
ruby, amethyst, shell.
28 × 15.3 × 12 cm
© Torben Hardenberg

444
Hartel, Ann-Kathrin
(b. 1984), DE
"Fremdkörper"
(Foreign body)
Brooch, 2016
Textile, steel.
10.5 × 8 × 4.5 cm
© Ann-Kathrin Hartel

181
Hedman, Hanna
(b. 1980), SE
"Potamonautes lividus"
from the series *While
They Await Extinction*
Brooch, 2011
Oxidised silver, indus-
trial varnished copper,
colour. 20 × 16 × 3 cm
© Hanna Hedman

182
Heikkilä, Kimmo
(b. 1970), FI
Pin, 2002
Silver. 2.5 × 2.5 × 3.7 cm
© Kimmo Heikkilä

183, 184
Hermsen, Herman
(b. 1953), NL
"Glass Ring"
Ring, 1986
Glass, silver.
3 × 3.6 × 3.5 cm
© Herman Hermsen

185, 186
Hermsen, Herman
(b. 1953), NL
"Brilliant Touch"
Brooch, 2006
Coloured plastic, glass.
10.3 × 7.7 cm
© Herman Hermsen

187
Hint, Nils (b. 1986), EE
"Shadow"
Brooch, 2014
Iron, ready-made
screws. 10 × 4.5 cm
© Nils Hint

188
Hochlin, Elsie-Ann
(b. 1961), NO
"Cashew Nut"
Earrings, 1991
Wood. 16.2 × 10 × 5 cm
© Elsie-Ann Hochlin/
BONO, Oslo 2021

189, 190, 191
Hochlin, Elsie-Ann
(b. 1961), NO
Earrings, 1994
Laminated stamps.
3 × 2.5 cm, 3.8 × 3.1 cm
© Elsie-Ann Hochlin/
BONO, Oslo 2021

547
Hodne, Olaf Tønnesland
(b. 1990), NO
"Window (rectangle)"
Brooch, 2018
Manufactured
quartz, steel, silver.
5.7 × 3.8 × 1.8 cm
© Olaf Hodne
Tønnesland

511
Holmsteen, Birgitte
(b. 1975), DK
"Love Thy Neighbour"
Brooch, 2011
Paper, split pin.
15 × 10.5 cm
© Birgitte Holmsteen

193
Hoogeboom, Peter
(b. 1961), NL
"Bouncing Balls"
Necklace, 1998
Rubber. 20 × 16.5 cm
© Peter Hoogeboom/
BONO, Oslo 2021

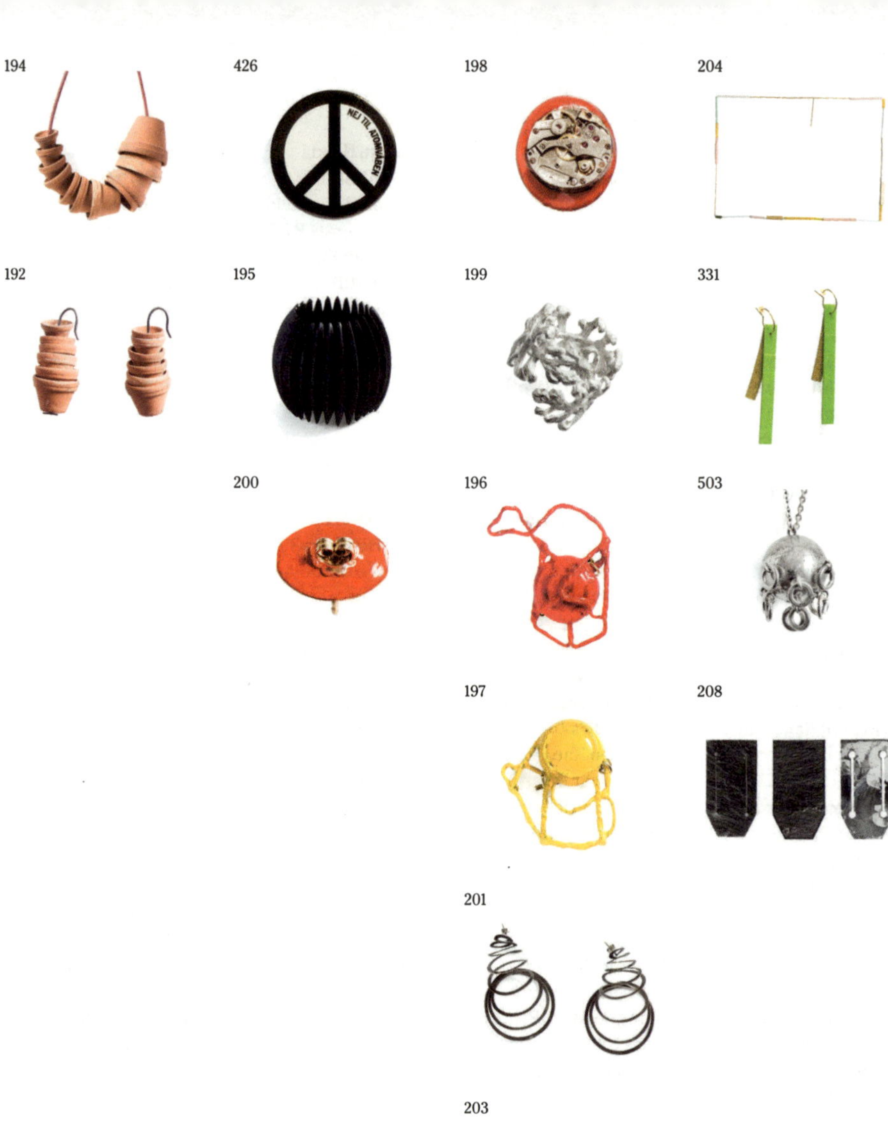

194

426

198

204

192

195

199

331

200

196

503

197

208

201

203

194
Hoogeboom, Peter
(b. 1961), NL
"Flowerpots"
Necklace, 2011
Terracotta, cord.
7.5 × 3.5 × 3.5 cm
© Peter Hoogeboom/
BONO, Oslo 2021
Made for Galerie Ra's
thirty-fifth anniversary,
for which the artists
were invited to create
a piece of jewellery
or object in a limited
edition.

192
Hoogeboom, Peter
(b. 1961), NL
"Pots"
Earrings, 2012
Terracotta, silver.
5.7 × 2.2 × 2.2 cm
© Peter Hoogeboom/
BONO, Oslo 2021
In the book *To Have and
to Hold. The Daalder
Collection of Contempo-
rary Jewellery* (2018),
Peter Hoogeboom says
about his choice of clay
as material: "Living in
a country built on clay
we reclaimed from the
sea made me realize I
worked with a material
far more precious than
gold or gems. And we
have been using clay
and ceramics to adorn
ourselves with from the
early dawn of man. It is
certainly not something
contemporary."

426
Holtom, Gerald
Campaign for Nuclear
Disarmament symbol
Ø 3,5 cm
Here with a text in
Danish text: "Nej til
atomvåben" (No to
nuclear weapon).
Badge, 1970s
In 1958 the British artist
Gerald Holtom designed
a symbol for the
Alderton march against
nuclear war. The logo
was a combination of
the letters "N" (two
arms outstretched
pointing down at 45
degrees) and "D" (one
arm raised above
the head) from the
semaphore alphabet
and quickly became the
symbol of the Campaign
for Nuclear Disarma-
ment. Soon it became
an international
emblem for anti-war
movements and was
universally associated
with peace.

195
Ijff, Janke (b. 1943), NL
Bracelet, 1985
Rubber. 10 × 12 cm
© Janke Ijff

200
Ishikawa, Mari
(b. 1964), JP/DE
"Memory"
Earrings, 2014
Clockwork, lacquer, 925
silver. 1.5 × 0.7 × 0.6 cm
© Mari Ishikawa

198
Ishikawa, Mari
(b. 1964), JP/DE
"Memory"
Pin, 2015
Clockwork,
lacquer, 925 silver.
2 × 1.5 × 0.5 cm
© Mari Ishikawa

199
Ishikawa, Mari
(b. 1964), JP/DE
"Shadow"
Ring, 2015
925 silver. H 1.5 cm
© Mari Ishikawa

196, 197
Ishikawa, Mari
(b. 1964), JP/DE
"Celebration"
Brooch, 2016
Champagne agrafe,
pigment, latex,
gold-plated brass.
5.5 × 5.5 × 1 cm
© Mari Ishikawa

201
Ishiyama, Reiko
(b. 1942), JP/US
Earrings, 1995
Silver. L 8 cm
© Reiko Ishiyama

203
Jilsøy, Grethe
(b. 1949), NO
"Show Off"
Ring, 1989
Rubber, acrylic.
17 × 4.6 × 5 cm
© Grethe Jilsøy/
BONO, Oslo 2021

204
Johansson, Karin
(b. 1964), SE
"Shortcut II"
Necklace, 2013
Gold, enamel, recon-
structed material,
acrylic. L 54 cm
© Karin Johansson/
BONO, Oslo 2021

331
Johansson, Karin
(b. 1964), SE
Earrings, 2016
Gold, acrylic. L 8 cm
© Karin Johansson/
BONO, Oslo 2021

503
Juhls Silver Gallery, NO
"Šiella" (Protection)/
"Komsekule"
(Cradle ball)
Necklace, 1960–/1985
925 silver. Ball Ø 3 cm
Juhls Silver Gallery
was established in
Kautokeino (Guovda-
geaidnu in Sami) in
Finnmark in 1959 by
Regine Juhls (b. 1939)
of Germany and Frank
Juhls (1931–2020) of
Denmark. "Komsekule"
is today associated
with Sami culture and
tradition and is used as
an amulet.
© Juhls Sølvsmie

208
Jung, Junwon
(b. 1978), KR/DE
Brooch, 2014
Titanium, zinc,
slate, silver, steel.
9.5 × 5.5 × 10.1 cm
© Junwon Jung

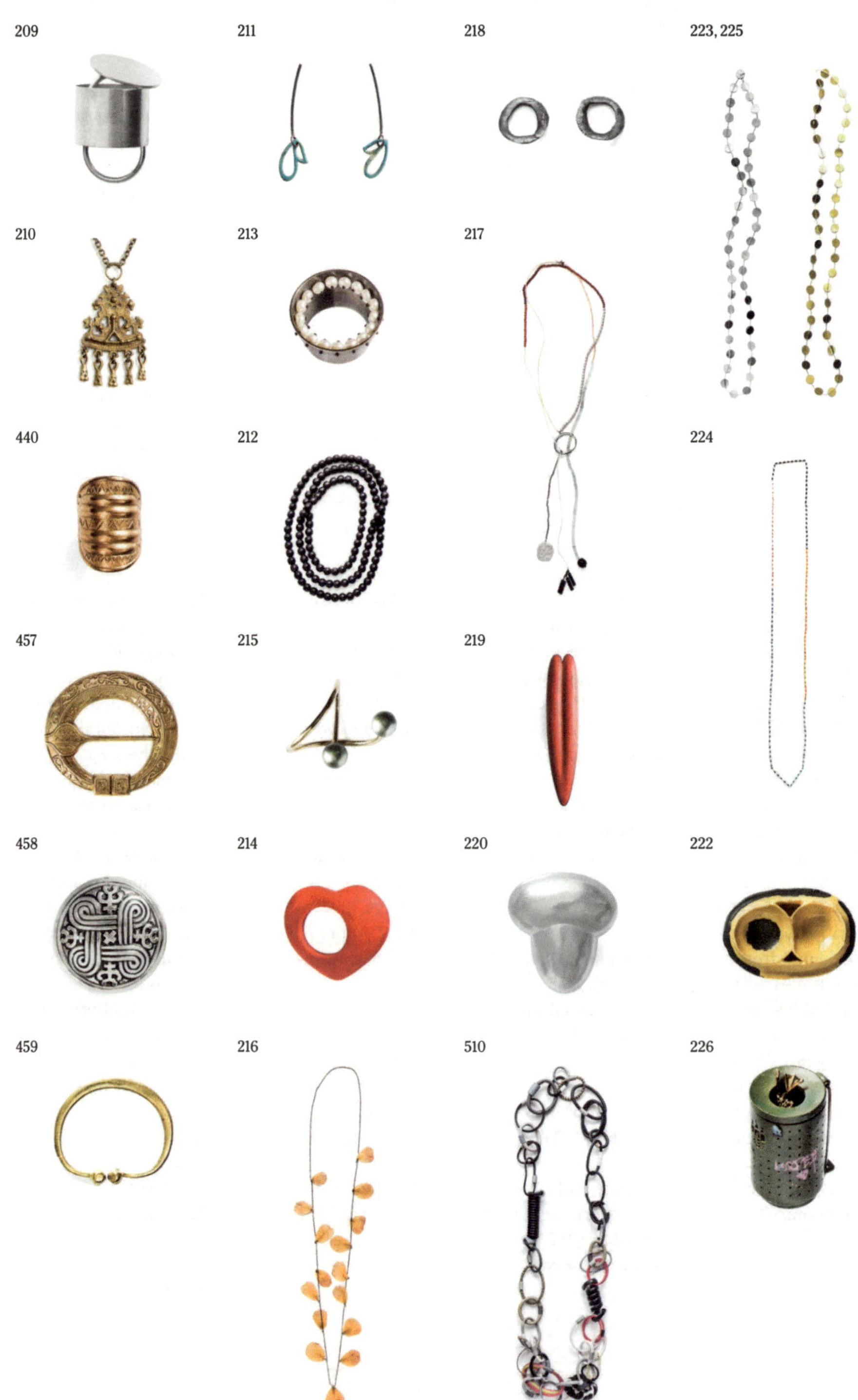

209

210

211

213

218

217

223, 225

440

212

224

457

215

219

458

214

220

222

459

216

510

226

518

209
Jung, Junwon
(b. 1978), KR
Ring, 2016
Silver. H 2 cm, Ø 2.5 cm
© Junwon Jung
Junwon Jung is famous
for his works of techni-
cal refinement: there is
a surprising effect when
the box turns into a ring.
The ring can be worn
with and without the
cylinder shape.

210
Kalevala Koru, FI
"Karkun riipus"
(Runaway pendant)
Necklace, 1971
Bronze. L 67 cm,
pendant 5.5 × 8 cm

440
Kalevala Koru, FI
Ring 111, 1970s
Bronze. H 2.7 cm
The ring is based on a
ring from the 12th cen-
tury found in Yliskylä,
Perniö, in Finland.

457
Kalevala Koru, FI
Brooch/fibula 169, 1970s
Bronze. 7.3 × 8 cm

458
Kalevala Koru, FI
Brooch, 1970s
925 silver. Ø 5.3 cm

459
Kalevala Koru, FI
Fibula, 1970s
Bronze. 5 × 6 cm

211
Kerr, Susan
(b. 1980), UK
Earrings, 2004
Silver, enamel. L 4 cm
© Susan Kerr

213
Klemm, Susanne
(b. 1965), CH/NL
"Conic" from the series
Deep Blue
Ring, 2003
Pearls, silver.
H 1.2 cm, Ø 2.5 cm
© Susanne Klemm

212
Klemm, Susanne
(b. 1965), CH/NL
"Caviar"
Necklace, 2011
Polyolefin. L 300 cm
© Susanne Klemm

215
Kløve, Jytte
(b. 1949), DK
"Two-Finger-Ring", 2007
Gold, Tahiti pearls.
4 × 4 × 4 cm
© Jytte Kløve/
BONO, Oslo 2021

214
Kløve, Jytte
(b. 1949), DK
"Heart Ring", 2011
Rubber. 3.8 × 4.5 × 1.5 cm
© Jytte Kløve/
BONO, Oslo 2021

216
Knobel, Esther
(b. 1949 PL), IL
Necklace, 1994
Laminated rose petals,
silver chain. L 62 cm
Unlimited edition
© Esther Knobel

218
Koh, Heeseung
(b. 1967), KR
Earrings, 2008
Oxidised silver. Ø 2 cm
© Heeseung Koh

217
Koh, Heeseung
(b. 1967), KR
Necklace, 2008
Glass beads, oxidised
silver. L 59 cm
© Heeseung Koh

219
Korssjøen, Synnøve
(b. 1949), NO
Brooch, 1992
Copper, enamel.
11.5 × 2.5 × 0.6 cm
© Synnøve Korssjøen/
BONO, Oslo 2021

220
Korssjøen, Synnøve
(b. 1949), NO
Brooch, 2000
Silver. 5.5 × 5.4 × 1.5 cm
© Synnøve Korssjøen/
BONO, Oslo 2021

510
Koshenkova, Maria
(b. 1981), RU/DK
"Voltage"
Necklace, 2009–12
Recycled plastic wires
and cables. L 46 cm
© Maria Koshenkova

223, 225
Kouswijk, Manon van
(b. 1967), NL/AU
"Paper Pearls"
Neckpiece, 2000/2013
Paper. L 35 cm
© Manon van Kouswijk

224
Kouswijk, Manon van
(b. 1967), NL/AU
"Out of the Office"
Necklace, 2012
Cotton, plastic sheath-
ing from industrially
produced paperclips.
L 40 cm
Multiple
© Manon van Kouswijk
Manon van Kouswijk
straightens the
paperclips, removes
the plastic covers,
cuts them into pieces
and strings them on
a thread, a working
method she has
described as goldsmith-
ing with stationery.

222
Kouswijk, Manon van
(b. 1967), NL/AU
"Ornamental Residue"
Brooch, 2013
Porcelain. 3.5 × 5.5 cm
© Manon van Kouswijk

226
Kristensen, Marie-
Louise (b. 1971), DK
"Cph: Faire la fête –
et après"
Brooch, 2011
Second-hand 14 ct
gold ring, brass.
4 × 2.2 × 2.5 cm
© Marie-Louise
Kristensen

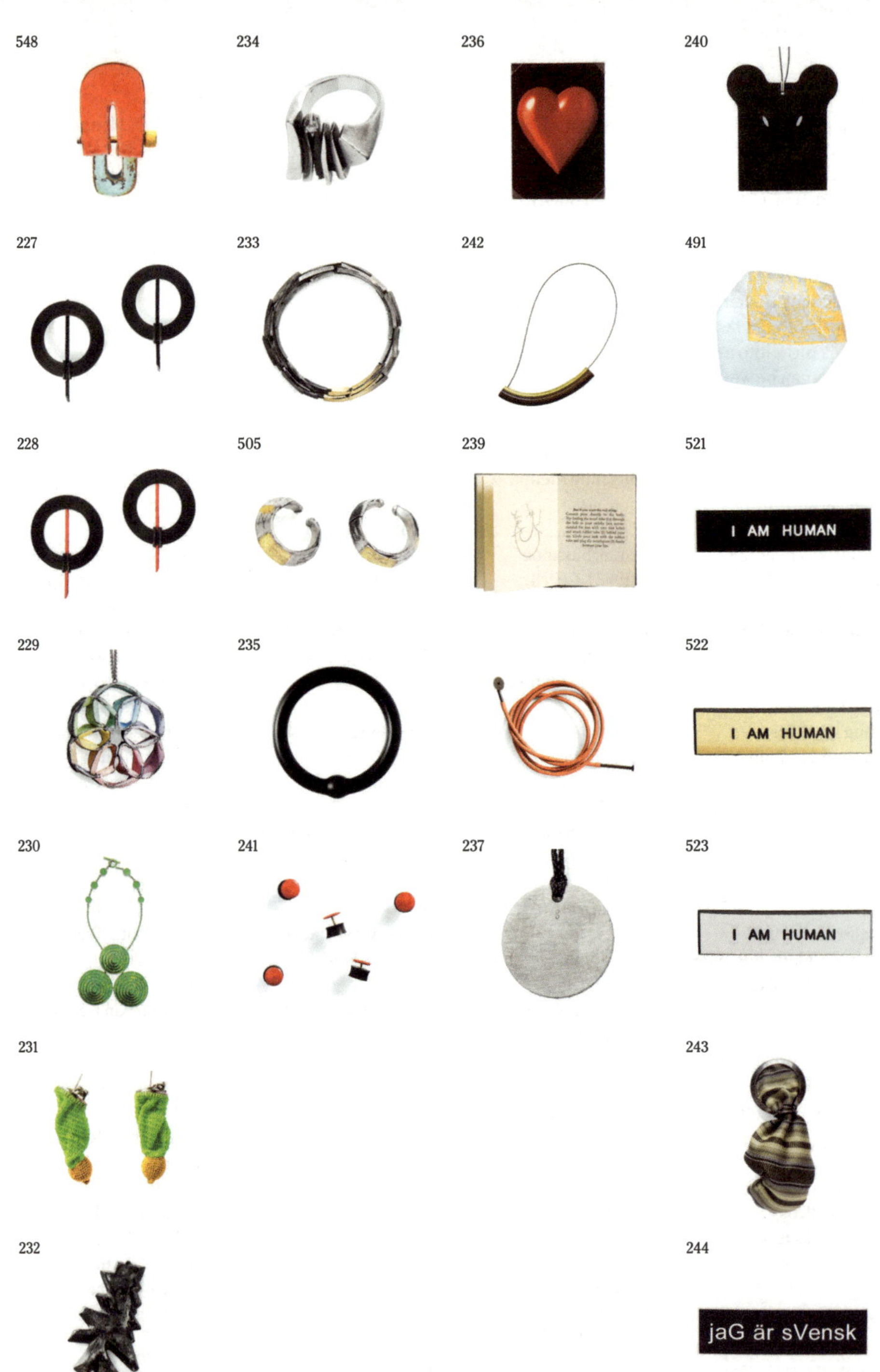

548
234
236
240
227
233
242
491
228
505
239
521
I AM HUMAN
229
235
522
I AM HUMAN
230
241
237
523
I AM HUMAN
231
243
232
244
jaG är sVensk

548
Kroeger, Jamie R.
(b. 1976), CA
"Linked 1"
Brooch, 2019
Copper, enamel.
10 × 6.2 × 2.5 cm
© Jamie R. Kroeger

227, 228
Krogh, Fie von
(b. 1956), NO
Earrings, 1991
Wood, rubber.
8.8 × 6.5 cm
© Fie von Krogh/
BONO, Oslo 2021

229
Kruger, Daniel
(b. 1951), ZA/DE
Necklace, 2011
Silver, pigment.
2.5 × 8 × 8 cm
© Daniel Kruger

230
Kruger, Daniel
(b. 1951), ZA/DE
Necklace, 2011
Silver, pigment.
14 × 12 × 3.5 cm
© Daniel Kruger

231
Kruger, Daniel
(b. 1951), ZA/DE
Earrings, 2016
Crocheted silk, glass
balls, silver. 5.5 × 2 cm
© Daniel Kruger

232
Krüger, Winfried
(b. 1944), DE
Brooch, 1984
Papier-mâché.
24 × 12 cm
© Winfried Krüger

234
Kræn, Anette
(b. 1945), DK
Ring, 1995
Diamond, silver, gilt
silver. 2 × 2.2 × 2.6 cm
© Anette Kræn

233
Kræn, Anette
(b. 1945), DK
"The Play of Light in the
Sea When the Eyes Are
Narrowed"
Necklace, 1999
Horsehair, oxidised
silver, lacquer, gold leaf.
Ø 17 cm
© Anette Kræn

505
Kræn, Anette
(b. 1945), DK
Earrings, 2000
Silver, gold leaf.
2.7 × 2.7 × 0.9 cm
© Anette Kræn

235
Künzli, Otto
(b. 1948), CH/DE
"Gold Makes You Blind"
Bracelet, 1980–
Synthetic rubber over
18 ct gold sphere.
Ø 8.3 cm
© Otto Künzli/
BONO, Oslo 2021

241
Künzli, Otto
(b. 1948), CH/DE
"The Red Dot"
Pin, 1980–
Drawing pin, rubber.
Ø 0.9 cm
© Otto Künzli/
BONO, Oslo 2021

236
Künzli, Otto
(b. 1948), CH/DE
"Postcard Brooch", 1981
Paper, plastic,
elastic, metal.
14.8 × 10.5 × 0.6 cm
© Otto Künzli/
BONO, Oslo 2021
The motive on the
postcard is the brooch
"Heart" by Künzli from
1985.

242
Künzli, Otto
(b. 1948), CH/DE
"Fragment"
Necklace, 1986
Demolished picture
frame, wood, gold leaf.
39 × 25 × 3 cm
© Otto Künzli/
BONO, Oslo 2021

239
Künzli, Otto
(b. 1948), CH/DE
"The Manhattan Piece",
no. 178 (out of 350)
Body piece, 1987
Dannemann cigarillos
box, brass, rubber, resin
(Ureol), paper, linen
(book). 11.3 × 8.7 × 1.5 cm
© Otto Künzli/
BONO, Oslo 2021

237
Künzli, Otto
(b. 1948), CH/DE
"Change"
Pendant, 2003–05
Silver. Ø 3.5 cm
© Otto Künzli/
BONO, Oslo 2021

240
Künzli, Otto
(b. 1948), CH/DE
"Blape pendant", 2010
MDF, "Faluner" Black,
lace. 9.5 × 8.5 × 0.4 cm
Edition of 40
© Otto Künzli/
BONO, Oslo 2021

491
Kuramoto, Yoko
(b. 1972), JP
Brooch, 2002
Glass, gold leaf.
6.5 × 6 cm
© Yoko Kuramoto

521, 522, 523
Laitinen, Auli
(b. 1967), SE
"I Am Human"
Brooch, 2001
Plastic, steel. 2 × 6.5 cm
© Auli Laitinen/
BONO, Oslo 2021

243
Laitinen, Auli
(b. 1967), SE
Brooch, 2004
Textile (tie), silver.
L 14 cm
© Auli Laitinen/
BONO, Oslo 2021

244
Laitinen, Auli
(b. 1967), SE
"Jag är svensk"
(I Am Swedish)
Brooch, 2012
Plastic, steel. 2.2 × 8 cm
© Auli Laitinen/
BONO, Oslo 2021

245   248   250   254

247   246   253   256

258

529   252   257

249   251   259

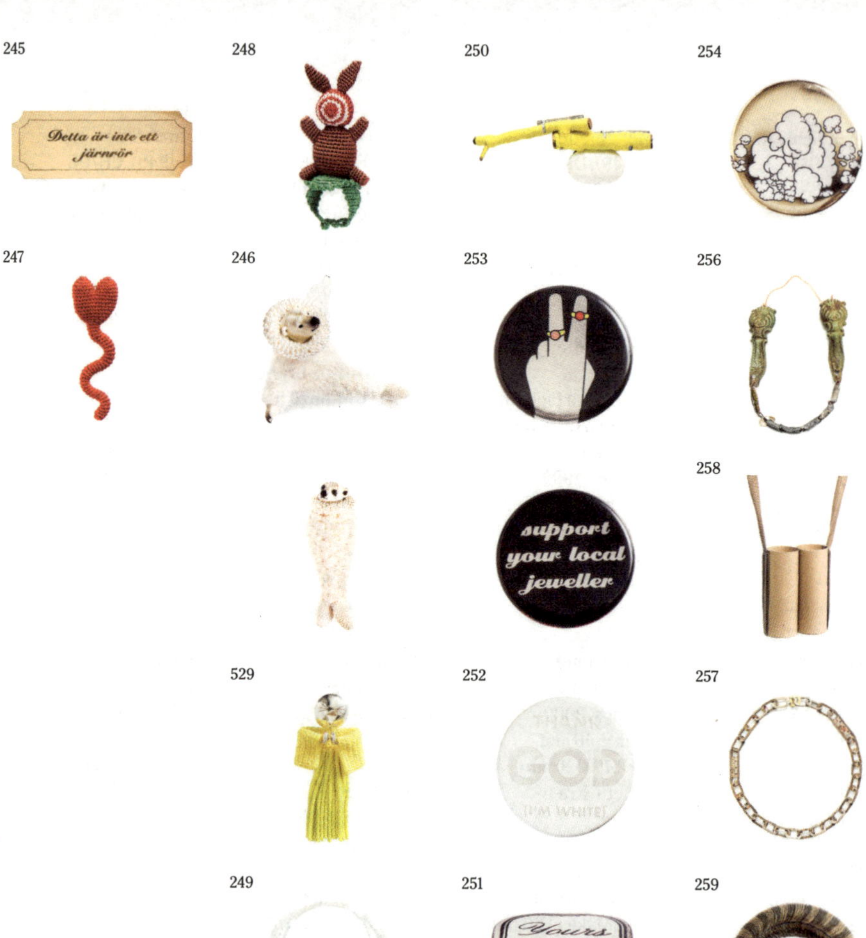

245
Laitinen, Auli
(b. 1967), SE
"Detta är inte ett
järnrör" (This Is Not
an Iron Pipe)
Brooch, 2016
Brass. 2.5 × 6.5 cm
© Auli Laitinen/
BONO, Oslo 2021
The text on the brooch
refers to the "Iron pipe
scandal" in Sweden.
In 2012 the newspaper
Expressen revealed how
three leading politicians
from the right-wing
party Sverigedemokra-
terna had ventured out
one night two years
before. With iron pipes
in their hands and with
racist and derogatory
words, they threat-
ened the comedian
Soran Ismail and his
friends as well as a very
intoxicated man for no
reason. Full of lies, they
initially rejected the
claims of provocative
behaviour, but their
own mobile recordings
revealed them.

247
Leest, Felieke van der
(b. 1968), NL/NO
"Sperm Heart"
Brooch, 1996–
Textiles, rubber, metal
safety pin. 8 × 2.5 × 1 cm
Unlimited edition
© Felieke van der Leest

248
Leest, Felieke van der
(b. 1968), NL/NO
"Target Rabbit"
Ring, 2002
Textiles. 8 × 3 × 2.5 cm
© Felieke van der Leest

246
Leest, Felieke van der
(b. 1968), NL/NO
"Pregnant Polar Bear"
Object with brooch,
2005
Textiles, plastic
animals, silver, plastic
beads. 14 × 11.5 × 4, bear
cub 10 × 3.5 × 3.5 cm
© Felieke van der Leest

529
Leest, Felieke van der
(b. 1968), NL/NO
"Canary"
Brooch, 2018
Textiles, glass beads,
silver. 8.5 × 4 × 2 cm
© Felieke van der Leest
Written on the reverse:
"Jorunn Veiteberg
Honourable Member of
Felieke's Canary Choir"

249
Lefebvre, Lise
(b. 1984), FR/NL
"Colier de perles"
Necklace, 2007
Textiles. 27.5 × 25.7 cm
© Lise Lefebvre
The pearl necklace is an
iconic classic necklace;
here it is translated
into a flat, laser-cut
textile version. Using
a digitally controlled
laser beam, the edges of
the necklace are melted
away from the textile.

250
Lehtinen, Helena
(b. 1952), FI
From the series
Landscapes
Brooch, 2009
Wood, thread, silver,
stone. 15 × 6.5 × 3 cm
© Helena Lehtinen

253
Lignel, Benjamin
(b. 1972), FR
"Support your
Local Jeweller"
Set of two badges, 2006
Aluminium, steel,
acetate. Ø 3 cm
© Benjamin Lignel

252
Lignel, Benjamin
(b. 1972), FR
"Manifest (Thank God)"
Badge, 2008
Gold-plated metal,
acetate, paper. Ø 5.6 cm
© Benjamin Lignel

251
Lignel, Benjamin
(b. 1972), FR
"Manifest (I Am)"
Set of two brooches, to
be worn separately or
one inside the other,
2009. Second-hand
metal box (screen-
printed), steel, fine gold.
3.3 × 4 × 1.5 cm
© Benjamin Lignel

254
Lignel, Benjamin
(b. 1972), FR
"La Disparition,
Saison 2, épisode 2"
(The Disappearance,
Season 2, Episode 2)
Brooch/badge, 2010
Steel, gold, industrial
paint, screen-printing
ink, acetate. Ø 5.6 cm
© Benjamin Lignel

256
Lillebostad, Sissel
(b. 1958), NO
Necklace, 2015
Found materials from
the beach. 40 × 24 × 4 cm
© Sissel Lillebostad

258
Lindberg, Kajsa
(b. 1980), SE
"Every Day –
Binoculars"
Necklace, 2008
Copper, textile, paint.
40 × 8 × 4 cm
© Kajsa Lindberg/
BONO, Oslo 2021

257
Lindberg, Kajsa
(b. 1980), SE
"Standard Graphs"
Necklace, 2012–13
Reworked folding rule.
L 33 cm
© Kajsa Lindberg/
BONO, Oslo 2021

259
Linssen, Nel
(1935–2016), NL
Bracelet, 1996
Paper. H 2.3 cm, Ø 9 cm
© Heirs of Nel Linssen

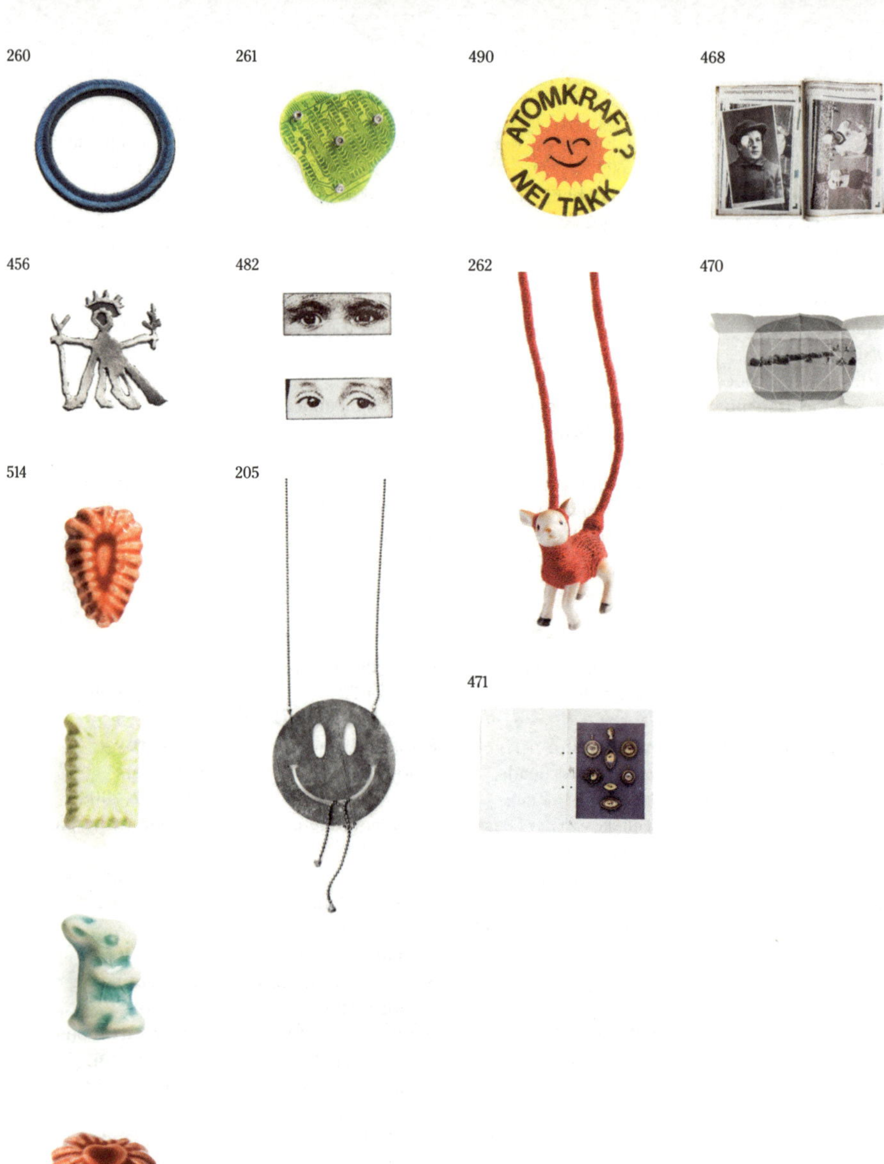

260
261
490
ATOMKRAFT ?
NEI TAKK
468
456
482
262
470
514
205
471
524

260
Linssen, Nel
(1935–2016), NL
Necklace, 2004
Paper. H 1.6 cm, Ø 19 cm
© Heirs of Nel Linssen

456
LOOC/
Lillehammer OL, NO
"Máhttaráhkku"
(Mother Earth)
Pin, 1993
Metal. 3.2 × 2.5 cm
During the 1994 Winter
Olympics in Lilleham-
mer, Norway, it became
very popular to collect
pins. This was the pin
for the Olympics cul-
tural programme.

514
Lothe, Linda Jansson
(b. 1963), SE/NO
"Sweets"
Three brooches and
one ring, 1999
Porcelain, metal.
Brooches 3 × 2 cm,
ring 3 × 3 cm
© Linda Jansson Lothe/
BONO, Oslo 2021

261
Luihn, Camilla
(b. 1968), NO
"Intercom"
Brooch, 1996/97
Paper, plastic.
5 × 5 × 1 cm
© Camilla Luihn/
BONO, Oslo 2021
The brooch is affixed to
the skin with a sticker.
It was part of the group
exhibition *Asteroids
– An Extraterrestrial
Exhibition* at RAM
gallery in Oslo in 1997.
The exhibition was rich
in references to science
fiction, video games,
comic books and NASA
reports, and the jewel-
lery was displayed in
UFO-like containers and
in luminous globes.

482
Luihn, Camilla
(b. 1968), NO
"The Aleppo Piece"
Two brooches, 2016
Enamel, mixed media.
1.5 × 4 cm
© Camilla Luihn/
BONO, Oslo 2021

205
Luihn, Camilla
(b. 1968), NO
"Places I've Been,
Things I've Seen"
Pendant, 2018/2020
Recycled, oxidised zinc,
oxidised silver. L 50 cm,
pendant 8 cm
© Camilla Luihn/
BONO, Oslo 2021

490
Lund, Anne (f, 1954), DK
«Atomkraft? Nei takk»
Jakkemerke, 1975
Ø 3,8 cm
The smiling sun is the
logo of the Danish
Organisation OOA
– Organisationen til
Oplysning om Atom-
kraft (Organisation
for Information about
Nuclear Power). It is
today used at protests
all over the world. Anne
Lund was only a 21 years
old student and activist
when she designed the
symbol.

262
Løvhaug, Anne Lene
(b. 1974), NO
"Trophy"
Necklace, 2003
Porcelain figure, wool.
L 34 cm
© Anne Lene Løvhaug

471
Mackert, Suska
(b. 1969), DE
"Atlas 15"
From the series *Eine
Ordnung des Glanzes*
Printed object, 2014
29 × 21 cm
Graphic design:
Christine Alberts
© Suska Mackert
Every effort has been
made by the artist to
credit the authors of all
the photographs and
images reproduced
from these publica-
tions. In most cases,
the images were cut-out
from daily newspapers.

468
Mackert, Suska
(b. 1969), DE
"Augen" (Eyes)
From the series *Eine
Ordnung des Glanzes*
Printed object, 2014
42 × 28.5 cm
Photography: Johannes
Kersting
Graphic design:
Christine Alberts
© Suska Mackert
The image pictured
is a photo of Anton
Tschechow from 1883,
when he was 23 years
old. Original news-
paper image source:
*Frankfurter Allgemeine
Zeitung*, culture images.

470
Mackert, Suska
(b. 1969), DE
"Diamond"
From the series *Eine
Ordnung des Glanzes*
Printed object, 2014
21 × 14.6 cm
Edition 17/80
Image source: Archives
Groupe De Beers,
Kimberley
Graphic design:
Christine Alberts
© Suska Mackert

469 264 280 273

263 271 272

274 281

279 275

276

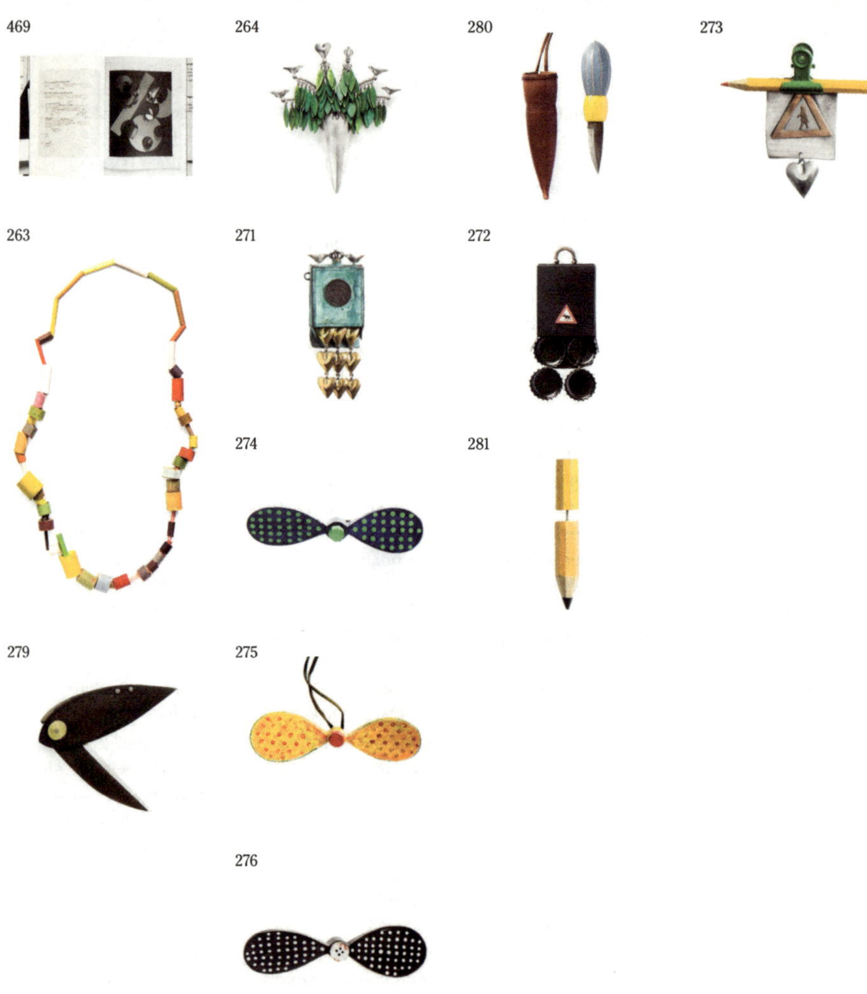

469
Mackert, Suska
(b. 1969), DE
"The Andy Warhol
Collection"
From the series *Eine
Ordnung des Glanzes*
Printed object, 2014
28.6 × 22 cm
Edition 17/80
Photography:
Johannes Kersting/
Gert Jan van Rooij
Graphic design:
Christine Alberts
© Suska Mackert

263
Marsland, Sally
(b. 1969), AU
Necklace, 2013
Polyurethane resin,
powdered pigment.
L 57 cm
© Sally Marsland

279
Mehus, Konrad
(b. 1941), NO
"Jackknife", 1985
Old file, steel, brass.
2.2 × 7.6 × 0.6 cm,
unfolded 11.1 cm
© Konrad Mehus/
BONO, Oslo 2021
Knife-smiths regard file
steel as good steel for
blades. But making a
good jackknife is easier
said than done. The
folding mechanism
requires a spring made
from sprung steel,
and this steel needs
to be tempered very
precisely if it is to serve
its purpose.

264
Mehus, Konrad
(b. 1941), NO
"Carrot *sølje*"
Brooch, 1991
Silver, wood.
13.4 × 13.5 × 1.2 cm
© Konrad Mehus/
BONO, Oslo 2021

271
Mehus, Konrad
(b. 1941), NO
"Poor Man's Silver with
Golden Hearts"
Brooch, 1991
Patinated copper, silver,
coin. 11.7 × 5 × 1.8 cm
© Konrad Mehus/
BONO, Oslo 2021

274, 275
Mehus, Konrad
(b. 1941), NO
"Propeller"
Bow tie, 1991
Painted wood,
leather cord. Blue
3.5 × 13.5 × 2 cm,
yellow 4.1 × 13.5 × 2 cm
© Konrad Mehus/
BONO, Oslo 2021

276
Mehus, Konrad
(b. 1941), NO
"Propeller"
Bow tie, 1991
Painted wood, mother-
of-pearl button, leather
cord. 4.2 × 15 × 2.2 cm
© Konrad Mehus/
BONO, Oslo 2021

280
Mehus, Konrad
(b. 1941), NO
"Sheath Knife", 1991
Leather, steel, painted
wood. 16.5 × 4.3 × 3.8 cm
© Konrad Mehus/
BONO, Oslo 2021

272
Mehus, Konrad
(b. 1941), NO
"Temporary Brooch"
from the series *Poor
Man's Silver*, 1991
Painted cardboard,
painted beer-bottle
caps, wood, safety pin.
14 × 6 × 2 cm
© Konrad Mehus/
BONO, Oslo 2021

281
Mehus, Konrad
(b. 1941), NO
"Ear Pencil", 1992
Ready-made pencil.
L 5.2 cm
© Konrad Mehus/
BONO, Oslo 2021

273
Mehus, Konrad
(b. 1941), NO
"Lotte, Lotte liten"
Brooch, 1992
Silver, copper, ready-
mades. 7.5 × 7.5 × 2 cm
© Konrad Mehus/
BONO, Oslo 2021
This brooch is Mehus's
comment to a negative
newspaper review he
received from the critic
Lotte Sandberg. The
brooch is shaped like
a writing pad. A red
pencil is also in place.
Everything is ready
for the critic to start
writing. But a heart
hangs from the writing
pad to remind the critic
to write from the heart.
A road sign depicting
a walking female figure
warns road users to
display caution when
the critic is out and
about. On the back
of the brooch, he has
engraved the words
"Lotte, Lotte liten"
(Lotte, Little Lotte). The
phonetic resemblance
evokes associations
with the chorus of the
Norwegian children's
song "Lasse, Lasse
liten":

*The world is so big,
so big,
Lasse, little Lasse
Much bigger than
you think,
Lasse, little Lasse.*

266

278

283

284

282a

267

269

282b

268

270

282c

277

265

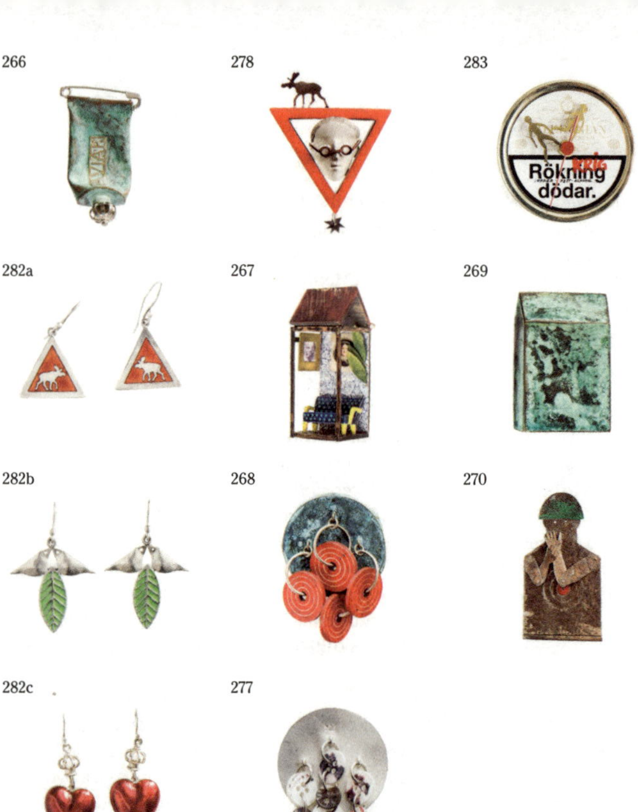

266
Mehus, Konrad
(b. 1941), NO
"Food Container"
from the series
Poor Man's Silver
Brooch, 1993
Patinated copper.
7.7 × 5.1 × 2.3 cm
© Konrad Mehus/
BONO, Oslo 2021

282
Mehus, Konrad
(b. 1941), NO
Earrings, 1994
925 silver, enamel.
Sign 2 × 2 cm, heart
4.5 × 2.5 × 1.2 cm,
bird 3.5 × 3 cm
Design for David-
Andersen
© Konrad Mehus/
BONO, Oslo 2021

265
Mehus, Konrad
(b. 1941), NO
"Valium" from the series
*Norwegian Popular
Medicine*
Brooch, 1998
Silvered bronze.
11.5 × 4.3 × 1.5 cm
© Konrad Mehus/
BONO, Oslo 2021
Medicine is a very
private matter. Going
around with a pill box
on one's chest that con-
tains clear information
about one's diagnosis
and dosage is to make
something intimate
and secret visible to
everyone. The text on
this box reads: "Konrad
Mehus: 1 tablet if
needed up to 3 times
daily".

278
Mehus, Konrad
(b. 1941), NO
"Warning Sign"
Brooch, 1998
Silver, copper, perspex.
8.6 × 6.7 × 0.3 cm
© Konrad Mehus/
BONO, Oslo 2021
A self-portrait of the
artist.

267
Mehus, Konrad
(b. 1941), NO
"Mark Replies: Two
Rooms and a Kitchen"
Brooch, 1999
Copper, wood, paper.
11.5 × 4.6 × 4 cm
© Konrad Mehus/
BONO, Oslo 2021

268
Mehus, Konrad
(b. 1941), NO
"Box *sølje*, red"
Brooch, 2005
Patinated copper, wood.
Ø 6.1 × 2.4 cm
© Konrad Mehus/
BONO, Oslo 2021

277
Mehus, Konrad
(b. 1941), NO
"Children *sølje*"
Brooch, 2010
Silver, mother-of-pearl
buttons. Ø 4.5 cm
© Konrad Mehus/
BONO, Oslo 2021

283
Mehus, Konrad
(b. 1941), NO
"Death and the Curse"
Wall clock, 2011
Box for pipe tobacco,
clockwork, brass.
Ø 10 cm
© Konrad Mehus/
BONO, Oslo 2021

269
Mehus, Konrad
(b. 1941), NO
"House"
Brooch, 2011
Patinated copper, silver.
5.3 × 3 × 2 cm
© Konrad Mehus/
BONO, Oslo 2021

270
Mehus, Konrad
(b. 1941), NO
"Bullet Catcher"
Brooch, 2020
Iron, paint, brass.
9.6 × 5.2 cm
© Konrad Mehus/
BONO, Oslo 2021

284
Melland, Nanna
(b. 1969), NO
"Swarm"
Brooch, 2012
Aluminium. 7.6 × 6 cm
© Nanna Melland/
BONO, Oslo 2021
In January 2013,
Melland made an
installation with 5,500
aeroplane forms at
Deichmanske, Oslo
Public Library. A much
smaller version was
exhibited at *Schmuck
2013*. The viewers were
invited to purchase a
piece from the instal-
lation, pin it on their
clothing and move back
into the world with a
heightened sense of
their place within the
global mass, the very
fragility of co-exist-
ence and a symbiotic
relationship to others
who have been engaged
in the same action.
The artist claims that
the airplane motif isn't
just about the theme of
global air traffic, since
flying is a corollary
to human existence,
through birds, through
the longing for freedom,
and today it is part of
everyday life.

518

450

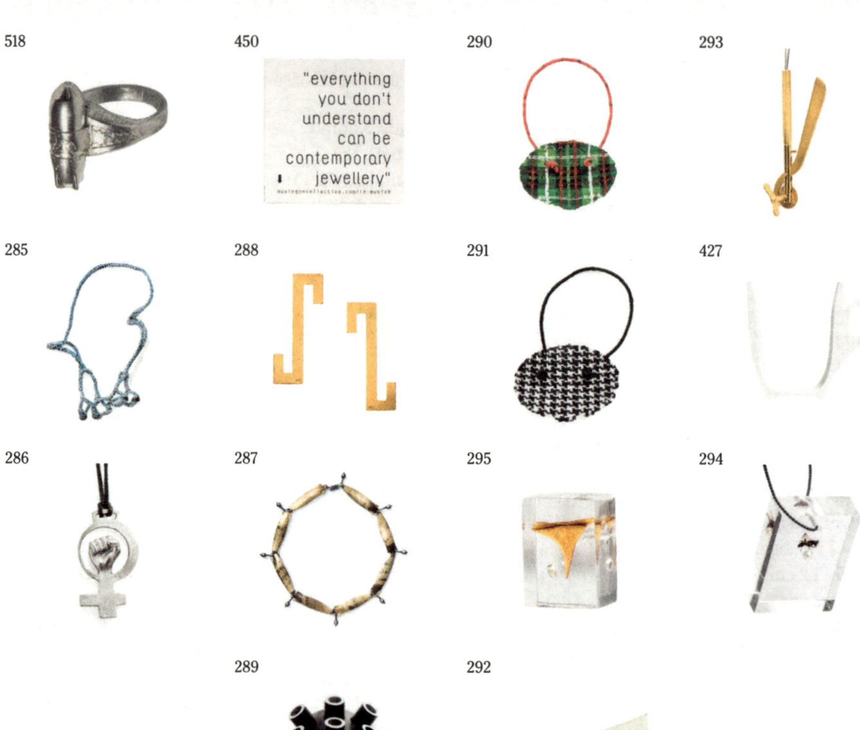

290

293

285

288

291

427

286

287

295

294

289

292

518
Melland, Nanna
(b. 1969), NO
"Ring of Ignorance",
2018
Tin. 3 × 2.5 cm
© Nanna Melland/
BONO, Oslo 2021
The ring is a cast of the
original "Lone Ranger
Atomic Ring" from 1947.

285
Minewaki, Mikiko
(b. 1967), JA
"Dino"
Necklace, 2015
Toy animal (dinosaur).
L 28 cm
© Mikiko Minewaki

286
Misje, B., NO
Women's Liberation
Symbol
Pendant, 1975
Tin. L 7.5 cm

450
Moving On Collective,
UK
"Everything You
Don't Understand
Can Be Contemporary
Jewellery"
Sticker, 2013
10 × 9.5 cm
The Collective was
started by students
on the MA Goldsmith-
ing, Silversmithing,
Metalwork & Jewellery
course at the Royal
College of Art in London
in the spring of 2013.
Their aim was to open
up the discussion about
the knowledge and
accessibility of art jew-
ellery through different
types of events.

288
Naur, Mikala
(b. 1957), NO
Earrings, 1987
Gilded brass. L 6.7 cm
© Mikala Naur

287
Naur, Mikala
(b. 1957), NO
Necklace, 1993
Brass (Abu Garcia
Toby 7g lures made in
Taiwan), freshwater
pearls, silver. Ø 17 cm
© Mikala Naur

289
Nippierd, Louise
(b. 1962), NO
Ring, 1999
Aluminium.
2.8 × 2.6 × 3.5 cm
© Louise Nippierd

290
Norton, Shelley
(b. 1961), NZ
"Breastplate"
Necklace, 2014
Plastic.
27.5 × 18 cm,
plate 12.5 × 18 cm
© Shelley Norton

291
Norton, Shelley
(b. 1961), NZ
"Breastplate
(Houndstooth)"
Necklace, 2014
Plastic.
28 × 20 cm,
plate 14 × 20 cm
© Shelley Norton

295
Noten, Ted (b. 1956), NL
"Piepjes" (Pip)
Pin, 1995–
Rose thorn, dia-
mond, acrylic, steel.
1.2 × 0.9 × 0.6 cm
Unlimited edition
© Ted Noten/
BONO, Oslo 2021

292
Noten, Ted (b. 1956), NL
"Mercedes Benz Brooch
no. 152"
Brooch, 2001
Steel. 2.8 × 7.5 × 1.4 cm
© Ted Noten/
BONO, Oslo 2021
The piece is cut out
by hand from a new
Mercedes-Benz E-class
210, 2001.

293
Noten, Ted (b. 1956), NL
"Necklace for an
Obsessed Ring Lover",
aka "My Most Criminal
Piece"
Necklace, 2003
24 ct gold-plated ready-
made tool, steel wire.
13 × 2.5 × 3 cm, exclud-
ing the wire
© Ted Noten/
BONO, Oslo 2021

427
Noten, Ted (b. 1956), NL
"Coffee Cup Brooch"
no. 137, 2004
Aluminium, porcelain.
8 × 9 × 1 cm
Unlimited edition
© Ted Noten/
BONO, Oslo 2021

294
Noten, Ted (b. 1956), NL
"Fred"
Necklace, 2004
Fly, pearl, acrylic.
3.5 × 2.5 × 1 cm
Limited edition
© Ted Noten/
BONO, Oslo 2021

298 550 431 421

296 501 302 304

299 300 303

297 301 472

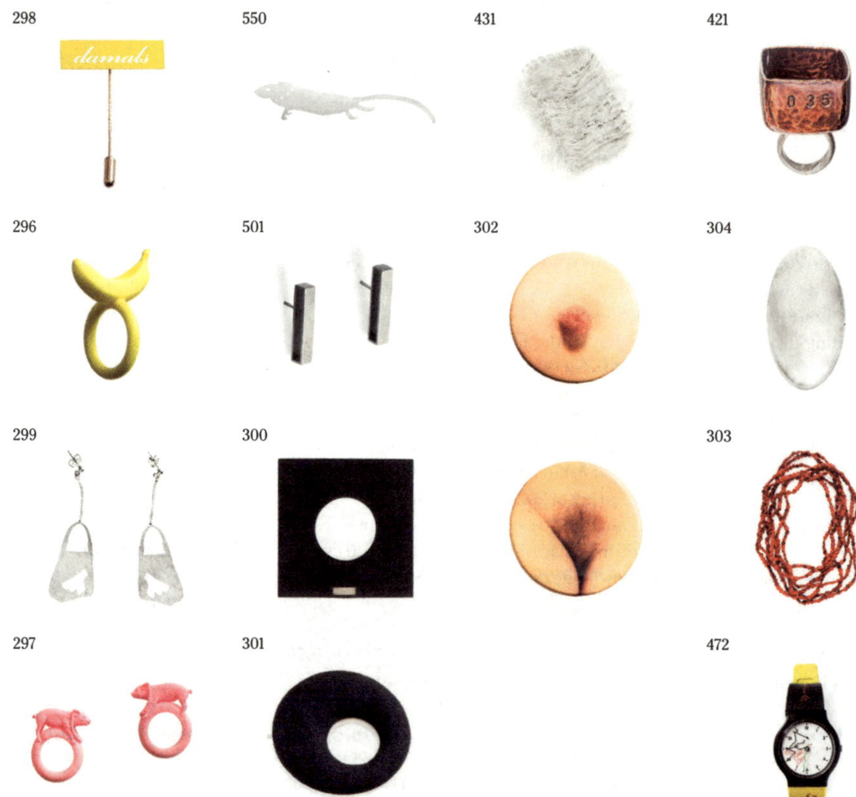

298
Noten, Ted (b. 1956), NL
"Damals" (Back Then)
Pin, 2007
Anodised aluminium.
5 × 3.6 cm
Edition of 100
© Ted Noten/
BONO, Oslo 2021
Liesbeth den Besten
asked Ted Noten to
make this pin for Think
Thank, A European
Initiative for the Applied
Arts meeting and
exhibition in 2007 with
the theme *Gift*. Every
participant received a
pin for free.

296
Noten, Ted (b. 1956), NL
"Banana"
Ring, 2008
3D printed nylon.
3.1 × 2.5 × 4 cm
Unlimited edition
© Ted Noten/
BONO, Oslo 2021

299
Noten, Ted (b. 1956), NL
"Icon"
Earrings, 2008
Silver. 7 × 2.3 cm
Edition of 5 and 1 AP
© Ted Noten/
BONO, Oslo 2021

297
Noten, Ted (b. 1956), NL
"Miss Piggy"
2 rings, 2008/2012
3D printed nylon with
glass fibre. 4 × 3 × 1 cm
Unlimited edition
© Ted Noten/
BONO, Oslo 2021

550
Noten, Ted (b. 1956), NL
"Little Princess"
Pin, 2012
Acrylic. 1.5 × 6 × 0.4 cm
Edition of 100
© Ted Noten/
BONO, Oslo 2021
The pin was given to
all new and renewing
Art Jewellery Forum
(AJF) supporters in
2012 as an exclusive
benefit. Noten's design
for AJF was inspired
by a conceptual
piece he designed in
1995 that gained him
international notoriety:
"The Turbo Princess",
a pendant featuring a
black mouse wearing a
pearl necklace encased
in acrylic.

501
Noyons, Karina
(b. 1964), DK
Earrings, 1990s
Silver. 3.5 × 0.5 × 0.5 cm
© Karina Noyons

300
Noyons, Karina
(b. 1964), DK
Bracelet no. 8 of 75
Rubber, silver. 11 × 11 cm
© Karina Noyons

301
Noyons, Karina
(b. 1964), DK, and
Lindqvist, Inge
(b. 1958), DK
Bracelet Bag no. 2, 2003
Felt, silver. Ø 6.5 cm
© Karina Noyons and
Inge Lindqvist

431
Olsen, Mette
(b. 1953), DK
"Housewife/Sunday"
Bracelet/object, 2015
Second-hand table run-
ners (Danish: *lyseduge*).
9.5 × 12.5 × 12.5 cm
© Mette Olsen

302
Ono, Yoko
(b. 1933), JP/US
"My Mummy Was
Beautiful"
Two badges, 2004
Paper, acetate, metal
pin. 3.8 × 3.8 × 0.6 cm
© Yoko Ono
The badges were made
for the 2004 Liverpool
Biennial. The publicity
coup for that particular
biennial was Yoko Ono's
city-wide project "My
Mummy Was Beautiful".
This was a series of
posters, badges and
carrier bags which
sported the image of a
female breast or pubis.
As expected, it caused
a storm and generated
a lot of free advertising
in tabloid news around
the world. In the spring
of 2005, the badges
were sold at the Astrup
Fearnley Museum in
Oslo in connection with
Yoko Ono's exhibition
Horizontal Memories.

421
Park, Soung-Chuel
(b. 1970), KR
Ring/pendant no. 035,
2015
Copper plate, covered
with several layers of
ott-chill (traditional
Korean varnishing tech-
nique). 3.5 × 3.5 × 4.5 cm
© Soung-Chuel Park

304
Passama, Noon
(b. 1983), TH/NL
"Extra Button"
Brooch, 2011
Galvanised copper,
car paint, acrylic
plate, button pins.
8.7 × 4.5 × 1.5 cm
© Noon Passama

303
Paumen, Hanneke
(b. 1956), NL
Neckpiece, 2006
Felt, silk. L 292 cm
© Hanneke Paumen

472
Penck, A.R.
(1939–2017), DE
"Animal Watch", 1992
Quartz watch, plastic
bracelet, waterproof
and shockproof
replacement bat-
tery (manufacturer
clockwork: Junghans).
24 × 3.6 cm
© A.R. Penck/
BONO, Oslo 2021

305

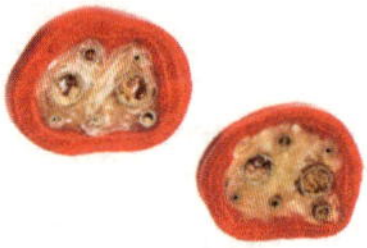

309

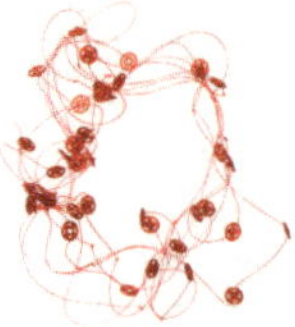

315

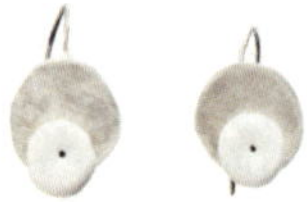

483

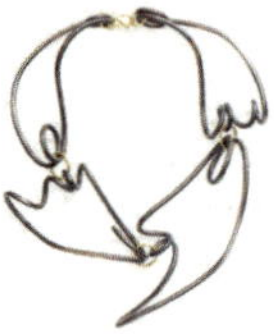

306

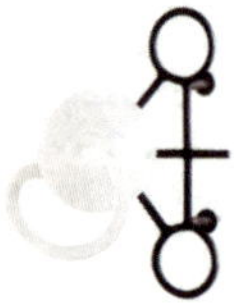

312

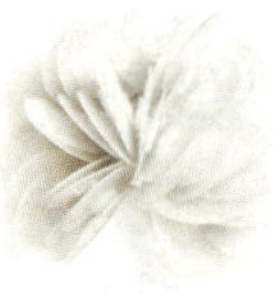

313

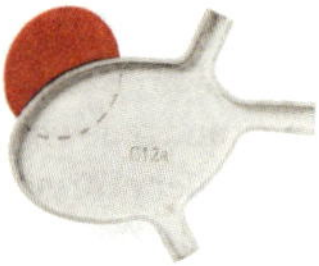

486

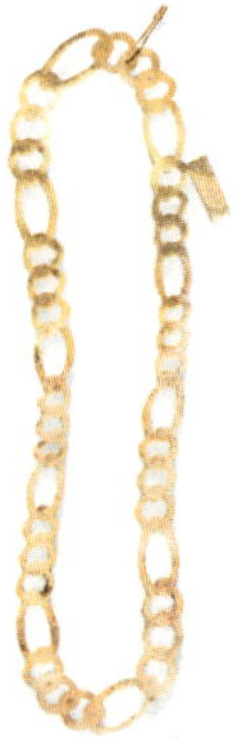

307

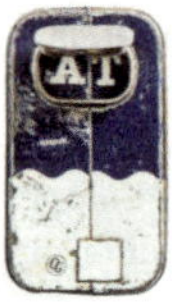

310

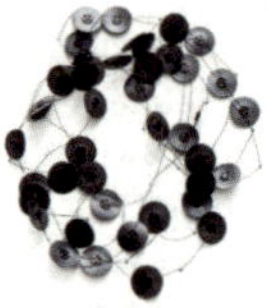

316

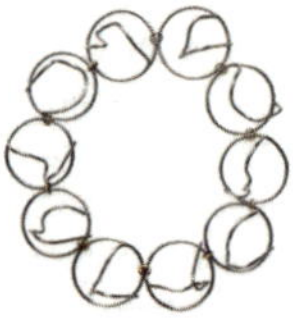

308

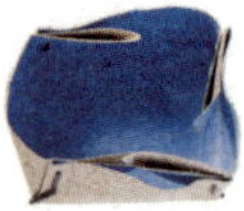

311

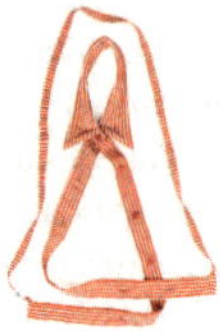

317

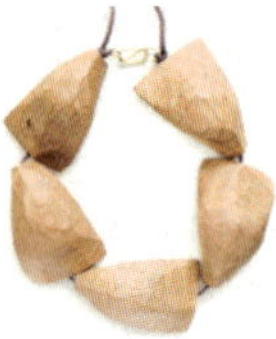

318

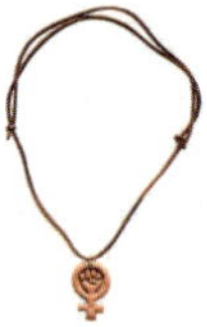

314

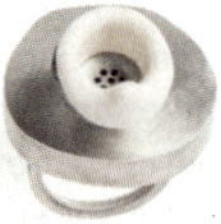

484

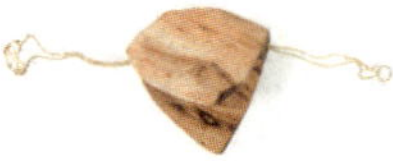

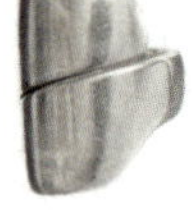

319

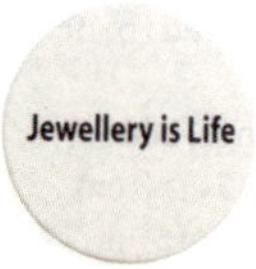

500

305
Peters, Ruudt
(b. 1950), NL
"Iosis"
Brooch, 2002
Silver, silk, polyester.
3.2 × 3.2 × 0.4 cm
© Ruudt Peters/
BONO, Oslo 2021

306
Peters, Ruudt
(b. 1950), NL
"Sefiroth"
Brooch, 2006
Silver, glass.
5.7 × 4 × 4 cm
© Ruudt Peters/
BONO, Oslo 2021
The brooch came in a
special box including
an edition of the book
Sefiroth, for which I
wrote an article.

307
Pond, Jo (b. 1968), UK
"Made in Great Britain"
Brooch, 2013
Steel, iron, repurposed
Elastoplastic tin.
9 × 5.2 × 1.7 cm
© Jo Pond

308
Pontoppidan, Karen
(b. 1968), DK/DE
"Context"
Brooch, 2013
Silver, canvas, paint.
5 × 4 × 3.5 cm
© Karen Pontoppidan

309
Prasch, Camilla
(b. 1967), DE/DK
"Knot Chain"
Bracelet/necklace, 2002
Silicone discs, plastic
snaps. Ø 11 cm
© Camilla Prasch

312
Prasch, Camilla
(b. 1967), DE/DK
"All Around"
Ring, 2005
Silicone. 5 × 6.5 × 4.5 cm
© Camilla Prasch

310
Prasch, Camilla
(b. 1967), DE/DK
Necklace, 2006
Silicone discs, plastic
snaps. Ø 18 cm
© Camilla Prasch

311
Prasch, Camilla
(b. 1967), DE/DK
"Lady Manhattan"
From the series
Ordnung Lass' Sein
Necklace, 2017
Cotton. Flexible length,
max. 118 cm
© Camilla Prasch

314
Prins, Katja
(b. 1970), NL
"Inventarium"
Ring, 2002
Silver, porcelain.
4 × 3.5 × 3.5 cm
© Katja Prins

315
Prins, Katja
(b. 1970), NL
"Inventarium"
Earrings, 2002
Silver, porcelain.
L 2.5 cm
© Katja Prins

313
Prins, Katja
(b. 1970), NL
"Nexus"
Brooch, 2009
Silver, recon-
structed red coral.
5.8 × 6 × 0.4 cm
© Katja Prins

316
Prühl, Dorothea
(b. 1937), DE
"Swans"
Necklace, 2005
Titanium, gold.
36 × 23 × 5 cm
© Dorothea Prühl

317
Prühl, Dorothea
(b. 1937), DE
"Birds in Winter"
Necklace, 2016
Cherrywood, gold.
L 25 cm, each element
9.5 cm
© Dorothea Prühl

484
Prühl, Dorothea
(b. 1937), DE
"Moth"
Pendant, 2017
Elm wood, gold.
L solid form 12 cm
© Dorothea Prühl

483
Prühl, Dorothea
(b. 1937), DE
"Night Birds"
Necklace, 2017
Titanium, gold. Four
elements each between
16–23 cm long
© Dorothea Prühl

486
PXL-MAD School of
Arts, BE
Brooch, 2015
Gilded and laser-cut
neoprene. 21.8 × 7 cm
Promo brooch made
by master students
from Hasselt as part
of their performance
"MAD Exhibitionists"
at *Schmuck 2015* in
Munich.

318
R., Jan, NO
Women's Liberation
Movement symbol,
ca. 1975
Unglazed ceramics.
L 5.5 cm

319
Rana, Mah (b. 1964), UK
"Jewellery Is Life"
Badge, 2001
Steel, paper. 2.5 × 2.5 cm
© Mah Rana

500
Ransby, Jørgen, DK
Ring, 1982
Silver. H 3.6 cm
© Jørgen Ransby

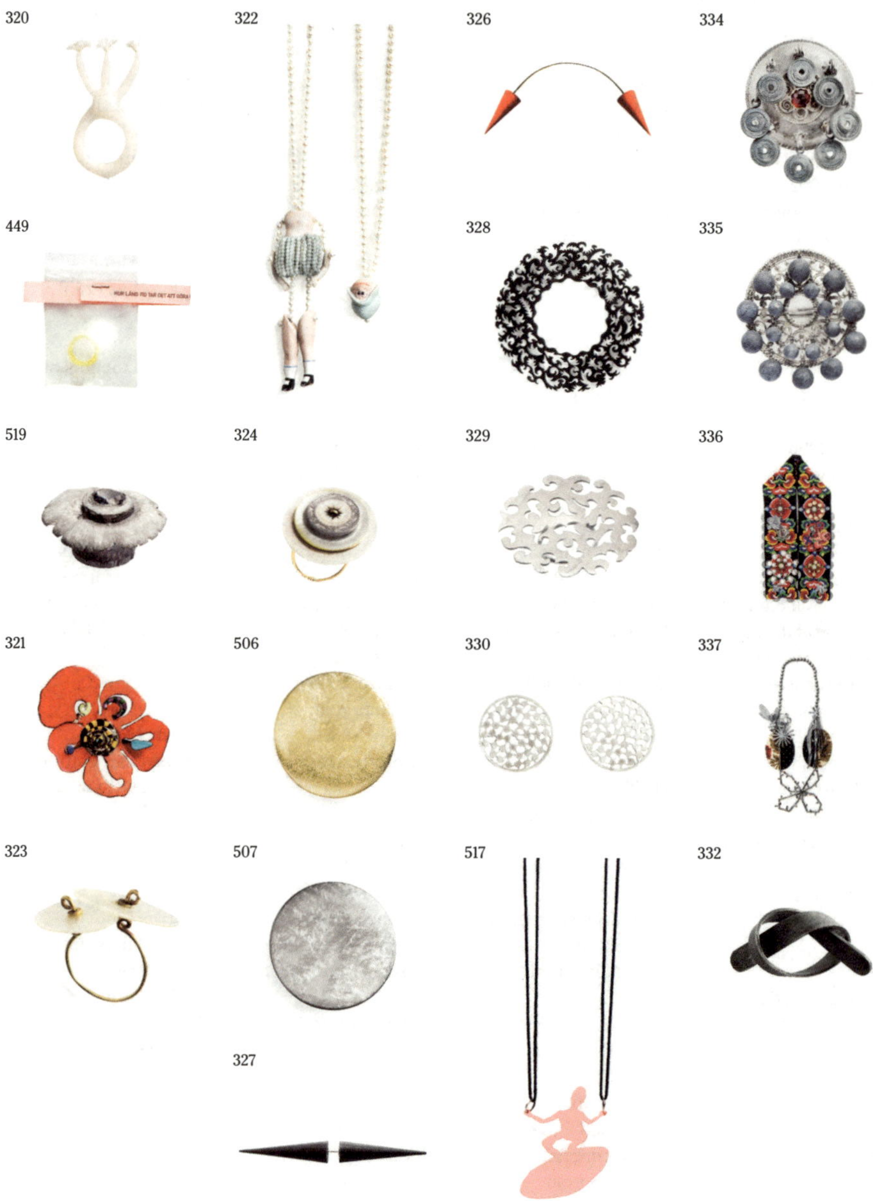

320
449
519
321
323
536
322
324
506
507
327
326
328
329
330
517
334
335
336
337
332

320
Rinman, Cathrine
(b. 1971), SE
Ring, 2000–04
Stearin. L 6 cm
© Cathrine Rinman

449
Rinman, Cathrine
(b. 1971), SE
"Soap Ring", 2001
Soap. Ø 2.5 cm
© Cathrine Rinman
The ring came in a
plastic bag with the
text: "Hur lång tid tar
det att göra en ring?"
(How long does it take
to make a ring?).

519
Roux-Fouillet, David
(b. 1978), DK/FR/UK
"Shoot"
Jewel, 2011
Lead, synthetic
corundum. Ø 1 cm
© David Roux-Fouillet

321
Rudjord, Alida
(b. 1966), NO
Brooch, 1994
Enamel. 7.5 × 9.3 × 2 cm
© Alida Rudjord/
BONO, Oslo 2021

323
Saabye, Mette
(b. 1969), DK
"Drops of Dew"
Ring, 2002
Gold, mother-of-pearl.
3 × 2.5 × 2.7 cm
© Mette Saabye

322
Saabye, Mette
(b. 1969), DK
"Jewellery Artist"
Necklace, 2002
Pearls, porcelain, glass
beads. L 55 cm
© Mette Saabye

324
Saabye, Mette
(b. 1969), DK
"Layer Cake"
Ring, 2006
Gold, second-hand
mother-of-pearl
buttons. Ø 3 cm
© Mette Saabye

506
Saabye, Mette
(b. 1969), DK
"The Gold Badge", 2008
White metal, plastic,
24 ct gold leaf.
7.5 × 7.5 × 0.3 cm
© Mette Saabye

507
Saabye, Mette
(b. 1969), DK
"The Silver Badge", 2017
White metal,
plastic, silver leaf.
7.5 × 7.5 × 0.3 cm
© Mette Saabye

327
Sand, Ella Heidi
(b. 1957), NO
Earrings, 1984
Ebony, silver, rubber.
L 10.5 cm
© Heidi Sand/
BONO, Oslo 2021

326
Sand, Ella Heidi
(b. 1957), NO
Earring, 1987
Silver, wood. L 10 cm
© Ella Heidi Sand/
BONO, Oslo 2021

328
Sand, Ella Heidi
(b. 1957), NO
Bracelet, 1989
Anodised aluminium.
Ø 13 cm
© Ella Heidi Sand/
BONO, Oslo 2021

329
Sand, Ella Heidi
(b. 1957), NO
Ring, 1992
Silver. Ø 4.5 cm
© Ella Heidi Sand/
BONO, Oslo 2021

330
Sand, Ella Heidi
(b. 1957), NO
Earrings, 2002
Silver. Ø 5 cm
© Ella Heidi Sand/
BONO, Oslo 2021

517
Sand, Ella Heidi
(b. 1957), NO
"Comment"
Pendant, 2015
Laser-cut steel, spray
paint. 3.7 × 3.5 cm
© Ella Heidi Sand/
BONO, Oslo 2021

334
Sarneel, Lucy
(1961–2020), NL
"Family Heirloom"
Brooch, 2008
Silver, zinc, glass.
Ø 4.5 cm
© Lucy Sarneel/
BONO, Oslo 2021

335
Sarneel, Lucy
(1961–2020), NL
"Family Heirloom"
Brooch, 2008
Silver, zinc. Ø 7 cm
© Lucy Sarneel/
BONO, Oslo 2021

336
Sarneel, Lucy
(1961–2020), NL
"Family Heirloom"
Neckpiece, 2008
Wool embroidery, zinc,
silver. 43 × 21 cm
© Lucy Sarneel/
BONO, Oslo 2021

337
Sarneel, Lucy
(1961–2020), NL
"La Double Vie"
Necklace, 2009
Zinc, nylon thread,
old textiles on rubber,
paint. 42 × 22 cm
© Lucy Sarneel/
BONO, Oslo 2021

332
Sarneel, Lucy
(1961–2020), NL
"Knot"
Pin, 2012
Zinc, acrylic paint,
varnish. 2.2 × 2.3 × 1.7 cm
Multiple of 10 pins
© Lucy Sarneel/
BONO, Oslo 2021

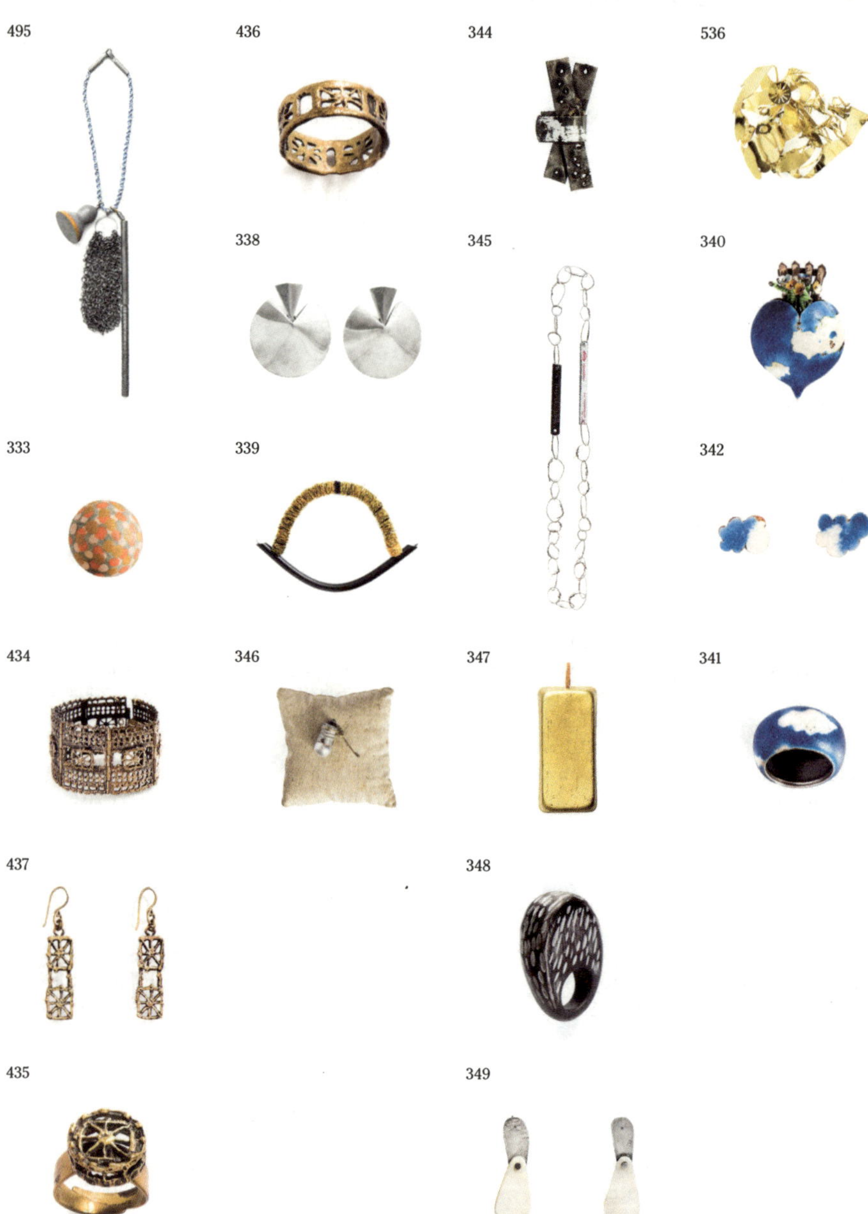

495
436
344
536
338
345
340
333
339
342
434
346
347
341
437
348
435
349

495
Sarneel, Lucy
(1961–2020), NL
"Daily Offer # 8"
Necklace, 2015
Zinc, calabash, wood,
epoxy, plastic raffia.
60 × 12 × 6.3 cm
© Lucy Sarneel/
BONO, Oslo 2021

333
Sarneel, Lucy
(1961–2020), NL
Pin, 2017
Zinc, acrylic paint,
varnish. Ø 1 cm
© Lucy Sarneel/
BONO, Oslo 2021

434
Sarpaneva, Pentti
(1925–1978), FI
"Pitsi" (Lace)
Bracelet, 1967–
Bronze. H 4.3 cm
Designed for Turun
Hopea Finland

437
Sarpaneva, Pentti
(1925–1978), FI
"Pitsi" (Lace)
Earrings, ca. 1970
Bronze. L 3 cm
Designed for Turun
Hopea Finland

435
Sarpaneva, Pentti
(1925–1978), FI
"Pitsi" (Lace)
Ring, ca. 1970
Bronze. Ø 1.6 cm
Designed for Turun
Hopea Finland

436
Sarpaneva, Pentti
(1925–1978), FI
"Pitsi" (Lace)
Ring, ca. 1970
Bronze. H 0.7 cm
Designed for Turun
Hopea Finland

338
Scharff, Allan
(b. 1946), DK
Earrings, ca. 1986
Silver. Ø 5 cm
Designed for
Georg Jensen
© Allan Scharff

339
Schei, Jorun Cathrine
Riiser (b. 1956), NO
Necklace, 1998
Paper, rubber, silver.
18 × 26 × 2 cm
© J. Cathrine Riiser
Schei/BONO, Oslo 2021

346
Schobinger, Bernhard
(b. 1946), CH
"Ersatzlampe"
(Replacement Lamp)
Brooch, 2009
Haiti pearl, gold,
textile. Two brooches
in one, with needle pad
7.3 × 7.3 × 4 cm, without
2.3 × 1 × 1 cm
© Bernhard Schobinger/
BONO, Oslo 2021

344
Schobinger, Bernhard
(b. 1946), CH
"Crossed Saws"
Ring, 2013
Steel saw blade, raw
diamond, paint.
6.2 × 2.6 × 2.3 cm
© Bernhard Schobinger/
BONO, Oslo 2021

345
Schobinger, Bernhard
(b. 1946), CH
"In – Yang Kette"
Necklace, 2013
Steel, stainless steel.
L 58 cm
© Bernhard Schobinger/
BONO, Oslo 2021

347
Schrijer, Moniek
(b. 1983), NZ
"Gold Bar Pendant"
Necklace, 2014
Cork, plaster, sand,
brass, leather, spray-
paint. 13 × 5.5 × 3 cm
No. 17/72
© Moniek Schrijer

348
Schrijer, Moniek
(b. 1983), NZ
"Rain Ring", 2014
Manuka wood, ink,
paint. 5.5 × 3.8 × 1.5 cm
© Moniek Schrijer

349
Schrijer, Moniek
(b. 1983), NZ
"Pearl Drop"
Earrings, 2015
Mother-of-pearl,
sterling silver. L 4.7 cm
© Moniek Schrijer

536
Schrijer, Moniek
(b. 1983), NZ
"Space Junk"
Brooch, 2018
Recycled laquered
brass, steel wire.
5 × 6.5 × 2 cm
Series of 180
© Moniek Schrijer

340
Schønberg, Lise
(b. 1945), NO
"Partly Cloudy
Weather"
Brooch, 2002
Silver, enamel.
6 × 4 × 1.7 cm
© Lise Schønberg/
BONO, Oslo 2021

342
Schønberg, Lise
(b. 1945), NO
"Partly Cloudy
Weather"
Earrings, 2002
Silver, enamel. 1.6 × 1.2,
1.8 × 1.9 cm
© Lise Schønberg/
BONO, Oslo 2021

341
Schønberg, Lise
(b. 1945), NO
"Partly Cloudy
Weather"
Ring, 2002
Silver, enamel. H 1.2 cm
© Lise Schønberg/
BONO, Oslo 2021

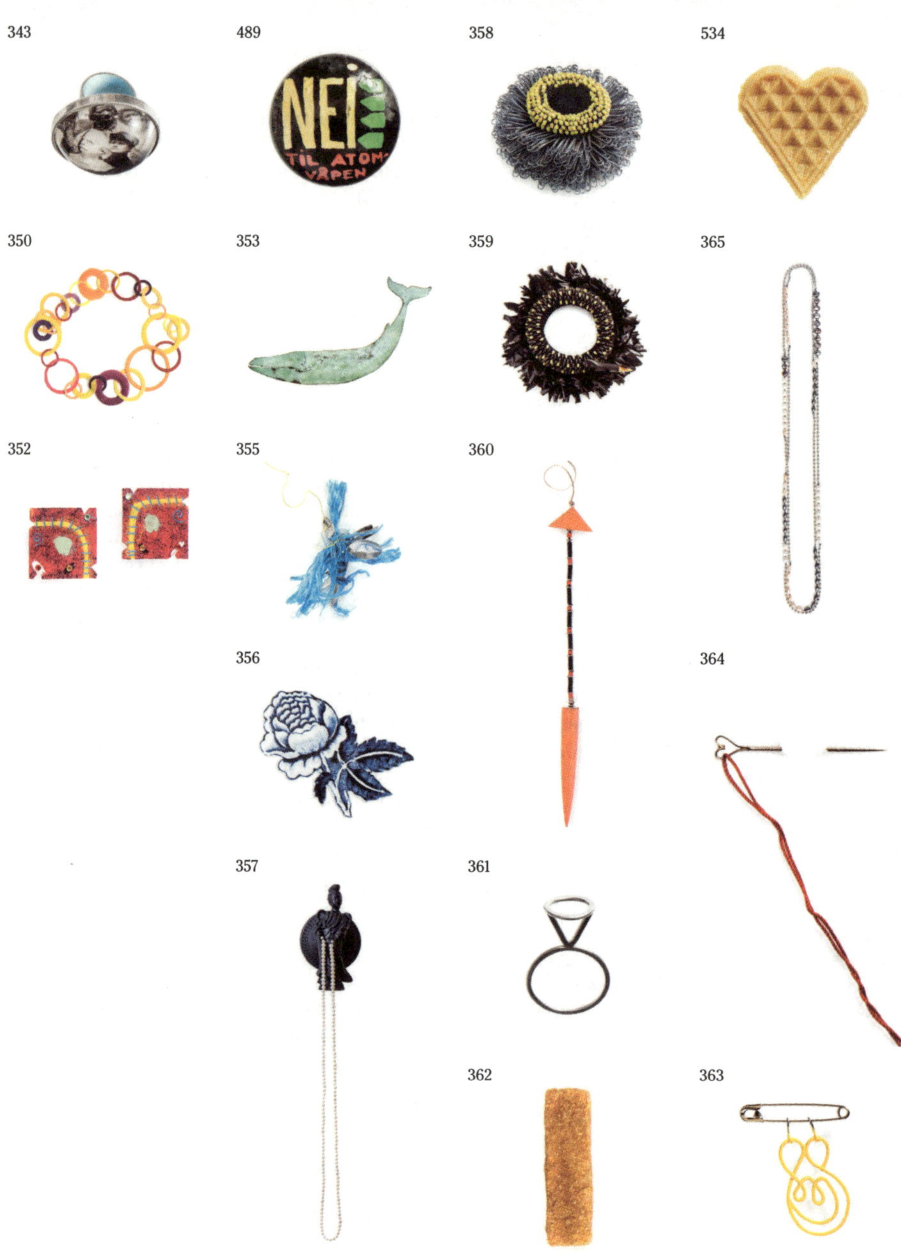

343
489
NEi
TIL ATOM-
VÅPEN
358
534
350
353
359
365
352
355
360
356
357
361
362
363
364

343
Schønberg, Lise
(b. 1945), NO
Ring, 2009
Silver, plastic, photo.
Ø 4.3 cm
© Lise Schønberg/
BONO, Oslo 2021
The photos are taken
from the biography
*Ambrosia Tønnesen
"Stenhugger i det
fine"* (2009), which I
authored. In front is the
bust of the composer
Edvard Grieg, just
behind him the sculptor
Ambrosia Tønnesen
with a hat. The ring was
a gift from her relatives
and has the following
inscription on the
reverse: "Til Jorunn for-
sker i det fine 2009. Fra
familien Des Bouvrie"
(To Jorunn researcher
in the fine [arts] 2009.
From the Des Bouvrie
family).

350
Seufert, Karin
(b. 1966), DE
Necklace in plastic
no. 373.18, 2013
Recycled plastic.
Ø 32 cm
© Karin Seufert

352
Sherburne, Annie
(b. 1957), UK
Earrings, 1986
Veneer, glass stones.
5.2 × 5.2 cm
© Annie Sherburne

489
Siri, NO
"Nei til atomvåpen"
(No to Nuclear
Weapons)
Badge, ca. 1980
Hand-painted wood.
Ø 4 cm

353
Slagsvold, Esther Helén
(b. 1956), NO
Brooch, 1991
Copper. 16.2 × 2.8 cm
© Esther Helén
Slagsvold

355
Slettemark, Kjartan
(1932–2008), NO/SE
Brooch, 1988
Plastic rope, teaspoons,
plastic plug, metal
string, telephone cord.
12 × 20 × 7.5 cm
© The estate of Kjartan
Slettemark

356
Slotte, Caroline
(b. 1975), FI
Brooch, 2005
Ceramics. 6.3 × 4.3 cm
© Caroline Slotte
The flower has
been sawn out of a
second-hand dish.

357
Smith, Matt (b. 1971), UK
"Wunderkammer 10"
Object, 2017
Black Parian ware,
freshwater pearls.
55 × 12 × 10 cm
© Matt Smith

358
Solgaard, Anne-Karine
(b. 1952), NO
Bracelet, 1988
Paper clips, plastic
beads. Ø 16, H 6.5 cm
© Anne-Karine Solgaard/
BONO, Oslo 2021

359
Solgaard, Anne-Karine
(b. 1952), NO
Bracelet, 1988
Plastic from garbage
bag, plastic beads,
wood. Ø 16, H 15 cm
© Anne-Karine Solgaard/
BONO, Oslo 2021

360
Solgaard, Anne-Karine
(b. 1952), NO
Earring, 1988
Plastic, painted wood,
silver. L 24 cm
© Anne-Karine Solgaard/
BONO, Oslo 2021

361
Sonne, Bo Kristine
(b. 1970), DK
"So Big a Diamond"
Ring, 2006
Silver. 3.3 × 1.2 cm
© Bo Sonne

362
Stach, Gisbert
(b. 1963), DE
"Gold Fingers"
Brooch, 2015
Baltic amber, silicone.
2.7 × 8.7 × 1.8 cm
© Gisbert Stach

534
Stach, Gisbert
(b. 1963), DE
"Herzwaffel"
(Heart Waffle)
Brooch, 2019
Baltic amber, silicone.
8.2 × 8.2 × 1.3 cm
© Gisbert Stach

365
Stofer, Hans
(b. 1957), CH/UK
"Drain Chain"
Necklace, 2003
Ball chain, freshwater
pearls. L 88 cm
© Hans Stofer

364
Stofer, Hans
(b. 1957), CH/UK
"Passion Pin", 2006
Needle, thread.
4.5 × 0.7 cm
Edition of 4
© Hans Stofer

363
Stofer, Hans
(b. 1957), CH/UK
Brooch, 2010
Wire, safety pin. 7 × 6 cm
© Hans Stofer

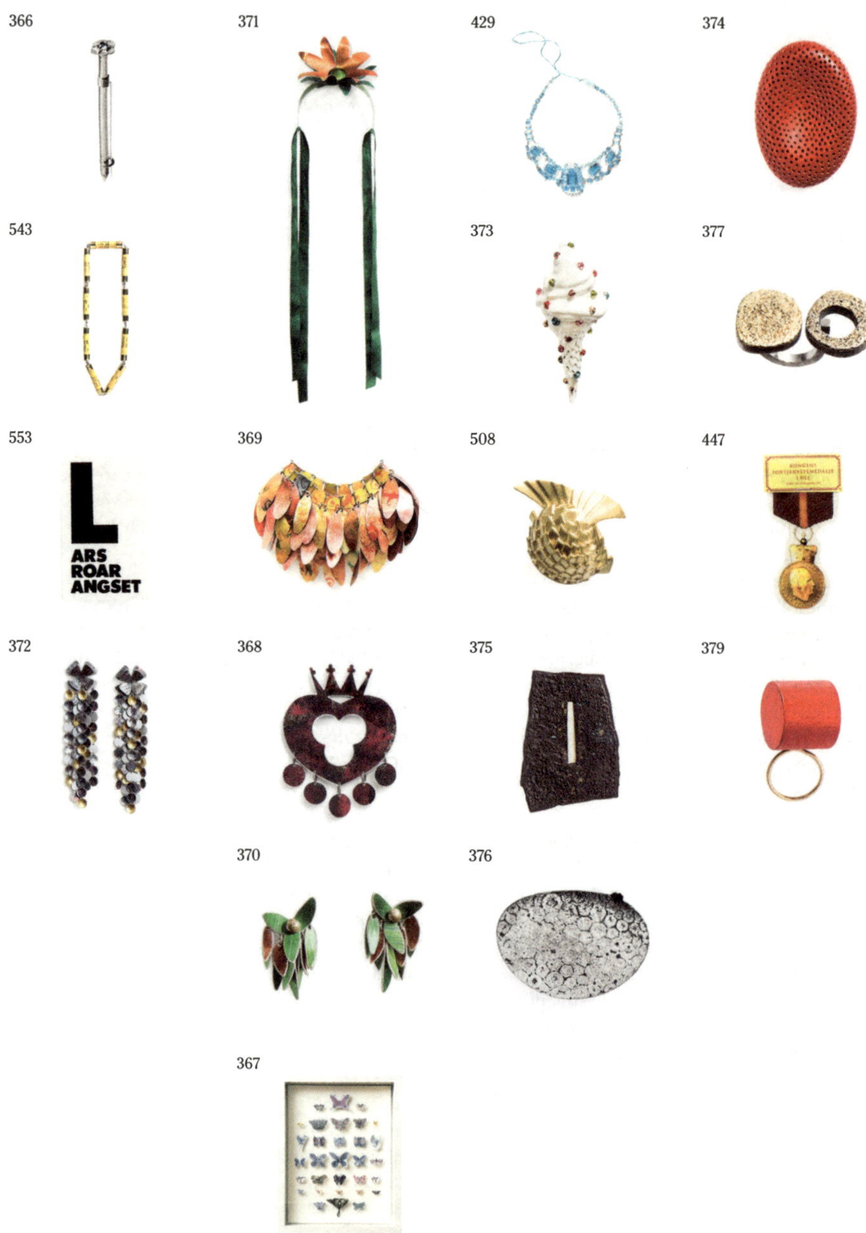

366

543

553

372

370

367

371

369

368

429

373

508

370

376

374

377

447

379

542

366
Stofer, Hans
(b. 1957), CH/UK
"Nägeli"
Brooch, 2017
Stainless steel,
Swarovski crystal.
L 5 cm
© Hans Stofer
The title plays on both
the German word for
nails, *Nägel*, and the
name of the Swiss bot-
anist Carl Wilhelm von
Nägeli (1817–1891), who
is considered one of
the founders of modern
botany.

543
Stofer, Hans
(b. 1957), CH/UK
"Diane"
Necklace, 2019
Shotgun cartridges.
L 40.5 cm
© Hans Stofer

553
Stuntpoetane, NO
"L"
Badge, 1985
Paper. 9.7 × 6 cm

372
Sture, Lars (b. 1961), NO
Earrings, 1991
Anodised aluminium.
22 × 7 cm
© Lars Sture/
BONO, Oslo 2021

371
Sture, Lars (b. 1961), NO
Headband, 1991
Anodised aluminium,
silk ribbon.
18 × 15.5 × 15.5 cm
© Lars Sture/
BONO, Oslo 2021

369
Sture, Lars (b. 1961), NO
Necklace, 1991
Anodised aluminium.
Ø 46 cm
© Lars Sture/
BONO, Oslo 2021

368
Sture, Lars (b. 1961), NO
"*Sølje*" (Brooch),
1991/92
Anodised aluminium.
13 × 10.5 cm
© Lars Sture/
BONO, Oslo 2021

370
Sture, Lars (b. 1961), NO
Earrings, 1995
Anodised aluminium.
4.2 × 2.5 × 1 cm
© Lars Sture/
BONO, Oslo 2021

367
Sture, Lars (b. 1961), NO
Object, 1998
Paper, wood. 50 × 40 cm
© Lars Sture/
BONO, Oslo 2021
A butterfly collection
based on clippings from
auction catalogues of
brooches covered with
gems and shaped like
butterflies.

429
Sture, Lars (b. 1961), NO
Necklace, 2001–02
Paper clippings from
auction catalogues.
17 × 14 cm
© Lars Sture/
BONO, Oslo 2021

373
Sun, Jie (b. 1984), CN/NL
"Young and Beautiful"
Brooch, 2015
Mixed materials,
Swarkovski crystals.
12 × 5 × 4.5 cm
© Jie Sun

508
Sun, Jie (b. 1984), CN/NL
"Big Fish"
Pin, 2016
Gold-plated silver.
2 × 3.5 × 2.5 cm
Edition of 100
Produced by NoCC/
Tongji University
© Jie Sun

375
Suntum, Per
(b. 1944), DK
Brooch, 1995
Silver, niello, walrus
tooth. 6.6 × 4.9 cm
© Per Suntum

376
Suntum, Per
(b. 1944), DK
Brooch, 2000
Silver, niello, steel, iron.
5 × 7 × 1 cm
© Per Suntum

374
Suntum, Per
(b. 1944), DK
"Kytos"
Brooch, 2001
Reconstructed coral,
gold. 5 × 7.2 × 2 cm
© Per Suntum
Kytos is Greek for cell,
and with its red colour
and biconcave shape
this work refers to our
vital red blood cells.
One of the microscopic
phenomena we have
inside us is thus high-
lighted and made into a
visible and poetic sign
to wear on the body.

377
Suntum, Per
(b. 1944), DK
"Fungi trio no. 2"
Ring, 2005
Patinated silver, 24 ct
gold. 2.4 × 4.5 × 3.5
© Per Suntum

447
Supernøtt Popsløyd, NO
"Kongens fortjenest-
emedalje i ull" (The
King's Medal of Merit
in Wool)
Brooch, 2005
Print on felt. H 12 cm

379
Svensson, Tore
(b. 1948), SE
"Inside Tube"
Ring, 2012
Wood, paint, 18 ct gold.
3.2 × 2 × 4 cm
© Tore Svensson/
BONO, Oslo 2021

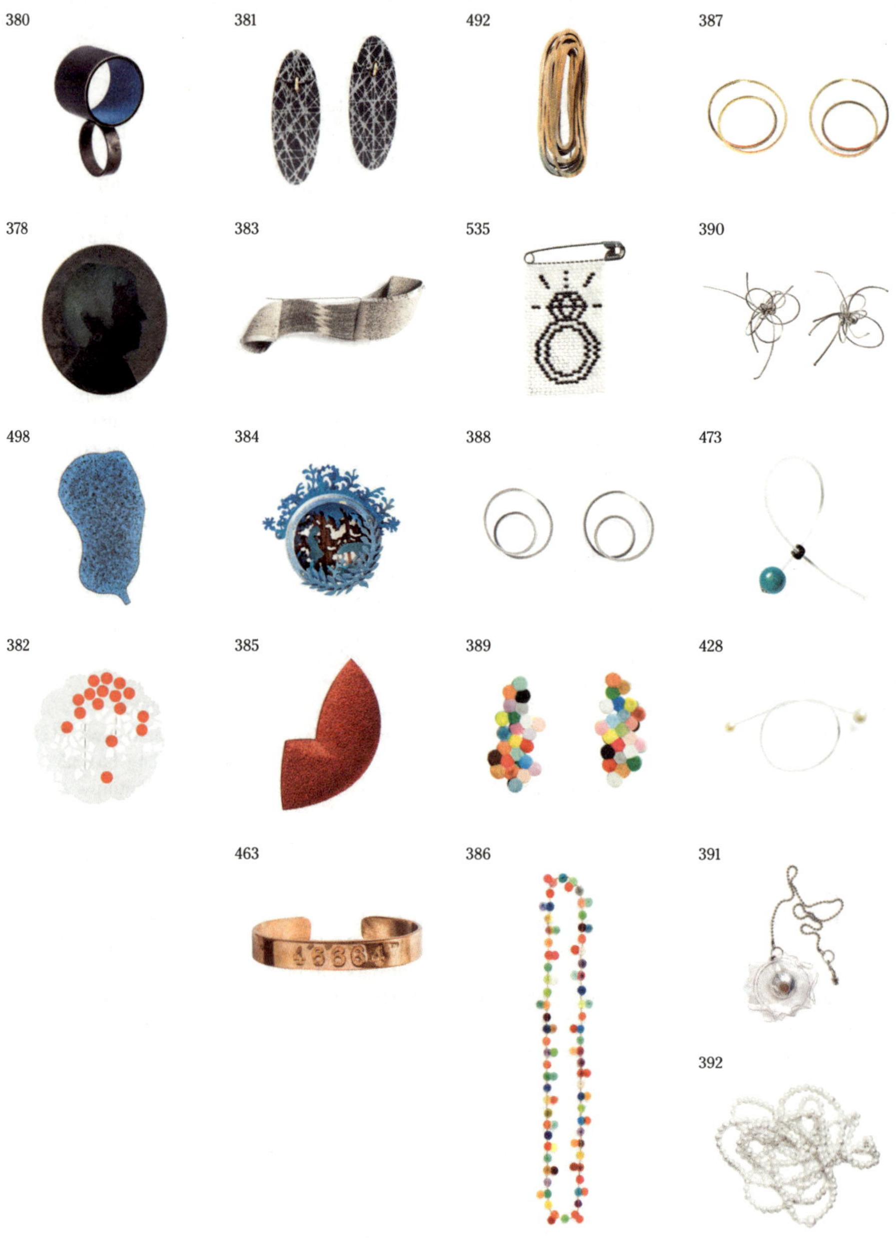

380
381
492
387
378
383
535
390
498
384
388
473
382
385
389
428
463
386
391
392

380
Svensson, Tore
(b. 1948), SE
"Tube"
Ring, 2012
Steel, paint.
2.5 × 2 × 4.5 cm
© Tore Svensson/
BONO, Oslo 2021

378
Svensson, Tore
(b. 1948), SE
"Jorunn"
Brooch, 2013
Steel, gilt, paint.
5 × 4.5 cm
© Tore Svensson/
BONO, Oslo 2021

498
Svensson, Tore
(b. 1948), SE
"Spegeldammen"
(The Mirror Pond)
Brooch, 2018
Steel. 10.5 × 6 cm
© Tore Svensson/
BONO, Oslo 2021
In the *Lake* series,
Svensson uses existing
shapes he finds on
Google Maps. He copies
a lake, prints it out
and makes a brooch in
steel from it. Spegel-
dammen is a lake in
Norra Djurgården in
Stockholm, Sweden.

382
Swärd, Ulrika
(b. 1966), SE
"Very Sold"
Brooch, 2007
Silver, paper. Ø 8.7 cm
© Ulrika Swärd/
BONO, Oslo 2021

381
Swärd, Ulrika
(b. 1966), SE
"Perstorp"
Earrings, 2008
Formica laminate, silver.
5 × 1.9 cm
© Ulrika Swärd/
BONO, Oslo 2021
The pattern used here is
a Swedish design icon,
Virrvarr, designed by
Sigvard Bernadotte in
1958. It is still in use in a
lot of different products
from the Perstorp
company.

383
Syvänoja, Janna
(b. 1960), FI
Brooch, 1992
Paper from a Finnish
telephone directory,
plastic, steel needle.
19.5 × 7.2 × 3 cm
© Janna Syvänoja

384
Talbot, Anna
(b. 1978), NO
"Blue Wolf"
Brooch, 2013
Second-hand tin box.
9.6 × 9.2 × 3 cm
© Anna Talbot

385
Teunen, Michiel
(b. 1957), NL
Brooch, 1992
Steel wire, polyure-
thane. 13 × 7 × 4 cm
© Michiel Teunen

463
The Nelson Mandela
Foundation, ZA
"46664 Bangle", 2009
Copper. Ø 6.5 cm

492
Tiitsar, Ketli
(b. 1972), EE
"Second Nature 1"
Brooch, 2016
Cherrywood, pigment,
silver. 14.5 × 5 cm
© Ketli Tiitsar

535
Tinsel Gallery, ZA
"Logo"
Brooch, 2019
Glass seed beads, safety
pin. 6 × 3.5 cm
The South African
jewellery gallery Tinsel,
based in Johannesburg
since 2006, has adapted
the Zulu tradition of
love letters to feature
their contemporary
logo.

388
Torkos, Karola
(b. 1975), DE
"Swirl", small
Earrings, 2010
Oxidised silver. Ø 3.8 cm
© Karola Torkos

389
Torkos, Karola
(b. 1975), DE
Earrings, 2011
Plastic. 7.5 × 3.6 cm
© Karola Torkos

386
Torkos, Karola
(b. 1975), DE
Necklace, 2011
Plastic, metal. L 41 cm
© Karola Torkos

387
Torkos, Karola
(b. 1975), DE
"Swirl", large
Earrings, 2011
Gold-plated silver,
ceramite. Ø 5.3 cm
© Karola Torkos

390
Trier, Trine (b. 1970), DK
Earrings, 2004–
Silver. 4 × 5.7 × 2.5 cm
© Trine Trier

473
Trier, Trine (b. 1970), DK
"Anarchist"
Ring, 2009
Nylon, plastic bead.
L 5 cm
© Trine Trier

428
Trier, Trine (b. 1970), DK
"The Anarchist's
Pearl Ring"
Ring, 2009
Nylon, pearls. L 4.5 cm
© Trine Trier

391
Tvedt, Tina (b. 1974), NO
"For the Diving Lady"
Necklace, 2001
PVC plastic, aluminium,
ball chain. L 66 cm
© Tina Tvedt/
BONO, Oslo 2021

392
Usel, Julie
(b. 1982), CH/UK
"Cling Film Collection"
Necklace, 2010
Cellophane. L 136 cm
© Julie Usel

546	502	400	406
441	396	408	404
393	397	405	409
394	398	403	411
395	399	407	
474	401, 402		

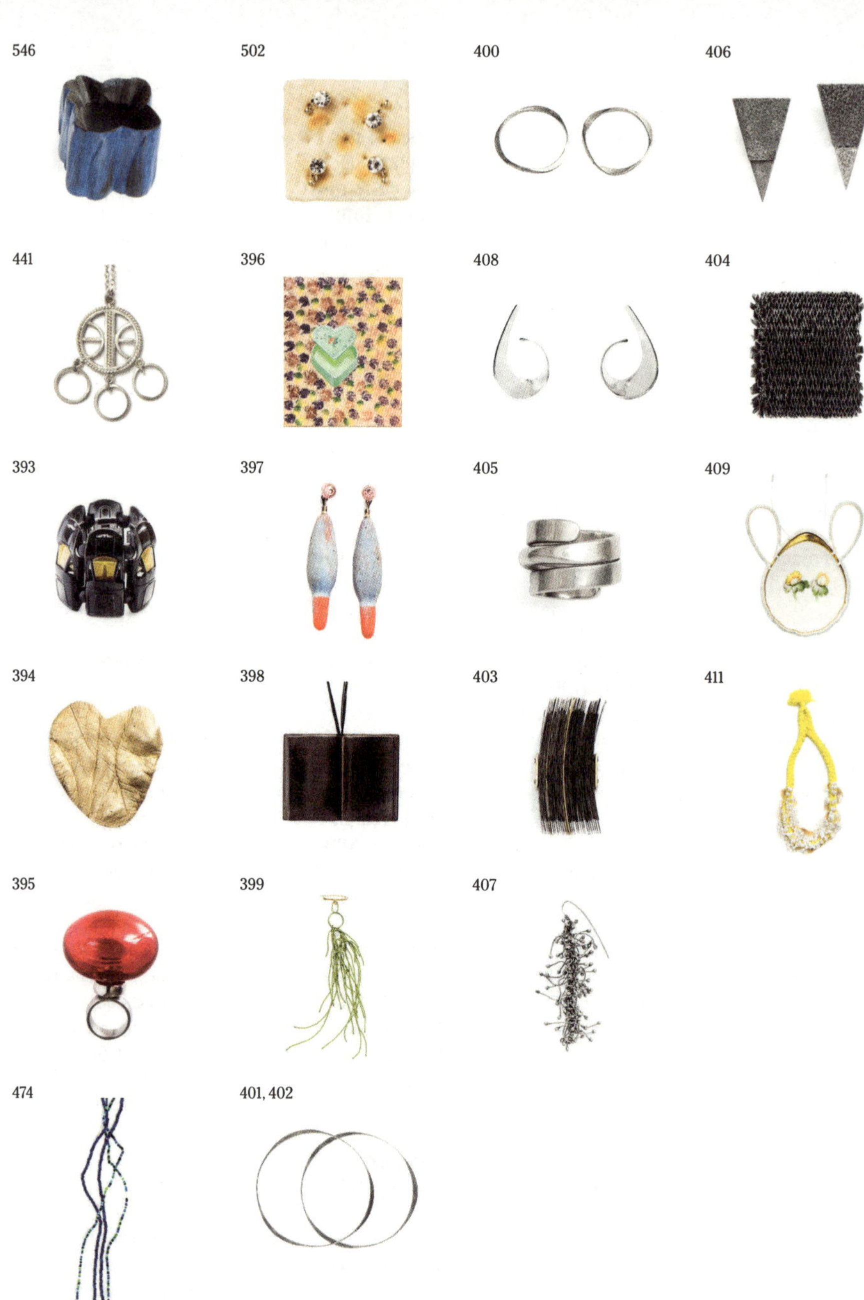

546
Vági, Flora (b. 1978), HU
Colour ring, 2016
Ebony, acrylic paint.
2.5 × 2.7 × 3 cm
© Flora Vági

441
Valdres sølvsmie, NO
Necklace, 1960s
925 silver. L 33.5,
L pendant 5.6 cm

393
Vallejo, Carolina
(b. 1966), GR/DK
"Racelet"
Bracelet, 1992
Toy cars, wooden
beads, elastic. H 7 cm
© Carolina Vallejo

394
Vallejo, Carolina
(b. 1966), GR/DK
"Compassion"
Brooch, 2003
24 ct gold-plated silver.
5.5 × 5 cm
© Carolina Vallejo

395
Vallejo, Carolina
(b. 1966), GR/DK
"Happiness"
Ring, 2003
Rubin gold glass, 925
silver. 4 × 4.5 × 6 cm
© Carolina Vallejo

474
Veiteberg, Jorunn
(b. 1955), NO/DK
Two necklaces, ca. 1970
Glass beads. L 60–65 cm
© Jorunn Veiteberg

502
Vemren, Hilde
(b. 1953), NO
Brooch, 1988
Plastic, glass stones,
metal. 5 × 5 cm
© Hilde Vemren/
BONO, Oslo 2021

396
Vemren, Hilde
(b. 1953), NO
"Memory"
Painting, 1990–92
Oil on canvas.
70 × 57 cm
© Hilde Vemren/
BONO, Oslo 2021

397
Veenre, Tanel
(b. 1977), EE
Earrings, 2010
Wood, zirconia, silver,
cosmic dust. 8 × 1.5 cm
© Tanel Veenre

398
Veenre, Tanel
(b. 1977), EE
"In the Beginning
Was the Word"
Necklace, 2011
Jet, threads.
13 × 10 × 2 cm
© Tanel Veenre

399
Vilhena, Manuel
(b. 1967), PT
Brooch, 2007
Gold, cotton. L 27 cm
© Manuel Vilhena

401, 402
Vigeland, Pål
(b. 1944), NO
Bracelet, 1981
Silver. Ø 6.8 cm
© Pål Vigeland/
BONO, Oslo 2021

400
Vigeland, Pål
(b. 1944), NO
Two rings, 1981
Silver. Ø 1.8 cm
© Pål Vigeland/
BONO, Oslo 2021

408
Vigeland, Tone
(b. 1938), NO
"Sling"
Earrings, 1958–
925 silver. 5 × 4 × 1.3 cm
Produced by PLUS
Applied Art Centre in
Fredrikstad, Norway
© Tone Vigeland/
BONO, Oslo 2021

405
Vigeland, Tone
(b. 1938), NO
Ring, 1973
Sterling silver. H 1.5 cm
Produced by PLUS
Applied Art Centre in
Fredrikstad, Norway
© Tone Vigeland/
BONO, Oslo 2021

403
Vigeland, Tone
(b. 1938), NO
Ring, 1982
Steel, gold, silver.
4.7 × 2.2 × 2.2 cm
© Tone Vigeland/
BONO, Oslo 2021

407
Vigeland, Tone
(b. 1938), NO
Earrings, 1988
Silver. L 9.3 cm
© Tone Vigeland/
BONO, Oslo 2021

406
Vigeland, Tone
(b. 1938), NO
Earrings, 1989
Steel, silver. 8.6 × 5.7 cm
© Tone Vigeland/
BONO, Oslo 2021

404
Vigeland, Tone
(b. 1938), NO
Bracelet, ca. 1991/92
Oxidised silver.
H 8 cm, Ø 8 cm
© Tone Vigeland/
BONO, Oslo 2021

409
Vivelsted, Mette
(b. 1967), DK
"Porcelain Mascot"
Necklace, 2008–10
Porcelain, glass beads,
silver. L 12 × 10.5 × 3 cm,
L with chain 48 cm
© Mette Vivelstad
The porcelain plate with
eranthis decoration was
produced by the Danish
company Bing & Grøn-
dahl and symbolises the
norms and values of the
artist's home country.
At the same time, the
plate has been trans-
formed into a mascot
inspired by Japanese
kawaii. In this way the
necklace can function
as a personal communi-
cation travel accessory
in a globalised world.

411
Walker, Lisa
(b. 1967), NZ
Necklace, 2006
Freshwater pearls, glue,
wool. L 35 cm
© Lisa Walker

410 499 416 418

412 415 417 467

413 525 432 422

414 419

445 551 515

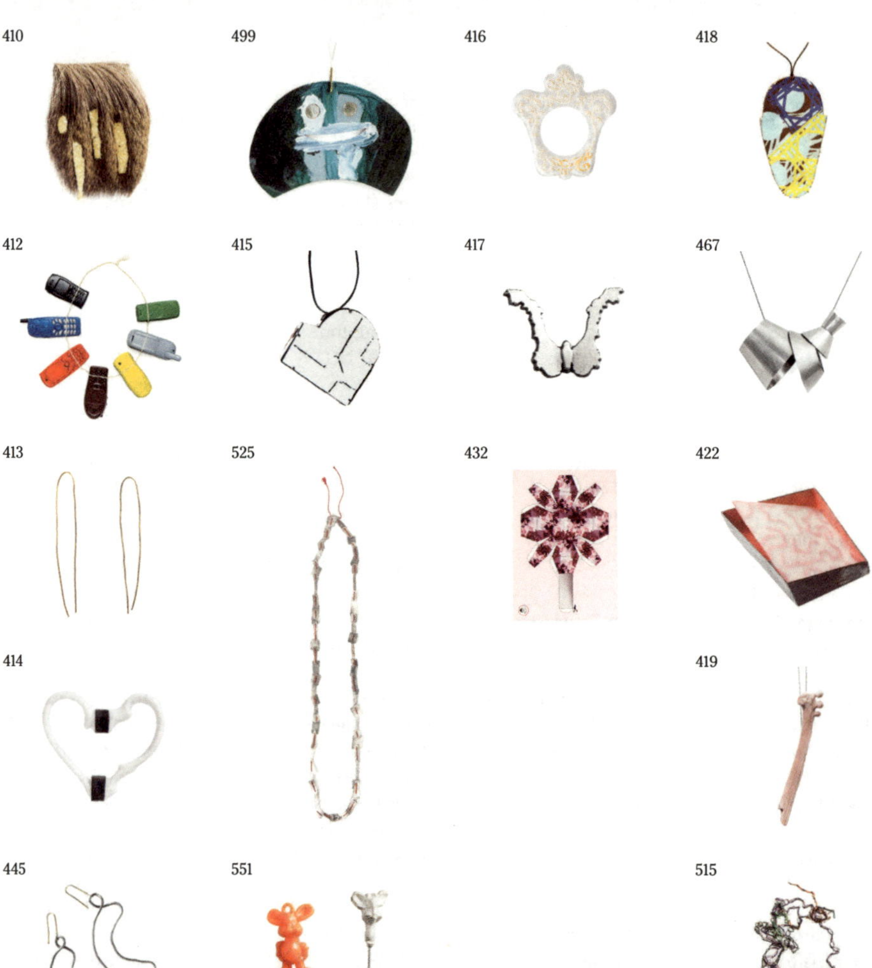

410
Walker, Lisa
(b. 1967), NZ
Brooch, 2008
Deer fur, fabric,
glue, 18 ct gold leaf.
10 × 7.5 cm
© Lisa Walker

412
Walker, Lisa
(b. 1967), NZ
Necklace, 2010
Mobile phones, lacquer
paint, thread. Ø 35 cm
© Lisa Walker
The seven phones
are each painted in a
different colour: green,
grey, yellow, brown, red,
blue and black.

413
Walker, Lisa
(b. 1967), NZ
Earrings, 2015
9 ct gold. L 10 cm
© Lisa Walker

414
Wallström, Mona
(b. 1956), SE
"Brooch Heart", 2015
Porcelain.
5.5 × 5 × 0.8 cm
© Mona Wallström/
BONO, Oslo 2021

445
Walter, Julia
(b. 1979), DE/NL
"Bananas"
Earrings, 2017
925 silver, 585 gold.
9 × 2 cm, 8 × 2 cm
© Julia Walter

499
Walter, Julia
(b. 1979), DE/NL
"Happy Face"
Necklace, 2017
Paint on chipboard,
soapstone inlays
(in collaboration with
F.O. De Bruyn Kops).
19 × 27 cm
© Julia Walter

415
Walz, Silvia
(b. 1965), DE/ES
"Porta Sky"
Pendant, 2016
Enamel on steel.
5.5 × 5.5 × 1 cm
© Silvia Walz

525
Wang, Hongxia
(b. 1971), CN/DK
Necklace, 2018
Silver, silk cord. L 44 cm
© Hongxia Wang

551
Wang, Hongxia
(b. 1971), CN/DK
Pin, 2019
925 silver. 2 × 1.5 × 0.1 cm
© Hongxia Wang
I love party crackers,
and at our New Year's
party in 2018 Hongxia
collected the plastic
figures that come inside
them. For the party the
following year, she had
made a silver cast of
one of them, a rabbit,
and mounted it on a
needle; she then hid a
copy of it in a cracker
for each of the eleven
guests.

416
Westerberg, Sissi
(b. 1975), SE
"Princess"
Ring, 2001
Acrylic. 4 × 3.7 cm
© Sissi Westerberg

417
Wolgers, Dan
(b. 1955), SE
"June 7th 1905"
Pin, 2005
Oxidised aluminium.
1.6 × 1.2 × 1.2 cm
© Dan Wolgers
The motive of this
memorial pin is the map
of Norway mirrored
to make the wings of a
butterfly. It is a minia-
ture version of Dan
Wolgers's public art-
work at the Svinesund
border station, between
Norway and Sweden,
where a swarm of
butterflies had landed
on the building. The
title refers to the date
when the Norwegian
parliament decided to
leave the union with
Sweden.

432
Wöhlke, Nina
(b. 1975?), DE
"Make Your Own
Diamond Ring"
Postcard, 2010
Paper. 15 × 10.5 cm
© Nina Wöhlke

418
Yamamoto, Kiyoshi
(b. 1983), JP/BR/NO
Necklace, 2011
Leather. 14.7 × 8 cm
© Kiyoshi Yamamoto

467
Yang, Jing (b.1987), CN
"I Am Not a Vase"
Necklace, 2015
Silver. 6 × 4 × 4 cm
© Jing Yang

422
Zanella, Annamaria
(b. 1966), IT
"Elena"
Brooch, 2018
Silver, perspex, niello
gold, resin, pigment,
acrylic. 4.5 × 4.5 × 2 cm
© Annamaria Zanella
The title refers to the
main character in Elena
Ferrante's *Neapolitan
Novels*.

419
Zellweger, Christoph
(b. 1962), CH
"Relic Rosé" from the
series *Ossarium Rosé*
Neckpiece, 2006
Mixed media, flock,
silver. L 23 cm,
L chain 60 cm
© Christoph Zellweger

515
Zhang, Xiaorui
(b. 1987), CN/UK
Necklace, 2010
Dyed rubber gloves,
metal. Ca. 160 × 30 cm
© Xiaorui Zhang

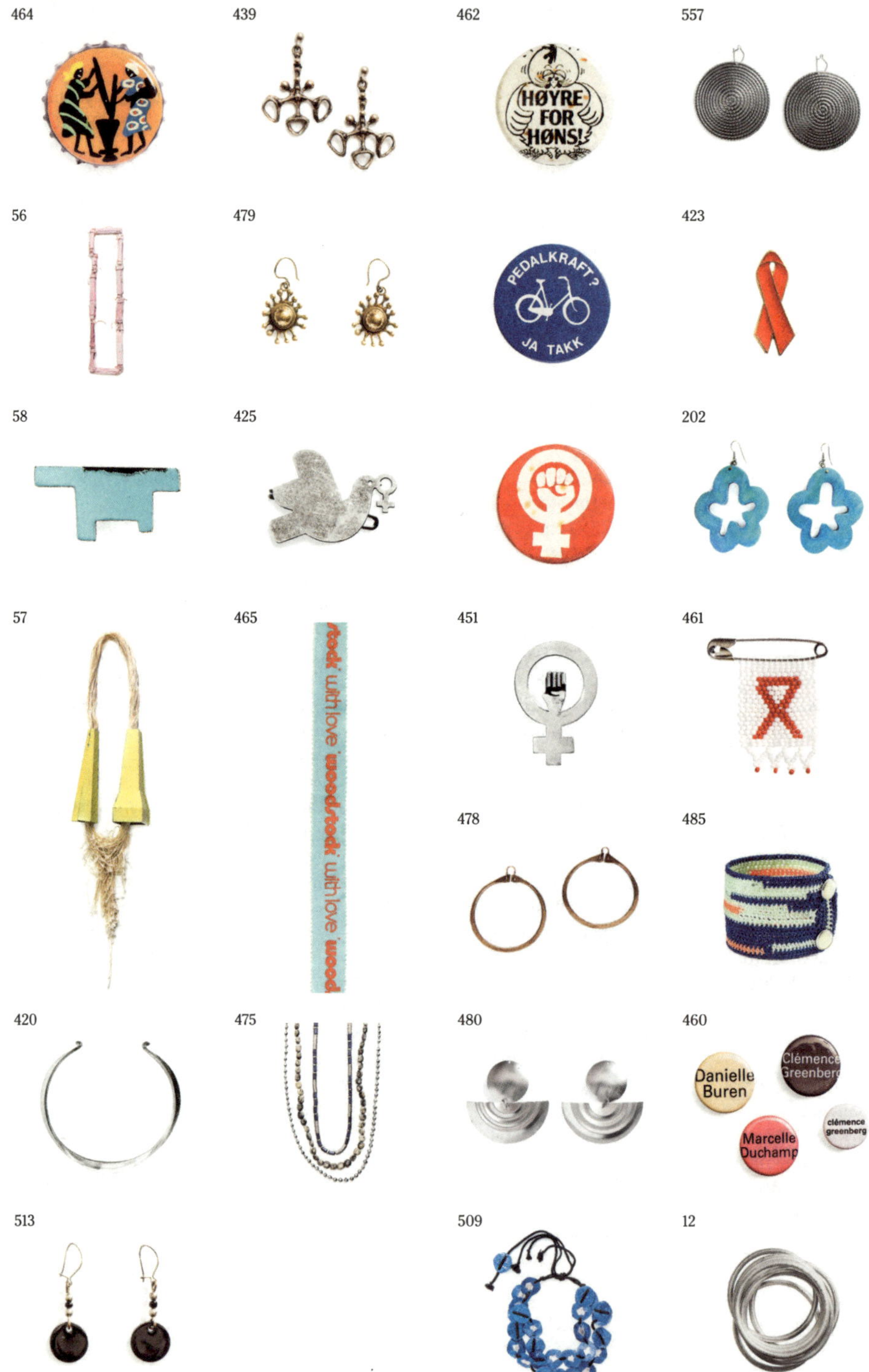

464
439
462
557
56
479
423
58
425
202
57
465
451
461
478
485
420
475
480
460
513
509
12
HØYRE FOR HØNS!
PEDALKRAFT? JA TAKK
Danielle Buren
Clémence Greenberg
Marcelle Duchamp
clémence greenberg

464
Zozmeo, ZA
"Bottle Top Brooch",
1998
Metal, paint. Ø 3 cm

56
Älgå, Sara Borgegård
(b. 1976), SE
"Pink"
Necklace, 2008
Pinewood, masking
tape, acrylic paint,
gouache, warp thread.
L 52 cm
© Sara Borgegård Älgå

58
Älgå, Sara Borgegård
(b. 1976), SE
Pin, 2014
Metal. 2.4 × 1.2 cm
© Sara Borgegård Älgå

57
Älgå, Sara Borgegård
(b. 1976), SE
Necklace, 2014
Warp thread, metal.
L 46 cm
© Sara Borgegård Älgå

420
Østern, Bjørn Sigurd
(b. 1935), NO
Neckpiece, 1974
925 silver. 13 × 14.2 cm
Produced by David-
Andersen

513
Unknown
Earrings, 1970s
Painted coin, metal.
L 3 cm

439
Unknown, FI
Earrings, 1970s
Bronze. L 3.5 cm

479
Unknown, FI
Earrings, 1970s
Bronze. L 3 cm

425
Unknown
Women's International
League for Peace and
Freedom, WILPF
Brooch, 1970s
Metal. 2 × 2.6 cm

465
Unknown, UK
"'woodstock' with love"
Headband, 1970
Cotton. L 86 cm

475
Unknown
3 necklaces, 1970–75
L 47, 54, 70 cm

462
Unknown
Political badges,
1970–81
Ø 2,5–4,5 cm

451
Unknown, NO
Women's Liberation
Symbol
Brooch, 1974
Silver. L 4 cm

478
Unknown
Earrings, ca. 1974–77
Copper. Ø 4 cm

480
Unknown, GB
Earrings, 1985
Tin. 7.5 × 7.8 cm

509
Unknown, IT
Necklace, 2005
Metal from tea lights,
cotton cord. L 50 cm
Bought from the Bien-
nale Store at the Venice
Biennale 2005.

557
Unknown
Earrings, 1988
Metal. Ø 5.5 cm

423
Unknown
Red ribbon pin, 1990s
Enamelled metal.
H 2.5 cm

202
Unknown
Earrings, ca. 1990
Wood, metal. 7 × 6.5 cm

461
Unknown, ZA
AIDS campaign symbol
Brooch, 1998
Pearl embroidery,
safety pin. 5 × 5 cm

485
Unknown, US
Armpiece, 2006
Textile, push buttons.
5.7 × 20 cm

460
Unknown, FR
Badges, 2009
Produced by Centre
Pompidou in connec-
tion with the exhibition
*Women Artists/elles@
centrepompidou*, 2009

12
Unknown, LA
Bracelets, 2013
Aluminium from UXOs.
Ø 7 cm
Produced in Ban Napia,
also called Bomb City,
in the Xiengkhouang
Province, Laos

L

M

N

W

Y

Z

© Jorunn Veiteberg, Rune Døli, Guri Dahl,
arnoldsche Art Publishers

www.arnoldsche.com

Author and editor
Jorunn Veiteberg

Concept
Guri Dahl and Rune Døli

Translator
Peter Cripps, The Wordwrights ANS

Copy editor
Wendy Brouwer

Graphic design
Modest [Rune Døli], Oslo

arnoldsche project management
Matthias Becher

Printed by
Schleunung, Marktheidenfeld

Bound by
Hubert & Co., Göttingen

Paper
90 gsm Munken Pure Rough
100 gsm Arctic the Volume White
80 gsm Munken Print White

Bibliographic information published by
the Deutsche Nationalbibliothek
The Deutsche Nationalbibliothek lists this
publication in the Deutsche Nationalbibliografie;
detailed bibliographic data are available at
www.dnb.de.

ISBN 978-3-89790-619-8

Made in Europe, 2021

**This book has been produced by
the generous support of**
Arts Council Norway
The Fritt Ord Foundation
Nordic Artists' Centre Dale
Norwegian Crafts
Ministry of Foreign Affairs Norway

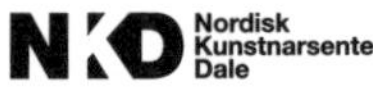

**Norwegian
Crafts**

Photo Credits
Photo Collection and photo montages
Guri Dahl, with the exception of
Jorunn Veiteberg p. 257 **[422]**, p. 174 **[332]**
Ole John Aandal p. 12
Marita Aarekol p. 482
Guri Dahl pp. 462, 463, 465
Elisa Helland-Hansen p. 476
Casper Helmer p. 488
Wil Lee-Wright p. 487
Gurli Nielsen p. 479
Nora Lodberg Nordskov p. 486
Private pp. 458, 461, 468, 469, 471, 472, 473,
474, 475, 477, 478, 480, 481, 483, 484, 485
Unknown pp. 457, 459, 460, 464, 466, 467